Beowulf to Beatles & Beyond

Beowulf to Beatles & Beyond

The Varieties of Poetry

David R. Pichaske

Macmillan Publishing Co., Inc.
NEW YORK

This book is for *Don and Martha,*
and *Ann, Pete, Sue and Joanne.*

MACMILLAN PUBLISHING CO., INC.
866 THIRD AVENUE, NEW YORK, NEW YORK 10022

COLLIER MACMILLAN CANADA, LTD.

LIBRARY OF CONGRESS CATALOGING IN PUBLICATION DATA

Pichaske, David R
Beowulf to Beatles and beyond.

"A select list of recordings of poems and songs": p.
Bibliography: p.
Includes index.
1. American poetry. 2. English poetry.
3. Poetics. I. Title.
PS586.P45 1981 821'.008 80-14796
ISBN 0-02-395380-2

PRINTING: 5 6 7 8 YEAR: 7 8

ISBN 0-02-395380-2

Acknowledgments

Acknowledgment is gratefully made to the following authors and publishers for permission to reprint copyrighted material:

Michael Anania: *Riversongs,* copyright © 1978 by The University of Illinois Press. Used by permission of the author and The University of Illinois Press.

John Ashbery: "Our Youth," copyright © 1957 by John Ashbery. Reprinted from *The Tennis Court Oath* by permission of Wesleyan University Press.

Margaret Atwood: "A Place: Fragments" from *The Circle Game* (Toronto: House of Anansi Press, 1967).

Margaret Avison: "New Year's Poem" from *Winter Sun* (Toronto: University of Toronto Press, 1960). Reprinted by permission of the author.

W. H. Auden: "Paysage Moralisé" copyright 1937 and renewed 1965 by W. H. Auden; "In Memory of W. B. Yeats" and "As I walked out one evening" copyright 1940 and renewed 1968 by W. H. Auden. Reprinted from *W. H. Auden: Collected Poems,* by W. H. Auden edited by Edward Mendelson, by permission of Random House, Inc.

Joan Baez: "Diamonds and Rust" copyright © 1975 Chandos Music (ASCAP). Reprinted by permission. All rights reserved.

James Ballowe: "The Doughboy" reprinted by permission of the author, from *The Coal Miners* (Peoria: Spoon River Poetry Press, 1979).

John Berryman: "Dream Songs" #1 and #69 from *77 Dream Songs.* Copyright © 1959, 1962, 1963, 1964 by John Berryman; "11 Addresses to the Lord" from *Love and Fame.* Copyright © 1970 by John Berryman. Reprinted with the permission of Farrar, Straus and Giroux, Inc.

Norbert Blei: Concrete Poems reprinted by permission of the author.

Robert Bly: "Asian Peace Offers Rejected Without Publication" from *The Light Around the Body* by Robert Bly. Copyright © 1966 by Robert Bly. Reprinted by permission of Harper & Row, Publishers, Inc.

Gwendolyn Brooks: "I Love Those Little Booths at Benvenuti's" Copyright © 1949 by Gwendolyn Brooks Blakely. "The Preacher: Ruminates Behind the Sermon"; "Sadie and Maud" Copyright © 1945 by Gwendolyn Brooks Blakely; "We Real Cool: The Pool Players. Seven at the Golden Shovel" Copyright © 1959 by Gwendolyn Brooks. Reprinted by permission of Harper & Row, Publishers, Inc.

Jackson Browne: "The Pretender" 1976, 1977 Swallow Turn Music. All rights administered by WB Music Corp. All rights reserved. Used by permission.

John Ciardi: "Men Marry What They Need. I Marry You." from *I Marry You* by John Ciardi. Copyright 1958 by Rutgers, The State University. Reprinted by permission of the author.

Leonard Cohen: "Suzanne" © 1966 by Project Seven Music, a division of Continental Total Media Project, Inc., 515 Madison Avenue, Suite 2205, New York, N.Y. 10022.

Wesli Court: "Confessional" by Charles D'Orleans, trans. by Wesli Court. Copyright © 1979 by *The Spoon River Quarterly.* Used by permission.

Charles Creed: "Jan Jensen/Raku Jar". Used by permission of the author. Copyright © 1979 by *The Spoon River Quarterly.*

Robert Creeley: "I Know a Man" from *For Love* by Robert Creeley. Used by permission of Charles Scribner's Sons. Copyright © 1962 Robert Creeley.

Jim Croce: "Time in a Bottle"; "You Don't Mess Around with Jim" © Copyright 1971, 1972 in U.S.A. and Canada. Blendingwell Music, Inc. and American Broadcasting Music, Inc. c/o Publishers' Licensing Corporation, 488 Madison Avenue, New York, N.Y. 10022. All rights reserved. Used by permission.

E. E. Cummings: "anyone lived in a pretty how town." Copyright 1944 by E. E. Cummings; renewed 1968 by Marion Morehouse Cummings. Reprinted from *Complete Poems 1913–1962* by E. E. Cummings by permission of Harcourt Brace Jovanovich, Inc. "Buffalo Bill's" from *Tulips & Chimneys,* edited by George James Firmage, by permission of Liveright Publishing Corporation. Copyright 1923, 1925 and renewed 1951, 1953, by E. E. Cummings. Copyright © 1973, 1976 by Nancy T. Andrews. Copyright © 1973, 1976 by George James Firmage. "next to of course god america i" from *Is* 5 Poems by E. E. Cummings, by permission of Liveright Publishing Corporation. Copyright 1926 by Horace Liveright. Copyright renewed 1953 by E. E. Cummings. "Plato told." Copyright 1944 by E. E. Cummings; renewed 1972 by Nancy T. Andrews. Reprinted from *Complete Poems 1913–1962* by permission of Harcourt Brace Jovanovich, Inc. "r-p-o-p-h-e-s-s-a-g-r" from *No Thanks,* edited by George James Firmage. By permission of Liveright Publishing Corporation. Copyright 1935 by E. E. Cummings. Copyright © 1968 by Marion Morehouse Cummings. Copyright © 1973, 1978 by Nancy T. Andrews. Copyright © 1973, 1978 by George James Firmage. "she being Brand" from *Is* 5 Poems by E. E. Cummings, by permission of Liveright Publishing Corporation. Copyright 1926 by Horace Liveright. Copyright renewed 1953 by E. E. Cummings.

Phil Dacey: "Looking at Models in the Sears Catalogue." Reprinted from *How I Escaped from the Labyrinth,* 1977, and used by permission of University of Pittsburgh Press.

Idris Davies: "The Bells of Rhymney" from *The Collected Poems of Idris Davies,* Gomer Press, J. D. Lewis & Sons. Reprinted by permission of the publisher.

Walter de la Mare: "Silver" reprinted with the permission of The Literary Trustees of Walter de la Mare, and The Society of Authors as their representative.

Emily Dickinson: "This was a Poet—It is That" copyright 1929 by Martha Dickinson Bianchi. Copyright © 1957 by Mary L. Hampson. By permission of Little, Brown and Company.

Alan Dugan: "Love Song: I and Thou" from *Collected Poems* (New Haven: Yale University Press, 1969). Reprinted by permission of the author.

Bob Dylan: "All Along the Watchtower," copyright © 1968 by Dwarf Music; "Desolation Row," © 1965 Warner Bros. Inc. All rights reserved. Used by permission; "I Pity the Poor Immigrant," copyright © 1968 by Dwarf Music; "John Wesley Harding," copyright © 1968 by Dwarf Music; "The Lonesome Death of Hattie Carroll," © 1964 and 1967 Warner Bros. Inc. All rights reserved. Used by permission; "Mr. Tamburine Man," © Warner Bros. Inc. All rights reserved. Used by permission; "Restless Farewell," © 1964 and 1966 Warner Bros. Inc. All rights reserved. Used by permission; "Sad-Eyed Lady of the Lowlands," copyright © 1966 by Dwarf Music; "Subterranean Homesick Blues," © 1965 Warner Bros. Inc. All rights reserved. Used by permission.

Richard Eberhart: "The Groundhog" from *Collected Poems 1930–1976* by Richard Eberhart. Copyright 1960, 1976 by Richard Eberhart. Reprinted by permission of Oxford University Press, Inc.

T. S. Eliot: "Macavity: The Mystery Cat," from *Old Possum's Book of Practical Cats,* copyright 1939 by T. S. Eliot; renewed 1967, Esme Valerie Eliot. Reprinted by permission of Harcourt Brace Jovanovitch, Inc.

Dave Etter: "Green-Eyed Boy After Reading Whitman and Sandburg," reprinted by permission of the author.

Achilles Fang (translator): Excerpts from the *Wen-fu* by Lu Chi, from "Rhymeprose on Literature: The *Wen-fu* of Lu Chi (A.D. 261–303)," *Harvard Journal of Asiatic Studies* 14 (1951) 527–556. Reprinted by permission of the Harvard-Yenching Institute.

Mimi Farina: "In the Quiet Morning," copyright © 1971 Almo Music Corp. and Chandos Music (ASCAP). International Copyright Secured. Made in U.S.A. All Rights Reserved.

Don Felder, Don Henley, and Glenn Frey: "Hotel California," words and music by Don Henley, Glenn Frey, and Don Felder. © 1976 and 1977 Cass Country Music and Red Cloud Music and Fingers Music.

Lawrence Ferlinghetti: "Constantly risking absurdity and death," "I have not lain with beauty," and "Sometime during eternity" from *A Coney Island of the Mind,* copyright © 1958 by Lawrence Ferlinghetti. Reprinted by permission of New Directions Publishing Corporation.

Robert Francis: "Silent Poem," copyright © 1970 by Robert Francis, reprinted from *Robert Francis: Collected Poems, 1936-1976* (University of Massachusetts Press, 1976).

Robert Frost: "After Apple-Picking," "The Death of the Hired Man," "Mending Wall," "Provide, Provide," from *The Poetry of Robert Frost* edited by Edward Connery Lathem. Copyright 1930, 1939, © 1969 by Holt, Rinehart and Winston, Inc.; copyright 1936, © 1958 by Robert Frost; copyright © 1964, 1967 by Lesley Frost Ballantine. Reprinted by permission of Holt, Rinehart and Winston, Publishers.

Allen Ginsberg: "America" from *Howl and Other Poems,* copyright © 1956, 1959 by Allen Ginsberg; "First Party at Ken Kesey's with Hell's Angels" from *Planet News,* copyright © 1974 by Allen Ginsberg; "Funny Death" from *Reality Sandwiches,* copyright © 1963 by Allen Ginsberg; "Going to Chicago" from *Fall of America,* copyright © 1972 by Allen Ginsberg; "Howl" from *Howl and Other Poems,* copyright © 1956, 1959 by Allen Ginsberg. Reprinted by permission of City Lights Books.

Steve Goodman: "The City of New Orleans," copyright © 1970, 1971 Buddah Music, Inc. and Turnpike Tom Music. All rights administered by United Artists Co., Inc.

Woody Guthrie: "Pretty Boy Floyd," © copyright 1961 by Fall River Music Inc. All rights reserved. Used by permission. "Tom Joad," words and music by Woody Guthrie, TRO © copyright 1960 and 1963 Ludlow Music, Inc., New York, N.Y. Used by permission.

James Haining: "There is no squash like a book." Copyright © 1978 by *The Spoon River Quarterly.* Used by permission of the author.

George Harrison: "Within You Without You." Copyright © 1967 Northern Songs Limited. All rights for the U.S.A., Mexico and the Philippines controlled by Maclen Music, Inc. c/o ATV Music Corp. Used by permission. All rights reserved.

A. E. Housman: "Eight O'Clock," from *The Collected Poems of A. E. Housman.* Copyright 1922 by Holt, Rinehart and Winston. Copyright 1950 by Barclays Bank Ltd. Reprinted by permission of Holt, Rinehart and Winston, Publishers. "Loveliest of Trees, the Cherry Now" and "To an Athlete Dying Young" from "A Shropshire Lad"—Authorized Edition—from *The Collected Poems of A. E. Housman.* Copyright © 1939, 1940, 1965 by Holt, Rinehart and Winston, copyright 1967, 1968 by Robert E. Symons. Reprinted by permission of Holt, Rinehart and Winston, Publishers.

Langston Hughes: "Young Gal's Blues" copyright 1927 by Alfred A. Knopf, Inc.; "Little Lyric" copyright 1942 by Alfred A. Knopf, Inc. and renewed by Arna Bontemps and George Houston Bass; "October 16" copyrighted 1948 by Alfred A. Knopf, Inc. Reprinted from *Selected Poems of Langston Hughes* by Langston Hughes. By permission of Alfred A. Knopf, Inc.

Janis Ian: "This Must Be Wrong." Reprinted by permission of Mine Music Ltd.

Mick Jaggar and Keith Richard: "No Expectations" copyright © 1968 Abkco Music Inc.; "Honky Tonk Women" copyright © 1969 Abkco Music Inc. Used by permission. All rights reserved. International copyright secured.

Robinson Jeffers: "Shine, Perishing Republic" copyright 1925 and renewed 1953 by Robinson Jeffers; "To the Stone-Cutters" copyright 1924 and renewed 1952 by Robinson Jeffers. Reprinted from *The Selected Poetry of Robinson Jeffers* by permission of Random House, Inc.

Billy Joel: "Honesty" © 1978 by Impulsive Music and April Music Inc. "My Life" © 1978 by Impulsive Music and April Music Inc. "Only the Good Die Young" © 1977, 1978 by Impulsive Music and April Music Inc. "She's Always a Woman" © 1977, 1978 by Impulsive Music and April Music Inc. Rights in the U.S.A. and Canada administered by April Music Inc. Used by permission. All rights reserved.

John Judson: "The Lineage of Indian Ponies" is from the book *Routes from the Onion's Dark,* published by Pentagram Press and copyrighted in 1976 by John Judson.

Galway Kinnell: "The Bear" from *Body Rags* by Galway Kinnell. Copyright © 1967 by Galway Kinnell. Reprinted by permission of Houghton Mifflin Company.

Martin Luther King, Jr.: "I Have a Dream" reprinted by permission of Joan Daves. Copyright © 1963 by Martin Luther King.

John Knoepfle: "The Farmer and the Owl" from *The Intricate Land* (New York: New Rivers Press, 1970). Reprinted by permission of the author.

Kris Kristofferson: "Me and Bobby McGee" © copyright 1969 by Combine Music Corp. International copyright secured. All rights reserved.

Greg Kuzma: "Nebraska" from *Nebraska* (Crete, Nebraska: The Best Cellar Press, 1977). Reprinted by permission of the author.

Don L. Lee: "But He Was Cool" from *Don't Cry, Scream,* copyright © 1969 by Don L. Lee. Reprinted by permission of Broadside Press.

John Lennon: "Working Class Hero," copyright © 1967 Northern Songs Limited. All rights for the U.S.A., Mexico and the Philippines controlled by Maclen Music, Inc. c/o ATV Music Corp. Used by permission. All rights reserved.

John Lennon and Paul McCartney: "All You Need Is Love." Copyright © 1967 Northern Songs Limited. "Being for the Benefit of Mr. Kite." Copyright © 1967 Northern Songs Limited. "A Day in the Life." Copyright © 1967 Northern Songs Limited. "Eleanor Rigby." Copyright © 1966 Northern Songs Limited. "Fixing a Hole." Copyright © 1967 Northern Songs Limited. "Getting Better." Copyright © 1967 Northern Songs Limited. "Good Morning, Good Morning." Copyright © 1967 Northern Songs Limited. "Let It Be." Copyright © 1970 Northern Songs Limited. "Lovely Rita." Copyright © 1967 Northern Songs Limited. "Lucy in the Sky with Diamonds." Copyright © 1967 Northern Songs Limited. "Norwegian Wood (This Bird Has Flown)." Copyright © 1965 Northern Songs Limited. "Oh! Darling." Copyright © 1969 Northern Songs Limited. "Penny Lane." Copyright © 1967 Northern Songs Limited. "Sgt. Pepper's Lonely Hearts Club Band." Copyright © 1967 Northern Songs Limited. "She's Leaving Home." Copyright © 1967 Northern Songs Limited. "Strawberry Fields Forever." Copyright © 1967 Northern Songs Limited. When I'm Sixty Four." Copyright © 1967 Northern Songs Limited. "With a Little Help from My Friends." Copyright © 1967 Northern Songs Limited. All rights for the U.S.A., Mexico and the Philippines controlled by Maclen Music, Inc. c/o ATV Music Corp. Used by permission. All rights reserved. "I Am the Walrus." Copyright © 1967 Northern Songs Limited. All rights for the U.S.A., Mexico and the Philippines controlled by Comet Music Corp. c/o ATV Music Corp. Used by permission. All rights reserved.

Denise Levertov: "The Altars in the Street," from *The Sorrow Dance,* copyright © 1956 by Denise Levertov. "One A.M.," from *The Jacob's Ladder,* copyright © 1958 by Denise Levertov Goodman. Reprinted by permission of New Directions.

Laurence Lieberman: "God's Measurements" from *God's Measurements.* Reprinted by permission of Macmillan Publishing Co., Inc. Copyright © 1979, 1980 by Laurence Lieberman. Originally appeared in *The New Yorker.* "Lobsters in the Brain Coral," from *The Osprey Suicides.* Reprinted by permission of Macmillan Publishing Co., Inc. Copyright 1970, 1973 by Laurence Lieberman. Originally appeared in *Poetry.*

Gordon Lightfoot: "Wreck of the Edmund Fitzgerald." Published by Moose Music, Inc. Reprinted by permission of Gordon Lightfoot.

Vachel Lindsay: "Bryan, Bryan, Bryan, Bryan," "The Little Turtle," "On the Building of Springfield," from *Collected Poems* reprinted with permission of Macmillan Publishing Co., Inc. Copyright 1920 by Macmillan Publishing Co., Inc, renewed 1948 by Elizabeth C. Lindsay.

Dorothy Livesay: "Going to Sleep," from *Collected Poems: The Two Seasons* by

Dorothy Livesay. Copyright © Dorothy Livesay, 1972. Reprinted by permission of McGraw-Hill Ryerson Limited.

Kerry Livgren: "Dust in the Wind" © 1977, 1980 Don Kirshner Music/Blackwood Music Publishing. c/o Kirshner/CBS Music Publishing. All rights reserved. Used by permission.

John Logan: "Love Poem," from *The Zigzag Walk* by John Logan. Copyright 1963, 1964, 1964, 1966, 1967, 1968, 1969 by John Logan. Reprinted by permission of the publisher, E. P. Dutton.

Robert Lowell: "Inauguration Day, 1953," from *Life Studies*. Copyright © 1956, 1959 by Robert Lowell. "Robert Frost" from *History* © 1967, 1968, 1969, 1970, 1973. Reprinted with permission of Farrar, Straus and Giroux, Inc.

Archibald MacLeish: "Ars Poetica" and "You, Andrew Marvell" from *The Collected Poems of Archibald MacLeish, 1917-1952*, copyright 1952 by Archibald MacLeish. Reprinted by permission of the publisher, Houghton Mifflin Company.

Edgar Lee Masters: "Aner Clute" from the *Spoon River Anthology* by Edgar Lee Masters, published by Macmillan Publishing Co., Inc., and reprinted by permission of Ellen C. Masters. Copyright Ellen C. Masters.

Thomas McGrath: from *Letter to an Imaginary Friend*—Part I, (Chicago: The Swallow Press, 1962). Reprinted by permission of the author.

Judith Minty: "The End of Summer" reprinted from *Heartland II: Poets of the Midwest*, edited by Lucien Stryk, copyright © 1975 by Northern Illinois University Press. Reprinted by permission of the publisher.

Joni Mitchell: "Blue Motel Room," © Crazy Crow Music. "Woodstock," © 1969 Siquomb Publishing Corp. "You Turn Me On, I'm a Radio," 1972 Crazy Crow Music. Used by permission. All rights reserved.

Marianne Moore: "The Fish" reprinted with permission of Macmillan Publishing Co., Inc. from *Collected Poems* by Marianne Moore. Copyright 1935 by Marianne Moore, renewed 1963 by Marianne Moore and T. S. Eliot.

Jim Morrison/The Doors: "Horse Latitudes" and "Twentieth Century Fox"—words by The Doors. © 1967 Doors Music Co. Used by permission of Author and Publisher.

Lisel Mueller: "First Snow in Lake Country" from *Dependencies* by Lisel Mueller, © 1957, 1958, 1959, 1960, 1961, 1962, 1963, 1964, 1965 by Lisel Mueller. Reprinted by permission of The University of North Carolina Press.

Alan O'Day: "Angie Baby" © 1974 WB Music Corp. All rights reserved. Used by permission.

Charles Olson: "Further Completion of Plat" from *Maximus Poems IV, V, VI* published by Viking Press, 1968 by Charles Olson. Reprinted by permission of the Estate of Charles Olson.

Sylvia Plath: "The Applicant" and "Lady Lazarus" from *Ariel* by Sylvia Plath. Copyright © 1963 by Ted Hughes. Reprinted by permission of Harper & Row, Publishers, Inc.

Po Chu-I: "The Flower Market" copyright 1919 and renewed 1947 by Arthur Waley. Reprinted from *A Hundred and Seventy Chinese Poems*, trans. by Arthur Waley. By permission of Alfred A. Knopf, Inc.

Ezra Pound: "Ballad of the Goodly Fere" from *Personnae*. Copyright 1937 by Ezra Pound. Reprinted by permission of New Directions.

John Crowe Ransom: "Bells for John Whiteside's Daughter" copyright 1924 by Alfred A. Knopf, Inc. and renewed 1952 by John Crowe Ransom. Reprinted from *Selected Poems* by permission of the publisher.

Keith Reid and Gary Brooker: "A Whiter Shade of Pale." Words and music by Keith Reid and Gary Brooker. © Copyright 1967 Essex Music International Ltd., London, England. TRO—Essex Music, Inc., New York, controls all publication rights for the U.S.A. and Canada. Used by permission.

Robbie Robertson: "Daniel and the Sacred Harp" © 1970 Canaan Music, Inc. "The Night They Drove Old Dixie Down" © 1969 Canaan Music, Inc. "The Rumor" © 1970 Canaan Music, Inc. Used by permission. All rights reserved.

Edwin Arlington Robinson: "Karma" copyright 1925 by Edwin Arlington Robinson, renewed 1952 by Ruth Nivison and Barbara R. Holt; "Mr. Flood's Party," copyright 1921 by Edwin Arlington Robinson, renewed 1949 by Ruth Nivison. Reprinted from *Collected Poems* by permission of The Macmillan Company. "The House on the Hill" and "Oh, For A Poet" from *The Children of Night* are used by permission of Charles Scribner's Sons and are fully protected by copyright.

Theodore Roethke: "Elegy for Jane" copyright © 1955 by The New Republic, Inc. Reprinted from *The Collected Poems of Theodore Roethke* by permission of Doubleday & Company, Inc.

Raymond Roseliep: "Thoreauhaiku" from *The Spoon River Quarterly,* Vol. III, Number 2, Spring 1978. Reprinted by permission of the author.

Carl Sandburg: "Gone" from *Chicago Poems* by Carl Sandburg, copyright 1916 by Holt, Rinehart and Winston, Inc.; renewed 1944 by Carl Sandburg. Reprinted by permission of Harcourt Brace Jovanovich, Inc.

Amy Jo Schoonover: "Rondel: An Un-Love Song." Copyright © 1978 by *The Spoon River Quarterly.* Reprinted by permission of the author.

Pete Seeger: "Waist Deep in the Big Muddy" TRO—copyright © 1967 Melody Trails, Inc., New York, New York. Used by permission.

Karl Shapiro: "The Bourgeois Poet #27" copyright © 1962 by Karl Shapiro. Reprinted from *Collected Poems,* 1940–1978, by Karl Shapiro. By permission of Random House, Inc.

Carly Simon: "That's the Way I've Always Heard It Should Be" © 1970 Quakenbush Music, Inc. "You're So Vain" © 1972 Quakenbush Music, Inc. Used by permission. All rights reserved.

Paul Simon: "American Tune" © 1973 Paul Simon; "El Condor Pasa (If I Could)" © 1933, 1963, 1970 Edward B. Marks Music Corp. and Jorge Milchberg, English lyric © 1970 Paul Simon; "Fifty Ways to Leave Your Lover" © 1975 Paul Simon; "So Long, Frank Lloyd Wright" © 1969, 1970 Paul Simon. International copyright secured. All rights reserved.

Louis Simpson: "American Poetry" Copyright © 1960, 1963 by Louis Simpson. Reprinted from *At The End of the Open Road* by permission of Wesleyan University Press.

Grace Slick: "White Rabbit" copyright © 1967 Irving Music, Inc. (BMI). International Copyright Secured. Made in U.S.A. All Rights Reserved.

Stephen Spender: "I Think Continually of Those Who Were Truly Great" from *Collected Poems* by Stephen Spender. Reprinted by permission of Faber and Faber Ltd.

William Stafford: "Now" and "The Stick in the Forest" from *Someday, Maybe* by William Stafford. Copyright © 1969 by William Stafford. Reprinted by permission of Harper & Row, Publishers, Inc.

Wallace Stevens: "Anecdote of the Jar," "Fabliau of Florida," "Nomad Exquisite," and "High Toned Old Christian Woman" copyright 1923 and renewed 1951 by Wallace Stevens; "The Idea of Order at Key West," copyright 1936 by Wallace Stevens and renewed 1964 by Holly Stevens Stephenson. Reprinted from *The Collected Poems of Wallace Stevens* by permission of Alfred A. Knopf, Inc.

Dylan Thomas: "Do Not Go Gentle Into That Good Night" from *The Poems of Dylan Thomas.* Copyright 1952 by Dylan Thomas. Reprinted by permission of New Directions. "Fern Hill" and "Prologue" from *The Poems of Dylan Thomas.* Copyright 1952 by Dylan Thomas. Copyright 1946 by New Directions Publishing Corporation.

Arthur Waley: "The Flower Market" by Po Chu-I. Copyright 1919 and renewed 1947 by Arthur Waley. Reprinted from *A Hundred and Seventy Chinese Poems,* translated by Arthur Waley, by permission of Alfred A. Knopf, Inc.

Richard Wilbur: "A Wood" copyright © 1967 by Richard Wilbur. "The Lilacs"

© 1963 by Richard Wilbur. Reprinted from his volume *Walking to Sleep* by permission of Harcourt Brace Jovanovich, Inc.

William Carlos Williams: "Dedication for a Plot of Ground," "Portrait of a Woman in Bed," and "The Red Wheelbarrow" from *Collected Earlier Poems* by William Carlos Williams. Copyright 1938 by New Directions Publishing Corporation.

Warren Woessner: "How the West Was Won." Copyright © 1979 by Warren Woessner. Reprinted from *No Hiding Place* (Peoria: Spoon River Poetry Press, 1979).

James Wright: "Autumn Begins in Martins Ferry, Ohio" Copyright © 1962 by James Wright. Reprinted from *Collected Poems* by permission of Wesleyan University Press.

William Butler Yeats: "Crazy Jane Talks with the Bishop" and "Dialogue of Self and Soul" copyright 1933 by The Macmillan Company, renewed 1961 by Bertha Georgie Yeats; "Leda and the Swan" copyright 1928 by The Macmillan Company, renewed 1956 by Georgie Yeats; "The Magi" "That the Night Come" copyright 1912 by The Macmillan Company, renewed 1940 by Bertha Georgie Yeats; "When You Are Old" copyright 1906 by The Macmillan Company, renewed 1934 by William Butler Yeats. From the *Collected Poems of William Butler Yeats.* Reprinted by permission of The Macmillan Company.

When You Are Old

When you are old and grey and full of sleep,
And nodding by the fire, take down this book,
And slowly read, and dream of the soft look
Your eyes had once, and of their shadows deep;

How many loved your moments of glad grace,
And loved your beauty with love false or true,
But one man loved the pilgrim soul in you,
And loved the sorrows of your changing face;

And bending down beside the glowing bars,
Murmur, a little sadly, how Love fled
And paced upon the mountains overhead
And hid his face amid a crowd of stars.

—*William Butler Yeats*

Preface to the First Edition

Laughter and unqualified ridicule are the usual reactions within the halls of academia to any mention of rock and roll lyrics as poetry, although it would appear that such reactions are no longer entirely justified. Over the past few years there has indeed emerged something we can call "the poetry of rock," something that can at times be quite good. The beginnings, of course, were far from promising. Despite the fertile sources on which rock music of the 1950's drew, it was musically innovative and vibrant but lyrically almost unrelievedly banal and trivial. If it contained any poetry at all, that poetry was pedestrian, adolescent doggerel full of unrefined slang and trite neoromantic convention. But in the early 1960's there burst upon the scene a number of exceptionally talented artists, perhaps even poets, who managed to bring together in various degrees all the many elements of what we now call rock and to make of them something of quality. It is true that Bob Dylan and Paul Simon and John Lennon in their early years were not much of an improvement over Buddy Holly or Elvis Presley, but they grew rapidly, sorting and mixing and improvising until things like "Sad-Eyed Lady of the Lowlands" and "Bleecker Street" and the lyrics of *Sergeant Pepper's Lonely Hearts Club Band* demonstrated that rock musicians could be poets too; that there could be and in fact was a poetry of rock as deserving of respect as the poetry of the English Renaissance or of the early Romantic period. Suddenly rock has become respectable—as respectable as rock can be—and it is fashionable to quote rock, to "study" rock, to criticize rock as one would criticize new volumes of poetry or new symphonic performances. There now exists a substantial and growing body of what we might call rock criticism, and one expects—or fears—that it will not be too many years before critics and criticians will be crawling over the still-living bodies of Bob Dylan and Paul Simon, just as they now crawl over the still-warm corpses of Eliot and Frost. Rock poetry has arrived, although many are still unaware of its arrival. Perhaps it is already departing.

This book accepts the idea of a poetry of rock and uses that poetry in conjunction with the poetry traditionally taught in poetry courses. It accepts the fact that most rock is bad poetry; but so also is 50 per cent of all published poetry, and so too was most of what was written during that incredibly productive decade of English literature between 1590 and 1600. And as we know only too well from experience, even bad poetry can serve a pedagogical purpose. Those who are unwilling to accept the idea of a poetry of rock may still find it useful to use rock as a vehicle into more traditional material, which is also contained in this volume. Whatever we wish to discuss about poetry, be it imagery and metaphor, alliteration and euphony, dramatic monologue and complaint, or simply the careful use of language in all its many aspects, we can find that in rock. What is more important, the idea of poetry becomes more immediate when it is demonstrated that everything we designate as "poetic" is to be found in rock lyrics, because the college generation is most obviously "into" rock. To approach poetry through rock has the advantage of demonstrating the relevance of poetry and poetic criticism to a generation that is highly skeptical about everything its fathers and grandfathers found worth studying. Poetry suddenly becomes not a thing far removed from the ordinary sphere of human experience, but a thing at the center of our lives, a thing with which we are all familiar—which is, of course, what poetry always was and still is (despite the opinions of the majority of Americans to the contrary).

Some will agree with Robert Christgau's dictum that "poems are read or said. Songs are sung," and go on to argue that this fundamental distinction between music and poetry ought to be made, and that this distinction invalidates the entire idea of a poetry of rock. But such an attitude is narrow and historically inaccurate. Virtually all early poetry was sung, or at least chanted to some kind of musical accompaniment. Many medieval poems were written to be sung, including that most treasured lyric, "Summer is icumen in." Those lyrics in Shakespeare's plays were songs before they were poems, as were the ballads we read in poetry anthologies. The fact is that lyrics make good poems, just as poems make good lyrics for musical compositions, and the distinction is not as easily drawn as Cristgau would have us believe. Hearing Vachel Lindsay perform his poems on records, one would begin to doubt that any distinction at all exists.

Others will quarrel with the organization of this anthology, arguing that it is impossible to find good poetry that relies exclusively on, say, alliteration or metaphor; that poetry really cannot be dissociated into component parts; that some method of structuring an anthology that does not break poetry into pieces would better fit the purposes of a college course. There is a certain amount of truth to that argument, of course, but the alternatives are not at all attractive. Either we must forget about some very useful critical terminology entirely, or we must use it haphazardly, as the individual poems demand. Neither of these approaches is pedagogically useful or sound, and I have accepted the structure I use as the most useful of all possibilities, even with its limitations. This structure allows the student to discuss poets and poetry in general, examine words as symbols and as sounds, engage in generic criticism, develop the ability to read poems in aggregations, and, finally, to form some qualitative judgments about individual poems.

Some people will argue that if poetry is at all like music, then it ought to be heard, not read. I agree entirely, and for that reason have provided an Appendix of recordings of the songs *and poems* contained in this volume. At a relatively modest cost, a department can build a substantial library of recorded poetry—students are usually more than willing to loan rock albums—which can be used either in a listening room of the library or on tape in a language lab to supplement the printed words that appear in this book. Frequently I have referred to recorded versions of both poems and songs in the discussions of this book; on such occasions tapes or records might with considerable profit be brought into the classroom to provide the basis for discussion.

A brief note on the texts of the rock lyrics. Only one who has dealt with these lyrics as poems can fully understand the textual problems they present—problems complicated beyond all telling by the fact that they, like medieval lyrics and ballads, seem invariably to have been sung before or as they were written; by the fact that those who compose them in a recording studio seem to take only the most casual interest in their publication in printed form; by the fact that music indicates no line lengths and frequently no punctuation; by the fact that transcription from recording to printed version (as on the jacket of *Sergeant Pepper*) is done in the most careless manner imaginable; by the fact that manuscript versions of some lyrics (Bob Dylan's "All Along the Watchtower," for example) serve to confuse rather than clarify problems; and by the fact that every time a lyric is printed somewhere it appears in a slightly different version. It is also apparent that rock singers have a distressing tendency to forget lyrics (sometimes their own) or to improvise upon the spot, so that what is sung on a record is not necessarily what appears on the lead sheet, and vice versa (Judy Collins' "Story of Isaac" and Leonard Cohen's lyric are virtually two different poems). This is not to chastise the composers and the singers; it is merely to observe some of the difficulties involved when one attempts to set an oral culture in print. Suffice it to say that when the variorum Bob Dylan appears, it will be a very sizeable volume. Meanwhile, we all labor in a cloud of unknowing.

And a final note concerning the selections. I have tried to strike a reasonable balance between the contemporary and the traditional, the fresh and the familiar, the sacred and the profane, in both rock and poetry. If that balance seems to favor the contemporary, the fresh, and the profane, it is because I believe that such a proportion is necessary to correct an imbalance other textbooks have created in favor of the traditional, the familiar (even stale), and the sacred—an imbalance that I believe has contributed greatly to the current American distaste for poetry of all kinds.

For their help in preparing this volume I owe special thanks to Tom Kent, Charles Clancy, Jack Carey, David Isaacson, and Robert C. Albrecht, who read the original manuscript and offered many valuable and insightful suggestions; Suzie Gordon and Cindy Newman, who did a great deal of typing; Bradley University, which provided a grant that paid for much of the typing and Xerox work; Dick Stewart of Irving Music, who has been most helpful and civil in all things; Byerly Music of Peoria, Illinois, which helped me with both sheet music and recordings; RCA, Vanguard, Caedmon Records, who donated or loaned many records; Free Press editors Pat Vitacco and Tom Gay, whose assistance was invaluable; and Elaine, my wife, for spending many nights alone while I worked in my office. And of course to Bob Dylan, Phil Ochs, The Beatles, Leonard Cohen, and Peter, Paul, and Mary—all brothers and sisters of mercy, bringers of comfort and song.

Preface to the Revised Edition

Looking back across the seventies to the months of 1970 and '71 when *Beowulf to Beatles* first came together, I am overwhelmed by the great zero of the decade. Advances on one front or another seem insignificant when compared to the stagnation, even regression in large areas of the social, political, literary, musical, and educational worlds: everywhere you turn it looks like one version or another of "back to the basics." Under the surface of this retreat to fundamentals, however, especially in education and literature, it seems to me that some profound changes have taken place, not so much along the cutting edge (where all the action was during the sixties), as in the fundamental assumptions with which we go about our daily business. Rather than found or feed a revolution, we have settled quite imperceptibly into consolidating a revolution socially, politically, educationally, and poetically. All the cries of "it's been the fifties all over" ought not to delude us: we have come a long way since 1959 and, I think, since 1969.

Rereading the preface to the first edition of *Beowulf to Beatles,* I am struck most of all by a strident, polemical tone that seems unnecessary, even embarassing ten years later. We've grown accustomed to the idea of poem as sound, for example, and of poem as song. We have accustomed ourselves to Charles Olson's "the HEAD, by way of the EAR, to the SYLLABLE/the HEART, by way of the BREATH, to the LINE." Ginsberg and Corso and Ferlinghetti and the whole school of non- or antiacademic poets have found their way into the respectability of literature textbooks. Records and tapes of songs and sung poems and read poems, and even lectures on poetry and interviews with poets have proliferated into "Spoken Arts treasuries" and "Cassette Curricula." Not that the Whitman-Sandburg-Williams tradition of poem as spoken word burst suddenly upon the world during the 1970s; on the contrary, the rebirth of that poetic tradition was taking place back in the sixties, even during the fifties. But only after living with this new poetry for some time have we been able to lock that rebirth into literary history. So today a poem is sung *or* said, and Bob Dylan is a poet after all, and you *can* read a serious paper on his work at the Midwest Popular Culture Association or the Modern Language Association convention without discomfort or sidewise glances. The decline in importance of imagism and irony—qualities of words as cognitive symbols—and the emergence of sound—of word as word—was one of the most significant developments of poetry during the sixties, was consolidated during the seventies, is something of a commonplace today. I like to think that the first edition of *Beowulf to Beatles* played some small role in that consolidation, although in so doing it made itself obsolete.

The seventies have seen the consolidation of other important developments in poetry and the way poetry is handled in the classroom. Primary among these, I think, is the death of the New Criticism. New Criticism had lost its preeminence among modes of criticism long before 1970, of course, but it lived on in second- and third-generation textbooks. During the seventies, however, teachers of literature seemed increasingly to understand what many poets and some critics had for a long while been complaining: that by stripping a poem of biographical and social context, New Criticism—while sharpening our reading and analysis—divested the poem of much that was meaningful; and by overvaluing such qualities as complexity, ambiguity, irony and tension, the New Critics impressed upon poetry that was brought to the public's attention a certain cool, intellectual, distanced quality that might not necessarily have been healthy for the art. Poets had been writing even in the forties and fifties poems that refused to conform to New Criticism's rules, infusing the poet's own self into the poem, insisting on direct and unequivocable statements, making a shambles of conventional form. During the sixties developments in poetry began to unravel the New Critical hegemony, and by the seventies they finally caught up with teachers, with the result that so-called "critical apparatus" has increasingly disappeared from textbooks and anthologies, and (more lamentably) introduction to poetry classes have disappeared from college curricula.

The third major development of the seventies was the passing of the classical "modern" greats—Yeats, Eliot, Frost, Pound, Robinson—into literary history. The giants are suddenly no longer contemporary; in some respects they seem as remote as Browning and Wordsworth. Under old copyright laws, much of Yeats, Sandburg, and even Eliot would be today in the public domain, including "The Wasteland." And the new poets, while nodding deferentially to the old titans (especially Ezra Pound), have owned new gods: William Carlos Williams, with Walt Whitman to the rear and Charles Olson to the front.

What has in fact been happening is an explosion of experimentation in which no poet, no school, no influence predominates. The dominant myths have been the poet as sooth-sayer and explorer, pressing further and then further against the frontiers of language, myth, sound, and structure. The seventies may have retreated from the outer edge of experimentation, but in retreat they consolidated our position well beyond traditional verse forms, metaphor as it had commonly been understood, generic distinctions, and the old ambiguities and complexities.

One thing which fueled and continues to fuel innovation is the proliferation of small presses throughout the country, most of them privately owned and operating at a loss, printing three or four books a year, books that the big publishing houses refuse to touch: poetry that is too far out of step with traditional or dominant canons of criticism to find a large audience . . . or poetry that is simply bad, or worse, poetry that is merely competent. Despite the fact that the poet commands today neither wealth nor respect among the laity, the contemporary American poet is publishing a prodigious amount of poetry. He publishes more freely, in fact, than ever before. He and she, for feminist presses are prominent among small presses, and feminist poetry as well—and Chicano poetry, gay poetry, black poetry, you name it. We are inundated with poetry despite the facts that few people read it and nobody's buying it. And because even first-rate poets cannot find a publisher among the major houses today, a reader simply must wade through the flood of small press offerings to discover what's going on in poetry. It may, in fact, be the age of the amateur, but let that pass.

All of these developments leave us in something of a quandary when it comes to teaching poetry. We have a new *kind* of poetry, a dozen new kinds of poetry which we do not entirely understand, and which resist almost by design the critical tools we bring to bear on them. I myself am confused, and I suspect from conversations and letters that my confusion is shared by many others both in and outside of the college classroom. My uncertainty stems from experience—experiences in teaching and writing poetry these past ten years, in editing *The Spoon River Quarterly*, in wading through small press offerings. Increasingly as I teach contemporary poetry and read criticism of contemporary poetry and hear the statements of contemporary poets, as I open the daily submissions to the quarterly, as I think self-consciously about my own poetry, I am aware of remarkable disparity between what I see, what I read, what I do, and poetry as I thought I understood it. Imagism is dead. Metaphor is shunned. Meter—there is none. Nor any rhyme either. Alliteration is underplayed. The symbol is avoided. Statement is either explicit or so oblique as nearly to be missed. Rhythm is complex and subtle in a way that excites me, but defies schematization. Allusion is gone. Everywhere and on every point the poetry I read seems to utterly different from the poetry of Browning, Yeats, Frost, Pound, or Eliot, that I am tempted to cry out, like Allen Tate on first seeing Lowell's *Life Studies,* "But, Cal, it's not *poetry!*" I also begin to doubt the tools of analysis, except as they can be applied to a poetry that seems increasingly dated, if not irrelevant. Indeed, the new poetry can make us look foolish as critics—it plays games with us, undermines our best intentions, subverts our best efforts. We find critics sounding less and less incisive, more and more "opaque" (read "unintelligible"), pompous, and—ultimately—inane. We read poems we do not understand, and then explications of those poems that we do not understand, and we wonder. In practical terms, we find ourselves left with two options: stick with traditional poetry, even if it does seem to ignore modern reality; or discard criticism and let the poem be a poem.

In putting together this second edition of *Beowulf to Beatles*, I have tried to accommodate as much as possible these various developments. First, and most importantly, I have attempted to synthesize everything I can imagine about the whole sweep of poetry into a single statement that might give some order to the chaos we see around us and relate the new poetry to the old. That statement is this: "A poem is a thing, a form, a voice, and a statement." You can push poetry in any one of those directions you wish, but the best poetry is that which encompasses all four, and those four qualities are what we're really talking about when we begin criticizing a poem. This is conservative enough, but it is functional: in teaching literature and in writing workshops I have found this simple reduction a useful slogan on which to base an exploration of poetry. The "critical apparatus" of this book is little more than an elaboration on thing, form, voice, and statement. It is true that this structure allows a good poem to fit into any one of four slots (as well as into Chapters 1 and maybe 6). But this structure also makes *Beowulf to Beatles II* the kind of book that a teacher or student could put next to any anthology or collection of poems, from a survey textbook to the latest collections of William Stafford or Robert Bly, and find it opens doors into the poetry. Some subsections of these four divisions will sound familiar to teachers and readers of other texts; others will sound new and perhaps odd. Especially necessary, I think, is more attention to the matter of voice, where we have simply failed for too long to draw fine distinctions or even to listen with an attentive ear.

Second, insofar as permissions fees have allowed, I have tried to apportion the contents of *Beowulf to Beatles II* equally among three main classes of poetry: (1) traditional poetry, defined to include the modern greats, Robinson, Pound, Eliot, Yeats, and Frost; (2) rock poetry, so as to preserve the most distinctive feature of the original *Beowulf to Beatles,* as well as to give fair representation to a number of first-rate poets whose work is sung, not said; and (3) "new poets," contemporaries, some belonging to the small press world only, so various and so teeming. In this last I have been bound only by my own instincts, which do not necessarily accord with current critical tastes, and by a desire to choose contemporary poetry that is in some way accessible to the college student. If *Beowulf to Beatles I* opened the classroom door to the poetry of rock, *Beowulf to Beatles II* is intended to open that door to at least some of the varieties of contemporary poetry.

Third, I have tried to make the voice of the editor less prominent than it was in the first edition, partly because such is the mode of the times, partly because I no longer have the assurance of youth that seems to underlie pronouncements on matters such as these. I'm less certain than I once was of what a poem is and how to talk about a poem. Increasingly, in class and in writing, I find myself reduced to the vaguenesses I so deprecated as an undergraduate: effusion, harangues, reading the poem again and again. "Wow!" enthuses Robert Bly at a reading. "What a re*mark*able poem!" And I echo him.

Fourth, I have relied increasingly on read or sung poetry. Except for the very obscure poems used often as illustrations of poetic faults, and the very contemporary poems, all of the poetry contained in this collection can be heard on record or on tape. I have worked from these recordings, listed in the discography section, in making my selections and in developing some of the apparatus that surrounds them in the text (and, to a much greater extent, in the teacher's manual). Some of these poems, in fact, are here *only* because of the way they sound: I heard them before I read them, and my initial impression was auditory. The difference in the way one perceives a poem is startling, and I commend the experiment to everyone.

Finally, I commend this text to you as a whole. I am sure some teachers, and many students, will be tempted to skip the traditional poetry in favor of the rock lyrics or the contemporary selections. Some selections contained in this book are very much out of style: the Pope, the Dryden, Emerson, and Holmes. They are not much to my taste either, but they are poetry, and the aim of this book is to give a student a sense, as the subtitle puts it, of "the varieties of poetry." To this end, Emerson's "Concord Hymn" or Pope's "Essay on Man" is as important as Ginsberg's "Howl" or Bob Dylan's "Mr. Tambourine Man."

For their important contributions to this book, I would like to thank Michael Hayes, Kathy Magee, April O'Marah, Terry Symonds, Mike Shea, Bradley University's Dr. John Hitt, John Nemo, and all my students in the seminar of the spring of 1979.

D.R.P

Contents

W. B. Yeats, *When You Are Old* **xii**

Preface to the First Edition **xiii**
Preface to the Revised Edition **xvii**

1 / The Roles of the Poet *1*

1. The Poet as Wordsmith 2

Jim Morrison, *Twentieth Century Fox* 4
A. E. Housman, *Loveliest of Trees, the Cherry Now* 5
W. B. Yeats, *That the Night Come* 6
e. e. cummings, *r-p-o-p-h-e-s-s-a-g-r* 8

2. The Poet as Historian 8

Homer, from *The Iliad* (trans. W. C. Bryant) 10
Alfred, Lord Tennyson, *The Passing of Arthur* 12
Woody Guthrie, *Pretty Boy Floyd* 24
Charles Olson, *Further Completion of Plat* 26
Allen Ginsberg, *First Party at Ken Kesey's with Hell's Angels* 28

3. The Poet as Entertainer 28

from *Beowulf* 30
Bernart de Ventadorn, *To Bel Vezer on Her Dismissal of the Poet* (trans. Ida Farnell) 33

T. S. Eliot, *Macavity: The Mystery Cat* 34
Vachel Lindsay, *The Little Turtle* 35
Bob Dylan, *Mr. Tambourine Man* 36
Lawrence Ferlinghetti, *Constantly risking absurdity* 38
anonymous, *Bring Us in Good Ale* 39

4. The Poet as Conscience **40**

Bob Dylan, *The Lonesome Death of Hattie Carroll* 42
Po Chu-I, *The Flower Market* (trans, Arthur Waley) 43
William Blake, *London* 44
John Lennon, *A Working Class Hero* 45
Percy Bysshe Shelley, *Sonnet: England in 1819* 45
Robert Bly, *Asian Peace Offers Rejected Without Publication* 46
James Wright, *Autumn Begins in Martins Ferry, Ohio* 47

5. The Poet as Visionary **48**

Edwin Arlington Robinson, *Sonnet: Oh for a Poet* 49
Vachel Lindsay, *On the Building of Springfield* 50
John Dryden, from *Annus Mirabilis* 52
W. C. Bryant, *To a Waterfowl* 53
Henry Wadsworth Longfellow, *A Psalm of Life* 54
Lennon-McCartney, *All You Need Is Love* 55
William Wordsworth, *The World Is Too Much with Us* 56
Robbie Robertson, *The Rumor* 57
Stephen Spender, *I Think Continually of Those Who Were Truly Great* 58
David Etter, *Green-Eyed Boy After Reading Whitman and Sandburg* 59

6. The Poet as Commemorator **60**

Ben Jonson, *Inviting a Friend to Supper* 61
William Cowper, *On the Burning of Lord Mansfield's Library* 63
Ralph Waldo Emerson, *Hymn Sung at the Completion of the Concord Monument, April 19, 1836* 63
Carly Simon, *You're So Vain* 64
A. E. Housman, *To an Athlete Dying Young* 65

Langston Hughes, *October 16* 67
Allen Ginsberg, *Going to Chicago* 68

7. The Poet as Myth Maker 68

Ovid, *Pygmalion and the Statue* (trans. John Dryden) 71
Bob Dylan, *John Wesley Harding* 73
Samuel Taylor Coleridge, *The Rime of the Ancient Mariner* 74
Billy Joel, *She's Always a Woman to Me* 94
Galway Kinnell, *The Bear* 95
Robert Bly, *Where We Must Look for Help* 98

8. The Poet as Artificer 99

Lu Chi, *Wen Fu* (trans. Achilles Fang) 101
William Shakespeare, *Sonnet 55* 102
Robinson Jeffers, *To the Stone-Cutters* 103
Wallace Stevens, *The Idea of Order at Key West* 103
Robert Herrick, *Delight in Disorder* 105
Margaret Atwood, *A Place: Fragments* 106

9. The Poet as Explorer 109

Emily Dickinson, *This Was a Poet* 111
e. e. cummings, *Buffalo Bill's* 112
William Carlos Williams, *Portrait of a Woman in Bed* 113
Warren Woessner, *How the West Was Won* 115
John Ashbery, *Our Youth* 115

10. The Poet as Sociologist/Psychologist 117

Walt Whitman, from *Song of Myself* (sections 7–12) 119
Theodore Roethke, *Elegy for Jane* 123
Paul Simon, *American Tune* 124
Matthew Arnold, *Dover Beach* 126
Robinson Jeffers, *Shine, Perishing Republic* 128
The Eagles, *Hotel California* 129
Billy Joel, *Only the Good Die Young* 130
Percy Bysshe Shelley, *Ode to the West Wind* 131
Jackson Browne, *The Pretender* 134
Sylvia Plath, *Lady Lazarus* 136
Bob Dylan, *Desolation Row* 139

2 / A Poem Is a Thing 143

Walt Whitman, from *Song of Myself* (section 15) 144

1. A Thing: Story 147

Thomas Hardy, *Her Death and After* 148
anonymous, *Sir Patrick Spence* 153
Robert Frost, *The Death of The Hired Man* 154
Jim Croce, *You Don't Mess Around with Jim* 159
John Keats, *La Belle Dame Sans Merci* 161
Edwin Arlington Robinson, *Karma* 162
Alan O'Day, *Angie Baby* 163
William Stafford, *The Stick in the Forest* 165

2. A Thing: Character 165

Lennon–McCartney, *Eleanor Rigby* 167
Carl Sandburg, *Gone* 169
Edwin Arlington Robinson, *Mr. Flood's Party* 169
Ben Jonson, *To Fine Lady Would-be* 171
Ben Jonson, *On English Mounsieur* 171
Mimi Farina, *In the Quiet Morning* 172
Robert Lowell, *Robert Frost* 173
John Wilmot, *On King Charles* 174
Billy Joel, *My Life* 175
Robert Browning, *My Last Duchess* 176
Joni Mitchell, *Blue Motel Room* 178
John Berryman, *'The Prisoner of Shark Island'* 179

3. A Thing: Place 181

Lennon–McCartney, *Penny Lane* 182
Robert Bly, *Driving Toward the Lac Qui Parle River* 183
Wallace Stevens, *Fabliau of Florida* 183
William Wordsworth, *Lines: Composed a few miles above Tintern Abbey* 184
Greg Kuzma, from *Nebraska* 188

4. A Thing: History 192

Robbie Robertson, *The Night They Drove Old Dixie Down* 194

Denise Levertov, *The Altars in the Street* 195
Thomas McGrath, from *Letter to an Imaginary Friend* 196
Alfred, Lord Tennyson, *The Charge of the Light Brigade* 200
Alfred, Lord Tennyson, *Ulysses* 201

5. A Thing: Event **203**

Joni Mitchell, *Woodstock* 204
Robert Lowell, *Inauguration Day: January, 1953* 205
John Milton, *On the Late Massacre in Piedmont* 206

6. A Thing: Object **207**

Steve Goodman, *The City of New Orleans* 208
Laurence Lieberman, *God's Measurements* 209
James Ballowe, *The Doughboy* 213
John Keats, *Ode on a Grecian Urn* 214
Wallace Stevens, *Anecdote of the Jar* 215
Richard Eberhart, *The Groundhog* 216

7. A Thing: Image **217**

William Carlos Williams, *The Red Wheelbarrow* 218
William Shakespeare, *Spring* 219
William Shakespeare, *Winter* 219
Leonard Cohen, *Suzanne* 221
Andrew Marvell, *To His Coy Mistress* 223
Walter de la Mare, *Silver* 225
Denise Levertov, *One* A.M. 226
Lennon-McCartney, *I Am the Walrus* 226
Samuel Taylor Coleridge, *Kubla Khan* 228
William Shakespeare, from *Romeo and Juliet* 230

8. A Thing: Simile, Metaphor, Symbol **237**

anonymous, *Come All You Fair and Tender Ladies* 239
Robert Herrick, *To Blossoms* 240
John Donne, *A Valediction: Forbidding Mourning* 240
Jagger-Richards, *No Expectations* 243
Paul Simon, *El Condor Pasa* 243
Louis Simpson, *American Poetry* 244
e. e. cummings, *she being Brand* 245

Joni Mitchell, *You Turn Me On, I'm a Radio* 246
Emily Dickinson, *"Hope" is the thing with feathers* 247
Walt Whitman, from *Song of Myself* (section 6) 248
Gerard Manley Hopkins, *The Windhover* 250
William Blake, *The Lamb* 251
William Blake, *The Tyger* 252

9. A Thing: Allusion **253**

Grace Slick, *White Rabbit* 255
Alan Dugan, *Love Song: I and Thou* 256
Archibald MacLeish, *You, Andrew Marvell* 257
Lawrence Ferlinghetti, *I have not lain with beauty* 259
James Haining, *Another* 260
William Blake, *Mock On, Mock On, Voltaire, Rousseau* 261

3 / A Poem Is a Voice ***262***

1. A Voice: Diction **264**

Kristofferson–Foster, *Me and Bobby McGee* 265
Lawrence Ferlinghetti, *Sometime during eternity* 266
Edgar Lee Masters, *Ode to Autumn* 268
Edgar Lee Masters, *Aner Clute* 270
John Knoepfle, *Farmer and the Owl* 271
Sir Thomas Wyatt, *They Flee from Me* 271
John Berryman, *Dream Song #1* 272

2. A Voice: Tone **273**

Jagger–Richards, *Honky Tonk Women* 275
Thomas Hardy, *Neutral Tones* 275
Robert Frost, *Provide, Provide* 276
Robert Herrick, *To the Virgins, to Make Much of Time* 278
Sylvia Plath, *The Applicant* 278
Robert Southey, *The Old Man's Comforts* 280
Lewis Caroll, *You Are Old, Father William* 281

3. A Voice: Assonance and Alliteration **282**

Bob Dylan, *Sad-Eyed Lady of the Lowlands* 283
Alfred, Lord Tennyson, *The Lotos-Eaters* 285

Wallace Stevens, *Nomad Exquisite* 287
Gerard Manley Hopkins, *Pied Beauty* 288
William Stafford, *Now* 289

4. A Voice: Rhyme **289**

Bob Dylan, *Subterranean Homesick Blues* 291
Janis Ian, *This Must Be Wrong* 294
Gwendolyn Brooks, *We Real Cool* 295
Gwendolyn Brooks, *I Love Those Little Booths at Benvenuti's* 296
Emily Dickinson, *I Like to See It Lap the Miles* 298
Thomas Hood, *Bridge of Sighs* 298
Ben Jonson, *A Fit of Rhyme Against Rhyme* 302

5. A Voice: Euphony and Cacophony **303**

Dylan Thomas, *Fern Hill* 305

6. A Voice: Meter and Rhythm **307**

Emily Dickinson, *Because I Could Not Stop for Death* 315
Gerard Manley Hopkins, *Spring and Fall: To a Young Child* 316
W. H. Auden, *As I Walked Out One Evening* 317

7. A Voice: Pitch **319**

Dylan Thomas, *Prologue* 322
William Carlos Williams, *Dedication for a Plot of Ground* 325

8. A Voice: Tempo **326**

A. E. Housman, *Eight O'Clock* 328
Lennon-McCartney, *Strawberry Fields* 329
Don L. Lee, *But He Was Cool* 330
Percy Bysshe Shelley, *Lines: When the Lamp Is Shattered* 331
Vachel Lindsay, *Bryan, Bryan, Bryan, Bryan* 332

4 / A Poem Is a Structure 340

Bob Dylan, from *A Restless Farewell* 341

1. A Structure: Stanza 343

George Herbert, *Virtue* 344
Bob Dylan, *I Pity the Poor Immigrant* 348
anonymous, *Lord Randall* 349
John Donne, *Song* (Go and catch a falling star) 349
William Shakespeare, *Under the Greenwood Tree* 350
John Ciardi, *Men Marry What They Need. I Marry You* 351

2. A Structure: Generic Forms 352

Sir Thomas Wyatt, *My Galley Charged with Forgetfulness* 354
William Shakespeare, *Sonnet 18* 355
William Shakespeare, *Sonnet 73* 356
John Donne, *Death, Be Not Proud* 356
William Wordsworth, *London, 1802* 357
William Butler Yeats, *Leda and the Swan* 357
e. e. cummings, *next to of course god* 358
Gerard Manley Hopkins, *Carrion Comfort* 358
Dylan Thomas, *Do Not Go Gentle into That Good Night* 360
Edwin Arlington Robinson, *The House on the Hill* 360
anonymous, *A flea and a fly and a flue* 362
anonymous, *A limerick gets laughs anatomical* 362
anonymous, *There was an old lady from Kent* 362
anonymous, *There was a young lady from Kent* 362
Edward Lear, *There was an old man with a beard* 362
anonymous, *There once was a lad from Peoria* 362
W. H. Auden, *Paysage Moralisé* 363
Rudyard Kipling, *Sestina of the Tramp-Royal* 365
Langston Hughes, *Little Lyric (Of Great Importance)* 366
Ben Jonson, *An Old Colt* 366
Robert Herrick, *Presence and Absence* 366
anonymous, *Seven Wealthy Towns* 367
Dorothy Livesay, *Going to Sleep* 367
Idris Davies, *The Bells of Rhymney* 367
Alexander Pope, from *Essay on Criticism* 368

3. A Structure: Music-Related Forms 373

Charles d'Orleans, *Confessional* (trans. Wesli Court) 374
Amy Jo Schoonover, *Rondel: An Un-Love Song* 374
Geoffrey Chaucer, from *The Parliment of Fowls* 375
anonymous, *The House of the Rising Sun* 378
anonymous, *Barbara Allan* 380
Gordon Lightfoot, *The Wreck of the* Edmund Fitzgerald 381
Woody Guthrie, *Tom Joad* 383
Ezra Pound, *Ballad of the Goodly Fere* 386
Langston Hughes, *Young Gal's Blues* 389
Billy Joel, *Honesty* 390

4. A Structure: Blank Verse 390

Robert Frost, *Mending Wall* 393
Robert Browning, *The Bishop Orders His Tomb at Saint Praxed's Church* 394

5. A Structure: Alliterative Structure 398

Alfred, Lord Tennyson, *The Battle of Brunanburh* 399
Richard Wilbur, *The Lilacs* 403

6. A Structure: Syllabic and Line Count 404

Algernon Charles Swinburne, *Hendecasyllabics* 405
Raymond Roseliep, *Thoreauhaiku* 406
Marianne Moore, *The Fish* 407
Judith Minty, *The End of Summer* 409
Robert Creeley, *The Language* 410

7. A Structure: Rhetorical Structure 411

Rev. Martin Luther King, Jr., *I Have a Dream* 414
Walt Whitman, *A Noiseless Patient Spider* 416
Psalm 150 416
Joan Baez, *Diamonds and Rust* 417

8. A Structure: Free Verse 418

Jim Morrison, *Horse Latitudes* 420
Philip Dacey, *Looking at Models in the Sears Catalogue* 421
John Logan, *Love Poem* 423
Allen Ginsberg, *Howl* 423

9. A Structure: Prose Poetry 433

Robert Bly, *Fall* 434
Karl Shapiro, *The Bourgeois Poet #27* 434

10. A Structure: Concrete Poetry 435

George Herbert, *Easter Wings* 435
Allen Ginsberg, *Funny Death* 436
Robert Francis, *Silent Poem* 438
Norbert Blei, *Four Concrete Poems* 439

5 / A Poem Is a Statement *443*

1. A Statement: Theme 445

Oliver Wendall Holmes, *The Chambered Nautilus* 446
Carly Simon, *The Way I've Always Heard It Should Be* 447
Mao Tse-tung, *Ode to the Plum Blossom* 450
Robert Frost, *After Apple-Picking* 451
Lennon-McCartney, *Norwegian Wood* 452
Richard Wilbur, *A Wood* 452
Lisel Mueller, *First Snow in Lake County* 453
Thomas Hardy, *Channel Firing* 454

2. A Statement: Allegory 455

Pete Seeger, *Waist Deep in the Big Muddy* 456
anonymous, *The Corpus Christi Carol* 458
e. e. cummings, *anyone lived in a pretty how town* 459
William Blake, *A Poison Tree* 460
Bob Dylan, *All Along the Watchtower* 461
Robbie Robertson, *Daniel and the Sacred Harp* 462

3. A Statement: Philosophy 463

Kerry Livgren, *Dust in the Wind* 464
Sir Edward Dyer, *My Mind to Me a Kingdom Is* 465
Alexander Pope, from *An Essay on Man* 466
Christopher Marlowe, *The Passionate Shepherd to His Love* 468
Sir Walter Raleigh, *The Nymph's Reply to the Shepherd* 469
Gwendolyn Brooks, *The Preacher: Ruminates Behind the Sermon* 470
Margaret Avison, *New Year's Poem* 470
William Butler Yeats, *A Dialogue of Self and Soul* 471

4. A Statement: Surrealistic Poetry 473

John Judson, *The Lineage of Indian Ponies* 475
Laurence Lieberman, *Lobsters in the Brain Coral* 476

5. A Statement: Paradox, Ambiguity, and Irony 479

John Crowe Ransom, *Bells for John Whiteside's Daughter* 480
John Donne, *Batter My Heart, Three-Personed God* 481
William Butler Yeats, *Crazy Jane Talks with the Bishop* 481
Emily Dickinson, *These Are the Days When Birds Come Back* 482
Lennon-McCartney, *Let It Be* 483
Sarah Cleghorn, *The Golf Links* 485
Gwendolyn Brooks, *Sadie and Maud* 486
Charles Kingsley, *Young and Old* 486

6. A Statement: Poetry as Aesthetic Statement 487

Wallace Stevens, *A High-Toned Old Christian Woman* 488
Paul Simon, *So Long, Frank Lloyd Wright* 489
Charles Creed, *Jan Jensen/Raku Jar/1977* 490
William Wordsworth, *Nuns Fret Not at Their Convent's Narrow Room* 491
Archibald MacLeish, *Ars Poetica* 492
W. H. Auden, *In Memory of W. B. Yeats* 493

7. A Statement: Wit **496**

Paul Simon, *Fifty Ways to Leave Your Lover* 497
Ben Jonson, *On My First Daughter* 499
John Wilmot, *On King Charles* 499
William Cowper, *On the Burning of Lord Mansfield's Library* 499
Alexander Pope, Lines: *On Dullness* 500
John Dryden, *Epigram on Milton* 501

8. A Statement: Antistatement **501**

Reid-Brooker, *A Whiter Shade of Pale* 502
Robert Creeley, *I Know a Man* 503

9. A Statement: Poetry of Statement **504**

Lennon-McCartney, *Oh Darling* 505
Jim Croce, *Time in a Bottle* 505
e. e. cummings, *plato told* 506
John Berryman, from *Eleven Addresses to the Lord,* #1 507

6 / Sustained Performances ***509***

The Beatles, *Sergeant Pepper's Lonely Hearts Club Band* 510
John Donne, *La Corona* 523
Michael Anania, *The Riversongs of Arion* 526
William Wordsworth, *Ode: Intimations of Immortality* from *Recollections of Early Childhood* 542

A Select Bibliography of Rock Criticism **549**

Oral Poetry: A List of Recorded Poems and Songs ***552***

Index ***561***

1 The Roles of the Poet

The poet does not count for much in modern America. Outside the university and small colonies of artists his voice is seldom heard, except in certain tedious public ceremonies when resonant passages from William Shakespeare or Robert Frost may be used to embellish the occasion.

It's not a matter of the poet being free to write his mind; rather, it is a matter of audience and, thereby, of self-respect. "In America especially," poet Gregory Corso wrote unhappily a couple of decades ago, "the poet is more likely to be bereft of respect and honor" than of freedom to write. He explained: "The sad thing about respect and honor in America is that it takes money to have them; therefore the American poet who wishes respect and honor is defeated before he starts, because money is a very difficult thing to obtain, and for a poet it is almost virtually impossible. A fool and his money are soon parted, but a poet and money never meet to be parted."

Things have changed some in America in the recent past, but not in this regard: poets still find themselves without audience apart from their fellow poets, and thus without money and without honor. They live by contrived life supports—a college teaching job or government grant—and know only too well that unless they "go commercial" they stand virtually no chance of penetrating the consciousness of a nation given over to sports, politics, Chevy vans, *Playboy* magazine, bad movies, and worse television. America still has little use for its poets.

This situation is unfortunate for the nation as well as for the poet, because, contrary to popular opinion, the poet has several uses. Historically the poet has been honored, respected, and rewarded on a level with the priest and the warrior, if not the ruler himself. "The poet is a light and winged and holy thing," said Plato. Renaissance courtier Sir Philip Sidney thought poetry "the first light-giver to ignorance," and argued that "no philosopher's precepts can sooner make you an honest man, than the reading of Virgil." Shelley, himself a poet and therefore not entirely impartial, declared flatly, "Poets are the unacknowledged legislators of the world." Poetess Hilda Doolittle wrote, "he takes precedence of the priest, / stands second only to the pharoah."

It is perhaps best to let pass such claims to the divinity of poets—they sound a bit self-serving and a bit hollow, as well as precipitating the interesting question of whether Plato et al overvalued poets even more than moderns undervalue them—and focus our attention on some of the specific roles that a poet, given the chance, might play in modern society: historian, entertainer, social conscience, visionary, commemorator, myth-maker, artificer, explorer, sociologist, psychologist. These are important jobs, ones often assigned to or appropriated by poets in other cultures. Modern poets seem especially eager to play the social conscience and the sociologist-psychologist, and while no poet plays every role, poets can and do play several. And other possibilities also exist: the poet as spokesman for conventional societal wisdom, for example (or as party spokesman, as in Soviet Russia). In fact, useful jobs for poets can be invented almost ad infinitum. This handful of functions will, however, more than justify poets and, more important, will provide a context within which to place the poems they write. Because, as Gregory Corso also noted, "Poetry and the poet are inseparable." The first step toward understanding what a poem attempts to do is perceiving what role the poet was playing. Especially today, when the poet's chief subject is often the poet and the voice of the poem is often the poet's own, poem and poet are often the same thing.

1. The Poet as Wordsmith

"A poet," someone has said, in what must be one of the most concise definitions on record, "is someone who's careful with words." Here is a definition that comes directly to the heart of the matter. For no matter what else poets are, they are wordsmiths, people who make things out of words. And because they work constantly with words, they are especially sensitive to various shades of meanings, to the feel and the touch of words, to the possibilities inherent in all language.

In this sense anyone who works with words can be a poet, including the writers of popular songs. Good songs live as much because of their lyrics as their music, and the songs of Bob Dylan, the Beatles, Robbie Robertson, Jim Morrison, and other careful rock writers can make as much claim to being poetry as the work of traditional poets like Housman and cummings and Yeats.

Words have many qualities, all of which the poet may use in fashioning the poem. The most obvious of these is meaning—both denotative and connotative—which plays such an important role in Jim Morrison's "Twentieth Century Fox" and A. E. Housman's "Loveliest of Trees." But denotative and connotative meaning are but one aspect of words a poet may find useful. Words also have sounds that can be used very effectively by a poet. Everyone knows that Poe played with sound combinations of the words to "The Bells" to make his verse evoke the sounds of the various bells he described, and we all can think of a number of other lines of poetry that are memorable more for the way they sound than for what they actually say. Some of the lines in "Twentieth Century Fox," for example, are memorable in this manner: "No tears, / No fears, / No ruined years." Clever rhymes. The phrase "wearing white" from Housman's poem sticks in our minds long after we have put the poem away because of the alliteration of the "w" sound in "wearing" and "white." The very successful advertisement "Pepsi pours it on" owed its appeal as much to the repetition of the "p" sound in "Pepsi pours" as to the pun in "pours it on." We are used to listening to rock songs and television advertisements, so we may be aware of the sound value of words in a Doors lyric or a soft drink commercial, but poetry has become in some circles too much a thing of the printed page for us to be fully attuned to the word sounds of a poem. But poetry should not—perhaps it can not—be read silently, like a textbook or a newspaper, just as we would never dream of *reading* an Elton John song silently to ourselves. Poetry should be read aloud and listened to, because in poetry as in rock songs, the music of the lines is important. The great poets, even in an age of printed books, in the days before records and tape recorders, never lost their ears, as William Butler Yeats's "That the Night Come" shows.

Words also have shape, at least when they are printed. *Playboy* magazine exploits this aspect of words when it prints "wordplays" like BOSOM or TALL. Advertising uses words as shapes when it prints something like *The* **HOMESTEAD** in an attempt to sell readers a piece of real estate. Notice how the large block letters of *homestead* emphasize the connotations of solidarity and tradition already built into the word itself, while the elegant script of *the* lends a note of class and luxury. A few poets have experimented with visual, or concrete poetry, making designs out of the words on the page, or twisting letters or typography into strange shapes. Some of this concrete poetry is even quite literally cast in concrete or etched in glass or painted on canvas. The poet e. e. cummings is famous for disarraying the typography of his poems, either to convey meaning or to catch the reader's attention. Sometimes the arrangement of words and letters in one of his poems is so important that it becomes the whole poem.

Conservative artists and critics have been at times critical of "concrete poetry'' and of sound-oriented poetry as well, as they tend increasingly to become visual arts and music. In the twentieth century, however, distinctions between prose and poetry, between literature and music and graphic art, between art and reality have all largely broken down. We are confronted with visual poetry, or pieces of sculpture that make noise, move, or even self-destruct, or ''happenings'' that are neither stage drama nor real life. Many of the old distinctions lose their meaning in the face of such experiments, and we are forced to invent new terms like ''visual poetry'' or ''happening'' or ''sung poetry'' to describe what we have experienced. It seems quite as sensible, on balance, to admit that words have shape and sound, just as they have meaning, and that as a poet uses meaning to create his poem, he may also use shape and sound. It is all, in the end, a matter of being careful with words.

Twentieth Century Fox

Well, she's fashionably lean
And she's fashionably late.
She'll never wreck a scene,
She'll never break a date;
But she's no drag
Just watch the way she walks,
She's a twentieth century fox.

She's a twentieth century fox;
No tears, no fears,
No ruined years,
No clocks;
She's a twentieth century fox.

She's the queen of cool,
And she's the lady who waits,
Since her mind left school,
It never hesitates;
She won't waste time
On elementary talk,
She's a twentieth century fox.

She's a twentieth century fox.
Got the world
Locked up

Inside a plastic box;
She's a twentieth century fox.

—Jim Morrison

At first glance the song appears to be something of a love poem to a girl of the twentieth century. Morrison appears to complement her in the opening lines: "She'll never wreck a scene, / She'll never break a date; / But she's no drag / Just watch the way she walks." But some very important words undercut that first impression and turn this love song into a harsh satire on modern women. "Plastic," for instance: what are the connotations of plastic? Could the word ever be used in a complimentary manner in reference to a woman? Or "fashionably." All we know of Morrison's attitude toward what is fashionable in morals, dress, and behavior makes it clear that this word is used pejoratively. The title phrase calls to mind a Hollywood film company and plays on the associations of false glamour that any mention of Hollywood and filmdom is bound to carry. The colloquial "fox" may suggest the modern American woman-as-predator, source of all kinds of sexual and psychological problems in both men and women resulting from this reversal of traditional male-female roles. It does not take very long before the connotation of the language of this song makes us very much aware that this is certainly no love lyric to the modern American woman. In fact, the connotation of the language makes it exactly the opposite.

Listen to The Doors' performance of this song. To what extent does the music—the two drum beats before "twentieth century fox," the insistence on that phrase achieved by the regularity of its rhythm contrasted to the rhythm of the initial four lines, the tone of Morrison's voice, his pronunciation—supplement the connotative meaning of the lyrics?

Loveliest of Trees, the Cherry Now

Loveliest of trees, the cherry now
Is hung with bloom along the bough,
And stands about the woodland ride
Wearing white for Eastertide.

Now, of my threescore years and ten,
Twenty will not come again,

5. *threescore years and ten:* the biblical life-span of man.

And take from seventy springs a score,
It only leaves me fifty more.

And since to look at things in bloom
Fifty springs are little room,
About the woodlands I will go
To see the cherry hung with snow.

—*A. E. Housman*

This is one of the most well-known of all A. E. Housman's lyrics—perhaps known to the point of being worn out. The subject is not complicated: a young man of twenty contemplates the freshness of spring, calculates that he has but fifty or so more years left in his life, and concludes that this time is "little room" to absorb "things in bloom." The thought is not profound; it might be even a bit maudlin and sentimental, but it strikes a responsive chord in even the most jaded of us. What makes the poem memorable, however, is the single word "snow," and the wealth of conflicting connotative meanings it is made to carry. On one level the poet is comparing the white of the cherry blossoms to the white of snow—an apt if trite comparison. On another level, "snow" echoes the thought of death in the second stanza, and carries connotations of mortality and death at the very moment it is being used to connote the life and rebirth of spring blossoms. We had nearly forgotten the unpleasant business of line 7 in the descriptions of the final stanza, but the last word of the poem brings it startlingly back into our minds in a fashion we simply cannot forget.

That the Night Come

She lived in storm and strife,
Her soul had such desire
For what proud death may bring
That it could not endure
The common good of life,
But lived as 'twere a king
That packed his marriage day
With banneret and pennon,
Trumpet and kettledrum,
And the outrageous cannon,
To bundle time away
That the night come.

—*William Butler Yeats*

If we read this poem, or listen to it read, we notice that Yeats settles early into a pattern of three strong beats or accents to the line. And we notice that those three strong beats are each separated by one weak beat, so as to form a very pleasant, regular pattern of alternative weak and strong syllables:

```
u   /    u  /    u   /
She lived in storm and strife,
 u   /  u   /   u /
Her soul had such desire
```

As the poem develops, however, that regularity begins to disintegrate, until by lines 8–10 it is virtually abandoned:

```
 u   /  u u  u  / u
With banneret and pennon,
 /   u  u  /  u u
Trumpet and kettledrum,
 u   u  u / u  / u
And the outrageous cannon,
```

Interestingly this confusion comes precisely as Yeats is talking about the king who, in his eagerness to hasten marriage day to marriage evening, filled it with noise and distraction. Then it's another relatively regular line, and out to a very irregular, but somehow perfectly appropriate

```
 u  u   /   /
That the night come.
```

Those two final beats of the two final words, like a couple of final whacks on the kettledrum, bring the poem dramatically together, the way "snow" finished off Housman's "Loveliest of Trees." But here the effect is achieved more by the *sound* of the poet's words than by his *sense*.

r-p-o-p-h-e-s-s-a-g-r

r-p-o-p-h-e-s-s-a-g-r
who
a) s w (e loo) k
upnowgath
PPEGORHRASS
eringint(o-
aThe):l
eA
!p:
S   a
(r
rIvInG   .gRrEaPsPhOs)
to
rea(be)rran(com)gi(e)ngly
,grasshopper;

—*e. e. cummings*

The poet is trying to capture on paper that instant when you have been thinking of nothing in particular and looking at nothing in particular, and suddenly out of nowhere something springs out at you. At first you are not sure just what it might be—only that it is indeed something, and that it has leaped up with great energy. Not until it lands, "rearranges itself" as cummings puts it, do you actually discover that it's a grasshopper. The successive rearrangements of the word "grasshopper," each more recognizable than the preceding, are clearly attempts by cummings to show this process of gradual recognition, and the typography of "leaps," with its arc and its exclamation point, is meant to suggest the actual startling leap of the insect. Here is a poem that depends almost entirely on the way it appears on a page for its meaning; it could probably never even be read aloud. Is this merely clever, or is the poet doing something significant? (Critics of cummings usually emphasize his "cleverness" as if he were in fact *merely* clever.) Are the clever and the significant necessarily mutually exclusive?

2. The Poet as Historian

In primitive cultures where written records are virtually unknown, one of the poet's most important functions has been and continues to be that of historian. In long narrative poems spun afresh each time he recites them, around complicated plot outlines stored in his head, the poet pours out the history of his people. Sometimes these poems can run to thousands of lines and take hours to recite. And they are the entire history of that culture: the remembered stories and poems of the poet, passed from generation to generation, from poet to poet, until finally they come to be written down or, more likely, forgotten. *Beowulf,* the great Icelandic sagas, the *Iliad* and *Odyssey* of Homer are all examples of the poet as historian. As we read those early poems we notice all the marks of history: a concern for genealogy that reduces some passages to little more than the recitation of names and relationships; a geographic particularity that is remarkable for its accuracy despite the intervening centuries (modern archaeologists are increasingly prone to trust the factualness of poems hundreds, even thousands, of years old); and a recounting of those adventures that constitute a people's finest moments and worst disasters.

One important aspect of all these narratives is interpretation. The poet as a historian is not content simply to recount facts; he wishes to explain them. Most frequently his explanation takes a theological form, as the wrath or favor of the gods—and their direct intervention in human lives—is used to explain the fortunes of human history. But note: while the gods may be capricious in dealing with men, they are more often doling out just rewards and punishments for man's own behavior. Thus the poet as historian often becomes something of a priest . . . and a moralist and philosopher as well. And thus Virgil, whose *Aeneid* is but a literary example of the poet as historian, will do more toward making one a moral individual than all the philosophers' writings put together.

With the advent of writing and then printing, and the emergence of prose (which invariably *follows* poetry in the literary development of a culture), poets relinquished some of their job as historians. Throughout the Middle Ages and the Renaissance, however, long poetic recountings of Greek, Roman, French, Germanic, biblical, and other histories—with increasing amounts of fiction added—continued to be popular. In the middle of the seventeenth century poet John Milton turned biblical historian to "justify the ways of God to men." For Milton, at least, the poem was as much history as theology. More recently Stephen Vincent Benet undertook to write a history of the Civil War in a long collection of poems titled *John Brown's Body.* And periodically, even today, poets turn to history for subject matter in poems of greater or shorter length.

In the twentieth century, however, it has been folk poets, amateur and frequently unschooled, who function most significantly as historians, recording a history that would otherwise be lost or giving us a unique perspective on communal history. Many amateur poets turn to local history for their subject matter, and many a folk song, like Guthrie's "Pretty Boy Floyd," contains social history.

The modern poet-historian has two options really: he can record history as it unfolds around him, or like Tennyson in *Idyls of the King* he can turn to past history and construct his poem out of the prose chronicles of "professional" historians (and letters, memoirs, and artifacts of long-dead people). American poets especially have been much attracted to the questions "What is this place, America? What does it mean to be American?" and often find themselves entangled in the web of history. William Carlos Williams' "Paterson" and Charles Olson's "Maximus Poems" both represent extended attempts to come to grips with the American experience by examining under a poetic microscope historical evidence gleaned from a particular geography (Paterson, New Jersey, and Gloucester, Massachusetts, respectively). Less given to *overt* philosophy in his poetry than many of his predecessors, Olson often fills his poem with vaulting fragments of history that are—neither more nor less—just good solid, informative history, interesting for its antiquity but not particularly different from the curious lore of the old oral epic.

At the other end of the spectrum, Allen Ginsberg, being very much a participant in the social and cultural history of the fifties and sixties, has recorded much of it in short poems: "Grant Park: August 28, 1968," "Rising Over Night-Blackened Detroit Streets," "D.C. Mobilization," "First Party at Ken Kesey's with Hell's Angels." Ginsberg, Guthrie, Olson—many modern poets have proved again and again that when it comes to selecting what is and is not of historical importance poets make very good historians indeed.

from The Iliad, *book 1*

O Goddess! sing the wrath of Peleus' son,
Achilles; sing the deadly wrath that brought
Woes numberless upon the Greeks, and swept
To Hades many a valiant soul, and gave
Their limbs a prey to dogs and birds of air,—
For so had Jove appointed,—from the time
When the two chiefs, Atrides, king of men,
And great Achilles, parted first as foes.
    Which of the gods put strife between the chiefs,
That they should thus contend? Latona's son
And Jove's. Incensed against the king, he bade
A deadly pestilence appear among
The army, and the men were perishing.
For Atreus' son with insult had received
Chryses the priest, who to the Grecian fleet
Came to redeem his daughter, offering
Uncounted ransom. In his hand he bore

The fillets of Apollo, archer-god,
Upon the golden sceptre, and he sued
To all the Greeks, but chiefly to the sons
Of Atreus, the two leaders of the host:—
"Ye sons of Atreus, and ye other chiefs,
Well-greaved Achaians, may the gods who dwell
Upon Olympus give you to o'erthrow
The city of Priam, and in safety reach
Your homes; but give me my beloved child,
And take her ransom, honoring him who sends
His arrows far, Apollo, son of Jove."
Then all the other Greeks, applauding, bade
Revere the priest and take the liberal gifts
He offered, but the counsel did not please
Atrides Agamemnon; he dismissed
The priest with scorn, and added threatening words:—
"Old man, let me not find thee loitering here,
Beside the roomy ships, or coming back
Hereafter, lest the fillet thou dost bear
And sceptre of thy god protect thee not.
This maiden I release not till old age
Shall overtake her in my Argive home,
Far from her native country, where her hand
Shall throw the shuttle and shall dress my couch.
Go, chafe me not, if thou wouldst safely go."
He spake; the aged man in fear obeyed
The mandate, and in silence walked apart,
Along the many-sounding ocean-side,
And fervently he prayed the monarch-god,
Apollo, golden-haired Latona's son:—
"Hear me, thou bearer of the silver bow,
Who guardest Chrysa, and the holy isle
Of Cilla, and art lord in Tenedos,
O Smintheus! if I ever helped to deck
Thy glorious temple, if I ever burned
Upon thy altar the fat thighs of goats
And bullocks, grant my prayer, and let thy shafts
Avenge upon the Greeks the tears I shed."
So spake he supplicating, and to him
Phœbus Apollo hearkened. Down he came,
Down from the summit of the Olympian mount,
Wrathful in heart; his shoulders bore the bow
And hollow quiver; there the arrows rang
Upon the shoulders of the angry god,

As on he moved. He came as comes the night,
And, seated from the ships aloof, sent forth
An arrow; terrible was heard the clang
Of the resplendent bow. At first he smote
The mules and the swift dogs, and then on man
He turned the deadly arrow. All around
Glared evermore the frequent funeral piles.
Nine days already had his shafts been showered
Among the host, and now, upon the tenth,
Achilles called the people of the camp
To council.

—translated by W. C. Bryant

In these opening lines of the *Iliad,* Homer tells the story of how Agamemnon, the Greek leader, refused to return to her father, a Trojan priest of Apollo, his daughter, whom the Greeks had taken captive and who was serving at the time as Agamemnon's concubine. Cryses, the priest, has offered liberal ransoms, and the rest of the Greeks urge Agamemnon to return her, but he will have none of it. So Cryses brings the wrath of Apollo upon the Greeks, precipitating a council, and thereafter a great falling out between Agamemnon and Achilles, which sends Achilles sulking to his tent, and nearly loses the war. How much of this story is true, we have no way of knowing; but note the intervention of god Apollo into the war between Greeks and Trojans once a priest of his is dishonored and, by implication, Apollo himself is insulted. History, Homer suggests, teaches us again and again that the gods cannot be insulted without penalty.

The Passing of Arthur

That story which the bold Sir Bedivere,
First made and latest left of all the knights,
Told, when the man was no more than a voice
In the white winter of his age, to those
With whom he dwelt, new faces, other minds.

For on their march to westward, Bedivere,
Who slowly paced among the slumbering host,
Heard in his tent the moanings of the King:

"I found Him in the shining of the stars,
I mark'd Him in the flowering of His fields,
But in His ways with men I find Him not.

I waged His wars, and now I pass and die.
O me! for why is all around us here
As if some lesser god had made the world,
But had not force to shape it as he would,
Till the High God behold it from beyond,
And enter it, and make it beautiful?
Or else as if the world were wholly fair,
But that these eyes of men are dense and dim,
And have not power to see it as it is—
Perchance, because we see not to the close;—
For I, being simple, though to work His will,
And have but stricken with the sword in vain,
And all whereon I lean'd in wife and friend
Is traitor to my peace, and all my realm
Reels back into the beast, and is no more.
My God, thou hast forgotten me in my death!
Nay—God my Christ—I pass but shall not die."

Then, ere that last weird battle in the west,
There came on Arthur sleeping, Gawain kill'd
In Lancelot's war, the ghost of Gawain blown
Along a wandering wind, and past his ear
Went shrilling: "Hollow, hollow all delight!
Hail, King! to-morrow thou shalt pass away.
Farewell! there is an isle of rest for thee.
And I am blown along a wandering wind,
And hollow, hollow, hollow all delight!"
And fainter onward, like wild birds that change
Their season in the night and wail their way
From cloud to cloud, down the long wind the dream
Shrill'd; but in going mingled with dim cries
Far in the moonlit haze among the hills,
As of some lonely city sack'd by night,
When all is lost, and wife and child with wail
Pass to new lords; and Arthur woke and call'd:
"Who spake? A dream. O, light upon the wind,
Thine, Gawain, was the voice—are these dim cries
Thine? or doth all that haunts the waste and wild
Mourn, knowing it will go along with me?"

This heard the bold sir Bedivere and spake:
"O me, my King, let pass whatever will,
Elves, and the harmless glamour of the field;
But in their stead thy name and glory cling

To all high places like a golden cloud
For ever; but as yet thou shall not pass.
Light was Gawain in life, and light in death
Is Gawain, for the ghost is as the man;
And care not thou for dreams from him, but rise—
I hear the steps of Modred in the west,
And with him many of thy people, and knights
Once thine, whom thou hast loved, but grosser grown
Than heathen, spitting at their vows and thee.
Right well in heart they know thee for the King.
Arise, go forth and conquer as of old.''

Then spake King Arthur to Sir Bedivere:
''Far other is this battle in the west
Whereto we move than when we strove in youth,
And brake the petty kings, and fought with Rome,
Or thrust the heathen from the Roman wall,
And shook him thro' the north. Ill doom is mine
To war against my people and my knights.
The king who fights his people fights himself.
And they my knights, who loved me once, the stroke
That strikes them dead is as my death to me.
Yet let us hence, and find or feel a way
Thro' this blind haze which, ever since I saw
One lying in the dust at Almesbury,
Hath folded in the passes of the world.''

Then rose the King and moved his host by night,
And ever push'd Sir Modred, league by league,
Back to the sunset bound of Lyonnesse—
A land of old upheaven from the abyss
By fire, to sink into the abyss again;
Where fragments of forgotten peoples dwelt,
And the long mountains ended in a coast
Of ever-shifting sand, and far away
The phantom circle of a moaning sea.
There the pursuer could pursue no more,
And he that fled no further fly the King;
And there, that day when the great light of heaven
Burn'd at his lowest in the rolling year,
On the waste sand by the waste sea they closed.
Nor ever yet had Arthur fought a fight
Like this last, dim, weird battle of the west.
A death-white mist slept over sand and sea,

Whereof the chill, to him who breathed it, drew
Down with his blood, till all his heart was cold
With formless fear; and even on Arthur fell
Confusion, since he saw not whom he fought.
For friend and foe were shadows in the mist,
And friend slew friend not knowing whom he slew;
And some had visions out of golden youth,
And some beheld the faces of old ghosts
Look in upon the battle; and in the mist
Was many a noble deed, many a base,
And chance and craft and strength in single fights,
And ever and anon with host to host
Shocks, and the splintering spear, the hard mail hewn,
Shield-breakings, and the clash of brands, the crash
Of battle-axes on shatter'd helms, and shrieks
After the Christ, of those who falling down
Look'd up for heaven, and only saw the mist;
And shouts of heathen and the traitor knights,
Oaths, insult, filth, and monstrous blasphemies,
Sweat, writhings, anguish, laboring of the lungs
In that close mist, and cryings for the light,
Moans of the dying, and voices of the dead.

Last, as by some one death-bed after wail
Of suffering, silence follows, or thro' death
Or death-like swoon, thus over all that shore,
Save for some whisper of the seething seas,
A dead hush fell; but when the dolorous day
Grew drearier toward twilight falling, came
A bitter wind, clear from the north, and blew
The mist aside, and with that wind the tide
Rose, and the pale King glanced across the field
Of battle. But no man was moving there;
Nor any cry of Christian heard thereon,
Nor yet of heathen; only the wan wave
Brake in among dead faces, to and fro
Swaying the helpless hands, and up and down
Tumbling the hollow helmets of the fallen,
And shiver'd brands that once had fought with Rome,
And rolling far along the gloomy shores
The voice of days of old and days to be.

Then spake King Arthur to Sir Bedivere,
And whiter than the mist that all day long
Had held the field of battle was the King:

"Hearest thou this great voice that shakes the world,
And wastes the narrow realm whereon we move,
And beats upon the faces of the dead,
My dead, as tho' they had not died for me?—
O Bedivere, for on my heart hath fallen
Confusion, till I know not what I am,
Nor whence I am, nor whether I be king;
Behold, I seem but king among the dead."

Then spoke the bold Sir Bedivere: "My King!
King everywhere! and so the dead have kings,
There also will I worship thee as king.
Yet still thy life is whole, and still I live
Who love thee; but who hates thee, he that brought
The heathen back among us, yonder stands,
Modred, unharm'd, the traitor of thine house."

Then spake the King: "My house hath been my doom.
But call not thou this traitor of my house
Who hath but dwelt beneath one roof with me.
My house are rather they who sware my vows,
Yea, even while they brake them, own'd me king.
And well for thee, saying in my dark hour,
When all the purport of my throne hath fail'd,
That quick or dead thou holdest me for king.
King am I, whatsoever be their cry;
And one last act of kinghood shalt thou see
Yet, ere I pass." And uttering this the King
Made at the man. Then Modred smote his liege
Hard on that helm which many a heathen sword
Had beaten thin; while Arthur at one blow,
Striking the last stroke with Excalibur,
Slew him, and, all but slain himself, he fell.

So all day long the noise of battle roll'd
Among the mountains by the winter sea,
Until King Arthur's Table, man by man,
Had fallen in Lyonnesse about their lord,
King Arthur; then, because his wound was deep,
The bold Sir Bedivere uplifted him,
And bore him to a chapel nigh the field,
A broken chancel with a broken cross,
That stood on a dark strait of barren land.
On one side lay the Ocean, and on one
Lay a great water, and the moon was full.

Then spake King Arthur to Sir Bedivere:
"The sequel of to-day unsolders all
The goodliest fellowship of famous knights
Whereof this world holds record. Such a sleep
They sleep—the men I loved. I think that we
Shall never more, at any future time,
Delight our souls with talk of knightly deeds,
Walking about the gardens and the halls
Of Camelot, as in the days that were.
I perish by this people which I made,—
Tho' Merlin sware that I should come again
To rule once more—but let what will be be,
I am so deeply smitten thro' the helm
That without help I cannot last till morn.
Thou therefore take my brand Excalibur,
Which was my pride; for thou rememberest how
In those old days, one summer noon, an arm
Rose up from out the bosom of the lake,
Clothed in white samite, mystic, wonderful,
Holding the sword—and how I row'd across
And took it, and have worn it, like a king;
And, wheresoever I am sung or told
In aftertime, this also shall be known.
But now delay not; take Excalibur,
And fling him far into the middle mere;
Watch what thou seest, and lightly bring me word."

To him replied the bold Sir Bedivere:
"It is not meet, Sir King, to leave thee thus,
Aidless, alone, and smitten thro' the helm—
A little thing may harm a wounded man;
Yet I thy hest will all perform at full,
Watch what I see, and lightly bring thee word."

So saying, from the ruin'd shrine he stept,
And in the moon athwart the place of tombs,
Where lay the mighty bones of ancient men,
Old knights, and over them the sea-wind sang
Shrill, chill, with flakes of foam. He, stepping down
By zigzag paths and juts of pointed rock,
Came on the shining levels of the lake.

There drew he forth the brand Excalibur,
And o'er him, drawing it, the winter moon,
Brightening the skirts of a long cloud, ran forth

And sparkled keen with frost against the hilt;
For all the haft twinkled with diamond sparks,
Myriads of topaz-lights, and jacinth-work
Of subtlest jewellery. He gazed so long
That both his eyes were dazzled as he stood,
This way and that dividing the swift mind,
In act to throw; but at the last it seem'd
Better to leave Excalibur conceal'd
There in the many-knotted water-flags,
That whistled stiff and dry about the marge.
So strode he back slow to the wounded King.

Then spake King Arthur to Sir Bedivere:
"Hast thou perform'd my mission which I gave?
What is it thou hast seen? or what hast heard?"

And answer made the bold Sir Bedivere:
"I heard the ripple washing in the reeds,
And the wild water lapping on the crag."

To whom replied King Arthur, faint and pale:
"Thou hast betray'd thy nature and thy name,
Not rendering true answer, as beseem'd
Thy fealty, nor like a noble knight;
For surer sign had follow'd, either hand,
Or voice, or else a motion of the mere.
This is a shameful thing for men to lie.
Yet now, I charge thee, quickly go again,
As thou art lief and dear, and do the thing
I bade thee, watch, and lightly bring me word."

Then went Sir Bedivere the second time
Across the ridge, and paced beside the mere,
Counting the dewy pebbles, fixt in thought;
But when he saw the wonder of the hilt,
How curiously and strangely chased, he smote
His palms together, and he cried aloud:

"And if indeed I cast the brand away,
Surely a precious thing, one worthy note,
Should thus be lost for ever from the earth,
Which might have pleased the eyes of many men.
What good should follow this, if this were done?
What harm, undone? Deep harm to disobey,

Seeing obedience is the bond of rule.
Were it well to obey then, if a king demand
An act unprofitable, against himself?
The King is sick, and knows not what he does.
What record or what relic of my lord
Should be to aftertime, but empty breath
And rumors of a doubt? But were this kept,
Stored in some treasure-house of mighty kings,
Some one might show it at a joust of arms,
Saying: "King Arthur's sword, Excalibur,
Wrought by the lonely Maiden of the Lake.
Nine years she wrought it, sitting in the deeps
Upon the hidden bases of the hills.'
So might some old man speak in the aftertime
To all the people, winning reverence.
But now much honor and much fame were lost."

So spake he, clouded with his own conceit,
And hid Excalibur the second time,
And so strode back slow to the wounded King.

Then spoke King Arthur, breathing heavily:
"What is it thou hast seen? or what hast heard?"

And answer made the bold Sir Bedivere:
"I heard the water lapping on the crag,
And the long ripple washing in the reeds."

To whom replied King Arthur, much in wrath:
"Ah miserable, and unkind, untrue,
Unknightly, traitor-hearted! Woe is me!
Authority forgets a dying king,
Laid widow'd of the power in his eye
That bow'd the will. I see thee what thou art,
For thou, the latest-left of all my knights,
In whom should meet the offices of all,
Thou wouldst betray me for the precious hilt;
Either from lust of gold, or like a girl
Valuing the giddy pleasure of the eyes.
Yet, for a man may fail in duty twice,
And the third time may prosper, get thee hence;
But, if thou spare to fling Excalibur,
I will arise and slay thee with my hands."

Then quickly rose Sir Bedivere, and ran,
And, leaping down the ridges lightly, plunged
Among the bulrush beds, and clutch'd the sword,
And strongly wheel'd and threw it. The great brand
Made lightnings in the splendor of the moon,
And flashing round and round, and whirl'd in an arch,
Shot like a streamer of the northern morn,
Seen where the moving isles of winter shock
By night, with noises of the Northern sea.
So flash'd and fell the brand Excalibur;
But ere he dipt the surface, rose an arm
Clothed in white samite, mystic, wonderful,
And caught him by the hilt, and brandish'd him
Three times, and drew him under in the mere.
And lightly went the other to the King.

Then spoke King Arthur, drawing thicker breath:
"Now see I by thine eyes that this is done.
Speak out; what is it thou hast heard, or seen?"

And answer made the bold Sir Bedivere:
"Sir King, I closed mine eyelids, lest the gems
Should blind my purpose, for I never saw,
Nor shall see, here or elsewhere, till I die,
Not tho' I live three lives of mortal men,
So great a miracle as yonder hilt.
Then with both hands I flung him, wheeling him;
But when I look'd again, behold an arm,
Clothed in white samite, mystic, wonderful,
That caught him by the hilt, and brandish'd him
Three times, and drew him under in the mere."

And answer made King Arthur, breathing hard:
"My end draws nigh; 't is time that I were gone.
Make broad thy shoulders to receive my weight,
And bear me to the margin; yet I fear
My wound hath taken cold, and I shall die."

So saying, from the pavement he half rose,
Slowly, with pain, reclining on his arm,
And looking wistfully with wide blue eyes
As in a picture. Him Sir Bedivere
Remorsefully regarded thro' his tears,
And would have spoken, but he found not words;

Then took with care, and kneeling on one knee,
O'er both his shoulders drew the languid hands,
And rising bore him thro' the place of tombs.

But, as he walk'd, King Arthur panted hard,
Like one that feels a nightmare on his bed
When all the house is mute. So sigh'd the King,
Muttering and murmuring at his ear, "Quick, quick!
I fear it is too late, and I shall die."
But the other swiftly strode from ridge to ridge,
Clothed with his breath, and looking, as he walk'd,
Larger than human on the frozen hills.
He heard the deep behind him, and a cry
Before. His own thought drove him like a goad.
Dry clash'd his harness in the icy caves
And barren chasms, and all to left and right
The bare black cliff clang'd round him, as he based
His feet on juts of slippery crag that rang
Sharp-smitten with the dint of armed heels—
And on a sudden, lo, the level lake,
And the long glories of the winter moon!

Then saw they how there hove a dusky barge,
Dark as a funeral scarf from stem to stern,
Beneath them; and descending they were ware
That all the decks were dense with stately forms,
Black-stoled, black-hooded, like a dream—by these
Three queens with crowns of gold—and from them rose
A cry that shiver'd to the tingling stars,
And, as it were one voice, an agony
Of lamentation, like a wind that shrills
All night in a waste land, where no one comes,
Or hath come, since the making of the world.

Then murmur'd Arthur, "Place me in the barge."
So to the barge they came. There those three queens
Put forth their hands, and took the King, and wept.
But she that rose the tallest of them all
And fairest laid his head upon her lap,
And loosed the shatter'd casque, and chafed his hands,
And call'd him by his name, complaining loud,
And dropping bitter tears against a brow
Striped with dark blood; for all his face was white
And colorless, and like the wither'd moon

Smote by the fresh beam of the springing east;
And all his greaves and cuisses dash'd with drops
Of onset; and the light and lustrous curls—
That made his forehead like a rising sun
High from the dais-throne—were parch'd with dust,
Or, clotted into points and hanging loose,
Mixt with the knightly growth that fringed his lips.
So like a shatter'd column lay the King;
Not like that Arthur who, with lance in rest,
From spur to plume a star of tournament,
Shot thro' the lists at Camelot, and charged
Before the eyes of ladies and of kings.

Then loudly cried the bold Sir Bedivere:
"Ah! my Lord Arthur, whither shall I go?
Where shall I hide my forehead and my eyes?
For now I see the true old times are dead,
When every morning brought a noble chance,
And every chance brought out a noble knight.
Such times have been not since the light that led
The holy Elders with the gift of myrrh.
But now the whole Round Table is dissolved
Which was an image of the mighty world;
And I, the last, go forth companionless,
And the days darken round me, and the years,
Among new men, strange faces, other minds."

And slowly answer'd Arthur from the barge:
"The old order changeth yielding place to new,
And God fulfils himself in many ways,
Lest one good custom should corrupt the world.
Comfort thyself; what comfort is in me?
I have lived my life, and that which I have done
May He within himself make pure! but thou,
If thou shouldst never see my face again,
Pray for my soul. More things are wrought by prayer
Than this world dreams of. Wherefore, let thy voice
Rise like a fountain for me night and day.
For what are men better than sheep or goats
That nourish a blind life within the brain,
If, knowing God, they lift not hands of prayer
Both for themselves and those who call them friend?
For so the whole round earth is every way

Bound by gold chains about the feet of God.
But now farewell, I am going a long way
With these thou seest—if indeed I go—
For all my mind is clouded with a doubt—
To the island-valley of Avilion;
Where falls not hail, or rain, or any snow,
Nor ever wind blows loudly; but it lies
Deep-meadow'd, happy, fair with orchard lawns
And bowery hollows crown'd with summer sea,
Where I will heal me of my grievous wound.''

So said he, and the barge with oar and sail
Moved from the brink, like some full-breasted swan
That, fluting a wild carol ere her death,
Ruffles her pure cold plume, and takes the flood
With swarthy webs. Long stood Sir Bedivere
Revolving many memories, till the hull
Look'd one black dot against the verge of dawn,
And on the mere the wailing died away.

But when that moan had past for evermore,
The stillness of the dead world's winter dawn
Amazed him, and he groan'd, ''The King is gone.''
And therewithal came on him the weird rhyme,
''From the great deep to the great deep he goes.''

Whereat he slowly turn'd and slowly clomb
The last hard footstep of that iron crag,
Thence mark'd the black hull moving yet, and cried:
''He passes to be king among the dead,
And after healing of his grievous wound
He comes again; but—if he come no more—
O me, be yon dark queens in yon black boat,
Who shriek'd and wail'd, the three whereat we gazed
On that high day, when, clothed with living light,
They stood before his throne in silence, friends
Of Arthur, who should help him at his need?''

Then from the dawn it seem'd there came, but faint
As from beyond the limit of the world,
Like the last echo born of a great cry,
Sounds, as if some fair city were one voice
Around a king returning from his wars.

Thereat once more he moved about, and clomb
Even to the highest he could climb, and saw,
Straining his eyes beneath an arch of hand,
Or thought he saw, the speck that bare the King,
Down that long water opening on the deep
Somewhere far off, pass on and on, and go
From less to less and vanish into light.
And the new sun rose bringing the new year.

—Alfred, Lord Tennyson

This long poem, a fragment of a projected history of the round table, is above all else a good story of knights and kings and adventures and the passing of King Arthur. It has what all good narrative and good history require: important deeds done by important people. But notice that Tennyson, although writing in the late nineteenth century, when priests, historians, poets, and philosophers had all gone their separate ways, cannot help raising in his history some important questions about the meaning behind human existence, which lead him inevitably—through his characters—to speculate on matters theological and philosophical. "I found Him in the shining stars," says Arthur of God, "But in His ways with men I find Him not." Somewhat further on he sounds like a modern existentialist philosopher: "King am I, whatsoever be their cry; / And one last act of kinghood shalt thou see / Yet, ere I pass." As the poem closes Tennyson has Arthur tell Bedivere, "More things are wrought by prayer / Than this world dreams of," a preachy statement even if it had not been sloganized on a hundred thousand billboards and bumper stickers. History becomes a vehicle for speculation. And, it would seem, Tennyson's vision of the powers that shape men's lives seems scarcely darker than that of the *Boewulf* poet.

Pretty Boy Floyd

If you'll gather 'round me, children,
A story I will tell,
About Pretty Boy Floyd, an outlaw,
Oklahoma knew him well.

It was in the town of Shawnee
On a Saturday afternoon,
His wife beside him in the wagon
As into town they rode.

There a deputy sheriff reproached him
In a manner rather rude
Using vulgar words of anger,
And his wife she overheard.

Pretty Boy grabbed a log chain,
The deputy grabbed his gun,
And in the fight that followed,
He laid that deputy down.

Then he took to the trees and timber
And lived a life of shame,
Every crime in Oklahoma
Was added to his name.

Yes, he took to the river bottom
Along the river shore,
And Pretty Boy found a welcome
At every farmer's door.

The papers said that Pretty Boy
Had robbed a bank each day,
While he was setting in some farmhouse
Three hundred miles away.

There's many a starving farmer
The same old story told
How the outlaw paid their mortgage
And saved their little home.

Others tell you 'bout a stranger
That came to beg a meal
And when the meal was finished
Left a thousand-dollar bill.

It was in Oklahoma City,
It was on Christmas Day,
There come a whole carload of groceries
With a note to say:

"You say that I'm an outlaw,
You say that I'm a thief.
Here's a Christmas dinner
For the families on relief."

Yes, as through this world I ramble,
I see lots of funny men,
Some will rob you with a six gun,
And some with a fountain pen.

But as through your life you'll travel,
Wherever you may roam,
You won't never see an outlaw
Drive a family from their home.

—*Woody Guthrie*

"This book," wrote Woody Guthrie in notes for this song in *Hard Hitting Songs for Hard-Hit People,* "just got some songs wrote by some people. Real people." Little people, he might have added, did add elsewhere. The book and the song are little people's history, with Guthrie as poet-historian. Nor is Guthrie shy about making his case, about laying his interpretation of history on the events he records. (In fact, whether Pretty Boy Floyd was hero or outlaw, victim or murderer is something we will never know, and something that even Guthrie himself could not have told us.) It is worth noting that, like the history of Homer's *Iliad* and the ballad singers, this song spent some time in the memory of its composer and his disciples before it was copyrighted in Guthrie's name, finally, in 1958.

Further Completion of Plat

Lt James Davis 14 acres 1717 and to share 4
more 1728/9 with his son-in-law James
Stanwood—all on the east side of the lower
road, defining therefore that stretch: the first
10 acres, May 23, 1717, are "of land and Rocks
between Joseph Ingarsons and Bryants."
Ingarson Ingersoll, and Bryant tied, as
Smallman, and James Stanwood is to be,
to Falmouth (Portland's) rearising

James Demerit,
the other later surviving one, with Ingersoll,
on the E side altogether—to Smallmans—
married Mary Briant and seems therefore
(as James Stanwood) to have come on,
as the fishermen and mariners did, to take over

earlier pasture uses of this higher land
up above Mill River. For, besides James Davis
his brother Ebenezer, and James' own son Elias,
also had acres, intermingled with John Day's
and Ezekiel Days',

                    and as the Days, but
as ship-owners, at the head of Mill River the Davises
were, like Captain Andrew Robinson, evidence how
quickly fishing came up in the 1st quarter of
the 18th century. And flushed their children
into Dogtown. Ebenezer died in 1732 leaving £3047
and Elias, coming on so fast the guess is he
was to be the strongest man in Gloucester, died
at 40 and already at sd age was worth

                    £4500

With a wharf at Canso (a fishing room);
with 6 schooners,

John, Mary, Molly, Flying Horse
& 3/4s of Greyhound and Elizabeth

                    [More on Joseph Ingersoll
to follow; and on the other side of the lower road,
Deacon Joseph Winslow, who bought from his father-in-law
Day, in 1724

—*Charles Olson*

Charles Olson's *Maximus Poems,* from which this fragment is taken, give off the sense of having some grand, overriding design, as if they were part of a weird, modern, distorted saga or *Iliad.* Into *Maximus* Olson threw everything: himself, the objective world of Gloucester, Massachusetts, local and national history. Sometimes the history shows up in great vaulting fragments that appear to have no *meaning* other than that they are curious fragments of America's—and Gloucester's—past.

First Party at Ken Kesey's with Hell's Angels

Cool black night thru the redwoods
cars parked outside in shade
behind the gate, stars dim above
the ravine, a fire burning by the side
porch and a few tired souls hunched over
in black leather jackets. In the huge
wooden house, a yellow chandelier
at 3AM the blast of loudspeakers
hi-fi Rolling Stones Ray Charles Beatles
Jumping Joe Jackson and twenty youths
dancing to the vibration thru the floor,
a little weed in the bathroom, girls in scarlet
tights, one muscular smooth skinned man
sweating dancing for hours, beer cans
bent littering the yard, a hanged man
sculpture dangling from a high creek branch,
children sleeping softly in their bedroom bunks.
And 4 police cars parked outside the painted
gate, red lights revolving in the leaves.

—*Allen Ginsberg*

History need not be grand when it is presented by the poet. In this short lyric Allen Ginsberg recreates a scene that will be familiar to those who have read Tom Wolfe's *The Electric Kool-Aid Acid Test:* a great moment in countercultural history, the first party at the home of novelist-turned-seer Ken Kesey with his Merry Pranksters, California acid heads, and the California Hell's Angels. Notice, however, that Ginsberg chooses *not* to interpret. He presents, or recreates, making permanent the ephemeral moment. Forever the four police cars, "red lights revolving" stand posed ironically against the male and female bodies, the damned juxtaposed against the elect, really not so different after all, fire in the lights, fire beside the porch, fire in the minds and hearts.

3. The Poet as Entertainer

A second role traditionally assigned to the poet is that of entertainer. In fact, in early societies it was the poet's function as historian that made him an entertainer because, as all writers know, people are enormously entertained by the artful telling and retelling of their own history. Celebrations in the old epic poems are always full of three kinds of entertainment: athletic competitions, races and games; food and drink; and the recitation of historical poems by a bard accompanying himself on a harp.

Poets entertain with many other kinds of poems, however. Tales of the mysterious, the supernatural, and the tragic have always been popular, as the border ballads make clear. The love song has a tradition quite as honorable as the epic poem, and over the long run it has proven far more durable: people still write love poems in an age of printed poetry, whereas epics—both written and oral—are largely dead. Even in the Middle Ages, however, love poems were still being sung by itinerant poets the likes of Bernart de Ventadorn, who wandered the countryside singing their love (and drinking) songs to the accompaniment of their own guitars for food, shelter, coins, or the favor of a beautiful woman.

Modern poets, perhaps overly impressed with other roles they think they ought to be playing, sometimes seem to resent any hint that they are in the entertainment business, although watching them pose at public readings one cannot help but realize they also perform, each in his own way. Dylan Thomas, Allen Ginsberg, Robert Bly, Lawrence Ferlinghetti, Robert Frost—to name only those who come most readily to mind—have been great performers of their work, as have been, naturally, such poets as Bob Dylan, John Lennon, Paul McCartney, Leonard Cohen, Joni Mitchell, who sing their work on stage and record. But even T. S. Eliot, who was usually insufferably stuffy in his Anglican high seriousness, could toss off *Old Possum's Book of Practical Cats,* filled with clever stories well-told, like "Macavity: The Mystery Cat."

One thing modern poets have been willing to enjoy, however, is "children's verse," which often seems little more than an excuse for light entertainment. And the more serious the poet, the more prone he seems to be to the lure of children's verse. Woody Guthrie and Carl Sandburg, who both might at times in their careers have been accused of almost ideological attachment to socialist reform, and whose work frequently burns with invective and demands for reform, wrote dozens of children's pieces. Vachel Lindsay, the poet-visionary who dedicated his life to leveling and then rebuilding (more beautifully) his home town of Springfield, Illinois, is best remembered today not for the town he built in his imagination, or the beautiful poetry he substituted for actual reconstruction, but for the entertaining little children's poem "I Have a Little Turtle."

Sometimes when poets comment on their own art they borrow the language of entertainment. "Poetry is like sports," Frost used to say—it's a play, a game, a performance. Bob Dylan, singing about art in "Mr. Tambourine Man," borrows the metaphor of a musical performer; Lawrence Ferlinghetti uses the metaphor of the trapeze artist, the acrobat, the circus performer in his poem "Constantly risking absurdity and death." As poets increasingly abandon their books to meet audiences face to face in readings, they realize more and more that, whatever else it may be, poetry is in part entertainment, and that poet goes unattended who cannot make at least a little show.

from Beowulf *(lines 1063–1164)*

Then song and revelry rose in the hall;
Before Healfdene's leader the harp was struck
And hall-joy wakened; the song was sung,
Hrothgar's gleeman rehearsed the lay
Of the sons of Finn when the terror befell them:

Hnaef of the Scyldings, the Half-Dane, fell in the Frisian slaughter;
Nor had Hildeburh cause to acclaim the faith of the Jutish folk,
Blameless, bereft of her brothers in battle, and stripped of her sons
Who fell overcome by their fate and wounded with spears!
Not for nothing Hoc's daughter bewailed death's bitter decree,
In the dawn under morning skies, when she saw the slaughter of kinsmen
In the place where her days had been filled with the fairest delights of the world.
Finn's thanes were slain in the fight, save only a few;
Nor could he do battle with Hengest or harry his shattered host;
And the Frisians made terms with the Danes, a truce, a hall for their dwelling,
A throne, and a sharing of rights with the sons of the Jutes,
And that Finn, the son of Folcwalda, each day would honor the Danes,
The host of Hengest, with gifts, with rings and guerdon of gold,
Such portion of plated treasure as he dealt to the Frisian folk
When he gladdened their hearts in the hall. So both were bound by the truce.

And Finn swore Hengest with oaths that were forceful and firm
He would rightfully rule his remnant, follow his council's decree,
And that no man should break the truce, or breach it by word or by will,
Nor the lordless in malice lament they were fated to follow
The man who had murdered their liege; and, if ever a Frisian
Fanned the feud with insolent speech, the sword should avenge it.
Then a funeral pyre was prepared, and gold was drawn from the hoard,
The best of the Scylding leaders was laid on the bier;
In the burning pile was a gleaming of blood-stained byrnies,
The gilded swine and the boar-helm hard from the hammer,
Many a warrior fated with wounds and fallen in battle.
And Hildeburh bade that her son be laid on the bier of Hnæf,
His body consumed in the surging flame on his uncle's shoulder.
Beside it the lady lamented, singing her mournful dirge.
The hero was placed on the pyre; the greates of funeral flames
Rolled with a roar to the skies at the burial barrow.
Heads melted with gashes gaped, the mortal wounds of the body,
Blood poured out in the flames; the fire, most greedy of spirits,
Swallowed up all whom battle had taken of both their peoples.
Their glory was gone! The warriors went to their homes,
Bereft of their friends, returning to Friesland, to city and strong-hold.
Then Hengest abode with Finn all the slaughter-stained winter,
But his heart longed ever for home, though he could not launch on the sea
His ring-stemmed ship, for the billows boiled with the storm,
Strove with the wind, and the winter locked ocean in bonds of ice;
Till a new spring shone once more on the dwellings of men,
The sunny and shining days which ever observe their season.
The winter was banished afar, and fair the bosom of earth.
Then the exile longed to be gone, the guest from his dwelling,
But his thoughts were more on revenge than on voyaging over the wave,
Plotting assault on the Jutes, renewal of war with the sword.
So he spurned not the naked hint when Hunlafing laid in his lap

The battle-flasher, the best of blades, well known to the Jutes!
In his own home death by the sword befell Finn, the fierce-
hearted,
When Guthlaf and Oslaf requited the grim attack,
The woe encountered beyond the sea, the sorrow they suffered,
Nor could bridle the restive spirits within their breasts!
Then the hall was reddened with blood and bodies of
foemen,
Finn killed in the midst of his men, and the fair queen taken.
The Scylding warriors bore to their ships all treasure and
wealth,
Such store as they found in the home of Finn of jewels and
gems.
And the noble queen they carried across the sea-paths,
Brought her back to the Danes, to her own dear people.

So the song was sung, the lay recited,
The sound of revelry rose in the hall.
Stewards poured wine from wondrous vessels;
And Wealhtheow, wearing a golden crown,
Came forth in state where the two were sitting,
Courteous comrades, uncle and nephew,
Each true to the other in ties of peace.

—*trans. Charles Kennedy*

In this poem within a poem the *Beowulf* poet describes the feast at Heorot (the Danes' assembly hall) on the day after Beowulf has killed the monster Grendel. There is eating and drinking, and the usual horse races, and then the court poet, in entertaining the Haelfdanes and their heroic visitor, retells a bit of Danish history, the story of a feud between the Frisians and the Danes, in which a company of Danes under their king Hnaef are treacherously set upon inside the Frisian's hall at Finnsburgh while on an apparently peaceful visit. The battle lasts for five days, but at length Hnaef is killed and the survivors, lead by Hengest, sue for peace with the exhausted Finns. The dead on both sides are burned, and Danes and Frisians settle in for an uneasy winter. The feud smolders through the dark months, as these things have a way of doing, and in the spring Hengest avenges the events of the previous year, killing Finn and taking his wife—a Dane—and much plunder back with him to Denmark.

As you read over this section of *Beowulf,* you will note that only the second half of this history is told by the court poet quoted by the *Beowulf* poet. Apparently his audience was familiar enough with the tale that he could begin with the funeral of the slain Hnaef, and everyone knew what he was talking about. (The beginning of the story we know because the history survived in another written fragment of Anglo-Saxon poetry called, not surprisingly, "The Fight at Finnsburgh." It too is incomplete, so we are still missing many of the details of this feud.) You may also catch the suggestion that the poet at Hoerot was singing his poem to the accompaniment of a harp. This was standard practice in early times, and the remains of such a harp were found in an Anglo-Saxon burial ship unearthed in this century at Sutton Hoo, England. The ancient poet, singing his history, is not so very different from a modern folk singer like Woody Guthrie, singing his own histories, half historian, half entertainer.

To Bel Vezer on Her Dismissal of the Poet

In vain at Ventadorn full many a friend
    Will seek me, for my lady doth refuse me,
And thither small I wish my way to wend,
    If ever thus despitefully she use me.
On me she frowningly her brow doth bend,
For why? My love to her hath ne'er an end,
    But of no other crime can she accuse me.

The fish full heedless falleth on the prey,
    And by the hook is caught; e'en so I found me
Falling full heedless upon love one day,
    Nor knew my plight till flames raged high around me,
That fiercer burn than furnace by my fay;
Yet ne'er an inch from them can I away,
    So fast the fetters of her love have bound me.

I marvel not her love should fetter me,
    Unto such beauty none hath e'er attained;
So courteous, gay, and fair, and good, is she,
    That for her worth all other worth hath waned;
I cannot blame her, she of blame is free,
Yet I would gladly speak if blame there be,
    But finding none, from speaking have refrained.

I send unto Provence great love and joy,
    And greater joy than ever tongue expresseth,
Great wonders work thereby, strange arts employ,
    Since that I give my heart no whit possesseth.

—Bernart de Ventadorn (trans. Ida Farnell)

3. *wend:* go. 12. *fay:* faith.

In this song Bernart complains of his love for lady Bel Vezer and of her cruelty in dismissing him from court, casting him out into the world to wander on down the line. In writing the poem (or song), however, the poet was undoubtedly addressing himself more to the lady than to his friends, making one last plea, as it were, for his cause . . . and seeking food, shelter, a few coins, and the lady's "favor." Notice the comparisons: the poet in love is caught like a fish on a hook; he burns like fire; he is bound in fetters. Some things have changed since the twelfth century, but not love.

Macavity: The Mystery Cat

Macavity's a Mystery Cat: he's called the Hidden Paw—
For he's the master criminal who can defy the Law.
He's the bafflement of Scotland Yard, the Flying Squad's despair:
For when they reach the scene of crime—*Macavity's not there!*

Macavity, Macavity, there's no one like Macavity,
He's broken every human law, he breaks the law of gravity.
His powers of levitation would make a fakir stare,
And when you reach the scene of crime—*Macavity's not there!*
You may seek him in the basement, you may look up in the air—
But I tell you once and once again, *Macavity's not there!*

Macavity's a ginger cat, he's very tall and thin;
You would know him if you saw him, for his eyes are sunken in.
His brow is deeply lined with thought, his head is highly domed;
His coat is dusty from neglect, his wiskers are uncombed.
He sways his head from side to side, with movements like a snake;
And when you think he's half asleep, he's always wide awake.

Macavity, Macavity, there's no one like Macavity,
For he's a fiend in feline shape, a monster of depravity.
You may meet him in a by-street, you may see him in the square—
But when a crime's discovered, then *Macavity's not there!*

He's outwardly respectable. (They say he cheats at cards.)
And his footprints are not found in any file of Scotland Yard's.
And when the larder's looted, or the jewel-case is rifled,
Or when the milk is missing, or another Peke's been stifled,
Or the greenhouse glass is broken, and the trellis past repair—
Ay, there's the wonder of the thing! *Macavity's not there!*

And when the Foreign Office find a Treaty's gone astray,
Or the Admiralty lose some plans and drawings by the way,
There may be a scrap of paper in the hall or on the stair—
But it's useless to investigate—*Macavity's not there!*
And when the loss has been disclosed, the Secret Service say:
"It *must* have been Macavity!"—but he's a mile away.
You'll be sure to find him resting, or a-licking of his thumbs,
Or engaged in doing complicated long division sums.

Macavity, Macavity, there's no one like Macavity,
There never was a Cat of such deceitfulness and suavity.
He always has an alibi, and one or two to spare:
At whatever time the deed took place—MACAVITY WASN'T THERE!
And they say that all the Cats whose wicked deeds are widely known
(I might mention Mungojerrie, I might mention Griddlebone)
Are nothing more than agents for the Cat who all the time
Just controls their operations: the Napoleon of Crime!

—*T. S. Eliot*

"What is all this?" you might well ask of the poet who wrote "The Waste Land" and *Christianity and Culture.* "A good performance" is the only possible answer, some carefully contrived and—to judge from the audience's reaction to Eliot's reading of the poem—a magnificently performed piece of pure entertainment.

The Little Turtle

(A Recitation for Martha Wakefield, Three Years Old)

There was a little turtle.
He lived in a box.
He swam in a puddle.
He climbed on the rocks.

He snapped at a mosquito.
He snapped at a flea.
He snapped at a minnow.
And he snapped at me.

He caught the mosquito.
He caught the flea.
He caught the minnow.
But he didn't catch me.

—*Vachel Lindsay*

What makes this poem so cute? What makes little kids enjoy it? Does it have any significance/meaning at all for adults? Is it poetry?

Mr. Tambourine Man

Hey! Mr. Tambourine Man, play a song for me,
I'm not sleepy and there is no place I'm going to.
Hey! Mr. Tambourine Man, play a song for me,
In the jingle jangle morning I'll come followin' you.

Though I know that evenin's empire has returned into sand,
Vanished from my hand,
Left me blindly here to stand but still not sleeping.
My weariness amazes me, I'm branded on my feet,
I have no one to meet
And the ancient empty street's too dead for dreaming.

Hey! Mr. Tambourine Man, play a song for me,
I'm not sleepy and there is no place I'm going to.
Hey! Mr. Tambourine Man, play a song for me,
In the jingle jangle morning I'll come followin' you.

Take me on a trip upon your magic swirlin' ship,
My senses have been stripped, my hands can't feel to grip,
My toes too numb to step, wait only for my boot heels
To be wanderin'.
I'm ready to go anywhere, I'm ready for to fade
Into my own parade, cast your dancing spell my way,
I promise to go under it.

Hey! Mr. Tambourine Man, play a song for me,
I'm not sleepy and there is no place I'm going to.
Hey! Mr. Tambourine Man, play a song for me,
In the jingle jangle morning I'll come followin' you.

Though you might hear laughin', spinnin', swingin' madly
across the sun,
It's not aimed at anyone, it's just escapin' on the run
And but for the sky there are no fences facin'.
And if you hear vague traces of skippin' reels of rhyme
To your tambourine in time, it's just a ragged clown behind,
I wouldn't pay it any mind, it's just a shadow you're
Seein' that he's chasing.

Hey! Mr. Tambourine Man, play a song for me,
I'm not sleepy and there is no place I'm going to.
Hey! Mr. Tambourine Man, play a song for me,
In the jingle jangle morning I'll come followin' you.

Then take me disappearin' through the smoke rings of my
mind,
Down the foggy ruins of time, far past the frozen leaves,
The haunted, frightened trees, out to the windy beach,
Far from the twisted reach of crazy sorrow.
Yes, to dance beneath the diamond sky with one hand waving
free,
Silhouetted by the sea, circled by the circus sands,
With all memory and fate driven deep beneath the waves,
Let me forget about today until tomorrow.

Hey! Mr. Tambourine Man, play a song for me,
I'm not sleepy and there is no place I'm going to.
Hey! Mr. Tambourine Man, play a song for me,
In the jingle jangle morning I'll come followin' you.

—Bob Dylan

"Do you consider yourself primarily a poet?" Nora Ephron once asked Bob Dylan in an interview. "No," he answered, objecting to her definition of "poet"; "I'm a trapeze artist."

This song says a great deal about music and the state of Dylan's own head. But it makes some statements about poetry as well: the magic swirling ship is Dylan's own art, and it's all a trip, and that trip is able to transport both the song writer and his audience from the nightmare of reality into a dreamworld of oblivion and beauty.

Constantly risking absurdity

Constantly risking absurdity
and death
whenever he performs
above the heads
of his audience
the poet like an acrobat
climbs on rime
to a high wire of his own making
and balancing on eyebeams
above a sea of faces
paces his way
to the other side of day
performing entrechats
and sleight-of-foot tricks
and other high theatrics
and all without mistaking
any thing
for what it may not be

For he's the super realist
who must perforce perceive
taut truth
before the taking of each stance or step
in his supposed advance
toward that still higher perch
where Beauty stands and waits
with gravity
to start her death-defying leap

And he
a little charleychaplin man
who may or may not catch
her fair eternal form
spreadeagled in the empty air
of existence

—*Lawrence Ferlinghetti*

Here is Dylan's trapeze artist in action. Behind Ferlinghetti's metaphor, however, are some fairly important statements about art, what it is, how it behaves. What does the poet have to say about his subject, about his art?

Bring Us in Good Ale

Bring us in good ale, and bring us in good ale;
For our Blessed Lady's sake, bring us in good ale!

Bring us no brown bread, for that is made of bran;
Nor bring us no white bread, for therein is no game;
    But bring us in good ale.

Bring us in no beef, for there are many bones;
But bring us in good ale, for that goes down at once;
    And bring us in good ale.

Bring us in no bacon, for that is passing fat;
But bring us in good ale, and give us enough of that;
    And bring us in good ale.

Bring us in no mutton, for that is often lean;
Nor bring us in no tripe, for they be seldom clean;
    But bring us in good ale.

Bring us in no eggs, for there are many shells;
But bring us in good ale, and give us nothing else;
    And bring us in good ale.

Bring us in no butter, for therein are many hairs;
Nor bring us in no pig's flesh, for that will make us boars;
    But bring us in good ale.

Bring us in no capon's flesh, for that is often dear;
Nor bring us in no duck's flesh, for they slobber in the mere;
    But bring us in good ale.

—*anonymous*

21. *dear:* expensive. 22. *mere:* pond.

Here is an old drinking song from the Middle Ages, sung no doubt by many a student in the small hours of the morning when they had better have been studying. Clearly it was a song: its first two lines are a refrain to follow each stanza as another stein of ale was poured down. Just as clearly, it makes precious little claim to being "poetry" in the high sense: it lacks profundity as well as sophistication. The meter is rough, the rhymes (even in the original Middle English) only approximate. Is it a poem? Is it art? Is there any reason for calling this poetry?

4. The Poet as Conscience

Many people are offended by the notion of poetry as "mere entertainment" or "mere art for art's sake" because they think the poet should function as a moral force in society, a sort of social critic who speaks out broadly for charity and responsibility and "the humanistic virtues," and particularly on specific events and issues as they present themselves. It is the poet's job to instill in a reader Virtue with the capital *V,* to make him in Sir Philip Sidney's words "a moral individual." And it's the poet's job to cry out against human injustice, against the innumerable (and, alas, omnipresent) examples of man's inhumanity to man.

At its worst, this view reduces the poet to a moral booster, a preacher or a school teacher who gives rhymed instructions on the necessity for being good, or the evils of sloth, capitalism, or John D. Rockefeller. Poets, being sensitive and intelligent people, resist oversimplification. They dislike seeing things in blacks and whites, and most of all they resist impressment into ideologies, be they capitalism, socialism, or Republicanism. So while most poets are sensitive to any form of human suffering, many have serious reservations about playing the role of conscience, even when a social and moral conscience is desperately needed. Particularly in the twentieth century poets have resisted this role, partly in reaction against the extreme moralism of nineteenth-century poetry (Tennyson's "more things are wrought by prayer/ Than this world dreams of" is but one example, and that among the least offensive), partly because poetry has removed itself to the colleges and universities, where detachment prevails.

However, always just below the surface of the poet's skin lurks the capacity for moral outrage and the impetus to cry out in broader or more specific terms. The 1960s were a period of great social and political turmoil, when hundreds of thousands of persons took to the streets, when songs *and poems* of moral indignation became quite popular. "We want 'poems that kill.' / Assassin poems," wrote Imamu Amiri Baraka (LeRoi Jones) in "Black Art."

The most obvious form of poet as conscience is the protest poem: a poem occasioned by a particular event designed specifically to call attention to the moral outrage that event represents. Among more detached critics these topical poems (songs) are supposed to be an embarrassment once the cause for which they were written has dropped out of the public consciousness. In fact, the poems / songs are supposed to have short lives, and thus lack the "timelessness" required of great poetry. Perhaps. But fifteen years after Dylan first sang "The Lonesome Death of Hattie Carroll" folksinger Jim Craig was singing it in a Chicago coffee house, introducing it with both an apology and a warning: "This is an old song, you might have forgotten about it. I haven't sung it for a long time myself, but this stuff is still going on and somebody ought to be talking about it." Causes may die; man being what he is, social injustice never seems to.

In fact, the poet has played the public conscious for any number of centuries, in any number of cultures. Early in ninth-century China, Po Chü-I recounted his visit to the flower market in which he was struck by the great and immoral difference between rich and poor. During the nineteenth century Percy Shelley and William Blake were ripping George III and English politicians in criticism to rival the worst anyone said about Lyndon Johnson and Vietnam. Early in the twentieth century Edwin Arlington Robinson was protesting callous robber barons, and Carl Sandburg and Edgar Lee Masters were bitterly attacking bankers, lawyers, railroad magnates, all the pillars of the economic establishment. Social injustices, and poetic outrage over social injustices, had been going on long, long before Dylan wrote "The Lonesome Death . . ." or Robert Bly wrote "Asian Peace Offers Rejected Without Publication."

The greatest social injustice, the greatest immorality is always the death of the human soul. Specific instances of justice miscarried, the rich squandering their wealth while the poor starve, a war fought brutally and stupidly are all but manifestations of this unhappy smallness of spirit, this blindness, this proclivity toward violence buried in the human spirit. All poems of protest and moral outrage work toward this root from specific causes and events. But it's possible for a poet to come directly to the root of the matter, and treat the issue of good and evil directly—or indirectly by choosing a more innocent metaphor. In "Autumn Begins in Martins Ferry, Ohio," for example, James Wright looks at football. But football to Wright is only a symbol of some innate tendency in Americans toward violence and destruction, frequently self-destruction. And it is the same violence, grafted in our bones, that created the Vietnam War. And a poem about football becomes a poem in protest against the War and finds itself in Robert Bly and David Ray's *A Poetry Reading Against the Vietnam War.*

Songwriters too can be subtle in their social statements. In the broadest sense of "protest songs," the very best work of Paul Simon, Bob Dylan, and the Beatles is social protest: "The Boxer" and "American Tune," *Sgt. Pepper's Lonely Hearts Club Band, John Wesley Harding,* many, many other songs and albums. And the music of protest continued from the sixties into the seventies, less direct, usually, than "The Lonesome Death of Hattie Carroll" or "A Working Class Hero," but significant acts of songwriting-poet acting as moral conscience. The blindness of Elton John's song "Daniel," for example, is a kind of analogue for social and moral blindness, the pain of having seen so much that one simply cannot bear to look at anything else.

The Lonesome Death of Hattie Carroll

William Zanzinger killed poor Hattie Carroll
With a cane that he twirled around his diamond ring finger
At a Baltimore hotel society gath'rin'.
And the cops were called in and his weapon took from him
As they rode him in custody down to the station
And booked William Zanzinger for first-degree murder.
But you who philosophize disgrace and criticize all fears,
Take the rag away from your face.
Now ain't the time for your tears.

William Zanzinger, who at twenty-four years
Owns a tobacco farm of six hundred acres
With rich wealthy parents who provide and protect him
And high office relations in the politics of Maryland,
Reacted to his deed with a shrug of his shoulders
And swear words and sneering, and his tongue it was snarling,
In a matter of minutes on bail was out walking.
But you who philosophize disgrace and criticize all fears,
Take the rag away from your face.
Now ain't the time for your tears.

Hattie Carroll was a maid of the kitchen.
She was fifty-one years old and gave birth to ten children
Who carried the dishes and took out the garbage
And never sat once at the head of the table
And didn't even talk to the people at the table
Who just cleaned up all the food from the table
And emptied the ashtrays on a whole other level,
Got killed by a blow, lay slain by a cane
That sailed through the air and came down through the room,
Doomed and determined to destroy all the gentle.
And she never done nothing to William Zanzinger.
But you who philosophize disgrace and criticize all fears,
Take the rag away from your face.
Now ain't the time for your tears.

In the courtroom of honor, the judge pounded his gavel
To show that all's equal and that the courts are on the level
And that the strings in the books ain't pulled and persuaded
And that even the nobles get properly handled
Once that the cops have chased after and caught 'em
And that the ladder of law has no top and no bottom,
Stared at the person who killed for no reason
Who just happened to be feelin' that way without warnin'.
And he spoke through his cloak, most deep and distinguished,
And handed out strongly, for penalty and repentance,
William Zanzinger with a six-month sentence.
Oh, but you who philosophize disgrace and criticize all fears,
Bury the rag deep in your face
For now's the time for your tears.

—Bob Dylan

Abstract the story of Hattie Carroll and William Zanzinger from Dylan's protest song. What happened? What does Dylan find most objectionable in the whole story? Is this stuff still going on?

The Flower Market

In the Royal City spring is almost over:
Tinkle, tinkle—the coaches and the horsemen pass.
We tell each other "This is the peony season":
And follow with the crowd that goes to the Flower Market.
"Cheap and dear—no uniform price:
The cost of the plant depends on the number of blossoms.
For the fine flower,—a hundred pieces of damask:
For the cheap flower,—five bits of silk.
Above is spread an awning to protect them;
Around is woven a wattle fence to screen them.
When they are transplanted, they will not lose their beauty."
Each household thoughtlessly follows the custom,
Man by man, no one realizing.
There happened to be an old farm labourer
Who came by chance that way.
He bowed his head and sighed a deep sigh:
But this sigh nobody understood.
He was thinking, "A cluster of deep-red flowers
Would pay the taxes of ten poor houses."

—Po Chu-I (translated by Arthur Waley)

London

I wander through each charter'd street,
Near where the charter'd Thames does flow,
And mark in every face I meet
Marks of weakness, marks of woe.

In every cry of every Man,
In every Infant's cry of fear,
In every voice, in every ban
The mind-forg'd manacles I hear.

How the chimney-sweeper's cry
Every black'ning church appalls;
And the hapless soldier's sigh
Runs in blood down palace walls.

But most through midnight streets I hear
How the youthful harlot's curse
Blasts the new-born infant's tear,
And blights with plagues the marriage hearse.

—*William Blake*

Blake's critique of London in the late eighteenth century lists several specific situations crying aloud for remedy: the chimney sweeps, young children blackened with soot and subjected not only to hard work but to lung diseases as well; the soldier, impressed against his will and killed so that some noble might live extravagantly; the young prostitute, whose curse blights both marriage and childbirth. Only in the first case does life seem to have changed significantly in the intervening century and a half, and in much of the world children still spend their time working instead of learning or playing.

But what bothers Blake more seems to be the "built in" nature of this corruption. The marks of weakness and woe seem to stem from structure and organization, oppressive organization, which blights imagination and freedom of spirit. By this definition, of course, modern American education is quite as objectionable as sweeping chimneys. And by this definition repression is just as built into the streets, into society, into human life today as it was in 1894. The chains that bind us remain—and they are "mind-forg'd," a result as much of our own thinking as anything else.

A Working Class Hero

As soon as you're born they make you feel small.
By giving you no time instead of it all.
Till the pain is so big you feel nothing at all.
A working class hero is something to be.
A working class hero is something to be.

They hurt you at home and they hit you at school.
They hate you if you're clever and they despise a fool.
Till you're so fucking crazy you can't follow their rules.
A working class hero is something to be.
A working class hero is something to be.

When they've tortured and scared you for twenty odd years,
Then they expect you to pick a career.
When you can't really function you're so full of fear.
A working class hero is something to be.
A working class hero is something to be.

Keep you doped with religion and sex on TV.
And you think you're so clever and classless and free,
But you're still fucking peasants as far as I can see.
A working class hero is something to be.
A working class hero is something to be.

There's room at the top they are telling you still,
But first you must learn how to smile as you kill,
If you want to be like the folks on the hill,
A working class hero is something to be.

A working class hero is something to be,
If you want to be a hero well just follow me,
If you want to be a hero well just follow me.

—*John Lennon*

Sonnet: England in 1819

An old, mad, blind, despised, and dying king,—
Princes, the dregs of their dull race, who flow
Through public scorn,—mud from a muddy spring,—
Rulers who neither see, nor feel, nor know,

But leech-like to their fainting country cling,
Till they drop, blind in blood, without a blow,—
A people starved and stabbed in the untilled field,—
An army, which liberticide and prey
Makes as a two-edged sword to all who wield,—
Golden and sanguine laws which tempt and slay;
Religion Christless, Godless—a book sealed;
A Senate,—Time's worst statute unrepealed,—
Are graves, from which a glorious Phantom may
Burst, to illumine our tempestuous day.

—*Percy Bysshe Shelley*

1. *dying king:* George III, who died the year after Shelley wrote this poem. 12. *Time's worst statue:* the law which penalized Roman Catholics for being Roman Catholics.

This sonnet certainly rivals even the most uncomplimentary things said about Lyndon Johnson during the 1960s, the high point in our times of the poet as conscience. What specific charges does Shelley level against his government? How would you interpret "golden and sanguine laws which tempt and slay"? What effect does Shelley get in line one by stringing together a series of short adjectives separated by commas? What comparisons does he use to degrade king and nobility?

It is worth noting that for all its topicality, this poem has endured for a century and a half, and is printed in most selected poems of Shelley. Why do you think it has stayed in the public consciousness so long?

Asian Peace Offers Rejected Without Publication

These suggestions by Asians are not taken seriously.
We know Rusk smiles as he passes them to someone.
Men like Rusk are not men:
They are bombs waiting to be loaded in a darkened hangar.
Rusk's assistants eat hurriedly,
Talking of Teilhard de Chardin,
Longing to get back to their offices
So they can cling to the underside of the steel wings shuddering faintly in the high altitudes.
They land first and hand the coffee mug to the drawn pilot.
They start the projector, and show the movie about the mad professor.

Lost angels huddled on a night branch!
The waves crossing
And recrossing beneath,
The sound of the rampaging Missouri—
Bending the reeds again and again—something inside us
Like a ghost train in the Rockies
About to be buried in snow!
Its long hoot
Making the owl in the Douglas fir turn his head . . .

—*Robert Bly*

2. *Rusk:* Dean Rusk, Secretary of State under Lyndon Johnson. 6. *Teilhard de Chardin:* French Jesuit priest, geologist and philosopher (1881–1955), author of *The Phenomenon of Man,* which achieved considerable popularity among middle brows during the sixties.

Speaking about the assassination of John F. Kennedy in 1963, Bly once told a group of college students that in the great public lament for the dead president he heard a cry of despair over the whole country, a kind of "Ooooh, here it all goes!" To what extent is that idea contained in this poem about unpublished peace proposals? Do you think Bly was right? If the rejection out of hand of peace proposals is, like the Kennedy assassination, but a symptom for some deeper malaise, what might that deeper problem be? What does Bly think it is? Is America essentially healthier or sicker than it was fifteen years ago?

Autumn Begins in Martins Ferry, Ohio

In the Shreve High Football stadium,
I think of Polacks nursing long beers in Tiltonsville,
And gray faces of Negroes in the blast furnace at Benwood,
And the ruptured night watchman of Wheeling Steel,
Dreaming of heroes.

All the proud fathers are ashamed to go home.
Their women cluck like starved pullets,
Dying for love.

Therefore,
Their sons grow suicidally beautiful
At the beginning of October,
And gallop terribly against each other's bodies.

—*James Wright*

Martins Ferry, Ohio, is not far from the area in western Pennsylvania in which the 1979 movie *The Deer Hunter* was set. You might wish to compare and contrast those statements on the Vietnam War, both in their metaphors and in their techniques.

5. The Poet as Visionary

One reason poets are so sensitive to the injustice and absurdity of what is, is that they usually have very strong senses of what might be or what ought to be. While poets, these days at least, are not much for practical programs of social improvement, they often dream brave and idealistic dreams of the future. For all their impracticalities and reluctance to be ideological and programmatic, poets provide an extraordinary source of vision.

Singing songs of the spirit, however, can be a risky business for any number of reasons. First, vision—especially if it gets preachy—can be as irritating as the stinging criticism of the poet-as-conscience, which may account for the general rejection of such poetry by American readers. Second, vision may seem too impractical, and the poet may find himself ridiculed into silence (or suicide) by his more sensible countrymen. Vachel Lindsay was in his day a great mystical visionary with brave plans for quite literally reconstructing his world. When New York defeated him, he returned to Illinois and settled for rebuilding his home town of Springfield. When Springfield defeated him (and, to be fair, other aspects of his life as well), he drank a bottle of Lysol.

Or a poet may succumb to the constant pressures to become a spokesman for the moral and ethical norms of his society, to reinforce what is rather than paint what might be. Certainly this is more lucrative, even if it is an end to visions. So the poet ends up, like Dryden in "Annus Mirabilis," sounding like a spokesman for the king, the president, or the chamber of commerce.

A fourth problem with poets as visionaries is that they often sound romantic and sentimental, and given over to "the power of positive thinking." Most offensive in this case is so-called "inspirational verse," which usually ends up sounding like a parody of itself:

When skies are dark and the night is deep,
When nightmares keep me from my sleep,
When the mountain is too high and steep,
When dangers all around me creep,
And troubles pile up in a heap,
I think of what my mother said,
With hairs of gray upon her head,

As she lay dying on her bed:
"The world has much of gold and lead;
Some days it's steak and some days bread.
But here's the way to get ahead:
When you're beset by doubts and dread,
And you've no place to lay your head,
No tears of sad self-pity shed,
But look to God and press ahead instead."

We might go on like this. Or we might look instead at the sermon William Cullen Bryant gave us in "To a Waterfowl," or Longfellow's "A Psalm of Life," either of which might be regarded as a paradigm of inspirational verse.

Still, people need vision, and poets will dream. "You may say I'm a dreamer," John Lennon sang in "Imagine," "but I'm not the only one." And he persisted in his vision, the same vision he expressed in "Mind Games," a vision for children of the sixties (and seventies, and eighties) to live by. Yes is the answer. And somewhere down the road, it may just happen that the visions of Lennon, like the visions of Whitman in Dave Etter's poem "Green-Eyed Boy After Reading Whitman and Sandburg," will help someone reconstruct his work, fish for his lost soul.

It is not even necessary for poetic visions to preach to us at all. In "The Rumor," Robbie Robertson (of the Band) had a dream that amounted to nothing more than "let the fog roll away." Still, that dream is as compelling as the visions with which Wordworth was trying to inspire us in "The World Is Too Much with Us," or of which Lennon sang in his songs. Usually poets are understated in their vision, prefering to extol, rather than preach about, what ought to be, what once was, what could be again. And in reminding us of "the soul's history / Through corridors of light" (the phrase is Spender's), they play a very essential role in any society.

Sonnet: Oh for a Poet

Oh for a poet—for a beacon bright
To rift this changless glimmer of dead gray;
To spirit back the Muses, long astray,
And flush Parnassus with a newer light;
To put these little sonnet-men to flight
Who fashion, in a shrewd mechanic way,
Songs without souls, that flicker for a day,
To vanish in irrevocable night.

What does it mean, this barren age of ours?
Here are the men, the women, and the flowers,
The seasons, and the sunset, as before.
What does it mean? Shall there not one arise
To wrench one banner from the western skies,
And mark it with his name forevermore?

—*Edwin Arlington Robinson*

4. *Parnassus:* a mountain in southern Greece sacred in Greek mythology to Apollo, the god of wisdom, and the Muses, who presided over the arts.

On the Building of Springfield

Let not our town be large, remembering
That little Athens was the Muses' home,
That Oxford rules the heart of London still,
That Florence gave the Renaissance to Rome.

Record it for the grandson of your son—
A city is not builded in a day:
Our little town cannot complete her soul
Till countless generations pass away.

Now let each child be joined as to a church
To her perpetual hopes, each man ordained:
Let every street be made a reverent aisle
Where Music grows and Beauty is unchained.

Let Science and Machinery and Trade
Be slaves of her, and make her all in all,
Building against our blatant, restless time
An unseen, skillful, medieval wall.

Let every citizen be rich toward God.
Let Christ the beggar, teach divinity.
Let no man rule who holds his money dear.
Let this, our city, be our luxury.

We should build parks that students from afar
Would choose to starve in, rather than go home,
Fair little squares, with Phidian ornament,
Food for the spirit, milk and honeycomb.

Songs shall be sung by us in that good day,
Songs we have written, blood within the rhyme
Beating, as when Old England still was glad,—
The purple, rich Elizabethan time.

. . . .

Say, is my prophecy too fair and far?
I only know, unless her faith be high,
The soul of this, our Nineveh, is doomed,
Our little Babylon will surely die.

Some city on the breast of Illinois
No wiser and no better at the start
By faith shall rise redeemed, by faith shall rise
Bearing the western glory in her heart.

The genius of the Maple, Elm and Oak,
The secret hidden in each grain of corn,
The glory that the prairie angels sing
At night when sons of Life and Love are born,

Born but to struggle, squalid and alone,
Broken and wandering in their early years.
When will they make our dusty streets their goal,
Within our attics hide their sacred tears?

When will they start our vulgar blood athrill
With living language, words that set us free?
When will they make a path of beauty clear
Between our riches and our liberty?

We must have many Lincoln-hearted men.
A city is not builded in a day.
And they must do their work, and come and go,
While countless generations pass away.

—*Vachel Lindsay*

23. *Phidius:* an Athenian sculptor (around 450 B.C.). 31. *Nineveh:* city in Assyria to which Jonah was sent as an apostle of reform. 32. *Babylon:* the capital of ancient Babylonia, but here more a symbol of luxury and corruption. 49. *Lincoln-hearted:* Abraham Lincoln spent his maturity in Springfield, before being elected President, and is buried there.

Lindsay's vision of the New Springfield came complete with illustrations and plans, both physical and metaphysical. Notice the comparisons, both favorable and unfavorable, to such cities as Babylon, Nineveh, Athens, Oxford, Florence: Lindsay had high aspirations. Most importantly, however, notice that for Lindsay, as for most poets, the soul is the important thing, and that the rebuilding he is thinking of is as much a spiritual as a physical affair.

from Annus Mirabilis

Me-thinks already, from this Chymick flame,
    I see a City of more precious mold:
Rich as the Town which gives the *Indies* names,
    With Silver pav'd, and all divine with Gold.

Already, Labouring with a mighty fate,
    She shakes the rubbish from her mounting brow,
And seems to have renew'd her Charters date,
    Which Heav'n will to the death of time allow.

More great than humane, now, and more *August,*
    New deifi'd she from her fires does rise:
Her widening streets on new foundations trust,
    And, opening, into larger parts she flies.

Before, she like some Shepherdess did show,
    Who sate to bathe her by a River's side:
Not answering to her fame, but rude and low,
    Nor taught the beauteous Arts of Modern pride.

Now, like a Maiden Queen, She will behold,
    From her high Turrets, hourly Sutors come:
The East with Incense, and the West with Gold,
    Will stand, like Suppliants, to receive her doom.

—*John Dryden*

1. *Chymick:* alchemical. 3. *Indies:* Mexico. 8. *August:* Augusta was the old name of London. 19. *doom:* judgment.

The *Annus Mirabilis,* or "year of wonders," was 1666, a year of plague, war, and the Great Fire of London, which literally burned the town down. These various disasters were widely interpreted as God's wrath being visited upon England for the unholy reign of Charles II.

However, Dryden took a different line: "Never had prince or people more mutual reason to love each other," he wrote, "if suffering for each other can endear affection." The fire would, Dryden predicted, create a new and more beautiful London, and a new and more powerful England. His vision, it need scarcely be mentioned, was more nearly realized than Lindsay's in the century that followed his poem.

To a Waterfowl

Whither, 'midst falling dew,
While glow the heavens with the last steps of day,
Far, through their rosy depths, dost thou pursue
Thy solitary way?

Vainly the fowler's eye
Might mark thy distant flight to do thee wrong,
As, darkly painted on the crimson sky,
Thy figure floats along.

Seek'st thou the plashy brink
Of weedy lake, or marge of river wide,
Or where the rocking billows rise and sink
On the chafed ocean side?

There is a Power whose care
Teaches thy way along that pathless coast,—
The desert and illimitable air,—
Lone wandering, but not lost.

All day thy wings have fann'd
At that far height, the cold thin atmosphere;
Yet stoop not, weary, to the welcome land,
Though the dark night is near.

And soon that toil shall end,
Soon shalt thou find a summer home, and rest,
And scream among thy fellows; reeds shall bend
Soon o'er thy sheltered nest.

Thou'rt gone, the abyss of heaven
Hath swallowed up thy form; yet, on my heart
Deeply hath sunk the lesson thou hast given,
And shall not soon depart.

He, who, from zone to zone,
Guides through the boundless sky thy certain flight,
In the long way that I must tread alone,
Will lead my steps aright.

—*William Cullen Bryant*

9. *plashy:* marshy.

Do you think this poem would have been strengthened or weakened if the final stanza had been omitted?

A Psalm of Life

I

Tell me not, in mournful numbers,
Life is but an empty dream!
For the soul is dead that slumbers,
And things are not what they seem.

II

Life is real—life is earnest—
And the grave is not its goal:
Dust thou art, to dust returnest,
Was not spoken of the soul.

III

Not enjoyment, and not sorrow,
Is our destin'd end or way;
But to *act,* that each to-morrow
Find us farther than to-day.

IV

Art is long, and time is fleeting,
And our hearts, though stout and brave,
Still, like muffled drums, are beating
Funeral marches to the grave.

V

In the world's broad field of battle,
In the bivouac of Life,
Be not like dumb, driven cattle!
Be a hero in the strife!

VI

Trust no Future, howe'er pleasant!
Let the dead Past bury its dead!
Act—act in the glorious Present!
Heart within, and God o'er head!

VII

Lives of great men all remind us
We can make *our* lives sublime,
And, departing, leave behind us
Footsteps on the sands of time.

VIII

Footsteps, that, perhaps another,
Sailing o'er life's solemn main,
A forlorn and shipwreck'd brother,
Seeing, shall take heart again.

IX

Let us then be up and doing,
With a heart for any fate;
Still achieving, still pursuing,
learn to labor and to wait.

—*Henry Wadsworth Longfellow*

1. *numbers:* metered verses; poems. 13. *Art is long, and time is fleeting:* a translation of a line from Seneca.

All You Need Is Love

There's nothing you can do that can't be done
Nothing you can sing that can't be sung
Nothing you can say but you can learn how to play the game
It's easy
All you need is love
All you need is love
All you need is love, love,
That is all you need

There's nothing you can make that can't be made
Noone you can save that can't be saved
Nothing you can do but you can learn how to be in time
It's easy
All you need is love
All you need is love
All you need is love, love,
That is all you need.

There's nothing you can know that isn't known
Nothing you can see that isn't shown
Nowhere you can be that isn't where you're meant to be
It's easy
All you need is love
All you need is love
All you need is love, love,
That is all you need.

—John Lennon & Paul McCartney

Compare and contrast Longfellow's poem and the Beatles' song. At first this might appear an exercise in absurdity, so completely different do they seem; yet when you come down to it, how different are the aims of each?

Listen closely to the Beatles recording of "All You Need is Love." Notice the musical phrases borrowed from other popular songs (among them the Beatles' own "She Loves You") woven into the swirling cyclone of music at the song's conclusion. Notice the curious time signature, alternating 3/4 and 4/4 time. Can you draw any correlations between the collage of musical phrases and the syncopated tempo and the song's theme?

The World Is Too Much with Us

The world is too much with us; late and soon,
Getting and spending, we lay waste our powers:
Little we see in Nature that is ours;
We have given our hearts away, a sordid boon!
This Sea that bares her bosom to the moon;
The winds that will be howling at all hours,
And are up-gathered now like sleeping flowers;
For this, for every thing, we are out of tune;
It moves us not.—Great God! I'd rather be
A Pagan suckled in a creed outworn;

So might I, standing on this pleasant lea,
Have glimpses that would make me less forlorn;
Have sight of Proteus rising from the sea;
Or hear old Triton blow his wreathèd horn.

—*William Wordsworth*

Trace the root of Wordsworth's discontent with the world around him. Is it society? Government? What does he mean by "too much with us"? By "getting and spending"? What solutions does he see to the problem? Is he really advocating a return to pagan religion in lines 10 following?

The Rumor

Now when the rumor comes to your town,
where it started no one knows;
some of your neighbors, well it might have been them.
Maybe it's a lie, even if it's a sin,
they'll repeat the rumor again.
Close your eyes, hang down your head
until the fog blows away, let it blow away;
Open up your arms and feel the good;
it's a-coming, a brand-new day.

Big men, little men turn into dust,
neighbors all informed, didn't mean to ruin no one.
Could there be someone here among this crowd
who's been accused, had his name misused,
and his privacy refused?
Close your eyes, hang down your head
until the fog blows away, let it blow away.
Open up your arms and feel the good;
it's a-coming, a brand-new day.

Now all you vigilantes want to make a move?
Maybe they won't; you know I sure hope they don't.
For whether this rumor proves true or false,
you can forgive, or you can regret,
but you can never, never forget.
Close your eyes, hang down your head
until the fog blows away, let it roll away.
Open up your arms and feel the good;
it's a-coming, a brand-new day.

—*Robbie Robertson*

In much of the Band's music there is an impulse toward transcending the merely temporal for—well, for a kind of mystical transcendence that does not easily translate from the language of poetry into that of criticism. This song moves from malice, character assassination, and generally injured feelings to an unclear but rich kind of affirmation: "Open up your arms . . . it's a-coming, a brand-new day." Rather than complain of injustices, even when the complaints are justified, we are advised to let the fog roll away—it *will* roll away—and work toward a better day. The vision is understated, fuzzy, unschematic, but it is undeniably there. And "The Rumor" is undeniably a very affirmative song.

I Think Continually of Those Who Were Truly Great

I think continually of those who were truly great.
Who, from the womb, remembered the soul's history
Through corridors of light where the hour are suns
Endless and singing. Whose lovely ambition
Was that their lips, still touched with fire,
Should tell of the Spirit clothed from head to foot in song.
And who hoarded from the Spring branches
The desires falling across their bodies like blossoms.

What is precious is never to forget
The essential delight of the blood drawn from ageless springs
Breaking through rocks in worlds before our earth;
Never to deny its pleasure in the simple morning light,
Nor its grave evening demand for love;
Never to allow gradually the traffic to smother
With noise and fog the flowering of the spirit.

Near the snow, near the sun, in the highest fields
See how these names are fêted by the waving grass,
And by the streamers of white cloud,
And whispers of wind in the listening sky;
The names of those who in their lives fought for life,
Who wore at their hearts the fire's center.
Born of the sun they traveled a short while towards the sun,
And left the vivid air signed with their honour.

—Stephen Spender

It is an old Platonic convention, used by Wordsworth among others in his famous "Intimations Ode," that our souls exist long before our bodies in a state of blessed innocence and joy, the sense of which we lose gradually as our soul languishes in the prison of the body during this life on earth. The child, being closer to this prenatal blessedness, has a purer vision than his father, and "age," as Thoreau put it, "is scarcely so well qualified a teacher as youth." Spender draws on this convention in his poem, and views poets (among other artists) as those who preserve this vision, singing all their lives of the Spirit, and refusing to forget. It is these visionaries who are really in tune with the world, and the natural world—if not human society—rings with their praise. Notice that in this definition, "poet" has almost nothing at all to do with words. A poet is he who best preserves his vision.

Green-Eyed Boy After Reading Whitman and Sandburg

Beyond the empty crossroads store
and the stubble of new-cut weeds
a man in a rough shirt and wide straw hat
whistles me to a long morning walk.
Clean smell of hay. This joyful flesh.
The sweet sound of the hermit thrush.
A virgin river sings in my free-verse head.

Deep in the honeysuckle shade
we fish for our lost American souls.

Yes, I'm sure there's a place for me
in this knockabout, haphazard world.

Oh, but look how the summer wind
bends the branches of the sycamore trees.

A black dog howls behind the barn.

—*Dave Etter*

lines 1–4: these lines draw heavily on phrases and images used by Whitman in "Song of Myself."

How does the green-eyed boy's reading of Whitman and Sandburg affect his perception of himself and his world? Is it only good things that he sees in a new light, or is the black dog just as much a part of this new world as the hermit thrush? Read some of the Whitman and Sandburg in this book and see if they affect your life.

6. The Poet as Commemorator

One reason politicians and commencement speakers use quotations from Shakespeare and Frost to ornament otherwise tedious speeches is that Shakespeare and Frost were, after all, very fine artists, and the decorative quality of their art embellishes the occasion. One function of art is always to decorate, to enrich our otherwise drab lives with a little color. The quoted poetry, along with music and song and all the on-stage decorations, make something beautiful, interesting, and entertaining out of a potentially tedious event.

But poetry—serious poetry—has a certain gravity to it that goes beyond entertainment and into ceremony. Nobody would accuse a high mass of being "entertainment," although it is full of show and ornamentation and what was called in previous centuries "spectacle." All the finery of language and clothing and music are present not so much to entertain as to underscore the importance of the occasion, to heighten the ceremony and thus the solemnity. Poetry can work this way too, especially if a poem is written specifically for or about a particular event. Then that occasion is singled out as something extra special, and it has the permanence and the dignity of art. Like a high mass, or a formal dinner with silver and china and crystal and men dressed in tuxedos, it has importance.

Thus poets are frequently called upon, or feel impelled, to commemorate in poetry such occasions as anniversaries, retirements, centennials, inaugurations, births, weddings, deaths. Just as frequently they will knock off a short piece for a less momentous occasion: a birthday, a sexual encounter, a pleasant evening on the town, the opening (or closing) of a play, a dinner invitation. The collected works of most poets are full of such verse, and—while much of it makes no pretense to greatness and some, especially the commissioned poems, is often quite bad—occasional poetry has its place in the scheme of things.

Like poets, song writers are constantly composing impromptu songs, most of which get sung only once. "I wrote seven songs last night," Bob Dylan announces on one of his bootlegged albums. "I gave them all away, though. They were just about things that were happening around the stage, about my friends and all." Every now and then, however, an occasional song seems just too good to throw away and finds its way onto an album, and thus to the public. Ricky Nelson's "Garden Party," about his performance at one of the rock-n-roll revival shows in Madison Square Garden, and Carly Simon's "You're So Vain" (which is said to be about a party at which Warren Beatty appeared) are good examples.

"You're So Vain" is a clever song that moves beyond the immediate occasion to make a statement on human foibles and vanities and life among the jet set. It almost reaches the level of social criticism; certainly it critiques human nature. The best occasional songs (Joni Mitchell's "Woodstock," for example, or Neil Young's "Four Dead in Ohio") and the best occasional poems (Robert Lowell's "Inauguration Day: January, 1953") use the events they commemorate as an excuse for personal statement. That statement may concern the times, human nature, art, or—as in the case of Emerson's "Concord Hymn"—remarks on the passing of time. The poet may even wish to issue a warning, like Langston Hughes in "October 16." In a casual, deliberately off-hand manner, Hughes begins, "Perhaps you will remember John Brown. . . ." By the close of his poem commemorating the centennial of Brown's raid on the federal arsenal at Harpers Ferry, Hughes's off-hand remark has become an admonition that events were to prove quite timely: "You *will* recall John Brown."

In contrast to Hughes, Allen Ginsberg is anything but subtle in his poem occasioned by the Democratic National Convention of 1968, held in Chicago, Illinois, during which Chicago police clubbed and gassed demonstrators, observers, reporters, political aides, and citizens, while Hubert Humphrey received the blessings of Lyndon Johnson and Chicago boss Richard Daley . . . and the presidential nomination over peace candidate Gene McCarthy. In the images Ginsberg pastes together in a verbal collage, he makes clear his contempt for both the police and the establishment politicians they protected, and his vision of the convention as the death of modern America. Like Hughes, then, Ginsberg sounds a warning in his commemorative poem. The occasion provides him with an excuse for making a statement.

Inviting a Friend to Supper

Tonight, grave sir, both my poor house and I
    Do equally desire your company:
Not that we think us worthy such a guest,
    But that your worth will dignify our feast
With those that come; whose grace may make that seem
  Something, which else could hope for no esteem.
It is the fair acceptance, Sir, creates
    The entertainment perfect: not the cates.
Yet shall you have, to rectify your palate,
    An olive, capers, or some better salad
Ushering the mutton; with a short-legged hen,
    If we can get her, full of eggs, and then
Lemons and wine for sauce; to these, a coney
    Is not to be despaired of for our money;

And though fowl now be scarce, yet there are clerks,
    The sky not falling, think we may have larks.
I'll tell you of more, and lie, so you will come:
    Of partridge, pheasant, wood-cock, of which some
May yet be there; and godwit if we can,
    Knot, rail, and ruff, too. Howsoe'er, my man
Shall read a piece of Virgil, Tacitus,
    Livy, or of some better book to us,
Of which we'll speak our minds amidst our meat;
    And I'll profess no verses to repeat.
To this, if aught appear which I not know of,
    That will the pastry, not my paper, show off.
Digestive cheese and fruit there sure will be;
    But that which most doth take my muse and me
Is a pure cup of rich Canary wine,
    Which is the Mermaid's now, but shall be mine;
Of which, had Horace or Anacreon tasted,
    Their lives, as do their lines, till now had lasted.
Tobacco, Nectar, or the Thespian spring
    Are all but Luther's beer to this I sing.
Of this we will sup free but moderately,
    And we will have no Pooly or Parrot by,
Nor shall our cups make any guilty men,
    But at our parting we shall be as when
We innocently met. No simple word
    That shall be uttered at our mirthful board
Shall make us sad next morning; or affright
    The liberty that we'll enjoy tonight.

—*Ben Jonson*

8. *cates:* dishes. 13. *coney:* rabbit. 19–20. *dogwit, knot, rail, ruff:* curlew, snipe, sandpiper, and corn rake (all game birds). 24. *profess:* promise. 29. *Canary:* a sweet wine from the Canary Island. 30. *Mermaid:* a tavern popular with poets in the early seventeenth century. 31. *Horace:* Latin poet; *Anacreon:* Greek poet famous for poems in praise of wine. 33. *Thespian:* dramatic. 36. *Pooly and Parrot:* actual names of government spies.

This is a dinner invitation written by the poet-playwright Ben Jonson in 1616. It is carefully polished, witty, full of learned references to other poets and places, obviously the product of much thought and labor . . . and yet it is obviously nothing more than a dinner invitation, promising good food (olives, salad, lamb, chicken, rabbit, perhaps partridge or pheasant or some other game birds), pleasant entertainment (a reading of Virgil, Tacitus, or Livy—Jonson modestly promises *not* to read his own work), fine wine, and good company. Best of all, no fear of morning anxieties over what went on the night before. The *idea* of such an evening, and the *fact* of such a civil invitation constitute, perhaps, a theme: the desirability of "gracious living." But this is to read the occasion surrounding the poem and not the poem itself, which remains, for all its craft, only a well-wrought invitation to dinner.

On the Burning of Lord Mansfield's Library, Together with his Manuscripts, by the Mob in the Month of June 1780.

So then—the Vandals of our isle,
　　Sworn foes to sense and law,
Have burnt to dust a nobler pile
　　Than ever Roman saw!

And Murray sighs o'er Pope and Swift,
　　And many a treasure more,
The well-judged purchase, and the gift
　　That graced his letter'd store.

Their pages mangled, burnt, and torn,
　　The loss was his alone;
But ages yet to come shall mourn
　　The burning of his own.

—*William Cowper*

5. *Murray:* Lord Mansfield.

Had Cowper never written his poem, the burning of Lord Mansfield's library would, no doubt, now be forgotten. And indeed, Cowper being a minor poet, even the immortality his poem confers upon the event is severely limited. Nevertheless, something is better than nothing, and the poem—as well as the compliment paid Lord Mansfield in the final two lines—is some small recompense for the loss of a library.

Hymn Sung at the Completion of the Concord Monument, April 19, 1836

By the rude bridge that arched the flood,
　　Their flag to April's breeze unfurled,
Here once the embattled farmers stood,
　　And fired the shot heard round the world.

The foe long since in silence slept;
Alike the conqueror silent sleeps;
And Time the ruined bridge has swept
Down the dark stream which seaward creeps.

On this green bank, by this soft stream,
We set to-day a votive stone;
That memory may their deed redeem,
When, like our sires, our sons are gone.

Spirit, that made those heroes dare
To die, or leave their children free,
Bid time and Nature gently spare
The shaft we raise to them and thee.

—*Ralph Waldo Emerson*

What could be more appropriate to the dedication of a memorial than the nicely turned thought of Emerson's closing lines: ''Bid Time and Nature gently spare / The shaft we raise to them and thee''? The poem looks ahead at the very moment it looks behind, and reminds everyone who hears it or reads it (it is now cast in bronze beside the reconstructed ''rude bridge'' across the river at Concord) that all men and all man's works are mortal.

There is an interesting footnote to this occasional poem, however: ''the shot heard round the world'' was fired not at Concord but up the road at Lexington. Whether Emerson was deliberately rewriting history or just got confused, his inaccurate poem has come to prevail over historical reality: most Americans today believe that the opening shots of the American Revolution were in fact fired at Concord.

You're So Vain

You walked into the party
like you were walking onto a yacht,
your hat strategically dipped below one eye,
your scarf it was apricot;
you had one eye in the mirror
as you watched yourself gavotte;
and all the girls dreamed that they'd be your partner,
they'd be your partner and
you're so vain, you probably think this song is about you;
you're so vain, you probably think this song is about you,
don't you, don't you?

Well I hear you went up to Saratoga
and your horse naturally won;
then you flew your Lear jet to Nova Scotia
to see a total eclipse of the sun.
You're where you should be all the time
and when you're not,
you're with some underworld spy or the wife of a close friend,
wife of a close friend and
you're so vain, you probably think this song is about you;
you're so vain, you probably think this song is about you,
don't you, don't you?

Well you had me several years ago
when I was still quite naive,
and you said we made such a pretty pair
that you would never leave;
but you gave away the things you loved,
and one of them was me;
I had some dreams, they were clouds in my coffee,
clouds in my coffee and
you're so vain, you probably think this song is about you;
you're so vain, you probably think this song is about you,
don't you, don't you?

—*Carly Simon*

"You're So Vain" is an interesting song for several reasons, not the least of which is the pure technical feat of rhyming "yacht" with "apricot" and "gavotte"—something you don't see every day, which alone would make the song remarkable. It is also a clever song in that it turns upon itself: if you think the song's about *you,* then it is, because you're so vain, as proven by the fact that you thought the song was for you.

To an Athlete Dying Young

The time you won your town the race
We chaired you through the market-place;
Man and boy stood cheering by,
And home we brought you shoulder-high.

To-day, the road all runners come,
Shoulder-high we bring you home,
And set you at your threshold down,
Townsman of a stiller town.

Smart lad, to slip betimes away
From fields where glory does not stay
And early though the laurel grows
It withers quicker than the rose.

Eyes the shady night has shut
Cannot see the record cut,
And silence sounds no worse than cheers
After earth has stopped the ears:

Now you will not swell the rout
Of lads that wore their honours out,
Runners whom renown outran
And the name died before the man.

So set, before its echoes fade,
The fleet foot on the sill of shade,
And hold to the low lintel up
The still-defended challenge-cup.

And round that early-laurelled head
Will flock to gaze the strengthless dead.
And find unwithered on its curls
The garland briefer than a girl's.

—*A. E. Houseman*

2. *chaired:* carried on one's shoulders. 23. *lintel:* a horizontal support above a door or window.

"To an Athlete Dying Young" was written, obviously, on the occasion of a death, one of the most common occasions for commemorative poetry. As such, it belongs to a literary genre called the *elegy,* a poem written to eulogize someone who has just died. The elegy has no specific structure, but does require that the poet, in some way or another, move from grief to joy or consolation. That is what Housman does here.

Housman's elegy is short, but it is very polished and elegant, and it breaks cleanly into three distinct divisions: the initial two stanzas present the subject by drawing a comparison between a victory parade and a funeral; the middle three stanzas present three different but related reasons why the athlete should not mind dying; and the final two stanzas manage some genuine affirmation in the form of the challenge-cup and the garland. Notice the way in which Housman moves from the past tense in stanza one to the present for the main portion of the poem to the future in the last, affirmative stanza. The change of tenses works to associate sorrow with the present and affirmation with the future, thereby emphasizing the development of his argument. Probably the calm, reserved tone of the poem produced by the measured, polished lines lends its own affirmative dignity to the effect of the imagery, argument, and tense sequence. Most impressive, however, is the classical simplicity of the poem: there is no riotous profusion of similes and metaphors, no intricately Latinate diction, no self-indulgent emotionalism—just a clean, decorous, elegantly simple poem. And like the simple laurel wreath of victory that the athlete once wore to mark his triumph in the foot race he won on earth, this simple poem is a very appropriate mark of triumph in the race of life.

October 16

Perhaps
You will remember
John Brown.

John Brown
Who took his gun,
Took twenty-one companions
White and black,
Went to shoot your way to freedom
Where two rivers meet
And the hills of the
North
And the hills of the
South
Look slow at one another—
And died
For your sake.

Now that you are
Many years free,
And the echo of the Civil War
Has passed away,
And Brown himself
Has long been tried at law,
Hanged by the neck,
And buried in the ground—
Since Harpers Ferry
Is alive with ghosts today,
Immortal raiders
Come again to town—

Perhaps
You will recall
John Brown.

—*Langston Hughes*

Going to Chicago

22,000 feet over Hazed square Vegetable planet Floor
Approaching Chicago to Die or flying over Earth another 40 years
to die—Indifferent, and Afraid, that the bone-shattering bullet
be the same as the vast evaporation-of-phenomena Cancer
Come true in an old man's bed. Or Historic
Fire-Heaven Descending 22,000 years End th' Atomic Aeon

The Lake's blue again, Sky's the same baby, tho' papers & Noses
rumor tar spread through the Natural Universe'll make Angel's feet sticky.
I heard the Angel King's voice, a bodiless tuneful teenager
Eternal in my own heart saying "Trust the Purest Joy—
Democratic Anger is an Illusion, Democratic Joy is God
Our Father is baby blue, the original face you see Sees You—"

How, thru Conventional Police & Revolutionary Fury
Remember the Helpless order the Police Armed to protect,
The Helpless Freedom the Revolutionary Conspired to honor—
I am the Angel King sang the Angel King
as mobs in Amphitheaters, Streets, Colosseums Parks and offices
Scream in despair over Meat and Metal Microphone

—*Allen Ginsberg*

12. *baby blue:* a reference, perhaps, to Bob Dylan's song "It's All Over Now, Baby Blue." Baby Blue represents the straight, middle-class, wholesome values of Lyndon Johnson's society.

7. The Poet as Myth-Maker

To most people the word *myth* means simply "something that is not true: a made-up story or a fictitious character; a lie." The cowboy as portrayed in standard American westerns is a myth, which is to say cowboys did not spend their time riding around on white horses, six-guns blazing, rescuing fair ladies, capturing horse thieves, and riding off into the sunset singing "Happy Trails to You." When somebody says the story of Ulysses' travels, or Beowulf's fight, or Noah's ark is a myth, he means that the story is a fabrication, not historically true. No cyclops and no sirens and no ten years wandering around the Mediterranean Sea after the Trojan War. Perhaps no Ulysses. No ark, no forty days and forty nights of rain, no flood, no rainbow as God's promise to man never again to destroy the world by water. Myths are assumed to be in a category with dreams: wild imaginings without basis in historical fact.

It is also assumed that because the myth has no historical validity it has no metaphysical validity either. To deny the actual historical existence of Ulysses and his adventures is also to deny the proposition embedded in the record of his travels that the gods, or some supernatural forces somewhere, actively intervene in the lives of mortals to assist or thwart their efforts. For another example, to deny that God actually told Noah to build an ark and bring with him pairs of every kind of animal is also to deny the theological point of the Noah's ark story: that God cares for his people and judges them, and will act to punish the evil and protect the good. Or, to take a more recent and secular myth, when someone points out that Horatio Alger's *Ragged Dick* is a myth, a made-up story, he is also assumed to deny the notion contained in *Ragged Dick* that poor young boys can rise from shining shoes to positions of wealth and power just by honesty, hard work, and clean living.

Theologians, poets, social historians and others have been quick to point out, however, that denying the historical reality of a myth does not necessarily invalidate the theological, poetic, or social truth of the myth. In fact, an ability to dissociate the matter of historical truth from the issue of metaphysical truth is the cornerstone of the literary sensibility. Perhaps Noah and his ark were not historical realities; nevertheless it may well be that God *does* act in human history to punish sinners and save the righteous. *Ragged Dick* was just a made-up character in a made-up story; nevertheless, it just may be that in America you *can* rise in the manner of Ragged Dick from poverty to wealth through hard work and honesty and a bit of good luck. Then again, perhaps you can't. The point is this: the poetic or social or psychological and theological truth of the myth is to be judged independently of its historical truth or falsehood.

Poets come to myth on two different and sometimes contradictory levels. On the simplest level, poets are always looking for characters and stories out of which to develop poems. So they may use a Beowulf or a Noah to make a poem or a play or even a song. In this sense they are interested in myth because a good myth has action and suspense and a sense of the supernatural, and is therefore attractive to audiences. No doubt there are many poets who make up myths with only this aim in mind: to find something commercial, something to sell.

Most poets, however, want a *true* myth, true in the sense that, like the Noah's ark story to the writer of Genesis, it contains an assessment of mankind and his world that the poet can hold up to his audience as valid. So Samuel Taylor Coleridge can make up the myth of the Ancient Mariner, a story which cannot possibly have any historical accuracy, to embody important (and, the consensus of opinion has been, valid) perceptions about mankind, guilt, repentence, and salvation. So Bob Dylan can create a John Wesley Harding who, while he may lack historical reality, is the embodiment of certain very true perceptions about American men: they like to think of themselves as outlaws, they want to rob the rich and help the poor, they use guns as a first, not a last resort.

In this sense the poet becomes not only an entertainer and a storyteller, but a kind of truth-seeker. Many people are making myths today who are not poets, of course, and many poets who use myth do so only on the superficial level of an entertainer looking for a good story. However, increasingly poets are accepting the role of myth-maker, with all the responsibility for truth (in the larger, nonhistorical sense of the word) that the role implies.

Evaluating myths is difficult, especially since many tend, like dreams, to lack literal sense. A coherent narrative line (realistic character motivation explainable in rational terms, cause and effect relationships, a plausible geographical and chronological sequence) is as unnecessary to a good myth as historical truth. Does the myth illuminate an aspect of yourself and your world which had been puzzling or confusing? Is there an insight in the myth that *feels* right? Myth derives from that dark side of our consciousness (or subconsciousness) from which come also emotions, intuitions, premonitions, and probably dreams. The poet, when he writes, gropes his way toward a realization that perhaps even he does not entirely understand. The reader also gropes, intuiting what is right and true, relying on instincts and sensibilities, knowing in his bones what is accurate.

You can eliminate immediately, of course, all myths like those of the McDonald's Corporation, the United States government, advertisers, and other agents of power which seem deliberately contrived to portray mankind in a manner obviously advantageous to the myth-maker. Distrust myths that serve the myth-maker, even if it is a poet making a myth that turns poets into seers, wise men, rulers, gods, or spokesmen of the gods. Do not rule out the old myths, even those which obviously lack historical truth, because some elements in human nature change slowly if at all. Recognize the fact that some myths explain some aspects of human nature, other myths others, even though set side by side the myths may be contradictory (the human mind is large; it has much space inside). Beyond that, you must proceed largely on intuition, sensing what there is—if anything—in the myths of Ovid, Coleridge, Bly, Kinnell, Dylan, and other myth-makers in this book that feels right for the modern world.

Pygmalion and the Statue

Pygmalion loathing their lascivious Life,
Abhorr'd all Womankind, but most a Wife:
So single chose to live, and shunn'd to wed,
Well pleas'd to want a Consort of his Bed.
Yet fearing Idleness, the Nurse of Ill,
In Sculpture exercis'd his happy Skill;
And carv'd in Iv'ry such a Maid, so fair,
As Nature could not with his Art compare,
Were she to work; but in her own Defence
Must take her Pattern here, and copy hence.
Pleas'd with his Idol, he commends, admires,
Adores; and last, the Thing ador'd, desires.
A very Virgin in her Face was seen,
And had she mov'd, a living Maid has been:
One wou'd have thought she cou'd have stirr'd; but strove
With Modesty, and was asham'd to move.
Art his with Art, so well perform'd the Cheat,
It caught the Carver with his own Deceit:
He knows 'tis Madness, yet he must adore,
And still the more he knows it, loves the more:
The Flesh, or what so seems, he touches oft,
Which feels so smooth, that he believes it soft.
Fir'd with this Thought, at once he strain'd the Breast,
And on the Lips a burning Kiss impress'd.
'Tis true, the harden'd Breast resists the Gripe,
And the cold Lips return a Kiss unripe:
But when, retiring back, he look'd agen,
To think it Iv'ry, was a Thought too mean:
So wou'd believe she kiss'd, and courting more,
Again embrac'd her naked Body o'er;
And straining hard the Statue, was afraid
His Hands had made a Dint, and hurt his Maid:
Explor'd her, Limb by Limb, and fear'd to find
So rude a Gripe had left a livid Mark behind:
What Flatt'ry now, he seeks her Mind to move,
And now with Gifts, (the pow'rful Bribes of Love:)
He furnishes her Closet first; and fills

The crowded Shelves with Rarities of Shells;
Adds Orient Pearls, which from the Conchs he drew,
And all the sparkling Stones of various Hue:
And Parrots, imitating Humane Tongue,
And Singing-birds in Silver Cages hung;
And ev'ry fragrant Flow'r, and od'rous Green,
Were sorted well, with Lumps of Amber laid between:
Rich, fashionable Robes her Person deck,
Pendants her Ears, and Pearls adorn her Neck:
Her taper'd Fingers too with Rings are grac'd,
And an embroider'd Zone surrounds her slender Waste.
Thus like a Queen array'd, so richly dress'd,
Beauteous she shew'd, but naked shew'd the best.
Then, from the Floor, he rais'd a Royal Bed,
With Cov'rings of *Sydonian* Purple spread:
The Solemn Rites perform'd, he calls her Bride,
With Blandishments invites her to his Side,
And as she were with Vital Sense possess'd,
Her Head did on a plumy Pillow rest.
The Feast of *Venus* came, a Solemn Day,
To which the *Cypriots* due Devotion pay;
With gilded Horns, the Milk-white Heifers led,
Slaughter'd before the sacred Altars, bled:
Pygmalion off'ring, first, approach'd the Shrine,
And then the Pray'rs implor'd the Pow'rs Divine,
Almighty Gods, if all we Mortals want,
If all we can require, be yours to grant;
Make this fair Statue mine, he wou'd have said,
But chang'd his Words, for shame; and only pray'd,
Give me the Likeness of my Iv'ry Maid.
The Golden Goddess, present at the Pray'r,
Well knew he meant th' inanimated Fair,
And gave the Sign of granting his Desire;
For trice in chearful Flames ascends the Fire.
The Youth, returning to his Mistress, hies,
And impudent in Hope, with ardent Eyes,
And beating Breast, by the dear Statue lies
He kisses her white Lips, renews the Bliss,
And looks, and thinks they redden at the Kiss;
He thought them warm before: Nor longer stays,
But next his Hand on her hard Bosom lays:
Hard as it was, beginning to relent,
It seem'd, the Breast beneath his Fingers bent;
He felt again, his Fingers made a Print,
'Twas Flesh, but Flesh so firm, it rose against the Dint:

The pleasing Task he fails not to renew;
Soft, and more soft at ev'ry Touch it grew;
Like pliant Wax, when chafing Hands reduce
The former Mass to Form, and frame for Use.
He would believe, but yet is still in pain,
And tries his Argument of sense again,
Presses the Pulse, and feels the leaping Vein.
Convinc'd, o'erjoy'd, his studied Thanks and Praise,
To her who made the Miracle, he pays:
Then Lips to Lips he join'd; now freed from Fear,
He found the Savour of the Kiss sincere:
At this the waken'd Image op'd her Eyes,
And view'd at once the Light and Lover, with surprise.
The Goddess present at the Match she made,
So bless'd the Bed, such Fruitfulness convey'd,
That e'er ten Moons had sharpen'd either Horn,
To crown their Bliss, a lovely Boy was born;
Paphos his Name, who grown to Manhood, wall'd
The City *Paphos,* from the Founder call'd.

—*Ovid (trans. John Dryden)*

28. *mean:* base; low. 48. *zone:* a wide belt or girdle. 52. *Sydonian:* from Sidon, ancient seaport in Phonecia, famous for its purple cloth.

The story of Pygmalion and his statue is, of course, fictional—but like all myths it contains a philosophical truth about artists and their relationship with their art. Pygmalion's attachment to, his belief in his statue is so great that, in the story at least, it comes alive. Is Ovid suggesting that an artist's energies can actually give life to his creation, or that artists sometimes get so wrapped up in their work that they go a little screwball? Can the truth content of this myth be extended beyond the world of art and applied to other areas of life? If you have ever seen *My Fair Lady* you may find a comparison between that play/movie and the myth of Pygmalion illuminating.

John Wesley Harding

John Wesley Harding
Was a friend to the poor,
He trav'led with a gun in ev'ry hand.
All along this countryside,
He opened a many a door,
But he was never known
To hurt a honest man.

'Twas down in Chaynee County,
A time they talk about,
With his lady by his side
He took a stand.
And soon the situation there
Was all but straightened out,
For he was always known
To lend a helping hand.

All across the telegraph
His name it did resound,
But no charge held against him
Could they prove.
And there was no man around
Who could track or chain him down,
He was never known
to make a foolish move.

—*Bob Dylan*

"John Wesley Harding" represents an interesting combination of the Methodist John Wesley on the one hand, and the Texas outlaw John Hardin on the other. As a myth, he embodies two contradictory characteristics: a concern for morality and justice, and an outlaw violence. On the one hand John Wesley Harding is always known to lend a helping hand and never hurts an honest man; on the other, he travels with gun in hand and is on the "most wanted" list. This combination is peculiarly American: we have a long tradition of regarding outlaws as more honest and more generous than law officials (see "Tom Joad" and "Pretty Boy Floyd," both by Woody Guthrie, in this regard), and in a country founded on revolution, we are sometimes quite willing to see more justice in an outlaw / thief / murderer than in the forces of law and order. What other examples of this myth can you think of? (Robin Hood comes immediately to mind.) How does Dylan's treatment of that myth compare to those interpretations?

The Rime of the Ancient Mariner

Part I

An ancient Mariner meeteth three Gallants bidden to a wedding-feast, and detaineth one.

It is an ancient Mariner,
And he stoppeth one of three.
"By thy long grey beard and glittering eye,
Now wherefore stopp'st thou me?

The Bridegroom's doors are opened wide,
And I am next of kin;
The guests are met, the feast is set:
May'st hear the merry din."

He holds him with his skinny hand,
"There was a ship," quoth he.
"Hold off! uphand me, grey-beard loon!"
Eftsoons his hand dropt he.

The Wedding-Guest is spell-bound by the eye of the old seafaring man, and constrained to hear his tale.

He holds him with his glittering eye—
The Wedding-Guest stood still,
And listens like a three years' child:
The Mariner hath his will.

The Wedding-Guest sat on a stone:
He cannot choose but hear;
And thus spake on that ancient man,
The bright-eyed Mariner.

"The ship was cheered, the harbour cleared,
Merrily did we drop
Below the kirk, below the hill,
Below the lighthouse top.

The Mariner tells how the ship sailed southward with a good wind and fair weather, till it reached the line.

The Sun came up upon the left,
Out of the sea came he!
And he shone bright, and on the right
Went down into the sea.

Higher and higher every day,
Till over the mast at noon—"
The Wedding-Guest here beat his breast,
For he heard the loud bassoon.

The Wedding-Guest heareth the bridal music; but the Mariner continueth his tale.

The bride hath paced into the hall,
Red as a rose is she;
Nodding their heads before her goes
The merry minstrelsy.

The Wedding-Guest he beat his breast,
Yet he cannot choose but hear;
And thus spake on that ancient man,
The bright-eyed Mariner.

The ship driven by a storm toward the south pole.

"And now the STORM-BLAST came, and he
Was tyrannous and strong:
He struck with his o'ertaking wings,
And chased us south along.

With sloping masts and dipping prow,
As who pursued with yell and blow
Still treads the shadow of his foe,
And forward bends his head,
The ship drove fast, loud roared the blast,
And southward aye we fled.

And now there came both mist and snow,
And it grew wondrous cold:
And ice, mast-high, came floating by,
As green as emerald.

The land of ice, and of fearful sounds where no living thing was to be seen.

And through the drifts the snowy clifts
Did send a dismal sheen:
Nor shapes of men nor beasts we ken—
The ice was all between.

The ice was here, the ice was there,
The ice was all around:
It cracked and growled, and roared and howled,
Like noises in a swound!

Till a great sea-bird called the Albatross, came through the snow-fog, and was received with great joy and hospitality.

At length did cross an Albatross,
Thorough the fog it came;
As if it had been a Christian soul,
We hailed it in God's name.

It ate the food it ne'er had eat,
And round and round it flew.
The ice did split with a thunder-fit;
The helmsman steered us through!

And lo! the Albatross proveth a bird of good omen, and followeth

And a good south wind sprung up behind;
The Albatross did follow,
And every day, for food or play,
Came to the mariner's hollo!

the ship as it returned northward through fog and floating ice.

In mist or cloud, on mast or shroud,
It perched for vespers nine;
Whiles all the night, through fog-smoke white,
Glimmered the white Moon-shine."

The ancient Mariner inhospitably killeth the pious bird of good omen.

"God save thee, ancient Mariner!
From the fiends, that plague thee thus!—
Why look'st thou so?"—With my cross-bow
I shot the ALBATROSS.

PART II

The Sun now rose upon the right:
Out of the sea came he,
Still hid in mist, and on the left
Went down into the sea.

And the good south wind still blew behind,
But no sweet bird did follow,
Nor any day for food or play
Came to the mariners' hollo!

His shipmates cry out against the ancient Mariner, for killing the bird of good luck.

And I had done a hellish thing,
And it would work 'em woe:
For all averred, I had killed the bird
That made the breeze to blow.
Ah wretch! said they, the bird to slay,
That made the breeze to blow!

But when the fog cleared off, they justify the same, and thus make themselves accomplices in the crime.

Nor dim nor red, like God's own head,
The glorious Sun uprist:
Then all averred, I had killed the bird
That brought the fog and mist.
'Twas right, said they, such birds to slay,
That bring the fog and mist.

The fair breeze continues; the ship enters the Pacific Ocean, and sails northward, even till it reaches the Line.

The fair breeze blew, the white foam flew,
The furrow followed free;
We were the first that ever burst
Into that silent sea.

The ship hath been suddenly becalmed.

Down dropt the breeze, the sails dropt down,
'Twas sad as sad could be;
And we did speak only to break
The silence of the sea!

All in a hot and copper sky,
The bloody Sun, at noon,
Right up above the mast did stand,
No bigger than the Moon.

Day after day, day after day,
We stuck, nor breath nor motion;
As idle as a painted ship
Upon a painted ocean.

And the Albatross begins to be avenged.

Water, water, every where,
And all the boards did shrink;
Water, water, every where,
Nor any drop to drink.

The very deep did rot: O Christ!
That ever this should be!
Yea, slimy things did crawl with legs
Upon the slimy sea.

About, about, in reel and rout
The death-fires danced at night;
The water, like a witch's oils,
Burnt green, and blue and white.

A Spirit had followed them; one of the invisible inhabitants of this planet, neither departed souls nor angels; concerning whom the learned Jew, Josephus, and the Platonic Constantinopolitan, Michael Psellus, may be consulted. They are very numerous, and there is no climate or element without one or more.

And some in dreams assuréd were
Of the Spirit that plagued us so;
Nine fathom deep he had followed us
From the land of mist and snow.

And every tongue, through utter drought,
Was withered at the root;
We could not speak, no more than if
We had been choked with soot.

The shipmates, in their sore distress, would fain throw the whole guilt on the ancient Mariner: in sign whereof they hang the dead sea-bird round his neck.

Ah! well a-day! what evil looks
Had I from old and young!
Instead of the cross, the Albatross
About my neck was hung.

Part III

There passed a weary time. Each throat
Was parched, and glazed each eye.
A weary time! a weary time!
How glazed each weary eye,
When looking westward, I beheld
A something in the sky.

The ancient Mariner beholdeth a sign in the element afar off.

At first it seemed a little speck,
And then it seemed a mist;
It moved and moved, and took at last
A certain shape, I wist.

A speck, a mist, a shape, I wist!
And still it neared and neared:
As if it dodged a water-sprite,
It plunged and tacked and veered.

At its nearer approach, it seemeth him to be a ship; and at a dear ransom he freeth his speech from the bonds of thirst.

With throats unslaked, with black lips baked,
We could nor laugh nor wail;
Through utter drought all dumb we stood!
I bit my arm, I sucked the blood,
And cried, A sail! a sail!

With throats unslaked, with black lips baked,
Agape they heard me call:
Gramercy! they for joy did grin,
And all at once their breath drew in,
As they were drinking all.

A flash of joy;

And horror follows. For can it be a ship that comes onward without wind or tide?

See! see! (I cried) she tacks no more!
Hither to work us weal;
Without a breeze, without a tide,
She steadies with upright keel!

The western wave was all a-flame.
The day was well nigh done!
Almost upon the western wave
Rested the broad bright Sun;
When that strange shape drove suddenly
Betwixt us and the Sun.

It seemeth him but the skeleton of a ship.

And straight the Sun was flecked with bars,
(Heaven's Mother send us grace!)
As if through a dungeon-grate he peered
With broad and burning face.

Alas! (thought I, and my heart beat loud)
How fast she nears and nears!
Are those *her* sails that glance in the Sun,
Like restless gossameres?

And its ribs are seen as bars on the face of the setting Sun.

Are those *her* ribs through which the Sun
Did peer, as through a grate?
And is that Woman all her crew?
Is that a DEATH? and are there two?
Is DEATH that woman's mate?

The Spectre-Woman and her Deathmate, and no other on board the skeleton ship.

Her lips were red, *her* looks were free,
Her locks were yellow as gold:
Her skin was as white as leprosy,
The Night-mare LIFE-IN-DEATH was she,
Who thicks man's blood with cold.

Like vessel, like crew!

Death and Life-in-Death have diced for the ship's crew, and she (the latter) winneth the ancient Mariner.

The naked hulk alongside came,
And the twain were casting dice;
"The game is done! I've won! I've won!"
Quoth she, and whistles thrice.

No twilight within the courts of the Sun.

The Sun's rim dips; the stars rush out:
At one stride comes the dark;
With far-heard whisper, o'er the sea,
Off shot the spectre-bark.

At the rising of the Moon,

We listened and looked sideways up!
Fear at my heart, as at a cup,
My life-blood seemed to sip!
The stars were dim, and thick the night,
The steersman's face by his lamp gleamed white;
From the sails the dew did drip—
Till clomb above the eastern bar
The hornéd Moon, with one bright star
Within the nether tip.

One after another,

One after one, by the star-dogged Moon,
Too quick for groan or sigh,
Each turned his face with a ghastly pang,
And cursed me with his eye.

His shipmates drop down dead.

Four times fifty living men,
(And I heard nor sigh nor groan)
With heavy thump, a lifeless lump,
They dropped down one by one.

But Life-in-Death begins her work on the ancient Mariner.

The souls did from their bodies fly,—
They fled to bliss or woe!
And every soul, it passed me by,
Like the whizz of my cross-bow!

Part IV

The Wedding-Guest feareth that a Spirit is talking to him;

"I fear thee, ancient Mariner!
I fear thy skinny hand!
And thou art long, and lank, and brown,
As is the ribbed sea-sand.

I fear thee and thy glittering eye,
And thy skinny hand, so brown."—

But the ancient Mariner assureth him of his bodily life, and proceedeth to relate his horrible penance.

Fear not, fear not, thou Wedding-Guest!
This body dropt not down.

Alone, alone, all, all alone,
Alone on a wide wide sea!
And never a saint took pity on
My soul in agony.

He despiseth the creatures of the calm,

The many men, so beautiful!
And they all dead did lie:
And a thousand thousand slimy things
Lived on; and so did I.

And envieth that *they* should live, and so many lie dead.

I looked upon the rotting sea,
And drew my eyes away;
I looked upon the rotting deck,
And there the dead men lay.

I looked to heaven, and tried to pray;
But or ever a prayer had gusht,
A wicked whisper came, and made
My heart as dry as dust.

I closed my lids, and kept them close,
And the balls like pulses beat;
For the sky and the sea, and the sea and the sky
Lay like a load on my weary eye,
And the dead were at my feet.

But the curse liveth for him in the eye of the dead men.

The cold sweat melted from their limbs,
Nor rot nor reek did they:
The look with which they looked on me
Had never passed away.

An orphan's curse would drag to hell
A spirit from on high;
But oh! more horrible than that
Is the curse in a dead man's eye!
Seven days, seven nights, I saw that curse,
And yet I could not die.

The moving Moon went up the sky,
And no where did abide:
Softly she was going up,
And a star or two beside—

Her beams bemocked the sultry main,
Like April hoar-frost spread;
But where the ship's huge shadow lay,
The charméd water burnt alway
A still and awful red.

In his loneliness and fixedness he yearneth towards the journeying Moon, and the stars that still sojourn, yet still move onward; and everywhere the blue sky belongs to them, and is their appointed rest, and their native country and their own natural homes, which they enter unannounced, as lords that are certainly expected and yet there is a silent joy at their arrival.

By the light of the Moon he beholdeth God's creatures of the great calm.

Beyond the shadow of the ship,
I watched the water-snakes:
They moved in tracks of shining white,
And when they reared, the elfish light
Fell off in hoary flakes.

Within the shadow of the ship
I watched their rich attire:
Blue, glossy green, and velvet black,
They coiled and swam; and every track
Was a flash of golden fire.

Their beauty and their happiness.

O happy living things! no tongue
Their beauty might declare:
A spring of love gushed from my heart,
And I blessed them unaware:
Sure my kind saint took pity on me,
And I blessed them unaware.

He blesseth them in his heart.

The spell begins to break.

The self-same moment I could pray;
And from my neck so free
The Albatross fell off, and sank
Like lead into the sea.

PART V

Oh sleep! it is a gentle thing,
Beloved from pole to pole!
To Mary Queen the praise be given!
She sent the gentle sleep from Heaven,
That slid into my soul.

By grace of the holy Mother, the ancient Mariner is refreshed with rain.

The silly buckets on the deck,
That had so long remained,
I dreamt that they were filled with dew;
And when I awoke, it rained.

My lips were wet, my throat was cold,
My garments all were dank;
Sure I had drunken in my dreams,
And still my body drank.

I moved, and could not feel my limbs:
I was so light—almost
I though that I had died in sleep,
And was a blesséd ghost.

He heareth sounds and seeth strange sights and commotions in the sky and the element.

And soon I heard a roaring wind:
It did not come anear;
But with its sound it shook the sails,
That were so thin and sere.

The upper air burst into life!
And a hundred fire-flags sheen,
To and fro they were hurried about!
And to and fro, and in and out,
The wan stars danced between.

And the coming wind did roar more loud,
And the sails did sigh like sedge;
And the rain poured down from one black cloud;
The Moon was at its edge.

The thick black cloud was cleft, and still
The Moon was at its side:
Like waters shot from some high crag,
The lightning fell with never a jag,
A river steep and wide.

The bodies of the ship's crew are inspired [inspirited, *S. L.*] and the ship moves on;

The loud wind never reached the ship.
Yet now the ship moved on!
Beneath the lightning and the Moon
The dead men gave a groan.

They groaned, they stirred, they all uprose,
Nor spake, nor moved their eyes;
It had been strange, even in a dream,
To have seen those dead men rise.

The helmsman steered, the ship moved on;
Yet never a breeze up-blew;
The mariners all 'gan work the ropes,
Where they were wont to do;
They raised their limbs like lifeless tools—
We were a ghastly crew.

The body of my brother's son
Stood by me, knee to knee:
The body and I pulled at one rope,
But he said nought to me.

But not by the souls of the men, nor by dæmons of earth or middle air, but by a blessed troop of angelic spirits, sent down by the invocation of the guardian saint.

"I fear thee, ancient Mariner!"
Be calm, thou Wedding-Guest!
'Twas not those souls that fled in pain,
Which to their corses came again,
But a troop of spirits blest:

For when it dawned—they dropped their arms,
And clustered round the mast;
Sweet sounds rose slowly through their mouths,
And from their bodies passed.

Around, around, flew each sweet sound,
Then darted to the Sun;
Slowly the sounds came back again,
Now mixed, now one by one.

Sometimes a-dropping from the sky
I heard the sky-lark sing;
Sometimes all little birds that are,
How they seemed to fill the sea and air
With their sweet jargoning!

And now 'twas like all instruments,
Now like a lonely flute;
And now it is an angel's song,
That makes the heavens be mute.

It ceased; yet still the sails made on
A pleasant noise till noon,
A noise like of a hidden brook
In the leafy month of June,
That to the sleeping woods all night
Singeth a quiet tune.

Till noon we quietly sailed on,
Yet never a breeze did breathe:
Slowly and smoothly went the ship,
Moved onward from beneath.

The lonesome Spirit from the south-pole carries on the ship as far as the Line, in obedience to the angelic troop, but still requireth vengeance.

Under the keel nine fathom deep,
From the land of mist and snow,
The spirit slid: and it was he
That made the ship to go..
The sails at noon left off their tune,
And the ship stood still also.

The Sun, right up above the mast,
Had fixed her to the ocean:
But in a minute she 'gan stir,
With a short uneasy motion—
Backwards and forwards half her length
With a short uneasy motion.

Then like a pawing horse let go,
She made a sudden bound:
It flung the blood into my head,
And I fell down in a swound.

The Polar Spirit's fellow-dæmons, the invisible inhabitants of the element, take part in his wrong; and two of them relate, one to the other, that penance long and heavy for the ancient Mariner hath been accorded to the Polar Spirit, who returneth southward.

How long in that same fit I lay,
I have not to declare;
But ere my living life returned,
I heard and in my soul discerned
Two voices in the air.

"Is it he?" quoth one, "Is this the man?
By him who died on cross,
With his cruel bow he laid full low
The harmless Albatross.

The spirit who bideth by himself
In the land of mist and snow,
He loved the bird that loved the man
Who shot him with his bow."

The other was a softer voice,
As soft as honey-dew:
Quoth he, "The man hath penance done,
And penance more will do."

Part VI

First Voice

"But tell me, tell me! speak again,
Thy soft response renewing—
What makes that ship drive on so fast?
What is the ocean doing?"

Second Voice

"Still as a slave before his lord,
The ocean hath no blast;
His great bright eye most silently
Up to the Moon is cast—

If he may know which way to go;
For she guides him smooth or grim.
See, brother, see! how graciously
She looketh down on him."

The Mariner hath been cast into a trance; for the angelic power causeth the vessel to drive northward faster than human life could endure.

First Voice

"But why drives on that ship so fast,
Without or wave or wind?"

Second Voice

"The air is cut away before,
And closes from behind.

Fly, brother, fly! more high, more high!
Or we shall be belated:
For slow and slow that ship will go,
When the Mariner's trance is abated."

The super-natural motion is retarded; the Mariner awakes, and his penance begins anew.

I woke, and we were sailing on
As in a gentle weather:
'Twas night, calm night, the moon was high;
The dead men stood together.

All stood together on the deck,
For a charnel-dungeon fitter:
All fixed on me their stony eyes,
That in the Moon did glitter.

The pang, the curse, with which they died,
Had never passed away:
I could not draw my eyes from theirs,
Nor turn them up to pray.

The curse is finally expiated.

And now this spell was snapt: once more
I viewed the ocean green,
And looked far forth, yet little saw
Of what had else been seen—

Like one, that on a lonesome road
Doth walk in fear and dread,
And having once turned round walks on,
And turns no more his head;
Because he knows, a frightful fiend
Doth close behind him tread.

But soon there breathed a wind on me,
Nor sound nor motion made:
Its path was not upon the sea,
In ripple or in shade.

It raised my hair, it fanned my cheek
Like a meadow-gale of spring—
It mingled strangely with my fears,
Yet it felt like a welcoming.

Swiftly, swiftly flew the ship,
Yet she sailed softly too:
Sweetly, sweetly blew the breeze—
On me alone it blew.

And the ancient Mariner beholdeth his native country.

Oh! dream of joy! is this indeed
The light-house top I see?
Is this the hill? is this the kirk?
Is this mine own countree?

We drifted o'er the harbour-bar,
And I with sobs did pray—
O let me be awake, my God!
Or let me sleep alway.

The harbour-bay was clear as glass,
So smoothly it was strewn!
And on the bay the moonlight lay,
And the shadow of the Moon.

The rock shone bright, the kirk no less,
That stands above the rock:
The moonlight steeped in silentness
The steady weathercock.

And the bay was white with silent light,
Till rising from the same,
Full many shapes, that shadows were,
In crimson colours came.

The angelic spirits leave the dead bodies,

A little distance from the prow
Those crimson shadows were:
I turned my eyes upon the deck—
Oh, Christ! what saw I there!

And appear in their own forms of light.

Each corse lay flat, lifeless and flat,
And, by the holy rood!
A man all light, a seraph-man,
On every corse there stood.

This seraph-band, each waved his hand:
It was a heavenly sight!
They stood as signals to the land,
Each one a lovely light;

This seraph-band, each waved his hand,
No voice did they impart—
No voice; but oh! the silence sank
Like music on my heart.

But soon I heard the dash of oars,
I heard the Pilot's cheer;
My head was turned perforce away
And I saw a boat appear.

The Pilot and the Pilot's boy,
I heard them coming fast:
Dear Lord in Heaven! it was a joy
The dead men could not blast.

I saw a third—I heard his voice:
It is the Hermit good!
He singeth loud his godly hymns
That he makes in the wood.
He'll shrieve my soul, he'll wash away
The Albatross's blood.

Part VII

The Hermit of the Wood,

This Hermit good lives in that wood
Which slopes down to the sea.
How loudly his sweet voice he rears!
He loves to talk with marineres
That come from a far countree.

He kneels at morn, and noon, and eve—
He hath a cushion plump:
It is the moss that wholly hides
The rotted old oak-stump.

The skiff-boat neared: I heard them talk,
"Why, this is strange, I trow!
Where are those lights so many and fair,
That signal made but now?"

Approacheth the ship with wonder.

"Strange, by my faith!" the Hermit said—
"And they answered not our cheer!
The planks looked warped! and see those sails,
How thin they are and sere!
I never saw aught like to them,
Unless perchance it were

Brown skeletons of leaves that lag
My forest-brook along;
When the ivy-tod is heavy with snow,
And the owlet whoops to the wolf below,
That eats the she-wolf's young."

"Dear Lord! it hath a fiendish look—
(The Pilot made reply)
I am a-feared"—"Push on, push on!"
Said the Hermit cheerily.

The boat came closer to the ship,
But I nor spake nor stirred;
The boat came close beneath the ship,
And straight a sound was heard.

The ship suddenly sinketh.

Under the water it rumbled on,
Still louder and more dread:
It reached the ship, it split the bay;
The ship went down like lead.

The ancient Mariner is saved in the Pilot's boat.

Stunned by that loud and dreadful sound,
Which sky and ocean smote,
Like one that hath been seven days drowned
My body lay afloat;
But swift as dreams, myself I found
Within the Pilot's boat.

Upon the whirl, where sank the ship,
The boat spun round and round;
And all was still, save that the hill
Was telling of the sound.

I moved my lips—the Pilot shrieked
And fell down in a fit;
The holy Hermit raised his eyes,
And prayed where he did sit.

I took the oars: the Pilot's boy,
Who now doth crazy go,
Laughed loud and long, and all the while
His eyes went to and fro.
"Ha! ha!" quoth he, "full plain I see.
The Devil knows how to row."

And now, all in my own countree,
I stood on the firm land!
The Hermit stepped forth from the boat,
And scarcely he could stand.

The ancient Mariner earnestly entreateth the Hermit to shrieve him;

"O shrieve me, shrieve me, holy man!"
The Hermit crossed his brow.
"Say quick," quoth he, "I bid thee say—
What manner of man art thou?"

and the penance of life falls on him.

Forthwith this frame of mine was wrenched
With a woful agony,
Which forced me to begin my tale;
And then it left me free.

And ever and anon through out his future life an agony constraineth him to travel from land to land;

Since then, at an uncertain hour,
That agony returns:
And till my ghastly tale is told,
This heart within me burns.

I pass, like night, from land to land;
I have strange power of speech;
That moment that his face I see,
I know the man that must hear me:
To him my tale I teach.

What loud uproar bursts from that door!
The wedding-guests are there:
But in the garden-bower the bride
And bride-maids singing are:
And hark the little vesper bell,
Which biddeth me to prayer!

O Wedding-Guests! this soul hath been
Alone on a wide wide sea:
So lonely 'twas, that God himself
Scarce seeméd there to be.

O sweeter than the marriage-feast,
'Tis sweeter far to me,
To walk together to the kirk
With a goodly company!—

To walk together to the kirk,
And all together pray,
While each to his great Father bends,
Old men, and babes, and loving friends
And youths and maidens gay!

And to teach, by his own example, love and reverence to all things that God made and loveth.

Farewell, farewell! but this I tell
To thee, thou Wedding-Guest!
He prayeth well, who loveth well
Both man and bird and beast.

He prayeth best, who loveth best
All things both great and small;
For the dear God who loveth us,
He made and loveth all.

The Mariner, whose eye is bright,
Whose beard with age is hoar,
Is gone: and now the Wedding-Guest
Turned from the bridegroom's door.

He went like one that hath been stunned,
And is of sense forlorn:
A sadder and a wiser man.
He rose the morrow morn.

—*Samuel Taylor Coleridge*

2. *stoppeth one of three:* at .333, surely one of the worst fielding percentages in English Literature. 12. *elftsoons:* at once. 23. *kirk:* church. 55. *clifts:* cliffs. 62. *swound:* swoon. 128. *death-fires:* St. Elmo's fire, an electrical phenomenon believed to portend disaster. 152. *wist:* knew. 164. *gramercy:* thanks. 184. *gossameres:* thin cobwebs. 314. *sheen:* shone. The fire-flags are the southern lights, the Aurora Australis. 348. *corses:* corpses. 362. *jargonings:* warbling. 489. *holy rood:* the cross. 535. *ivy tod:* clump of ivy.

1. The primary focus in this poem is the Ancient Mariner himself. Recount his experience. What did he do? What happened to him? Why? How has he changed? Why?

2. What does the albatross seem to represent in this poem? Why does the mariner commit such a terrible crime as killing the albatross apparently is? Or *is* killing the albatross his crime?

3. Why was the mariner's life spared? Or did he die and return to life? Does he deserve resurrection? Why?

4. A secondary focus in this poem is the wedding guest. What is his reaction to the mariner's tale? Why does Coleridge have him going to a wedding feast when he is stopped by the mariner?

5. Can you relate the myth of the Ancient Mariner to any other religious stories you know? In what ways does Coleridge's poem seem to be a reworking of other religious myths?

6. What truths about human behavior do you find embodied in Coleridge's poem?

7. What tricks does Coleridge use to give his poem a mysterious, supernatural coloring? What legitimacies do the supernatural elements in the tale give to its myth?

She's Always a Woman to Me

She can kill with a smile
She can wound with her eyes
She can ruin your faith with
Her casual lies
And she only reveals what she
Wants you to see
She hides like a child
But she's always a woman to me.

She can lead you to love
She can take you or leave you
She can ask for the truth
But she'll never believe you
And she'll take what you give her
As long as it's free
She steals like a thief
But she's always a woman to me.

Oh—she takes care of herself
She can wait if she wants
She's ahead of her time.
Oh—and she never gives out
And she never gives in
She just changes her mind.

She will promise you more
Than the Garden of Eden
Then she'll carelessly cut you
And laugh while you're bleedin'
But she'll bring out the best
And the worst you can be
Blame it all on yourself
Cause she's always a woman to me.

Oh—she takes care of herself
She can wait if she wants
She's ahead of her time
Oh—and she never gives out
And she never gives in
She just changes her mind.

She is frequently kind
And she's suddenly cruel
She can do as she pleases
She's nobody's fool
But she can't be convicted
She's earned her degree
And the most she will do
Is throw shadows at you
But she's always a woman to me.

—*Billy Joel*

In this song Billy Joel attempts a new definition of woman, a new myth for women of the late 1970s and the 1980s. He creates a mythical person against whom real women can measure themselves. She is paradoxical, much like Dylan's "Sad-Eyed Lady of the Lowlands," and she is enormously attractive. What do you think of her? Is she too liberated? Is she, underneath the surface of things, the same old woman, the conception, really, of a male-chauvinist mind? How different is this woman of 1978 from the woman of 1968 or 1955? Of 1920? Of 1880?

The Bear

1

In late winter
I sometimes glimpse bits of steam
coming up from
some fault in the old snow
and bend close and see it is lung-colored
and put down my nose
and know
the chilly, enduring odor of bear.

2

I take a wolf's rib and whittle
it sharp at both ends
and coil it up
and freeze it in blubber and place it out
on the fairway of the bears.

And when it has vanished
I move out on the bear tracks,
roaming in circles
until I come to the first, tentative, dark
splash on the earth.

And I set out
running, following the splashes
of blood wandering over the world.
At the cut, gashed resting places
I stop and rest,
at the crawl-marks
where he lay out on his belly
to overpass some stretch of bauchy ice
I lie out
dragging myself forward with bear-knives in my fists.

3

On the third day I begin to starve,
at nightfall I bend down as I knew I would
at a turd sopped in blood,
and hesitate, and pick it up,
and thrust it in my mouth, and gnash it down,
and rise
and go on running.

4

On the seventh day,
living by now on bear blood alone,
I can see his upturned carcass far out ahead, a scraggled,
steamy hulk,
the heavy fur riffling in the wind.

I come up to him
and stare at the narrow-spaced, petty eyes,
the dismayed
face laid back on the shoulder, the nostrils
flared, catching
perhaps the first taint of me as he
died.

I hack
a ravine in his thigh, and eat and drink,
and tear him down his whole length
and open him and climb in
and close him up after me, against the wind,
and sleep.

5

And dream
of lumbering flatfooted
over the tundra,
stabbed twice from within,
splattering a trail behind me,
splattering it out no matter which way I lurch,
no matter which parabola of bear-transcendence,
which dance of solitude I attempt,
which gravity-clutched leap,
which trudge, which groan.

6

Until one day I totter and fall—
fall on this
stomach that has tried so hard to keep up,
to digest the blood as it leaked in,
to break up
and digest the bone itself: and now the breeze
blows over me, blows off
the hideous belches of ill-digested bear blood
and rotted stomach
and the ordinary, wretched odor of bear,

blows across
my sore, lolled tongue a song
or screech, until I think I must rise up
and dance. And I lie still.

7

I awaken I think. Marshlights
reappear, geese
come trailing again up the flyway.
In her ravine under old snow the dam-bear
lies, licking

lumps of smeared fur
and drizzly eyes into shapes
with her tongue. And one
hairy-soled trudge stuck out before me,
the next groaned out,
the next,
the next,
the rest of my days I spend
wandering: wondering
what, anyway,
was that sticky infusion, that rank flavor of blood, that poetry, by
    which I lived?

—*Galway Kinnell*

This poem, Kinnell once wrote, had its beginning in a bit of Indian legend: that in hunting a bear the young brave was required to eat its droppings. This and other literal details of the bear hunt are contained in the poem. But the bear has significance beyond that of mere prey hunted by Indians; it is, in fact, nearly a symbol. What does it signify? Well, in part at least, it represents our own animal instincts and nature. In hunting the bear, in eating its flesh and drinking its blood, in climbing into the bear's skin, the poet becomes the bear, takes on his instincts . . . and thereby reclaims a part of himself. By implication, of course, Kinnell's readers are invited to look for the bear inside themselves, and the process by which that bear has been purged or covered up, and the process by which it can be reclaimed. Kinnell may almost be said to assert the necessity of reclaiming our own inner beasts as well as hunters.

What do you think of this idea?

Where We Must Look for Help

The dove returns: it found no resting place;
It was in flight all night above the shaken seas;
Beneath ark eaves
The dove shall magnify the tiger's bed;
Give the dove peace.
The split-tail swallows leave the sill at dawn;
At dusk, blue swallows shall return.
On the third day the crow shall fly;
The crow, the crow, the spider-colored crow,
The crow shall find new mud to walk upon.

—*Robert Bly*

In introducing this poem at a reading, Bly called it a poem of the dark or shadow side of the personality, the side which is hidden from us, to which belong our sense of tragedy, our emotions, and intuitive knowledge. What elements of this poem seem to come from the light and dark sides of our personalities respectively?

The myth Bly uses in this poem is an older Babylonian version of the Noah story, in which not one bird but three were sent out to search for land. Why is this older version of the myth more useful to Bly than the story recorded in the Bible? Where must we, according to Bly, look "for help"? For help in what?

8. The Poet as Artificer

One of mankind's most psychologically compelling drives is his need to make some sense out of his world. We need order, we seek order . . . and once we settle on an order we cling to it tenaciously. People ask themselves the ultimate question "Why?" and turn to their own experiences and thoughts for answers. Once they have come to conclusions, they then tend to order future experiences according to their own point of view. Young people, who have yet to discover answers to their ultimate questions, are notoriously more open to experimentation than their parents, who often select and edit according to preconceived views of the world developed in their own more open youth.

All of this is to say that early training dies hard, even in the face of facts, and that order, once discovered, is not easily let loose. It is also to note that poets perform a function that is of considerable interest to all of us, that of discovering the order in chaos and, occasionally, the chaos in old orders. A successful poem "ends in a clarification of life," Frost said, "in a momentary stay against confusion." "Poetry should make order out of the poet's private chaos and chaos out of the world's mechanical order," said Thomas McGrath. "But it should be a 'purer chaos,' one which gives man a new vision and a sense of his forgotten powers, a chaos from which a new Creation can be made." The poet is an artificer, someone who creates new structures, new shapes, new orders.

One aspect of this ordering, of course, is simply the process of selecting experience and fashioning a poem out of it. The content of a poem is admitted because it hangs together in some more or less discernible relationship—and in that relationship exists an order (or a new and purer chaos). One of the poet's gifts is the ability to see relationships where other people see nothing, and thereby, to offer insight.

The poet also imposes order on his work by arranging something first, then second, then third, establishing a series of sequential relationships that can be philosophically enlightening, aesthetically satisfying, or both. In finding phrases, words, pieces to the verbal puzzle that is his poem, the poet creates harmony or order in his style. Finally, the poet may choose to impose a form on his work: regular meter, a pattern of rhymes, an arrangement of similarly phrased sentences or lines with similar length or beats or even syllable counts. While structural forms have loosened considerably in the twentieth century, form still plays an important role in the way a poet imposes order on what appears to be random.

Some cautions are in order here. First, there is a constant temptation even among poets to rely on old orders—philosophical or structural—and to give in to habit and formula. Poetic traditions, like people, grow old and tend to come to new experiences in terms of old solutions. The history of poetry is in one sense little more than a long sequence of solutions to the old question "Why?" This book is full of solutions from various poets of various centuries. But each new poem, as Eliot noted in "East Coker," is a new venture, a new raid upon the inarticulate and the chaotic, in which the old solutions no longer hold. However, as Chaucer wrote some centuries before Eliot, out of these old fields comes new grain; and out of the old solutions come the germs of new ideas. What is needed is the candor to confront an experience that does not conform to the old solutions—to open up content and form to experience that poetry did not previously encompass. And here especially there are arguments among poets, between the youngsters and their elders, and literary modes swing back and forth.

This raises another caution: some poets, like so many of the rest of us, discover in their quest for order nothing more than randomness and disorder, or the inadequacy of old answers. They are not really comforting poets to read if what we seek in poetry is reassurance. A line like Frost's famous "If design govern in a thing so small," or a title like Margaret Atwood's "A Place: Fragments," or the disintegration of form in contemporary poetry can be disconcerting in their indications of an order not found. However, chaos can be exhilarating and the stuff from which a new creation can be made.

Conversely, to raise the third caution, in a curious way the poet sometimes creates in the very act of searching for order and permanence the order and permanence he seeks. It is possible that the ultimate realities *are* in ideas, that the poet, by changing our ideas, can in fact reorder the nature of things. "When she sang," Wallace Stevens wrote in his famous poem "The Idea of Order at Key West," "the sea, / Whatever self it had, became the self / That was her song." Art may be not only a mirror to life, not only an ideal against which we can measure reality, but a *shaper* of life . . . and the poet an artificer not only of poetry, but of perception and experience as well.

Wen-fu

Taking his position at the hub of things, [the writer] contemplates the mystery of the universe; he feeds his emotions and his mind on the great works of the past.
Moving along with the four seasons, he sighs at the passing of time; gazing at the myriad objects, he thinks of the complexity of the world.
He sorrows over the falling leaves in virile autumn; he takes joy in the delicate bud of fragrant spring.
With awe at heart, he experiences chill; his spirit solemn, he turns his gaze to the clouds.
He declaims the superb works of his predecessors; he croons the clean fragrance of past worthies.
He roams in the Forest of Literature, and praises the symmetry of great art.
Moved, he pushes his books away and takes the writing-brush, that he may express himself in letters.
At first he withholds his sight and turns his hearing inward; he is lost in thought, questioning everywhere.
His spirit gallops to the eight ends of the universe; his mind wanders along vast distances.
In the end, as his mood dawns clearer and clearer, objects, clean-cut now in outline, shove one another forward.
He sips the essence of letters; he rinses his mouth with the extract of the Six Arts.
Floating on the heavenly lake, he swims along; plunging into the nether spring, he immerses himself.
Thereupon, submerged words wriggle up, as when a darting fish, with the hook in its gills, leaps from a deep lake; floating beauties flutter down, as when a high-flying bird, with the harpoon-string around its wings, drops from a crest of cloud.
He gathers words never used in a hundred generations; he picks rhythms never sung in a thousand years.
He spurns the morning blossom, now full blown; he plucks the evening bud, which has yet to open.
He sees past and present in a moment; he touches the four seas in a twinkling of an eye.
Now he selects ideas and fixes them in order; he examines words and puts them in their places.

He taps at the door of all that is colorful; he chooses from among everything that rings.
Now he shakes the foliage by tugging the twig; now he follows back along the waves to the fountainhead of the stream.
Sometimes he brings out what was hidden; sometimes, looking for an easy prey, he bags a hard one.
Now, the tiger puts in new stripes, to the consternation of other beasts; now, the dragon emerges, and terrifies all the birds.
Sometimes things fit together, are easy to manage; sometimes they jar each other, are awkward to manipulate.
He empties his mind completely, to concentrate his thoughts; he collects his wits before he puts words together.
He traps heaven and earth in the cage of form; he crushes the myriad objects against the tip of his brush.
At first they hesitate upon his parched lips; finally they flow through the well-moistened brush.
Reason, supporting the matter [of the poem], stiffens the trunk; style, depending from it, spreads luxuriance around.
Emotion and expression never disagree: all changes [in his mood] are betrayed on his face.
If the thought touches on joy, a smile is inevitable; no sooner is sorrow spoken of than a sigh escapes. . . .

—*Lu Chi*
(translated by *Achilles Fang*)

11. *Six Arts:* ceremonial observances, music, archery, writing, mathematics, and charioteering.

1. Upon what resources does the poet, according to Lu Chi, draw in composing his poem?
2. How important does form in poetry appear to be to Lu Chi?
3. How—if at all—does the role of the poet in Chinese society differ from the poet's role in American culture?

Sonnet 55

Not marble, nor the gilded monuments
Of princes, shall outlive this powerful rhyme;
But you shall shine more bright in these contents
Than unswept stone, besmeared with sluttish time.
When wasteful war shall statues overturn,
And broils root out the work of masonry,
Nor Mars his sword nor war's quick fire shall burn
The living record of your memory.

'Gainst death and all oblivious enmity
Shall you pace forth; your praise shall still find room
Even in the eyes of all posterity
That wear this world out to the ending doom.
So, till the judgment that yourself arise,
You live in this, and dwell in lovers' eyes.

—*William Shakespeare*

6. *broils:* quarrels, tumults. 7. *Mars his:* Mars'. 13. *that:* when.

One quality of poem as artifice, of course, is permanence. It is amazing how the poet's order, and the philosopher's, have a way of outlasting the contrivances of nature and even the monuments of man.

To the Stone-Cutters

Stone-cutters fighting time with marble, you foredefeated
Challengers of oblivion
Eat cynical earnings, knowing rock splits, records fall down,
The square-limbed Roman letters
Scale in the thaws, wear in the rain. The poet as well
Builds his monument mockingly;
For man will be blotted out, the blithe earth die, the brave sun
Die blind, his heart blackening:
Yet stones have stood for a thousand years, and pained
  thoughts found
The honey peace in old poems.

—*Robinson Jeffers*

Still, not even poems last forever. In "To the Stone-Cutters" Jeffers begins with an implicit contrast: we think quietly to ourselves as we read those initial five lines, "But poems do not crack or scale or split. Poems are forever." Then Jeffers moves to a comparison: poems are, in fact, like monuments, because eventually it all falls down. Finally Jeffers offers a guarded affirmation of permanence and order: stones last thousands of years, and old poems still work their healing on newly pained hearts.

The Idea of Order at Key West

She sang beyond the genius of the sea.
The water never formed to mind or voice,
Like a body wholly body, fluttering

Its empty sleeves; and yet its mimic motion
Made constant cry, caused constantly a cry,
That was not ours although we understood,
Inhuman, of the veritable ocean.

The sea was not a mask. No more was she.
The song and water were not medleyed sound
Even if what she sang was what she heard,
Since what she sang was uttered word by word.
It may be that in all her phrases stirred
The grinding water and the gasping wind;
But it was she and not the sea we heard.
For she was the maker of the song she sang.
The ever-hooded, tragic-gestured sea
Was merely a place by which she walked to sing.
Whose spirit is this? we said, because we knew
It was the spirit that we sought and knew
That we should ask this often as she sang.

If it was only the dark voice of the sea
That rose, or even colored by many waves;
If it was only the outer voice of sky
And cloud, of the sunken coral water-walled,
However clear, it would have been deep air,
The heaving speech of air, a summer sound
Repeated in a summer without end
And sound alone. But it was more than that,
More even than her voice, and ours, among
The meaningless plungings of water and the wind,
Theatrical distances, bronze shadows heaped
On high horizons, mountainous atmospheres
Of sky and sea.
It was her voice that made
The sky acutest at its vanishing.
She measured to the hour its solitude.
She was the single artificer of the world
In which she sang. And when she sang, the sea,
Whatever self it had, became the self
That was her song, for she was the marker. Then we,
As we beheld her striding there alone,
Knew that there never was a world for her
Except the one she sang and, singing, made.

Ramon Fernandez, tell me, if you know,
Why, when the singing ended and we turned

Toward the town, tell why the glassy lights,
The lights in the fishing boats at anchor there,
As the night descended, tilting in the air,
Mastered the night and portioned out the sea,
Fixing emblazoned zones and fiery poles,
Arranging, deepening, enchanting night.
Oh! Blessed rage for order, pale Ramon,
The maker's rage to order words of the sea,
Words of the fragrant portals, dimly-starred,
And of ourselves and of our origins,
In ghostlier demarcations, keener sounds.

—*Wallace Stevens*

43. Ramon Fernandez: a Spanish critic and aesthetician.

Stevens presents us with two seas: one surrounding Key West, and one created in the song of the female singer. The relationship between the two is somewhat unclear in the first four sections of the poem, but begins to emerge in the fifth: "And when she sang, the sea, / Whatever self it had, became the self / That was her song." The artist, according to Stevens, takes natural phenomena and transforms them into something different. And when the audience turns from the sea of the song to the sea in the harbor, it finds that latter sea transformed: "The lights . . . / Mastered the night and portioned out the sea." The natural sea is magically ordered after the production of the poem, apparently as a result of the process of poetic creation. So too, Stevens implies, the artist orders experience for his audience, first in his poem and afterwards in the arrangement the artistic construct imposes on natural phenomena.

Delight in Disorder

A sweet disorder in the dress
Kindles in clothes a wantonness.
A lawn about the shoulders thrown
Into a fine distraction;
An erring lace, which here and there
Enthralls the crimson stomacher;
A cuff neglectful, and thereby
Ribbons to flow confusedly;
A winning wave (deserving note)
In the tempestuous petticoat;
A careless shoestring, in whose tie

I see a wild civility:
Do more bewitch me than when art
Is too precise in every part.

—*Robert Herrick*

2. *wantonness:* gaiety. 3. *lawn:* linen scarf. 4. *distraction:* confusion. 6. *stomacher:* an ornamental garment worn under the lacing of the bodice.

Sometimes what is interesting is disorder. Especially in a world of strict order, or a world where things (or ideas) seem too carefully arranged, a little chaos seems more attractive, somehow more *true,* than the order it disrupts. This is Herrick's point in "Delight in Disorder," where his subject is as much philosophical as physical, and his delight is at least as aesthetic as sensual.

A Place: Fragments

i)

Here on the rim, cringing
under the cracked whip of winter
we live
in houses of ice,
but not because we want to:
in order to survive
we make what we can and have to
with what we have.

ii)

Old woman I visited once
out of my way
in a little-visited province:

she had a neat
house, a clean parlour
though obsolete and poor:

a cushion with a fringe;
glass animals arranged
across the mantlepiece (a swan, a horse,
a bull); a mirror;
a teacup sent from Scotland;
several heraldic spoons;

a lamp; and in the center
of the table, a paperweight:
hollow glass globe
filled with water, and
a house, a man, a snowstorm.

The room was as
dustless as possible
and free of spiders.
I
stood in the door-
way, at the fulcrum where

this trivial but
stringent inner order
held its delicate balance
with the random scattering or
clogged merging of
things: ditch by the road; dried
reeds in the wind; flat
wet bush, grey sky
sweeping away outside.

iii)

The cities are only outposts.

Watch that man
walking on cement as though on snowshoes:
senses the road
a muskeg, loose mat of roots and brown
vegetable decay
or crust of ice that
easily might break and
slush or water under
suck him down

The land flows like a
sluggish current.

The mountains eddy slowly towards the sea.

iv)

The people who come here also
flow: their bodies becoming
nebulous, diffused, quietly
spreading out into the air across
these interstellar sidewalks

v)

This is what it must be
like in outer space
where the stars are pasted flat
againt the total
black of the expanding
eye, fly-
specks of burning dust

vi)

There is no center;
the centers
travel with us unseen
like our shadows
on a day when there is no sun.

We must move back:
there are too many foregrounds.

Now, clutter of twigs
across our eyes, tatter
of birds at the eye's edge; the straggle
of dead treetrunks; patch
of lichen
and in love, tangle
of limbs and fingers, the texture
of pores and lines on the skin.

vii)

An other sense tugs at us:
we have lost something,
some key to these things
which must be writings
and are locked against us
or perhaps (like a potential
mine, unknown vein

of metal in the rock)
something not lost or hidden
but just not found yet

that informs, holds together
this confusion, this largeness
and dissolving:

not above or behind
or within it, but one
with it: an

identity:
something too huge and simple
for us to see.

—*Margaret Atwood*

11. *province:* Ms. Atwood is Canadian. 44. *muskeg:* swamp.

Poets do not always find the order they seek. In her visit to one of Canada's more rural provinces, Atwood discovers an order in the home of the old woman she visits, a "stringent inner order" with a "delicate balance." But it is an old order, a leftover from another world or another century, holding together just a little longer, but doomed to crumble like the monuments of Jeffers's stonecutters. For Atwood this old order is already gone, and for the world outside the old woman's house as well, we suspect. Cities provide only "outposts" of civilization, and immediately beneath the veneer of the city (the cement sidewalk) lurks a swamp of confusion that will suck a person under. "There is no center," Atwood concludes somewhat pessimistically, echoing William Butler Yeats's line "The center cannot hold," and voicing the consensual opinion of the twentieth century. In the final section of her poem Atwood speaks of a key to these things which we sense but cannot discover: what she is looking for, of course, is the new creation which, in McGrath's words, should be possible out of this chaos.

It is worth noting, as a final comment on this poem, that Atwood's poetic form—the disjointed way she arranges words and lines on the page—is a very close analogue to her statement.

9. The Poet as Explorer

In the purest sense every poem, every work of art that is not a patent plagiarism is exploratory, a new arrangement of words, of phrases, of images and observations, a new attempt at meaning. The same might be said of common prose, even of everyday speech: the situation—and the words—are never *exactly* the same on any two occasions, and always we must fashion something new out of something old. Even in our letters to our mothers we are exploring new ways of saying things.

Usually, however, we create the new out of the old: words we've read, expressions we've heard, language we've learned. Poets too learn from each other and the world around them, and it's not difficult once you know enough to concoct whole dialogues, whole poems built of phrases quoted from here or there. Poets can be "traditional," using conventional forms, conventional images, conventional language to express conventional thoughts.

But not modern poets. One of the severest criticisms that can be leveled at a contemporary poet is the charge that his work is conventional; no serious artist likes to think that his work is not unique, the uniquer the better. Poets speak of "finding their own voice" or "discovering their own matter"; what they mean is that they want to distinguish themselves from all other poets past and present, either by covering new ground or by seeing familiar objects in a fresh light. Even critics these days are more impressed with the exploratory than the conventional, and in our histories and anthologies of literature we tend to value artists more according to how innovative they were than according to how popular they were when they lived. John Donne, Gerard Manley Hopkins, and Emily Dickinson (who published only seven poems during her lifetime, some of them "reworked" by editors to "smooth them out") are all conspicuous examples here. Walt Whitman, generally considered to be the father of modern American poetry, was not popular in his day. But each of these poets looked forward to developments in poetry that we find particularly modern, and for their innovation they are remembered. Conversely, many poets popular in their day have virtually dropped from the public consciousness.

This distrust of convention, this rage for innovation has its advantages and its disadvantages. On the one hand, it tempts poets too far from the center, makes them reluctant to borrow from their predecessors and their contemporaries, and discourages a great poet from looking around him, picking up the best of what's already going on, and putting everything together in a summary of the age. Poets would rather father movements than encapsulate them. Sometimes poetry becomes faddish and directionless. Its thrust is lost in splinter groups and internal aesthetic arguments. A mode of expression is no sooner discovered than it is exploited, no sooner exploited than forgotten. Finally, in their quest for innovation and individuality poets sometimes transcend the sublime into the ridiculous. Almost always they transcend their audiences.

On the other hand, contemporary poetry is rarely dull. The poet, more than anyone else, is aware of the enormous range of possibilities in language and vision, in subject and expression. Like artists in other media, contemporary poets are continuously making art from any kind of language, myth, or cultural artifact that happens to fall into their hands. They explore constantly the outer limits of sound, meaning, tone, denotation, and connotation, mining the incredible richness of the English language. "We've got language we're not even using," said poet George Starbuck. They explore Indian, oriental, Mayan mythologies and report their discoveries to the rest of us. They tune their ears to the world around them, listening for "found poems," poems that just happen to happen on television or in conversation or in ordinary newspaper prose. "I like to steal poems from my students," confessed poet Sandra Cisnaros, "because they're always talking poems, and if nobody else is going to use them, I will." Some poets have even experimented with "significant compositional use of blank space," printing a single line (for example, Dennis Phillips's "At crossroads: no signs only voices," in his book *The Frontier*) on one large sheet of paper, making the page more empty paper than ink. And a few poets have gone so far as to cut poems or prose into tiny pieces of a word or two, toss them into the air, and see what came out as the words settled themselves onto the carpet in relationships and meanings of their own.

If this kind of exploration unsettles our notions of poetry, and disrupts our conventional orders, so much the better says the modern poet. New orders and new explanations can be constructed to accommodate the new discoveries. If critics don't like it, or the old folks, nevermind: look at all the criticism of Whitman, look at that review of Wordsworth's *Lyrical Ballads* that began, "This will never do." If our vision is blurred for the moment, always there is the faith that a new sense will emerge, a new key will be found, a new model constructed, and in the final analysis a new, more encompassing, and more valid vision will emerge. The poet should no more desist from exploring language than the scientist from exploring the world around him.

This Was a Poet

This was a Poet—It is That
Distills amazing sense
From ordinary Meanings—
And Attar so immense

From the familiar species
That perished by the Door—
We wonder it was not Ourselves
Arrested it—before—

Of Pictures, the Discloser—
The Poet—it is He—
Entitles Us—by Contrast—
To ceaseless Poverty—

Of Portion—so unconscious—
The Robbing—could not harm—
Himself—to Him—a Fortune—
Exterior—to Time—

—Emily Dickinson

4. *attar:* a fragrant oil or perfume distilled from the petals of flowers. 8. *arrested:* sensed, perceived.

Dickinson, in her poem on poets, sees the poet as one who perceives the miraculous in the ordinary. She uses several comparisons: he distills mystery from experience the way one distills perfume from flower petals; he reveals the hidden meaning of allegories (probably the best translation of "pictures" is not "paintings" or "photographs," but "depictions," in the sense of allegorical depictions); he is so rich as never to notice us stealing a bit of his metaphysical fortune. This view of the poet as one who could see the extraordinary in the common, and the notion that the extraordinary was to be found in the common, were both widely held during the nineteenth century.

Buffalo Bill's

Buffalo Bill's
defunct
        who used to
        ride a watersmooth-silver
                                                  stallion
and break onetwothreefourfive pigeonsjustlikethat
                                                                                Jesus

he was a handsome man
                                        and what i want to know is
how do you like your blueeyed boy
Mister Death

—e. e. cummings

Although we've accustomed ourselves somewhat to the idiosyncrasies of e. e. cummings's poetry over the last few decades, much of his work seemed disconcertingly, inaccessibly experimental when he was writing during the twenties and the thirties. Even today people accustomed to prose or traditional poetry find cummings's work unusual. Compare this poem with a poem by, say, Frost or Yeats, and point out the features of cummings's work that seem innovative. Apart from the mere innovation of it all, can you think of any reason why cummings might want to run together "onetwothreefourfive" and "pigeonsjustlikethat"? Why "Jesus" has its own exclusive line?

Portrait of a Woman in Bed

There's my things
drying in the corner:
that blue skirt
joined to the grey shirt—

I'm sick of trouble!
Lift the covers
if you want me
and you'll see
the rest of my clothes—
thought it would be cold
lying with nothing on!

I won't work
and I've got no cash.
What are you going to do
about it?
—and no jewelry
(the crazy fools)

But I've my two eyes
and a smooth face
and here's this! look!
it's high!

There's brains and blood
in there—
my name's Robitza!
Corsets
can go to the devil—
and drawers along with them—
What do I care!

My two boys?
—they're keen!
Let the rich lady
care for them—
they'll beat the school
or
let them go to the gutter—
that ends trouble.

This house is empty
isn't it?
Then it's mine
because I need it.
Oh, I won't starve
while there's the bible
to make them feed me.

Try to help me
if you want trouble
or leave me alone—
that ends trouble.

The country physician
is a damned fool
and you
can go to hell!

You could have closed the door
when you came in;
do it when you go out.
I'm tired.

—*William Carlos Williams*

William Carlos Williams was another twentieth-century innovator. He was especially influential in infusing into poetry the language and speech patterns of the American street. If you compare this poem with a poem by, say, Frost, you will see immediately what this means. What words and phrases sound especially like "street talk"? What do you think of this woman—is she heroic or despicable, or merely "there"? Is she what you expected when you read the title of the poem?

How the West Was Won

(Lines found on "The Westerners," NBC-TV)

"You ain't gonna make it, Injiun.
See them buzzards hangin' up there
waitin' for you?

You ain't the same Apache.
You turnin' into a dead man."

—*Warren Woessner*

1. This is, as its epigraph indicates, a "found poem," an artifact that Woessner picked up from an NBC-TV script writer and presents to us just about as he found it. Do you find any art—any structure, any form, any artifice—in the poem?

2. Woessner leaves us to draw our own meanings from this cultural artifact, either on the assumption that its significance is so obvious we can't miss it, or because he views it as having no significance at all. Which do you think?

3. In what way is Woessner acting as historian here, as well as explorer?

Our Youth

Of bricks . . . Who built it? Like some crazy balloon
When love leans on us
Its nights . . . The velvety pavement sticks to our feet.
The dead puppies turn us back on love.
Where we are. Sometimes
The brick arches led to a room like a bubble, that broke when
 you entered it
And sometimes to a fallen leaf.
We got crazy with emotion, showing how much we knew.

The Arabs took us. We knew
The dead horses. We were discovering coffee,
How it is to be drunk hot, with bare feet
In Canada. And the immortal music of Chopin

Which we had been discovering for several months
Since we were fourteen years old. And coffee grounds,
And the wonder of hands, and the wonder of the day
When the child discovers her first dead hand.

Do you know it? Hasn't she
Observed you too? Haven't you been observed to her?
My, haven't the flowers been? Is the evil
In't? What window? What did you say there?

Heh? Eh? Our youth is dead.
From the minute we discover it with eyes closed
Advancing into mountain light.
Ouch . . . You will never have that young boy,

That boy with the monocle
Could have been your father
He is passing by. No, that other one,
Upstairs. He is the one who wanted to see you.

He is dead. Green and yellow handkerchiefs cover him.
Perhaps he will never rot, I see
That my clothes are dry. I will go.
The naked girl crosses the street.

Blue hampers . . . Explosions,
Ice . . . The ridiculous
Vases of porphyry. All that our youth
Can't use, that it was created for.
It's true we have not avoided our destiny
By weeding out the old people.
Our faces have filled with smoke. We escape
Down the cloud ladder, but the problem has not been solved.

—*John Ashbery*

"Most of my poems," John Ashbery has said, "are about the experience of experience." On another occasion he explained that each poem was but "a snapshot of whatever is going through my mind at the time." This is certainly experimental, and quite explanatory of the almost total randomness of his poems. What specific features of this poem make it difficult to understand? Can you make any rational sense at all of it? If a poem can offer no mythical coherence, no rational sense, no continuity of structure or theme, what can it offer in compensation? Is it "explanation" enough of such a poem to point out that in resisting so successfully the tools of analysis, it reflects the confusion of modern life?

10. The Poet as Sociologist/Psychologist

A good poem, as we shall see, has four components: thing (its subject matter), voice (the sound of the poet speaking), form (the poem's structure), and statement (its meaning). We are usually attracted first to a poem by either its subject or the voice of the poet; what makes the poem memorable, however, is usually its statement or its performance, the *way* the poet goes about turning thing into statement. At one time it was more or less assumed that the primary purpose of a poem was to instruct, and any poem that did not make you a better person wasn't really worth your time. Modern poets generally rebel against such ideas, against audiences in search of important statements on important subjects, but it is a fact that even modern poets *do* make statements and offer insights that make their poetry instructive as well as beautiful.

A poem's statement may, of course, be on any subject imaginable, but the favorite topic of all poets seems to be man—either alone or in society. Long before the pseudo-sciences of psychology and sociology were invented, poets were playing the psychologist and the sociologist, analyzing in their own intuitive manner human behavior and motivation. This habit has persisted, although the modern world—given over as it is to abstract statistics, steeped in rules of probability and statistically valid samples, and skeptical about observation with the naked eye (or heart)—pays scant attention to the views of poets, who are most often written off as unreliable dreamers or, worse, madmen. The poet who speaks out on the world around him, especially if he plays the social conscience and criticizes, is told to get back to his poetry and leave the social analysis to "experts." The truth of the matter is that poets are among the most reliable of all commentators on human nature and society and—except when lobbying for their own importance in the scheme of things—are most to be trusted. They have no vested interest, they have great sensitivity, and they deal in specifics, in *things,* not in abstract generalizations and percentages. They are closer in this to people like you and me, who are concretions, not abstractions. In the myths they create to help man understand himself and in the statements they make in their poems, poets—rightly understood—can offer more insight than even philosophers.

Four things cloud the statements of poets as sociologists and psychologists. First, modern poets tend to understate their case, gambling everything on one fragile case, even on a word or a phrase. They would a hundred times rather their statement be lost in subtleties than have to preach in the manner of Emerson and Longfellow. Thus their statement is often lost in the inattentive ear, or may take several readings to perceive.

Second, poets often use similes and metaphors—comparisons—to make their point. Talking about a bear or a tree or a fox, they may be making a point about human nature in a poem that you will think is just about a bear or a tree or a fox.

Third, and very common among contemporary poets especially, poets often talk about others by examining themselves. They speak about mankind in general by looking inward in particular. So-called "confessional poets" make a habit of stripping in public, baring their souls to us, so that we can easily miss the universality of their lives, the "poet as everyman," and thereby miss the comment they make on the human situation. Even though the main subject of many contemporary poets is themselves, and *I*'s dot the page like bits of pepper and crystals of salt, we ought not to assume that the confessional poet is analyzing only himself, or speaking only of and to his own situation. As the Beatles once put it, "I am he as you are he as you are me and we are all together." Of all modern poets, confessional poets most play the roles of sociologist and psychologist.

The fourth caution, however, is that this I-is-you equation is sometimes inaccurate. Professional psychologists have discovered that writing poetry (or dancing or painting) has a certain therapeutic value, and one treatment for some mentally disturbed people is to get them to write poetry. (Many modern poets have spent time in mental hospitals, which might lead one to the overly simple conclusion that since they found poetry therapeutic, what works for them might work for others.) Large numbers of even ordinary people have taken to writing poems "to express themselves" and "to relieve tensions." Some people look for "poetry groups" the way they'd look for group therapy sessions, and bleed for each other regularly once a week, Friday night at eight, bring your own beer. Poetry *looks* easy, especially contemporary poetry which has legitimized the self as subject, the language of everyday speech as voice, and free verse as a structure. And so you find enormous amounts of amateur poetry that is in reality social or psychological therapy: bleeding on the page.

The problem with this kind of poetry is that it ignores its audience. Because there is no obligation to consider the reader, there is no obligation to affect the reader. It is usually trivial, because most of our private lives are trivial. Disregarding its personal value, this poetry might function as evidence in a psychological or sociological case study—which is exactly how psychologists and sociologists view it. Or it is gossip.

It's difficult to determine the boundary between "confessional poetry" (where the poet's self stands for all of us, and a legitimate social or psychological point is made) and poetry as therapy. Sometimes even Dylan, Plath, Sexton, Ginsberg seem to step far over the line. But the distinction is critical, for it is all the difference between a real hamburger and a McDonald's imitation.

from Song of Myself

7. Has any one supposed it lucky to be born?
I hasten to inform him or her it is just as lucky to die, and
 I know it.

I pass death with the dying and birth with the new-wash'd
 babe, and am not contain'd between my hat and boots,
And peruse manifold objects, no two alike and every one
 good,
The earth good and the stars good, and their adjuncts all
 good.

I am not an earth nor an adjunct of an earth,
I am the mate and companion of people, all just as immor-
 tal and fathomless as myself,
(They do not know how immortal, but I know.)

Every kind for itself and its own, for me mine male and
 female,
For me those that have been boys and that love women,
For me the man that is proud and feels how it stings to be
 slighted,
For me the sweet-heart and the old maid, for me mothers
 and the mothers of mothers,
For me lips that have smiled, eyes that have shed tears,
For me children and the begetters of children.

Undrape! you are not guilty to me, nor stale nor dis-
 carded,
I see through the broadcloth and gingham whether or no,
And am around, tenacious, acquisitive, tireless, and cannot
 be shaken away.

8. The little one sleeps in its cradle,
I lift the gauze and look a long time, and silently brush away
 flies with my hand.

The youngster and the red-faced girl turn aside up the bushy hill,
I peeringly view them from the top.

The suicide sprawls on the bloody floor of the bedroom,
I witness the corpse with its dabbled hair, I note where the pistol has fallen.

The blab of the pave, tires of carts, sluff of boot-soles, talk of the promenaders,
The heavy omnibus, the driver with his interrogating thumb, the clank of the shod horses on the granite floor,
The snow-sleighs, clinking, shouted jokes, pelts of snow-balls,
The hurrahs for popular favorites, the fury of rous'd mobs,
The flap of the curtain'd litter, a sick man inside borne to the hospital,
The meeting of enemies, the sudden oath, the blows and fall,
The excited crowd, the policeman with his star quickly working his passage to the centre of the crowd,
The impassive stones that receive and return so many echoes,
What groans of over-fed or half-starv'd who fall sunstruck or in fits,
What exclamations of women taken suddenly who hurry home and give birth to babes,
What living and buried speech is always vibrating here, what howls restrain'd by decorum,
Arrests of criminals, slights, adulterous offers made, acceptances, rejections with convex lips,
I mind them or the show or resonance of them—I come and I depart.

9. The big doors of the country barn stand open and ready,
The dried grass of the harvest-time loads the slow-drawn wagon,
The clear light plays on the brown gray and green intertinged,
The armfuls are pack'd to the sagging mow.

I am there, I help, I came stretch'd atop of the load,
I felt its soft jolts, one leg reclined on the other,
I jump from the cross-beams and seize the clover and timothy,
And roll head over heels and tangle my hair full of wisps.

10. Alone far in the wilds and mountains I hunt,
Wandering amazed at my own lightness and glee,
In the late afternoon choosing a safe spot to pass the night,
Kindling a fire and broiling the fresh-kill'd game,
Falling alseep on the gather'd leaves with my dog and gun by my side.

The Yankee clipper is under her sky-sails, she cuts the sparkle and scud,
My eyes settle the land, I bend at her prow or shout joyously from the deck.

The boatmen and clam-diggers arose early and stopt for me,
I tuck'd my trouser-ends in my boots and went and had a good time;
You should have been with us that day round the chowder-kettle.

I saw the marriage of the trapper in the open air in the far west, the bride was a red girl,
Her father and his friends sat near cross-legged and dumbly smoking, they had moccasins to their feet and large thick blankets hanging from their shoulders,
On a bank lounged the trapper, he was drest mostly in skins, his luxuriant beard and curls protected his neck, he held his bride by the hand,
She had long eyelashes, her head was bare, her coarse straight locks decended upon her voluptuous limbs and reach'd to her feet.

The runaway slave came to my house and stopt outside,
I heard his motions crackling the twigs of the woodpile,
Through the swung half-door of the kitchen I saw him limpsy and weak,
And went where he sat on a log and led him in and assured him,
And brought water and fill'd a tub for his sweated body and bruis'd feet,
And gave him a room that enter'd from my own, and gave him some coarse clean clothes,
And remember perfectly well his revolving eyes and his awkwardness,
And remember putting plasters on the galls of his neck and ankles;

He staid with me a week before he was recuperated and pass'd north,
I had him sit next me at table, my fire-lock lean'd in the corner.

11. Twenty-eight young men bathe by the shore,
Twenty-eight young men and all so friendly;
Twenty-eight years of womanly life and all so lonesome.

She owns the fine house by the rise of the bank,
She hides handsome and richly drest aft the blinds of the window.

Which of the young men does she like the best?
Ah the homeliest of them is beautiful to her.

Where are you off to, lady? for I see you,
You splash in the water there, yet stay stock still in your room.

Dancing and laughing along the beach came the twenty-ninth bather,
The rest did not see her, but she saw them and loved them.

The beards of the young men glisten'd with wet, it ran from their long hair,
Little streams pass'd all over their bodies.

An unseen hand also pass'd over their bodies,
It descended tremblingly from their temples and ribs.

The young men float on their backs, their white bellies bulge to the sun, they do not ask who seizes fast to them,
They do not know who puffs and declines with pendant and bending arch,
They do not think whom they souse with spray.

12. The butcher-boy puts off his killing-clothes, or sharpens his knife at the stall in the market,
I loiter enjoying his repartee and his shuffle and break-down.

Blacksmiths with grimed and hairy chests environ the
anvil,
Each has his main-sledge, they are all out, there is a great
heat in the fire.

From the cinder-strew'd threshold I follow their
movements,
The lithe sheer of their waists plays even with their
massive arms,
Overhand the hammers swing, overhand so slow, overhand
so sure,
They do not hasten, each man hits in his place.

—*Walt Whitman*

26. *omnibus:* bus, here a horse-drawn bus. 51. *scud:* wind-driven mist. 62. *limpsy:* limping or swaying. 89. *shuffle and break-down:* two dances popular in minstrel shows.

"Every atom belonging to me as good belongs to you," sang Walt Whitman at the outset of "Song of Myself," thereby making his poem the quintessence of everyman. "Song of Myself" is a great encyclopaedia of Whitman's various selves, incorporating man and woman, hireling and tradesman and slave, everyone Whitman had ever met or could think of meeting. But behind the great catalogue lies an implicit statement of acceptance, which the poet states clearly: "you are not guilty to me, nor stale nor discarded." All are equal, and all equally important (in section 15, another list of people and professions, Whitman places the president immediately after the prostitute—a characteristic bit of humor). Whitman's statement, then, is nothing less than the American dream of equality for all and social justice.

But Whitman is psychologist as well as sociologist. Notice especially section 11. Psychoanalyze this twenty-eight-year-old woman. What does she want? What fears inhibit her? What does Whitman have to say about all this?

Elegy for Jane

My student, thrown by a horse

I remember the neckcurls, limp and damp as tendrils;
And her quick look, a sidelong pickerel smile;
And how, once startled into talk, the light syllables leaped for
her,
And she balanced in the delight of her thought,

A wren, happy, tail into the wind,
Her song trembling the twigs and small branches.
The shade sang with her;
The leaves, their whispers turned to kissing,
And the mould sang in the bleached valleys under the rose.

Oh, when she was sad, she cast herself down into such a pure depth,
Even a father could not find her:
Scraping her cheek against straw,
Stirring the clearest water.

My sparrow, you are not here,
Waiting like a fern, making a spiney shadow.
The sides of wet stones cannot console me,
Nor the moss, wound with the last light.

If only I could nudge you from this sleep,
My maimed darling, my skittery pigeon.
Over this damp grave I speak the words of my love:
I, with no rights in this matter,
Neither father nor lover.

—*Theodore Roethke*

At first glance it is difficult to see in this poem the poet as sociologist. What we have here is a commemorative poem occasioned by the death of Roethke's student. But consider the matter for a moment, those last few lines. Implicit in them is a comment about the relationship between Roethke and Jane: what it was and what it might have been. For professional reasons the poet has no rights at all in this matter: he can be neither father nor lover, and if he becomes too much of either he may breach certain trusts. But as a human being and as a poet Roethke breaks through those roles to become (at the risk of sounding clichéd) one person caring for another. "Elegy for Jane" is an elegy for a dead girl, certainly; but it is also a commentary on the way human relationships may be repressed in the roles we are forced to play with each other.

American Tune

Many's the time I've been mistaken
And many times confused
Yes, and I've often felt forsaken

And certainly misused
But I'm all right, I'm all right
I'm just weary to my bones
Still, you don't expect to be
Bright and bon vivant
So far away from home, so far away from home

And I don't know a soul who's not been battered
I don't have a friend who feels at ease
I don't know a dream that's not been shattered
Or driven to its knees
But it's all right, it's all right
We've lived so well so long
Still, when I think of the road
We're traveling on
I wonder what went wrong
I can't help it, I wonder what went wrong

And I dreamed I was dying
And I dreamed that my soul rose unexpectedly
And looking back down on me
Smiled reassuringly
And I dreamed I was flying
And high up above my eyes could clearly see
The Statue of Liberty
Sailing away to sea
And I dreamed I was flying

We come on the ship they call the Mayflower
We come on the ship that sailed the moon
We come in the age's most uncertain hour
And sing an American tune
But it's all right, it's all right
You can't be forever blessed
Still, tomorrow's going to be another working day
And I'm trying to get some rest
That's all I'm trying to get some rest

—*Paul Simon*

In this song, one of the most important songs of the 1970s, Paul Simon takes a look at the world around him, at the stagnation which seems to have set in after the intense social and political activism of the sixties, at "the Great Sleep" as it were, and asks himself what's gone wrong with society. What answers does he give?

Dover Beach

The sea is calm to-night.
The tide is full, the moon lies fair
Upon the straits;—on the French coast the light
Gleams and is gone; the cliffs of England stand,
Glimmering and vast, out in the tranquil bay.
Come to the window, sweet is the night-air!
Only, from the long line of spray
Where the sea meets the moon-blanch'd land,
Listen! you hear the grating roar
Of pebbles which the waves draw back, and fling,
At their return, up the high strand,
Begin, and cease, and then again begin,
With tremulous cadence slow, and bring
The eternal note of sadness in.

Sophocles long ago
Heard it on the Ægean, and it brought
Into his mind the turbid ebb and flow
Of human misery; we
Find also in the sound a thought,
Hearing it by this distant northern sea.

The Sea of Faith
Was once, too, at the full, and round earth's shore
Lay like the folds of a bright girdle furl'd.
But now I only hear
Its melancholy, long, withdrawing roar,
Retreating, to the breath
Of the night-wind, down the vast edges drear
And naked shingles of the world.

Ah, love, let us be true
To one another! for the world, which seems
To lie before us like a land of dreams,
So various, so beautiful, so new,
Hath really neither joy, nor love, nor light,
Nor certitude, nor peace, nor help for pain;

And we are here as on a darkling plain
Swept with confused alarms of struggle and flight,
Where ignorant armies clash by night.

—*Matthew Arnold*

15. *Sophocles:* Greek tragedian, author of *Oedipus Rex.*

This poem is a "dramatic monologue," the name given to a certain type of poem, in which the poet pretends to be someone else, and the entire poem is "spoken" in the persona of that other character. We will be more interested in the form of dramatic monologues when we talk about a person as the subject of the poem. What interests us here is the way Arnold uses the *persona* speaking this poem as a vehicle for speculation on the world around him. Gradually sociology emerges out of a dramatic situation.

The dramatic situation in which the speaker confronts us can be reconstructed from hints in his speech by a little ingenuity on our part. A man is looking out of a window (line 6) at Dover Beach (title) and beyond it to France (line 3). He muses on the tranquility of the night, the beauty of the cliffs and the bay and the glimmering lights on the opposite coast, and listens pensively to the "tremulous cadence" of the ocean. The tide is going out, and the waves pick up pebbles as they approach the shore, then fling them back along the sand as they break. The sound of the grating pebbles is all that undercuts the magic of the moonlight night along the spectacular cliffs of Dover.

But the pebbles are enough to set the speaker thinking; they bring in, as he puts it, a note of sadness. Just what the speaker means by this note of sadness is not yet clear (either to himself or to us), but it starts him thinking of Sophocles, the Greek tragedian, whose primary concern was, as the speaker sees it, the ebb and flow of human sadness. Perhaps the speaker is projecting his own views onto Sophocles; perhaps he sees in the Greek a man from a distant time and culture who shares something of his own outlook on the human situation. In any event, we begin to understand now the note of human sadness in line 14. Then the speaker develops his thought further by comparing the sea before him and faith (lines 21ff.). By line 28 his thoughts have wandered a long way, geographically and philosophically, from the beginning of the poem, and we are snapped back to reality in line 29. The speaker addresses his love (we do not know whether it is his wife or not) and suggests that in the face of a world in which ignorance, confusion, and darkness prevail, a world without faith, all that is left is for lovers to be true to one another. The closing image—the darkling plain upon which ignorant armies clash—finally defines for us what Arnold meant by the note of sadness and the sea of faith: faith amounts to certitude and love and joy and peace and light—all the things absent now; the note of sadness is a note of regret at the loss of all these marks of civilized society. The realization, which has dawned on the speaker as gradually as it dawns on us, brings the poem to a rather somber conclusion.

Shine, Perishing Republic

While this America settles in the mold of its vulgarity, heavily
thickening to empire,
And protest, only a bubble in the molten mass, pops and sighs
out, and the mass hardens,

I sadly smiling remember that the flower fades to make fruit,
the fruit rots to make earth.
Out of the mother; and through the spring exultances, ripeness
and decadence; and home to the mother.

You make haste on decay: not blameworthy; life is good, be it
stubbornly long or suddenly
A mortal splendor: meteors are not needed less than mountains:
shine, perishing republic.

But for my children, I would rather have them keep their
distance from the thickening center; corruption
Never has been compulsory, when the cities lie at the monster's
feet there are left the mountains.

And boys, be in nothing so moderate as in love of man, a
clever servant, insufferable master.
There is the trap that catches noblest spirits, that caught—they
say—God, when he walked on earth.

—*Robinson Jeffers*

How would you compare Jeffers's assessment of American society with Whitman's? With Paul Simon's? (With the Eagles' in "Hotel California" that follows? With Arnold's view of nineteenth-century England?) Has something happened to America between 1855, when Whitman was writing "Song of Myself," and the twentieth century, when Jeffers and Simon were writing? Or is the difference in views merely a matter of temperament?

Hotel California

On a dark desert highway, cool wind in my hair,
Warm smell of colitas rising up through the air,
Up ahead in the distance I saw a shimmering light,
My head grew heavy and my sight grew dim,
I had to stop for the night.

There she stood in the doorway; I heard the mission bell
And I was thinking to myself,
"This could be Heaven or this could be hell."
Then she lit up a candle and she showed me the way
There were voices down the corridor,
I thought I heard them say,

"Welcome to the Hotel California,
Such a lovely place (such a lovely face);
Plenty of room at the Hotel California
Any time of year, you can find it here."

Her mind is Tiffany-twisted, she got the Mercedes bends,
She got a lot of pretty, pretty boys
That she calls friends.
How they dance in the courtyard,
Sweet summer sweat,
Some dance to remember,
Some dance to forget.

So I called up the captain,
"Please bring me my wine."
He said, "We haven't had that spirit here
Since nineteen sixty-nine."
And still those voices are calling from far away,
Wake you up in the middle of the night
Just to hear them say,

"Welcome to the Hotel California,
Such a lovely place (such a lovely face);
They livin' it up at the Hotel California;
What a nice surprise, bring your alibis."

Mirrors on the ceiling, the pink champagne on ice,
And she said, "We are all just prisoners here,
Of our own device."
And in the master's chambers
They gathered for the feast;
They stab it with their steely knives,
But they just can't kill the beast.

Last thing I remember I was
Running for the door.
I had to find the passage back
To the place I was before.
"Relax," said the night man,
"We are programmed to receive.
You can check out any time you like,
But you can never leave."

—Felder, Henley, Frey

In this surrealistic vision of "Hotel California," the Eagles speak out on the world they see around them. Here is a portrait of modern America (or is it only California? or is California just a metaphor for America?). What does this song say about contemporary American society? Is it in your view heaven or hell? What particular aspects of American (California) life style are specifically commented upon in this song?

Only the Good Die Young

Come out, Virginia, don't let me wait
You Catholic girls start much too late
But sooner or later it comes down to fate
I might as well be the one
They showed you a statue and told you to pray
They built you a temple and locked you away
But they never told you the price that you pay
For things that you might have done
Only the good die young.

You might have heard I run with a dangerous crowd
We might be laughing a bit too loud
But that never hurt no one
Come on Virginia show me a sign
Send up a signal, I'll throw you the line

The stained glass curtain you're hiding behind
Never lets in the sun
And only the good die young.

You got a nice white dress and
A party on your confirmation
You got a brand-new soul and a cross of gold
But Virginia they didn't give you quite enough information
You didn't count on me
When you were counting on your rosary
They say there's a heaven for those who will wait
Some say it's better but I say it ain't,
I'd rather laugh with the sinners than cry with the saints
Sinners have much more fun
And only the good die young.

You say your mother told you all
that I could give you was a bad reputation
She never cared for me
But did she ever say a prayer for me?

—Billy Joel

In this boy's monologue to a girl, what social institutions does Billy Joel seem to be attacking? What arguments does he use? With whom do you side? Apart from satirizing the hypocrisy and sterility of a social institution, how does "Only the Good Die Young" provide insight into human foibles, wishes, behavior? What comment does it make on people as well as institutions?

Ode to the West Wind

1

O wild West Wind, thou breath of Autumn's being,
Thou, from those unseen presence the leaves dead
Are driven, like ghosts from an enchanter fleeing,

Yellow, and black, and pale, and hectic red,
Pestilence-striken multitudes: O thou,
Who chariotest to their dark wintry bed

The wingèd seeds, where they lie cold and low,
Each like a corpse within its grave, until
Thine azure sister of the Spring shall blow

Her clarion o'er the dreaming earth, and fill
(Driving sweet buds like flocks to feed in air)
With living hues and odours plain and hill:

Wild Spirit, which art moving everywhere;
Destroyer and preserver; hear, oh, hear!

2

Thou on whose stream, 'mid the steep sky's commotion,
Loose clouds like earth's decaying leaves are shed,
Shook from the tangled boughs of Heaven and Ocean,

Angels of rain and lightning: there are spread
On the blue surface of thine airy surge,
Like the bright hair uplifted from the head

Of some fierce Mænad, even from the dim verge
Of the horizon to the zenith's height
The locks of the approaching storm. Thou dirge

Of the dying Year, to which this closing night
Will be the dome of a vast sepulchre,
Vaulted with all thy congregated might

Of vapours, from whose solid atmosphere
Black rain, and fire, and hail will burst: oh, hear!

3

Thou who didst waken from his summer dreams
The blue Mediterranean, where he lay,
Lulled by the coil of his crystalline streams,

Beside a pumice isle in Baia's bay,
And saw in sleep old palaces and towers
Quivering within the wave's intenser day,

All overgrown with azure moss and flowers
So sweet, the sense faints picturing them! Thou
For whose path the Atlantic's level powers

Cleave themselves into chasms, while far below
The sea-blooms and the oozy woods which wear
The sapless foliage of the ocean, know

Thy voice, and suddenly grow gray with fear,
And tremble and despoil themselves: oh, hear!

4

If I were a dead leaf thou mightest bear;
If I were a swift cloud to fly with thee;
A wave to pant beneath thy power, and share

The impulse of thy strength, only less free
Than thou, O uncontrollable! If even
I were as in my boyhood, and could be

The comrade of thy wanderings over Heaven,
As then, when to outstrip thy skiey speed
Scarce seemed a vision; I would ne'er have striven

As thus with thee in prayer in my sore need.
Oh, lift me as a wave, a leaf, a cloud!
I fall upon the thorns of life! I bleed!

A heavy weight of hours has chained and bowed
One too like thee: tameless, and swift, and proud.

5

Make me thy lyre, even as the forest is:
What if my leaves are falling like its own!
The tumult of thy mighty harmonies

Will take from both a deep, autumnal tone,
Sweet though in sadness. Be thou, Spirit fierce,
My spirit! Be thou me, impetuous one!

Drive my dead thoughts over the universe
Like withered leaves to quicken a new birth!
And, by the incantation of this verse,

Scatter, as from an unextinguished hearth
Ashes and sparks, my words among mankind!
Be through my lips to unawakened Earth

The trumpet of a prophecy! O Wind,
If winter comes, can Spring be far behind?

—*Percy Bysshe Shelley*

21. *Maenad:* a female attendant of Bacchus, hence, any wild or frenzied woman. 32. Baia: an ancient resort city in southwest Italy. 57. *lyre:* an aeolian harp, played by the wind passing over its strings.

This well known poem, obviously written at a time when the poet was feeling depressed, depleted, and generally unhappy, is an invocation to the west wind begging for inspiration and reanimation. The poet wishes he were a dead leaf, a cloud, a wave (lines 42–45 and stanzas one, two, and three respectively) so that the wind might stir his lethargic self into action. Although the poem is about personal depression, it has meaning for us, because we too have our moments of depression, and the poem is not so personalized that it makes Shelley's own experience unrelated to the general human condition of exhaustion. In psychoanalyzing himself, then, Shelley can psychoanalyze us in our depressed phases.

Implicit in this invocation to the wind is a neo-Platonic theory of art, in which the artist (or the individual) is but a tool or an instrument played upon by some spirit, from which comes inspiration and art and vision. Do you find this to be the case in your own life, when you write (or play sports) or think?

The poem is not particularly optimistic, in that the inspiration Shelley is looking for never comes. But he leaves himself with some hope: "If winter comes, can Spring be far behind?" Is this enough for you in your darker moments?

The Pretender

I'm going to rent myself a house
In the shade of the freeway
I'm going to pack my lunch in the morning
And go to work each day
And when the evening rolls around
I'll go on home and lay my body down
And when the morning light comes streaming in
I'll get up and do it again
Amen.

I want to know what became of the changes
We waited for love to bring
Were they only the fitful dreams
Of some greater awakening
I've been aware of the time going by
They say in the end it's the wink of an eye
And when the morning light comes streaming in
You'll get up and do it again
Amen.

Caught between the longing for love
And the struggle for the legal tender
Where the sirens sing and the church bells ring
And the junkman pounds his fender
Where the veterans dream of the fight
Fast asleep at the traffic light
And the children solemnly wait
For the ice cream vendor
Out into the cool of the evening
Strolls the pretender
He knows that all his hopes and dreams
Begin and end there.

Ah the laughter of the lovers
As they run through the night
Leaving nothing for the others
But to choose off and fight
And tear at the world with all their might
While the ships bearing their dreams
Sail out of sight.

I'm going to find myself a girl
Who can show me what laughter means
And we'll fill in the missing colors
In each other's paint by number dreams
And then we'll put our dark glasses on
And we'll make love until our strength is gone
And when the morning light comes streaming in
We'll get up and do it again
Get it up again.

I'm going to be a happy idiot
And struggle for the legal tender
Where the ads take aim and lay their claim

To the heart and the soul of the spender
And believe in whatever may lie
In those things that money can buy
Thought true love could have been a contender
Are you there?
Say a prayer for the pretender
Who started out so young and strong
Only to surrender.

—Jackson Browne

What Jackson Browne is tracing in "The Pretender" is the death of dreams in modern America. The world of this song is the world of Bob Seger's "Night Moves," a world of frustration and dead ends. The Pretender knows some part of him is dead, but that doesn't make it any more alive. Love has failed (we're not told why), and that was his last hope.

In part this song is a sociological analysis of modern civilization; in part it's a psychological analysis of one particular person. How would you analyze the speaker in this song? Does he give in too easily? Is he just not tough enough? Is he, in fact, still free, because he is not deluded into believing in the materialistic world that surrounds him? What options does he have, psychologically and sociologically?

Lady Lazarus

I have done it again.
One year in every ten
I manage it—

A sort of walking miracle, my skin
Bright as a Nazi lampshade,
My right foot

A paperweight,
My face a featureless, fine
Jew linen.

Peel off the napkin
O my enemy.
Do I terrify?

The nose, the eye pits, the full set of teeth?
The sour breath
Will vanish in a day.

Soon, soon the flesh
The grave cave ate will be
At home on me

And I a smiling woman.
I am only thirty.
And like the cat I have nine times to die.

This is Number Three.
What a trash
To annihilate each decade.

What a million filaments.
The peanut-crunching crowd
Shoves in to see

Them unwrap me hand and foot—
The big strip tease.
Gentleman, ladies,

These are my hands,
My knees.
I may be skin and bone,

Nevertheless, I am the same, identical woman.
The first time it happened I was ten.
It was an accident.

The second time I meant
To last it out and not come back at all.
I rocked shut

As a seashell.
They had to call and call
And pick the worms off me like sticky pearls.

Dying
Is an art, like everything else.
I do it exceptionally well.

I do it so it feels like hell.
I do it so it feels real.
I guess you could say I've a call.

It's easy enough to do it in a cell.
It's easy enough to do it and stay put.
It's the theatrical

Comeback in broad day
To the same place, the same face, the same brute
Amused shout:

"A miracle!"
That knocks me out.
There is a charge

For the eyeing of my scars, there is a charge
For the hearing of my heart—
It really goes.

And there is a charge, a very large charge,
For a word or a touch
Or a bit of blood

Or a piece of my hair or my clothes.
So, so, Herr Doktor.
So, Herr Enemy.

I am your opus,
I am your valuable,
The pure gold baby

That melts to a shriek.
I turn and burn.
Do not think I underestimate your great concern.

Ash, Ash—
You poke and stir.
Flesh, bone, there is nothing there—

A cake of soap,
A wedding ring,
A gold filling.

Herr God, Herr Lucifer,
Beware
Beware.

Out of the ash
I rise with my red hair
And I eat men like air.

—*Sylvia Plath*

Sylvia Plath was one of the most intensely personal poets of the post-World War II period, turning again and again to herself and her own psychological problems as the subject of her poetry. The brutality and the pain of her self-analyses are almost unbearable at times, but they also contain some elements of (black) humor—the final lines of "Lady Lazarus," for example, with the grisly warning to her persecutors "I eat men like air."

But beyond her preoccupation with herself, Plath touches upon a number of important concerns of everyone living in America of the fifties, sixties, seventies, and eighties: our preoccupation with spectacle and show; the Nazi horror and our awareness that there's a little Nazi in all of us; the women's movement and its issues; and the distractions that pressure all of us constantly, even if they do not drive us to suicide.

Plath has developed an enormous cult following in the past decade or so, especially among women. How much do you empathize with her? How meaningful is her private life to you? Do you find "Lady Lazarus" a statement of your own darker thoughts, or just the raving of some crazy woman who was too self-pitying for her own good?

Desolation Row

They're selling postcards of the hanging
They're painting the passports brown
The beauty parlor is filled with sailors
The circus is in town
Here comes the blind commissioner
They've got him in a trance
One hand is tied to the tight-rope walker
The other is in his pants
And the riot squad they're restless
They need somewhere to go
As Lady and I look out tonight
From Desolation Row

Cinderella, she seems so easy
"It takes one to know one," she smiles
And puts her hands in her back pockets
Bette Davis style

And in comes Romeo, he's moaning
"You Belong to Me I Believe"
And someone says," You're in the wrong place, my friend
You better leave"
And the only sound that's left
After the ambulances go
Is Cinderella sweeping up
On Desolation Row

Now the moon is almost hidden
The stars are beginning to hide
The fortunetelling lady
Has even taken all her things inside
All except for Cain and Abel
And the hunchback of Notre Dame
Everybody is making love
Or else expecting rain
And the Good Samaritan, he's dressing
He's getting ready for the show
He's going to the carnival tonight
On Desolation Row

Now Ophelia, she's 'neath the window
For her I feel so afraid
On her twenty-second birthday
She already is an old maid
To her, death is quite romantic
She wears an iron vest
Her profession's her religion
Her sin is her lifelessness
And though her eyes are fixed upon
Noah's great rainbow
She spends her time peeking
Into Desolation Row

Einstein, disguised as Robin Hood
With his memories in a trunk
Passed this way an hour ago
With his friend, a jealous monk
He looked so immaculately frightful
As he bummed a cigarette
Then he went off sniffing drainpipes
And reciting the alphabet
Now you would not think to look at him
But he was famous long ago

For playing the electric violin
On Desolation Row

Dr. Filth, he keeps his world
Inside of a leather cup
But all his sexless patients
They're trying to blow it up
Now his nurse, some local loser
She's in charge of the cyanide hole
And she also keeps the cards that read
"Have Mercy on His Soul"
They all play on penny whistles
You can hear them blow
If you lean your head out far enough
From Desolation Row

Across the street they've nailed the curtains
They're getting ready for the feast
The Phantom of the Opera
A perfect image of a priest
They're spoonfeeding Casanova
To get him to feel more assured
Then they'll kill him with self-confidence
After poisoning him with words
And the Phantom's shouting to skinny girls
"Get Outa Here If You Don't Know
Casanova is just being punished for going
To Desolation Row"

Now at midnight all the agents
And the superhuman crew
Come out and round up everyone
That knows more than they do
Then they bring them to the factory
Where the heart-attack machine
Is strapped across their shoulders
And then the kerosene
Is brought down from the castles
By insurance men who go
Check to see that nobody is escaping
To Desolation Row

Praise be to Nero's Neptune
The Titanic sails at dawn

And everybody's shouting
"Which Side Are You On?"
And Ezra Pound and T. S. Eliot
Fighting in the captain's tower
While calypso singers laugh at them
And fishermen hold flowers
Between the windows of the sea
Where lovely mermaids flow
And nobody has to think too much
About Desolation Row

Yes, I received your letter yesterday
(About the time the door knob broke)
When you asked how I was doing
Was that some kind of joke?
All these people that you mention
Yes, I know them, they're quite lame
I had to rearrange their faces
And give them all another name
Right now I can't read too good
Don't send me no more letters no
Not unless you mail them
From Desolation Row

—*Bob Dylan*

2 A Poem Is a Thing

The difference between a poet and a philosopher is that a poet expresses his speculations in the hard concretions, while the philosopher is apt to slip off into airy abstractions. Whatever statements a poet may wish to make about life, human nature, God, good, evil, time, his own art, he makes them with one foot firmly planted in the world. "No ideas but in things," the modern American poet William Carlos Williams said in "Paterson," and the phrase has become something of a slogan to contemporary poets. Partly in reaction to schools of poetry which overemphasized the idea and underplayed the thing, partly as an assertion of thingness against the general abstracting tendencies of the twentieth century, modern poets have hammered away at thingness, sometimes at the expense of statement and idea. If some contemporary painters, to deemphasize the importance of representational painting, could state flatly "painting is paint," some poets are content to say flatly "writing is words."

One aspect of words as words is, of course, their sound and their shape on the printed page, and contemporary poets are increasingly aware of those values of words. But what Williams was looking at, and the aspect of language most important to the poet, is the way a word calls to our minds a solid, concrete object: *hammer, Chevrolet, cheerleader, butterfly, desert.* These words have a hard reality to them that contrasts sharply with words like, say, *holiness, idea, eternity,* and the favorites of amateur poets *somethingness, emptiness, loneliness.* Even verbs and adjectives, once you move away from the fuzziness of *go* and *do,* of *whole* and *pretty,* can have this concreteness: *tackle, squeeze, boisterous, fleshy, burgundy.* And words can be used to recreate for the reader characters and stories and events, so that the poet does not so much *talk about* them as *present* them to his audience for their own inspection. It is around this thing—the image, the myth, the symbol, the literal leg of the metaphor, the story, the character—that the poem weaves itself. "So much depends,'' Williams also said, ''upon a red wheelbarrow.'' The whole poem hangs on its own thing.

And he was correct. It is the thing of the poem which first attracts us, about which we feel most confident and most comfortable, which first gives us access to the poem. We may be unable to say exactly what Coleridge means in ''The Rime of the Ancient Mariner,'' his statement may be elusive and unclear, but one thing is certain: he tells a hell of a good story. Whatever else the Beatles might be using ''Penny Lane'' to represent, it is still a street in Liverpool, with a barber shop and fire station and a nurse selling poppies. Whatever Blake's tiger and Hopkins's windhover represent symbolically, they are a real tiger and a real falcon respectively, and we envision them burning at us or circling above us. A symbol or metaphor may insist on something abstract as well as that concrete image, but always there is the palpable reality of the tangible object. While we may be unable to grasp the abstraction between thumb and finger, we can nail down that thing and feel it and see it and touch it and smell it. And that's very comfortable.

American poets especially seem strong on thing in their poetry. ''Whatever it is,'' wrote Louis Simpson in a poem titled ''American Poetry,'' ''it must have/ A stomach that can digest/ Rubber, coal, uranium, moons, poems.'' Perhaps Americans emphasize concretions because the American is an outdoorsman and many American writers started out not in school, but by working a variety of jobs; not by reading books in the library, but by writing for newspapers. Walt Whitman—probably the greatest of nineteenth-century American poets and perhaps the greatest American poet ever—was such a person. His experiences as a reporter trained his eye to see in precise, almost photographic detail, detail that his poetry never lost, detail that sometimes reduces a passage to a heap of Things, one piled upon each other, a kind of collage of persons, places, events, and stories, what Emerson called ''an auctioneer's inventory of a warehouse.''

from Song of Myself

15. The pure contralto sings in the organ loft,
The carpenter dresses his plank, the tongue of his
foreplane whistles its wild ascending lisp,
The married and unmarried children ride home to their
  Thanksgiving dinner,
The pilot seizes the king-pin, he heaves down with a strong
  arm,
The mate stands braced in the whale-boat, lance and
  harpoon are ready,

The duck-shooter walks by silent and cautious stretches,
The deacons are ordain'd with cross'd hands at the altar,
The spinning-girl retreats and advances to the hum of the
 big wheel,
The farmer stops by the bars as he walks on a First-day
 loafe and looks at the oats and rye,
The lunatic is carried at last to the asylum a confirm'd
 case,
(He will never sleep any more as he did in the cot in his
 mother's bedroom;)
The jour printer with grey head and gaunt jaws works at
 his case,
He turns his quid of tobacco while his eyes blur with the
 manuscript;
The malform'd limbs are tied to the surgeon's table,
What is removed drops horribly in a pail;
The quadroon girl is sold at the auction-stand, the
 drunkard nods by the bar-room stove,
The machinest rolls up his sleeves, the policeman travels
 his beat, the gate-keeper marks who pass,
The young fellow drives the express-wagon. (I love him,
 though I do not know him;)
The half-breed straps on his light boots to compete in the
 race,
The western turkey-shooting draws old and young, some
 lean on their rifles, some sit on logs,
Out from the crowd steps the marksman, takes his
 position, levels his piece;
The groups of newly-come immigrants cover the wharf
 or levee,
As the woolly-pates hoe in the sugar-field, the overseer
 views them from his saddle,
The bugle calls in the ball-room, the gentlemen run for
 their partners, the dancers bow to each other,
The youth lies awake in the cedar-roof'd garret and harks
 to the musical rain,
The Wolverine sets traps on the creek that helps fill the
 Huron,
The squaw wrapt in her yellow-hemm'd cloth is offering
 moccasins and bead-bags for sale,
The connoisseur peers along the exhibition-gallery with
 half-shut eyes bent sideways,
As the deck-hands make fast the steamboat the plank is
 thrown for the shore-going passengers,

The younger-sister holds out the skein while the elder sister winds it off in a ball, and stops now and then for the knots,
The one-year wife is recovering and happy having a week ago borne her first child.
The clean-hair'd Yankee girl works with her sewing-machine or in the factory or mill,
The paying-man leans on his two-handed rammer, the reporter's lead flies swiftly over the note-book, the sign-painter is lettering with blue and gold,
The canal boy trots on the tow-path, the book-keeper counts at his desk, the shoemaker waxes his thread,
The conductor beats time for the band and all the performers follow him,
The child is baptized, the convert is making his first professions,
The regatta is spread on the bay, the race is begun, (how the white sails sparkle!)
The drover watching his drove sings out to them that would stray,
The pedler sweats with his pack on his back, (the purchaser higgling about the odd cent;)
The bride unrumples her white dress, the minute-hand of the clock moves slowly.
The opium-eater reclines with rigid head and just-open'd lips,
The prostitute draggles her shawl, her bonnet bobs on her tipsy and pimpled neck,
The crowd laugh at her blackguard oaths, the men jeer and wink to each other,
(Miserable! I do not laugh at your oaths nor jeer you;)
The President holding a cabinet council is surrounded by the great Secretaries,
On the piazza walk three matrons stately and friendly with twined arms,
The crew of the fish-smack pack repeated layers of halibut in the hold,
The Missourian crosses the plains toting his wares and his cattle,
As the fare-collector goes through the train he gives notice by the jingling of loose change,
The floor-men are laying the floor, the tinners are tinning the roof, the masons are calling for mortar,
In single file each shouldering his hod pass onward the laborers;

Seasons pursuing each other the indescribable crowd is
 gather'd, it is the fourth of Seventh-month, (what salutes
 of cannon and small arms!)
Seasons pursuing each other the plougher ploughs, the
 mower mows, and the winter-grain falls in the ground;
Off on the lakes the pike-fisher watches and waits by the
 hole in the frozen surface,
The stumps stand thick round the clearing, the squatter
 strikes deep with his axe,
Flatboatmen make fast towards dusk near the cotton-wood
 or pecan-trees,
Coon-seekers go through the regions of the Red river or
 through those drain'd by the Tennessee, or through
 those of the Arkansas,
Torches shine in the dark that hangs on the Chattahooche
 or Altamahaw,
Patriarchs sit at supper with sons and grandsons and great-
 grandsons around them,
In walls of adobie, in canvas tents, rest hunters and
 trappers after their day's sport,
The city sleeps and the country sleeps,
The living sleep for their time, the dead sleep for their
 time,
The old husband sleeps by his wife and the young husband
 sleeps by his wife;
And these tend inward to me, and I tend outward to them,
And such as it is to be of these more or less I am,
And of these one and all I weave the song of myself.

—*Walt Whitman*

9. *bars:* the posts of a rail fence. *First-day:* Sunday. 12. *jour:* journeyman. 16. *Wolverine:* inhabitant of Michigan. 24. *paving-man:* someone who lays or repairs street pavement.

1. A Thing: Story

Traditionally poetry is divided into three classifications: dramatic, narrative, and lyric. Dramatic poetry, as you might have guessed, is poetry used in dramatic presentations, which may vary in length from a short "dramatic monologue," delivered by one speaker to a very specific, implied audience, to a full-scale play, publicly produced in front of whoever pays his money. Narrative poetry is poetry that tells a story, long or short, fiction or nonfiction, anything from a brief ballad to great historical epics such as *Beowulf* or *The Odyssey.* Lyric poetry is poetry that expresses a mood, makes a short philosophical speculation, paints a picture, presents a myth. Lyric poems are short, and the voice of the poet is prominent.

These distinctions have fallen largely out of use in the twentieth century, because most modern plays (in contrast to dramas written through the nineteenth century) are written in prose. Long narratives are usually also in prose—novels or short stories—and that has pretty much finished narrative poetry. Three centuries ago, James Michner's *Centennial* and Arthur Haley's *Roots* would have been long poems instead of novels. The stories that do get told in verse tend to be more reflective, making narrative poetry a form of lyric poetry. And increasingly story or dramatic situation is used as the basis for speculation: that is the story is told not for its own sake, or the drama played as a working out of conflict, but implied behind some picture painting or meditation.

Still, there are holdouts. Robert Frost's "The Death of the Hired Man," one of the most famous poems of the twentieth century, is a narrative poem. In the "foreword" to his *Selected Poems,* Robinson Jeffers wrote, "Long ago . . . it became evident to me that poetry—if it was to survive at all—must reclaim some of the power and reality that it was so hastily surrendering to prose. . . . The most 'modern' of the English poetry . . . was becoming slight and fantastic, abstract, unreal, eccentric; and it was not even saving its soul, for these are generally anti-poetic qualities. It must reclaim substance and sense, and physical and psychological reality. This feeling has been basic in my mind since then. It led me to write narrative poetry, and to draw subjects from contemporary life." The new lyric poetry was too slight, too abstract, and too unreal for Jeffers. Those are "anti-poetic" qualities, the logical answer to which was real story with real people. Something concrete, something people could understand.

So story remains with us, not prominent as it once was, but not lost entirely. We have story poems, and we have story songs, and we are likely to have them for some time to come, because they do have, as Jeffers suggested, a physical and psychological reality which makes them accessible and attractive.

Her Death and After

The summons was urgent: and forth I went—
By the way of the Western Wall, so drear
On that winter night, and sought a gate,
Where one, by Fate,
Lay dying that I held dear,

And there, as I paused by her tenement,
And the trees shed on me their rime and hoar,
I thought of the man who had left her lone—
Him who made her his own
When I loved her, long before.

The rooms within had the piteous shine
That home-things wear when there's aught amiss;
From the stairway floated the rise and fall
Of an infant's call,
Whose birth had brought her to this.

Her life was the price she would pay for that whine—
For a child by the man she did not love.
"But let that rest for ever," I said,
And bent my tread
To the bedchamber above.

She took my hand in her thin white own,
And smiled her thanks—though nigh too weak—
And made them a sign to leave us there,
Then faltered, ere
She could bring herself to speak.

"Just to see you—before I go—he'll condone
Such a natural thing now my time's not such—
When Death is so near it hustles hence
All passioned sense
Between woman and man as such!

"My husband is absent. As heretofore
The City detains him. But, in truth,
He has not been kind. . . . I will speak no blame,
But—the child is lame;
O, I pray she may reach his ruth!

"Forgive past days—I can say no more—
Maybe had we wed you would now repine! . . .
But I treated you ill. I was punished. Farewell!
—Truth shall I tell?
Would the child were yours and mine!

"As a wife I was true. But, such my unease
That, could I insert a deed back in Time,
I'd make her yours, to secure your care;
And the scandal bear,
And the penalty for the crime!"

—When I had left, and the swinging trees
Rang above me, as lauding her candid say,
Another was I. Her words were enough:
Came smooth, came rough,
I felt I could live my day.

Next night she died; and her obsequies
In the Field of Tombs where the earthworks frowned
Had her husband's heed. His tendance spent,
I often went
And pondered by her mound.

All that year and the next year whiled,
And I still went thitherward in the gloam;
But the Town forgot her and her nook,
And her husband took
Another Love to his home.

And the rumour flew that the lame lone child
Whom she wished for its safety child of mine,
Was treated ill when offspring came
Of the new-made dame,
And marked a more vigorous line.

A smarter grief within me wrought
Than even at loss of her so dear
That the being whose soul my soul suffused
Had a child ill-used,
While I dared not interfere!

One eve as I stood at my spot of thought
In the white-stoned Garth, brooding thus her wrong,
Her husband neared; and to shun his nod
By her hallowed sod
I went from the tombs among

To the Cirque of the Gladiators which faced—
That haggard mark of Imperial Rome,
Whose Pagan echoes mock the chime
Of our Christian time
From its hollows of chalk and loam.

The sun's gold touch was scarce displaced
From the vast Arena where men once bled,
When her husband followed; bowed; half-passed
With lip upcast;
Then halting sullenly said:

'It is noised that you visit my first wife's tomb.
Now, I gave her an honoured name to bear
While living, when dead. So I've claim to ask
By what right you task
My patience by vigiling there?

"There's decency even in death, I assume;
Preserve it, sir, and keep away;
For the mother of my first-born you
Show mind undue!
—Sir, I've nothing more to say"

A desperate stroke discerned I then—
God pardon—or pardon not—the lie;
She had sighed that she wished (lest the child should pine
Of slights) 'twere mine,
So I said: "But the father I.

"That you thought it yours is the way of men;
But I won her troth long ere your day:
You learnt how, in dying, she summoned me?
'Twas in fealty.
—Sir, I've nothing more to say,

"Save that, if you'll hand me my little maid,
I'll take her, and rear her, and spare you toil.
Think it more than a friendly act none can;
I'm a lonely man,
While you've a large pot to boil.

"If not, and you'll put it to ball or blade—
To-night, to-morrow night, anywhen—
I'll meet you here. . . . But think of it,
And in season fit
Let me hear from you again."

—Well, I went away, hoping; but nought I heard
Of my stroke for the child, till there greeted me
A little voice that one day came
To my window-frame
And babbled innocently:

"My father who's not my own, sends word
I'm to stay here, sir, where I belong!"
Next a writing came: "Since the child was the fruit
Of your lawless suit,
Pray take her, to right a wrong."

And I did. And I gave the child my love,
And the child loved me, and estranged us none.
But compunctions loomed; for I'd harmed the dead
By what I said
For the good of the living one.

—Yet though, God wot, I am sinner enough,
And unworthy the woman who drew me so,
Perhaps this wrong for her darling's good
She forgives, or would,
If only she could know!

—*Thomas Hardy*

6. *tenement:* house. 35. *ruth:* pity 53. *tendance:* attention, attendance at the grave. 111. *ball or blade:* a duel by pistols (ball) or swords (blade). 131. *wot:* knows.

"Her Death and After" is never going to be a great poem by anybody's standards: its characters are thinly drawn; it is too sentimental by half; and the moralizing of the final stanza is obnoxious to anyone except a reprobate from late Victorian England. And yet. Yet the poem tells a good story, and it carries a reader. For all its failures of voice and statement, this poem works, because its story carries it. While it may not be a great poem, it's a good example of just how far a good story can carry a poem.

Sir Patrick Spence

The king sits in Dumferling toune,
  Drinking the blude-reid wine:
"O whar will I get guid sailor,
  To sail this schip of mine?"

Up and spak an eldern knicht,
  Sat at the kings richt kne:
"Sir Patrick Spence is the best sailor
  That sails upon the se."

The king has written a braid letter,
  And signed it wi' his hand,
And sent it to Sir Patrick Spence,
  Was walking on the sand.

The first line that Sir Patrick red,
  A loud lauch lauched he;
The next line that Sir Patrick red,
  The teir blinded his ee.

"O wha is this has done this deid,
  This ill deid don to me,
To send me out this time o' the yeir,
  To sail upon the se?!

"Mak hast, mak hast, my mirry men all,
  Our guid schip sails the morne:"
"O say na sae, my master deir,
  For I feir a deadlie storme.

Late late yestreen I saw the new moone,
  Wi' the auld moone in hir arme,
And I feir, I feir, my deir master,
  That we will cum to harme."

O our Scots nobles were richt laith
  To weet their cork-heild schoone;
Bot lang owre a' the play wer playd,
  Thair hats they swam aboone.

O lang, lang, may their ladies sit,
  Wi' thair fans into their hand,
Or eir they se Sir Patrick Spence
  Cum sailing to the land.

O lang, lang, may the ladies stand,
  Wi' thair gold kems in their hair,
Waiting for their ain deir lords,
  For they'll se thame na mair.

Have owre, have owre to Aberdour,
  It's fiftie fadom deip,
And thair lies guid Sir Patrick Spence,
  Wi' the Scots lords at his feit.

—*anonymous*

3. *guid:* good. 9. *braid:* broad? 30. *cork-heild schoone:* cork-heeled shoes.

1. Summarize the plot of this story. The tale is sparsely told, and many details are omitted. How important to the poem's appeal is what's left out of the telling?

2. Why did Sir Patrick Spence first laugh, then cry when he read the king's letter?

3. Why did the old nobleman volunteer Sir Patrick for this mission? Do you suspect any old emnity between them, or between the court and Sir Patrick?

4. What commentary does this poem make on human nature, politics, life in general?

The Death of the Hired Man

Mary sat musing on the lamp-flame at the table,
Waiting for Warren. When she heard his step,
She ran on tiptoe down the darkened passage
To meet him in the doorway with the news
And put him on his guard. "Silas is back."
She pushed him outward with her through the door
And shut it after her. "Be kind," she said.
She took the market things from Warren's arms
And set them on the porch, then drew him down
To sit beside her on the wooden steps.

"When was I ever anything but kind to him?
But I'll not have the fellow back," he said.
"I told him so last haying, didn't I?
If he left then, I said, that ended it.
What good is he? Who else will harbor him
At his age for the little he can do?
What help he is there's no depending on.
Off he goes always when I need him most.
He thinks he ought to earn a little pay,
Enough at least to buy tobacco with,
So he won't have to beg and be beholden.
'All right,' I say, 'I can't afford to pay
Any fixed wages, though I wish I could.'
'Someone else can.' 'Then someone else will have to.'
I shouldn't mind his bettering himself
If that was what it was. You can be certain,
When he begins like that, there's someone at him
Trying to coax him off with pocket money—
In haying time, when any help is scarce.
In winter he comes back to us. I'm done."

"Sh! not so loud: he'll hear you," Mary said.

"I want him to: he'll have to soon or late."

"He's worn out. He's asleep beside the stove.
When I came up from Rowe's I found him here,
Huddled against the barn door fast asleep,
A miserable sight, and frightening, too—
You needn't smile—I didn't recognize him—
I wasn't looking for him—and he's changed.
Wait till you see."
"Where did you say he'd been?"

"He didn't say. I dragged him to the house,
And gave him tea and tried to make him smoke.
I tried to make him talk about his travels.
Nothing would do: he just kept nodding off."

"What did he say? Did he say anything?"

"But little."

"Anything? Mary, confess
He said he'd come to ditch the meadow for me."

"Warren!"

"But did he? I just want to know."

"Of course he did. What would you have him say?
Surely you wouldn't grudge the poor old man
Some humble way to save his self-respect.
He added, if you really care to know,
He meant to clear the upper pasture, too.
That sounds like something you have heard before?
Warren, I wish you could have heard the way
He jumbled everything. I stopped to look
Two or three times—he made me feel so queer—
To see if he was talking in his sleep.
He ran on Harold Wilson—you remember—
The boy you had in haying four years since.
He's finished school, and teaching in his college.
Silas declares you'll have to get him back.
He says they two will make a team for work:
Between them they will lay this farm as smooth!
The way he mixed that in with other things.
He thinks young Wilson a likely lad, though daft
On education—you know how they fought
All through July under the blazing sun,
Silas up on the cart to build the load,
Harold along beside to pitch it on."

"Yes, I took care to keep well out of earshot."

"Well, those days trouble Silas like a dream.
You wouldn't think they would. How some things linger!
Harold's young college-boy's assurance piqued him.
After so many years he still keeps finding
Good arguments he sees he might have used.
I sympathize. I know just how it feels
To think of the right thing to say too late.
Harold's associated in his mind with Latin.
He asked me what I thought of Harold's saying
He studied Latin, like the violin,
Because he liked it—that an argument!
He said he couldn't make the boy believe

He could find water with a hazel prong—
Which showed how much good school had ever done him.
He wanted to go over that. But most of all
He thinks if he could have another chance
To teach him how to build a load of hay—''

''I know, that's Silas' one accomplishment.
He bundles every forkful in its place,
And tags and numbers it for future reference,
So he can find and easily dislodge it
In the unloading. Silas does that well.
He takes it out in bunches like big birds' nests.
You never see him standing on the hay
He's trying to lift, straining to lift himself.''

''He thinks if he could teach him that, he'd be
Some good perhaps to someone in the world.
He hates to see a boy the fool of books.
Poor Silas, so concerned for other folk,
And nothing to look backward to with pride,
And nothing to look forward to with hope,
So now and never any different.''

Part of a moon was falling down the west,
Dragging the whole sky with it to the hills.
Its light poured softly in her lap. She saw it
And spread her apron to it. She put out her hand
Among the harplike morning-glory strings,
Taut with the dew from garden bed to eaves,
As if she played unheard some tenderness
That wrought on him beside her in the night.
''Warren,'' she said, ''he has come home to die:
You needn't be afraid he'll leave you this time.''

''Home,'' he mocked gently.

''Yes, what else but home?
It all depends on what you mean by home.
Of course he's nothing to us, any more
Than was the hound that came a stranger to us
Out of the woods, worn out upon the trail.''

''Home is the place where, when you have to go there,
They have to take you in.''

"I should have called it
Something you somehow haven't to deserve."

Warren leaned out and took a step or two,
Picked up a little stick, and brought it back
And broke it in his hand and tossed it by.
"Silas had better claim on us you think
Than on his brother? Thirteen little miles
As the road winds would bring him to his door.
Silas has walked that far no doubt today.
Why doesn't he go there? His brother's rich,
A somebody—director in the bank."

"He never told us that."

"We know it, though."

"I think his brother ought to help, of course.
I'll see to that if there is need. He ought of right
To take him in, and might be willing to—
He may be better than appearances.
But have some pity on Silas. Do you think
If he had any pride in claiming kin
Or anything he looked for from his brother,
He'd keep so still about him all this time?"

"I wonder what's between them."

"I can tell you.
Silas is what he is—we wouldn't mind him—
But just the kind that kinsfolk can't abide.
He never did a thing so very bad.
He don't know why he isn't quite as good
As anybody. Worthless though he is,
He won't be made ashamed to please his brother."

"*I* can't think Si ever hurt anyone."

"No, but he hurt my heart the way he lay
And rolled his old head on the sharp-edged chair-back.
He wouldn't let me put him on the lounge.
You must go in and see what you can do.
I made the bed up for him there tonight.
You'll be surprised at him—how much he's broken.
His working days are done; I'm sure of it."

"I'd not be in a hurry to say that."

"I haven't been. Go, look, see for yourself.
But, Warren, please remember how it is:
He's come to help you ditch the meadow.
He has a plan. You mustn't laugh at him.
He may not speak of it, and then he may.
I'll sit and see if that small sailing cloud
Will hit or miss the moon."

It hit the moon.
Then there were three there, making a dim row,
The moon, the little silver cloud, and she.

Warren returned—too soon, it seemed to her—
Slipped to her side, caught up her hand and waited.

"Warren?" she questioned.

"Dead," was all he answered.

—*Robert Frost*

Robert Frost's "The Death of the Hired Man" is one of the best known narrative poems in American literature. It tells two stories, really, the story of the hired man Silas, and the story of Mary and Warren. What kind of a man is Silas? Why did he leave? Why has he returned "home"? What kind of people are Mary and Warren? What tensions do you sense between them? On whose side of this domestic quarrel do you find yourself? Why?

In what sense is "The Death of the Hired Man" concerned with matters far weightier than an old and broken hired hand who comes home to die on some New England farm?

You Don't Mess Around with Jim

Uptown got its hustlers
Bowery got its bums
42nd Street got big Jim Walker
He a pool-shootin' son of a gun
Yea, he big and dumb as a man can come
But he stronger than a country hoss
And when the bad folks all get together at night
You know they all call big Jim "Boss" . . . just because . . .
and they say

You don't tug on Superman's cape
You don't spit into the wind
You don't pull the mask off the old Lone Ranger
And you don't mess around with Jim.

Well outa south Alabama come a country boy
He say I'm lookin' for a man named Jim
I am a pool-shootin' boy
My name Willie McCoy
But down home they call me Slim
Yea I'm lookin' for the king of 42nd Street
He drivin' a drop-top Cadillac
Last week he took all my money
And it may sound funny
But I come to get my money back
And everybody say, Jack . . . don't you know that
You don't tug on Superman's cape
You don't spit into the wind
You don't pull the mask off the old Lone Ranger
And you don't mess around with Jim.

Well a hush fell over the pool room
Jimmy come boppin' in off the street
And when the cuttin' were done
The only part that wasn't bloody
Was the soles of the big man's feet
Yea he were cut in 'bout a hundred places
And he were shot in a couple more
And you better believe
They sung a different kind of story
When big Jim hit the floor . . . now they say
You don't tug on Superman's cape
You don't spit into the wind
You don't pull the mask off the old Lone Ranger
And you don't mess around with Slim.

Yea, big Jim got his hat
Find out where it's at
And it's not hustling people strange to you
Even if you do got a two-piece custom-made
pool cue . . . yea.

—*Jim Croce*

What differences in technique—if any—can you find between this story-song of Jim Croce's and "The Ballad of Sir Patrick Spence"? How does Croce use language to give us a strong sense of character and place? How do these two elements contribute to the effectiveness of his story?

La Belle Dame Sans Merci

O what can ail thee, knight at arms,
  Alone and palely loitering?
The sedge has withered from the lake,
  And no birds sing!

O what can ail thee, knight at arms,
  So haggard and so woe-begone?
The squirrel's granary is full,
  And the harvest's done.

I see a lily on thy brow,
  With anguish moist and fewer dew;
And on thy cheeks a fading rose
  Fast withereth too.—

I met a lady in the meads,
  Full beautiful, a faery's child;
Her hair was long, her foot was light,
  And her eyes were wild.

I made a garland for her head,
  And bracelets, too, and fragrant zone;
She looked at me as she did love,
  And made sweet moan.

I set her on my pacing steed,
  And nothing else, saw all day long;
For sidelong would she bend, and sing
  A faery's song.

She found me roots of relish sweet,
  And honey wild, and manna dew;
And sure in language strange she said,
  "I love thee true."

She took me to her elfin grot,
  And there she wept and sighed full sore;
And there I shut her wild, wild eyes
  With kisses four.

And there she lullèd me alseep,
  And there I dreamed, ah woe betide!
The latest dream I ever dreamt,
  On the cold hillside.

I saw pale kings, and princes too,
  Pale warriors, death-pale were they all,
Who cried, "La Belle Dame sans Merci
  Thee hath in thrall!"

I saw their starved lips in the gloam
  With horrid warning gaped wide—
And I awoke and found me here,
  On the cold hill's side.

And this is why I sojourn here,
  Alone and palely loitering;
Though the sedge is withered from the lake,
  And no birds sing.

—*John Keats*

13. *meads:* meadows. 18. *fragrant zone:* girdle. 29. *grot:* grotto.

"La Belle Dame Sans Merci" is a literary ballad, the equivalent of "Sir Patrick Spence," but written by an educated poet conscious of himself as an artist. Again the tale is sparsely told. Characters are important here, and the tale is nearly a myth: an embodiment of some truths about the effects women may have on men. What is "La Belle Dame" like? What has she done to the speaker, the gentle knight at arms? Is the season of the year (note the closing stanzas of the poem) relevant to the poem? What effect does Keats get by repeating his first stanza as his last?

Karma

Christmas was in the air and all was well
With him, but for a few confusing flaws
In divers of God's images. Because

A friend of his would neither buy nor sell,
Was he to answer for the axe that fell?
He pondered; and the reason for it was,
Partly, a slowly freezing Santa Claus
Upon the corner, with his beard and bell.
Acknowledging an improvident surprise,
He magnified a fancy that he wished
The friend whom he had wrecked were here again.
Not sure of that, he found a compromise;
And from the fullness of his heart he fished
A dime for Jesus who had died for man.

—*Edwin Arlington Robinson*

Here is a short story compressed into a poem by Edwin Arlington Robinson. It is a social protest, not too much understated in its heavy irony, against big business and the way people stab even their friends in the back just to get ahead in the world. Notice, however, that this robber baron is not entirely conscious of what he's doing, and what success has done to him. The wish that the friend he ruined were alive once more (what has become of him we can only guess, but it seems that he either died poor or killed himself) is only half conscious, and certainly this man isn't aware of how trifling his contribution of "A dime for Jesus who had died for men" is. He is probably unaware that success has left him a hollow man, and he may in this respect be most to be pitied. Robinson titles this little tale "Karma," or destiny, as if to remind us of the Buddhist concept that the sum of a man's actions during his lifetime determines his future incarnations. This dime will not weigh very heavily in the balance.

Angie Baby

You live your life in the songs you hear
On the rock-and-roll radio,
And when a young girl doesn't have any friends
That's a really nice place to go.
Folks hopin' you'd turn out cool,
But they had to take you out of school.
You're a little touched, you know, Angie baby.

Lovers appear in your room each night
And they whirl you 'cross the floor,
But they always seem to fade away

When your daddy taps on your door.
Angie, girl, are you all right?
Tell the radio good-night.
Radio by your side, Angie baby.

Angie baby,
You're a special lady
Livin' in a world of make believe,
Well, maybe.

Stoppin' at her house is a neighbor boy
With evil on his mind,
'Cause he's been peakin' in Angie's room
At night through her window blind.
"I see your folks have gone away,
Would you dance with me today?
I'll show you how to have a good time, Angie baby."

When he walks in her room he feels confused
Like he walked into a play,
And the music's so loud it spins him around
'Til his soul has lost its way.
And as she turns the volume down,
he's getting smaller with the sound;
It seems to pull him off the ground.
Toward the radio he's bound, never to be found.

Angie baby,
You're a special lady
Livin' in a world of make believe
Well, maybe.

The headlines read that a boy disappeared,
And ev'ryone thinks he died
'Cept a crazy girl with a secret lover
Who keeps her satisfied.
It's so nice to be insane;
No one asks you to explain,
Radio by your side, Angie baby.

Angie baby,
You're a special lady
Livin' in a world of make believe
Well, maybe.

—*Alan O'Day*

Compare and contrast the stories of Big Jim, Angie, Sir Patrick, and La Belle Dame. What do they have in common that makes them good stories? Do you think they would be as interesting in prose as they are in ballad or song form? Why or why not?

The Stick in the Forest

A stick in the forest that pointed
where the center of the universe is
broke in the wind that started
its exact note of mourning
when Buddha's mother died.

Around us then a new crystal
began to form itself, and men—
awakened by what happened—
held precious whatever breathed:
we are all gestures that the world makes.

"Be, be," Buddha said.

—*William Stafford*

In reading this poem aloud for a Cassette Curriculum tape, the poet commented, "It's like a little story, it has some kind of narrative to sustain it. I must confess the story . . . doesn't come from anywhere, by which I mean, it's not a story that anyone told me, it's a story that the world began to tell me when I began to write the poem. It may not amount to much, but I have a suspicion that stories that are much greater must have come about in a way like this, a way of entering into an experience that you begin to have, as a consequence of trying to write something, so that you let the next thing occur, and the next thing, and the next thing." Stafford went on to title his collected poems (1977) *Stories That Could Be True.* What do you suppose he meant by his tape recorded comments and his title? What meaning, if any, does this narrative have for you? Is this perhaps more a myth than a story? Is Stafford more an explorer than a story teller? Do you think this is really how much greater stories were written?

2. A Thing: Character

Over the centuries people—in one form or another—have proven by far the most popular subjects for poets (as for all artists) . . . which is not surprising. The proper study of mankind is man, as Pope once observed.

In building poems around a person, the poet has several options. He may simply create a character who appeals to him either as a unique individual or a type. Chaucer's famous Canterbury pilgrims, Sandburg's Chick Lorimer, Robinson's Mr. Flood, the Beatles' Eleanor Rigby are all examples of such poem-people. The strength of such a poem depends largely on the poet's insight into his subject and his skill in creating character by using particularized details of conversation, description, and action. Normally such characters are fictitious, although they certainly have their roots in the poet's observation of actual people. Perhaps they are composites of several real people known to the poet, plus a little imagination. They may even be "type" characters: the dandy, the cheerleader, the businessman, the jock.

A second option the poet has is to write a kind of "public" poem on a public, or well-known person: Abraham Lincoln, Janis Joplin, Robert Frost. Both poet and audience know the poem's subject actually exists; the poet's job is to interpret the celebrity for his audience or, if the subject is not well known, to present him/her accurately. The poet's goal is truth here, not a flattering portrait. While poets often try to be kind, they can just as easily be the opposite, especially if the public personage is someone they consider bogus or self-impressed. Here the poet risks lawsuits, charges of libel, and general reprisals: Carl Sandburg was persuaded on these grounds to drop the name Billy Sunday (the Billy Graham of his times) from his poem "To a Contemporary Bunkshooter." Although everyone who read the poem knew whom he was talking about, Sandburg—and his editors—were legally safe. The feeling around Spoon River country was that Edgar Lee Masters based too many of his "fictional" characters in *Spoon River Anthology* too closely on real persons buried in the Petersburg and Lewiston graveyards . . . and Masters was bitterly resented for it. Modern courts, especially in America, have been easier on such matters than courts in England and earlier centuries; but truth, as the lawyers say, is an absolute defense against libel, and poets may owe their security more to their own truth-telling than to the protection of the courts. One thing is certain: with real persons, as with historical events, legitimate poets are rarely bought off by considerations of power and wealth. They call 'em as they see 'em, as Rochester's poem on King Charles shows, and poets who lie and flatter are held most in contempt by their fellow poets.

A third option in writing poems about people is for the poet to crawl into the skin of his subject—fictional or real, contemporary or historical—and speak the poem from the point of view and in the language of his subject. Such poems—like Browning's "My Last Duchess," Arnold's "Dover Beach," Billy Joel's song "My Life"—are called dramatic monologues and, to work successfully, require considerable skill. Not only must the poet adopt unaccustomed language and speech patterns, he must tell a story through a conversation, half of which he can present in the words of his character, and half of which he must imply (because he can neither record nor describe the reaction of whomever the character is addressing). Thus the dramatic monologue can become an artistic tour de force as well as a vivid presentation of character.

A fourth option, of course, is for the poet to use himself as the subject of his poem. How much the poet uses externals such as person, event, place, even story to write about himself and what really interests him—how much the poet is, in other words, writing about the poet no matter what his subject—is always a debatable question. The line between one's self and one's fictional characters is often thin: many "fictional" characters are but thinly veiled projections of the poet's or author's own psychological self. Poet Angela Jackson once defined a persona poem this way: "That's where you get to say what you want to say, and swear someone else said it."

In recent years the old "I-am-you" equation and increasing introspection have lead poets into so-called "confessional poetry," in which the person in the poem is virtually equivalent with the poet. Wordsworth started it all by writing his autobiographical "The Prelude: or Growth of a Poet's Mind," and romantic poets ever since have been more than willing to follow. Today confessional poets like Plath, Sexton, Lowell, and singer Bob Dylan are very popular indeed. Even when a modern poet creates a persona—like Berryman in *The Dream Songs*—those personae are often but poor disguises for the poet's own self.

Eleanor Rigby

Ah, look at all the lonely people!
Ah, look at all the lonely people!

Eleanor Rigby
Picks up the rice in the church where a wedding has been
Lives in a dream
Waits at the window
Wearing the face that she keeps in a jar by the door.
Who is it for?

All the lonely people,
Where do they all come from?
All the lonely people,
Where do they all belong?

Father McKenzie,
Writing the words of a sermon that no one will hear,
No one comes near
Look at him working,
Darning his socks in the night when there's nobody there
What does he care?

All the lonely people,
Where do they all come from?
All the lonely people,
Where do they all belong?

Ah, look at all the lonely people!
Ah, look at all the lonely people!

Eleanor Rigby,
Died in the church and was buried along with her name
Nobody came
Father McKenzie,
Wiping the dirt from his hands as he walks from the grave,
No one was saved.

All the lonely people,
Where do they all come from?
All the lonely people,
Where do they all belong?

Ah, look at all the lonely people!
Ah, look at all the lonely people!

—John Lennon–Paul McCartney

Lennon and McCartney manage, in three scenes of a very few words, to paint vivid pictures of two memorable characters in this song: Eleanor Rigby and Father McKenzie. Describe them as fully as you can, allowing your imagination to fill in where the poets leave blank space. What kind of lives do these people lead? What do they eat? What kind of clothes do they wear? What do they do on Friday night? Which details of the song's description are most memorable? (This song is, incidentally, almost a textbook lesson in making the minutest detail carry enormous significance.)

Listen to the Beatles' performance of this song. How does their performance reinforce the impressions created by the words of the song?

Gone

Everybody loved Chick Lorimer in our town.
Far off
Everybody loved her.
So we all love a wild girl keeping a hold
On a dream she wants.
Nobody knows now where Chick Lorimer went.
Nobody knows why she packed her trunk . . . a few old things
And is gone,
Gone with her little chin
Thrust ahead of her
And her soft hair blowing careless
From under a wide hat,
Dancer, singer, a laughing passionate lover.

Were there ten men or a hundred hunting Chick?
Were there five men or fifty with aching hearts?
Everybody loved Chick Lorimer.
Nobody knows where she's gone.

—*Carl Sandburg*

What does Chick Lorimer represent—to herself, to Sandburg, to the ten or a hundred men hunting her?

What happened to Chick Lorimer? Where has she gone? Why?

Mr. Flood's Party

Old Eben Flood, climbing alone one night
Over the hill between the town below
And the forsaken upland hermitage
That held as much as he should ever know
On earth again of home, paused warily.
The road was his with not a native near;
And Eben, having leisure, said aloud,
For no man else in Tilbury Town to hear:

"Well, Mr. Flood, we have the harvest moon
Again, and we may not have many more;
The bird is on the wing, the poet says,
And you and I have said it here before.
Drink to the bird." He raised up to the light

The jug that he had gone so far to fill,
And answered huskily: ''Well, Mr. Flood;
Since you propose it, I believe I will.''

Alone, as if enduring to the end
A valiant armor of scarred hopes outworn,
He stood there in the middle of the road
Like Roland's ghost winding a silent horn.
Below him, in the town among the trees,
Where friends of other days had honored him,
A phantom salutation of the dead
Rang thinly till old Eben's eyes were dim.

Then, as a mother lays her sleeping child
Down tenderly, fearing it may awake,
He set the jug down slowly at his feet
With trembling care, knowing that most things break;
And only when assured that on firm earth
It stood, as the uncertain lives of men
Assuredly did not, he paced away,
And with his hand extended paused again:

''Well, Mr. Flood, we have not met like this
In a long time; and many a change has come
To both of us, I fear, since last it was
We had a drop together. Welcome home!''
Convivially returning with himself,
Again he raised the jug up to the light;
And with an acquiescent quaver said:
''Well, Mr. Flood, if you insist, I might.

''Only a very little, Mr. Flood—
For auld lang syne. No more, sir; that will do.''
So, for the time, apparently it did,
And Eben evidently thought so too;
For soon amid the silver loneliness
Of night he lifted up his voice and sang,
Secure, with only two moons listening,
Until the whole harmonious landscape rang—

''For auld lang syne.'' The weary throat gave out,
The last word wavered; and the song being done,
He raised again the jug regretfully
And shook his head, and was again alone.

There was not much that was ahead of him,
And there was nothing in the town below—
Where strangers would have shut the many doors
That many friends had opened long ago.

—*Edwin Arlington Robinson*

This poem is a story of sorts, built around a single character, old Eben Flood. Look carefuly at the details of Robinson's poem: they are carefully contrived. Eben's name: what does it suggest about his character? The comparison of Eben drinking from his jug to Roland, the hero of the medieval French epic, blowing his horn: what does it suggest, both about Flood and about Robinson's attitude toward Flood? It's a humorous comparison, of course, but there's a bit of affection there, as elsewhere in the portrait. How about Flood's drinking: it suggests, as the psychologists would say, deep-seated emotional problems. What are they?

What is Robinson saying about the human condition here? Can you group Eleanor Rigby, Father McKenzie, Chick Lorimer, and Eben Flood together and make any generalization about them?

To Fine Lady Would-be

Fine Madam Would-be, wherefore should you fear,
That love to make so well, a child to bear?
The world reputes you barren, but I know
Your 'pothecarie, and his drugs says no.
Is it the pain affrights? That's soon forgot.
Or your complexion's loss? You have a pot,
That can restore that. Will it hurt your feature?
To make amends, yo'are thought a wholesome creature.
What should the cause be? Oh, you live at court:
And there's both loss of time, and loss of sport
In a great belly. Write, then on thy womb,
Of the not born, yet buried, here's the tomb.

—*Ben Jonson*

2. *make:* make love. 4. *'pothecarie:* apothecary, druggist. 6. *pot:* of makeup.

On English Mounsieur

Would you believe, when you this Mounsieur see,
That his whole body should speak French, not he?

That so much scarf of France, and hat, and feather,
And shoe, and tie, and garter should come hither,
And land on one, whose face durst never be
Toward the sea, farther than the half-way tree?
That he, untravelled, should be French so much,
As Frenchmen in his company, should seem Dutch?
Or had his father, when he did him get,
The French disease, with which he labours yet?
Or hung some Mounsieur's picture on the wall,
By which his damme conceived him clothes and all?
Or is it some French statue? No: 't doth move,
And stoop, and cringe. O then, it needs must prove
The new French tailor's motion, monthly made,
Daily to turn to Paul's, and help the trade.

—*Ben Jonson*

10. *French disease:* syphilis. 15. *motion:* puppet. 16. *Paul's:* St. Paul's Church, in London: the latest fashion is made in France, then imported immediately to London by puppets such as this to help the French balance of payments.

Here are two of Ben Jonson's livelier portraits of English court life in the early seventeenth century. While both poems may have been modeled on specific individuals, both are types, as their titles suggest: the woman who is bedding her way to influence at court, and the gentleman who has decided that clothes make the man. As you can see, Jonson had little use for such capons. As you can also see, both issues—abortion and fashion—are quite alive today, and both types are with us still.

In the Quiet Morning

In the quiet morning
There was much despair
And in the hours that followed
No one could repair

That poor girl
Tossed by the tides of misfortune
Barely here to tell her tale
Rolled in on a sea of disaster
Rolled out on a mainline rail

She once walked right at my side
I'm sure she walked by you
Her striding steps could not deny
Torment from a child who knew

That in the quiet morning
There would be despair
And in the hours that followed
No one could repair

That poor girl
She cried out her song so loud
It was heard the whole world round
A symphony of violence
The great southwest unbound

La La La La La La La
La La La La La La La
La La La La La La La La La
La La La La
La La La

—*Mimi Farina*

This song is about Janis Joplin, her life and her death. It is about a real person, a public person. How does Mimi Farina read the person of Janis Joplin? What discrepancies does she see between Janis's public self and her private self? What does she mean by "a symphony of violence / The great southwest unbound"? Is there a commentary here on American culture as well as on Janis Joplin? How true to your estimation of Janis's character is this song?

Robert Frost

Robert Frost at midnight, the audience gone
to vapor, the great act laid on the shelf in mothballs,
his voice is musical and raw—he writes in the flyleaf:
For Robert from Robert, his friend in the art.
"Sometimes I feel too full of myself," I say.
And he, misunderstanding, "When I am low,
I stray away. My son wasn't your kind. The night
we told him Merrill Moore would come to treat him,
he said, 'I'll kill him first.' One of my daughters thought
things,

thought every male she met was out to make her;
the way she dressed, she couldn't make a whorehouse."
And I, "Sometimes I'm so happy I can't stand myself."
And he, "When I am too full of joy, I think
how little good my health did anyone near me."

—*Robert Lowell*

Here is a poem about someone we all know—or think we know—poet Robert Frost. But this poem is designed to look behind "the great act" and show us another side. How different is the Frost who emerges in this poem from the Frost you thought you knew? How is he similar to his act?

On King Charles

For which he was banish'd the Court
and turn'd Mountebank

In the Isle of Great *Britain* long since famous known,
For breeding the best C[ully] in *Christendom;*
There reigns, and long may he reign and thrive,
The easiest Prince and best bred Man alive:
Him no ambition moves to seek Renown,
Like the *French* Fool to wander up and down,
Starving his Subjects, hazarding his Crown.
Nor are his high desires above his strength,
His Scepter and his P—— are of a length,
And she that plays with one may sway the other,
And make him little wiser than his Brother.
I hate all Monarchs and the Thrones they sit on,
From the Hector of *France* to the Cully of *Britain.*
Poor Prince, thy P—— like the Buffoons at Court,
It governs thee, because it makes thee sport;
Tho' Safety, Law, Religion, Life lay on't,
'Twill break through all to its way to C——.
Restless he rolls about from Whore to Whore,
A merry Monarch, scandalous and poor.
To *Carewell* the most Dear of all thy Dears,
The sure relief of thy declining Years;
Oft he bewails his fortune and her fate,
To love so well, and to be lov'd so late;
For when in her he settles well his T——,
Yet his dull graceless Buttocks hang an Arse.
This you'd believe, had I but time to tell you,

The pain it costs to poor laborious *Nelly,*
While she employs Hands, Fingers, Lips and thighs,
E're she can raise the Member she enjoys.

—*John Wilmot, Earl of Rochester*

13. *Cully:* fool.

Well! What more can be said? Except to note that this poem cost the Earl of Rochester dearly, as such scurrility is bound to do.

My Life

Got a call from an old friend
We used to be so close
Said he couldn't go on the American way
Closed the shop, sold the house
Bought a ticket to the West Coast
Now he gives them a stand-up routine in L.A.

I don't need you to worry for me 'cause I'm alright
I don't want you to tell me it's time to come home
I don't care what you say anymore, this is my life
Go ahead with your own life and leave me alone.

I never said you had to offer me a second chance
I never said I was a victim of circumstance
I still belong, don't get me wrong
And you can speak your mind
But not on my time.

They will tell you you can't sleep alone
In a strange place
Then they'll tell you you can't sleep
With somebody else
But sooner or later you sleep
In your own space
Either way it's okay
You wake up with yourself.

I don't need you to worry for me 'cause I'm alright
I don't want you to tell me it's time to come home
I don't care what you say anymore, this is my life
Go head with your own life and leave me alone.

—*Billy Joel*

Most of this song is put in the mouth of the singer's "old friend" who's decided to throw it all over and head out to L.A. How would you describe him, his values, his life? How much of yourself do you see in him? What is the "American way" he has given over? What "American way" has he adopted? What is the composer's attitude toward the values and arguments his friend gives him? How can you tell?

"You wake up with yourself"—does this sound like the Beatles, like Robinson, like any other contemporary poets? What social commentary is the poet making here?

My Last Duchess

Ferrara

That's my last Duchess painted on the wall,
Looking as if she were alive. I call
That piece a wonder, now: Frà Pandolf's hands
Worked busily a day, and there she stands.
Will't please you sit and look at her? I said
"Frà Pandolf" by design, for never read
Strangers like you that pictured countenance,
The depth and passion of its earnest glance,
But to myself they turned (since none puts by
The curtain I have drawn for you, but I)
And seemed as they would ask me, if they durst,
How such a glance came there; so, not the first
Are you to turn and ask thus. Sir, 'twas not
Her husband's presence only, called that spot
Of joy into the Duchess' cheek: perhaps
Frà Pandolf chanced to say, "Her mantel laps
Over my lady's wrist too much," or "Paint
Must never hope to reproduce the faint
Half-flush that dies along her throat": such stuff
Was courtesy, she thought, and cause enough
For calling up that spot of joy. She had
A heart—how shall I say?—too soon made glad,
Too easily impressed: she liked whate'er
She looked on, and her looks went everywhere.
Sir, 'twas all one! My favor at her breast,
The dropping of the daylight in the West,
The bough of cherries some officious fool
Broke in the orchard for her, the white mule
She rode with round the terrace—all and each
Would draw from her alike the approving speech,

Or blush, at least. She thanked men—good! but thanked
Somehow—I know not how—as if she ranked
My gift of a nine-hundred-years-old name
With anybody's gift. Who'd stoop to blame
This sort of trifling? Even had you skill
In speech—(which I have not)—to make your will
Quite clear to such an one, and say, "Just this
Or that in you disgusts me; here you miss,
Or there exceed the mark"—and if she let
Herself be lessoned so, nor plainly set
Her wits to yours, forsooth, and made excuse,
—E'en then would be some stooping; and I choose
Never to stoop. Oh sir, she smiled, no doubt,
Whene'er I passed her; but who passed without
Much the same smile? This grew; I gave commands;
Then all smiles stopped together. There she stands
As if alive. Will't please you rise? We'll meet
The company below, then. I repeat,
The Count your master's known munificence
Is ample warrant that no just pretence
Of mine for dowry will be disallowed;
Though his fair daughter's self, as I avowed
At starting, is my object. Nay, we'll go
Together down, sir. Notice Neptune, though,
Taming a sea-horse, thought a rarity,
Which Claus of Innsbruck cast in bronze for me!

—*Robert Browning*

Ferrara: Ruler and kingdom of Renaissance Italy. 3. *Fra Pandolf:* a fictional painter. The painting sounds suspiciously like the "Mona Lisa" of Da Vinci. 56. *Klaus of Innsbruck:* a fictional sculptor. Such a statue exists today in the Palace of the Doges, Venice.

This poem, although written by Robert Browning in Victorian England, is spoken by the Duke of Ferrara in Renaissance Italy. The Duke is entertaining an ambassador sent to negotiate a marriage agreement for some young lady soon to become the Duke's second wife. Ferrara, in passing through the palace with his guest, takes a moment to point out a painting of his last duchess, done by one Fra Pandolf. And in pointing out the painting he suggests, either intentionally or otherwise, some of the reasons she is a former duchess. By implication he is also laying down some guidelines his future wife will have to live by if she wishes not to become a former duchess also. Some lines of the poem, however, refer to actions the Duke takes as he chats with his guest; for example, the "Nay, we'll go/ Together down, sir," is an indication that the pair have come to a staircase and the ambassador has indicated to the Duke that, by virtue of rank, the Duke should precede him and he will follow. What other indications of action and interaction can you find in this poem?

What sort of person is the Duke? What remarks of his support your interpretation of his character? What does he expect of his wife? Of everyone around him? What do you make of lines 45–46: "I gave commands; Then all smiles stopped together"?

What sort of a person was the former duchess? Was she as innocent as we at first suspect, or do you think she and the painter (or she and some other men around the Duke's court) might have had something going? Why?

The Duke's closing remarks direct the ambassador's attention to a statue of Neptune, apparently a totally unrelated subject. Has the Duke revealed more than he intended, and is this—and the "Nay, we'll go/ Together down, sir"—a diversion? Or has he made satisfactorily clear the point he set out to make, so that he and the ambassador understand each other perfectly? Or might the statue be a kind of emblem of his character, and thus an apt summary of the poem?

Blue Motel Room

I've got a blue motel room
With a blue bedspread
I've got the blues inside and outside my head
Will you still love me
When I call you up when I'm down
Here in Savannah it's pouring down
Palm trees in the porch light like slick black cellophane
Will you still love me
when I call you up when I get back to town?
I know that you've got all those pretty girls coming on
Hanging on your boom-boom-pachyderm
Well you tell those girls that you've got German Measles
Honey, tell 'em you've got germs
I hope you'll be thinking of me
Because I'll be thinking of you
While I'm traveling home alone
Tell those girls that you've got Joni
She's coming back home.

I've got road maps
From two dozen states

I've got coast to coast just to contemplate
Will you still love me
When I get back to town?
It's funny how these old feelings hang around
You think they're gone
No, no
They just go underground
Will you still love me
When I get back to L.A. town?
You and me we're like America and Russia
We're always keeping score
We're always balancing the power
And that can get to be a cold cold war
We're going to have to hold ourselves a peace talk
In some neutral café
You lay down your sneaking around the town, honey,
And I'll lay down the highway.

I've got a blue motel room
With a blue bedspread
I've got the blues inside and outside my head
Will you still love me
When I get back to town?

—*Joni Mitchell*

Like many contemporary song writers, Joni Mitchell has a habit of putting herself and her loves into her poetry and songs. Especially when the subject is love, however, this easy equation of poet with song can be dangerous. "I was trying to write about an affair without letting my wife know it," John Lennon once said of "Norwegian Wood"; while that may be true, that song is certainly more than a song about an affair. Bob Dylan, in songs like "Sad-Eyed Lady of the Lowlands" and "It's All Over Now, Baby Blue" seems to be writing in part about himself and his friends, but he too transcends the merely personal. This song purports to be very personal: "Tell those girls that you've got Joni." To what extent does the poet rise above her own self and make a statement every woman (and man) can identify with?

'The Prisoner of Shark Island'

with Paul Muni

Henry is old, old; for Henry remembers
Mr Deeds' tuba, & the Cameo,

& the race in *Ben Hur,—The Lost World,* with sound,
& *The Man from Blankley's,* which he did not dig,
nor did he understand one caption of,
bewildered Henry, while the Big Ones laughed.

Now Henry is unmistakably a Big One.
Fúnnee; he don't féel so.
He just stuck around.
The German & the Russian films into
Italian & Japanese films turned, while many
were prevented from making it.

He wishing he could squirm again where Hoot
is just ahead of rustlers, where William S
forgoes some deep advantage, & moves on,
where Hashknife Hartley having the matter taped
the rats are flying. For the rats
have moved in, mostly, and this is for real.

—John Berryman

Title: a 1936 movie; Paul Muni played a very small role if he played one at all. 2–4. *Mr. Deeds,* etc.: Berryman lists a number of movies from the twenties and thirties, all of which date him. 13. *Hoot:* "Hoot" Gibson, cowboy actor. 14. *William S:* William S. Hart, cowboy actor.

In his *Dream Songs* sequence, Berryman created what he called a persona, "an imaginary character (not the poet, not me) named Henry, a white American in early middle age sometimes in blackface." Readers agree, however, that Henry is only Berryman in a disguise that fools nobody, an alter ego, not a persona. In this poem we learn some things about Berryman-Henry: he's getting old, and his age bothers him. What bothers him more, however, is knowing he's supposed to be "a Big One," and not feeling like a Big One. Berryman-Henry is insecure in his greatness and more than a little uncomfortable with the feeling of "having made it." He recalls with fondness the old days and the old films, where it was all play and make-believe, and you didn't stick around, and life was lived more on the edge. Now, this is depressingly, frighteningly "for real."

What Berryman reveals to us is not a love affair with the cheatin' man back home, sneaking around or riding the highway, but something quite as universal: old age creeping up, the awkward settled feeling of having made it when you don't really feel as if you've made it at all.

3. A Thing: Place

One of the more interesting aspects of American poetry (illustrated as well as anywhere in the Whitman passage quoted earlier) is its strong affinity for place. In every case the poet will substitute "Manito, Illinois," or "Wapakoneta, Ohio," for "one of those small midwestern towns," or "Gloucester, Massachusetts," for "an old New England fishing village." Poets like to be particular in place as in everything else. Sometimes they build whole poems around a Gloucester or a Paterson or a Manito, Illinois.

Part of the poet's fondness for place is particularity; another is verisimilitude: the more precise the description, the truer the poet's report sounds . . . and the more reliable. However, this strong demand for place permeates all American culture, not just our poetry, and one suspects a need more deep-seated than particularity or verisimilitude: one suspects a profound insecurity, bred in the bones of a people who were born on a boat headed for the New World, on a wagon train headed west, in a sod hut somewhere on the Nebraska prairie, in the back seat of a Greyhound bus rollin' down Highway 41. Americans move often, and have a lot of places to move to. Even today ours is a great and largely unsettled land, and we feel just a bit insecure in our heritage, uncertain of our roots. The vastness of the continent and the anxieties of the American spirit will, I suspect, explain the strong sense of place in New World poetry more than anything else.

Whatever the reason, this has been a fortunate development for poetry, because place, like narrative and character, presents an easy door into a poem. We may not know at first exactly what Robert Bly is up to in "Driving Toward the Lac Qui Parle River," but we can visualize the place, and that's attractive to us. Wordsworth's "Tintern Abbey" may be a poem about time and the passage of time, but it is also a fine description of a lovely place. And if we don't care much for Wordsworth's philosophizing, we can relate to his description. Likewise with Greg Kuzma's poem "Nebraska." "Penny Lane is a bus roundabout in Liverpool," Paul McCartney recalled, "and there's a barber shop showing photographs of every head he's had the pleasure to know—no that's not true, they're just photos of hairstyles, but all the people who come and go stop to say hello. It's part fact, part nostalgia for a place which is a great place, blue suburban skies as we remember it, and it's still there." The song is more than justified as a photograph of a particular place at a particular time.

Penny Lane

In Penny Lane there is a barber showing photographs
of ev'ry head he's had the pleasure to know.
And all the people that come and go
stop and say "hello."
On the corner is a banker with a motorcar
the little children laugh at him behind his back.
And the banker never wears a mac
In the pouring rain—very strange.
Penny Lane is in my ears and in my eyes,
there beneath the blue suburban skies
I sit and meanwhile back
In Penny Lane there is a fireman with an hourglass
and in his pocket is a portrait of the Queen.
He likes to keep his fire engine clean,
it's a clean machine.
Penny Lane is in my ears and in my eyes,
a four of fish and finger pies
in summer meanwhile back
Behind the shelter in the middle of the round-a-bout
The pretty nurse is selling poppies from a tray.
And though she feels as if she's in a play
she is anyway.
In Penny Lane, the barber shaves another customer,
we see the banker sitting waiting for a trim
and then the fireman rushes in
from the pouring rain—very strange.
Penny Lane is in my ears and in my eyes,
there beneath the blue suburban skies
I set and meanwhile back
Penny Lane is in my ears and in my eyes,
there beneath the blue suburban skies . . .
Penny Lane!

—John Lennon-Paul McCartney

What flavor do you get from this song about Penny Lane? Is it a prosperous section of town? What sort of people live there? What contrasts are implied between Penny Lane and other places? Is this song in any way more than a photograph of a pleasant time/place which may now no longer still be there?

Driving Toward the Lac Qui Parle River

I

I am driving; it is dusk; Minnesota.
The stubble field catches the last growth of sun.
The soybeans are breathing on all sides.
Old men are sitting before their houses on carseats
In the small towns. I am happy,
The moon rising above the turkey sheds.

II

The small world of the car
Plunges through the deep fields of the night,
On the road from Willmar to Milan.
This solitude covered with iron
Moves through the fields of night
Penetrated by the noise of crickets.

III

Nearly to Milan, suddenly a small bridge,
And water kneeling in the moonlight.
In small towns the houses are built right on the ground;
The lamplight falls on all fours in the grass.
When I reach the river, the full moon covers it;
A few people are talking low in a boat.

—*Robert Bly*

What details of Bly's poem help to particularize its place? Do these details concentrate themselves in any section of the poem? What is the poet's relationship with the landscape around him? Why in the final section is it *suddenly* a small bridge, the water, a few people talking low in a boat?

Fabliau of Florida

Barque of phosphor
On the palmy beach,

Move outward into heaven,
Into the alabasters
And night blues.

Foam and cloud are one.
Sultry moon-monsters
Are dissolving.

Fill your black hull
With white moonlight.

There will never be an end
To this droning of the surf.

—*Wallace Stevens*

This poem is a masterpiece of concise description, because it uses in every case exactly the right word to describe effects that are not very easy to describe: barque (ship) of phosphor, alabasters and night blues, sultry moon-monsters. But in tying the ship, the beach, and the waters to earth and sky, black and white, and the eternity of the surf, Stevens links geography to other, weightier matters, making place an excuse for statement. This poem transcends its graphically beautiful description and evokes an eternity in which everything is one, and all is fitting.

Lines

Composed a few miles above Tintern Abbey,
On revisiting the banks of the Wye during
a tour, July 13, 1798.

Five years have past; five summers, with the length
Of five long winters! and again I hear
These waters, rolling from their mountain-springs
With a soft inland murmur.—Once again
Do I behold these steep and lofty cliffs,
That on a wild secluded scene impress
Thoughts of more deep seclusion; and connect
The landscape with the quiet of the sky.
The day is come when I again repose
Here, under this dark sycamore, and view
These plots of cottage-ground, these orchard-tufts,
Which at this season, with their unripe fruits,
Are clad in one green hue, and lose themselves
'Mid groves and copses. Once again I see
These hedge-rows, hardly hedge-rows, little lines
Of sportive wood run wild: these pastoral farms,
Green to the very door; and wreaths of smoke
Sent up, in silence, from among the trees!

With some uncertain notice, as might seem
Of vagrant dwellers in the houseless woods,
Or of some Hermit's cave, where by his fire
The Hermit sits alone.
These beauteous forms,
Through a long absence, have not been to me
As is a landscape to blind man's eye:
But oft, in lonely rooms, and 'mid the din
Of towns and cities, I have owed to them
In hours of weariness, sensations sweet,
Felt in the blood, and felt along the heart;
And passing even into my purer mind,
With tranquil restoration:—feelings too
Of unremembered pleasure: such, perhaps,
As have no slight or trivial influence
On that best portion of a good man's life,
His little, nameless, unremembered, acts
Of kindness and of love. Nor less, I trust,
To them I may have owed another gift,
Of aspect more sublime; that blessed mood,
In which the burthen of the mystery,
In which the heavy and the weary weight
Of all this unintelligible world,
Is lightened:—that serene and blessed mood,
In which the affections gently lead us on,—
Until, the breath of this corporeal frame
And even the motion of our human blood
Almost suspended, we are laid asleep
In body, and became a living soul:
While with an eye made quiet by the power
Of harmony, and the deep power of joy,
We see into the life of things.
If this
Be but a vain belief, yet, oh! how oft—
In darkness and amid the many shapes
Of joyless daylight; when the fretful stir
Unprofitable, and the fever of the world,
Have hung upon the beatings of my heart—
How oft, in spirit, have I turned to thee,
O sylvan Wye! thou wanderer thro' the woods,
How often has my spirit turned to thee!
And now, with gleams of half-extinguished thought,
With many recognitions dim and faint,
And somewhat of a sad perplexity,

The picture of the mind revives again:
While here I stand, not only with the sense
Of present pleasure, but with pleasing thoughts
That in this moment there is life and food
For future years. And so I dare to hope,
Though changed, no doubt, from what I was when first
I came among these hills; when like a roe
I bounded o'er the mountains, by the sides
Of the deep rivers, and the lonely streams,
Wherever nature led: more like a man
Flying from something that he dreads, than one
Who sought the thing he loved. For nature then
(The coarser pleasures of my boyish days,
And their glad animal movements all gone by)
To me was all in all.—I cannot paint
What then I was. The sounding cataract
Haunted me like a passion: the tall rock,
The mountain, and the deep and gloomy wood,
Their colours and their forms, were then to me
An appetite; a feeling and a love,
That had no need of a remoter charm,
By thought supplied, nor any interest
Unborrowed from the eye.—That time is past,
And all its aching joys are now no more,
And all its dizzy raptures. Not for this
Faint I, nor mourn nor murmur; other gifts
Have followed; for such loss, I would believe,
Abundant recompense. For I have learned
To look on nature, not as in the hour
Of thoughtless youth; but hearing oftentimes
The still, sad music of humanity,
Nor harsh nor grating, though of ample power
To chasten and subdue. And I have felt
A presence that disturbs me with the joy
Of elevated thoughts; a sense sublime
Of something far more deeply interfused,
Whose dwelling is the light of setting suns,
And the round ocean and the living air,
And the blue sky, and in the mind of man;
A motion and a spirit, that impels
All thinking things, all objects of all thought,
And rolls through all things. Therefore am I still
A lover of the meadows and the woods,
And mountains; and of all that we behold

From this green earth; of all the mighty world
Of eye, and ear,—both what they half create,
And what perceive; well pleased to recognise
In nature and the language of the sense,
The anchor of my purest thoughts, the nurse,
The guide, the guardian of my heart, and soul
Of all my moral being.
Nor perchance,
If I were not thus taught, should I the more
Suffer my genial spirits to decay:
For thou art with me here upon the banks
Of this fair river; thou my dearest Friend,
My dear, dear Friend; and in thy voice I catch
The language of my former heart, and read
My former pleasures in the shooting lights
Of thy wild eyes. Oh! yet a little while
May I behold in thee what I was once,
My dear, dear Sister! and this prayer I make,
Knowing that Nature never did betray
The heart that loved her; 't is her privilege,
Through all the years of this our life, to lead
From joy to joy: for she can so inform
The mind that is within us, so impress
With quietness and beauty, and so feed
With lofty thoughts, that neither evil tongues,
Rash judgments, nor the sneers of selfish men,
Nor greetings where no kindness is, nor all
The dreary intercourse of daily life,
Shall e'er prevail against us, or disturb
Our cheerful faith, that all which we behold
Is full of blessings. Therefore let the moon
Shine on thee in thy solitary walk;
And let the misty mountain-winds be free
To blow against thee: and, in after years,
When these wild ecstasies shall be matured
Into a sober pleasure; when thy mind
Shall be a mansion for all lovely forms,
Thy memory be as a dwelling-place
For all sweet sounds and harmonies; oh! then,
If solitude, or fear, or pain, or grief,
Should be thy portion, with what healing thoughts
Of tender joy wilt thou remember me,
And these my exhortations! Nor, perchance—
If I should be where I no more can hear

Thy voice, nor catch from my wild eyes these gleams
Of past existence—wilt thou then forget
That on the banks of this delightful stream
We stood together; and that I, so long
A worshipper of Nature, hither came
Unwearied in that service; rather say
With warmer love—oh! with far deeper zeal
Of holier love. Nor wilt thou then forget,
That after many wanderings, many years
Of absence, these steep woods and lofty cliffs,
And this green pastoral landscape, were to me
More dear, both for themselves and for thy sake!

—*William Wordsworth*

1. What about this landscape attracts Wordsworth? Where does his description of the physical place concentrate itself? Is there a difference between the way he regarded this place five years before writing the poem, and at the time he wrote this poem? What is that difference?

2. Obviously Wordsworth is concerned here with much more than mere description of a place. What has this spot come to represent to him? What effect has his recollection of this place had on him elsewhere? Lines 88–102 seem especially important in describing Wordsworth's attitude toward place.

3. Wordsworth is particularly interested in man's relationship with nature, but he appears to contradict himself on this later. In lines 11–18 and 90–102 man is presented as being essentially in harmony with nature, while in 128–31 they are described as being in opposition. What do you think?

4. Wordsworth's "dear, dear Friend" is his sister Dorothy. What is their relationship? What does the poet wish for her? Not so much the ability to feel "a sense sublime/ Of something far more deeply interfused . . . a motion and a spirit" as simple, sustaining memory, like that Wordsworth expressed in lines 25 following of "Tintern Abbey."

from Nebraska

Nebraska's all dirt. I didn't find that
anything so strange, and might not mention it
at all in here except three years ago
I had the chance to make a turn
through New York State, the upper central part,
where I was born, and lived in blindness
twenty years, and drove, with my father,

on one of the best days we've had together,
up through the struggling farmland toward
the mountains. Out my left window as
I drove, I spied the fields scattered with
rocks, smallish ones, no bigger than
potatoes, most of them, which I mistook
for such,
until he quickly told me they were rocks.
Their like is not out here,
'cept now and then
my forking brings one up, or now and then
at the end of some humungous wheat field
there's a big one looking shy as sin.
What it comes to in comparison
is we have little to build walls or fences
with, so my short row of osage orange
out back's been bid for three times by
the local folk. They want its tardy rot
for fenceposts. But I didn't sell.

The garden grows most anything. I even
had luck with okra both last year
and the one before.
Had more
than we used, more than we needed, so I canned
two dozen pints. Out of them so far
I've launched a dozen soups, okra
making the stock more jellied, and more
full-bodied. Beets in abundance, tomatoes
sprawled all summer on the straw
I learned, from two bad years,
to spread out underneath them. Corn,
three good crops, though our plot is small,
tons of green beans (five weeks of
aching backs), cucumbers like submarines
under their leaves, all sorts of flowers,
zinnias my favorite for their hardiness.
Radishes early of course, and cauliflower
late, last year almost for Christmas
fresh out of the garden. Cutting the
last head December 15.

It sleeps now, the garden, and the cauliflower
this year, I confess, didn't make it,
getting perhaps too late a start,

I don't know,
or the bugs in it too fierce for me.
A rainy spring, and I didn't get the plants
in, or the dogs tracked them down.
Broccoli no better. But the snow now
over them both. After the
first freeze
they stink, the way they will if
half digested. As if the air were eating
them, which, I guess, it is.
Now there's no sign of them, the zinnia stalks
keeping the best lookouts
next to the pepper plants.
What they come down to, these plants,
is something I'd like for myself,
not to the bone, but to the sinews.
Lately I've gotten fat, so I mean this too,
but mainly I'd like to get lean again,
The way I was in high school or in college.
Being a father has meant
being a lap to sit on, so I am.
And Barb's the same. We think,
quite frequently,
it would be good to allow the wind a chance
to get at us, make us dance as it does
the trees, the crops, coyotes and the rest.
If not so much anymore to fit in better,
we've learned enough to know we've come to that,
but to last longer as we hope to be.

Lacking proper mountains, we must
do with hills. The golf course near our house
provides two fairly good ones for our
sleds and skis. The kids, at least,
are convinced. And when the snow's iced
it's even enough for me. Last week
one day it even got too much, the wind chill
taking zero down to twenty-five below,
my face recalled those winters with my Dad
and brother, skiing, cross country,
near Rome, New York, my old home. I miss
those days,
the woods that make them different days
than these. In summer,

the golf course does what it does best—
we play. The kids too young yet though
they go. They walk around behind us till they tire,
and then we walk them all the way
in spite of that.

Nebraska's farmers are like wheat.
They are the color of wheat, most of them,
and when they cough, for they are smokers,
many of them, they sound like wheat
when it is old and ready for cutting.
Their wives are often similar, though paler
for being indoors more.
Their children are like children anywhere—
we ought to know, our children bring them
home, weekdays or weekends, half the kids
of Crete, excepting the fact there is no big river
to fish in, as in Louisiana or Missouri,
excepting the fact that when they are Boy Scouts
and Girl Scouts
they have to go away to find the land.
It's here, the land, but put to use,
the farms great living rooms, all carpets.
Still, there are streetlights to explode,
cats to be rescued.

The cats in Nebraska are like other cats
in that they howl when hurt
or involved in love making.
Often the rest of the state at three AM
is silent
as if listening to them.
And where there is a dog nearby
it chases the cats
and sends them up trees.
Toward which, at odd hours,
a fire truck, usually a ladder truck,
speeds down streets which smell like cornflakes.
Often the cat is rescued, as elsewhere,
or climbs higher up, in which case the man
in the hat expresses dismay, then
driving off. They will come down, in time,
as in Connecticut.

Nebraska also has her hogs. If you
are slow on the road, if you are late
for work and you are in a hurry,
chances are that hogs will be ahead of you,
recently sold, or off to fattening,
or being moved for one or another or
another reason. Late for supper, the thick
sunset like pink cream on the horizon,
tell the wife, the husband,
there were hogs on the road. It is no lie.
There are hogs on the road as I write this.

—*Greg Kuzma*

"Nebraska" is poet Greg Kuzma's attempt to come to grips with the amplitudes and attitudes of the midwest after his transplant from the northeast. The poem takes the form of a report, or letter, from Kuzma in Crete, Nebraska, to a reader probably unfamiliar with the state, and thus the poet is given an opportunity to explain his geography (and, indirectly, himself). What is interesting is that even in explaining his surroundings Kuzma reflects them; in discussing his alienation he betrays his assimilation. For in the tone of his poem, in his language, in his casual voice and disarming frankness we hear the voice of Nebraska. Look at the details of geography contained in this poem; at the selection of subjects; at its organization; at the poet's voice. What kind of a state is Nebraska?

4. A Thing: History

When we speak of history being the thing out of which some poems are constructed, we are talking about two different situations really. In the first, the poet is himself an historian, recording history—public or private, personal or social—either objectively, as a photographer would take pictures, as one who sees but forms no opinions, or as a social scientist seeking to make some sense, and thereby some statement out of history. In either case the poet, whether contemporary with or distanced from the history he records, tries to be as true as possible to his matter, convinced that he can best succeed by coming as close as he can to what actually happened. Statement grows primarily out of subject matter.

A second use of history in poetry occurs when the poet develops a story around a historical character or situation. The prose equivalent of this type of history poem is not the nonfiction book of the professional historian or social scientist, but the historical novel. This kind of history poem, like the novel or short story, may have its own internal validity—the truth of its insights into human nature—and it may have the right historical flavor, but it is not reliable as a picture of "the way it really happened." The Duke of Ferrara, to draw an example from Browning's "My Last Duchess (Chapter 2, Section 1), did not have his first wife rubbed out for smiling at servants and the painter, and he did not negotiate as Browning described with the ambassador representing the father of his second wife. In poems of this type historical characters and situations are more vehicles for what the poet wishes to say than objective realities in their own right.

These two uses of history blur, of course, in practice, where writing "what really happened" often proves virtually impossible. Longfellow's famous "The Landlord's Tale" ("Listen, my children, and you shall hear/ Of the midnight ride of Paul Revere") manages to distort history considerably, and as we have already noted (Chapter 1, Section 6), "Hymn Sung at the Completion of the Concord Monument, April 19, 1836" contains a little historical inaccuracy. However, poetry enough of both types exists to allow us a working distinction between these two types of historical poems. Charles Olson, always interested in solid things, filled his *Maximus Poems* with bit and pieces of Gloucester history, solid historical facts researched out of old books and interviews. Denise Levertov records some Vietnam War history in her "The Altars in the Streets." Walt Whitman, who was an eyewitness to several Civil War battles and nursed many an injured soldier to health or the grave, recorded many of his experiences in his poetry. Thomas McGrath also used a personal history in part I of his *Letter to an Imaginary Friend;* nevertheless, he sounds most like a professional historian recounting tales of rural life before the War. Robbie Robertson, on the other hand, resurrects Robert E. Lee, Stoneman, and the Danville train in his song "The Night They Drove Old Dixie Down," but Virgil Caine is a fictional person, and the events recounted in his song never happened. The flavor is pleasant and the character feels "true," but the history of this song is a fabrication. Tennyson's depiction of Ulysses is pure fiction—true to the character of Ulysses, but without foundation in Homer or elsewhere. The poem is quite the opposite of his famous "The Charge of the Light Brigade," which recounts the disastrous charge of British troops against the Russian batteries at Balaclava (October 25, 1854) and was written within months of the battle.

Either way (or both ways together), history has as much appeal as place and character for the modern reader, who feels as cut off from his history as he is uprooted from his place and insulated from his fellow human beings. Interestingly, the modern poets of history, like William Carlos Williams (*Paterson*) and Charles Olson (*The Maximus Poems*) are often also poets of place; and songs of history—from "The Battle of

New Orleans'' to ''The Wreck of the Edmund Fitzgerald''—are almost as popular as place songs.

The Night They Drove Old Dixie Down

Virgil Caine is the name
And I served on the Danville train,
'Til Stoneman's Cavalry came
And tore up the tracks again.
In the winter of sixty-five,
We were hungry, just barely alive.
By May the tenth, Richmond had fell;
It's a time I remember, oh, so well.
The night they drove old Dixie down,
And all the bells were ringin',
The night they drove old Dixie down,
And the people were singin',
They went La, la, la, la, la, la,
La, la, la, la, la, la, la, la.

Back with my wife in Tennessee
When one day she called to me
''Virgil, quick, come see:
There goes Robert E. Lee!''
Now, I don't mind choppin' wood
And I don't care if the money's no good,
Ya take what ya need and ya leave the rest
But they should never have taken the very best.
The night they drove old Dixie down,
And all the bells were ringin',
The night they drove old Dixie down,
And all the people were singin',
They went La, la, la, la, la, la,
La, la, la, la, la, la, la, la.

Like my father before me
I will work the land
And like my brother above me
who took a rebel stand.
He was just eighteen, proud and brave,
But a Yankee laid him in his grave
I swear by the mud below my feet
You cain't raise a Caine back up

When he's in defeat.
The night they drove old Dixie down,
And all the bells were ringin',
The night they drove old Dixie down,
And all the people were singin',
they went La, la, la, la, la, la,
La, la, la, la, la, la, la, la.

—*Robbie Robertson*

This song comes from the Band's first album, *The Band,* which is filled with songs of the American past. In fact, the repertoire of the Band is heavy with songs of the past: "Across the Great Divide," "Caledonia Mission," "W. S. Walcott Medicine Show," "The Last of the Blacksmiths." What values do you find in this song, and in the reclamation of history in general? What sort of feeling do you get from this song?

The Altars in the Street

On June 17th, 1966, The New York Times *reported that, as part of the Buddhist campaign of passive non-resistance, Viet-Namese children were building altars in the streets of Saigon and Hue, effectively jamming traffic.*

Children begin at green dawn nimbly to build
topheavy altars, overweighted with prayers,
thronged each instant more densely

with almost-visible ancestors.
Where tanks have cracked the roadway
the frail altars shake; here a boy

with red stumps for hands steadies a corner,
here one adjusts with his crutch the holy base.
The vast silence of Buddha overtakes

and overrules the oncoming roar
of tragic life that fills alleys and avenues;
it blocks the way of pedicabs, police, convoys.

The hale and maimed together
hurry to construct for the Buddha
a dwelling at each intersection. Each altar

made from whatever stones, sticks, dreams, are at hand,
is a facet of one altar; by noon
the whole city in all its corruption,

all its shed blood the monsoon cannot wash away,
has become a temple,
fragile, insolent, absolute.

—*Denise Levertov*

Levertov records here a piece of historical evidence. Hers is a relatively objective account, and yet the poet's sympathies are obvious. What words, what details betray her? Is this an affirmative or a pessimistic poem? What elements in human nature does it affirm? Condemn? Look at the last line of the poem: "fragile, insolent, absolute." How do these words contradict each other? In what sense are they absolutely right?

from Letter to an Imaginary Friend

3.

The rites of passage toward the stranger's country,
The secret language foreign as a beard . . .
I turned in machine-made circles: first from the screaming red
Weather where the straw stack grew and the rattling thresher
  mourned;
Then to the rocking engine where the fly-wheel flashed and
  labored
And the drive-belt waxed and waned, the splices clapped at its
  cross
Ebbing and flowing, slack or taut as the spikers
Dropped the bivouaced wheat in the feeder's revolving throat.

Feathered in steam like a great tormented beast
The engine roared and laughed, dreamed and complained,
And the pet-cocks dropped and sizzled; and under its fiery gut
Stalactites formed from the hand-hold's rheumy slobbers.
—Mane of sparks, metallic spike of its voice,
The mile-long bacony crackle of burning grease!
There the engineer sat, on the high drivers,
Aloof as a God. Filthy. A hunk of waste
Clutched in one gauntleted hand, in the other the oil can
Beaked and long-necked as some exotic bird;
Wreathed in smoke, in the clatter of loose eccentrics.

And the water-monkey, back from the green quiet of the river
With a full tank, was rolling a brown quirrly
(A high school boy) hunkered in the dripping shade
Of the water-tender, in the tall talk and acrid sweat
Of the circle of spitting stiffs whose cloud-topped bundle-racks
Waited their turns at the feeder.
And the fireman: goggled, shirtless, a flashing-three tined fork,
Its handle charred, stuck through the shiny metallic
Lip of the engine, into the flaming, smoky
Fire-box of its heart.
Myself: straw-monkey. Jester at court.

So, dawn to dusk, dark to dark, hurried
From the booming furious brume of the thresher's back
To the antipodean panting engine. Caught in the first
Circle.

Was it hard? I don't know. It was terrifying.
The whistle snapped and I ran. The thresher moaned on its
  glut.
The Danaean rain of the wheat rained down.
Hard? No. Everyone wanted to help me.
My father, riding the grain-tanks from the field
To the town elevators, starting out in the chilly dawn
And home at the cold midnight, eating when time allowed,
Doing the work of a threshing hand and the chores of the farm
          to boot,
Harnessing the team I was too short to harness,
Helping me pick up a load when he got back from town
In the jolting musical empty grain tank.
                    He had boils that summer,
His neck was circled with ruby light, I remember.
Poulticed with heated bottles.
My mother helped. I had cookies stuffed in my pocket,
Ginger . . .
Their crumbly sweetness.
                    Worrying:
"Jim, is it too hard?
The boy's tired as a horse."
My grandfather too,
After the first week, when they found a man,
Came prancing and dancing, pulling his thin beard:
"Kate, let the boy be quitting.
It's hard, long hours. Let him quit."

My father came in the dark
(Where I'd gone into sleep, into the open flaming
Mouth of the dream, the whistle biting my ears,
The night vibrating,
In the fog of the red rust, steam, the rattle of concaves)
Came about midnight.
His last chore done, he led me into the bright
Kitchen. (The table was already set for breakfast;
The potatoes were sliced; the pie, cross cut; a cloth
Fenced out the flies.)
Then, his supper, we ate ice cream and cheese;
Sardines; crackers; tomatoes still wet with the night
Out of the garden; cucumbers crisp and salty
Cooled in the watertrough; bacon and watermelon
Left over from supper.
"Tom, Old Timer," he'd say. "Ain't you had enough?
This workin' won't get you nowheres. Let the job go.
We got a man for her now."
But I couldn't. No way to quit.
My hand was stuck to the plough and I cried to stay.
(As at morning, with the sleep stuck in my eyes and my morning breakfast
Dead in my stomach I cried for the day to be gone).

I couldn't quit. I came out of sleep at four
Dazed and dreaming and ate my food on the run,
And ran to the barn; the roan team knelt and dozed;
I clapped the harness on them and kicked them awake
And rode the off one, galloping, into the field
Where the engine slept in its heat.
The fireman grunted. He struck a match to his fork.
The crackling fireball, thrust to the metal heart,
Ignited the still dark day.

Sometimes, at night, after a long move to another farm,
Hours after the bundle-teams were gone and sleeping,
After we'd set the rig for the next day,
I rode the off-horse home.
Midnight, maybe, the dogs of the strange farms
Barking behind me, the river short-cut rustling
With its dark and secret life and the deep pools warm.
(I swam there once in the dead of night while the team
Nuzzled the black water).
Home then. Dead beat.

To quit was impossible once you had started.
All you could do was somehow to learn the ropes.
No one could teach you.
When you were late the whistle
Blasted you into the kingly estate
Of the daylight man. Responsibility. The hot foundries
Of the will.
But when, your load up, you squatted
In the spitting circle of stiffs, in the hot shade
Under the sky-piled bundle-racks waiting their turn at the
feeder,
Chewing on rose apples and bumming a smoke—
You were no man there.
A man to the engine's hunger, to the lash of the whistle,
But not to the tough young punks from Detroit or Chicago
Drifting the tide of the harvest the first time
And jealous of manhood.
Not to the old stiffs
Smoke shooters, their bindles weighted with dust
From Kansas to Calgary.
Not to your uncle surely
Boss of the rig who slapped you once when you swore,
Before the ritual was known or the language of men.

O great port of the Dream! Gate to the fearful country,
So near and magically far, what key will open?
Their alien smell, their talk, their foreign hungers,
And something awful, secret: I saw them, lost,
Borne on the fearful stream in a sinful valor
And longed to enter. To know. To burn in that fire.

—*Thomas McGrath*

37. *Danaean rain:* Zeus impregnated Danae in the form of a shower of gold. She gave birth later to Perseus.

In this section of *Letter to an Imaginary Friend* McGrath records experiences of his early youth, threshing grain on a midwestern farm. His memories are vivid, alive with detail. In the larger sense they are as much a part of our national history as of McGrath's own biography. But the poet does more than simply retell history, personal or public: he interprets the experience. Why did he insist on working such a hard, taxing job? What is the tension between him and his uncle, boss of the rig? Why does he say "To quit was impossible once you had started"? What's he trying to prove?

The Charge of the Light Brigade

I

Half a league, half a league,
Half a league onward,
All in the valley of Death
    Rode the six hundred.
"Forward the Light Brigade!
Charge for the guns!" he said.
Into the valley of Death
    Rode the six hundred.

II

"Forward, the Light Brigade!"
Was there a man dismay'd?
Not tho' the soldier knew
    Some one had blunder'd.
Theirs not to make reply,
Theirs not to reason why,
Theirs but to do and die.
Into the valley of Death
    Rode the six hundred.

III

Cannon to right of them,
Cannon to left of them,
Cannon in front of them
    Volley'd and thunder'd;
Storm'd at with shot and shell,
Boldly they rode and well,
Into the jaws of Death,
Into the mouth of hell
    Rode the six hundred.

IV

Flash'd all their sabres bare,
Flash'd as they turn'd in air
Sabring the gunners there,
Charging an army, while
    All the world wonder'd.
Plunged in the battery-smoke
Right thro' the line they broke;
Cossack and Russian
Reel'd from the sabre-stroke

Shatter'd and sunder'd.
Then they rode back, but not,
Not the six hundred.

V

Cannon to right of them,
Cannon to left of them,
Cannon behind them
Volley'd and thunder'd;
Storm'd at with shot and shell,
While horse and hero fell,
They that had fought so well
Came thro' the jaws of Death,
Back from the mouth of hell,
All that was left of them,
Left of six hundred.

VI

When can their glory fade?
O the wild charge they made!
All the world wonder'd.
Honor the charge they made!
Honor the Light Brigade,
Noble six hundred!

—*Alfred, Lord Tennyson*

What does this poetic recounting of the charge of the Light Brigade have that a prose report of the battle would lack?

Ulysses

It little profits that an idle king,
By this still hearth, among these barren crags,
Match'd with an aged wife, I mete and dole
Unequal laws unto a savage race,
That hoard, and sleep, and feed, and know not me.
I cannot rest from travel; I will drink
Life to the lees. All times I have enjoy'd
Greatly, have suffer'd greatly, both with those
That loved me, and alone; on shore, and when
Thro' scudding drifts the rainy Hyades
Vext the dim sea. I am become a name;
For always roaming with a hungry heart

Much have I seen and known,—cities of men
And manners, climates, councils, governments,
Myself not least, but honor'd of them all,—
And drunk delight of battle with my peers,
Far on the ringing plains of windy Troy.
I am a part of all that I have met;
Yet all experience is an arch wherethro'
Gleams that untravell'd world whose margin fades
For ever and for ever when I move.
How dull it is to pause, to make an end,
To rust unburnish'd, not to shine in use!
As tho' to breathe were life! Life piled on life
Were all too little, and of one to me
Little remains; but every hour is saved
From that eternal silence, something more,
A bringer of new things; and vile it were
For some three suns to store and hoard myself,
And this gray spirit yearning in desire
To follow knowledge like a sinking star,
Beyond the utmost bound of human thought.
  This is my son, mine own Telemachus,
To whom I leave the sceptre and the isle,—
Well-loved of me, discerning to fulfill
This labor, by slow prudence to make mild
A rugged people, and thro' soft degrees
Subdue them to the useful and the good.
Most blameless is he, centred in the sphere
Of common duties, decent not to fail
In offices of tenderness, and pay
Meet adoration to my household gods,
When I am gone. He works his work, I mine.
  There lies the port; the vessel puffs her sail;
There gloom the dark, broad seas. My mariners,
Souls that have toil'd, and wrought, and thought with me,—
That ever with a frolic welcome took
The thunder and the sunshine, and opposed
Free hearts, free foreheads,—you and I are old;
Old age hath yet his honor and his toil.
Death closes all; but something ere the end,
Some work of noble note, may yet be done,
Not unbecoming men that strove with Gods.
The lights begin to twinkle from the rocks;
The long day wanes; the slow moon climbs; the deep
Moans round with many voices. Come, my friends.

'T is not too late to seek a newer world.
Push off, and sitting well in order smite
The sounding furrows; for my purpose holds
To sail beyond the sunset, and the baths
Of all the western stars, until I die.
It may be that the gulfs will wash us down;
It may be we shall touch the Happy Isles,
And see the great Achilles, whom we knew.
Tho' much is taken, much abides; and tho'
We are not now that strength which in old days
Moved earth and heaven, that which we are, we are,—
One equal temper of heroic hearts,
Made weak by time and fate, but strong in will
To strive, to seek, to find, and not to yield.

—*Alfred, Lord Tennyson*

10. *Hyades:* an asterism of five stars in the constellation Taurus, supposed to indicate rain when they rise with the sun.

This poem is a dramatic monologue (see Chapter 1, Section 2) in which Tennyson projects himself into the historical (or pseudohistorical) character Ulysses. The time is some years after Ulysses has returned from Troy and his wanderings around the Mediterranean Sea, and he is getting bored with life in Ithica. He proposes to take to the road (or the sea) once more, in search of some last few adventures, some last greatness. More important to this poem than Greek history (we have no record of Ulysses leaving home once he had returned) is the myth of Ulysses: the wanderer, the explorer, the "name / For always roaming with a hungry heart." Why is Ulysses an appropriate historical character in whom to embody this myth? How tied to history is this character? What other embodiments of this same myth can you think of?

5. A Thing: Event

An important event in personal, social, or political history often forms the basis for a poem. Such poems, when they are not purely historical, usually fall into one of three categories. The first is the commemorative poem, usually commissioned to give permanence and ceremonial ornamentation to a public event. The second is the topical poem written on an event very much in the public consciousness, often expressing a strong political or social philosophy and urging a course of direct action. The third is a poem that views an event, usually after the fact, as being an important turning point in personal, social, or political history.

Overlap is, of course, sometimes possible, but not as much as you might suspect. The sad truth is that most events chosen for commemoration in officially sanctioned poems are simply not significant . . . or at least not in the sense that the people doing the commemorating want to think. Few poems are more dismal, and ultimately more irrelevant, than those written for Memorial Day celebrations, the U.S. centennial or bicentennial, or a presidential inauguration. And those commemorations of public events that are successful are usually successful on terms far different from those envisioned by the people who promote events. Robert Lowell's "Inauguration Day: January, 1953" is a case in point: the poem captures the significance of the event, all right, but it's a kind of counterinaugural poem that sees Eisenhower's inauguration more as the start of another ice age than as the dawning of the golden age that any new president likes to think will accompany his term in office.

Topical poems, for their part, usually fade with the memory of the events that spawned them. And topical poems fade very, very quickly. They may be redeemed in part by a remarkable display of poetic talent, but even Milton's "On the Late Massacre in Piedmont" and Bob Dylan's "The Lonesome Death of Hattie Carroll" turn yellow around the corners not ten years after being written.

Most events of real significance happen quite by accident, or their significance occurs quite by accident and becomes apparent only after the fact, after poets and social historians develop a perspective on history. Woodstock is a case in point: what was intended as nothing more than a big rock concert (with good times and lots of bucks for the promoters) turned into an emblem for all that was wonderful about a counterculture of the late sixties. Who would have thought it, out there in the rain and the mud? In poems of event, as in other matters, hindsight is usually better than foresight.

Woodstock

I came upon a child of God,
He was walking along the road.
And I asked him, "Where are you going?"
And this he told me:
"I'm going down to Yasgur's farm,
I'm going to join in a rock-n-roll band,
I'm going to camp out on the land

And try an' get my soul free."
  We are stardust,
  We are golden,
  And we've got to get ourselves
  Back to the garden.
"Than can I walk beside you?
I have come here to lose the smog,
And I feel to be a cog in something turning.
Well maybe it is just the time of year,
Or maybe it's the time of man,
I don't know who I am
But life is for learning."
  We are stardust,
  We are golden,
  And we've got to get ourselves
  Back to the garden.
By the time we got to Woodstock
We were half a million strong,
And everywhere there was song and celebration.
And I dreamed I saw the bombers
Riding shotgun in the sky,
And they were turning into butterflies
Above our nation.
  We are stardust,
  We are golden,
  And we've got to get ourselves
  Back to the garden.

—*Joni Mitchell*

5. *Yasgur's farm:* the farm near Woodstock where the rock festival was held. 12. *garden:* the Garden of Eden?

In retrospect, the great gathering at Woodstock has come to represent all the most positive aspects of the sixties: love, peace, freedom, music, grass, good vibrations. What specific elements of the event can you find in Joni Mitchell's song? Judging from the connotations of the words she uses, what would you take to be her attitude toward Woodstock? What did (does) the event mean to her?

Inauguration Day: January, 1953

The snow had buried Stuyvesant.
The subways drummed the vaults. I heard

the El's green girders charge on Third,
Manhattan's truss of adamant,
that groaned in ermine, slummed on want. . . .
Cyclonic zero of the word,
God of our armies, who interred
Cold Harbor's blue immortals, Grant!
Horseman, your sword is in the groove!

Ice, ice. Our wheels no longer move.
Look, the fixed stars, all just alike
as lack-land atoms, split apart,
and the Republic summons Ike,
the mausoleum in her heart.

—*Robert Lowell*

Title: President Eisenhower's first inauguration. 1. *Stuyvesant:* a housing project in New York. 8. *Cold Harbor:* the site of two Civil War battles involving General (later President) Grant; also a pun on New York harbor locked with ice. Grant is buried in a large mausoleum in Manhattan.

1. What *facts* about Inauguration Day, 1953, does Lowell's poem contain? How are these facts interpreted by the poet?
2. What aspects of New York City not directly relevant to the business of inaugurating a president does Lowell see fit to mention in his poem? Why? Is this a case of guilt by association?
3. Do you agree or disagree with Lowell's assessment of the Eisenhower years?

On the Late Massacre in Piedmont

Avenge, O Lord, thy slaughtered saints, whose bones
  Lie scattered on the Alpine mountains cold;
  Even them who kept thy truth so pure of old
  When all our fathers worshipped stocks and stones,
Forget not; in thy book record their groans
  Who were thy sheep and in their ancient fold
  Slain by the bloody Piedmontese that rolled
  Mother with infant down the rocks. Their moans
The vales redoubled to the hills, and they
  To heaven. Their martyred blood and ashes sow
  O'er all the Italian fields where still doth sway
The triple tyrant: that from these may grow

A hundredfold, who having learned thy way
Early may fly the Babylonian woe.

—*John Milton*

Title: The Waldenses, a heretical sect settled in northern Italy, had been given freedom of worship until 1655, when it was abruptly terminated. The massacre that resulted was vigorously protested by all the Protestant powers of Europe. 4. *stocks and stones:* graven images. 12. *triple tyrannt:* the Pope, so named because of his three-crowned tiara. 14. *Babylonian:* as allusion to the Babylonian captivity of the Jews and to the Babylonian Captivity of the Papacy, when the Pope resided for nearly a century in France rather than Rome.

How much history is recounted *in* Milton's poem (excluding the footnotes, of course)? How intelligible is the poem *without* the footnotes? How well has it weathered three centuries? How much evidence of artistic skill can you find in the poem?

6. A Thing: Object

While they may lack some of the attraction of place, story, and characters, simple objects sometimes serve as the subject around which a poet can spin a poem. Statues, jars, automobiles, trains, flowers—any common household object will do.

There are some differences, however. While a poet may occasionally be content just to present a character, relate a story, capture the mood of a place, mere description of an object is generally more successful as a painting or a photograph than as a poem. While "object poems" have been written, especially in the first half of the twentieth century, such poems grew more out of aesthetic theory than poetic practice: they were for the most part studied attempts to reassert objectiveness in a poetry that had gone philosophical and soft. In treating objects as subjects of their poems, most poets turn them into symbols or metaphors. The Grecian urn, for Keats, becomes a symbol of art, of things eternal, of a beauty that never even changes, let alone ages or dies. The city of New Orleans to Steve Goodman and the statue of the doughboy to James Ballowe represent those relics of the past, once important, now merely comfortable, that America has outgrown and tossed away and forgotten in the mad rush of things. The groundhog becomes for Eberhart a symbol for life (and passion) exterminated by the passage of time. And a common jar—a palpable and very real jar, whatever else the poem may say—becomes for Wallace Stevens . . . well, a symbol for a great many things that are much more than that. While a story may be only a good tale, and while place may be largely a mood or flavor, an object—except in the most self-conscious of modern poetry—is almost always infused with deeper meaning. Still objects are, like people, concrete and real, and we find in them a certain comfortable easiness, an easy door into the world of the poem.

The City of New Orleans

Ridin' on the City of New Orleans,
Illinois Central Monday mornin' rail.
Fifteen cars and fifteen restless riders,
Three conductors and twenty-five sacks of mail;
All along the southbound Odyssey, the train pulls out of
  Kankakee
And rolls along the houses, farms and fields.
Passin' towns that have no name and freightyards full of old
  black men,
And the graveyards of the rusted automobiles.

Good morning America, how are you?
Say, don't you know me, I'm your native son.
I'm the train they call the City of New Orleans.
I'll be gone five hundred miles when the day is done.

Dealin' card games with the old men in the club car,
Penny a point ain't no one keepin' score.
Pass the paper bag that holds the bottle;
Feel the wheels grumblin' 'neath the floor;
And the sons of pullman porters, and the sons of engineers
Ride their father's magic carpet made of steel.
Mothers with their babes asleep are rockin' to the gentle beat
And the rhythm of the rails is all they feel.

Good morning America, how are you?
Said don't you know me, I'm your native son.
I'm the train they call the City of New Orleans.
I'll be gone five hundred miles when the day is done.

Night time on the City of New Orleans,
Changin' cars in Memphis, Tennessee;
Halfway home, we'll be there by mornin',
Thru the Mississippi darkness rollin' down to the sea.
But all the towns and people seem to fade into a bad dream,
And the steel rail still ain't heard the news;

The conductor sings his songs again;
The passangers will please refrain,
This train's got the disappearin' railroad blues.

Good night, America, how are you?
Said don't you know me, I'm your native son.
I'm the train they call the City of New Orleans.
I'll be gone five hundred miles when the day is done.

—*Steve Goodman*

What specific details of Goodman's description of the train suggest uselessness and decay and contribute to the generally elegaic mood of the song? What is the purpose of changing the refrain line from "Good morning, America" to "Good night, America"? How important is place to the success of this song?

God's Measurements

(*Todaiji Temple, Nara*)

"The statue weighs 452 tons, measures 53.5 ft. in height, and has a face 16 ft. long by 9.5 ft. wide, eyes 3.9 ft. wide, a nose 1.6 ft. high, a mouth 3.7 ft. wide, ears 8.5 ft. long, hands 6.8 ft. long, and thumbs 4.8 ft. long. The materials employed are estimated as follows: 437 tons of bronze; 165 lbs. of mercury; 288 lbs. of pure gold; 7 tons of vegetable wax; and an amazing amount of charcoal and other materials."

As incense smoke thins, a stupendous,
wide, brooding face emerges above us. The long ribbon-
looped ears, ending in weighty teardrop-
fat lobes, slowly unravel from the wrappings of smoke trails
as we advance, the whole bronze olive-green head
mushrooming from its mask
of mist. It floats, hovers—balloonlike, isolate—
over the befogged shoulders. A cosmos
of global body,
seated cross-legged on a great lotus-
blossom bronze pedestal, ascends

into the clearing before us,
the pedestal in turn installed on a broader stone base
which knows touch of our hastily donned
slippers, blocking our passage. Not one forward step possible.

we backstep twice to see the more clearly
over the jutting head-
high edge of stone, the full figure now vivid
and preternaturally clear before us,
body draped in swirls
of cloud, itself cloud-shaped, cloud-alloyed,
growing into a mass, a solid—

if wavery—form. Still, it is the head,
so distant, holds us. Why do we so thrill at eye-guessed
estimates of measurements, measurements!
The eyes and mouth, wide as you are long, my son; the
length of ears makes two of you, the height of lofty face
three of me, and, yes,
you can ride lying on the thumb, your near mate
for length and width, the two of you nestled
together mimicking
a God's freakish double thumb! But, no, I
will not lift you to the stone ledge,

launching your unstoppable climb
to test my twin-thumbs caprice, despite your scandalous
wails
reverberating in the temple
upper chambers, strident in my ears; nor shall I scold
or muzzle you, but hoist you to my shoulders
where, first clasping hands
for lift and support as you unfold to your full
height above my head, I clench your ankles,
as much to steady
and balance you as to prevent surprise
leaps. Together, of a tallness

to match, or exceed, the whole hand's length,
let us promenade around His Excellency's right flank.
Now, wobblingly, we stalk: you, stiltjack,
in love with instant towers sprung from the idiot body's
endlessly stretchable elastic of flesh, I
half scaffold, half anchor,
the two of us a father-son hobbling hinge—
telescope of our bones, joined end to end,
not doubled up
in laughter or loss of balance but bending
and unbending into beatitudes . . . .

We look up, to scrutinize the Gold, stilt-
walking our charmed gavotte. Then, looking into each
other's eyes—
I staring up, you staring down—
we both shudder, communing between your flexed legs,
spread the width of my two shoulders: our four eyes,
riveted in silence,
agree! We have seen the bronze head nod. The eyelids
flutter. The bronze bosom draw breath. The tarnished
skins of metal wrinkling
into folds over charcoal hid ribs. Organs—
heart and lungs—of vegetable wax, waxen

liver, waxen pancreas. All glands,
mercury, but in pure form, not poisons fed upon by dying
fish hordes. Our eyes swear we both saw
bronze flesh breathe, bronze knees shift for comfort under all
that obese weight (no gold in the fat buttocks, fat
hips, we agree to that!),
grand flab he can never jog off in throes
of deep meditation. Does he diet, or fast?
Does he shed bronze, gold,
or weightless, sad wax only? We crane our necks
to see how he leans and sways, as we wend

our wide, counterclockwise, happy circle
around him, counting splendid curled petals of the great
lotus-
blossom seat, the petals alternately
pointing upward and curving downward, the puffed
whirlwinds of incense smoke eddying up, thinning out,
in sudden gusts and lulls,
as if the blossom itself exhaled the perfume
clouds submerging all but the Ancient's head, breath
after vaporous breath . . . .
We revolve, degree by slow degree, circling
the statue's base, half again wider

than the vast lotus throne half again
the diameter of the bloated God's girth, and we behold
the *thousand views* of the Buddha's
changing postures, the torso's bulk crafted by an army
of master sculptors. *Eight near-perfect castings
in three years. Aborted casts,*

unnumbered. No surmising how many dozens
of failed castings, cracked one-hundred-foot-wide
molds, collapsed scaffolds,
casters of irreplaceable genius crushed
in falling debris . . . . Sudden glare!

We squint, sun cascading into the hall
from hidden windows high in the temple cupola—
thousands
of sparkly points on the statue's
coruscating skull flare on, off, on, off, and I can see
great circles connecting all dots of light
on meticulously shaped
rondures of annealed jaw plates, shoulder plates, breast
plates, my sight travelling in arcs and swirls, curved
lines running in a mesh
of intersecting spirals dense as cross-
hatching in the divinely crafted

anatomies of Hieronymus Bosch
or the woodcut body dissections of Vesalius: God's
or human's, all the light-lines engraved
on the celestial body's grandly continuous surface
intersect. *Our body, a wing shining*
in the happy, happy
light of its wholeness. A moonlight angel's wing
in flight. Or underwater devil ray's
wing torchlit
by diver's forehead searchlight beam . . . .
High throne-back behind the Buddha's

head usurps our view while we wind
around his back side, topped not by headrest or flat
cushion,
as it had appeared to us wrongly
in profile, but a goldleaf-covered broad wooden halo
decorated with portraits of sixteen Bosatsu,
by our ambulatory
count, a troop of gilt sub-deities, satellites
in orbit perpetually—each a mirror,
or reflecting moon,
to the one Daibutsu . . . . *Oh, look! The whole halo*
is shimmering, dancing before our eyes!

—*Larry Lieberman*

Here is certainly thing: 452 tons of thing, the details of which Lieberman takes considerable pains to give us. What details of the Buddha do you find particularly memorable? Why? For all its vast bulk, however, the statue has its own chimerical airiness. Is it there or not? Is it alive? Is it possible for something so massive to be so ephemeral?

The Doughboy

In Memory of Our Heroic Dead
Veterans of the World War 1917–1918

For years he stalked the town until we noticed him
above the President who gave 'em the hell he knew so well.

Smack in the middle of Main Street,
Our first and only public sculpture,
green like money by World War II,
a public nuisance, the Doughboy
waved at arm's length a ripe grenade
like a pomegranate for all to see.

Automobiles chipped at his feet
or veered into the Herrin Supply.
Stoplights appeared
green, then yellow, then red
bombs bursting in air.
He was in another war,
his weapons obsolete.

He didn't know what hit him.

We have him where we want him now,
in the park by the city limits
where he stands among all the dead at war.
Leisurely we approach to read him.
His feet entangled in barbed wire,
His mouth agape, his eyes hollow,
he dies surprised from a wound to the heart.

—*James Ballowe*

What does Ballowe mean by his last line, "he died surprised from a wound to the heart"? Why is line 16 set apart from the rest of the poem? What suggestions can you draw from the similes "green like money" and "like a ripe pomegranate"?

Ode on a Grecian Urn

1

Thou still unravish'd bride of quietness.
Thou foster-child of silence and slow time.
Sylvan historian, who canst thus express
A flowery tale more sweetly than our rhyme:
What leaf-fring'd legend haunts about thy shape
Of deities or mortals, or of both,
In Tempe or the dales of Arcady?
What men or gods are these? What maidens loth?
What mad pursuit? What struggle to escape?
What pipes and timbrels? What wild ecstasy?

2

Heard melodies are sweet, but those unheard
Are sweeter; therefore, ye soft pipes, play on;
Not to the sensual ear, but, more endear'd,
Pipe to the spirit ditties of no tone:
Fair youth, beneath the trees, thou canst not leave
Thy song, nor ever can those trees be bare:
Bold lover, never, never canst thou kiss,
Though winning near the goal—yet, do not grieve;
She cannot fade, though thou hast not thy bliss,
For ever wilt thou love, and she be fair!

3

Ah, happy, happy boughs! that cannot shed
Your leaves, nor ever bid the spring adieu;
And, happy melodist, unwearied,
For ever piping songs for ever new;
More happy love! more happy, happy love!
For ever warm and still to be enjoy'd,
For ever panting, and for ever young;
All breathing human passion far above,
That leaves a heart high sorrowful and cloy'd,
A burning forehead, and a parching tongue.

4

Who are these coming to the sacrifice?
To what green altar, O mysterious priest,
Lead'st thou that heifer lowing at the skies,
And all her silken flanks with garlands drest?
What little town by river or sea shore,

Or mountain-built with peaceful citadel,
Is emptied of this folk, this pious morn?
And, little town, thy streets for evermore
Will silent be; and not a soul to tell
Why thou art desolate, can e'er return.

5

O Attic shape! Fair attitude! with brede
Of marble men and maidens overwrought,
With forest branches and the trodden weed;
Thou, silent form, dost tease us out of thought
As doth eternity: Cold Pastoral!
When old age shall this generation waste,
Thou shalt remain, in midst of other woe
Than ours, a friend to man, to whom thou say'st,
"Beauty is truth, truth beauty,"—that is all
Ye know on earth, and all ye need to know.

—*John Keats*

Describe in as much detail as you can the scenes depicted on the Grecian urn. As Keats notes, none of them will ever change: they are as eternal as they are beautiful. What advantages does this beauty have? Are there any disadvantages?

Anecdote of the Jar

I placed a jar in Tennessee,
And round it was, upon a hill.
It made the slovenly wilderness
Surround that hill.

The wilderness rose up to it,
And sprawled around, no longer wild.
The jar was round upon the ground
And tall and of a port in air.

It took dominion everywhere.
The jar was gray and bare.
It did not give of bird or bush,
Like nothing else in Tennessee.

—*Wallace Stevens*

Here is Wallace Stevens's tale of a jar in Tennessee. It hints in every line at allegory and hidden meaning, but it is first and always a simple jar. What definite statements can you make about this jar and its effects on its environment? What does the jar seem to you to represent? Read some of the other poems by Wallace Stevens in this book to see if their subjects, themes, and techniques help you interpret the significance of this curious jar in Tennessee.

The Groundhog

In June, amid the golden fields,
I saw a groundhog lying dead.
Dead lay he; my senses shook,
And mind outshot our naked frailty.
There lowly in the vigorous summer
His form began its senseless change,
And made my senses waver dim
Seeing nature ferocious in him.
Inspecting close his maggots' might
And seething cauldron of his being,
Half with loathing, half with a strange love,
I poked him with an angry stick.
The fever arose, became a flame
And Vigour circumscribed the skies,
Immense energy in the sun,
And through my frame a sunless trembling.
My stick had done nor good nor harm.
Then stood I silent in the day
Watching the object, as before;
And kept my reverence for knowledge
Trying for control, to be still,
To quell the passion of the blood;
Until I had bent down on my knees
Praying for joy in the sight of decay.
And so I left; and I returned
In Autumn strict of eye, to see
The sap gone out of the groundhog,
But the bony sodden hulk remained.
But the year had lost its meaning,
And in intellectual chains
I lost both love and loathing,
Mured up in the wall of wisdom.
Another summer took the fields again
Massive and burning, full of life,

But when I chanced upon the spot
There was only a little hair left,
And bones bleaching in the sunlight
Beautiful as architecture;
I watched them like a geometer,
And cut a walking stick from a birch.
It has been three years, now.
There is no sign of the groundhog.
I stood there in the whirling summer,
My hand capped a withered heart,
And thought of China and of Greece,
Of Alexander in his tent;
Of Montaigne in his tower,
Of Saint Theresa in her wild lament.

—Richard Eberhart

The key to this poem is not so much in the groundhog as in the poet's reaction to the groundhog. At first he is very moved by the rotting corpse, himself as seething as the decomposing groundhog and the stir in the air above it. On his second visit, the poet—like the decaying groundhog—is much more subdued; by the third visit, there is as little life in the poet as in the vanished animal. What do China, Greece, Alexander, Montaigne, and Theresa have to do with either groundhogs or the poet?

7. A Thing: Image

Some words, because they are concrete, because they name things, make a special appeal to one or more of our senses—usually the sense of sight, but sometimes smell, taste, hearing, even touch. Poetry, which is more concrete than most writing, makes a greater use of these sensuously appealing words than does prose, although it has no monopoly on imagery by any means. "Fire-engine red" is substantively different from "bright red," because the one phrase tells us how red the red is, while the other creates an image in our mind's eye and lets us *see* for ourselves how bright the red is. One phrase is diffuse, abstract, antipoetic; the other is concrete, visual, poetic. In the same way, "ghostly moan" and "mackerel-scented wharves" appeal to our senses of hearing and smell respectively—you'd be likely to find them in a poem somewhere.

An image is a thing: you can smell it, taste it, feel it, see it. A single image can be very powerful, although no matter how well examined, it can scarcely match the impact of a remarkable character carefully portrayed, or a suspenseful story artfully told. Collectively, however, a group or "cluster" of images can overpower the senses. By virtue of their collective connotative meaning and the associations they bring to the poem, they can even make a relatively definite statement. As modern poetry becomes compressed and modern poets turn away from narrative and "beautiful thoughts beautifully expressed" to rediscover "ideas in things," imagery has become increasingly important in poetry. Some modern poems are little more than collages of images that form a carefully modulated series of tones throughout the length of the poem, speaking to the reader on a prerational, intuitive level. A whole school of "imagism," developed shortly after World War I, was strong enough to tempt even a poet like Carl Sandburg into writing his famous—and entirely atypical—imagistic poem "Fog." The imagistic tradition, reinforced by Oriental poetry (heavy on images, and popular in America throughout the twentieth century) and the constant quest after compression and concision, make imagism a force even today.

In discussing poetry, critics also use the term "imagery" in a looser sense to refer to an extended series of words all derived from the same source. "trade," "get," "spend," and "toil" (in Wordsworth's sonnet "The World Is Too Much with Us") are referred to as "commercial imagery," because all the words have to do with commerce. "Holy," "saint," "prayer," "reverence," and "bless," although they are not concrete and do not appeal to any of our senses, might be called "religious imagery," because they are all words associated with religion. So too there might be a pattern of sexual imagery, or natural imagery, or light/dark imagery or winter imagery or whatever, spread across a section or the entire length of a poem. A clever poet can use such imagery to reinforce or play against the statement he's making in his poem.

The Red Wheelbarrow

so much depends
upon

a red wheel
barrow

glazed with rain
water

beside the white
chickens.

—William Carlos Williams

This poem, a classic of modern imagistic poetry, is something of an explanation of the art. "So much depends," Williams tells us, on the picture of the red wheelbarrow, glazed with rain water, beside the chickens. "What depends?" we want to know. This poem depends. For if we don't understand the primacy of that small photograph, then we've lost the poem. And by implication we have lost not only this poem but all poetry that depends on the concrete, visualizable thing that is the image.

Spring

When daisies pied and violets blue
  And lady-smocks all silver-white
And cuckoo-buds of yellow hue
  Do paint the meadows with delight,
The cuckoo then, on every tree,
Mocks married men; for thus sings he,
  Cuckoo!
Cuckoo, cuckoo! O, word of fear,
Unpleasing to a married ear!

When shepherds pipe on oaten straws,
  And merry larks are ploughmen's clocks,
When turtles tread, and rooks, and daws,
  And maidens bleach their summer smocks,
The cuckoo then, on every tree,
Mocks married men; for thus sings he,
  Cuckoo!
Cuckoo, cuckoo! O, word of fear,
Unpleasing to a married ear!

—*William Shakespeare*

9. *unpleasing:* the cuckoo (like the cowbird) lays its eggs in the nests of other birds, and its call resembles the English world "cuckold." For these reasons its call would be unpleasing to a married ear.

Winter

When icicles hang by the wall,
  And Dick the shepherd blows his nail,
And Tom bears logs into the hall,
  And milk comes frozen home in pail,

When blood is nipped and ways be foul,
  Then nightly sings the staring owl:
      "Tu-whit, tu-who!"
      A merry note,
While greasy Joan doth keel the pot.

When all aloud the wind doth blow,
  And coughing drowns the parson's saw,
And birds sit brooding in the snow,
  And Marian's nose looks red and raw,
When roasted crabs hiss in the bowl,
  Then nightly sings the staring owl:
      "Tu-whit, tu-who!"
      A merry note,
While greasy Joan doth keel the pot.

—*William Shakespeare*

9. *keel:* stir. 11. *saw:* proverb. 14. *crabs:* crab apples.

The imagery is complicated. On the simplest level the poems contain natural imagery appropriate to the season: daisies, violets, cuckoo-buds, straws, larks, turtledoves in spring; icicles, logs, owls, roasted crab apples in winter. The appropriateness of the natural imagery and the way it creates an immediate picture of the respective seasons have been much admired by readers over the last three centuries. But look again at the imagery. The cuckoo of "Spring" has obvious sexual overtones. The daisies are pied (multicolored) and have overtones of inconstancy. The other flowers also have sexual overtones: lady-smocks and cuckoo-buds. The oaten straws are phallic, and the treading turtles ("and rooks, and daws,/And maidens . . .") are overtly sexual, perhaps unpleasantly so. And the imagery of "Winter" is even more sexual and more unpleasant. It could be argued that the sexuality of Shakespeare's imagery is entirely unintentional—but anyone who knows his work well knows both his fondness for double meanings and his tendency to drop the most frightening obscenities into the middle of his most beautiful and tender passages. It is quite probable that we are justified in reading double meanings into his imagery in these two songs, especially since that of "Spring" is suggested overtly in lines 8–9 and 17–18 of the poem itself. Is that duplicity necessarily self-contradictory? Does the poet have a point he's trying to make by using such two-sided imagery? Or is he merely being perverse? In your spare time read over *Love's Labours Lost,* from which these two songs are taken, and consider their meaning when put in the context of the whole play.

Suzanne

Suzanne takes you down
To her place near the river
You can hear the boats go by
You can spend the night beside her.
And you know that she's half crazy
But that's why you want to be there
And she feeds you tea and oranges
That come all the way from China.
And just when you mean to tell her
That you have no love to give her
Then she gets you on her wavelength
And she lets the river answer
That you've always been her lover
And you want to travel with her
And you want to travel blind
And you know that she will trust you
For you've touched her perfect body with your mind.

And Jesus was a sailor
When he walked upon the water
And he spent a long time watching
From his lonely wooden tower.
And when he knew for certain
Only drowning men could see him
He said, "All men will be sailors then
Until the sea shall free them."
But he himself was broken
Long before the sky would open
Forsaken, almost human,
He sank beneath your wisdom like a stone.
And you want to travel with him
And you want to travel blind
And you think maybe you'll trust him
For he's touched your perfect body with his mind.

Now Suzanne takes your hand
And she leads you to the river
She is wearing rags and feathers
From Salvation Army counters.
And the sun pours down like honey
On our lady of the harbour;
And she shows you where to look

Among the garbage and the flowers.
There are heroes in the seaweed,
There are children in the morning,
They are leaning out for love
And they will lean that way forever
While Suzanne holds the mirror.
And you want to travel with her
And you want to travel blind
And you know that you can trust her
For she's touched your perfect body with her mind.

—*Leonard Cohen*

39. *our lady of the harbour:* many European harbor cities have large statues of Christ or Mary on a hill adjacent to the harbor to bless ships as they pass.

In moving from "Spring"' and "Winter" to Leonard Cohen's "Suzanne" we move from the profane to the sacred and from poetry that makes at least some kind of literal sense to poetry that is almost entirely dependent on the connotations and associations of its imagery and the responses produced in a listener by the successive images. No matter what we want to say about the suggestions of "When icicles hang by the wall,/And Dick the shepherd blows his nail," the lines have a literal sense that is absent in lines like "Forsaken, almost human,/He sank beneath your wisdom/Like a stone." Perhaps because the literal meaning is absent, perhaps because the imagery is richer and more complex, "Suzanne" demands more attention than either of Shakespeare's songs. Central to the poem's meaning is an understanding of Suzanne, Jesus, the person addressed by the poet, and the interrelationships among the three. Although nothing definite is said by Cohen, we can make some reasonably precise statements about all three, based on the imagery with which the poet surrounds each. Suzanne loves: she loves you even before she meets you, she loves you enough to offer you tea and oranges (luxury items in most economies, carrying connotations of great value). Perhaps because of her totally selfless love, the world considers her half crazy. The effect of her love is so strong that it transforms even the garbage world of the waterfront: there are heroes in the seaweed. There is something vaguely religious about Suzanne, for religious imagery surrounds her: "our lady of the harbour," "Salvation Army counters," most of all, "love." On the other hand, she wears rags and feathers and lives down by the river: she may be not only half crazy, but a tramp as well. You can spend the night beside her. Her character is both religious and sexual, much like Cohen's Sisters of Mercy.

Jesus, like Suzanne, is associated with the water: she lives near the water; he was a sailor and walked upon it. Just as our wisdom cannot fathom Suzanne and we suspect she's crazy, Jesus sank beneath our wisdom "like a stone." Suzanne wastes a lot of love on the waterfront bums; Jesus spent his time hanging around with "drowning men."

The indefinite "you" of the poem provides the measure of both Suzanne and Jesus, because it is upon this character that they act. He is in need of love, but by instinct distrustful, perhaps because of previous experiences. He is probably one of the "drowning men" of line 23. He is desperately in need of direction and help, which he gains as the poem progresses: the imagery of the final stanza is richly affirmative. So we may say that the experience here is roughly similar to that of "Sisters of Mercy": the poet and an indefinite "you" meet with a semireligious woman who is able to transform their depression into affirmation.

The presence of Jesus in the poem and the wealth of water imagery bring a strong religious element into "Suzanne." Does water have its Christian significance of baptism here? Is that what is going on in the final stanza? Or is the baptismal significance subsumed into a broader connotation of water, that of regeneration and life? Is Suzanne given religious overtones in an attempt to suggest the effect she has on a man, or is her effect due to her position as a human agent of the divine Jesus? Might Suzanne be a Salvation Army lass? These are all possibilities supported to some extent by the imagery, although the poet is so vague that we cannot affirm or deny any of them for sure. Clearly the man experiences some sort of converson, but the variety of the images for rebirth and the many images for death (drowning men) and life (the sun pouring down like honey) make it unclear whether the conversion is specifically Christian, broadly religious, or something else entirely.

To His Coy Mistress

Had we but world enough and time,
This coyness, lady, were no crime.
We would sit down and think which way
To walk, and pass our long love's day;
Thou by the Indian Ganges' side
Shouldst rubies find; I by the tide
Of Humber would complain. I would
Love you ten years before the Flood;
And you should, if you please, refuse
Till the conversion of the Jews.
My vegetable love should grow
Vaster than empires, and more slow.
An hundred years should go to praise

Thine eyes, and on thy forehead gaze;
Two hundred to adore each breast,
But thirty thousand to the rest;
An age at least to every part,
And the last age should show your heart.
For, lady, you deserve this state,
Nor would I love at lower rate.
  But at my back I always hear
Times wingèd chariot hurrying near;
And yonder all before us lie
Deserts of vast eternity.
Thy beauty shall no more be found,
Nor in thy marble vault shall sound
My echoing song; then worms shall try
That long preserved virginity,
And your quaint honor turn to dust,
And into ashes all my lust.
The grave's a fine and private place,
But none, I think, do there embrace.
  Now therefore, while the youthful hue
Sits on thy skin like morning dew,
And while thy willing soul transpires
At every pore with instant fires,
Now let us sport us while we may;
And now, like am'rous birds of prey,
Rather at once our time devour,
Than languish in his slow-chapt power,
Let us roll all our strength, and all
Our sweetness, up into one ball;
And tear our pleasures with rough strife
Through the iron gates of life.
Thus, though we cannot make our sun
Stand still, yet we will make him run.

—*Andrew Marvell*

1. *world:* space. 7. *Humber:* a river in England; *complain:* see the section on genres, "complaints." 29. *quaint:* quite possibly a pun on quaint = old and ME queynte = female private parts. 40. *chapt:* cracked, roughened.

1. This poem has a more definite literal meaning than "Suzanne." In fact, it reduces to a syllogism once the wealth of imagery is removed. What specifically is the argument? Is it valid?

2. How does the poet change the imagery of each section of the argument to accord with his various premises?

3. Is the poet entirely serious in his argument, apparently an attempt at seduction? Is there something mildly humorous about the incongruity of a cold, rational argument tricked out with lush, sensual imagery? Is the poet conscious of this?

4. Compare the thought of the last line with the thought expressed in Yeats' "That the Night Come" (Chapter 1, Section 1). Do you find this idea of rushing through life with a kind of savage eagerness for death reckless and grotesque, or is it something you too have felt at one time or another?

Silver

Slowly, silently, now the moon
Walks the night in her silver shoon;
This way, and that, she peers, and sees
Silver fruit upon silver trees;
One by one the casements catch
Her beams beneath the silvery thatch;
Couched in his kneel, like a log,
With paws of silver sleeps the dog;
From their shadowy cote the white breasts peep
Of doves in a silver-feathered sleep;
A harvest mouse goes scampering by,
With silver claws and a silver eye;
And moveless fish in the water gleam,
By silver reeds in a silver stream.

—*Walter de la Mare*

2. *shoon:* archaic plural of shoe. 9. *cote:* shelter for sleep.

1. Examine the images closely. At first they all appear to enchance the silvery quality of the landscape, and some of them—the water images especially—would definitely give off a silver shine in the moonlight. A few others might be silvery if seen in the proper light: the doves' white breasts, the eye of the mouse. Others, however, are not silver in any light: the fruit, the straw thatch of the house. Is this a failure on the poet's part or has he made a significant point about perception and the eye of the beholder?

2. Note the focus downward as the images proceed: from trees to housetop, to dog, to doves, to mouse, to fish. What does this add to the poem? To its message?

3. "Like a log" in line seven: is this trite and used merely for the sake of a rhyme for "dog," or is there something more to it?

One A.M.

The kitchen patio in snowy
moonlight.   That
snowsilence, that
abandon to stillness.
The sawhorse, the concrete
washtub, snowblue. The washline
bowed under its snowfur!
Moon has silenced
the crickets, the summer frogs
hold their breath.
Summer night, summer night, standing
one-legged, a crane
in the snowmarsh, staring
at snowmoon!

—Denise Levertov

1. What season of the year is it? How can you tell?
2. What qualities of snow are most important to Levertov's poem?
3. Summer night is compared to a crane, standing one-legged and staring at the moon. What connotations does the crane carry that might be applicable to the world at 1:00 A.M.?

I Am the Walrus

I am he as you are he as you are me and we are all together.
See how they run like pigs from a gun see how they fly,
I'm crying.
Sitting on a cornflake—waiting for the van to come.
Corporation teashirt, stupid bloody tuesday man you been a
    naughty boy you let your face grow long.
I am the eggman, they are the eggmen—I am the walrus
GOO GOO GOO JOOB.
City policeman sitting pretty little policeman in a row,
See how they fly like Lucy in the sky—see how they run
I'm crying—I'm crying.
Yellow matter custard dripping from a dead dog's eye.
Crabalocker fishwife pornographic priestess boy you been a
    naughty girl, you let your knickers down.
I am the eggman, they are the eggmen—I am the walrus.
GOO GOO GOO JOOB.
Sitting in an English garden waiting for the sun,

If the sun don't come, you get a tan from standing in the
English rain,
I am the eggman, they are the eggmen—I am the walrus.
GOO GOO GOO JOOB.
Expert texpert choking smokers don't you think the joker
laughs at you? Ha ha ha!
See how they smile, like pigs in a sty, see how they snied.
I'm crying.
Semolina pilchard climbing up the Eiffel Tower.
Elementary penguin singing Hare Krishna man you should
have seen them kicking
Edgar Allen Poe.
I am the eggman, they are the eggmen—I am the walrus.
GOO GOO GOO JOOB
GOO GOO GOO JOOB GOO GOO
GOOOOOOOOOOOJOOOOB

—John Lennon-Paul McCartney

Some people have argued that "I Am the Walrus" is a put-on, a meaningless collage of images designed to elicit absurd responses from overingenious listeners. Others view it as a good imagistic poem, as well as a good song. At the crux of the matter is just what the walrus represents, since we are all equal to I and "I am the walrus," and therefore we are all walruses. Popular mythology would have the walrus be slang for corpse, and the song about death. Many of the other images, however, apparently have little to do with death: pornographic priestess, pigs in a sty, the eggman. The music, from its opening wrenching cacophony to its cyclonic conclusion, is vaguely unpleasant, harsh, and perhaps terrifying—all of which may or may not suggest death. Someone appears to be chanting "Everybody's a hunchback" as the song swirls to its finish, and it very definitely ends with a quotation from Shakespeare's *King Lear,* act *IV,* scene 6.

EDGAR I know thee well—a serviceable villain,
As duteous to the vices of thy mistress
As badness would desire.
GLOUCESTER What, is he dead?
EDGAR Sit you down, father, rest you.

Lines 15–16 are set off from the rest of the song by virtue of their own unique musical setting—are they perhaps the key to unlocking the poem? Discuss the many images of the song, the effect they have on the senses, the effect the music has on them, and see if you can relate them coherently. Can anything be said about the theme of this poem, anything more definite than, "This is an extremely unpleasant poem about extreme unpleasantness?" Is that theme enough?

Kubla Khan

In Xanadu did Kubla Khan
A stately pleasure-dome decree:
Where Alph, the sacred river, ran
Through caverns measureless to man
Down to a sunless sea.
So twice five miles of fertile ground
With walls and towers were girdled round:
And here were gardens bright with sinuous rills,
Where blossomed many an incense-bearing tree,
And here were forests ancient as the hills,
Enfolding sunny spots of greenery.

But oh! that deep romantic chasm which slanted
Down the green hill athwart a cedarn cover!
A savage place! as holy and enchanted
As e'er beneath a waning moon was haunted
By woman wailing for her demon-lover!
And from this chasm, with ceaseless turmoil seething,
As if this earth in fast thick pants were breathing,
A mighty fountain momently was forced,
Amid whose swift half-intermitted burst
Huge fragments vaulted like rebounding hail,
Or chaffy grain beneath the tresher's flail:
And 'mid these dancing rocks at once and ever
It flung up momently the sacred river.
Five miles meandering with a mazy motion
Through wood and dale the sacred river ran,
Then reached the caverns measureless to man,
And sank in tumult to a lifeless ocean:
And 'mid this tumult Kubla heard from far
Ancestral voices prophesying war!

The shadow of the dome of pleasure
Floated midway on the waves;
Where was heard the mingled measure
From the fountain and the caves.
It was a miracle of rare device,
A sunny pleasure-dome with caves of ice!

A damsel with a dulcimer
In a vision once I saw:
It was an Abyssinian maid,
And on her dulcimer she played,
Singing of Mount Abora.
Could I revive within me
Her symphony and song,
To such a deep delight 'twould win me,
That music loud and long,
I would build that dome in air,
That sunny dome! those caves of ice!
And all who heard should see them there,
And all should cry, Beware! Beware!
His flashing eyes, his floating hair!
Weave a circle round him thrice,
And close your eyes with holy dread,
For he on honey-dew hath fed,
And drunk the milk of Paradise.

—*Samuel Taylor Coleridge*

Coleridge claimed that he literally dreamed this poem on an opium trip one day, wrote part of it down, then forgot the rest when interrupted in his study by a visitor. There is a lesson in all that if such was indeed the case. We have little reason to doubt Coleridge, although the process of composition had probably been at work long before the dream, deep in the poet's subconscious. So complex are the images and the sources of the images that it took John Livingston Lowes a full book (*The Road to Xanadu*) to discuss them, the process by which they worked themselves into Coleridge's subconscious, and the relationship of this poem to the rest of his work. What is Coleridge describing here? What images are associated with the pleasure dome? What images are associated with the chasm? What contrasts do you find between the two? What has all this to do with the poet and his vision?

The poem is undeniably impressive (the rock group Rush developed their song "Xanadu" from this poem, on the album *A Farewell to Kings,* and it is a staple of poetry courses everywhere); can any rational sense be made of it? Is it too much the mood piece and too imprecise?

Long poems, like "To His Coy Mistress," allow a poet to change imagery as his subject changes, or to play back and forth on several different imagistic themes. The longer the poem, of course, the greater the possibilities, and the imagery in a four-hundred-line poem like Eliot's "The Waste Land" or a several-thousand-line poem like Whitman's "Leaves of Grass" is so complex that extensive study is required before patterns begin to emerge. Many playwrights write in verse, and frequently that verse involves complex patterns of imagery of several varieties. Shakespeare was both a good poet and a first rate playwright, and the imagery and poetry of a play like *Romeo and Juliet* or *King Lear* are as fine as those of any poem in the English language. Act II, scenes 1 and 2 of *Romeo and Juliet* present a case in point. Shakespeare's imagery changes with his characters: Mercutio, who is exceptionally cynical and unromantic, uses considerable sexual imagery and many images of darkness. Romeo, whose love is sexual but romantic as well, uses sexual imagery of a more chaste nature, astronomical imagery, and extensive light imagery. Juliet echoes Romeo, and toward the end of the scene introduces falconry imagery. What is most important, however, is the pattern of light and dark imagery that pervades the speech of all the characters in these scenes—indeed—the whole play. The play is a battleground on which images of light war against images of darkness, and the wealth of connotative significance carried by light and darkness is what makes the play more than just a love story. It is not insignificant that the Prince of Verona begins the final speech of the play with the lines, "A glooming peace this morning with it brings,/ The Sun for sorrow will not show his head." Imagistically, light loses in the play. Trace the development of light and dark imagery, as well as other patterns of imagery, through these two scenes. Do they foreshadow imagistically the play's end, or do they imply an optimism here that is unwarranted by the play's conclusion?

Romeo and Juliet, Act II.

Scene I. A lane by the wall of Capulet's orchard.

[*Enter* ROMEO.]

ROMEO Can I go forward when my heart is here?
Turn back, dull earth, and find thy centre out.

[*He climbs the wall, and leaps down within it.*]
[*Enter* BENVOLIO *and* MERCUTIO]

BENVOLIO Romeo! my cousin Romeo!

MERCUTIO He is wise;
And, on my life, hath stol'n him home to bed.

BENVOLIO He ran this way, and leap'd this orchard wall:
Call, good Mercutio.

MERCUTIO Nay, I'll conjure too?
Romeo! humours! madman! passion! lover!
Appear thou in the likeness of a sigh:
Speak but one rhyme, and I am satisfied;

Cry but "Ay me!" pronounce but "love" and
"dove;"
Speak to my gossip Venus one fair word,
One nick-name for her purblind son and heir,
Young Adam Cupid, he that shot so trim,
When King Cophetua loved the begger-maid!
He heareth not, he stirreth not, he moveth not;
The ape is dead, and I must conjure him.
I conjure thee by Rosaline's bright eyes,
By her high forehead and her scarlet lip,
By her fine foot, straight leg and quivering thigh
And the demesnes that there adjacent lie,
That in thy likeness thou appear to us!

BENVOLIO And if he hear thee, thou wilt anger him.

MERCUTIO This cannot anger him; 'twould anger him
To raise a spirit in his mistress' circle
Of some strange nature, letting it there stand
Till she had laid it and conjured it down;
That were some spite: my invocation
Is fair and honest, and in his mistress' name
I conjure only but to raise up him.

BENVOLIO Come, he hath hid himself among these trees,
To be consorted with the humorous night:
Blind is his love and best befits the dark.

MERCUTIO If love be blind, love cannot hit the mark.
Now will he sit under a medlar tree,
And wish his mistress were that kind of fruit
As maids call medlars, when they laugh alone.
O, Romeo, that she were, O, that she were
An open et cætera, thou a poperin pear!
Romeo, good night: I'll to my truckle-bed;
This field-bed is too cold for me to sleep:
Come, shall we go?

BENVOLIO Go, then; for 'tis in vain
To seek him here that means not to be found.

[*Exeunt.*]

6. *conjure:* raise up by incantation, as if Romeo were a spirit. 7. *humours:* the bodily fluids, which men of the Renaissance assumed filled the body. In a healthy man the humors were in balance; in madmen, lovers, and sick people, the humors were out of balance. Love, insanity, sickness—it's all the same, Mercutio implies; he's "in a bad humour." 11. *gossip:* friend. 12. *purblind:* totally blind. 13. *Adam:* hypocritical. 14. *Cophetua:* a ballad character. 17. *Rosaline:* before he met Juliet, Romeo was in love with Rosaline. Mercutio is as yet unaware that the object of Romeo's affections has changed. 20. *demesnes:* estates, areas, regions. 22. *anger him:* because of the obscene puns Mercutio

has been making about a subject that to Romeo is sacred. 34. *medlar:* a small fruit resembling a brown apple. 39. *truckle-bed:* a small rollaway bed tucked under a standing bed during the day time. 40. *field-bed:* a bed on the bare ground.

Scene II. Capulet's orchard.

[*Enter* ROMEO.]

ROMEO He jests at scars that never felt a wound.

[JULIET *appears above at a window.*]

But, soft! what light through yonder window breaks?
It is the east, and Juliet is the sun.
Arise, fair sun, and kill the envious moon,
Who is already sick and pale with grief,
That thou her maid art far more fair than she:
Be not her maid, since she is envious;
Her vestal livery is but sick and green
And none but fools do wear it; cast it off.
It is my lady, O, it is my love!
O, that she knew she were!
She speaks, yet she says nothing: what of that?
Her eye discourses; I will answer it.
I am too bold, 'tis not to me she speaks:
Two of the fairest stars in all the heaven,
Having some business, do entreat her eyes
To twinkle in their spheres till they return.
What if her eyes were there, they in her head?
The brightness of her cheek would shame those stars,
As daylight doth a lamp; her eyes in heaven
Would through the airy region stream so bright
That birds would sing and think it were not night.
See, how she leans her cheek upon her hand!
O, that I were a glove upon that hand,
That I might touch that cheek!

JULIET Ay me!

ROMEO She speaks:

O, speak again, bright angel! for thou art
As glorious to this night, being o'er my head,
As is a wingèd messenger of heaven
Unto the white-upturnèd wondering eyes
Of mortals that fall back to gaze on him
When he bestrides the lazy-pacing clouds
And sails upon the bosom of the air.

JULIET O Romeo, Romeo! wherefore art thou Romeo?
Deny thy father and refuse thy name;
Or, if thou wilt not, be but sworn my love,
And I'll no longer be a Capulet.
ROMEO [*Aside*] Shall I hear more, or shall I speak at this?
JULIET 'Tis but thy name that is my enemy;
Thou art thyself, though not a Montague.
What's Montague? it is nor hand, nor foot,
Nor arm, nor face, nor any other part
Belonging to a man. O, be some other name!
What's in a name? that which we call a rose
By any other name would smell so sweet;
So Romeo would, were he not Romeo call'd,
Retain that dear perfection which he owes
Without that title. Romeo, doff thy name,
And for that name which is no part of thee
Take all myself.
ROMEO I take thee at thy word:
Call me but love, and I'll be new baptized;
Henceforth I never will be Romeo.
JULIET What man art thou that thus bescreen'd in night
So stumblest on my counsel?
ROMEO By a name
I know not how to tell thee who I am:
My name, dear saint, is hateful to myself,
Because it is an enemy to thee;
Had I it written I would tear the word.
JULIET My ears have not yet drunk a hundred words
Of that tongue's utterance, yet I know the sound:
Art thou not Romeo and a Montague?
ROMEO Neither, fair saint, if either thee dislike.
JULIET How camest thou hither, tell me, and wherefore?
The orchard walls are high and hard to climb,
And the place death, considering who thou art,
If any of my kinsmen find thee here.
ROMEO With love's light wings did I o'erperch these walls,
For stony limits cannot hold love out,
And what love can do that dares love attempt;
Therefore thy kinsmen are no let to me.
JULIET If they do see thee, they will murder thee.
ROMEO Alack, there lies more peril in thine eye
Than twenty of their swords: look thou but sweet,
And I am proof against their enmity.

JULIET I would not for the world they saw thee here.
ROMEO I have night's cloak to hide me from their sight;
And but thou love me, let them find me here:
My life were better ended by their hate,
Than death proroguèd, wanting of thy love.
JULIET By whose direction found'st thou out this place?
ROMEO By love, who first did prompt me to inquire;
He lent me counsel and I lent him eyes.
I am no pilot; yet, wert thou as far
As that vast shore wash'd with the farthest sea,
I would adventure for such merchandise.
JULIET Thou know'st the mask of night is on my face,
Else would a maiden blush bepaint my cheek
For that which thou hast heard me speak tonight.
Fain would I dwell on form, fain, fain deny
What I have spoke: but farewell compliment!
Dost thou love me? I know that wilt say "Ay."
And I will take thy word: yet, if thou swear'st,
Thou mayst prove false; at lovers' perjuries,
They say, Jove laughs. O gentle Romeo,
If thou dost love, pronounce it faithfully:
Or if thou think'st I am too quickly won,
I'll frown and be perverse and say thee nay,
So thou wilt woo; but else, not for the world.
In truth, fair Montague, I am too fond,
And therefore thou mayst think my 'haviour light:
But trust me, gentleman, I'll prove more true
Than those that have more cunning to be strange.
I should have been more strange, I must confess,
But that thou overheard'st, ere I was ware,
My true love's passion; therefore pardon me,
And not impute this yielding to light love,
Which the dark night hath so discovered.
ROMEO Lady, by yonder blessed moon I swear
That tips with silver all these fruit-tree tops—
JULIET O, swear not by the moon, the inconstant moon,
That monthly changes in her circled orb,
Lest that thy love prove likewise variable.
ROMEO What shall I swear by?
JULIET Do not swear at all;
Or, if thou wilt, swear by thy gracious self,
Which is the god of my idolatry,
And I'll believe thee.

ROMEO If my heart's dear love—
JULIET Well, do not swear: although I joy in thee,
I have no joy of this contract to-night:
It is too rash, too unadvised, too sudden;
Too like the lightning, which doth cease to be
Ere one can say "It lightens." Sweet, good night!
This bud of love, by summer's ripening breath,
May prove a beauteous flower when next we meet.
Good night, good night! as sweet repose and rest
Come to thy heart as that within my breast!
ROMEO O, wilt thou leave me so unsatisfied?
JULIET What satisfaction canst thou have tonight?
ROMEO The exchange of thy love's faithful vow for mine.
JULIET I gave thee mine before thou didst request it:
And yet I would it were to give again.
ROMEO Wouldst thou withdraw it? for what purpose, love?
JULIET But to be frank, and give it thee again.
And yet I wish but for the thing I have:
By bounty is as boundless as the sea,
My love as deep; the more I give to thee,
The more I have, for both are infinite.
[NURSE *calls within.*]
I hear some noise within; dear love, adieu!
Anon, good nurse! Sweet Montague, be true.
Stay but a little, I will come again.
[*Exit, above.*
ROMEO O blessèd, blessèd night! I am afear'd,
Being in night, all this but a dream,
Too flattering-sweet to be substantial.
[*Re-enter* JULIET, *above.*]
JULIET Three words, dear Romeo, and good night indeed.
If that thy bent of love be honourable,
Thy purpose marriage, send me word tomorrow,
By one that I'll procure to come to thee,
Where and what time thou wilt perform the rite;
And all my fortunes at thy foot I'll lay
And follow thee my lord throughout the world.
NURSE [*Within*] Madam!
JULIET I come, anon.—But if thou mean'st not well.
I do beseech thee—
NURSE [*Within*] Madam!
JULIET By and by, I come:—

To cease thy suit, and leave me to my grief:
To-morrow will I send.

ROMEO So thrive my soul—

JULIET A thousand times good night!

[Exit, above.

ROMEO A thousand times the worse, to want thy light.
Love goes toward love, as schoolboys from their books,
But love from love, toward school with heavy looks.

[Retiring.

[*Re-enter* JULIET, *above.*]

JULIET Hist! Romeo, hist! O, for a falconer's voice,
To lure this tassel-gentle back again!
Bondage is hoarse, and may not speak aloud;
Else would I tear the cave where Echo lies,
And make her airy tongue more hoarse than mine,
With repetition of my Romeo's name.

ROMEO It is my soul that calls upon my name:
How silver-sweet sound lovers' tongues by night,
Like softest music to attending ears!

JULIET Romeo!

ROMEO My dear?

JULIET At what o'clock to-morrow
Shall I send to thee?

ROMEO At the hour of nine.

JULIET I will not fail: 'tis twenty years till then.
I have forgot why I did call thee back.

ROMEO Let me stand here till thou remember it.

JULIET I shall forget, to have thee still stand there,
Remembering how I love thy company.

ROMEO And I'll still stay, to have thee still forget,
Forgetting any other home but this.

JULIET 'Tis almost morning; I would have thee gone:
And yet no further than a wanton's bird;
Who lets it hop a little from her hand,
Like a poor prisoner in his twisted gyves,
And with a silk thread plucks it back again,
So loving-jealous of his liberty.

ROMEO I would I were thy bird.

JULIET Sweet, so would I:
Yet I should kill thee with much cherishing.
Good night, good night! parting is such sweet sorrow,

That I shall say good night till it be morrow.
[*Exit, above.*

ROMEO Sleep dwell upon thine eyes, peace in thy breast!
Would I were sleep and peace, so sweet to rest!
Hence will I to my ghostly father's cell,
His help to crave, and my dear hap to tell.
[*Exit.*

4. *Moon:* the goddess of the sphere of the moon was Diana, also goddess of virginity. Romeo's imagery here is working on two levels. 8. *vestal:* virgin. 20. *eyes:* the sun was frequently called the heaven's eye or the heaven's mind in Neo-Platonic thought. Romeo is working on a contrast between ordinary stars, whose places in the heavens Juliet's eyes are taking temporarily, and her eyes, which seem more like the sun than a star. 66. *o'erperch:* fly over. 99. *light:* immodest. A pun is intended. 109. *the inconstant moon:* because the moon alone among heavenly bodies appeared to change size, its sphere was considered the dividing line between things mutable and things immutable. Cf. "sublunary love" in Donne's "A Valediction: Forbidding Mourning." 160. *tassel-gentle:* a male tercel falcon. 180. *gyves:* fetters. 190. *crave:* request; *hap:* fortune.

8. A Thing: Simile, Metaphor, Symbol

Traditionally the figures of speech most popular with poets have been similes, metaphors, and symbols, all devices for making one thing—usually something concrete and visualizable—represent something else—usually an abstraction or an idea. Rhetorically there is little difference among the three. "My love is like a red, red rose" is a simile; "the red rose of my love" is a metaphor; "a rose" might, in the right context, symbolize love. In practice, however, there is considerable difference, because metaphors tend to be more open-ended than similes, and symbols are the most open-ended of all. Thus symbols are "richer" than metaphors, which are in turn "richer" than similes. There is, of course, the disadvantage with open-endedness that there is little control over what a reader will "read into" the poem. Symbolism can be a bad disease, and symbol-hunting as well. For that reason, and because many contemporary poets have resisted the role of preacher and philosopher, the symbol—and to a lesser extent the metaphor and simile—have lost some of their popularity to the image, which is heavier on visualization, lighter on hidden meaning.

There are other differences between similes, metaphors, and symbols. Metaphoric poetry is different from symbolic poetry, with different strengths and defects. One problem with metaphor is its proclivity for cliché: "my faith is like an oak tree," "cool as cucumbers," or "lily-white face and ruby lips." These are flat comparisons, tired and by now meaningless, and they make very bad poetry. Another danger inherent in metaphor is the possibility of mixed metaphor: a comparison that contradicts itself. "We're going to take his record," said one politician of his opponent, "and cram it down his throat until he doesn't have a leg to stand on." These are two clichéed metaphors that contradict each other. The branches of Joyce Kilmer's famous trees ("I think that I shall never see/ A poem as lovely as a tree . . .") are in one line the tree's hair (full of robins' nests) and in another line "leafy hands" lifted to heaven to pray. They can't be both. In Paul Simon's song "A Bridge over Troubled Water" the poet is in one line a bridge over the water, in another a boat "sailing right behind." Can't be both, and the muddle hurts the poem.

Metaphorical poetry tends toward wit: verse becomes a game in which the poet, partly to explain his meaning but partly to show off what a clever fellow he is, extends a metaphor as far as he can, developing at great length obscure or unusual comparisons which we may never have thought of. How is a woman like a radio? Like a car? On the surface of it, there's no comparison, yet Joni Mitchell and e. e. cummings built very interesting poems around these metaphors.

A good metaphor has layers of meaning, has depth and resonance, and rewards many readings. It does not reveal itself all at once. A bad simile or metaphor is stale to begin with, reveals everything in an instant, or disintegrates into nonsense after a few moments' thought. One of the most common faults of bad poetry (as in that of Rod McKuen or Joyce Kilmer) is careless, inconsistent metaphor.

Symbolist poetry, on the other hand, tends less toward wit than to a mystical fuzziness, because the symbol is so much more open-ended than the metaphor. Take the rose, for example. It might symbolize love. It might also symbolize the House of Lancaster or York, the Virgin Mary, beauty, the Lutheran Church, virginity . . . or nothing at all. Moreover, because the rose has been made at one time or another to carry all these meanings and more, it brings with it into the poem associations of each, even when it's representing something else. Public symbols—symbols like the colors red and blue and green, objects like the Cadillac car or the dove or the swastika or the rose—have been so often used to represent certain values that they resist any poet's attempt to change their meaning, no matter what context they are put in. A dove is always going to represent peace, green will always represent jealousy or rebirth, the Cadillac will always represent ostentatious affluence. Even when a poet does not intend the dove or the Cadillac to be symbolic, they will be read as symbols and they will give off a vaguely symbolic flavor that confers on a poem a mystical, transcendent air, the hint of "something more here than meets the eye." The lamb and the tiger of Blake's poems are public symbols properly used; their effect on the atmosphere of the poem is obvious.

Nonce symbols are symbols a poet makes up for the duration of the poem. The grass becomes to Walt Whitman a remarkably open personal nonce symbol, an avenue into a new mode of perception. Hopkins's windhover is a nonce symbol. Seals and Crofts' popular song "Summer Breeze" is in some respects a symbol of all the refreshing, comfortable, easy familiarity of a stable marriage and good home life. Who would have thought that a simple summer breeze, a falcon, or the grass could mean so much? But this is characteristic of poets who dwell in symbolic landscapes: the commonest objects are invested with a nearly mystical meaning, so that their true reality is not what you see, but what hovers around them nearly unseen. Metaphorical poets are witty manipulators; symbolists are neo-Platonic metaphysicians.

Come All You Fair and Tender Ladies

Come all you fair and tender ladies,
Take warning how you court young men.
They're like the stars of a summer's morning,
First they'll appear and then they're gone.

If I had known before I courted
I never would have courted none.
I'd lave locked my heart in a box of golden
And fastened it up with a silver pin.

I wish I were some little swallow,
And I had wings and I could fly.
I'd fly away to my false true-lover
And when he'd speak I would deny.

But I am not a little swallow;
I have no wings, neither can I fly.
So I'll sit down here to weep in sorrow
And try to pass my troubles by.

—*anonymous*

1. What specifically has happened to the singer of this song? What is her attitude toward her experience?

2. What connotations do golden and silver have? How effective is the image of lines 7–8?

3. In what ways is the comparison between the lady and the swallow appropriate? And that between men and stars? Which do you think has more depth?

To Blossoms

Fair pledges of a fruitful tree,
Why do ye fall so fast?
Your date is not so past
But you may stay yet here a while,
To blush and gently smile,
And go at last.

What, were ye born to be
An hour or half's delight,
And so to bid good-night?
'Twas pity nature brought ye forth
Merely to show your worth,
And lose you quite.

But you are lovely leaves, where we
May read how soon things have
Their end, though ne'er so brave;
And after they have shown their pride,
Like you a while, they glide
Into the grave.

—*Robert Herrick*

15. *brave:* beautiful.

What simple comparison does Herrick set up in his poem? How original is it? What specific words in the first and second stanzas betray Herrick's comparison even before he draws it in stanza three? What effect does the poet get by making the last line of each stanza noticeably shorter than the others?

A Valediction: Forbidding Mourning

As virtuous men pass mildly away,
And whisper to their souls, to go,
Whilst some of their sad friends do say,
The breath goes now, and some say, no:

So let us melt, and make no noise,
No tear-floods, nor sigh-tempests move,
T'were profanation of our joys
To tell the laity our love.

Moving of th' earth brings harms and fears,
  Men reckon what it did and meant,
But trepidation of the spheres,
  Though greater far, is innocent.

Dull sublunary lovers' love
  (Whose soul is sense) cannot admit
Absence, because it doth remove
  Those things which elemented it.

But we by a love, so much refined
  That our selves know not what it is,
Inter-assurèd of the mind,
  Care less, eyes, lips, and hands to miss.

Our two souls therefore, which are one,
  Though I must go, endure not yet
A breach, but an expansion,
  Like gold to airy thinness beat.

If they be two, they are two so
  As stiff twin compasses are two,
Thy soul, the fixt foot, makes no show
  To move, but doth, if th' other do.

And though it in the center sit,
  Yet when the other far doth roam,
It leans, and hearkens after it,
  And grows erect, as that comes home.

Such wilt thou be to me, who must
  Like th' other foot, obliquely run;
Thy firmness makes my circle just,
  And makes me end, where I begun.

—*John Donne*

This poem contains some of the most complicated workings-out of similes in the English language. In the first two stanzas, the poet compares the parting of himself and his lover to the death of virtuous men: because they have nothing to fear in the afterlife, they make no noise or "sigh-tempests" when they die—in fact, their death is so calm that friends are unsure about the exact moment of death. Donne suggests that the parting of himself and his love be just as peaceful, because a telltale commotion would cheapen their love (7–8) and imply that they feared separation as virtueless men fear death. Next Donne compares the parting to the movement of the heavenly bodies of the Ptolemaic system: when earth, the lowest of the nine spheres, moves, it causes great commotion among men who fear the significance of such motion; but when the highest spheres move, they are unnoticed. Since Donne's love is of a higher nature, the departure should cause no commotion. Then the poet compares the stretching of their love to the stretching of gold as it is beaten to a foil, and finally to the movement of the two legs of a compass, an instrument used to draw circles in geometry and to mark distances by navigators. His love, he argues, remains fixed at home, while he moves away from her and around her (two motions are involved here). But even though the points move apart, the two legs remain attached at the top; so their spiritual love will bind them together, even though they move away from each other. Donne develops the argument further: when the one leg moves away from the other (as when the navigator uses the compass to mark distances), the other leg moves sympathetically with it, and the efficacy of the entire instrument is predicated on the fixedness (the constancy) of the two legs; so their love will remain constant even though they are separated. Moreover, the rigidity (constancy) of the compass (love) causes the outside leg to move in a perfect circle, so that it ends where it began (Donne returns to his love).

The similes are rhetorically complex, and Donne manages to suggest a great deal in a little space. But a rhetorical analysis does not exhaust the possibilities of the poem by any means. The circle is a particularly apt image for love, since it is continuous, perfect, and has no beginning or end. The simile involving the celestial bodies is similarly significant: men of the Middle Ages and Renaissance viewed change and mutability as the law of the world (a reasonable assumption, even today), observing that everything on earth changed from life to death, from joy to unhappiness, from wealth to poverty (and occasionally vice versa). So too the moon changed. But as far as they could see the other planets did not change, so quite obviously the realm of mutability was confined to the sphere of the moon and below. "Sublunary" in line 13 implies more than higher and lower love, then; it implies a changing, inconstant love as contrasted to a changeless love. Look carefully at some of the diction in the poem: "stiff," "foot," "grows erect," and "firmness." Some people find the obvious sexual connotations of these words incompatible with the celestial love that Donne has been talking about. What is your reaction? Does the vulgar destroy the celestial or do they complement each other? Might it be that the generation of the 1980s is in a better position to appreciate this poem of the 1600s than was the generation of the 1940s or the Victorian period in England?

No Expectations

Take me to the station
And put me on a train.
I've got no expectations
To pass through here again.

Once I was a rich man
And now I am so poor,
But never in my sweet, short life
Have I felt like this before.

Your heart is like a diamond,
You throw your pearls at swine,
And as I watched you leaving me
You packed my peace of mind.

Our love was like the water
That splashes on a stone,
Our love is like our music,
It's here and then it's gone.

So take me to the airport
And put me on a plane.
I've got no expectations
To pass through here again.

—Mick Jagger–Keith Richards

What situation underlies this song? What has happened to the speaker? How does he feel about it? What comparisons does he draw? How effective are the metaphors? How original?

El Condor Pasa

I'd rather be a sparrow than a snail.
Yes I would
If I could,
I surely would.

I'd rather be a hammer than a nail.
Yes I would.
If I only could,
I surely would.

Anyway, I'd rather sail away
Like a swan that's here and gone.
A man gets tied up to the ground,
He gives the world its saddest sound,
Its saddest sound.

I'd rather be a forest than a street.
Yes I would.
If I only could,
I surely would.

I'd rather feel the earth beneath my feet.
Yes I would.
If I only could,
I surely would.

—Paul Simon

In each stanza of this poem Paul Simon uses two metaphors, each a matched pair, one attractive, one unattractive. What brings sparrows and snails together? Hammers and nails? Swans and men? Forests and streets? What makes the first metaphor in each case so much more attractive than the second? What is the "message" of Simon's song? How does its music contradict or reinforce that statement?

American Poetry

Whatever it is, it must have
A stomach than can digest
Rubber, coal, uranium, moons, poems.

Like the shark, it contains a shoe.
It must swim for miles through the desert
Uttering cries that are almost human.

—Louis Simpson

In his statement on American poetry, Simpson uses metaphors to comment on the state of the art and the predicament of artists in contemporary America. Look over some of the poetry by American poets that you have already read, and compare this poem to it. Is it full of the thingness implied by "rubber, coal, uranium, moons, poems"? How is it like a shark? (What does Simpson mean by a shark with a shoe?) Gregory Corso's comments quoted at the beginning of Chapter 1 provide a good gloss on Simpson's desert. What does Simpson mean by "uttering cries that are *almost* human" (my italics)?

she being Brand

she being Brand

-new;and you
know consequently a
little stiff i was
careful of her and(having

thoroughly oiled the universal
joint tested my gas felt of
her radiator made sure her springs were O.

K.)i went right to it flooded-the-carburetor cranked her

up,slipped the
clutch(and then somehow got into reverse she
kicked what
the hell)next
minute i was back in neutral tried and

again slo-wly;bare,ly nudg.   ing(my

lev-er Right-
oh and her gears being in
A 1 shape passed
from low through
second-in-to-high like
greasedlightning)just as we turned the corner of Divinity

avenue i touched the accelerator and give

her the juice,good

                              (it
was the first ride and believe i we was
happy to see how nice she acted right up to
the last minute coming back down by the Public
Gardens i slammed on
the

internalexpanding
&
externalcontracting
brakes Bothatonce and

brought allofher tremB
-ling
to a:dead.

stand-
;Still)

—*e. e. cummings*

More sex here than in Shakespeare's "Winter" and "Spring," although a careful examination of the poem will demonstrate that the subject is never mentioned overtly. This poem is an extended metaphor; is it merely clever (or dirty), or does the poet make a statement about trying out women (or men) as one test drives a new car? What is the poet's attitude toward his speaker? Why? Is this a male-chauvinist poem?

Discuss cummings's use of typographic arrangement to enhance the effects of his poem.

You Turn Me On, I'm a Radio

If you're driving into town
With a dark cloud above you
Dial in the number
Who's bound to love you
Oh, honey, you turn me on
I'm a radio
I'm a country station
I'm a little bit corny
I'm a broadcasting tower
Waving for you
And I'm sending you out
This signal here
I hope you can pick it up
Loud and clear
I know you don't like weak women
You get bored so quick
And you don't like strong women
'Cause they're hip to your tricks

It's been dirty for dirty
Down the line
But if you've got too many doubts
If there's no good reception for me
Then tune me out, 'cause, honey
Who needs the static
It hurts the head
And you wind up cracking
And the day goes dismal
From "Breakfast Barney"
To the sign-off prayer
What a sorry face you get to wear
I'm going to tell you again now
If you're still listening there
If you're driving into town
With a dark cloud above you
Dial in the number
Who's bound to love you
If you're lying on the beach
With the transistor going
Kick off the sandflies, honey
The love's still flowing
If your head says forget it
But your heart's still smoking
Call me at the station
The lines are open.

—*Joni Mitchell*

Like cummings's poem, this song is an extended metaphor. How many separate radio phrases can you find in it? Is this merely clever, or does Joni Mitchell have a point to make about life in the seventies (and the eighties)? What is it?

Listen to Joni perform this song on record. How does her delivery approximate the sound of a radio announcer? What affect does this have on the poem?

"Hope" is the thing with feathers

"Hope" is the thing with feathers—
That perches in the soul—
And sings the tune without the words—
And never stops—at all—

And sweetest—in the Gale—is heard—
And sore must be the storm—
That could abash the little Bird
That kept so many warm—

I've heard it in the chillest land—
And on the strangest Sea—
Yet, never, in Extremity,
It asked a crumb—of Me.

—*Emily Dickinson*

In Dickinson's poem we have extended metaphor approaching symbol. Hope is compared to a bird; or rather, the little bird becomes a symbol for hope, singing as it does in the chillest land and needing no nourishment at all from the poet. What makes this poem more symbolism than metaphor is the feeling of a whole symbolic landscape: the bird, the gale, the land and sea are all symbols for hope on the one hand, adversity on the other. And the crumb, the tiny crumb on which Dickinson ends her poem, may be the most important symbol of all, for it represents that payment which we mortals do *not* have to make for this, the most valuable of gifts.

from Song of Myself

6. A child said What is the grass? fetching it to me with full hands;
How could I answer the child? I do not know what it is any more than he.

I guess it must be the flag of my disposition, out of hopeful green stuff woven.

Or I guess it is the handkerchief of the Lord,
A scented gift and remembrancer designedly dropt,
Bearing the owner's name someway in the corners, that we may see and remark, and say Whose?

Or I guess the grass is itself a child, the produced babe of the vegetation.

Or I guess it is a uniform hieroglyphic,
And it means, Sprouting alike in broad zones and narrow zones,

Growing among black folks as among white,
Kanuck, Tuckahoe, Congressman, Cuff, I give them the same, I receive them the same.

And now it seems to me the beautiful uncut hair of graves.

Tenderly will I use you curling grass,
It may be you transpire from the breasts of young men,
It may be if I had known them I would have loved them,
It may be you are from old people, or from offspring taken soon out of their mothers' laps,
And here you are the mothers' laps.

This grass is very dark to be from the white heads of old mothers,
Darker than the colorless beards of old men,
Dark to come from under the faint red roofs of mouths.
O I perceive after all so many uttering tongues,
And I perceive they do not come from the roofs of mouths for nothing.

I wish I could translate the hints about the dead young men and women,
And the hints about old men and mothers, and the offspring taken soon out of their laps.

What do you think has become of the young and old men?
And what do you think has become of the women and children?

They are alive and well somewhere,
The smallest sprout shows there is really no death,
And if ever there was it led forward life, and does not wait at the end to arrest it,
And ceas'd the moment life appear'd.

All goes onward and outward, nothing collapses,
And to die is different from what any one supposed, and luckier.

—*Walt Whitman*

The poet's own optimism, the Lord's presence, birth and youth, equality, and annihilation of death—the grass here is made to symbolize a multiplicity of things. How many different symbolic meanings for grass do you derive from this segment of the poem? How do you interpret "the handkerchief of the Lord"? "the beautiful uncut hair of graves"? Can these various symbolic significations of grass be subsumed under a single heading? How does Whitman move from the subject grass to the final two lines of this section of his poem?

The Windhover

To Christ Our Lord

I caught this morning morning's minion, king-
  dom of daylight's dauphin, dapple-dawn-drawn Falcon, in
  his riding
  Of the rolling level underneath him steady air, and striding
High there, how he rung upon the rein of a wimpling wing
In his ecstasy! then off, off forth on swing,
  As a skate's heel sweeps smooth on a bow-bend: the hurl and
  gliding
  Rebuffed the big wind. My heart in hiding
Stirred for a bird,—the achieve of, the mastery of the thing!

Brute beauty and valour and act, oh, air, pride, plume, here
  Buckle! AND the fire that breaks from thee then, a billion
Times told lovelier, more dangerous, O my chevalier!

  No wonder of it: sheer plod makes plough down sillion
Shine, and blue-bleak embers, ah my dear,
  Fall, gall themselves, and gash gold-vermilion.

—Gerard Manley Hopkins

The first step in discussing the symbolism of Hopkins's windhover is to straighten out the poem—no simple matter. The first three lines might be roughly paraphrased to read, "This morning I saw the morning's lord, the dauphin of the kingdom of daylight, the falcon who is dappled like the dawn, as he rode the air that was actually windy but seemed steady underneath him." Nothing particularly mysterious here, especially to those who know the windhover, a kind of falcon with an uncanny ability to hover in the air with its head to the wind, then glide quickly in a long arc ("swing / As a skate's heel sweeps smooth on a bow-bend") across the sky. The focus is on the apparent stasis, then the sudden motion, and on the swiftness with which the transition is made. This and other aspects of the bird are contrasted to the poet's own station: the freedom, grace, beauty, and swiftness provide a contrast to the poet's earthbound situation. The word "buckle" in line 10 is a problem: it might mean either "join together" or "collapse" —or both at once. The "thee" of that line is also a problem; does it address the windhover or "my chevalier?" Clearly there is a contrast between the falcon and "my chevalier," just as there is a contrast between the poet and the bird, although the nature of this contrast is different and serves to mitigate the feelings of inferiority the poet felt in the bird's presence. The poet draws on the strength of Christ, presumably his chevalier, who is a billion times lovelier than the windhover. In fact, in Christ even the menial labor of the earth-bound poet becomes beautiful, in much the same way that ashes when they fall break open to reveal a gold-vermillion inside.

The falcon is an old symbol for Christ (to whom the poem is dedicated), a symbol used widely during the Middle Ages with overtones of chivalry and feudalism. Is this traditional meaning the symbolic meaning of the windhover in this poem? How has Hopkins moved beyond traditional significations with his own personal signification? Is it possible for a symbol to function on a literal level as a contrast to the very thing it signifies on the symbolic level, as the windhover seems to in this poem? Is such complexity self-contradictory or enriching?

The Lamb

Little Lamb, who made thee?
Dost thou know who made thee?
Gave thee life, and bid thee feed
By the stream and o'er the mead;
Gave thee clothing of delight,
Softest clothing, wooly, bright;
Gave thee such a tender voice,
Making all the vales rejoice?
Little Lamb, who made thee?
Dost thou know who made thee?

Little Lamb, I'll tell thee,
Little Lamb, I'll tell thee:
He is callèd by thy name,
For he calls himself a Lamb.
He is meek, and he is mild;
He became a little child.
I a child, and thou a lamb,
We are callèd by his name.
Little Lamb, God bless thee!
Little Lamb, God bless thee!

—*William Blake*

1. Make a list of all the possible symbolic significations for "lamb." Which of them are operative in this poem? How can you be sure?

2. Could it be said that the poem tells us more about the speaker than about the animal itself? Do you suppose this is the poet's intention?

3. Do some of the lines, especially "He is meek and he is mild / He became a little child" remind you of a Sunday School hymn (for instance, "Jesus loves me, this I know / For the Bible tells me so")? Is the similarity accidental?

4. Discuss the relationships among the child who speaks the poem, the lamb to whom it is addressed, and God.

The Tyger

Tyger! Tyger! burning bright
In the forests of the night,
What immortal hand or eye
Could frame thy fearful symmetry?

In what distant deeps or skies
Burnt the fire of thine eyes?
On what wings dare he aspire?
What the hand dare seize the fire?

And what shoulder, and what art
Could twist the sinews of thy heart?
And when thy heart began to beat,
What dread hand? and what dread feet?

What the hammer? what the chain?
In what furnace was thy brain?
What the anvil? what dread grasp
Dare its deadly terrors clasp?

When the stars threw down their spears,
And water'd heaven with their tears,
Did he smile his work to see?
Did he who made the Lamb make thee?

Tyger! Tyger! burning bright
In the forests of the night,
What immortal hand or eye,
Dare frame thy fearful symmetry?

—*William Blake*

1. What does the tiger symbolize? Is it a vaguer symbol than the lamb?

2. What is the nature of the relationship between the lamb and the tiger? What questions about the nature of creation do the pair pose?

3. Much of the imagery of the poem suggests a forge, with its fires and anvil and furnace. What makes the forge an appropriate image in this poem?

4. Lines 17–18 may be a reference to the Fall of Adam and Eve, at which time, we have it on the best authority, all creation groaned aloud. Why would such a reference suit the poem's theme and subject?

5. The poem is a series of rhetorical questions, as is the first stanza of "The Lamb." But unlike the questions in that poem, those here are unanswered. There is only a significant shift from "Could frame thy fearful symmetry?" to "Dare frame thy fearful symmetry?" Why?

6. Consider for a moment the implications of "fearful symmetry." To what exactly does the phrase refer? What does it suggest? Is there anything inherently fearful about symmetry, or is it merely the tiger's symmetry that inspires terror?

9. A Thing: Allusion

Writers read. And because they read, travel, look, and think, their minds retain fragments of culture, some of which are bound to end up in their poems. The poet T. S. Eliot, in fact, thought that every poet should be a carrier of culture, and every poem should give evidence of not only the individual poet's talent, but the long literary tradition that lies behind a poem. Many poems of his contain lines borrowed directly or with only minor modifications from other poems.

Other poets do this too, unconsciously sometimes, but often quite deliberately. And often a poet will find reason to make some glancing reference to a person, historical event, or cultural artifact other than the immediate subject of his poem. Such allusions allow him to expand significantly the scope of his immediate subject by implying parallels or contrasts between it and whatever is alluded to. In "I Have Not Lain with Beauty," for example, Lawrence Ferlinghetti quotes, in a poem about poetry, bits of other poems about poetry, which represent the point against which he is arguing. Dylan Thomas sets the place of "Fern Hill," a poem recalling his own childhood and the loss of his own childish naivete, squarely on the farm in Wales where he grew up, but he alludes several times to Adam and Eve and the Garden of Eden, thereby tying his own loss of innocence to theirs, and making the poem as much a commentary on human experience as personal biography.

This kind of cross referencing, if you will, goes on in song as well. See, for example, Elton John's "Goodby Yellow Brick Road," an obvious allusion to *The Wizard of Oz,* Dylan's "Ezra Pound and T. S. Eliot / Fighting in the captain's tower" (in "Desolation Row"), and the Beatles' "Yer Blues," with the line "Just like Dylan's Mr. Jones."

Which raises the main problem of allusion: if the poet's audience does not know *The Wizard of Oz,* the poetry of Ezra Pound and T. S. Eliot, Bob Dylan's song "Ballad of a Thin Man" (in which Mr. Jones makes his appearance), then the nuance of the allusion is lost. In fact, the allusion may be not only lost, but the cause of some confusion. Allusions that require footnotes disrupt a poem more than they help it; and allusions that cannot be explained, even by the experts, suggest a poet who is so personal that he loses his audience. Such a poet is ultimately more bother than he's worth.

The problem of allusion is doubled, of course, when the allusion is so central to the poem that it constitutes an important part of the poem's meaning: miss the allusion, and you miss the poem. Such is the case with Grace and Darby Slick's "White Rabbit," Blake's "Mock On, Mock On, Voltaire, Rousseau," and Jim Haining's "Another." Here the cultural allusion constitutes the very matter of which the poem is built. Someone unfamiliar with Lewis Carroll's *Alice in Wonderland,* the writings of Voltaire and Rousseau, and Emily Dickinson's poem "There Is No Frigate Like a Book" will find those poems virtually meaningless.

What can a poet expect of an audience? What does an audience owe a poet? At one time, and not so very long ago, poets could legitimately expect their readers to come to a poem equipped with a working familiarity of Greek and Latin mythology and literature, the Bible, and the basic outline of Western civilization, which would enable them to recognize allusions to, for example, Mt. Olympus, Chartres cathedral, the Empress Josephine, and the Golden Hind. Today poets might better expect audiences steeped in "Sesame Street," baseball, and popular music, and responsive to Cookie Monster, Hank Aaron, and disco—although people who read *poetry* are perhaps more likely to read Greek tragedies than watch "Sesame Street." Though this assumes that poetry is an elitist art form, which may be an entirely false assumption. Maybe. The point: the contemporary poet has no idea, really, what to expect of his audience. As culture "opens up," poetry also opens up, to draw on movies, television programs, radio, popular music, comic strips, sports—every aspect of culture, high or low. But poets, knowing how this range has broadened, may be reluctant to rely too heavily on allusion in their poetry. There is very little these days of Greek and Roman mythology in poetry (once a poetic staple), and generally speaking there is less allusion than earlier in the twentieth century, especially among poets whose primary aim is to be understood by their audiences. And when they do make use of allusion, it is the kind of reference which will swim right by an unsuspecting reader without even breaking the surface of the water.

White Rabbit

One pill makes you larger
And one pill makes you small.
And the ones that mother gives you
Don't do anything at all.
Go ask Alice
When she's ten feet tall.

And if you go chasing rabbits
And you know you're going to fall,
Tell 'em a hookah smoking caterpillar
Has given you the call.
Call Alice
When she was just small.

When men on the chessboard
Get up and tell you where to go.
And you've just had some kind of mushroom,
And you mind is moving low.
Go ask Alice
I think she'll know.

When logic and proportion
Have fallen sloppy dead,
And the White Knight is talking backwards
And the Red Queen's lost her head.

Remember what the dormouse said:
"Feed your head.
Feed your head.
Feed your head."

—*Grace Slick*

9. *hookah:* a large water pipe.

1. What is the real subject of the song? What sort of pills confront the person to whom it is addressed?

2. How do you explain the wealth of allusion to Lewis Carroll's fiction? To what specific incidents does Slick allude? What about the subject of the song and the nature of the books makes the allusions appropriate?

3. What did the dormouse have to say in *Alice in Wonderland?* Of what relevance is that here? The song builds, somewhat like Ravel's "Bolero," to a spectacular conclusion in which Slick fairly shrieks at us on the record. This performance, coupled with the fact that the advice is repeated three times, places considerable emphasis on this line. Why?

Love Song: I and Thou

Nothing is plumb, level or square:
  the studs are bowed, the joists
are shaky by nature, no piece fits
  any other piece without a gap
or pinch, and bent nails
  dance all over the surfacing
like maggots. By Christ
  I am no carpenter. I built
the roof for myself, the walls
  for myself, the floors
for myself, and got
  hung up in it myself. I
danced with a purple thumb
  at this house-warming, drunk
with my prime whiskey: rage.
  Oh I spat rage's nails
into the frame-up of my work:
  it held. It settled plumb,
level, solid, square and true
  for that great moment. Then
it screamed and went on through,
  skewing as wrong the other way.
God damned it. This is hell,
  but I planed it, I sawed it,
I nailed it, and I
  will live in it until it kills me.
I can nail my left palm
  to the left-hand cross-piece but

I can't do everything myself.
  I need a hand to nail the right,
a help, a love, a you, a wife.

—Alan Dugan

This poem is built on a metaphor: the poet's house is the poet's life. He made it; it's all askew; and he's got only himself to blame, only "a help, a love, a you, a wife" to ask for help. Besides the metaphor, however, Dugan makes a fairly obvious allusion to Christ on the cross: "I can nail my left palm / to the left-hand cross-piece." How do you interpret this comparison of poet to Christ, this invitation to help / love / wife to help nail him up? How serious is the poet about himself, about his predicament?

You, Andrew Marvell

And here face down beneath the sun
And here upon earth's noonward height
To feel the always coming on
The always rising of the night:

To feel creep up the curving east
The earthly chill of dusk and slow
Upon those under lands the vast
And ever-climbing shadow grow

And strange at Ecbatan the trees
Take leaf by leaf the evening strange
The flooding dark about their knees
The mountains over Persia change

And now at Kermanshah the gate
Dark empty and the withered grass
And through the twilight now the late
Few travelers in the westward pass

And Baghdad darken and the bridge
Across the silent river gone
And through Arabia the edge
Of evening widen and steal on

And deepen on Palmyra's street
The wheel rut in the ruined stone
And Lebanon fade out and Crete
High through the clouds and overblown

And over Sicily the air
Still flashing with the landward gulls
And loom and slowly disappear
The sails above the shadowy hulls

And Spain go under and the shore
Of Africa the gilded sand
And evening vanish and no more
The low pale light across that land

Nor now the long light on the sea:
And here face downward in the sun
To feel how swift how secretly
The shadow of the night comes on . . .

—*Archibald MacLeish*

9. *Ecbatan:* once the capital of Media. 13. *Kermanshah:* ancient city in Iran. 21. *Palmyra:* ancient city in Syria.

Reread and digest Andrew Marvell's "To His Coy Mistress" if you do not remember it well. Then read "You, Andrew Marvell" again carefully. Obviously the two poems are not on the same subject: one is a seduction poem, the other has something to do with the decline of civilizations of the past and the probable decline of our own contemporary civilization. But some definite links exist. Both poems are concerned with the process of time and its ravages, and the position of MacLeish as he lies "face down beneath the sun" makes it obvious that it is "at his back" that he hears time's winged chariot hurrying near. The poem may also draw on a book by Oswald Spengler, *The Decline of the West,* in which the author argued that civilization, like the sun, moved from east to west, and that European and even American civilization were doomed to decline in the very near future. Why might MacLeish find it useful to recall Andrew Marvell's poem in his own?

I have not lain with beauty

I have not lain with beauty all my life
telling over to myself
its most rife charms

I have not lain with beauty all my life
and lied with it as well
telling over to myself
how beauty never dies
but lies apart
among the aborigines
of art
and far above the battlefields
of love
It is above all that
oh yes
It sits upon the choicest of
Church seats
up there where art directors meet
to choose the things for immortality
And they have lain with beauty
all their lives
And they have fed on honeydew
and drunk the wines of Paradise
so that they know exactly how
a thing of beauty is a joy
forever and forever
and how it never never
quite can fade
into a money-losing nothingness

Oh no I have not lain
on Beauty Rests like this
afraid to rise at night
for fear that I might somehow miss
some movement beauty might have made

Yet I have slept with beauty
in my own weird way
and I have made a hungry scene or two
with beauty in my bed

and so spilled out another poem or two
    and so spilled out another poem or two
                                        upon the Bosch-like world

—*Lawrence Ferlinghetti*

21. The line echoes "Kubla Khan," line 15. 24. The line echoes the first line of Keats's "Endymion": "A thing of beauty is a joy forever." 30. *Beauty Rest:* brand name of a mattress widely advertised in the late fifties. 40. *Bosch:* Renaissance painter whose landscapes are unusually grotesque and surrealistic.

What notions of art does Ferlinghetti argue against? Who holds them? What is his idea of art? What kind of people agree with him?

Look over the poem: Ferlinghetti covers several areas of culture in forty lines. One, obviously, is Fine Art; another is pop art; another banking and investment. How many others can you find? What is the point of this mix? What is the point of Ferlinghetti's broadly sexual language?

Another

There is no squash like a book.
There is no dress like the table.
There is no jelly for ideals.
There is no monotone like a neighbor.
There is no Emily like her.

—*James Haining*

The Emily of line 5 is poet Emily Dickinson, and Haining's first line is a parody of the first line of one of her poems, "There is no frigate like a book." What is Haining's attitude toward that poem? Toward that view of art? Toward Dickinson? What makes you think so?

Mock On, Mock On, Voltaire, Rousseau

Mock on, mock on, Voltaire, Rousseau:
Mock on, mock on: 'tis all in vain!
You throw the sand against the wind,
And the wind blows it back again.

And every sand becomes a Gem
Reflected in the beams divine;
Blown back they blind the mocking Eye,
But still in Israel's paths they shine.

The Atoms of Democritus
And Newton's Particles of light
Are sands upon the Red Sea shore,
Where Israel's tents do shine so bright.

—*William Blake*

1. *Voltaire:* eighteenth-century French dramatist, poet, essayist, and historian; *Rousseau:* eighteenth-century French educator and philosopher. 9. *Democritus:* Greek philosopher of the fifth century B.C., who first proposed the idea that all matter was made up of tiny particles called atoms. 10. *Newton:* British mathematician, physicist, and philosopher.

Blake covers a good deal of intellectual history in this poem, and modern readers may simply not be familiar with the work of Voltaire, Rousseau, Democritus, and Newton. To what extent does the poem explain its own allusions? Can you discern from Blake's argument against these scientists and philosophers what it is in their work that he objects to? Has this poem lost its audience by depending too much on material outside the poem?

3 A Poem Is a Voice

Only on rare occasions is the thing of a poem passed along to readers as is, in its raw, undigested state. While poets like Eliot and Olson may quote fragments of dialogue, history, or other poems directly in their own work, and while poets like Warren Woessner ("How the West Was Won," Chapter 1, Section 9) may copy down directly a "found poem" discovered in a movie, on television, or on the street corner, most poets impose upon their matter one or more of the three other major qualities of poetry: structure (form), statement (theme), and voice.

Of the three, voice might seem to be least important to the poem as a work of art with claims to significance and permanence, because voice is so "ornamental." Voice is, simply, a poet's own style—what makes a poem of Robert Frost's so unmistakably Frost, a song by the early Beatles so clearly early Beatles. We recognize instantly their choice of words, their rhythms and intonations, the peculiar pattern of their speech . . . their voice. And if the voice is pleasant, attractive, and we enjoy their performance, we come back to hear some more. But surely voice is more ornamentation than anything else.

Well. That is to take the short view of things. First, such elements of voice as tone and diction may constitute an important part of a poem's meaning, and thus be as important to its statement as to its voice. Irony, for example, is a quality of voice, a way of speaking; but it turns a statement inside out and makes a poem mean exactly the opposite of what it says. Such other elements of voice as meter and rhyme can be arranged in patterns that give a poem structure, which can, in turn, sometimes be a significant part of a poem's meaning. Frequently elements of voice—the poet's carefully chosen language, subtle variations of rhythm and tempo—can highlight certain aspects of his subject, coloring our view of the poem's subject and contributing significantly to its statement. William Butler Yeats's "That the Night Come" (Chapter

1, Section 1) provides a good example of rhythm contributing to statement.

Finally, it may be precisely this controlled use of language, and the ornamentation of rhyme and rhythm, alliteration, pitch, and tempo, that constitute the true essence of poetry. Philosophers make statements. Engineers create structures. Historians and photographers record stories, characters, events, and places. But only the poet speaks with a recognizably warm and human voice. It is not, after all, Chaucer's statements that first attract us to the *Canterbury Tales,* but his stories and his characters and the voice of his narrator. What made the Beatles popular in the early sixties was their sound. What makes a reading by Allen Ginsberg or Robert Bly memorable is, as much as anything else, the poet's own voice. Contemporary poets, incidentally, who have become accustomed to speaking as well as publishing their poems, have also become increasingly alert to the possibilities of voice and sensitive to subtleties of rhythm, pitch, tempo, rhyme, and alliteration.

We must be careful in the matter of voice, however, on two points. First, as it is possible for any clever musician to imitate the sound of the early Beatles, it is also easy for any clever poet to imitate the voices of great poets like Frost, Donne, Eliot, Williams, Whitman, Ginsberg, to name only a few of the most popular. And because poets, like musicians, are always learning from each other, they often unconsciously fall under the influence of a poet they particularly admire and may take to writing imitation Frost or imitation Williams. While this may fool some people, discerning audiences resent imitative styles and demand above all else that art be genuine. Nothing is more damning than for a reviewer to compare some new poet to one or two of the older, established poets; and there is no higher compliment than to say of a new poet, "She writes with her own voice." In fact, contemporary poets have sometimes strayed far into the realm of the idiosyncratic in their quest for a unique voice.

The other side of the coin is this curious fact: a good poet can speak in many voices, none of which happens to be the voice of the poet himself. A poet may, like an actor, adopt in a given poem a special role, including a special language and rhythms of speech. This is always the case in dramatic monologues and other "person poems," where the poet pretends to be someone else, but it may also be the case in poems where the "I" of the poem appears to be the poet. "The great act," Robert Lowell called Frost's voice in his poem "Robert Frost." Poets may speak of telling the truth and maintaining integrity, but they don't necessarily mean that what they present in a poem is themselves. The truth of which they speak is a poetic truth: the poem must be honest to itself, not to the poet, who just may, in another poem with another truth, adopt a very different way of looking at things . . . and a very different voice.

The poet's voice, then, is the voice he selects as being truthful in the context of the poem. There is a paradox here, of course: on the one hand we distrust poets (or singers) who manipulate too candidly their voices and styles, who are "mere artificers" in their poems, "mere stylists" in their songs. Yet we respect a multiplicity of truths and a multiplicity of voices, and find a poet (or singer) too simplistic and too narrow if he persists too long in the same voice. What we ought to require of the perfect poem is that the poet's voice in that particular poem, like the poet's structure, be appropriate to the subject and statement.

1. A Voice: Diction

The major determinant of a poet's voice, obviously, is the language he uses, his "diction." Although poets may vary their diction from poem to poem and from one time of their lives to another, most poets with a distinctive voice settle into a vocabulary that makes a listener think, "You know, that just *sounds* like Frost." Or Plath. Or Dylan. Or A. E. Housman.

While a poet's language is his own business, it can be colored by the age and geography in which he lives, and by public attitudes toward what is and what is not appropriate language for poetry. During the Middle Ages, and again during the eighteenth century, proper poetic diction was considered a matter of decorum. Poets used a language appropriate to their subjects: elegant, Latinate, "high" language for important or high subjects; simple, largely Anglo-Saxon, "low" language for common subjects. Poets varied their diction with their subjects. But because poetry was most likely to concern itself with elevated subjects, the high style predominated, and the language of poetry was during those times a pretty lofty language. The English Romantic poets, writing at the beginning of the nineteenth century, thought the language (and subject) of poetry should be "the common man," so they ignored high and low styles and wrote in what they considered the common language (but what sounds today more like a parody of the King James translation of the Bible). Their American counterpart Walt Whitman, following at a pace of several decades, was more successful in finding the language of the common man, and brought his voice (and his structure) more accurately into sympathy with his democratic subject. These reforms, however, were largely lost on both sides of the Atlantic by the end of the nineteenth century, when late Victorian poetic diction became self-consciously genteel, using only words that would not offend the ear of a well-bred lady. Victorian poetry tended in most cases to loftiness as well as to gentility.

Twentieth-century poets, however, have largely rejected as unnatural any constraints on poetic language, because they objected to the artificiality of the poetry produced (a good example of which can be found in Edgar Lee Masters's "Ode to Autumn," following), and because constraints restricted implicitly or explicitly the range of subjects they could write about. Modern poetry stems from Whitman, in subject and in language. Poetry during this century has seen a steady retreat from the notion of a lofty poetic diction. Edgar Lee Masters's collection *Spoon River Anthology,* from which "Aner Clute" comes, was a major step in that retreat, which has continued right down to . . . well, what people of breeding and education would call the language of the gutter. The last forces of "purity" were routed at the end of the 1950s in the now-famous obscenity trial involving Allen Ginsberg's "Howl," in which the poem was found to have redemptive social value. It was therefore not obscene, and therefore—if courts are to pass on such matters—legitimate art. Today we allow poets their choice of subject and language, from any of the four levels of diction: formal, informal, colloquial, and vulgar. And if John Knoepfle wants to write in a poem "birdshit . . . birdshit / dirty pious birdshit," we ask only that this words be appropriate to his purpose, that he be honest in his use of language. No words are proscribed from the poet's vocabulary, then. On the contrary, poets are free to achieve impressive effects by suddenly changing their level of diction or by using diction incongruous to their subject.

Me and Bobby McGee

Busted flat in Baton Rouge, headin' for the trains,
Feelin' nearly faded as my jeans,
Bobby thumbed a diesel down just before it rained:
Took us all the way to New Orleans.
I took my harpoon out of my dirty, red bandanna
And was blowin' sad while Bobby sang the blues
With them windshield wipers slappin' time and Bobby clappin'
  hands
We fin'ly sang up every song that driver knew;

Freedom's just another word for nothin' left to lose,
And nothin' ain't worth nothin', but it's free;

Feelin' good was easy, Lord, when Bobby sang the blues;
And, buddy, that was good enough for me;
Good enough for me and Bobby McGee.

From the coal mines of Kentucky to the California sun
Bobby shared the secrets of my soul;
Standin' right besides me, Lord, through everything I done,
And every night she kept me from the cold.
Then, somewhere near Salinas, Lord, I let her slip away
Lookin' for the home I hope she'll find;
And I'd trade all my tomorrows for a single yesterday;
Holdin' Bobby's body next to mine;

Freedom's just another word for nothin' left to lose,
And nothin' ain't worth nothin', but it's free;
Feeling good was easy, Lord, when Bobby sang the blues;
And, buddy, that was good enough for me;
Good enough for me and Bobby McGee.

—*Kris Kristofferson–Fred Foster*

How would you characterize the singer in this song? What kind of a person is he (or she—Janis Joplin made this song famous)? What kind of a life does he/she live? What became of Bobby McGee? What words do you find particularly memorable (one is definitely the first, "busted")? From what level of language do they come? What about the grammar of this song? How is this language appropriate to the character you imagine singing it? Compare Kristofferson's recording with Joplin's. Which do you find truer to the song?

Sometime during eternity

Sometime during eternity
some guys show up
and one of them
who shows up real late
is a kind of carpenter
from some square-type place
like Galilee
and he starts wailing
and claiming he is hip
to who made heaven
and earth
and that the cat

who really laid it on us
is his Dad

And moreover
he adds
It's all writ down
on some scroll-type parchments
which some henchmen
leave lying around the Dead Sea somewheres
a long time ago
and which you won't even find
for a coupla thousand years ago or so
or at least for
nineteen hundred and fortyseven
of them
to be exact
and even then
nobody really believes them
or me
for that matter

You're hot
they tell him

And they cool him

They stretch him on the Tree to cool

And everybody after that
is always making models
of this Tree
with Him hung up
and always crooning His name
and calling Him to come down
and sit in
on their combo
as if he is *the* king cat
who's got to blow
or they can't quite make it

Only he don't come down
from His Tree

Him just hang there
on His Tree
looking real Petered out
and real cool
and also
according to a roundup
of late world news
from the usual unreliable sources
real dead

—*Lawrence Ferlinghetti*

18. *scroll-type parchments:* the Dead Sea scrolls.

Much of the effect of this poem stems from its diction, from the great disparity between what most people would consider an appropriate kind of diction for a religious poem and the language Ferlinghetti uses. We are simply not used to hearing Christ referred to as "*the* king cat." Some readers find this language offensive, but Ferlinghetti has a point to make, which he suggests in his closing lines. If the sources are unreliable, then Christ is not dead. But in some circles he's gone for sure, the poet implies: exactly those circles that have codified religion into some "scroll-type parchments," have refined Christ to the safety of sterility (as singer Phil Ochs put it in his song "Crucifixion"). These are, ironically, the people most likely to be offended at hearing Christ talked about in the lively, contemporary language the poet uses. As Ferlinghetti shows, some people's attitude toward religious language is at times directly and inversely proportional to the depth of their religious conviction.

Ode to Autumn

Season of gusty days and cloudy nights,
The wind which showers wine apples to the ground
Blows at midday the long, pale, lunar lights
O'er weedy fields with melancholy sound.
Summer has gone, but she has left a show
Of downy clouds against the autumn sky,
Which the chill breezes chafe until they glow—
Ghosts of that luxury
Which now is by.

The golden trees against a sky of June
Seem like a life that is too soon grown gray;

Through smothering clouds the large autumnal moon
  Rolls argently her undiminished way.
The wonder of night's bright processional
  Abates not with the fading of the flowers,
Still glorious on all the earth doth fall—
  But for those withered bowers
  The pain is ours.

Here in my garden all the rich repose,
  The silence and the trance of summer eves
Has passed into a death presaging doze;
  The air is twinkling with the falling leaves
And sad elf-sighs do fill each little dell.
  Yet when the wind booms from the vale below
The moon is shaken like a cockleshell,
  Through the long, ragged bough
  That moans its woe.

If spring and summer by thy mask, O year,
  Which falls in autumn, leaving hideous
The thing we deemed was to our being dear,
  Then life may not be that it seems to us
In youth—but sometime may reveal—
  When the worn heart the shock can scarcely bear
A countenance to make the spirit reel,
  On reefs of keen despair,
  To perish there.

Ah, many a time and oft on nights like this
  The whip-poor-will has sent abroad her song
From depths of anguish and from heights of bliss.
  Now is it fancy? But methought along
The withered fringes of the tangled grass
  A few belated crickets sent a shrill
Of hesitating song—this, too, must pass;
  Their little voices still
  On mead and hill.

The night wind rises and the clouds which spume
  Dark from the faint and starry-lighted west
Are edged with fire against their heavy gloom.
  'Tis time that I should seek the thoughtless rest
Which day denies—much that we deeply prize
  Doth stir the mind's reflections and awake

The pains which else had slumbered—in such wise
  Rich, fruitful autumn, dear, for thine own sake
Through thy most fair disguise
We see Death's eyes.

—*Edgar Lee Masters (1898)*

Aner Clute

Over and over they used to ask me,
While buying the wine or the beer,
In Peoria first, and later in Chicago,
Denver, Frisco, New York, wherever I lived,
How I happened to lead the life,
And what was the start of it.
Well, I told them a silk dress,
And a promise of marriage from a rich man—
(It was Lucius Atherton).
But that was not really it at all.
Suppose a boy steals an apple
From the tray at the grocery store,
And they all begin to call him a thief,
The editor, minister, judge, and all the people—
"A thief," "a thief," "a thief," wherever he goes.
And he can't get work, and he can't get bread
Without stealing it, why the boy will steal.
It's the way the people regard the theft of the apple
That makes the boy what he is.

—*Edgar Lee Masters (1915)*

What an enormous difference between these two poems! One labors under the supposition that poetry has to be beautiful thoughts in beautiful language; the other sparkles with the candor of language—and thought—freed from formality. The adventure was, in 1915, a radical departure from poetic norms, and Masters first published the poems of *Spoon River Anthology* under a pseudonym, lest things like "Aner Clute" hurt his reputation as a poet and a lawyer. Point out characteristic diction in each poem, and then compare the old to the new. How has Masters's subject, as well as his language changed? Read some poems by Allen Ginsberg, William Carlos Williams, and some contemporary American poets in this book and decide for yourself what kind of revolution in poetic diction "Aner Clute" was a part of.

Farmer and the Owl

farmer said to this owl he caught
okay you skinny prophet
lets see how you light up the dark
theres your tailfeathers
diddled in kerosene
and struck to hells fire with my match
owl fussed and flared in the yard
screeched hoo hoo   hoo hoo hoo
o god of all owls
stiffen my bones with manganese
and you you son of a kansas fathead
bawl out loud when you see my revelations
here I go and haylofts to the last of me
o my virginal owlsoul
may you rise with a pure blue flame
from the ashes of this barn tonight
farmer watched his barn burn down
birdshit   he said birdshit
dirty pious birdshit   birdshit

—*John Knoepfle*

2. *prophet:* popular superstition has the owl a prophet of bad luck; it is for that reason still hunted and killed. 9–16. The owl's invocation recalls Matthew Arnold's poem "Empedocles on Etna."

The story of this poem is magnificent enough, but it is Knoepfle's remarkable diction that makes it truly great: the owl with his "you, you son of a kansas fathead" and then his invocation to his "god of all owls," the farmer with his "skinny prophet," the tail feathers "diddled" in kerosene, and finally his impotent mutterings of "birdshit . . . birdshit." Underneath all the story and the language, however, lies a weighty matter: the bird is obviously a Christ symbol (well, at least a prophet-martyr symbol), and the torching of bird and barn a kind of ritual sacrifice. What statement is the poet making, in his story and in his diction, about the myth of the martyr-prophet? What makes you think so?

They Flee from Me

They flee from me that sometime did me seek,
   With naked foot stalking in my chamber.

I have seen them gentle, tame, and meek,
That now are wild, and do not remember
That sometime they put themself in danger
To take bread at my hand; and now they range
Busily seeking with a continual change.

Thanked be Fortune, it hath been otherwise
Twenty times better; but once, in special,
In thin array, after a pleasant guise,
When her loose gown from her shoulders did fall,
And she me caught in her arms long and small,
Therewith all sweetly did me kiss,
And softly said, "Dear heart, how like you this?"

It was no dream; I lay broad waking.
But all is turned thorough my gentleness,
Into a strange fashion of forsaking;
And I have leave to go of her goodness,
And she also to use newfangleness.
But since that I so kindely am served,
I would fain know what she hath deserved.

—Sir Thomas Wyatt

8. *Fortune:* a semideific personification, popular in the Middle Ages and Renaissance, always associated with change and instability. 19. *kindely:* naturally. 21. *fain:* gladly, with pleasure.

In this poem Wyatt laments being forsaken by his women, one in particular, who have cleared out, bored with his "gentleness," to search for novelty and excitement elsewhere. He compares them with deer, formerly tame, now wild, who used to eat from his hand but now "range / Busily seeking with a continual change." Look at the language of the poem: how does it help to characterize the poet as someone gentle, for whom love is no game or "newfangleness," but an honest, sincere relationship?

Dream Song #1

Huffy Henry hid the day
unappeasable Henry sulked.
I see his point,—a trying to put things over.
It was the thought that they thought
they could *do* it made Henry wicked & away.
But he should have come out and talked.

All the world like a woolen lover
once did seem on Henry's side.
Then came a departure.
Thereafter nothing fell out as it might or ought.
I don't see how Henry, pried
open for all the world to see, survived.

What he has now to say is a long
wonder the world can bear & be.
Once in a sycamore I was glad
all at the top, and I sang.
Hard on the land wears the strong sea
and empty grows every bed.

—*John Berryman*

This is the first of a long sequence of *Dream Songs,* in which John Berryman—alias Henry—analyzes himself and, by implication and indirection, the world around him. The poems are complex mixtures of the poet, his persona, a black alter-ego named Mr. Bones, and the world. A variety of voices resounds through the collection, and through individual poems in the collection. In this poem, for example, "I see his point" sounds very simply, unartistically colloquial, while "made Henry wicked & away" has something of the obliqueness, the artistic spin of the poet. How many voices do you hear in this poem? Which lines would you assign to which voice?

The poem contains several metaphors: "like a woolen lover," "pried/ open for all the world to see." How do you interpret these? What about the strong sea, wearing against the land? The empty bed?

What is the effect in the final two lines of inverting the natural word order, so that instead of subject-verb-complement we get complement-verb-subject?

Look ahead to the discussion of assonance and alliteration in Chapter 3, Section 3. What examples of each can you find there?

2. A Voice: Tone

One important function of a poet's diction is to create a mood in a poem, a tone. Sometimes individual words provide a key to the poem's tone, like "plastic" in the Doors' "Twentieth Century Fox" (Chapter 1, Section 1). In other poems metaphors are important, as in Paul Simon's "I Am a Rock." Careful poets can use even the rhythm of a poem to create tone, or rhyme. Usually, however, tone emerges from diction and—when the poem is heard instead of read—from the poet's delivery.

Tone represents a poet's attitude toward his subject as it determines his diction and his intonation, and because the vocabulary and the sound of a poet's voice influence the audience's reaction, tone may also be said to be our own attitude toward the subject of the poem. Poems can be lightly or bombastically funny. They can be somber, sarcastic, bitter, angry, reflective, sentimental, ironic, solemn, or—as in Hardy's "Neutral Tones"—simply neutral.

Sometimes, of course, the tone intended by the poet is not what the audience heard. Such confusions usually arise when (a) the poet is too subtle or too ambivalent, or (b) the audience and the poet come from too-different cultures. *Rolling Stone* reviewer Jon Landau bombed Paul Simon's first solo album in an article titled "Everything Put Together Falls Apart," but Simon claimed that Landau didn't understand the songs: "A lot of the lyrics they thought depressed and pessimistic are really ironic and funny." And vice versa. "Mother and Child Reunion," for example, which you might have thought was a witty throw-away, is actually a song about death! One admirer of British poet A. E. Housman once told him he thought "1887," his poem commemorating the fiftieth anniversary of Queen Victoria's reign, was brilliant parody of the old British stiff-upper-lip thing: "Get you the sons your fathers got / And God will save the Queen." It turned out Housman was dead serious (and his admirer very much embarrassed). Randy Newman's song "Short People" created a sensation not too many years ago because it was not understood as parody (is it?); and the Rolling Stones had trouble with "Brown Sugar" and "Some Girls" for the same reason. The changing meaning of "gay" gives T. S. Eliot's line "Old Tom, gay Tom, Becket of London" a meaning—and a tone—entirely different from what he intended.

What you have in each case is a failure of tone. In some cases the fault may lie with the audience, in others with the poet, but in every case confusion is created. As long as people continue to live isolated, individual existences, as long as I am I and you are you, as long as pluralism survives in our culture (and pluralism *is* preferable to uniformity and conformity), then confusions of tone are going to happen. What is important in dealing with tone is that the audience try, for the sake of the poem, to put itself in the poet's position, and that the poet choose his diction carefully enough that he is in control of his language and his subject.

Honky Tonk Women

I met a gin-soaked, barroom queen in Memphis,
She tried to take me upstairs for a ride.
She had to heave me right across her shoulder
'Cause I just can't seem to drink you off my mind.
It's the Honky Tonk Women
Gimme the honky tonk blues.

I played a divorcee in New York City,
I had to put up some kind of a fight.
The lady then she covered me with roses,
She blew my nose and then she blew my mind.
It's the Honky Tonk Women
Gimme the honky tonk blues.

—Mick Jagger–Keith Richards

The singer in this song has lost his love and is trying to drink himself into oblivion to numb the pain. How many country and western songs are built around the same situation? And how weepy are they? But the Stones' song is not sentimental at all. In fact, the song is full of life—seedy life to be sure (the gin-soaked barroom queen, the honkey-tonk women)—but enormous activity and vitality. In fact, the song is nearly a parody of all those sentimental "lost my lady" laments you hear so often, because what this singer is doing, really, is not crying in his beer but reeling from one woman to another. The reaction of the speaker, like the tone of the song, is a refreshing change from the gush we'd expect to get in this situation.

Neutral Tones

We stood by a pond that winter day,
And the sun was white, as though chidden of God
And a few leaves lay on the starving sod;
  —They had fallen from an ash, and were gray.

Your eyes on me were as eyes that rove
Over tedious riddles of years ago;
And some words played between us to and fro
  On which lost the more by our love.

The smile on your mouth was the deadest thing
Alive enough to have strength to die;
And a grin of bitterness swept thereby
  Like an ominous bird a-wing. . . .

Since then, keen lessons that love deceives,
And wrings with wrong, have shaped to me
Your face, and the God-curst sun, and a tree,
  And a pond edged with grayish leaves.

—*Thomas Hardy*

2. *chidden:* scolded, faulted. 12. *ominous bird a-wing:* the Greeks and Romans believed that certain birds seen in certain positions indicated impending good fortune or disaster.

1. Read the poem carefully and describe the situation in which it is written. What people are involved? What is happening as the speaker says the poem? What has happened in the past to which he refers? How many different points in time does the poem involve?

2. Examine carefully the similes and metaphors: "white, as though chidden of God," "as eyes that rove / Over tedious riddles of years ago," "the deadest thing / Alive enough to have strength to die," "Like an ominous bird a-wing." How do they reflect back on the speaker or his former love, and to what times in their relationship do these similes and metaphors refer?

3. The title itself identifies the tone of this poem; why should it be "neutral"? What imagery contributes to this tone?

4. Does your own experience allow you to identify with this poem? Do you think love affairs of any consequence ever really burn out so entirely that there remains neither love nor hate, only nothing?

Provide, Provide

The witch that came (the withered hag)
To wash the steps with pail and rag,
Was once the beauty Abishag,

The picture pride of Hollywood.
Too many fall from great and good
For you to doubt the likelihood.

Die early and avoid the fate.
Or if predestined to die late,
Make up your mind to die in state.

Make the whole stock exchange your own!
If need be occupy a throne,
Where nobody can call *you* crone.

Some have relied on what they knew;
Others on being simply true.
What worked for them might work for you.

No memory of having starred
Atones for later disregard,
Or keeps the end from being hard.

Better to go down dignified
With boughten friendship at your side
Than none at all. Provide, provide!

—*Robert Frost*

Robert Frost is a master of tone, although he can be deceitfully ambiguous in all aspects of his art. On its surface, this poem is a cynical admonition to store up for ourselves treasures on earth, so that when things turn sour, we can take care of ourselves. Hollywood's beauties, grown old, find themselves scrubbing floors if they're not careful. Nor can lost beauty or the memory of having been great provide comfort in old age. Better die early, Frost suggests, or else sock plenty of money away against old age. Provide, provide. Better friends who love you for your bucks than no friends at all.

Underneath this cynical exterior, however, lurks a lightness of tone that undercuts the speaker's cynicism. Rhyme is very prominent in this poem, and the steady rhyme of "Hollywood," "good," and "likelihood," or "starred," "disregard," and "hard" make us think that Frost just might be putting us on. But then again, he might not: those final words "Provide, provide!" hang like a genial warning in the air after the rest of the poem disintegrates in smoke. Perhaps what amuses Frost is our surprise at this cynicism from such a comfortable, warm poet. Besides, as Chaucer told us, often many a serious thing is said in jest.

So we never really know about this poem; we're uncertain just where in this ambiguity of tones Frost stands. Which is probably precisely what the poet wanted.

To the Virgins, to Make Much of Time

Gather ye rosebuds while ye may,
  Old time is still a-flying;
And this same flower that smiles today,
  Tomorrow will be dying.

The glorious lamp of heaven, the sun,
  The higher he's a-getting,
The sooner will his race be run,
  And nearer he's to setting.

That age is best which is the first,
  When youth and blood are warmer,
But being spent, the worse, and worst
  Times still succeed the former.

Then be not coy, but use your time,
  And while ye may, go marry;
For having lost but once your prime,
  You may for ever tarry.

—*Robert Herrick*

What similarities of content and tone can you find between this poem and Frost's "Provide, Provide"? What differences? What argument is Herrick making here? How persuasive is he? How serious?

The Applicant

First, are you our sort of a person?
Do you wear
A glass eye, false teeth or a crutch,
A brace or a hook,
Rubber breasts or a rubber crotch,

Stitches to show something's missing? No, no? Then
How can we give you a thing?
Stop crying.
Open your hand.
Empty? Empty. Here is a hand

To fill it and willing
To bring teacups and roll away headaches
And do whatever you tell it.
Will you marry it?
It is guaranteed

To thumb shut your eyes at the end
And dissolve of sorrow.
We make new stock from the salt.
I notice you are stark naked.
How about this suit—

Black and stiff, but not a bad fit.
Will you marry it?
It is waterproof, shatterproof, proof
Against fire and bombs through the roof.
Believe me, they'll bury you in it.

Now your head, excuse me, is empty.
I have the ticket for that.
Come here, sweetie, out of the closet.
Well, what do you think of *that?*
Naked as paper to start

But in twenty-five years she'll be silver,
In fifty, gold.
A living doll, everywhere you look.
It can sew, it can cook,
It can talk, talk, talk.

It works, there is nothing wrong with it.
You have a hole, its a poultice.
You have an eye, it's an image.
My boy, it's your last resort.
Will you marry it, marry it, marry it.

—*Sylvia Plath*

What is Plath's applicant applying for? How does the poet view this sacred institution? What does marriage do to men and women? What is the reason for "it" in lines 14 and 15, 34–40? What is the tone of this poem? What words contribute to that tone? Listen to Plath read this poem and then ask yourself again about its tone and which words are most important.

The Old Man's Comforts

And How He Gained Them

''You are old, Father William,'' the young man cried,
''The few locks which are left you are gray;
You are hale, Father William, a hearty old man,
Now tell me the reason, I pray.''

''In the days of my youth,'' Father William replied,
''I remembered that youth would fly fast,
And abused not my health, and my vigor at first,
That I never might need them at last.''

''You are old, Father William,'' the young man cried,
''And pleasures with youth pass away;
And yet you lament not the days that are gone,
Now tell me the reason, I pray.''

''In the days of my youth,'' Father William replied,
''I remembered that youth could not last;
I thought of the future, whatever I did,
That I never might grieve for the past.''

''You are old, Father William,'' the young man cried,
''And life must be hastening away;
You are cheerful, and love to converse upon death,
Now tell me the reason, I pray.''

''I am cheerful, young man,'' Father William replied,
''Let the cause thy attention engage;
In the days of my youth I remember'd my God!
And He hath not forgotten my age.''

—*Robert Southey*

1. What kind of man is Father William? What do you think is Robert Southey's attitude toward him? How can you tell?

2. Read the poem aloud, noting the rhythm of the lines and the pattern of rhymes. Is there anything about this rhythm that undercuts the tone you thought Southey was trying to establish? Do you think this undercutting is intentional?

You Are Old, Father William

"You are old, Father William," the young man said
  "And your hair has become very white;
And yet you incessantly stand on your head—
  Do you think, at your age, it is right?"

"In my youth," Father William replied to his son,
  "I feared it might injure the brain;
But, now that I'm perfectly sure I have none,
  Why, I do it again and again."

"You are old," said the youth, "as I mentioned before.
  And have grown most uncommonly fat;
Yet you turned a back-somersault in at the door—
  Pray, what is the reason of that?"

"In my youth," said the sage, as he shook his grey locks,
  "I kept all my limbs very supple
By the use of this ointment—one shilling the box—
  Allow me to sell you a couple?"

"You are old," said the youth, "and your jaws are too weak
  For anything tougher than suet;
Yet you finished the goose, with the bones and the beak—
  Pray, how did you manage to do it?"

"In my youth," said his father, "I took to the law,
  And argued each case with my wife;
And the muscular strength, which it gave to my jaw
  Has lasted the rest of my life."

"You are old," said the youth, "one would hardly suppose
  That your eye was as steady as ever;
Yet you balanced an eel on the end of your nose—
  What made you so awfully clever?"

"I have answered three questions, and that is enough,"
  Said his father. "Don't give yourself airs!
Do you think I can listen all day to such stuff?
  Be off, or I'll kick you down-stairs!"

—*Lewis Carroll*

Here is a parody of Southey's poem written by Lewis Carroll. Note that its tone is light, and that it borrows phrases and entire lines from the original. How does Carroll create his humor? What is *his* attitude toward Southey's Father William? In what ways does Carroll's parody offer a comment on art and poetry?

3. A Voice: Assonance and Alliteration

A poet's voice depends a great deal on the sound of his poetry: not merely diction and pronunciation, but how often and what kind of rhyme is used, his rhythm and tempo, the pitch of his voice as he reads, the general patterns of sound in a line of poetry. Patterns of repeated sounds within lines of poetry are particularly effective in creating a memorable voice, because vowels and consonants used in sound patterns may be consciously or unconsciously chosen to create a desired tone. The triple "p" of the final line of Ramson's poem "Bells for John Whiteside's Daughter" (Chapter 5, Section 4), for example, brings that poem to an abrupt and perplexing conclusion: "we are vexed at her brown study, / Lying so primly propped." In other poems the sound of an "l" or an "m" or "n" might be used to create a smooth, pleasant, mellifluous tone, or the sounds of "k" and "f" to create a jarring, unpleasant tone. The long "o" moans; the nasal "a" whines; the short "i" spits. Of course words can be made up especially to imitate the sound they identify, such as *hoot, moo, heehaw,* or *choochoo;* and other words in common usage (like *babble, moan,* or *thud*) have such an onomatopoetic quality to them. But poets usually work with more ordinary nouns, adjectives, adverbs and verbs, working into their poetry patterns of repeated consonant sounds (alliteration) or vowel sounds (assonance) that will help them control tone.

Assonance and alliteration surround us. Madison Avenue advertisers and politicians know that alliterative phrases are both epigrammatic and catchy: "*P*e*p*si *p*ours it on," "*k*ooks and *c*ommies," "*p*eace, *p*rogress and *p*ros*p*erity." These make nice slogans. In poetry, assonance and alliteration can serve several functions. They can exist merely to attract a reader's attention. They can act as a unifying element, especially when spread across several lines, to knit areas together. They can contribute significantly to a poem's meaning by creating a mood appropriate to the poem's sense, or by accenting certain important words and phrases. Edgar Allan Poe, despite his monotonous rhythms and other weaknesses, had a real genius for *sound,* and both "The Raven" and "Bells," poems known to every high school student, allow him to show off his facility. In that famous line "the silken, sad, uncertain rustling," Poe's words actually rustle.

As poetic devices, assonance and alliteration go back a long way in English poetry. In fact, they antedate rhythm and rhyme: Old English poets counted four accents or beats to the line, and tried their best to make three and sometimes all four of those beats alliterate. Their poetry was extremely musical, even if they did have to strain the sense of their words sometimes to manage those alliterations. While few poets rely so heavily on alliteration today, some sense of the Old English music can be had by listening to the Gaelic poetry of Scotland and Ireland, or the great bardic poetry of Wales. Modern poets are content usually with a little assonance or alliteration, which has a little music and, in the words of William Stafford, "an effect" on their poetry.

Sad-Eyed Lady of the Lowlands

With your merc'ry mouth in the missionary times,
And your eyes like smoke and your prayers like rhymes,
And your silver cross, and your voice like chimes,
Oh, who do they think could bury you?
With your pockets well-protected at last,
And your streetcar visions which you place on the grass
And your flesh like silk, and your face like glass,
Who among them do they think could carry you?

Sad-eyed lady of the lowlands,
Where the sad-eyed prophet says that no man comes,
My warehouse eyes my Arabian drums
Should I put them by your gate,
Or sad-eyed lady, should I wait?

With your sheets like metal and your belt like lace
And your deck of cards missing the jack and the ace
And your basement clothes and your hollow face
Who among them can think he could outguess you?
With your silhouette when the sunlight dims
Into your eyes where the moonlight swims
And your matchbook songs and your gypsy hymns
Who among them could try to impress you?

The kings of Tyrus with their convict list
Are waiting in line for the geranium kiss

And you wouldn't know it would happen like this,
But who among them really wants just to kiss you?
With your childhood flames on your midnight rug.
With your Spanish manners and your mother's drugs
And your cowboy mouth and your curfew plugs,
Who among them do you think could resist you?

Oh, the farmers and the businessmen, they all did decide
To show you the dead angels that they used to hide,
But why did they pick you to sympathize with their side
Oh how could they ever stake you?
They wish you'd accepted the blame for the farm
But with the sea at your feet and the phony false alarm
And the child of the hoodlum wrapped up in your arms
How could they ever have persuaded you?

With your sheet metal memory of cannery row
And your magazine husband who one day just had to go
And your gentleness now which you just can't help but show
Who among them do you think would employ you?
Now you stand with your thief, you're on his parole
With your holy medallion which fingertips fold
And your saint-like face and your ghost-like soul
Oh who among them do you think could destroy you?

Sad-eyed lady of the lowlands,
Where the sad-eyed prophet said that no man comes,
My warehouse eyes my Arabian drums
Should I put them by your gate,
Or sad-eyed lady, should I wait?

—*Bob Dylan*

"Sad-Eyed Lady" is one of Dylan's most admired songs, although all attempts to explain the nature of its attraction have proven embarrassingly inadequate. Perhaps, as everyone assumes, the key to the poem is the profusion of images, similes, and metaphors (at times paradoxical and self-contradictory in their connotations) that fill the song almost, but not quite, to excess. But these images are a very mixed bag, sometimes banal ("With your silhouette when the sunlight dims"), sometimes startling in their freshness and insight ("mercury mouth," "magazine husband"), sometimes totally enigmatic ("missionary times," "matchbook songs"). Although they convey a generally smooth, saintly impression of the lady, they will not take us very far for all their wealth of connotative information. Perhaps the song is incapable of being grasped between the thumb and forefinger of rational, purely denotative discourse; perhaps it can only be "experienced," never explained. Or perhaps the right place to begin is not with the imagery but with the sound values of the words.

There is much alliteration in the song, mostly of the liquid "l" and the nasal "m" and "n" consonants. And there is much assonance: the long "a" in "Arabian," "Lady," and "gate" in the refrain; the long "i" of lines 22, 23, 24; the long "e" of line 35. But even vowel qualities that are not identical (those of the phrase "sad-eyed lady," for example) have an assonant effect because of the proximity of the sound and of the "a" of "sad" to that of the "a" of "lady." Both are liquid, soft and smooth. They are not sharp and do not hurt like the short "i" of "wit" or "sit." They do not whine like the "a" of "asp." The poem is filled with long, languid vowel sounds that reproduce in the ear the effect that images like silk and glass and sheet metal produce in the mind; to this extent sound follows sense. But it may well be that in this song sound precedes sense; that the most important aspect of "Sad-Eyed Lady of the Lowlands" is not the imagery but the sound; that the soft rich music of the words tells us more about Dylan's lady than all the images combined.

Listen carefully to the poet's own performance of the song, trying to determine exactly the poem's effect on a listener, and from what elements of the lyrics the effect derives. The song has also been recorded by Dylan's friend Joan Baez, whose voice is, according to many critics, tonally richer and "better" than Dylan's. Whose recording better captures the spirit of the poem?

The Lotos-Eaters

"Courage!" he said, and pointed toward the land,
"This mounting wave will roll us shoreward soon."
In the afternoon they came unto a land
In which it seemèd always afternoon.
All round the coast the languid air did swoon,
Breathing like one that hath a weary dream.
Full-faced above the valley stood the moon;
And like a downward smoke, the slender stream
Along the cliff to fall and pause and fall did seem.

A land of streams! some, like a downward smoke,
Slow-dropping veils of thinnest lawn, did go;
And some through wavering lights and shadows broke,
Rolling a slumbrous sheet of foam below.

They saw the gleaming river seaward flow
From the inner land; far off, three mountain-tops,
Three silent pinnacles of aged snow,
Stood sunset-flushed; and, dewed with showery drops,
Up-clomb the shadowy pine above the woven copse.

The charmèd sunset lingered low adown
In the red West; through mountain clefts the dale
Was seen far inland, and the yellow down
Bordered with palm, and many a winding vale
And meadow, set with slender galingale;
A land where all things always seemed the same!
And round about the keel with faces pale,
Dark faces pale against that rosy flame,
The mild-eyed melancholy Lotos-eaters came.

Branches they bore of that enchanted stem,
Laden with flower and fruit, whereof they gave
To each, but whoso did receive of them,
And taste, to him the gushing of the wave
Far far away did seem to mourn and rave
On alien shores; and if his fellow spake,
His voice was thin, as voices from the grave;
And deep-asleep he seemed, yet all awake,
And music in his ears his beating heart did make.

They sat them down upon the yellow sand
Between the sun and moon upon the shore;
And sweet it was to dream of Fatherland,
Of child, and wife, and slave; but evermore
Most weary seemed the sea, weary the oar,
Weary the wandering fields of barren foam.
Then someone said, "We shall return no more";
And all at once they sang, "Our island home
Is far beyond the wave; we will no longer roam."

—Alfred, Lord Tennyson

27. *Lotos-eaters:* The lotos-berry is about the size of an olive and tastes like a fig or date, Herodotus tells us. Tennyson's lotos (and Homer's) may well be the Arabic Sidr, used in the preparation of a rich amber liquor drunk today on the island of Djerba. Cf. Louis Golding. *Goodbye to Ithaca* (London, 1955) pp. 89–93.

The story recounted by Tennyson in his poem comes from book 10 of *The Odyssey,* in which Ulysses and his men, plagued by a nine-day storm and driven far off their course, arrive at the island of the lotos-eaters, a spaced-out people who fed on the fruit of forgetfulness that produces in them an enervation, lethargy, and euphoria similar to a marijuana high. These folk innocently give some of the fruit to a few of Ulysses's men, and only with great difficulty can he drag them back to his ship and embark for what proved to be the island of the Cyclops. What images does Tennyson use to convey the dreamlike effect of the lotos fruit? What sounds does Tennyson use to develop the dreamlike quality of the world seen through the eyes of a lotos-eater, and the slow pace of their lives? Analyze lines 27 and 45 closely; what patterns of assonance and alliteration do you find? How are the sounds used by Tennyson especially appropriate to the lines' meanings?

Nomad Exquisite

As the immense dew of Florida
Brings forth
The big-finned palm
And green vine angering for life,

As the immense dew of Florida
Brings forth hymn and hymn
From the beholder,
Beholding all these green sides
And gold sides of green sides,

And blessed mornings,
Meet for the eye of the young alligator,
And lightning colors
So, in me, come flinging
Forms, flames, and the flakes of flames.

—*Wallace Stevens*

Circle all alliterated consonants and all assonated vowels, and draw lines connecting all similar sounds. What function do you think this web of alliteration and assonance performs in this poem?

Listen to Stevens read this poem on record. What sound patterns did you catch in listening that you had missed in reading the poem to yourself? Have you changed your mind at all about the purpose of the alliteration?

Pied Beauty

Glory be to God for dappled things—
For skies of couple-colour as a brinded cow;
For rose-moles all in stipple upon trout that swim;
Fresh-firecoal chestnut-falls; finches' wings;
Landscape plotted and pieced—fold, fallow, and plough;
And áll trádes, their gear and tackle and trim.

All things counter, original, spare, strange;
Whatever is fickle, freckled (who knows how?)
With swift, slow; sweet, sour; adazzle, dim;
He fathers-forth whose beauty is past change:
Praise him.

—*Gerard Manley Hopkins*

"Pied Beauty" is another poem constructed on paradoxes: all things changing and various are the creations of a God who himself never changes, for which reason the poet bids us praise him. The command to praise is given twice; the majority of the poem is taken up with lists of the various dappled things created by God, a list that upon close examination appears much less varied than first impression makes it seem. The skies of line 2, the stream in which the trout of line 3 presumably swim, and the landscape of line 5 cover the three realms of life: air, sea, and land. The cow, the trout, and the finch survey the inhabitants of these realms. The plotted and pieced land suggests farming, and "all trades" suggests commerce; the two categories include most of the occupations known to man. Lines 7–9 enumerate several opposites, some obvious (swift and slow, sweet and sour), others more oblique (counter and original). And after this catalogue of all the variety of God's creation comes an affirmation of its togetherness and the sameness of the Creator. The paradox is startling here, especially in what it implies about apparently fickle and freckled human experience.

Hopkins is a very musical poet, and it is not surprising to find a considerable amount of alliteration in one of his poems. But could it be argued that in this poem the alliteration has a special function? The subject of the poem is the sameness in opposites, similarities in things that are dissimilar. Does the sameness of the sounds "a*d*azzle, *d*im" reflect similarity in dissimilar words? Might the insistence of the "f" sound throughout the whole poem be a verbal insistence on unity among a list of disparate elements? Reexamine carefully all the patterns of consonants in the poem, note how pervasive the alliteration is, and evaluate the sophistication of Hopkins's use of sound.

Now

Where we live, the teakettle whistles out
its heart. Fern arrives to
batter the window. Every day gets lost
in a stray sunset and little touches of air.
Someone opens a door. It is this year.

We hear crickets compute their brittle
almanac. A friend or a stranger
comes to the door; it is always "Hello" again,
but just a friend or a stranger.
We get up and look out: a good year?

God knows. People we meet look older.
They ask how we are. It is this year.

—*William Stafford*

Here is a little New Year's poem from William Stafford, a poem that emphasizes the way time and the passage of time have a habit of slipping between the cracks of day-to-day living: the teakettle, the fernlike patterns of ice condensing on a cold window, the sound of the crickets, the visits of friends. Always it is just "now," and we never really know what comes ahead (or, for that matter, what lies behind).

Read the poem carefully, looking for repeated word sounds. In reading it aloud for a Cassette Curriculum tape recording, the poet said this: "It occurred to me while I was reading this poem that something might be said about the recurrence of sounds. As I look at it, I look at it on the page, I see, Yes, there are some recurrences, but they are not exact recurrences like rhyme. Maybe 'air,' 'year,' 'door,' 'stranger,' 'older,' 'they ask how we are,' 'it is this year.' I don't want to overemphasize this matter of repetition of sounds, but it occurred to me to call attention to something that I hope was having an effect." Did you notice those recurrent sounds when first you read the poem? What effect do you think they have? Are they ornamental or functional?

4. A Voice: Rhyme

The single quality most associated with poetry in the popular imagination is rhyme. If it rhymes, it's poetry; if it's poetry, it's got to rhyme. People get annoyed with poetry that does not rhyme, and in amateur verse they are willing to engage in any distortion of rhythm, normal English word order, and even meaning just for the sake of a rhyme. In terms of twisted phrases, awkward rhythm, meaningless imagery, and pointless filler lines, rhyme is responsible for more bad poetry than any other trick of the poet's trade . . . which may explain why modern poets avoid it. Yet rhyme was a late development in English poetry; as we have noted, Old English poetry did not rhyme at all. Rhyme was introduced from French poetry (originally from the Latin), where it was used for ornamentation, and where the highly inflected nature of the language made finding rhymes less difficult than it is in English. In fact, Latin poetry—because Latin does not much care about word order, and because Latin has so many inflectional endings—often rhymed not only at the end of a line, but one or two places in the middle of the line as well. But English is a language different from French and Latin, and unless a poet is very clever, he must either distort normal word order in his sentences for the sake of getting a perfect rhyme at the end of the line or use *half rhymes, slant rhymes, near rhymes,* or *eye rhymes* like "over" and "lover," "same" and "gone," or "through" and "enough." Although poets sometimes deliberately use *near rhyme* to avoid those typewriter bells that ring at the end of a regularly metered and rhymed line, the profusion of near rhyme in English poetry is more often a result of difficulty in finding an appropriate perfect rhyme that does not sacrifice sense to sound. And half rhyme is not nearly so noticeable as you would at first think; it's used extensively in hymns and songs, where it slips by without much objection.

For two words to rhyme, it is necessary that their last *accented* syllables *and all syllables following* sound alike. Rhyme is relatively easy if
U / U
the rhymed words end in an accented syllable—"about" and "through-
/
out," for example—but more difficult when the last syllable of each
/ U / U
word is unaccented. "Quickly" and "slowly" do not rhyme, even through they have identical final syllables, because the "ly" is not ac-
/ U
cented. You would need two syllables of rhyme here, like "coming"
/ U
and "strumming." Rhymes of two syllables—or *feminine rhyme*—have a light, vaguely humorous quality, an element of wit and surprise that you do not find in one-syllable, or *masculine* rhyme. The effect of rhyme seems to be exponential, not arithmetic, for *triple* rhyme (three rhymed syllables) is always humorous, as these couplets from Byron's *Don Juan* should demonstrate:

For instance—passion in a lover's glorious,
But in a husband is pronounced uxorious.

He learn'd the arts of riding, fencing, gunnery,
And how to scale a fortress—or a nunnery.

But—oh! ye lords of ladies intellectual,
Inform us truly, have they not hen-peck'd you all?

Note, finally, that rhyme, while usually used to mark the end of a line of poetry, need not be relegated exclusively to that position in the poem. Internal rhyme is common in English:

Ah, distinctly I rem*ember* it was in the bleak Dec*ember,*
And each separate dying *ember* wrought its ghost upon the *floor.*
Eagerly I wished the m*orrow;*—vainly I had tried to b*orrow*
From my books surcease of s*orrow*—sorrow for the lost Le*nore*—
For the rare and radiant maiden whom the angels name Le*nore*—
Nameless here for ever*more.*

—Edgar Allan Poe ("*The Raven*")

Poets might also make use of random rhyme across a line or several lines of poetry (the "recurrences of sound" described by William Stafford might be considered randomly occurrences of near rhyme), or he might, like Algernon Charles Swinburne, string out a whole series of rhymed words in a single line: "Villon, our sad bad glad mad brother's name" ("A Ballad of François Villon").

Subterranean Homesick Blues

Johnny's in the basement
Mixing up the medicine
I'm on the pavement
Thinking about the government
The man in the trench coat,
Badge out, laid off
Says he's got a bad cough
Wants to get it paid off.
Look out, kid
It's somethin' you did
God knows when

But your're doin' it again
You better duck down the alley way
Lookin' for a new friend
The man in the coon-skin cap
By the big pen
Wants eleven dollar bills
You only got ten.

Maggie comes fleet foot,
Face full of black soot
Talkin' that the heat put
Plants in the bed but
The phone's tapped any-way
Maggie says that many say
They must bust in early May
Orders from the D. A.
Look out kid
Don't matter what you did
Walk on your tip toes
Don't try "No Doz"
Better stay away from those
That carry around a fire hose
Keep a clean nose
Watch the plain clothes
You don't need a weather man
To know which way the wind blows.

Get sick, get well
Hang around a ink well
Ring bell, hard to tell
If anything is goin' to sell
Try hard, get barred
Get back, write braille
Get jailed, jump bail
Join the army if you fail.
Look out kid, you're gonna get hit
But users, cheaters
Six time losers
Hang around the theatres
Girl by the whirlpool
Lookin' for a new fool
Don't follow leaders
Watch the parkin' meters.

Ah get born, keep warm
Short pants, romance, learn to dance
Get dressed, get blessed
Try to be a success
Please her, please him, buy gifts
Don't steal, don't lift
Twenty years of schoolin'
And they put you on the day shift.
Look out kid they keep it all hid
Better jump down a manhole
Light yourself a candle, don't wear sandals
Try to avoid the scandals
Don't wanna be a bum
You better chew gum
The pump don't work
'Cause the vandals took the handles.

—*Bob Dylan*

The pattern of rhymes in this poem is very rough, although rhymes themselves are plentiful. At the beginning of the second stanza, Dylan rhymes "foot," "soot," and "put," then half-rhymes "but." Those four rhymes are followed by four more: "way," "say," "May," and "A." It would appear here that Dylan is using four rhymes, followed by four more, and so forth. But the first stanza, even if we allow "medicine" and "basement" to be half rhymes (it's worth noting that "basement," "pavement," and "government" are also only approximate rhymes), throws in "trench coat," which rhymes with nothing at all. The third stanza gives us five rhymes initially, by virtue of the internal rhyme of line 39: "well," "well," "bell," "tell," and "sell." Clearly the poet is more interested in piling up rhymes of various sorts than he is in being regular in the pattern of his rhyme. In English poets of the past—notably John Skelton—such an arrangement was considered a defect of the poetry, but in this song the irregular profusion is largely responsible for what Dylan, with his pronunciation, would call the "suck-cess" of the song. Why?

Given another subject and another poem—say an elegy on the death of a friend—this irregular and incessant rhyming would probably destroy the poem. But Dylan is not writing an elegy. "Subterranean Homesick Blues" is not about death, unless it's the death of spirit that accompanies confusion and alienation; it's about life in the twentieth century as experienced by a young man originally from Minnesota who later migrated to New York City. Dylan is creating a kaleidoscopic view of life in modern America, and of the dangers and pitfalls and exploitations that surround every kid trying to grow up in this country. In a very few lines of idiosyncratic poetry he manages to say just about everything that Paul Goodman said a few years before him in his analysis of America during the fifties, *Growing Up Absurd:* youth is exploited economically, socially, educationally; it is put down, bought off, and most of all bribed-threatened-cajoled into staying in line. This kind of an existence is depressing, infuriating, but most of all confusing, because it comes to you from all sides at once. It is the element of confusion that Dylan manages to capture so well in his driving tempo and jangling rhymes, which complement each other. The rhymes of the poem are functional, then, something beyond mere embellishment. The sense of the poem is paralleled by the sound of the poem.

This Must Be Wrong

I gave a party
I said you could come
You showed up at my door
with all your leathers on
I said This must be wrong
It can't be right
How can you make love to me
dressed up for a fight?
Pick me up off the floor
No more—cause you surely
can't be mine.

Religion came
almost overnight
You were the high priest
I was the sacrifice
I said This must be wrong
This can't be right
Take off your stupid robe
and put down your knife
These ropes are getting tight
All right—you surely
can't be mine.

I came home half dead
Late on a Saturday night
You stand on the bed and you

tell me you're learning to fly
I said Take off your boots
Take off your cape
Throw away your long johns
I ain't no Lois Lane
Before I get my kryptonite
All right—'cause you surely
can't be mine.

I was ready for love
Big brass bed and all
I was ready for love
You said Let's talk about the war
I said What war?
What war?
Take off your clothes
and don't worry me no more
I ain't no fly by night
All right—you surely
can't be mine.

—Janis Ian

1. To what kind of a person is this song addressed? How secure is this individual? What is the relationship between speaker and the person addressed? Do they enjoy this relationship?

2. Explain the Lois Lane and kryptonite business. Why is an allusion to Superman appropriate to this song?

3. Glance down the words at the right end of each line: "party," "come," "door," "on," "wrong," "right," "me," "fight," etc. How many examples of rhyme can you find? How much does Ian rely on half rhyme? Listen to the song sung and decide whether the near rhyme works almost as well as rhyme, or if it's nearly invisible.

We Real Cool

The Pool Players.
Seven at the Golden Shovel.

We real cool. We
Left school. We

Lurk late. We
Strike straight. We

Sing sin. We
Thin gin. We

Jazz June. We
Die soon.

—*Gwendolyn Brooks*

Identify the patterns of rhyme and alliteration in this poem. Why is such a profusion of rhyme and alliteration appropriate to a poem on pool players at the Golden Shovel?

I Love Those Little Booths at Benvenuti's

They get to Benvenuti's. There are booths
To hide in while observing tropical truths
About this—dusky folk, so clamorous!
So colorfully incorrect,
So amorous,
So flatly brave!
Boothed-in, one can detect,
Dissect.

One knows and scarcely knows what to expect.

What antics, knives, what lurching dirt; what ditty—
Dirty, rich, carmine, hot, not bottled up,
Straining in sexual soprano, cut
And praying in the bass, partial, unpretty.

They sit, sup,
(Whose friends, if not themselves, arrange
To rent in Venice "a very large cabana,
Small palace," and eat mostly what is strange.)
They sit, they settle; presently are met
By the light heat, the lazy upward whine
And lazy croaky downward drawl of "Tanya."
And their interiors sweat.
They lean back in the half-light, stab their stares
At: walls, panels of imitation oak
With would-be marbly look; linoleum squares
Of dusty rose and brown with little white splashes,
White curls; a vendor tidily encased;
Young yellow waiter moving with straight haste,

Old oaken waiter, lolling and amused;
Some paper napkins in a water glass;
Table, initialed, rubbed, as a desk in school.

They stare. They tire. They feel refused,
Feel overwhelmed by subtle treasons!
Nobody here will take the part of jester.

The absolute stutters, and the rationale
Stoops off in astonishment.
But not gaily
And not with their consent,

They play "They All Say I'm The Biggest Fool"
And "Voo Me On The Vot Nay" and "New Lester
Leaps In" and "For Sentimental Reasons."

But how shall they tell people they have been
Out Bronzeville way? For all the nickels in
Have not bought savagery or defined a "folk."

The colored people will not "clown."

The colored people arrive, sit firmly down,
Eat their Express Spaghetti, their T-bone steak,
Handling their steel and crockery with no clatter,
Laugh punily, rise, go firmly out of the door.

—Gwendolyn Brooks

1. *Benvenuti's:* restaurant in Chicago.

Normally we expect a regular pattern of rhymes in poetry, although for no particular reason except habit. Read carefully through this poem and circle all the rhymes and half rhymes you notice. Can you find any pattern at all?

This is a poem about black society and white society, and the way whites view black society. With what expectations do white folk come to Benvenuti's? How do they feel while they're there? When they leave? What brings them here in the first place? This poem was first published in 1945; have things changed substantially since then?

Brooks uses the word "firmly" twice in her closing line. Why?

I Like to See It Lap the Miles

I like to see it lap the Miles—
And lick the Valleys up—
And stop to feed itself at Tanks—
And then—prodigious step

Around a Pile of Mountains—
And supercilious peer
In Shanties—by the sides of Roads—
And then a Quarry pare

To fit its sides
And crawl between
Complaining all the while
In horrid—hooting stanza—
Then chase itself down Hill—

And neigh like Boanerges—
Then—prompter than a Star
Stop—docile and omnipotent
At its own stable door—

—*Emily Dickinson*

14. *Boanerges:* the name given by Christ to John and James, meaning "sons of thunder."

1. This poem is built upon a simple extended metaphor: railroad train as horse. What lines in the poem develop which elements of that comparison? How apt is it? How fresh?

2. Dickinson often used half rhyme; in fact, she probably used more half rhyme than perfect rhyme. This poem is filled with it: "up" and "step," "peer" and "pare," "while" and "hill," "Star" and "door." Suppose these had been perfect rhymes; given the regularity of Dickinson's rhythm, do you think the poem would have sounded better or worse?

Bridge of Sighs

One more Unfortunate,
Weary of breath,
Rashly importunate,
Gone to her death!

Take her up tenderly,
Lift her with care;—
Fashion'd so slenderly,
Young, and so fair!

Look at her garments
Clinging like cerements;
Whilst the wave constantly
Drips from her clothing;
Take her up instantly,
Loving, not loathing.—

Touch her not scornfully;
Think of her mournfully,
Gently and humanly;
Not of the stains of her,
All that remains of her
Now, is pure womanly.

Make no deep scrutiny
Into her mutiny
Rash and undutiful;
Past all dishonour,
Death has left on her
Only the beautiful.

Still, for all slips of hers,
One of Eve's family—
Wipe those poor lips of hers
Oozing so clammily,
Loop up her tresses
Escaped from the comb,
Her fair auburn tresses;
Whilst wonderment guesses
Where was her home?

Who was her father?
Who was her mother?
Had she a sister?
Had she a brother?
Or was there a dearer one
Still, and a nearer one
Yet, than all other?

Alas! for the rarity
Of Christian charity
Under the sun!
Oh! it was pitiful!
Near a whole city full,
Home she had none.

Sisterly, brotherly,
Fatherly, motherly
Feelings had changed:
Love, by harsh evidence,
Thrown from its eminence,
Even God's providence
Seeming estranged.

Where the lamps quiver
So far in the river,
With many a light
From window and casement
From garret to basement,
She stood, with amazement,
Houseless by night.

The bleak wind of March
Made her tremble and shiver;
But not the dark arch,
Or the black flowing river:
Mad from life's history,
Glad to death's mystery,
Swift to be hurl'd—
Anywhere, anywhere
Out of the world!

In she plunged boldly,
No matter how coldly
The rough river ran,—
Over the brink of it,
Picture it—think of it,
Dissolute Man!
Lave in it, drink of it
Then, if you can!

Take her up tenderly,
Lift her with care;
Fashion'd so slenderly,
Young, and so fair!

Ere her limbs frigidly
Stiffen too rigidly,
Decently,—kindly,—
Smooth, and compose them;
And her eyes, close them,
Staring so blindly!

Dreadfully staring
Through muddy impurity,
As when with the daring
Last look of despairing
Fixed on futurity.

Perishing gloomily,
Spurred by contumely,
Cold inhumanity,
Burning insanity,
Into her rest,—
Cross her hands humbly,
As if praying dumbly,
Over her breast!
Owning her weakness,
Her evil behaviour,
And leaving, with meekness,
Her sins to her Saviour!

—*Thomas Hood*

Title: The Bridge of Sighs, in Venice, connects the Palace of the Doges, where criminals would be judged, to the prison, whence few ever returned. It is, however, an enclosed bridge, from which nobody could drown himself. 3. *importunate:* stubbornly persistent. 10. *cerements:* cloth coated with wax, used for wrapping the dead. 78. *lave:* bathe. 96. *contumely:* contempt.

In his essay "The Poetic Principle," Edgar Allan Poe held this poem up to readers as a remarkable poem. "The versification, although carrying the fanciful to the very range of the fantastic, is nevertheless admirably adapted to the wild insanity which is the thesis of the poem." Analyze the rhymes in the poem. What tone do they create? Do you think it is appropriate to the subject of the poem?

A Fit of Rhyme Against Rhyme

Rhyme, the rack of finest wits,
That expresseth but by fits,
True conceit,
Spoiling senses of their treasure,
Cozening judgement with a measure,
But false weight.
Wresting words, from their true calling;
Propping verse, for fear of falling
To the ground.
Jointing syllabes, drowning letters,
Fast'ning vowels, as with fetters
They were bound!
Soon as lazy thou wert known,
All good poetry hence was flown,
And art banished.
For a thousand years together,
All Parnassus' green did wither,
And wit vanished.
Pegasus did fly away,
At the wells no Muse did stay,
But bewailed
So to see the fountain dry,
And Apollo's music die,
All light failed!
Starveling rhymes did fill the stage,
Not a poet in an age,
Worth crowning;
Not a work deserving bays,
Nor a line deserving praise,
Pallas frowning.
Greek was free from rhyme's infection,
Happy Greek, by this protection,
Was not spoiled.
Whilst the Latin, queen of tongues,
Is not yet free from rhyme's wrongs,
But rests foiled.
Scarce the hill again doth flourish,
Scarce the world a wit doth nourish,
To restore
Phoebus to his crown again;
And the Muses to their brain;
As before.

Vulgar languages that want
Words and sweetness, and be scant
Of true measure,
Tyrant rhyme hath so abused,
That they long since have refused
Other ceasure.
He that first invented thee,
May his joints tormented be,
Cramped forever;
Still may syllabes jar with time,
Still may reason war with rhyme,
Resting never.
May his sense, when it would meet
The cold tumor in his feet,
Grow unsounder,
And his title be long fool,
That in rearing such a school,
Was the founder.

—Ben Jonson

1. *rack:* an instrument of torture that twists the body out of shape; hence, here, twister or distorter. 3. *conceit:* an ingenious or overly clever expression. 5. *cozening:* cheating. 10. *jointing:* combining, joining. 13. *wert:* were. 17. *Parnassus:* a mountain in southern Greece, believed to be the abode of Apollo and the muses. 28. *bays:* bay leaves, here a crown made of bay leaves given in classical times as a sign of honor. 30. *Pallas:* Athena, one of the Greek goddesses. 40. *Phoebus:* Apollo, god of wisdom and the arts.

What charges does Jonson level against rhyme in this poem? Why does he recall so favorably Greek poetry? How does the form of Jonson's poem illustrate the vices he claims rhyme inspires in poetry?

5. A Voice: Euphony and Cacophony

Sometimes lines that are not exactly alliterative or assonant, lines that have no rhyme or near rhyme or "patterns of repeated sounds," as Stafford put it, lines that resist reduction to these patterns of sound are simply pleasant or unpleasant to hear. We talk about their "music," by which we mean not a series of pitches and tones, but the rich structure of word sounds the poet has created. But we have no categories of analysis beyond saying that they are simply euphonic (pleasant sounding) or cacophonic (unpleasant sounding). The fourth stanza of Bob Dylan's "Mr. Tambourine Man" may function here as a good example:

Then take me disappearin' through the smoke rings of my
  mind
Down the foggy ruins of time
Far past the frozen leaves
The haunted, frightened trees
Out to the windy beach
Far from the twisted reach of crazy sorrow
Yes, to dance beneath the diamond sky with one hand wavin'
  free
Silhouetted by the sea,
Circled by the circus sands
With all memory and fate
Driven deep beneath the waves
let me forget about today until tomorrow.

Hey! Mister Tambourine Man play a song for me,
I'm not sleepy and there is no place I'm going to.
Hey! Mister Tambourine Man play a song for me
In the jingle jangle mornin' I'll come followin' you.

The poem certainly makes extensive use of both alliteration and assonance, and "jingle-jangle" is *onomatopoetic:* the word has no meaning other than the sound it makes. The title phrase represents a subtle combination of assonance and alliteration that goes far to account for the way it haunts a listener. But some sections of the poem are impressive in a way that cannot be adequately explained by alliteration or assonance. Look, for example, at lines 1–5. The passage begins with a series of pleasant-sounding vowel and consonant combinations. Line 2 picks up and echoes in "ruins" the "r" of "rings" and the "u" of "through." It echoes in "time" the "m" and "i" of "mind." Lines 2–3 use similar "f . . . e" patterns in "frozen leaves" and "frightened trees." But the lines are pleasantly musical beyond these patterns, and the music is appropriate to Dylan's description of the world into which he is escaping. When the poet looks back, however, he sees less pleasant things, and his language changes accordingly. From the attractive "smoke rings of my mind," the imagery of the poem turns to "the twisted reach of crazy sorrow"; the sound of the language becomes vaguely unpleasant and cacophonous in the consonants of "twisted reach" and "crazy." Sound mirrors sense in the change from euphony to cacophony, moving from the pleasant to the unpleasant.

John Milton, whose ear was probably as fine as that of any poet who has ever lived, used euphonic and cacophonic effects often, but nowhere more effectively than in the passage of *Paradise Lost* (I, 876–83) that describes the opening of the gates of Hell to let Satan fly up to earth to tempt Adam and Eve. Notice how the euphony of the lines turns to cacophony as the gates swing open and the harmony of creation is disturbed by the discord of Hell.

. . . then in the key-hole turns
Th' intricate wards, and every Bolt and Bar
Of massy iron or solid Rock with ease
Unfast'ns: on a sudden op'n fly
With impetuous recoil and jarring sound
Th' infernal doors, and on their hinges grate
Harsh Thunder, that the lowest bottom shook
Of *Erebus*.

Erebus: according to Hesiod, the first child of Chaos; here a dark, vast envelope of space and matter.

One of the most musical of modern poets was the Welshman Dylan Thomas. In fact, in reading he half-sang his poetry, in the old bardic tradition. Read—or, better still, listen to Thomas himself read on record or tape—"Fern Hill," an ode to his early childhood in Wales:

Fern Hill

Now as I was young and easy under the apple boughs
About the lilting house and happy as the grass was green,
    The night above the dingle starry,
        Time let me hail and climb
    Golden in the heydays of his eyes,
And honored among wagons I was prince of the apple towns
And once below a time I lordly had the trees and leaves
        Trail with daisies and barley
    Down the rivers of the windfall light.

And as I was green and carefree, famous among the barns
About the happy yard and singing as the farm was home,
    In the sun that is young once only,
        Time let me play and be
    Golden in the mercy of his means,
And green and golden I was huntsman and herdsman, the calves
Sang to my horn, the foxes on the hills barked clear and cold,
        And the sabbath rang slowly
    In the pebbles of the holy streams.

All the sun long it was running, it was lovely, the hay
Fields high as the house, the tunes from the chimneys, it was air
    And playing, lovely and watery
        And fire green as grass.
    And nightly under the simple stars
As I rode to sleep the owls were bearing the farm away,
All the moon long I heard, blessed among stables, the nightjars
    Flying with the ricks, and the horses
        Flashing into the dark.

And then to awake, and the farm, like a wanderer white
With the dew, come back, the cock on his shoulder: it was all
    Shining, it was Adam and maiden,
        The sky gathered again
    And the sun grew round that very day.
So it must have been after the birth of the simple light
In the first, spinning place, the spellbound horses walking warm
    Out of the whinnying green stable
        On to the fields of praise.

And honored among foxes and pheasants by the gay house
Under the new made clouds and happy as the heart was long,
    In the sun born over and over,
        I ran my heedless way,
    My wishes raced through the house high hay
And nothing I cared, at my sky blue trades, that time allows
In all his tuneful turning so few and such morning songs
    Before the children green and golden
        Follow him out of grace,

Nothing I cared, in the lamb white days, that time would take me
Up to the swallow thronged loft by the shadow of my hand,
    In the moon that is always rising,
        Not that riding to sleep
    I should hear him fly with the high fields
And wake to the farm forever fled from the childless land.
Oh as I was young and easy in the mercy of his means,
        Time held me green and dying
    Though I sang in my chains like the sea.

—*Dylan Thomas*

2. *lilting:* rhythmic, swinging. 3. *dingle:* a deep, narrow cleft between two hills. 25. *nightjars:* nocturnal European birds. 26. *ricks:* stacks of hay or straw.

What was the poet's life like when he was young? Where did he live? What did he do? What comparisons does he draw between his life and other moments in history? What did Thomas have as a child that he now lacks? On what does he blame his loss? How can he recover what he's lost?

How would you describe the poet's voice? What is the tone of this poem? What creates that tone? What examples of assonance, alliteration, rhyme, euphony, and cacophony can you find in this poem? How does the music of the poem enhance its meaning? How does the music of Thomas's reading enhance the music already built into the poem?

6. A Voice: Meter and Rhythm

Next to rhyme, a regular meter is most associated by readers with poetry. Prose is words without meter and rhyme; poetry has a regular pulse of *ta*s and *da*s, of unaccented and accented syllables, that form a smooth pattern called meter. You can tell a poem by its meter and rhyme: *ta-da, ta-da, ta-da, ta-spring; / ta-da, ta-da, ta-da, ta-thing; / ta-da, ta-da, ta-da, ta-glow; / ta-da, ta-da, ta-da, ta-grow*. And so forth. The more skillful the poet, the smoother the meter. The best poetry is that poetry with the most regular meter and the cleanest rhymes, according to some standards.

As we have seen, however, poetry is many things together, several of which have nothing to do with words as sound, and thereby nothing to do with rhyme and meter. Furthermore, although early poetry had pulse and rhythm, the regularities of meter built into that *ta-da, ta-da, ta-da, ta-da* scheme are a product largely of the last few centuries. It is quite possible to create impressive effects with rhythmic characteristics of language without resorting to the regularities of accentual meter—in fact, it seems that the more attuned poets are to words as sound, the more impatient they become with the narrow and unimaginative confines of traditional meter. They know that such meters are slightly artificial, and ours is not an age that admires artifice. They know that overly strict meter becomes monotonous, and that some meters, too carefully insisted upon, have a galloping tempo that makes them unsuitable for many subjects. They know that the most effective lines of some poems written in traditional meters are exactly those lines where regularity breaks down. Free verse, unmetered verse, is only a century or so old, really, but in the past few decades most serious poets have preferred free verse (which is not entirely free, since it usually creates its own pattern of phrases and lines, much like jazz rhythms) to traditional meters, about ten to one. In considering the rhythm of poetry, then, we must keep our ears attuned not only to regular patterns of accented and unaccented syllables, but to the loose rhythmic cadences of line and phrase that also constitute rhythm.

Generally speaking we can distinguish three different degrees of looseness in rhythm. Most strict, of course, is traditional meter, which measures (scans) each line according to its accented and unaccented syllables and requires a regular pattern of both. A second and looser pattern we might call pulse or beat, borrowing our terminology from music. Here the poet maintains a steady pulse or beat by maintaining a constant number of accented syllables per line. The number of short, or unaccented syllables, is largely irrelevant, however, and may vary from line to line. This may count three or four, or whatever, accents or pulses per line, and let the rest develop randomly. The third and loosest degree of rhythm maintains no constant meter, no constant pulse over the length of the poem, but constantly changes patterns of beat, accent, or phrase, so that the poet is free to adapt his rhythm to the demands of each individual line or group of lines.

First regular meter, as it has come to us from the eighteenth and nineteenth centuries.

Traditional meter can be justified—or at least explained—in several ways. One theory assumes that the poet's function is to impose an order on raw, chaotic experience: from an apparently disordered, capricious, random world unraveling at every corner, the poet draws from his experience a series of insights, patterns, interrelationships, which he communicates to his audience in his poem. Part of the construct of the poem—this ordered vision of things—is contained in the selection and arrangement of details, in metaphors, in symbols, in statements. Another part of the poet's ordered vision is to be found in the regular rhythm of the language he uses, in his meter.

A second explanation of traditional meter holds that order *is* inherent in the nature of things, and that the poet is reproducing in his art the rhythmic regularity he sees and feels in the natural world around him. This naturalist-biological justification sees poetic meter as a verbal correlative to such natural phenomena as the circling of planets, the beating of the heart, the turning of the seasons. Such a view of man, his universe, his nature, elevates poetry to the highest form of literary expression precisely because in its meter it is most sensitive to the natural pulses of life.

A third justification of traditional meter is the justification from difficulty: since it's harder to write regularly metered poetry than free verse, and since we take more pleasure in playing a difficult game than in playing a simple game, then it follows that poetry that succeeds at something difficult—regular meter, perfect rhymes—is going to be more pleasurable than simpler poetry. When asked about free verse, Robert Frost once remarked that he'd as soon play tennis without a net, indicating that for him at least part of the appeal of traditional meter was the way it challenged a poet's skill.

Perhaps the true explanation of regular meter in poetry is historical, profoundly unphilosophical, and really quite simple: in primitive societies poetry was sung, or at least accompanied by musical instruments while being chanted. Music has a rhythm of its own—a very regular rhythm in pretwentieth-century "classical" music, a looser rhythm in jazz songs and chants. The rhythm of music was naturally imposed upon the words of the poem, which were written down long before modern musical notation was developed. Thus the poem appeared to have a rough meter of its own, which in fact it had borrowed from music. In the eighteenth century this roughness was refined (the eighteenth century refined everything it touched), making metrics into a pseudoscience and requiring clocklike regularity in poetic meter.

Modern theories of meter grow out of Latin treatises on the subject (slightly misunderstood by medieval English and French scribes, but let it pass), and were developed largely after the English Renaissance. These classify all syllables as either accented or unaccented, and arrange the "longs" and the "shorts" into regular patterns of small units called *feet.* This simple division of syllables into accented and unaccented may be something of a fiction, since accent is often relative, and normally unaccented syllables may be given some soft stress in a particular phrase, but this simple approach works or most poetry. Hence, we would scan a line of English prose as follows:

/ u u / u / u / u / u / u
Hence, we would scan a line of English prose as follows.

An accented syllable, as is obvious, is designated with a /; an unaccented syllable is designated with a u . Out of the possible combinations of *accented* and *unaccented* syllables (or *longs* and *shorts,* as they are frequently called), any variety of units or poetic feet can be constructed. The most popular of these are the following:

u / u / u / u /
IAMB (u /): I think that I shall nev er see

u u / u u / u u /
ANAPEST (u u /): For I'm wear y with hunt in' and fain
u u /
would lay down.

/ u / u / u / u
TROCHEE (/ u): Once u pon a midnight dreary

/ u u / u u / u u
DACTYL (/ u u): Half a league, half a league half a league
/ u
onward

These feet account for about 95 per cent of all English feet, although occasionally in lines of mainly iamb*ic* or trocha*ic* or anapest*ic* or dactyl*ic* feet a few others occur:

/ /
SPONDEE (//): someday

u / u
AMPHIBRACH (u / u): condition

/ u /
AMPHIMACHER (/ u /): element

u / u u u / u u u / u
PYRRHUS (u u): Tomor row and tomor row and tomorrow

These feet are exceptional (probably designed to cover breakdowns in the qualitative scansion system); there is no such thing as a spond*aic* line or a phyrr*ic* line.

Lines of qualitatively scanned poetry are designated by an adjective describing the predominant foot followed by a noun indicating the number of feet in the line. For example, iambic pentameter is a line containing five iambic feet. The Greek prefixes are used to create the metrical designation: MONOMETER (one foot), DIMETER (two feet), TRIMETER (three feet), TETRAMETER (four feet), PENTAMETER (five feet), HEXAMETER (six feet), HEPTAMETER (seven feet). Monometer and dimeter are uncommon. Longer lines, like larger molecules, are unstable and tend to dissociate: the ballad stanza is essentially a heptameter couplet broken into four instead of two lines, with four, three, four, three feet in each line.

Turn to some poems in this book which appear to be written in traditional meters (they are usually characterized by lines of approximately equal length, with rhymes at the end of each line). Try scanning some of their lines to see what meter the poet was using. Then, and more significantly, discuss the appropriateness of the meter to the poem's subject. A random search may prove interesting, or you may wish to look specifically at Yeats's "That the Night Come," Housman's "Loveliest of Trees," Eliot's "Macavity: the Mystery Cat," Shelley's "England in 1819," Stevens's "The Idea of Order at Key West," Lennon and McCartney's "Being for the Benefit of Mr. Kite," Southey's "The Old Man's Comforts," and Bob Dylan's "Sad-Eyed Lady of the Lowlands." It might be especially interesting to listen to these poems read, either by the poets themselves or by professional readers, to see how oral performance enhances or underplays metrical structures of a poem. You will soon discover, for example, that no serious reader reads a poem in the lilting *ta-da, ta-da, ta-da, ta-da* voice used too often by amateurs, just as they do their best to underplay, not emphasize, the rhymes at the end of the lines.

Another thing listening to these poems may do is point out immediately deficiencies in traditional metrical analysis. The most obvious is that some lines like "Tomorrow and tomorrow and tomorrow" (probably intended as iambic pentameter) do not fit well into the system; others contain large numbers of imperfect or defective feet—feet with more or fewer short syllables than they should have. Another problem is the tendency of poets to invert feet, especially at the beginning of poems, thereby confusing the pattern.

/ u u / u / u /
Mark but this flea, and mark in this

(Donne, "The Flea")

/ u u / u / u / u /
Something there is that does not love a wall

(Frost, "Mending Wall")

In fact, the first stanza of any poem is notoriously unreliable as a guide to its metrical pattern.

In some instances punctuation or rhetorical considerations give an accent to a syllable that would not receive one according to an abstract metrical pattern.

// / u u /
O rose, thou art sick.

The syllable "O" picks up a secondary accent (as indicated) because of the rhetoric of the apostrophe, whereas normally it would be short. Or an accent may be said to hover somewhere around the two syllables "O rose," in which case it is marked as indicated. Neither scansion is very precise.

And finally, these are lines that simply resist the scansion a qualitative system would impose on them, like the third line of this stanza from Samuel Johnson's "On the Death of Mr. Robert Levet."

Well tried through many a varying year,
  See Levet to the grave descend,
Officious, innocent, sincere,
  Of every friendless name the friend.

The poem is written in iambic tetrameter, but the third line clearly breaks into a three-foot unit composed of one amphibrach, one dactyl, and one iamb:

u / u / u u u /
Officious, innocent, sincere,

Faced with these difficulties, modern methods of metrical analysis have become either incredibly complicated or very simple. Hopkins created for himself a system of poetics which is for all practical purposes unintelligible; Eliot has been accused of writing in something resembling simple Early English four-stress verse.

Old English metrics might, in fact, offer an entirely new means of measuring a poem's rhythm, a system much richer than traditional English metrics in that it allows for more variation and play on the poet's part. While we are not entirely certain how Anglo-Saxon poets structured their verse, it appears that they counted accented syllables only, using four stresses with an undetermined number of short, or unaccented syllables per line. Thus a few lines of Anglo-Saxon poetry might provide a pattern like this:

/ u / u u u / u /
u u/ u/ u / / u
/ u/ uu/ u u /
u u / u/u u u/ /

Such poetry obviously has pulse and rhythm, but it lacks regularity.

Another possibility is that Anglo-Saxon poetry should be measured musically, not in terms of accented and unaccented syllables, but in terms of the length of time it takes to say a syllable, and a line. One scholar has done exactly that, and created a system of measuring rhythm that could be extended to other poetry. For example, we might scan Emily Dickinson's famous poem "Because I Could Not Stop for Death" accentually into a series of alternating iambic tetrameter and iambic trimeter lines:

u / u / u / u /
Because I could not stop for Death,
u / u / u /
He kindly stopped for me;
u / u / u / u /
The carriage held but just ourselves
u / u /u/
And Immortality.

We might, however, also translate it into a series of four measures of simple 4/4 time, using a musical notation:

4/4

Because I could not stop for Death, He kindly stopped for me;

The carriage held but just ourselves And Immortality.

Note that such a musical notation accounts for the pause after "me" and "Immortality," pauses which are very definitely in Dickinson's poem, but which accentual scansion loses entirely. Note also that this scansion better explains "Immortality," which does not really, unless we stretch it, have the accent on its final syllable that the first scansion, the accentual scansion, forces it to have. While there may be further subtleties to the line that a sequence of simple eighth notes oversimplifies (one suspects, for example, that "Because" would be more accurately represented with a sixteenth note and a dotted eighth than by two eighth notes), the musical analysis gives a more realistic idea of what the poem sounds like.

To choose a second example, let us look at a stanza from W. H. Auden's "As I Walked Out One Evening." Accentual scansion will produce a rough pattern indeed, for the poem is full of extra "short" syllables:

u / u / u u / u
The glacier knocks in the cupboard,
u / u / u u /
The desert sighs in the bed,
u u / u u / u / u
And the crack in the teacup opens
u / u u / u u /
A lane to the land of the dead.

We might say simply that Auden uses lines of three accented syllables each, and let things go at that; or we might translate the stanza into musical notation, this more sophisticated than what we used for the Dickinson poem, using quarter notes, eighth notes, sixteenth notes, and rests to indicate pauses:

The glacier knocks in the cupboard, the desert sighs in the bed,

And the crack in the teacup opens a lane to the land of the dead.

Again there may be some oversimplification, but the point is that two sixteenth notes, and the two syllables that come with them ("in the," "cupboard," or "teacup") are easily exchangeable for one eighth note, an accomodation which is more readily explained using a musical notation than by traditional, accentual scansion. Exactly what a poet hears when writing a poem is difficult to say; however, the poet W. D. Snodgrass had this to say about one section of Walt Whitman's "Song of Myself":

> It's a 7/8 rhythm, oddly enough. My brother's a drummer, just as I used to be, and once we were working out a program of Whitman readings with drums. Boy, were we having fun with that. We were trying to notate the poem, when all of a sudden it hit us—it's a 7/8! And where would Whitman ever have heard of a 7/8? You know, he loved music, all kinds of performances, went to operas, concerts, band concerts, and loved all that kind of stuff. But he never would have heard of a 7/8 rhythm in his whole career. You'd hear it in belly dance joints and places like that. . . .

A third possibility is that poetry should be marked off in phrases to indicate the arc of rhythms inherent in the spoken sentence, rhythms which transcend both the accent and the duration of individual words. We might, for example, take Samuel Johnson's poem on Robert Levet and mark it off by phrases, not by poetic feet or musical pulse:

Well tried through many a varying year,
See Levet to the grave descend,
Officious, innocent, sincere,
Of every friendless name the friend.

So marked, the poem has a shape quite different from four lines of ∪ / ∪ / ∪ / ∪ / piled one on top of the other. Or consider the line from "Dover Beach" that described the breaking of successive waves upon the sand: "Begin, and cease, and then again begin." The metrics would be simple iambic pentameter, but the commas after "begin" and "cease" force pauses at these points, and the last three feet are very regular. There is a sharp break between the "e" of "cease" and the "a" of "and." The rhythm of the line looks something like this:

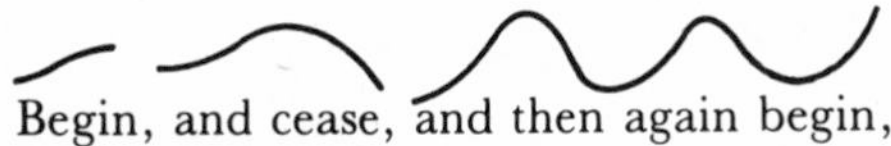

Begin, and cease, and then again begin,

Sound here parallels sense because of the rhythm. As the waves break and cease, the sound ceases; when the waves begin again, the sound begins its regular pulse again. It is the rhythm, not the meter of the poem, that makes this line impressive. And traditional systems of scansion cannot indicate this rhythm.

The remarkable thing about poetry, of course, is that all three forms of rhythm can be superimposed over each other in a single poem, making the voice of the poet very subtle and complex indeed. A poem does have a pattern of accented and unaccented syllables; it does have a musical pulse which depends more on duration than accent; and phrases do indeed exert an influence that can shape the rhythm of a poem. A careful poet, then, can play one rhythm against another, bringing occasionally one, then another to the surface of the poem, adding patterns of rhyme and alliteration, creating a very subtle and complex voice.

Examine carefully the meters and rhythms of the following poems. First look for patterns of accentual meter, paying special attention to variations in the established pattern and looking for *reasons* which might explain those variations. Then try your ear at counting musical pulses in the lines, paying attention to pauses or rests. Finally, try indicating the shape of phrases in each poem. When you have finished, a preliminary analysis, listen to the poem read on tape or record, and see how your ear compares with the voice of the poet or reader. You will soon discover that there is more than one way to read a line of poetry—which adds even more to the complexity of the poem's rhythm and voice.

Because I Could Not Stop for Death

Because I could not stop for Death,
He kindly stopped for me;
The carriage held but just ourselves
And Immortality.

We slowly drove, he knew no haste,
And I had put away
My labor, and my leisure too,
For his civility.

We passed the school where children played
At wrestling in a ring;
We passed the fields of gazing grain,
We passed the setting sun.

We paused before a house that seemed
A swelling of the ground;
The roof was scarcely visible,
The cornice but a mound.

Since then 'tis centuries; but each
Feels shorter than the day
I first surmised the horses' heads
Were toward eternity.

—Emily Dickinson

What simple comparisons does Dickinson make in this poem? How apt are they? What images do you find in this poem? Which are most memorable? What pauses seem especially important in this poem? How do they effect Dickinson's predominately iambic meter?

Spring and Fall: To a Young Child

Márgarét, are you griéving
Over Goldengrove unleaving?
Leáves, like the things of man, you
With your fresh thoughts care for, can you?
Áh! ás the heart grows older
It will come to such sights colder
By and by, nor spare a sigh
Though worlds of wanwood leafmeal lie;
And yet you wíll weep and know why.
Now no matter, child, the name:
Sórrow's spríngs áre the same,
Nor mouth had, no nor mind, expressed
What heart heard of, ghost guessed:
It is the blight man was born for,
It is Margaret you mourn for.

—Gerard Manley Hopkins

13. *ghost:* spirit.

1. What message does the poet have for young Margaret in this

poem? What do you suppose he means by "What heart heard of, ghost guessed"?

2. The image "worlds of wanwood leafmeal lie" has troubled many readers; how would you explain it?

3. What kind of rhymes can you find in this poem? How prominent are they? Does Hopkins's rhythm emphasize them or deemphasize them?

4. Is there any way this poem can be reduced to metrical regularity? Are some of Hopkins's rhythmic irregularities explainable in light of the meaning of his poem?

As I Walked Out One Evening

As I walked out one evening,
  Walking down Bristol Street,
The crowds upon the pavement
  Were fields of harvest wheat.

And down by the brimming river
  I heard a lover sing
Under an arch of the railway:
  "Love has no ending.

"I'll love you dear, I'll love you
  Till China and Africa meet,
And the river jumps over the mountain
  And the salmon sing in the street,

"I'll love you till the ocean
  Is folded and hung up to dry
And the seven stars go squawking
  Like geese about the sky.

"The years shall run like rabbits,
  For in my arms I hold
The Flower of the Ages,
  And the first love of the world."

But all the clocks in the city
  Began to whirr and chime:
"O let not Time deceive you,
  You cannot conquer Time.

"In the burrows of the Nightmare
  Where Justice naked is,
Time watches from the shadow
  And coughs when you would kiss.

"In headaches and in worry
  Vaguely life leaks away.
And Time will have his fancy
  To-morrow or to-day.

"Into many a green valley
  Drifts the appalling snow;
Time breaks the threaded dances
  And the diver's brilliant bow.

"O plunge your hands in water,
  Plunge them in up to the wrist;
Stare, stare in the basin
  And wonder what you've missed.

"The glacier knocks in the cupboard,
  The desert sighs in the bed,
And the crack in the tea-cup opens
  A lane to the land of the dead.

"Where the beggers raffle the banknotes
  And the Giant is enchanting to Jack,
And the Lily-white Boy is a Roarer,
  And Jill goes down on her back.

"O look, look in the mirror,
  O look in your distress;
Life remains a blessing
  Although you cannot bless.

"O stand, stand at the window
  As the tears scald and start;
You shall love your crooked neighbour
  With your crooked heart."

It was late, late in the evening,
  The lovers they were gone;
The clocks had ceased their chiming,
  And the deep river ran on.

—W. H. Auden

Discuss the connotations of each of the following metaphors and images: ''fields of harvest wheat,'' ''brimming river,'' ''salmon,'' ''geese across the sky,'' ''rabbits,'' ''clocks,'' ''life *leaks* away,'' ''green valleys,'' ''appalling snow,'' ''glacier,'' ''cupboard,'' ''tea-cup.'' What associations do they bring to the poem?

What clichés does Auden use in here? (One is ''I'll love you till the ocean/ Is folded and hung up to dry''; there are others.) What purpose does he have in using them?

What would you say is the tone of this poem? Where does it come from?

How does Auden feel about the plight of mankind? How are his feelings different from Hopkins's? How is the tone of this poem different from the tone of ''Spring and Fall''?

7. A Voice: Pitch

In a letter to John Bartlett, written way back in 1913, Robert Frost wrote about the sense of sound and the sound of sense:

> The best place to get the abstract sound of sense is from voices behind a door that cuts off the words. Ask yourself how these sentences would sound without the words in which they are embodied:
> You mean to tell me you can't read?
> I said no such thing.
> Well read then.
> You're not my teacher.

Then Frost went on to speak of a reader giving each of those sentences ''the proper posture,'' the proper inflection, the proper series of pitches. The first sentence is a series of modulating pitches, finally ascending on the word ''read.'' The second is a straight sequence of descending pitches. The third rises, then falls, ''read'' being a pitch or two higher than ''well'' and ''then.'' The fourth sentence descends, then rises.

We might plot them on a musical staff like this:

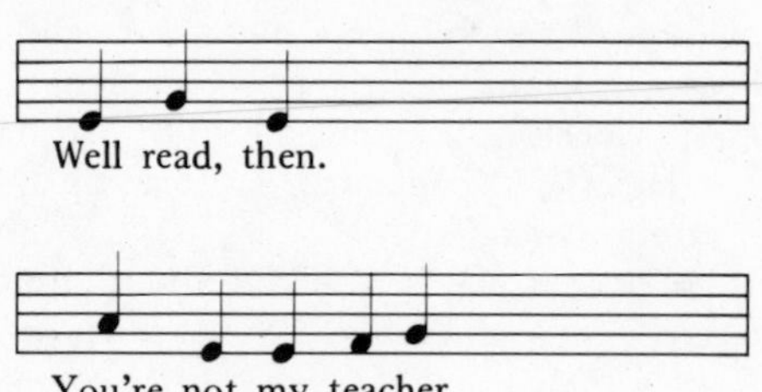

You can't fill a poem full of this kind of music, Frost claimed, but you can create remarkable effects of voice with an occasional "musical line."

Few poets, and even fewer critics, talk about the effect of a series of pitches in a poem. We have no system for structuring, or even indicating pitches, although many poets, when they *read* their poems, come quite close to singing. Some do in fact sing their poems—not only the poets of popular music, but poets like Vachel Lindsay, Allen Ginsberg, other so-called Beat poets. Robert Bly, Dylan Thomas come very, very close to song. And as poetry becomes increasingly audial, as more and more poets appear on record as well as (sometimes instead of) in print, considerations of music such as pitch and tempo become increasingly important to the discussion of poetry. Today more than at any time in its recent history, poetry approaches song—which brings it right back to the old days of *Beowulf,* wandering minstrels, and Shakespeare's plays, when poems were sung, and songs were poems, and the two art forms were closest of kin.

Of course it is possible to so order the pitches of a poem as to make up a little tune, and to write that tune out on a musical staff, and create thereby a song. This book is filled with musical poems, and the question "How does the tune of this song reinforce or undermine the meaning of the lyrics?" is one that should pass through your mind every time you read the lyrics of a Beatles song or a Joni Mitchell song or a poem by Bob Dylan. But let us pass the song-poems and focus our attention on poems that are spoken, but with such an inflection of the voice that a reader hears not only a pattern of accented and unaccented syllables, not only a pulse and a rhythm, not only assonances and alliterations, but pitches as well.

Like a good tune, a good series of pitches defies reduction to rules. We can, however, identify patterns.

First, a sequential falling or rising pattern:

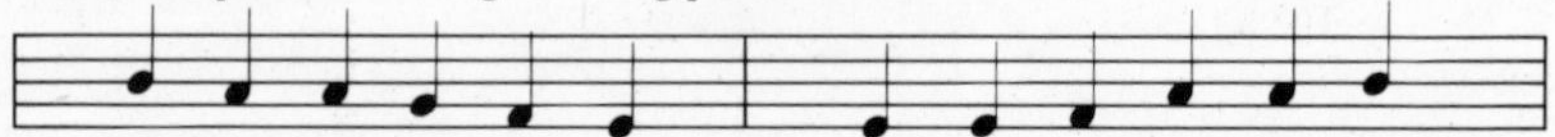

Then a rising-then-falling, or falling-then-rising pattern:

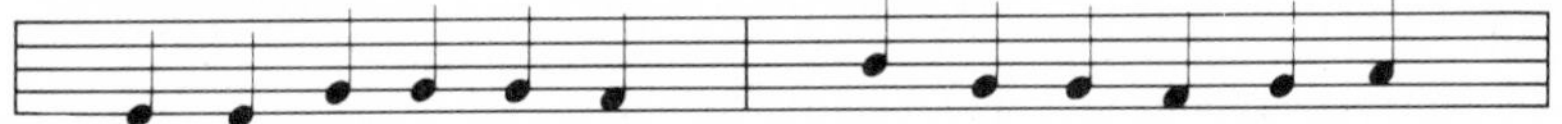

Finally, a long series of modulations with a rise at the end, or a series of modulations with a fall at the end:

Out of these basic patterns the poet is free to create his own structures, as the mood of the poem dictates. In some cases the poet may, in reading, wish simply to mark the close of each phrase with a drop in pitch, chanting his poem in the voice of an auctioneer, simply to create a rhetorical effect. It's not hard, for example, to imagine in the mind's ear old Walt Whitman reading these lines from "Salut au Monde!" as a series of incantations, longer, then shorter, then longer, each with a gradual rise in pitch, rounded off by a sudden drop, creating a grand, rolling, cumulative effect like the voice of an auctioneer or revivalist preacher:

I see male and female everywhere,

I see the serene brotherhood of philosophs,

I see the constructiveness of my race,

I see the results of the constructiveness and industry of my race,

I see ranks, colors, barbarisms, civilizations,

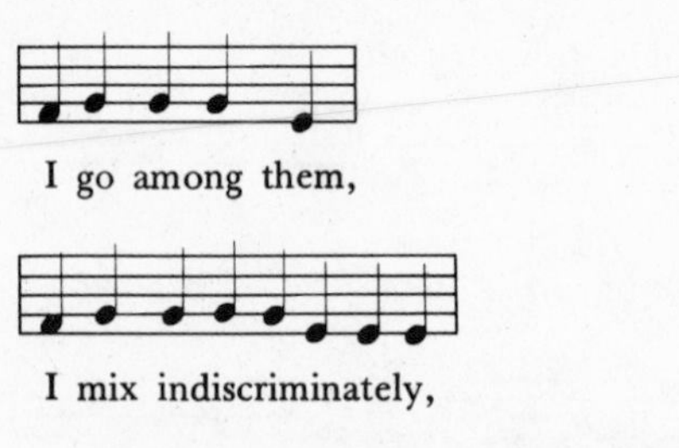

And I salute all the inhabitants of the earth.

There is, in fact, no better place to develop a sense for this incantatory pitching of language that at a fundamentalist church service, or an old fashioned auction, where English is not so much spoken as chanted.

A truly musical poet, however, creates complex patterns of pitch in his poems. Listen to Dylan Thomas reading the "Prologue" to his *Collected Poems,* on the Caedmon recording of *Dylan Thomas Reading His Collected Poems,* or to William Carlos Williams reading "Dedication for a Plot of Ground" on volume two of the Spoken Arts *Treasury of 100 American Poets Reading Their Poems.* Notice how each poet works the pattern of pitches in one line against the pattern of pitches in another, sometimes by way of contrast, sometimes by way of parallelism. Notice how pitch occasionally echoes the sense of the line (to take an obvious example, the pitches of Thomas's first line is a straight series of descending tones, which is obviously suited to the words "This day winding down now"). Notice the music of the reading, in Thomas's case a very beautiful, lofty music, in Williams's case a flat, "American," even New Jersey voice that sounds like the language of the street heard through a closed door that muffles some of the words.

Prologue

This day winding down now
At God speeded summer's end
In the torrent salmon sun,
In my seashaken house
On a breakneck of rocks
Tangled with chirrup and fruit,
Froth, flute, fin and quill
At a wood's dancing hoof,
By scummed, starfish sands

With their fishwife cross
Gulls, pipers, cockles, and sails,
Out there, crow black, men
Tackled with clouds, who kneel
To the sunset nets,
Geese nearly in heaven, boys
Stabbing, and herons, and shells
That speak seven seas,
Eternal waters away
From the cities of nine
Days' night whose towers will catch
In the religious wind
Like stalks of tall, dry straw,
At poor peace I sing
To you strangers (though song
Is a burning and crested act,
The fire of birds in
The world's turning wood,
For my sawn, splay sounds),
Out of these seathumbed leaves
That will fly and fall
Like leaves of trees and as soon
Crumble and undie
Into the dogdayed night.
Seaward the salmon, sucked sun slips,
And the dumb swans drub blue
My dabbed bay's dusk, as I hack
This rumpus of shapes
For you to know
How I, a spinning man,
Glory also this star, bird
Roared, sea born, man torn, blood blest.
Hark: I trumpet the place,
From fish to jumping hill! Look:
I build my bellowing ark
To the best of my love
As the flood begins,
Out of the fountainhead
Of fear, rage red, manalive,
Molten and mountainous to stream
Over the wound asleep
Sheep white hollow farms

To Wales in my arms.

Hoo, there, in castle keep,
You king singsong owls, who moonbeam
The flickering runs and dive
The dingle furred deer dead!
Huloo, on plumbed bryns,
O my ruffled ring dove
In the hooting, nearly dark
With Welsh and reverent rook,
Coo rooing the woods' praise,
Who moons her blue notes from her nest
Down to the curlew herd!
Ho, hullaballoing clan
Agape, with woe
In your beaks, on the gabbing capes!
Heigh, on horseback hill, jack
Whisking hare! who
Hears, there, this fox light, my flood ship's
Clangour as I hew and smite
(A clash of anvils for my
Hubbub and fiddle, this tune
On a tongued puffball)
But animals thick as thieves
On God's rough tumbling grounds
(Hail to His beasthood!).
Beasts who sleep good and thin,
Hist, in hogsback woods! The haystacked
Hollow farms in a throng
Of waters cluck and cling,
And barnroofs cockcrow war!
O kingdom of neighbours, finned
Felled and quilled, flash to my patch
Work ark and the moonshine
Drinking Noah of the bay,
With pelt, and scale, and fleece:
Only the drowned deep bells
Of sheep and churches noise
Poor peace as the sun sets
And dark shoals every holy field.
We will ride out alone, and then,
Under the stars of Wales,
Cry, Multitudes of arks! Across
The water lidded lands,
Manned with their loves they'll move,
Like wooden islands, hill to hill.

Huloo, my prowed dove with a flute!
Ahoy, old, sea-legged fox,
Tom tit and Dai mouse!
My ark sings in the sun
At God speeded summer's end
And the flood flowers now.

—*Dylan Thomas*

28 ascending. *splay:* clumsy. 47 descending. *dingle:* a small, wooded valley. 40 descending. *curlew:* a brownish, long-legged shore bird.

Notice the proliferation of imagery, assonance, alliteration, and music in this poem. It is a collage of sound and pictures, and the structure of the poem is more a device to carry images and sounds than a statement of purpose. Then again, the purpose of the prologue is not to make a statement, but to suggest, by offering a representative sampling, what is to come. In this respect, Thomas's prologue is more like a musical overture than anything else.

Dedication for a Plot of Ground

This plot of ground
facing the waters of this inlet
is dedicated to the living presence of
Emily Dickinson Wellcome
who was born in England, married,
lost her husband and with
her five-year-old son
sailed for New York in a two-master,
was driven to the Azores;
ran adrift on Fire Island shoal,
met her second husband
in a Brooklyn boarding house,
went with him to Puerto Rico
bore three more children, lost
her second husband, lived hard
for eight years in St. Thomas,
Puerto Rico, San Domingo, followed
the oldest son to New York,
lost her daughter, lost her "baby",
sized the two boys of
the oldest son by the second marriage
mothered them—they being

motherless—fought for them
against the other grandmother
and the aunts, brought them here
summer after summer, defended
herself here against thieves,
storms, sun, fire,
against flies, against girls
that came smelling about, against
drought, against weeds, storm-tides,
neighbors, weasels that stole her chickens,
against the weakness of her own hands,
against the growing strength of
the boys, against wind, against
the stones, against trespassers,
against rents, against her own mind.

She grubbed this earth with her own hands,
domineered over this grass plot,
blackguarded her oldest son
into buying it, lived here fifteen years,
attained a final loneliness and—

If you can bring nothing to this place
but your carcass, keep out.

—*William Carlos Williams*

How would you describe the tone of this poem? What details of Williams's description help create that tone? What specific words does he use that contribute to it? How does the voice he uses in reading the poem help to control our attitude toward Mrs. Wellcome?

What is the effect of the word "carcass" in the poem's last line?

8. A Voice: Tempo

Another musical term critics of poetry might profitably borrow is tempo: the relative speed at which a composition is played. In music tempo may be indicated broadly by such words as "andante" (slow, but not as slow as "adagio"), or "allegro" (fast, faster than "allegretto," but slower than "presto"), or tempo may be indicated very precisely with a metronome setting. Hymns often come with directions for tempo: "broadly, with grandeur," or "not too slow," or "brightly." But Vachel Lindsay is almost unique among poets in giving tempo instructions to readers of some of his poems: "To be sung or read with great speed"; "In an even, deliberate, narrative manner"; "Louder and louder, faster and faster"; "To be brawled in the beginning with a snapping explosiveness, ending in a langorous chant."

Indicated or not, tempo is an important part of the sound of a poem, of the voice of the poet when he reads. Usually poets control tempo without explicit directions by using words which—because of vowel and consonant sequences—can be spoken very quickly or must be spoken rather slowly. Tempo can also be controlled by appropriate assonances and alliterations, and by patterns of accentual meter. Even punctuation is useful. For example, these lines from Lindsay's poem "Bryan, Bryan, Bryan, Bryan" are slow lines:

The State House loomed afar,
A speck, a hive, a football,
A captive balloon!

The *reasons* these lines are slow are several and complicated. One is the vowel sequence of the first line, the "ou" of "house," the "oo" of "loomed," the second "a" of "afar": these vowels all take plenty of time to pronounce, as do the "a" of "football" and "captive" and the "oo" of "balloon." The consonants of some words also slow the lines down, especially the "m" of "loomed" and the "n" of "balloon." It takes time for the tongue to untwist from the final "t" of "State" and get swallowed for the "h" of "House." The final "d" on "loomed" takes time to get to, especially after the "m." The commas after "speck," "hive," and "football" slow down line two. The accentual pattern of line one, with its three accents in a row ("State House loomed") slows the sequence. And so forth.

By contrast, these lines, also from "Bryan, Bryan, Bryan, Bryan," move rather quickly:

Defeat of alfalfa and the Mariposa lily.
Defeat of the Pacific and the long Mississippi.
Defeat of the young by the old and silly.

Much of the speed comes from a change in meter: while the three lines quoted earlier were predominately iambic, these three lines are predominately anapestic, and they gallop. The earlier three contained extra accents; these contain extra short syllables. No commas break these lines. And notice how easily your mouth and tongue glide from "d" to "e" in "defeat," from "e" to "f" to "ea" to "t" to "a" to "l" to "f" to "a" to "l" to "f" to "a" to "nd." Moves right along.

More recently, poets have begun to control the tempo of their poems by typographical tricks. Cummings, in "Buffalo Bill's defunct," prints "onetwothreefourfive" and "pigeonsjustlikethat" to indicate a faster tempo. Conversely, Robert Creeley sometimes breaks words in half at the end of a line to slow things down. (And when he reads his poems, he reads those breaks, much to the vexation of an unaccustomed ear.)

What is more interesting than indicating or even controlling tempo is, of course, the appropriateness of tempo to the meaning of a poem. Here poets have been particularly unimaginative, for in almost every case they choose a tempo that reinforces the words' meaning. Willing to work with ironies and ambiguities everywhere else, poets have been generally reluctant to confuse meaning by an ironic tempo. Sound follows sense. Thus the pause after "cease" in Matthew Arnold's line "Begin, and cease, and then again begin." Thus the pause immediately before "and struck" in Housman's poem "Eight O'Clock." Thus a slowing of tempo at the close of Don L. Lee's "But He Was Cool," to emphasize the transition from cool to hot. Note, however, that in overlaying tempo on existing patterns of rhythm and meter, assonance, alliteration, rhyme, and pitch, poets can add one more element to the complex voice of their poems.

Eight O'Clock

He stood, and heard the steeple
  Sprinkle the quarters on the morning town.
One, two, three, four, to market-place and people
  It tossed them down.

Strapped, noosed, nighing his hour,
  He stood and counted them and cursed his luck;
And then the clock collected in the tower
  Its strength, and struck.

—A. E. Housman

1. What situation is described in the poem? From whose point of view?

2. Why the focus on the clock? Is it appropriate that the clock should almost take over the poem?

3. Housman's meter and rhythm are very complicated in this poem. Can you find any metrical pattern at all in the poem? Where is it most regular? Why? What rhythmic pulses does Housman lay on top of his basic meter? Why the heavy pulse of accents in lines three and five? Why does the rhythm of line 7 extend without pause into line 8? Why the slowing of tempo immediately before "and struck"?

Strawberry Fields

Let me take you down 'cause I'm going to
strawberry fields.
Nothing is real,
and nothing to get hung about.
Strawberry fields forever.

Living is easy with eyes closed,
misunderstanding all you see.
It's getting hard to be someone but it all works out.
It doesn't matter much to me.

Let me take you down 'cause I'm going to
strawberry fields.
Nothing is real,
and nothing to get hung up on.
Strawberry fields forever.

No one I think is in my tree—
I mean it must be high or low.
That is, you know you can't tune it but it's all right,
that is, I think it's not too bad.

Let me take you down 'cause I'm going to
strawberry fields.
Nothing is real,
and nothing to get hung up on.
Strawberry fields forever.

Always know, sometimes think it's me,
but you know I know and it's a dream.
I think I know of thee, ah, yes, but it's all wrong,
that is, I think I disagree.

Let me take you down 'cause I'm going to
strawberry fields.
Nothing is real,
and nothing to get hung up on.
Strawberry fields forever.

—John Lennon–Paul McCartney

Examine the lyrics and listen to a recording of this song, paying special attention to its tempo. How would you describe that tempo? Is there any particular reason why you think it especially appropriate (or inappropriate) to the lyrics?

But He Was Cool

or: he even stopped for green lights

super-cool
ultrablack
a tan/purple
had a beautiful shade.
he had a double-natural
that wd put the sisters to shame.
his dashikis were tailor made
& his beads were imported sea shells
  (from some blk/country i ever heard of)
he was triple-hip.

his tikis were hand carved
out of ivory
& came express from the motherland.
he would greet u in swahili
& say good-by in yoruba.
woooooooooooo-jim he bes so cool & ill tel li gent
        cool-cool is so cool he was un-cooled by
            other niggers' cool
        cool-cool ultracool was bop-cool/ice box
            cool as cool cold cool
        his wine didn't have to be cooled, him was
            air conditioned cool
        cool-cool/real cool made me cool—now
            ain't that cool
        cool-cool so cool him nick-named refrigerator.

cool-cool so cool
he didn't know,
after detroit, newark, chicago &c.,
we had to hip
    cool-cool/ super-cool/ real cool
  that
to be black
is
to be
very-hot

—*Don L. Lee*

Using a pen or pencil to mark arcs of phrasing, divide this poem into phrases. Notice how Lee's phrases grow and his tempo picks up speed as the poem progresses. Why does the poet do this? What specific devices does the poet use to increase or decrease his tempo?

This poem was written at the height of the 1960s; how valid is its statement today?

Lines: When the Lamp Is Shattered

I

When the lamp is shattered
The light in the dust lies dead—
When the cloud is scattered
The rainbow's glory is shed.
When the lute is broken,
Sweet tones are remembered not;
When the lips have spoken,
Loved accents are soon forgot.

II

As music and splendour
Survive not the lamp and the lute,
The heart's echoes render
No song when the spirit is mute:—
No song but sad dirges,
Like the wind through a ruined cell,
Or the mournful surges
That ring the dead seaman's kneel.

III

When hearts have once mingled
Love first leaves the well-built nest;
The weak one is singled
To endure what it once possessed.
O Love! who bewailest
The frailty of all things here,
Why choose you the frailest
For your cradle, your home, and your bier?

IV

Its passions will rock thee
As the storms rock the ravens on high;
Bright reason will mock thee,

Like the sun from a wintry sky.
  From thy nest every rafter
Will rot, and thine eagle home
  Leave thee naked to laughter,
When leaves fall and cold winds come.

—Percy Bysshe Shelley

Read through this poem casually, marking with pluses and minuses those passages which you think read quickly or slowly. Then reread it more carefully to verify your initial impressions. Look at those lines you found slow: what slows them down? *Why* might Shelley wish to slow his tempo here? Ask yourself the same questions for those passages you marked with a plus.

What metaphors does Shelley use in this poem? What statement about love and the death of love do they make? How fresh are his metaphors? How appropriate to his statement?

Bryan, Bryan, Bryan, Bryan

I

There are plenty of sweeping, swinging, stinging, gorgeous
  things to shout about,
And knock your old blue devils out.

I brag and chant of Bryan, Bryan, Bryan,
Candidate for president who sketched a silver Zion,
The one American Poet who could sing outdoors,
He brought in tides of wonder, of unprecedented splendor,
Wild roses from the plains, that made hearts tender,
All the funny circus silks
Of politics unfurled,
Bartlett pears of romance that were honey at the cores,
And torchlights down the street, to the end of the world.

There were truths eternal in the gab and tittle-tattle.
There were real heads broken in the fustian and the rattle.
There were real lines drawn:
Not the silver and the gold,
But Nebraska's cry went eastward against the dour and old,
The mean and cold.

It was eighteen ninety-six, and I was just sixteen
And Altgeld ruled in Springfield, Illinois,

When there came from the sunset Nebraska's shout of joy:
In a coat like a deacon, in a black Stetson hat
He scourged the elephant plutocrats
With barbed wire from the Platte.
The scales dropped from their mighty eyes.
They saw that summer's noon
The tribe of wonders coming
To a marching tune.

Oh, the longhorns from Texas,
The jay hawks from Kansas,
The plop-eyed bungaroo and giant giassicus,
The varmint, chipmunk, bugaboo,
The horned-toad, prairie-dog and ballyhoo,
From all the newborn states arow,
Bidding the eagles of the west fly on,
Bidding the eagles of the west fly on.
The fawn, prodactyl and thing-a-ma-jig,
The rakaboor, the hellangone,
The whangdoodle, batfowl and pig,
The coyote, wild-cat and grizzly in a glow,
In a miracle and health and speed, the whole breed abreast,
They leaped the Mississippi, blue border of the West,
From the Gulf to Canada, two thousand miles long:—
Against the towns of Tubal Cain,
Ah,—sharp was their song.
Against the ways of Tubal Cain, too cunning for the young,
The longhorn calf, the buffalo and wampus gave tongue.

These creatures were defending things Mark Hanna never dreamed:
The moods of airy childhood that in desert dews gleamed,
The gossamers and whimsies,
The monkeyshines and didoes
Rank and strange
Of the canyons and the range,
The ultimate fantastics
Of the far western slope,
And of prairie schooner children
Born beneath the stars,
Beneath falling snows,
Of the babies born at midnight
In the sod huts of lost hope,
With no physician there,

Except a Kansas prayer,
With the Indian raid a-howling through the air.

And all these in their helpless days
By the dour East oppressed,
Mean paternalism
Making their mistakes for them,
Crucifying half the West,
Till the whole Atlantic coast
Seemed a giant spiders' nest.

And these children and their sons
At last rode through the cactus,
A cliff of mighty cowboys
On the lope,
With gun and rope.
And all the way to frightened Maine the old East heard them call,
And saw our Bryan by a mile lead the wall
Of men and whirling flowers and beasts,
The bard and the prophet of them all.
Prairie avenger, mountain lion,
Bryan, Bryan, Bryan, Bryan,
Gigantic troubadour, speaking like a siege gun,
Smashing Plymouth Rock with his boulders from the West,
And just a hundred miles behind, tornadoes piled across the sky,
Blotting out sun and moon,
A sign on high.

Headlong, dazed and blinking in the weird green light,
The scalawags made moan,
Afraid to fight.

II

When Bryan came to Springfield, and Altgeld gave him greeting,
Rochester was deserted, Divernon was deserted,
Mechanicsburg, Riverton, Chickenbristle, Cotton Hill,
Empty: for all Sangamon drove to the meeting—
In silver-decked racing cart,
Buggy, buckboard, carryall,
Carriage, phaeton, whatever would haul,
And silver-decked farm-wagons gritted, banged and rolled,
With the new tale of Bryan by the iron tires told.

The State House loomed afar,
A speck, a hive, a football,
A captive balloon!
And the town was all one spreading wing of bunting, plumes, and sunshine,
Every rag and flag, and Bryan picture sold,
With the rigs in many a dusty line
Jammed our streets at noon,
And joined the wild parade against the power of gold.

We roamed, we boys from High School,
With mankind,
While Springfield gleamed,
Silk-lined.
Oh, Tom Dines, and Art Fitzgerald,
And the gangs that they could get!
I can hear them yelling yet.
Helping the incantation,
Defying aristocracy,
With every bridle gone,
Ridding the world of the low down mean,
Bidding the eagles of the West fly on,
Bidding the eagles of the West fly on,
We were bully, wild and woolly,
Never yet curried below the knees.
We saw flowers in the air,
Fair as the Pleiades, bright as Orion,
—Hopes of all mankind,
Made rare, resistless, thrice refined.
Oh, we bucks from every Springfield ward!
Colts of democracy—
Yet time-winds out of Chaos from the star-fields of the Lord.

The long parade rolled on. I stood by my best girl.
She was a cool young citizen, with wise and laughing eyes.
With my necktie by my ear, I was stepping on my dear,
But she kept like a pattern, without a shaken curl.

She wore in her hair a brave prairie rose.
Her gold chums cut her, for that was not the pose.
No Gibson Girl would wear it in that fresh way.
But we were fairy Democrats, and this was our day.

The earth rocked like the ocean, the sidewalk was a deck.
The houses for the moment were lost in the wide wreck.

And the bands played strange and stranger music as they trailed along.
Against the ways of Tubal Cain,
Ah, sharp was their song!
The demons in the bricks, the demons in the grass,
The demons in the bank-vaults peered out to see us pass,
And the angels in the trees, the angels in the grass,
The angels in the flags, peered out to see us pass.
And the sidewalk was our chariot, and the flowers bloomed higher,
And the street turned to silver and the grass turned to fire,
And then it was but grass, and the town was there again,
A place for women and men.

III

Then we stood where we could see
Every band,
And the speaker's stand.
And Bryan took the platform.
And he was introduced.
And he lifted his hand
And cast a new spell.
Progressive silence fell
In Springfield,
In Illinois,
Around the world.
Then we heard these glacial boulders across the prairie rolled:
"The people have a right to make their own mistakes. . . .
You shall not crucify mankind
Upon a cross of gold."

And everybody heard him—
In the streets and State House yard.
And everybody heard him
In Springfield,
In Illinois,
Around and around and around the world,
That danced upon its axis
And like a darling bronco whirled.

IV

July, August, suspense.
Wall Street lost to sense.

August, September, October,
More suspense,
And the whole East down like a wind-smashed fence.

Then Hanna to the rescue,
Hanna of Ohio,
Rallying the roller-tops,
Rallying the bucket-shops.
Threatening drouth and death,
Promising manna,
Rallying the trusts against the bawling flannelmouth;
Invading misers' cellars,
Tin-cans, socks,
Melting down the rocks,
Pouring out the long green to a million workers,
Spondulix by the mountain-load, to stop each new tornado,
And beat the cheapskate, blatherskite,
Populistic, anarchistic,
Deacon—desperado.

V

Election night at midnight:
Boy Bryan's defeat.
Defeat of western silver.
Defeat of the wheat.
Victory of letterfiles
And plutocrats in miles
With dollar signs upon their coats,
Diamond watchchains on their vests
And spats on their feet.
Victory of custodians,
Plymouth Rock,
And all that inbred landlord stock.
Victory of the neat.
Defeat of the aspen groves of Colorado valleys,
The blue bells of the Rockies,
And blue bonnets of old Texas,
By the Pittsburg alleys.
Defeat the alfalfa and the Mariposa lily.
Defeat of the Pacific and the long Mississippi.
Defeat of the young by the old and silly.
Defeat of tornadoes by the poison vats supreme.
Defeat of my boyhood, defeat of my dream.

VI

Where is McKinley, that respectable McKinley,
The man without an angle or a tangle,
Who soothed down the city man and soothed down the
  farmer,
The German, the Irish, the Southerner, the Northerner,
Who climbed every greasy pole, and slipped through every
  crack;
Who soothed down the gambling hall, the bar-room, the
  church,
The devil vote, the angel vote, the neutral vote,
The desperately wicked, and the victims on the rack,
The gold vote, the silver vote, the brass vote, the lead vote,
Every vote? . . .

Where is McKinley, Mark Hanna's McKinley,
His slave, his echo, his suit of clothes?
Gone to join the shadows, with the pomps of that time,
And the flame of that summer's prairie rose.

Where is Cleveland whom the Democratic platform
Read from the party in a glorious hour,
Gone to join the shadows with pitchfork Tillman,
And sledge-hammer Altgeld who wrecked his power.

Where is Hanna, bulldog Hanna.
Low-browed Hanna, who said: "Stand pat"?
Gone to his place with old Pierpont Morgan.
Gone somewhere . . . with lean rat Platt.

Where is Roosevelt, the young dude cowboy,
Who hated Bryan, then aped his way?
Gone to join the shadows with mighty Cromwell
And tall King Saul, till the Judgment day.

Where is Altgeld, brave as the truth,
Whose name the few still say with tears?
Gone to join the ironies with Old John Brown,
Whose fame rings loud for a thousand years.

Where is that boy, that Heaven-born Bryan,
That Homer Bryan, who sang from the West?
Gone to join the shadows with Altgeld the Eagle,
Where the kings and the slaves and the troubadours rest.

—*Vachel Lindsay*

3. *Bryan:* William Jennings Bryan, presidential candidate in 1896, 1900, and 1908. 4. *silver Zion:* Bryon was a free-silver man; that is, he advocated the unrestricted coinage of silver, especially at a fixed relationship to gold. Free silver was supported by the west; the gold standard was supported by east coast bankers and politicians, who considered free silver inflationary. 19. *Altgeld:* Democratic reformist governor of Illinois, 1892–96, champion of free silver, Bryan, labor, and farmers. 47. *Mark Hanna:* American industrialist, robber baron, and financier of Republican politicians and Republican causes. 87. *scalawags:* rascals. 95. *phaeton:* a light, open, four-wheeled carriage. 134. *Gibson Girl:* east coast illustrator Charles Dana Gibson made his "Gibson Girl" a standard for American women from 1890–1910. She was beautiful, athletic, stylish . . . and eastern. 163. *"cross of gold":* from Bryan's famous "Cross of Gold" speech, made at the Democratic National Convention in 1896, a major landmark in the free-silver cause. 224. *McKinley:* William McKinley, twenty-fifth president of the United States, Mark Hanna-financed from early in his career, a conservative Republican who defeated Bryan in the elections of 1896 and 1900. 228. *Cleveland:* Grover Cleveland, twenty-second and twenty-fourth president of the United States, 1885–89, 1893–97, a reform president. 230. *Tillman:* Southern politician who once threatened to "stick my pitchfork" through President Cleveland's ribs. 234. *Morgan:* mightiest banker on Wall Street; died in 1913. 235. *Platt:* conservative and perhaps corrupt Republican politician from New York (1833–1910). 236. *Roosevelt:* Theodore Roosevelt, twenty-sixth president of the United States (1901–09). 238. *Cromwell:* Oliver Cromwell (1599–1658), British military, religious, and political leader, between 1653–58 "Lord Protector of the Commonwealth." 242. *John Brown:* American abolitionist (1800–1859).

What roles is poet Vachel Lindsay playing in this poem? What does he expect his poem to do? What images does he use? What devices of voice does he use? How would you describe the tone of this long poem? Where does the tempo of the poem speed up? Where slow down? What causes shifts in the tempo? Why does Lindsay change his tempo (apart from the obvious reason that it adds variety)?

4 A Poem Is a Structure

Most poems, especially those written before the twentieth century, exhibit a clear architecture, some patterning of rhymes, accented syllables, or alliterations into lines and stanzas, some recognizable structure. Even in the twentieth century, with the breakdown of traditional meters and forms, most poetry exhibits some structure, although its design (like that of a modern home) may be relatively free-form.

The origins of structure in poetry are, as you might expect, a matter of speculation. Perhaps they stem from mankind's instinctive impulse to create pattern and order—in his buildings, in his drawings, in his life, in his poems. As we have already seen, the poet is in one sense an artificer, like all other artists.

Or perhaps the structure of poetry reflects, consciously or unconsciously, a natural order of the world and human society, just as the regular pulse of poetry may reflect a rhythm buried in nature. Earlier societies, after all, were much more structured than ours—or, rather, their structures seemed more fixed, more permanent.

Without discounting either of those possibilities, it seems more likely that structure in poetry came directly from two different conditions. First, poetry was early associated with music. For all the lyricist's freedom to substitute, say, two eighth notes (and thus two syllables of word) for one quarter (one syllable), it is a general rule of thumb that lines sung to the same tune will, when put on a printed page, look largely alike: they will have similar rhythmic patterns and generally similar lengths. And when the tune changes, the structure and shape of the line is likely to change as well. For example, the capital letters in the following stanza from Bob Dylan's "Restless Farewell" indicate tunes, not rhymes. Note that lines with similar melodies have similar lengths and rhythmic patterns, and even rhyming words at the end:

A Oh all the money that in my whole life I did spend, be it mine right or wrongfully,
A I let it slip gladly past the hands of my friends to tie up the time most forcefully.
B But the bottles are done,
B We've killed each one
C And the table's full and overflowed.
D And the corner sign
D Says it's closing time,
E So I'll bid farewell and be down the road

Every poetry was, as we have noted, sung or accompanied by musical instruments or dance—and the patterns of the music and dance undoubtedly imposed themselves on the poems (or, rather, the patterns of the song and the poem were one).

A second condition giving rise to structure in poetry is the oral nature of primitive culture. Without books, typewriters, or crib sheets, poets had to memorize their material or lose it entirely. And nice little structures of rhyme and meter and alliteration were much easier to remember than unpatterned prose. Even today we turn to "Thirty days hath September" or "*i* before *e*, except after *c*" when we want to find out how many days in August, or how to spell "neither." Even the bardic poets, who apparently recomposed *Beowulf* or the *Iliad* each time they sang them, wrote their epics not from scratch, but from a great vocabulary of alliterative phrases, which they had memorized, and which they pieced together into a poem, as a builder of modular homes pieces together structures built back in the factory.

Whatever—structure as an artifice, as a mnemonic device, as a reflection of music and dance—most poetry before the twentieth century has structure of an easily recognized nature. That nature can vary, however. It may be a simple pattern of accented syllables. It may be a more precise pattern of accented *and* unaccented syllables, built with the help of rhyme into stanzas. It may be a stanza-and-refrain structure. It may amount simply to lines of similar length or a prescribed number of syllables. It may be a loose pattern of repeated rhythms or phrases. It may be a design, in words, on the page. In the twentieth century, as our social and political structure—as our entire civilization—seems to crumble around us, and order seems to dissolve on every side, poetry may be nonstructured or a very free-form design made either with the sound of a poem's words or the arrangement of words and letters on the page. Some modern lyric poets have even joined dramatic poets and epic poets in discarding pattern entirely and writing what they candidly call "prose poetry."

Structure, whether rigid or loose, always poses one critical question to both poet and critic, and that is the old chicken-or-the-egg problem: which comes first, a poem's content or its shape? Ideally, of course, form and content are one. Both work to the same goal, and each is in harmony with the other. Anyone who has written poetry, however, knows that the poem does not usually begin as a harmony of form and structure—most often it begins with one or the other and works from there. And along the way accommodations must inevitably be made, either form to content, or content to form. If the poet, for example, has opted for a form which demands a line end in an iambic foot rhyming with "trout," and he has found a perfectly natural, exact expression of the idea he wants to communicate that ends with the word "snowing," then he's got a problem. Either he must fiddle around with his words (and probably his meaning, since no two words ever mean exactly the same thing) until the meter and rhyme are straightened out, or he can stick with "snowing" and let form be damned. And at the beginning of any poem, the poet faces an even more fundamental choice: should the poem begin with form or idea? Should the poet say (to take a relatively demanding form), "Okay, look, I want to write a sonnet. A sonnet has fourteen lines of iambic pentameter, rhymed a b a b c d c d e f e f g g. It breaks into three four-line units of thought, and has a two-line summary at the end. It looks like this:

U / U / U / U / U / a
U / U / U / U / U / b
U / U / U / U / U / a
U / U / U / U / U /. b
U / U / U / U / U / c
U / U / U / U / U / d
U / U / U / U / U / c
U / U / U / U / U /. d
U / U / U / U / U / e
U / U / U / U / U / f
U / U / U / U / U / e
U / U / U / U / U /. f
U / U / U / U / U / g
U / U / U / U / U /. g

Now how am I going to fill up all those U's and /'s, and how am I going to find a nice four-line block of idea, and what rhymes can I use for the *a, b, c, d, e, f,* and *g* rhymes?" Or does the poet say, "Okay, look, I want to write a love poem to my boyfriend, and I want to compare him to a snow flurry (because he's so cool and gentle). Now what sort of form would go along with that idea?" Or does the poet write her images and metaphors, her thoughts and patterns of sound, worry about the thing of the poem, voice, and statement, letting the structure of the poem emerge as it will? Increasingly poets are unwilling to compromise elements of matter, voice, or statement to structure. Structure, they argue, is organic—it grows naturally out of content. Try to find the perfectly symmetrical leaf or flower—it's a freak. The perfectly symmetrical poem is a freak too, and often it's not worth the distortion of the rest of the poem. Perhaps such poets are merely less competent than their predecessors. Perhaps they have a point: poetry of the eighteenth and seventeenth centuries, which almost invariably began in form and stuck close to the form it began with, does distort sense and narrow the range of its voice considerably. Perhaps they are merely breaking out of one structure and into others, for language is as much a prison as poetic form. In any case, today free verse and "organic form" predominate, and structure is not one of a poem's major elements.

1. A Structure: Stanza

The most commonly used method of imposing structure on a short lyric poem is to pattern the accented and unaccented syllables into iambic, or dactylic, or trochaic, or anapestic feet, and pattern the feet into lines of similar length, and mark the end of lines with a rhyme, and create thereby a stanza. This stanza is repeated, without variation, to the end of the poem. A poet might, for example, settle on four lines of iambic tetrameter, rhyming "sing," "go," "spring," "slow." Designating the accented syllables with a / and the unaccented syllables with a U, and making the first rhyme *a* and the second rhyme *b,* the stanzaic pattern would look like this in the abstract:

U / U / U / U / a
U / U / U / U / b
U / U / U / U / a
U / U / U / U / b

Fleshed out with words, such an abstract pattern might produce, for example, this stanza by William Morris:

But I shall die unless you stand,
—Half lying now, you are so weak,—
Within my arms, unless your hand
Pass to and fro across my cheek.

Four-line stanzas, called *quatrains,* are quite common in English. They aren't difficult to write, and they can be varied to suit a poet's purposes and whims. The rhyme scheme, for example, might run *a b b a* instead of *a b a b,* or perhaps *a a b b.* The meter might be iambic trimeter, or iambic pentameter, or anapestic trimeter, or whatever. Perhaps a poet would like to do three lines of iambic tetrameter, followed by a fourth of iambic dimeter:

Sweet day, so cool, so calm, so bright,	U / U / U / U /	a
The bridal of the earth and sky:	U / U / U / U /	b
The dew shall weep thy fall tonight;	U / U / U / U /	a
For thou must die.	U / U /	b

A poet might shorten the second and fourth lines by one foot, making alternate lines of iambic tetrameter and iambic trimeter, and rhyme only the second and the fourth line. This form of the quatrain is very common in poetry, and is called the ballad stanza (because, in case you couldn't guess, most sung ballads take this form):

There lived a wife at Usher's Well,	U / U / U / U /	x
And a wealthy wife was she;	U / U / U /	a
She had three stout and stalwart sons,	U / U / U / U /	x
And sent them o'er the sea.	U / U / U /	a

Further variations on the quatrain are possible. A poet might want to use the same line to close each stanza, or a variation on a theme, thereby allowing that line to grow in meaning and importance as the poem unfolds. George Herbert's poem "Virtue," the first stanza of which we looked at earlier, is such a poem. It contains four stanzas, the first three ending in variations of "thou must die," the final stanza (which contrasts the immortal soul to a day, a rose, and spring) reversing the thought to "Then chiefly lives":

Virtue

Sweet day, so cool so calm, so bright,
  The bridal of the earth and sky;
The dew shall weep thy fall tonight;
  For thou might die.

Sweet rose, whose hue, angry and brave
  Bids the rash gazer wipe his eye:
Thy root is ever in its grave,
  And thou must die.

Sweet spring, full of sweet days and roses,
A box where sweets compacted lie;
My music shows ye have your closes,
And all must die.

Only a sweet and virtuous soul,
Like seasoned timber, never gives;
But though the whole world turn to coal,
Then chiefly lives.

—*George Herbert*

2. *bridal:* marriage. 5. *brave:* splendid. 10. *sweets:* perfumes. 15. *coal:* ashes.

Sometimes a poet, or singer, likes to repeat the fourth line of the quatrain, making a five-line stanza:

Joe Hill came over from Sweden's shore,
Looking for some work to do,
And the Statue of Liberty waved him by
As Joe come asailing through, Joe Hill,
As Joe came asailing through.

—Phil Ochs, *Joe Hill*

Finally, the quatrain—or any other stanzaic pattern for that matter—may be followed by a refrain, or chorus, which may have the same or a different form (some choruses are only a single line long) and is sung or read after each stanza. Refrains are more common in songs than in written poetry.

The quatrain is not, of course, the only possible stanzaic structure. Rhyme royal, a verse form introduced into English by Geoffrey Chaucer and so named because King James I of Scotland used it in his poem, *The Kinges Quair,* consists of seven lines of iambic pentameter rhymed ababbcc. Here is one stanza of Chaucer's *Parliament of Fowls,* written in rhyme royal:

For out of olde feeldes, as men saith,
Cometh al this newe corn from yer to yere,
And out of olde books, in good feith,
Cometh al this newe science that men lere.
But now to purpos as of this matere:
To rede forth so gan me to delite
That al that day me thoughte but a lite.

2. *corn:* grain. 4. *science:* learning, knowledge. 6. "I began so to delight in reading." 7. *lite:* little.

Abstracted, the form looks like this:

U / U / U / U / U / a
U / U / U / U / U / b
U / U / U / U / U / a
U / U / U / U / U / b
U / U / U / U / U / b
U / U / U / U / U / c
U / U / U / U / U / c

Spenserean stanza has also been popular with English and American poets, although it is relatively difficult to write, because it requires nine lines per stanza and allows only three rhyming sounds:

So th'one for wrong, the other strives for right,
And each to deadly shame would drive his foe:
The cruel steel so greedily doth bite
In tender flesh, that streams of blood down flow,
With which the arms, that erst so bright did show,
Into a pure vermillion now are dyed:
Great ruth in all the gazers' hearts did grow,
Seeing the gored wounds to gape so wide,
That victory they dare not wish for either side.

—*Edmund Spenser,* The Faerie Queene

5. *erst:* at first, once. 7. *ruth:* sorrow.

Abstracted, Spenserean stanza looks like this:

U / U / U / U / U / a
U / U / U / U / U / b
U / U / U / U / U / a
U / U / U / U / U / b
U / U / U / U / U / b
U / U / U / U / U / c
U / U / U / U / U / b
U / U / U / U / U / c
U / U / U / U / U / U / c

Note, incidentally, that the first eight lines of this stanza are iambic pentameter, while the last line is iambic hexameter.

Another stanzaic pattern that has been popular with English poets is *terza rima,* a three-line form borrowed from the Italian poets. While its meter is up to the poet, usually poets prefer iambic pentameter. The interesting feature of *terza rima* is its interlocking rhymes: the second line rhyme of one stanza becomes the first and third line rhyme of the next, and so on: *a b a, b c b, c d c, d e d,* etc. Shelley used *terza rima* in "Ode to the West Wind," printed in full in Chapter 1, Section 10.

O wild West Wind, thou breath of Autumn's being,
Thou, from whose unseen presence the leaves dead
Are driven, like ghosts from an enchanter fleeing,

Yellow, and black, and pale, and hectic red,
Pestilence-stricken multitudes: O thou
Who chariotest to their dark wintry bed

The winged seeds, where they lie cold and low
Each like a corpse within its grave, until
Thine azure sister of the Spring shall blow . . .

Terza rima has been used, sometimes with minor variation, by Milton, Byron, MacLeish, Auden, and Eliot as well as Shelley.

Of course the poet is always free to make up his own stanzaic pattern, which can be as simple or as complicated as he wants. In "To a Skylark," Shelley used a stanza of four lines of iambic trimeter followed by one line of iambic hexameter, rhymed *a b a b b:*

Like a Poet hidden
  In the light of thought,
Singing hymns unbidden,
  Till the world is wrought
To sympathy with hopes and fears it heeded not.

Shakespeare used a very complicated stanzaic pattern for "Under the Greenwood Tree," a poem sung in his play *As You Like It.*

It is usually understood that once a poet has settled on a stanzaic pattern, each stanza will follow whatever he has chosen. However, this is not always the case. Wordsworth used a varying stanzaic pattern in his famous "Ode: Intimations of Immortality," so that each stanza seems almost a fresh invention. Other poets have seen fit to change their stanzaic pattern in mid-poem, when the purpose suited them. In the final section of "Bryan, Bryan, Bryan, Bryan," for example, Lindsay slipped from the loose, rambling free form he had used in the rest of his poem into more stately, more elegaic, more commemorative quatrains, a trick also used by W. H. Auden in his poem "In Memory of W. B. Yeats."

I Pity the Poor Immigrant

I pity the poor immigrant
Who wishes he would've stayed home,
Who uses all his power to do evil
And in the end is always left alone.
That man who with his fingers cheats
And who lies with ev'ry breath,
Who passionately hates his life
And likewise fears his death.

I pity the poor immigrant
Whose strength is all in vain
Whose heaven is like Ironsides,
Whose tears are like rain;
Who eats but is not satisfied,
Who hears but does not see,
Who falls in love with wealth itself,
And turns his back on me.

I pity the poor immigrant
Who tramples through the mud,
Who fills his mouth with laughing
And who builds his town with blood;
Whose visions in their final end
Must shatter like the glass,
I pity the poor immigrant
When his gladness comes to pass.

—*Bob Dylan*

1. Identify Dylan's stanzaic pattern by reducing it to a set of U's, /'s and letters, signifying unaccented syllables, accented syllables, and rhymes. Dylan has used three stanzas, but each stanza can be divided into four- and even two-line units. Would you say this structure is fluid or fixed, kinetic or static, open or closed?

2. What kind of person is the immigrant? What do you make of the line "who builds his town with blood"? Or "whose heaven is like Ironsides"? These are metaphors, of course, and need careful interpretation. Why does the immigrant wish he had stayed home?

3. We must assume that the immigrant is attached to his hopes and dreams, his "visions," as Dylan calls them in line 20, no matter how corrupt and corrupting they may be. Why, then, should the destruction of those visions be "gladness" (line 24)? And if the shattering of illusions is beneficial, why should Dylan pity the immigrant?

4. How much of yourself, of modern America, do you see in this song?

Lord Randall

"O where hae ye been, Lord Randall, my son?
O where hae ye been, my handsome young man?"
"I hae been in the wildwood; mother, make my bed soon,
For I'm weary wi' hunting, and fain wald lie down."

"What gat ye to your dinner, Lord Randall, my son?
What gat ye to your dinner, my handsome young man?"
"I gat eels boiled in broo; mother, make my bed soon,
For I'm weary wi' hunting, and fain wald lie down."

"What became of your bloodhounds, Lord Randall, my son?
What became of your bloodhounds, my handsome young
man?"
"O they swell'd and they died; mother, make my bed soon,
For I'm weary wi' hunting, and fain wald lie down."

"O I fear ye are poisoned, Lord Randall, my son!
O I fear ye are poisoned, my handsome young man!"
"O yes! I am poisoned; mother make my bed soon,
For I'm sick at the heart, and I fain wald lie down."

—*anonymous*

1. *hae:* have. 4. *fain wald:* would like to.

How does the anonymous poet of "Lord Randall" adapt the ballad stanza to make his poem more effective? The poem is very sparse, especially given the repetitions used by the poet: Lord Randall, his mother, his "love." Important details are left hanging, and some of the characters seem fuzzy. What do you think about this true love: a witch or merely a bitch? Has Lord Randall actually been poisoned, or is he just bummed out because his girl has dumped on him?

Song

Go and catch a falling star,
 Get with child a mandrake root,
Tell me where all past years are,
 Or who cleft the devil's foot,

Teach me to hear mermaids singing,
Or to keep off envy's stinging,
    And find
    What wind
Serves to advance an honest mind.

If thou beest born to strange sights,
  Things invisible to see,
Ride ten thousand days and nights,
  Till age snow white hairs on thee.
Thou, when thou return'st, wilt tell me
All strange wonders that befell thee,
    And swear
    No where
Lives a woman true and fair.

If thou find'st one, let me know:
  Such a pilgrimage were sweet;
Yet do not; I would not go,
  Though at next door we might meet.
Though she were true when you met her,
And last till you write your letter,
    Yet she
    Will be
False, ere I come, to two, or three.

—*John Donne*

Reduce this poem to a pattern of U's, /'s, and letters. (Note, incidentally, that "find" and "wind" would, when Donne wrote the poem, have been a perfect rhyme). It is a very idiosyncratic form; might that be one reason Donne calls his poem "Song"? The last line is interrupted by three commas. What effect does this have on the statement Donne is making in the poem?

Under the Greenwood Tree

    Under the greenwood tree
    Who loves to lie with me,
    And turn his merry note
    Unto the sweet bird's throat,
Come hither, come hither, come hither:
    Here shall he see
    No enemy
But winter and rough weather.

Who doth ambition shun
And loves to live i'the sun,
Seeking the food he eats,
And pleased with what he gets,
Come hither, come hither, come hither:
Here shall he see
No enemy
But winter and rough weather.

—*William Shakespeare*

This song is for all practical purposes a stanza and refrain. What kinds of images are presented in the first four lines of each stanza? In the refrain lines? What contrasts does Shakespeare set up? Would you say this song has a message? What is it?

Men Marry What They Need. I Marry You

Men marry what they need. I marry you,
morning by morning, day by day, night by night,
and every marriage makes this marriage new.

In the broken name of heaven, in the light
that shatters granite, by the spitting shore,
in air that leaps and wobbles like a kite,

I marry you from time and a great door
is shut and stays shut against wind, sea, stone,
sunburst, and heavenfall. And home once more

inside our walls of skin and struts of bone,
man-woman, woman-man, and each the other,
I marry you by all dark and all dawn

and lean to let time spend. Why should I bother
the flies about me? Let them buzz and do.
Men marry their queen, their daughter, or their mother

by names they prove, but that thin buzz whines through:
when reason falls to reasons, cause is true.
Men marry what they need. I marry you.

—*John Ciardi*

What is the form of this poem? Is it particularly effective in a poem on love and marriage? Notice that Ciardi links the final stanza to the first by repeating line one as line 18. What effect does this have on the poem? The poem is a web of images and metaphors: morning, day, night, "light that shatters granite," "spitting shore," kite, door, wind, sea, stone, sunburst, and heavenfall. Then the flies. What do all these images and metaphors contribute to the poem?

2. A Structure: Generic Forms

Genre is a literary term used to describe a class or a subclass of literature. *Poetry* is a generic term, as are *prose* and *drama;* but so too are *lyric* and *epic* (kinds of poetry), *comedy* and *tragedy* (kinds of drama), and *novel, short story,* and *novella* (types of fiction). On a still finer scale, epic poetry may be divided into *folk epic, literary epic, romance,* or *chanson de geste.* Lyric poetry may be divided into *ballad, ballade, ode, sonnet, dramatic monologue, complaint,* or any one of a bundle of other types. Genre may designate, then, a kind of literature on either the broad or the narrow scale.

The idea of literary genres is an old one, a leftover from critical thought of the pre-Romantic period, rearticulated (without much effect) at the beginning of the twentieth century. It presupposes a certain number of types of literature, each with its own formal characteristics, style, and appropriate subject matter. When a poet writes, he selects a particular form and adopts the style, language, stanzaic patterns, subjects, and other conventions appropriate to that genre. A good poet is one who is proficient in all the traditional genres. And something of the tradition of a chosen genre is poured into his poem—while, conversely, his new poem develops ever so slightly the tradition of the genre. It is this reciprocity between the individual poem and the tradition that makes a working familiarity with literary genres useful to readers of poetry. This and the fact that genre structures poems.

In the loosest sense the requirements of a genre provide form simply by saying what subjects a poet should and should not write about, and what should happen with those subjects over the course of the poem. The requirement, for example, that an elegy move from sorrow to affirmation or transcedence imposes a certain order and perhaps even a selection of detail on the poem. The requirement of a sestina that all six of the key words repeated at the end of each line of each stanza appear in the closing three lines of the poem certainly imposes itself upon the poet's thoughts. The ballad's preference for stories of domestic tragedy or the supernatural, the dramatic monologue's requirement that a poet speak only in the voice of a persona—these, by circumscribing the poet's freedom to write whatever he wants however he wants, impose an order.

Other genres impose very strict requirements of meter and rhyme scheme on a poem. The sonnet, the villanelle, the limerick, the sestina, the rondeau, the couplet, the ballad—these are as much metrical forms as anything else. (Conversely, such genres as the complaint, the dream vision, the debate, the verse epistle tend to describe what's going on in the poem, without reference to metrical pattern.) They very much impose a structure upon the poem.

In examining the genres that follow, you should bear two things in mind. First, some genres (the dramatic monologue, for example, or the ballad) are discussed elsewhere in this book (Chapter 2, Section 2 and Chapter 4, Section 3 respectively), because, genre being a loose enough term, they were naturally appropriate to other discussions. Second, there exist in the history of English literature many more genres than you will find here. Several have had periods of popularity, others have been always obscure. Because the concept of genre is not popular among contemporary poets, discussion here limits itself to only the most popular, and to only those that impose structure on a poem.

Sonnet

The sonnet was imported to England from Italy during the early Renaissance, around 1500 A.D. Although unusually demanding in its rhyme scheme, it has proven by far the most popular and enduring of all English genres. The early sonnet—the *Petrarchan* or *Italian sonnet* as it is called—is a poem of fourteen lines of iambic pentameter broken into two units: an octet (consisting of eight lines) and a sestet (the remaining six). The octet always rhymes *a b b a a b b a;* the sestet may rhyme in a variety of ways: *c d c c d c, c d e c d e, c d c d c d.* The natural division falls between the octet and the sestet. Frequently, the one poses a paradox that the other resolves, or a question that is answered, or a problem that is solved. Obviously a verse form this tight, which gives a poet only four or five sounds on which to construct fourteen rhymes, is much more difficult in English, an uninflected language, than in Italian, where the inflectional endings can be used for rhymes. Less than a century after the sonnet's introduction into England, Shakespeare was busy popularizing the *English* or *Shakespearean sonnet,* which allows seven different sounds in its rhyme scheme: a series of three quatrains (four-line units) followed by a couplet, usually rhymed *a b a b c d c d e f e f g g.* The natural division of the Shakespearean sonnet is different from that of the Italian: it breaks cleanly into three major units that may be used to develop three parallel paradoxes (or pose three parallel questions) and a couplet that may then resolve, recapitulate, or answer. The major break is between line 12 and line 13, although the breaks between quatrains are usually observed, at least by some form of punctuation. On rare occasions an ambitious English poet attempts a *Spenserean sonnet,* which combines Italian and English rhymes in an *a b a b b c b c c d c d e e* pattern.

Part of the success of the sonnet is due to its amazing versatility, a versatility that makes the rules we have been discussing almost an exercise in pedantry. Poets vary rhyme schemes, ignore the obvious breaking points, experiment in meters other than pentameter and in feet other than iambic. It always surprises some people to discover that many poems by e. e. cummings, one of the freest of all modern English poets, are really sonnets in disguise. The following selections, coupled with a glance back and a glance ahead at some of the other sonnets in this book, should demonstrate some of the versatility of the form. Study the rhyme schemes, the organization of the material within the form, the use of form to supplement and even to convey the major part of a poem's meaning. Observe how a good poet like Wordsworth or Milton is at home within the apparently narrow confines of fourteen lines. And perhaps, merely as an exercise in appreciation of other poems, try composing a sonnet of your own.

My Galley Charged with Forgetfulness

My galley, chargèd with forgetfulness,
Thorough sharp seas in winter nights doth pass
'Tween rock and rock; and eke mine enemy, alas!
That is my Lord, steereth with cruelness;
And every oar a thought in readiness,
As though that death were light in such a case.
An endless wind doth tear the sail apace
Of forcèd sighs, and trusty fearfulness;
A rain of tears, a cloud of dark disdain,
Hath done the wearèd cords great hinderance,
Wreathèd with error and eke with ignorance.
The stars be hid that led me to this pain.
Drownèd is reason that should me comfort,
And I remain despairing of the port.

—*Sir Thomas Wyatt*

1. *charged:* laden. 3. *eke:* also.

The comparison between a despairing lover and a ship lost in a storm at sea is traditional, and can be traced through the Middle Ages to classical literature. This ship, "charged with forgetfulness" (i.e., laden with neglect—his lady's neglect), is steered by the poet's cruel enemy, his disdainful mistress, who guides him from one sorrow to another. Wyatt works out his metaphor at considerable length: the ship's oars are his thoughts, the storm is his sighs, the rain is his tears, the clouds are his lady's disdain. Most significant, however, are the stars of line 12, probably the eyes of his lady. It was a convention of medieval and Renaissance iconography that love proceeded from the eyes of the beloved through the eyes of the lover; but it was probably the eyes of his lady that first attracted Wyatt. They are now hid (presumably behind her disdainful behavior), and the poet is without guidance. The eye as the source of knowledge is also a neo-Platonic convention: to see is to know. The blinding, then, is metaphysical, as Wyatt goes on to point out in the final two lines of the sonnet: reason is drowned, it does not function. And unless reason functions, Wyatt the man and the lover can never hope to achieve the self-control that will bring him to port (that is, a state of emotional stability). The metaphor is complicated, but the metaphysics of the poem are even more complicated.

Look at the rhyme scheme of the sonnet. The obvious breaking points are after lines 4, 8, and 12, but Wyatt's punctuation and thought force breaks after lines 3, 6, 11, and 12. Just as the lover is somewhat disjointed, the sonnet is a bit disjointed. Contrast the divisions of thought in this poem with those in the next two sonnets by Shakespeare. Note how Shakespeare, in contrast to Wyatt, ends each quatrain with a colon or a period. But then, he does not have Wyatt's reasons for irregularity.

Sonnet 18

Shall I compare thee to a Summer's day?
Thou art more lovely and more temperate:
Rough winds do shake the darling buds of May,
And Summer's lease hath all too short a date:
Sometime too hot the eye of heaven shines,
And often is his gold complexion dimm'd,
And every fair from fair sometime declines,
By chance, or nature's changing course, untrimm'd;
But thy eternal Summer shall not fade,
Nor lose possession of that fair thou ow'st,
Nor shall Death brag thou wander'st in his shade,
When in eternal lines to time thou grow'st:
   So long as men can breathe, or eyes can see,
   So long lives this, and this gives life to thee.

—*William Shakespeare*

Sonnet 73

That time of year thou mayest in me behold
When yellow leaves, or none, or few, do hang
Upon those boughs which shake against the cold,
Bare ruined choirs, where late the sweet birds sang.
In me thou seest the twilight of such day
As after sunset fadeth in the west,
Which by and by black night doth take away,
Death's second self, that seals up all in rest.
In me thou seest the glowing of such fire
That on the ashes of his youth doth die,
As the death-bed whereon it must expire,
Consumed with that which it was nourished by.
  This thou perceiv'st, which makes thy love more strong,
  To love that well which thou must leave ere long.

—*William Shakespeare*

Look carefully at the divisions of *thought* in each sonnet. Both break nicely into units of 4, 4, 4, and 2, but in Sonnet 18 the real shift comes in line 9, where Shakespeare turns from natural beauty to the beauty of his love as eternalized in this sonnet, whereas in Sonnet 73 the break comes in line 13, where Shakespeare turns to summarize the previous three quatrains.

Death, Be Not Proud

Death, be not proud, though some have called thee
Mighty and dreadful, for thou art not so,
For those whom thou think'st thou dost overthrow
Die not, poor Death, nor yet canst thou kill me.
From rest and sleep, which but thy pictures be,
Much pleasure, then from thee much more must flow;
And soonest our best men with thee do go—
Rest of their bones and souls' delivery!
Thou'rt slave to fate, chance, kings and desperate men,
And dost with poison, war, and sickness dwell,
And poppy or charms can make us sleep as well,
And better than thy stroke; why swell'st thou then?
One short sleep past, we wake eternally,
And death shall be no more: Death, thou shalt die!

—*John Donne*

11. *poppy:* the source of opium. 12. *swell'st:* swell (with pride).

1. What specific reasons does the poet give why Death should not be proud? Death is usually called the Grim Reaper; here Death is "poor Death." This is certainly startling; is it convincing?

2. Donne loved paradox in all his writing and his poetry. What paradoxes does he explore here?

3. Do you find Donne's meter, and his form, rougher or smoother than Shakespeare's? In what ways? Which do you more admire, this sonnet or those of Shakespeare? Why?

London, 1802

Milton! thou shouldst be living at this hour:
England hath need of thee: she is a fen
Of stagnant waters: altar, sword, and pen,
Fireside, the heroic wealth of hall and bower,
Have forfeited their ancient English dower
Of inward happiness. We are selfish men;
Oh! raise us up, return to us again;
And give us manners, virtue, freedom, power.
Thy soul was like a Star, and dwelt apart;
Thou hadst a voice whose sound was like the sea:
Pure as the naked heavens, majestic, free,
So didst thou travel on life's common way,
In cheerful godliness; and yet thy heart
The lowliest duties on herself did lay.

—*William Wordsworth*

What role is the poet playing in this poem? How does Wordsworth's assessment of England in the early nineteenth century compare with Shelley's and Blake's (Chapter 1, Section 4)? Notice that while Shelley and Blake look to externals, Wordsworth looks inside. Do all three come to roughly the same conclusions?

Leda and the Swan

A sudden blow: the great wings beating still
Above the staggering girl, her thighs caressed
By the dark webs, her nape caught in his bill,
He holds her helpless breast upon his breast.

How can those terrified vague fingers push
The feathered glory from her loosening thighs?

And how can body, laid in that white rush,
But feel the strange heart beating where it lies?

A shudder in the loins engenders there
The broken wall, the burning roof and tower
And Agamemnon dead.
                                        Being so caught up,
So mastered by the brute blood of the air,
Did she put on his knowledge with his power
Before the indifferent beak could let her drop?

—*William Butler Yeats*

Title: the subject of the poem is the rape of Leda by Jupiter, disguised as a swan.

next to of course god

"next to of course god america i
love you land of the pilgrims' and so forth oh
say can you see by the dawn's early my
country 'tis of centuries come and go
and are no more what of it we should worry
in every language even deafanddumb
thy sons acclaim your glorious name by gorry
by jingo by gee by gosh by gum
why talk of beauty what could be more
beautiful than these heroic happy dead
who rushed like lions to the roaring slaughter
they did not stop to think they died instead
then shall the voice of liberty be mute?"

He spoke. And drank rapidly a glass of water

—*e. e. cummings*

In whose voice does cummings speak the first thirteen lines of his poem? What clichés of patriotic speech does he use? What is his attitude toward the speaker? What is the tone of this poem?

How orthodox is this sonnet structurally?

Carrion Comfort

Not, I'll not, carrion comfort, Despair, not feast on thee;
Not untwist—slack they may be—these last strands of man

In me or, most weary, cry *I can no more.* I can;
Can something, hope, wish day come, not choose not to be.
But ah, but O thou terrible, why wouldst thou rude on me
Thy wring-world right foot rock? lay a lionlimb against me?
  scan
With darksome devouring eyes my bruisèd bones? and fan,
O in turns of tempest, me heaped there; me frantic to avoid
  thee and flee?
  Why? That my chaff might fly; my grain lie, sheer and clear.
Nay in all that toil, that coil, since (seems) I kissed the rod,
Hand rather, my heart lo! lapped strength, stole joy, would
  laugh, chéer.
Cheer whom though? the hero whose heaven-handling flung
  me, foot trod
Me? or me that fought him? O which one? is it each one? That
  night, that year
Of now done darkness I wretch lay wrestling with (my God!)
  my God.

—*Gerard Manley Hopkins*

5. *rude:* roughly. 10. *coil:* disturbance. 14. *wrestling:* the allusion is to Jacob wrestling with the angel in Genesis 18.

Describe the voice of this poem. Discuss its subject. Now turn to its structure. Look down the right-hand margin, at the final words of each line; clearly this is a sonnet, and insofar as rhymes are concerned, a very tight sonnet. Try scanning Hopkins's meter. How about his rhythm? Can you think of any reason why, given the voice and the subject of this poem, its structure should be so wracked?

Villanelle

The villanelle was imported into English from the French during the middle ages. It is nowhere near as popular as the sonnet, perhaps because of its exceptionally difficult rhyme scheme, and because it is usually an artificial sounding form. The villanelle consists of six stanzas, the first five containing three lines each, the sixth having four lines. Only two rhymes are used across the entire nineteen lines: *a b a a b a a b a a b a a b a a b a a.* Not only that, line 1 is repeated in its entirity as lines 6, 12, and 18, and line 3 is repeated in its entirity to form lines 9, 15, and 19. Not only is the form artificial, it can become monotonous.

Curiously, the two great modern villanelles, by Robinson and Thomas respectively, have none of the form's characteristic lightness. Nor do they seem unduly repetitious, all things considered.

Do Not Go Gentle into That Good Night

Do not go gentle into that good night,
Old age should burn and rave at close of day;
Rage, rage against the dying of the light.

Though wise men at their end know dark is right,
Because their words had forked no lightning they
Do not go gentle into that good night.

Good men, the last wave by, crying how bright
Their frail deeds might have danced in a green bay,
Rage, rage against the dying of the light.

Wild men who caught and sang the sun in flight,
And learn, too late, they grieved it on its way,
Do not go gentle into that good night.

Grave men, near death, who see with blinding sight
Blind eyes could blaze like meteors and be gay,
Rage, rage against the dying of the light.

And you, my father, there on the sad height,
Curse, bless, me now with your fierce tears, I pray.
Do not go gentle into that good night.
Rage, rage against the dying of the light.

—Dylan Thomas

Why, does Thomas suggest, should we rage against death? Wise men, good men, wild men, grave men—all find cause to feel cheated. Is there any way to win at this game?

The House on the Hill

They are all gone away,
  The House is shut and still,
There is nothing more to say.

Through broken walls and gray
  The winds blow bleak and shrill
They are all gone away.

Nor is there one to-day
  To speak them good or ill:
There is nothing more to say.

Why is it then we stray
  Around the sunken sill?
They are all gone away,

And our poor fancy-play
  For them is wasted skill:
There is nothing more to say.

There is ruin and decay
  In the House on the Hill:
They are all gone away,
There is nothing more to say.

—*Edwin Arlington Robinson*

Here is an interesting little poem that makes a success out of saying nothing, and saying nothing again and again. "There is nothing more to say," Robinson tells us candidly; it is all ruin and decay. All of us have had this feeling of futility, usually after hearing of the death of someone we loved. And there *is* nothing, really, to be said, except that you're sorry and what can you say? In treating this subject and this mood with this form, Robinson makes the repetition of lines 1 and 3 work for him: in the monotony of the poem lies its statement.

Limerick

Another very tight form, but one which has proven infinitely more popular than the villanelle, is the limerick. Sprung from unknown origins, the limerick first made its appearance in 1820. It is always a humorous form, probably because of its propensity to use anapestic feet and the prominence of its rhymes, which are frequently feminine. The shortness of its lines (trimeter and dimeter) serves to enhance the lightness of its meter and rhyme. While iambic feet may be substituted at almost any point for the anapestic, the basic form of the limerick is this:

U U / U U / U U / (U) a
U U / U U / U U / (U) a
U U / U U / (U) b
U U / U U / (U) b
U U / U U / U U / (U) a

Fleshed out with words, this form might produce any one of the following poems.

A flea and a fly in a flue
Were imprisoned, so what could they do?
Said the fly, "Let us flee!"
Said the flea, "Let us fly!"
So they flew through a flaw in the flue.

—*anonymous*

A limerick gets laughs anatomical
Into space that is quite economical.
But the good ones I've seen
So seldom are clean,
And the clean ones are seldom so comical.

—*anonymous*

There was an old lady from Kent
Whose nose was most awfully bent.
She followed her nose
One day, I suppose,
And no one knows which way she went.

—*anonymous*

There was a young lady from Kent
Who said that she knew what it meant
When men asked her to dine,
Gave her cocktails and wine;
She knew what it meant—but she went.

—*anonymous*

There was an old man with a beard,
Who said, "It is just as I feared!
Two owls and a hen,
Four larks and a wren
Have all built nests in my beard."

—*Edward Lear*

There once was a lad from Peoria
Who said to his girl, "I want more o'ya."
Said she, "That's too bad,
What there is you have had,
You and the others before ya."

—*anonymous*

Sestina

The sestina is one of the more interesting forms in poetry because it structures itself not by meter and rhyme, but by meter and repeated words. The poem consists of six stanzas of six lines each, rounded off with a three-line envoy. While the length of the line is not restricted to iambic pentameter, the form does require strict attention to the last word of each line of each stanza, which are always the same six words in each stanza, but rearranged in accordance with a strict sequence. If we number the end words of the first stanza 1, 2, 3, 4, 5, and 6 respectively, then in the second stanza we will fine the same words in this sequence: 6, 1, 5, 2, 4, 3. In the third stanza they will appear 3, 6, 4, 1, 2, and 5. And so on, beginning each new stanza with the last word of the last line of the preceding stanza, then to the last word of the first line of preceding stanza, then last word of next-to-last line, then last word of next-to-first line, then third-from-last, and finally the last word of the third-from-first line of the preceding stanza. Not only that, the three-line envoy must contain the 5, 3, and 1 words at the end of each of its three lines . . . with the 2, 4, and 6 words buried in the *middle* of those three lines. Obviously the form is a challenge, and a very difficult challenge at that. But Swinburne, Kipling, Auden, and Bishop have all written sestinas in English.

Paysage Moralisé

Hearing of harvests rotting in the valleys,
Seeing at end of street the barren mountains,
Round corners coming suddenly on water,
Knowing them shipwrecked who were launched for islands,
We honour founders of these starving cities
Whose honour is the image of our sorrow,

Which cannot see its likeness in their sorrow
That brought them desperate to the brink of valleys;
Dreaming of evening walks through learned cities
They reined their violent horses on the mountains,
Those fields like ships to castaways on islands,
Visions of green to them who craved for water.

They built by rivers and at night the water
Running past windows comforted their sorrows;
Each in his little bed conceived of islands
Where every day was dancing in the valleys

And all the green trees blossomed on the mountains
Where love was innocent, being far from cities.

But dawn came back and they were still in cities;
No marvellous creatures rose up from the water;
There was still gold and silver in the mountains
But hunger was a more immediate sorrow,
Although to moping villagers in valleys
Some waving pilgrims were describing islands . . .

"The gods," they promise, "visit us from islands,
Are stalking, head-up, lovely, through our cities;
Now is the time to leave your wretched valleys
And sail with them across the lime-green water,
Sitting at their white sides, forget your sorrow,
The shadow cast across your lives by mountains."

So many, doubtful, perished in the mountains,
Climbing up crags to get a view of islands,
So many, fearful, took with them their sorrow
Which stayed them when they reached unhappy cities,
So many, careless, dived and drowned in water,
So many, wretched, would not leave their valleys.

It is our sorrow. Shall it melt? Ah, water
Would gush, flush, green these mountains and these valleys,
And we rebuild our cities, not dream of islands.

—*W. H. Auden*

1. List the symbolic meanings of the elements of this "moralised landscape." Are they traditional symbolic values, or nonce usages? What other symbols are used in the poem?

2. Auden makes a distinction between "our sorrow" (lines 6, 27) and "their sorrow" (lines 7, 14). Who are "they" and "we"? Are the respective sorrows different? In what ways?

3. What transformation takes place in the fourth stanza? Are the men of this stanza the same men who "reined their violent horses on the mountains" and "built by rivers"? What has happened allegorically?

4. What kind of misdirected effort is suggested in the sixth stanza? If these responses to sorrow are ill-conceived and inadequate, what would be the appropriate response? Does Auden give us a suggestion in the final three lines?

5. Would you call the poem entirely optimistic, guardedly hopeful,

or totally pessimistic in its final conclusions? Have the situation described by the poet and the possibilities for regeneration changed much since the poem was written?

Sestina of the Tramp-Royal

Speakin' in general, I 'ave tried 'em all—
The 'appy roads that take you o'er the world.
Speakin' in general, I 'ave found them good
For such as cannot use one bed too long,
But must get 'ence, the same as I 'ave done,
An' go observin' matters till they die.

What do it matter where or 'ow we die,
So long as we've our 'ealth to watch it all—
The different ways that different things are done,
An' men an' women lovin' in this world;
Takin' our chances as they come along,
An' when they ain't, pretendin' they are good?

In cash or credit—no, it aren't no good;
You 'ave to 'ave the 'abit or you'd die,
Unless you lived your life but one day long,
Nor didn't prophesy nor fret at all,
But drew your tucker some'ow from the world,
An' never bothered what you might ha' done.

But, Gawd, what things are they I 'aven't done!
I've turned my 'and to most, an' turned it good,
In various situations round the world—
For 'im that doth not work must surely die;
But that's no reason man should labour all
'Is life on one same shift—life's none so long.

Therefore, from job to job I've moved along.
Pay couldn't 'old me when my time was done,
For something in my 'ead upset it all,
Till I 'ad dropped whatever 't was for good,
An', out at sea, be'eld the dock-lights die,
An' met my mate—the wind that tramps the world!

It's like a book, I think, this bloomin' world,
Which you can read and care for just so long,

But presently you feel that you will die
Unless you get the page you're readin' done,
An' turn another—likely not so good;
But what you're after is to turn 'em all.

Gawd bless this world! Whatever she 'ath done—
Excep' when awful long—I've found it good.
So write, before I die, "'E liked it all!"

—*Rudyard Kipling*

Many modern readers think that Kipling's poetry is just too damned cheerful. After meeting this character, do you agree?

Couplet

A couplet is simply two lines of the same meter ending in similar rhymed words. The lines may be of any length, but they must rhyme, and there must be only two of them:

Little Lyric (Of Great Importance)

I wish the rent
Was heaven sent.

—*Langston Hughes*

An Old Colt

For all night-sins, with others' wives, unknown,
Colt, now, doth daily penance in his own.

—*Ben Jonson*

Presence and Absence

When what is lov'd, is Present, love doth spring;
But being absent, Love lies languishing,

—*Robert Herrick*

Seven Wealthy Towns

Seven wealthy towns content for Homer dead
Through which the living Homer begged his bread.

—anonymous

Going to Sleep

I shall lie like this when I am dead—
But with one more secret in my head.

—Dorothy Livesay

Couplets have a compressed, epigrammatical, vaguely witty quality that makes them especially effective expressions of pithy wisdom:

Early to bed and early to rise,
Makes a man healthy, wealthy and wise.

—Ben Franklin

Early to rise and early to bed
Makes a man wise and wealthy and dead.

—anonymous

Although originally used to refer only to two-line poems complete within themselves, couplet as a form was long ago extended to cover poems of any length, as long as they rhymed *a a b b c c d d e e f f* etc. Such couplets can be subdivided into closed couplets (in which the thought comes complete in two lines, the end of which is marked with a period, colon, semicolon, or a comma) and open couplets (in which the sense of the poem extends through the end of one couplet and into the next. Couplets became the dominant form of poetry in the seventeenth century, when Pope and Dryden developed the *heroic couplet* (iambic pentameter couplets) first used by Chaucer and popularized in the seventeenth century, into a highly refined form sensitive to subtle variations in voice. Since then the couplet went out of favor (during the nineteenth century) and has never returned to the preeminence it once knew.

The Bells of Rhymney

"Oh what will you give me?"
Say the sad bells of Rhymney.

"Is there hope for the future?"
Say the brown bells of Merthyr.
"Who made the mine owner?"
Say the black bells of Rhondda.
And "Who robbed the miners?"
Say the grim bells of Blaina.

"They will plunder willy nilly,"
Say the bells of Caerphilly.
"They have fangs, they have teeth,"
Say the loud bells of Neath.
"Even God is uneasy,"
Say the moist bells of Swansea.
And "What will you give me?"
Say the sad bells of Rhymney.

"Throw the vandals in court,"
Say the bells of Newport.
"All would be well if, if, if, if . . ."
Say the green bells of Cardiff.
"Why so worried, sisters, why?"
Sang the silver bells of Wye.
"Oh, what will you give me?"
Say the sad bells of Rhymney.

—*Idris Davies*

This song is a series of couplets, rhyming on various cities in the southern (mining) part of Wales. What role is the poet playing here? What is his voice? Listen to Pete Seeger sing this poem: how does Seeger's melody enhance the statement of the poem?

from Essay on Criticism

A perfect judge will read each work of wit
With the same spirit that its author writ:
Survey the whole, nor seek slight faults to find
Where nature moves, and rapture warms the mind;
Nor lose, for that malignant dull delight,
The gen'rous pleasure to be charmed with wit.
But in such lays as neither ebb nor flow,
Correctly cold, and regularly low,
That, shunning faults, one quiet tenor keep,
We cannot blame indeed—but we may sleep.

In wit, as nature, what affects our hearts
Is not th' exactness of peculiar parts;
'Tis not a lip or eye we beauty call,
But the joint force and full result of all.
Thus when we view some well proportioned dome
(The world's just wonder, and ev'n thine, O Rome!)
No single parts unequally surprise;
All comes united to th' admiring eyes;
No monstrous height or breadth or length appear;
The whole at once is bold, and regular.
  Whoever thinks a faultless piece to see,
Thinks what ne'er was, nor is, nor e'er shall be.
In ev'ry work regard the writer's end,
Since none can compass more than they intend;
And if the means be just, the conduct true,
Applause, in spite of trivial faults, is due.
As men of breeding, sometimes men of wit,
T' avoid great errors must the less commit,
Neglect the rules each verbal critic lays,
For not to know some trifles is a praise.
Most critics, fond of some subservient art,
Still make the whole depend upon a part;
They talk of principles, but notions prize,
And all to one loved folly sacrifice.
  Once on a time La Mancha's knight, they say,
A certain bard encount'ring on the way,
Discoursed in terms as just, with looks as sage,
As e'er could Dennis, of the Grecian stage;
Concluding all were desp'rate sots and fools
Who durst depart from Aristotle's rules.
Our author, happy in a judge so nice,
Produced his play, and begged the knight's advice;
Make him observe the subject and the plot,
The manners, passions, unities—what not?
All which exact to rule were brought about,
Were but a combat in the lists left out.
"What! leave the combat out?" exclaims the knight.
"Yes, or we must renounce the Stagirite."
"Not so, by heav'n!" he answers in a rage;
"Knights, squires, and steeds must enter on the stage."
"So vast a throng the stage can ne'er contain."
"Then build a new, or act it in a plain."
  Thus critics of less judgment than caprice,
Curious, not knowing, not exact but nice,

Form short ideas, and offend in arts
(As most in manners) by a love to parts.
  Some to conceit alone their taste confine,
And glitt'ring thoughts struck out at ev'ry line;
Pleased with a work where nothing's just or fit,
One glaring chaos and wild heap of wit.
Poets, like painters, thus unskilled to trace
The naked nature and the living grace,
With gold and jewels cover ev'ry part,
And hide with ornaments their want of art.
True wit is nature to advantage dressed,
What oft was thought, but ne'er so well expressed;
Something whose truth convinced at sight we find,
That gives us back the image of our mind.
As shades more sweetly recommend the light,
So modest plainness sets off sprightly wit;
For works may have more wit than does 'em good,
As bodies perish through excess of blood.
  Others for language all their care express,
And value books, as women men, for dress.
Their praise is still, "The style is excellent."—
The sense they humbly take upon content.
Words are like leaves; and where they most abound,
Much fruit of sense beneath is rarely found.
False eloquence, like the prismatic glass,
Its gaudy colors spreads on ev'ry place;
The face of nature we no more survey:
All glares alike, without distinction gay.
But true expression, like th' unchanging sun,
Clears and improves whate'er it shines upon;
It gilds all objects, but it alters none.
Expression is the dress of thought, and still
Appears more decent as more suitable;
A vile conceit in pompous words expressed
Is like a clown in regal purple dressed;
For diff'rent styles with diff'rent subjects sort,
As sev'ral garbs with country, town, and court.
Some by old words to fame have made pretense,
Ancients in phrase, mere moderns in their sense;
Such labored nothings, in so strange a style,
Amaze th' unlearn'd, and make the learned smile.
Unlucky as Fungoso in the play,
These sparks with awkward vanity display
What the fine gentleman wore yesterday;

And but so mimic ancient wits, at best,
As apes our grandsires, in their doublets dressed.
In words as fashions the same rule will hold,
Alike fantastic if too new or old:
Be not the first by whom the new are tried,
Nor yet the last to lay the old aside.
  But most by numbers judge a poet's song,
And smooth or rough with them is right or wrong:
In the bright Muse though thousand charms conspire,
Her voice is all these tuneful fools admire;
Who haunt Parnassus but to please their ear,
Not mend their minds; as some to church repair,
Not for the doctrine, but the music there.
These equal syllables alone require,
Though oft the ear the open vowels tire;
While expletives their feeble aid do join,
And ten low words oft creep in one dull line;
While they ring round the same unvaried chimes,
With sure returns of still-expected rimes:
Where'er you find "the cooling western breeze,"
In the next line it "whispers through the trees";
If crystal streams "with pleasing murmurs creep,"
The reader's threatened (not in vain) with "sleep";
Then, at the last and only couplet fraught
With some unmeaning thing they call a thought,
A needless Alexandrine ends the song,
That, like a wounded snake, drags its slow length along.
Leave such to tune their own dull rimes, and know
What's roundly smooth or languishingly slow;
And praise the easy vigor of a line
Where Denham's strength and Waller's sweetness join.
True ease in writing comes from art, not chance,
As those move easiest who have learned to dance.
'Tis not enough no harshness gives offense;
The sound must seem an echo to the sense.
Soft is the strain when zephyr gently blows,
And the smooth stream in smoother numbers flows;
But when loud surges lash the sounding shore,
The hoarse, rough verse should like the torrent roar.
When Ajax strives some rock's vast weight to throw,
The line too labors, and the words move slow;
Not so when swift Camilla scours the plain,
Flies o'er the unbending corn, and skims along the main.
Hear how Timotheus' varied lays surprise,

And bid alternate passions fall and rise!
While, at each change, the son of Libyan Jove
Now burns with glory and then melts with love;
Now his fierce eyes with sparkling fury glow,
Now sighs steal out and tears begin to flow:
Persians and Greeks like turns of nature found,
And the world's victor stood subdued by sound!
The pow'r of music all our hearts allow,
And what Timotheus was, is Dryden now.

—*Alexander Pope*

35. *La Mancha's knight:* Don Quixote. The episode Pope describes is not from the original, but from a spurious continuation. 38. *Dennis:* a popular critic (1657–1734). 57. *conceit:* metaphor, usually overly clever or ingenious. 76. *upon content:* on trust. 90. *sort:* consort, harmonize, are appropriate. 96. *Fungoso:* the foppish butt of many of Jonson's jokes in *Every Man Out Of His Humor.* 105. *numbers:* versification. Note how Pope makes the lines exemplify the defects of sound they condemn, just as many of his previous lines exemplified the defects of sense they attacked. 124. *Alexandrine:* a line of six iambic feet—like the line following. 129. *Denham . . . and Waller:* minor poets influential in the development of the heroic couplet in which Pope is writing. 138. *Ajax:* a Greek hero, characterized in English literature from the Renaissance on as exceptionally strong and exceptionally thick-witted. 140. *Camilla:* a woman who fought against the Trojans after they arrived in Italy (cf. *Aeneid* VII. 808 ff.). 142. *Timotheus:* a musician of Alexander the Great. The reference may be to Dryden's "Alexander's Feast." 151. *Dryden:* a major British poet, contemporary of Pope.

This passage is excerpted from a long poetic essay in which Alexander Pope laid down the canons of taste for the end of the eigthteenth century. In a review of the poem, Joseph Addison said the poem assembles the "most known and most received observations on the subject of literature and criticism." In other words, not much in the poem was new with Pope; he drew on his own age and classical Greek and Roman theorists. In part one of the poem Pope constructs a harmonious system of art and life, based largely on compromise and the ideal of a golden mean. In part two, from which these lines are taken, he analyzes the causes of bad criticism. What guidelines does he set for being a good reader? What excesses and errors of thought does he caution against? What aspects of bad poetry seem most to have offended Pope?

Look carefully at Pope's couplets. They are uniformedly closed couplets; that is, each is self-contained within two lines. Rhymes are perfect, meter regular. This could become very monotonous very quickly. And yet it doesn't. Pope uses one device after another of voice—rhythm, pitch, tempo, assonance, alliteration, euphony, and cacophony—to create variety, which might otherwise be missing. To take a couple of obvious examples, look at lines 127 and 128, in which Pope smooths and slows the line about "roundly smooth" and "languishingly slow'' poetry, and accelerates the tempo of the line about poetry of ''easy vigor.'' Notice variations in Pope's placement of the pause, or *caesura,* that usually comes somewhere in the middle of a line of iambic pentameter: sometimes it comes early in the line, sometimes late, sometimes marked with a comma, sometimes unmarked . . . and sometimes it comes not at all. Notice subtle variations in the regular iambic meter, and places where rhythm and phrasing work against the monotony of U / U / U / U / U /. Pope gets a great deal of voice modulation into an otherwise monotonous form.

3. A Structure: Music-Related Forms

Because poetry was and continues to be closely associated with music, the shapes of music often impose themselves on poetry, not only in terms of pulse and meter, but in the arrangement of lines, the length of lines, and development of rhyme schemes. As we noted earlier in regard to Bob Dylan's ''Restless Farewell,'' lines sung to the same or similar tunes are quite likely to have similar rhythmic and metrical patterns, and to rhyme. And when the tune changes, so also does the metrical structure of the line. In many medieval poetic forms, and in some modern poetic forms as well, we can see very clearly the impression left upon poetry by musical structure.

Rondel

The *rondel,* along with variations like the rondeau, the roundel, and the roundelay, was a musical form popular in medieval France. All are relatively loose forms, in that the number of lines they contain may vary, depending on what the poet decides to do for a refrain. Characteristically the rondel consists of thirteen or fourteen lines, rhymed *a b b a a b a b a b b a a* or *a b b a a b a b a b b a a b.* The first two lines provide a refrain that is repeated in lines 7 and 8, and again in lines 13 and 14. At the end of the poem, however, the poet may wish to repeat only the first line of the refrain, in which case the rondel contains 13, not 14 lines. The form is loose, however, and might better be designated this way: *R a b R a b b R,* where *R* indicates a refrain of an unspecified number of lines (usually two, possibly three) repeated in whole or in part as indicated. Chaucer, for example, called the song sung by the birds at the close of his ''Parliament of Fowls'' a rondel, even though it contains a three-line refrain. The point is, of course, that the refrain is a device of music, not of poetry, and the repetition designated by *R* may be a random number of measures—and thus a varying number of lines of poetry.

Confessional

My ghostly father, let me confess,
First to God and then to you,
That at a window—do you know how?—
I stole a kiss of great sweetness.

It was done without advisedness,
But it is done, not undone now.
My ghostly father, let me confess,
First to God and then to you.

But it shall be restored, doubtless,
For kisses one should rebestow,
And that to God I make this vow,
Otherwise I ask forgiveness.
My ghostly father, let me confess,
First to God and then to you.

—Charles d'Orleans (trans. Wesli Court)

Notice especially the tone in this poem: light, witty, a kind of mock confession to a good-natured confessor (the "ghostly"—holy—father) who will certainly approve the stolen kiss unless it is returned. The *rondel* is a light form, both because of its artificiality and because it grew up in a light, pleasant, courtly environment.

Rondel: An Un-Love Song

Among the other things that do not matter
I hear you boasting your unending love.
That trap, at least, I know to rise above
As quicksand lie or envy's brittle patter.

While dreams decay and lifetime idols shatter
What in the world can you be thinking of?
Among the other things that do not matter
I hear you boasting your unending love.

I watch the rosy petals fall and scatter
And listen for the melancholy dove:
He does not mourn his poor rejected love!
You mimic now the squirrel's antic chatter
Among the other things that do not matter.

—*Amy Jo Schoonover*

In several respects this "un-love song" works against the nature of its form: where we would expect artificial, good-natured trivialities, "sweet nothings" as the expression goes, this poem urges the lover to put away such nonsense as things that do not matter. What *does* matter? Is this poem, for all its hard-nosed tone, affirmative or pessimistic?

from The Parliament of Fowls

Now welcome, summer, with thy sunne softe,
That hast these winter's wedres overshake,
And driven away the large nights blake.

Saint Valentine, that art full high on loft,
Thus singen smalle foules for thy sake:
Now welcome, summer, with thy sunne softe,
That hast these winter's wedres overshake,
And driven away the large nights blake.

Well han they cause for to gladen ofte,
Sith each of hem recovered hath his make;
Ful blissful mowe they singe whan they wake:
Now welcome, summer, with thy sunne softe,
That hast these winter's wedres overshake,
And driven away the large nights blake.

—*Geoffrey Chaucer*

1. *summer:* warm weather, not necessarily summer. In fact, since this is a Valentine's Day poem, probably spring. 2. *wedres:* storms. *overshake:* dispelled. 3. *blake:* black. 9. *han:* have; *gladen:* rejoice. 10. *hem:* them; *make:* mate. 11. *mowe:* might.

This little piece of joy and cotton candy is a celebration of spring in the best and most conventional medieval tradition. Its tone is light; its content is conventional; and it has nothing more profound to say than "Summer's here and the time is right for dancing in the streets!"

Ballad

The ballad is the most popular of musical forms to be assimilated into written poetry, probably because it is an easy form within which to work, and it lends itself well to story telling and character presentation. While the term *ballad* may be used poetically to refer simply to any short narrative poem designed to be sung (and musically to refer to any sung narrative poem, in any of a variety of tempos and forms), in the narrower sense ballad means a quite specific form, containing four lines, eight measures of music. The four lines of poetry have four stresses, three stresses, four stresses, and three; the music is usually in 4/4 time, with each stressed syllable and following unaccented syllables receiving a half note's worth time. Rests or a full half note absorb the space left at the end of the second and fourth lines. Poetically the form looks like this:

u / u / u / u u /
It fell about a Martinmas time,
u u / u / u / u
When the green leaves were a-fallin',
u / u u / u u / u /
That Sir John Graeme from the West country
u u / u / u / u
Fell in love wi' Bawbie Allan.

Musically the form looks like this:

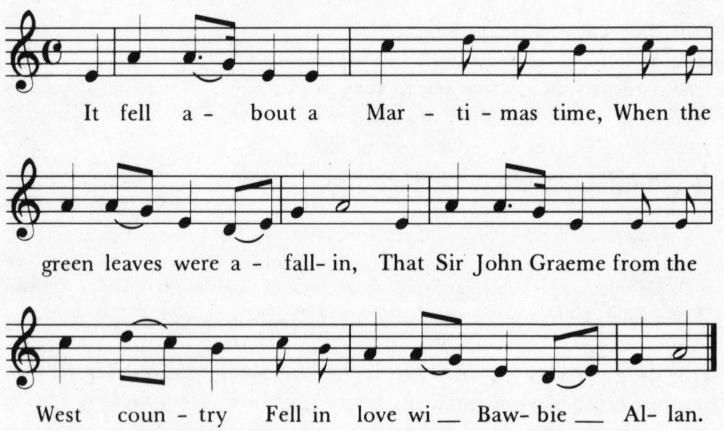

The ballad, as you will note, is a loose form metrically, counting accents but allowing one, two, even three unaccented syllables between the accents. It rhymes only the second and fourth stanza, although a clever poet may wish to make lines one and three rhyme internally:

The gypsy rover come over the hill,
Down to the valley shady;
And he whistled and he sang 'til the green woods rang,
And he won the heart of a lady.

It is this looseness and flexibility which make the ballad so popular, among folk singers and educated poets alike. And note: the ballad stanza, smoothed out in meter and rhyme, forms the structure of many, many hymns: one line of iambic tetrameter, one of iambic trimeter, one tetrameter, one trimeter; 8 syllables, then 7, then 8, then 7:

Joy to the world! The Lord is come;
Let earth receive her king;
Let every heart prepare him room
And heav'n and nature sing.

—*Isaac Watts*

O God, our help in ages past,
Our hope for years to come,
Our shelter from the stormy blast,
And our eternal home:

Under the shadow of Thy throne
Thy saints have dwelt secure;
Sufficient is Thine arm alone
And our defense is sure.

—*Isaac Watts*

So common is this form in hymn tunes that it is called "common meter." Hymnody was an important influence on the American poet Emily Dickinson, and many of her poems are in common meter (see "Because I Could Not Stop for Death," Chapter 3, Section 6).

As a literary genre, the ballad has a long history, dating to the later middle ages, to songs that were sung along the Scottish border. These songs were usually of domestic tragedy, political or social issues, or injustices and crimes—all subjects that subsequent ballads have found particularly attractive. They are told sparsely, with important details implied or left out entirely, so that the ballad has a picked, skeletal atmosphere. Understatement is more common that overstatement. Transitions are quick. Characterization is thin. Dialogue is common, as are repetition and refrains. The people we meet in ballads tend to be low-life characters, or nobility out of favor at court. There is a strong sense of social justice in the border ballad.

Subsequent development of the ballad, both as printed on broadsides in sixteenth-century England, and developed in the oral folk culture of the American south and west during the eighteenth and nineteenth centuries, has tended to reinforce these characteristics of the ballad as a genre. And when the ballad was resurrected early in the sixties as a vehicle for protest (marching and singing went hand in hand), it was because the genre's history, as well as its form, suited the ballad to the purposes of folk singer-demonstrators like Pete Seeger, Phil Ochs, and Bob Dylan.

The ballad has spent most of its life as a folk art form; that is, it is especially popular with poets and composers who cannot read or write music or poetry. For that reason ballads have a kind of homemade feel to them that is partially a matter of meter, partially a result of language, partially just an atmosphere or tone. (This is a direct contrast to the sonnet, which is a very sophisticated form used only by educated poets.) In fact, in the hands of an educated poet the ballad loses some of its roughness and honesty, and never seems to work well. While virtually all poets—except those of the late seventeenth century, who were locked into heroic couplets—have fiddled around with ballads, few have been able to match folk ballads like "Barbara Allan" or "The House of the Rising Sun."

The House of the Rising Sun

There is a house in New Orleans,
They call the Rising Sun.
It has been the ruin of many a poor girl,
And me, oh Lord, was one.

If I had listened to what mama said,
I'd be at home today.
But being so young and foolish, poor girl,
Let a gambler lead me astray.

My mother is a tailor,
She sews those new blue jeans.
My sweetheart is a drunkard, Lord,
Down in New Orleans.

The only thing a drunkard needs
Is a suitcase and a trunk.
The only time he's satisfied
Is when he's on a drunk.

He'll fill his glasses to the brim,
He passes them around,
And the only pleasure he gets out of life
Is bumming from town to town.

Go tell my baby sister,
Never do like I have done.
To shun that house in New Orleans
They call The Rising Sun.

It's one foot on the platform,
And the other one on the train.
I'm going back to New Orleans
To wear the ball and chain.

I'm going back to New Orleans,
My race is almost run.
I'm going back to spend my life
Beneath that Rising Sun.

—*anonymous*

Title: There is no specific house in New Orleans called The Rising Sun, although the sign as a symbol for a bawdy house is frequent in America and England.

Read this ballad over several times, or listen to it performed on record. Notice, incidentally, that recorded versions vary significantly and are similar to the one printed here only in broad outline. The ballad is spoken in the first person by a young girl who ran away from home, was seduced and abandoned in the finest melodramatic manner by a good-for-nothing gambler, and is now returning to New Orleans and the House of the Rising Sun. Many of the details are not especially clear: the house itself has been the ruin of many women, but does that necessarily make it a bawdy house? The suggestion is strong, but not so strong as to be conclusive. And the ball and chain of line 28: are they metaphorical (suggesting that try as she may, the girl cannot escape her way of life) or literal (suggesting that she has been arrested and is being sent to a New Orleans jail)? And the rising sun beneath which she will spend the rest of her life: is that the sign of the house or is that the heavenly body under which she will be buried after her race is run? Or is it perhaps both at once?

But ballads always have an aura of mystery to them, a vague indefinite quality to their narrative that allows the listener to sketch in details for himself. In its paucity of definite detail "The House of the Rising Sun" is typical of its genre, and we should expect rather than criticize the vagueness we find in it. Notice, though, the scope of the poem, the amount of information it does convey in thirty-two short lines. We meet the girl, her mother and sister, her lover, and the Rising Sun, and get a very good idea of the way all these elements have come together in the life of the speaker. The poem has scope but lacks precision. Notice also the colloquial simplicity, the roughness of the meter, the tragedy implicit in the story: all these are also to be expected in a ballad, and we should not be especially critical of expressions like "me, oh Lord, was" or "Never do like I have done" because they are grammatically incorrect or poetically unpolished. This is what ballads are like, as the remaining poems in this section should make abundantly clear.

Barbara Allan

It was in and about the Martinmas time,
  When the green leaves were a-falling,
That Sir John Graeme in the west country
  Fell in love with Barbara Allan.

He sent his man down through the town,
  To the place where she was dwelling,
"O haste and come to my master dear,
  Gin ye be Barbara Allan."

O slooly, slooly rose she up,
  To the place where he was lying,
And when she drew the curtain by—
  "Young man, I think you're dying."

"O it's I'm sick, and very, very sick,
  And 'tis a' for Barbara Allan."
"O the better for me ye's never be,
  Tho' your heart's blood were a-spilling.

"O dinna ye mind, young man," said she,
"When ye was in the tavern a-drinking,
That ye made the healths gae round and round,
And slighted Barbara Allan."

And slowly, slowly raise she up,
And slowly, slowly left him;
And singing, said she cou'd not stay,
Since death of life had reft him.

She had not gane a mile but twa,
When she heard the dead-bell ringing,
And every jow that the dead-bell geid,
It cry'd, Woe to Barbara Allan.

"O mother, mother, make my bed,
O make it saft and narrow,
Since my love died for me today,
I'll die for him tomorrow.

—*anonymous*

1. Martinmas: St. Martin's Day, November 11. 26. *dead-bell:* the death bell, which tolled to mark a death in the community.

The Wreck of the *Edmund Fitzergald*

The legend lives on from the Chippewa on down
Of the big lake they called Gitche Gumee;
The lake it is said never gives up her dead
When the skies of November turn gloomy.

With a load of iron ore 26,000 tons more
Than the *Edmund Fitzgerald* weighed empty
That good ship and true was a bone to be chewed
When the gales of November came early.

The ship was the pride of the American side
Comin' back from some mill in Wisconsin;
As the big freighters go it was bigger than most
With a crew and good captain well seasoned.

Concluding some terms with a couple of steel firms
When they left fully loaded for Cleveland;
And later that night when the ship's bell rang:
Could it be the north wind they'd been feelin'?

The wind in the wires made a tattletale sound
And a wave broke over the railing;
And every man knew as the captain did too
'Twas the witch of November come stealin'.

The dawn came late and the breakfast had to wait
When the gales of November came slashin'
When afternoon came it was freezin' rain
In the face of a hurricane west wind.

When suppertime came the old cook came on deck
Sayin', "Fellas, it's too rough to feed ya."
At seven P.M. a main hatchway caved in,
He said, "Fellas, it's been good to know ya."

The captain wired in he had water comin' in
And the good ship and crew was in peril,
And later that night 'is lights went out of sight,
Came the wreck of the *Edmund Fitzgerald.*

Does anyone know where the love of God goes
When the waves turn the minutes to hours?
The searchers all say they'd have made Whitefish Bay
If they'd put fifteen more miles behind 'er.

They might have split up or they might have capsized,
They may have broke deep and took water,
And all that remains is the faces and the names
Of the wives and the sons and the daughters.

Lake Huron rolls, Superior sings,
In the rooms of her ice water mansion;
Old Michigan steams like a young man's dreams;
The islands and bays are for sportsmen;

And further below Lake Ontario
Takes in what Lake Erie can send her,
And the iron boats do as the mariners all know
With the gales of November remembered.

In a musty old hall in Detroit they prayed
In the maritime sailors' cathedral.
The church bell chimed 'til it rang twenty-nine times
For each man on the *Edmund Fitzgerald.*

The legend lives on from the Chippewa on down
Of the big lake they called Gitche Gumee;
Superior they said never gives up her dead
When the gales of November come early.

—*Gordon Lightfoot*

2. *Gitche Gumee:* Lake Superior.

"The Wreck of the *Edmund Fitzgerald*" is no folk ballad, composed by an unknown and illiterate folksinger and handed down from generation to the next, like "Barbara Allan." It was written by an educated modern about a giant ore carrier that went down in November, 1975. How well has Lightfoot managed to capture the feeling of an authentic folk ballad? What qualities of the folk ballad—other than its stanzaic form, of course—do you find in this song? How does it compare with "The House of the Rising Sun," or with Woody Guthrie's "Tom Joad"?

The Grapes of Wrath

Tom Joad

Tom Joad got out of the old McAllister pen,
And there he got his parole,
After four long years on a man-killin charge,
Tom Joad came awalking down the road, poor boy,
Tom Joad came awalking down the road.

It was there he met a truck-driving man
And there he caught him a ride,
Said, I just got out of the old McAllister pen
Charge called "homicide,"
Charge called "homicide."

That truck rolled away in a big cloud of dust,
Tommy turned his face toward home
Met Preacher Casey and they had a little drink
But he found that his family they was gone, Tom Joad,
He found that his family they was gone.

Found his mother's old-fashioned shoe
He found his daddy's hat,
Found little Muley, and little Muley said,
They been tractored out by the "cats," Tom,
They been tractored out by the "cats."

Tom Joad went down to the neighboring farm
There he found his family.
They took Preacher Casey and loaded in a car,
His mother said, we got to get away, Tom,
His mother said, we got to get away.

The twelve of the Joads made a mighty heavy load
Grandpaw Joad did cry.
He took up a handful of land in his hand,
Said I'm sticking with the farm till I die,
I'm sticking with the farm till I die.

They fed him short-ribs, coffee, and soothing syrup,
And Grandpaw Joad did die.
They buried Grandpaw on the Oklahoma road,
Grandmaw on the California side,
Grandmaw on the California side.

They stood on a mountain and looked to the west,
It looked like the promised land
A bright green valley with a river runnin' through,
There was work for every single hand, they thought,
There was work for every single hand.

The Joads rolled into a jungle camp
And there they cooked a stew,
And the hungry little kids of the jungle camp
Said, we'd like to have some, too, yes,
We'd like to have some, too.

A deputy sheriff cut loose at a man,
He shot a woman in the back,
Before he could take his aim again,
Preacher Casey dropped him in his tracks, good boy,
Preacher Casey dropped him in his tracks.

They handcuffed Casey and took him to jail,
And then he got away,
He met Tom Joad by the old river bridge,
And these few words he did say, Preacher Casey,
And these few words he did say.

Well, I preached for the Lord for a mighty long time,
Preached about the rich and the poor,
Us working folks has got to stick together,
Or we ain't got a chance any more, Lord knows,
Or we ain't got a chance any more.

The deputies come, and Tom and Casey run
To a place where the water run down,
A vigilante thug killed Casey with a club,
And laid Preacher Casey on the ground, poor boy,
And laid Preacher Casey on the ground.

Tom Joad, he grabbed that vigilante's club
He brought it down on his head,
Tom Joad took flight that dark rainy night,
A deputy and a preacher layin' dead, two men,
A deputy and a preacher layin' dead.

Tommy run back where his mama was asleep
He woke her up out of bed,
He kissed goodbye to the mother that he loved,
And he said what Preacher Casey said, Tom Joad,
He said what Preacher Casey said.

Everybody might be just One Big Soul
It looks thataway to me,
Everywhere you look in the day or night,
That's where I'm agonna be, maw,
That's where I'm agonna be.

Wherever little children are hungry and cry,
Wherever people ain't free,
Wherever men are fighting for their rights,
That's where I'm agonna be, maw,
That's where I'm agonna be.

—*Woody Guthrie*

This song provides one example after another of the roughness of ballad meter, and of the ability of music to compress two, three, four syllables into one short pulse. The first line, for example, looks as if it would contain five stresses, looks as if there is no way it *cannot* contain five stresses, and thus five musical beats:

```
     /          /         /      /      /
Tom Joad got out of the old McAllister pen
```

Nevertheless, when sung, the line has only four musical beats:

```
     /          /         /             /
Tom Joad got out of the old McAllister pen
```

Four quick eighth and sixteenth notes are snuck in there between "old" and "pen." In what other ways is "Tom Joad" characteristic of the ballad as a genre?

Ballad of the Goodly Fere

Simon Zelotes speaketh it somewhile after the Crucifixion

Ha' we lost the goodliest fere o' all
For the priests and the gallows tree?
Aye, lover he was of brawny men,
O' ships and the open sea.

When they came wi' a host to take Our Man
His smile was good to see,
"First let these go!" quo' our Goodly Fere,
"Or I'll see ye damned," says he.

Aye, he sent us out through the crossed high spears,
And the scorn of his laugh rang free,
"Why took ye not me when I walked about
Alone in the town?" says he.

Oh we drank his "Hale" in the good red wine
When we last made company,
No capon priest was the Goodly Fere
But a man o' men was he.

I ha' seen him drive a hundred men
Wi' a bundle o' cords swung free,
When they took the high and holy house
For their pawn and treasury.

They'll no get him a' in a book I think
Thought they write it cunningly;
No mouse of the scrolls was the Goodly Fere
But aye loved the open sea.

If they think they ha' snared our Goodly Fere
They are fools to the last degree.
"I'll go to the feast," quo' our Goodly Fere,
"Though I go to the gallows tree."

"Ye ha' seen me heal the lame and the blind,
And wake the dead," says he,
"Ye shall see one thing to master all:
'Tis how a brave man dies on the tree."

A son of God was the Goodly Fere
That bade us his brothers be.
I ha' seen him cow a thousand men.
I ha' seen him upon the tree.

He cried no cry when they drave the nails
And the blood gushed hot and free,
The hounds of the crimson sky gave tongue
But never a cry cried he.

I ha' seen him cow a thousand men
On the hills o' Galilee,
They whined as he walked out calm between,
Wi' his eyes like the gray o' the sea.

Like the sea that brooks no voyaging
With the winds unleashed and free,
Like the sea that he cowed at Gennesaret
Wi' twey words spoke' suddenly.

A master of men was the Goodly Fere,
A mate of the wind and sea,
If they think they ha' slain our Goodly Fere
They are fools eternally.

I ha' seen him eat o' the honey-comb
Sin' they nailed him to the tree.

—*Ezra Pound*

7. *Fere:* companion. 17ff.: Cf. Mark 11:15, 16. 47. *Gennesaret:* Cf. Matthew 8:24ff.

This ballad was written by Ezra Pound in the early twentieth century. In what ways does the highly educated Pound try to capture the rough, unself-conscious feeling of the ballad? How successful is he? How does he portray Christ? Simon Zelotes? Might his characterization of Simon and Christ have something to do with his choice of the ballad form for this poem?

The Blues

Blues, like ballad, can refer simply to any song of a troubled mind sung in a wracked voice to smokey tunes filled with notes that slip somewhere between the keys of the piano. Or, in its formal sense, it can refer to a twelve-measure pattern of music broken into a regular progression of chords and producing a poetical structure of three lines. Usually the first and second lines are identical or similar, and the third provides a kind of resolution or answer to those initial two calls. The structure has been called a "call, call, response" arrangement, and looks something like this:

I'm goin' to leave here walkin', goin' down highway 61;
Yes I'm goin' to leave here walkin', goin' down highway 61.
If I run up on my no good Joanie, I declare we'll have some fun.

—*Memphis Willie B.*

Hey, I'm old bumble bee, a stinger just long as my arm.
I'm an old bumble bee, a stinger just long as my arm.
I sting the good-looking women everywhere I goes along.

—*Bo Carter*

As a genre the blues is originally a black form, but it has been used by many, many white musicians, and is quite common in all pop music today. While few poets have used the form, except for poems that are songs, Langston Hughes published in his *Selected Poems* "Young Gal's Blues":

Young Gal's Blues

I'm gonna walk to the graveyard
'Hind ma friend Miss Cora Lee.
Gonna walk to the graveyard
'Hind ma dear friend Cora Lee
Cause when I'm dead some
Body'll have to walk behind me.

I'm goin' to the po' house
To see ma old Aunt Clew.
Goin' to the po' house
To see ma old Aunt Clew.
When I'm old an' ugly
I'll want to see somebody, too.

The po' house is lonely
An' the grave is cold.
O, the po' house is lonely,
The graveyard grave is cold.
But I'd rather be dead than
To be ugly an' old.

When love is gone what
Can a young girl do?
When love is gone, O,
What can a young gal do?
Keep on alovin' me, daddy,
Cause I don't want to be blue.

—*Langston Hughes*

Tin Pan Alley Form

A second form popular in contemporary music is the old Tin Pan Alley form of melody A, followed by melody A, followed by melody B, followed by melody A again (with, perhaps a return to B, and then A). Both melodies may extend for several measures, and be quite complicated. And they may, quite accidentally, contain tunes—and thus lines of poetry—of approximately the same length and shape. More often the B melody, and the poetry that comes with it, will be significantly shorter than the A melody, producing a pattern of poetry that can be puzzling to somebody unfamiliar with music. If the A melody is both stanza and refrain, and the B melody is both shorter and lacks a refrain, the resultant pattern can be especially confusing:

Honesty

If you search for tenderness, it isn't hard to find
You can have the love you need to live,
But if you look for truthfulness, you might just as well be blind
It always seems to be so hard to give.
Honesty is such a lonely word, everyone is so untrue;
Honesty is hardly ever heard and mostly what I need from you.

I can always find someone to say they sympathize
If I wear my heart out on my sleeve;
But I don't want some pretty face to tell me pretty lies
All I want is someone to believe.
Honesty is such a lonely word, everyone is so untrue;
Honesty is hardly ever heard and mostly what I need from you.

I can find a lover
I can find a friend
I can have security
Until the bitter end
Anyone can comfort me
With promises again
I know,
I know

When I'm deep inside of me don't be too concerned
I won't ask for nothin' while I'm gone
When I want sincerity tell me where else can I turn,
'Cause you're the one that I depend upon.
Honesty is such a lonely word, everyone is so untrue;
Honesty is hardly ever heard and mostly what I need from you.

—*Billy Joel*

We might note, incidentally, that if some of the structures of Shakespeare's poems, or Donne's, or other Renaissance lyricists look odd to us, their structures are surely no odder than this song's. And it may well be that the key to their curious shape is to be found in the music—now in many cases lost—which accompanied them.

4. A Structure: Blank Verse

Blank verse is not, as many people believe, the same thing as free verse. Blank verse is unrhymed iambic pentameter: line after line of

U / U / U / U / U / U / U / U / . As innocuous looking as this form may appear, it has proven remarkably attuned to the natural inflection of the English language (we all tend to speak naturally in iambic feet), and has long been a favorite of poets, especially in longer narrative or dramatic poems. Shakespeare used blank verse for much of his plays, Wordsworth used blank verse for his long autobiographical poem "The Prelude," Frost used blank verse in his famous "The Death of the Hired Man." It seems to have just the right degree of structure, just the right degree of freedom for English poetry.

Lines of blank verse are unrhymed, and as often as not, have no punctuation to mark the end of one line and the beginning of the next. They might just as well, then, be no lines at all, in infinity of U / U / U / U / U / U / U / U / U / U / U / U /. In dramatic poetry, one line of blank verse may even be shared by two, even three actors, and thus fragmented quite beyond recognition. Shakespeare opened act II scene ii of *Romeo and Juliet,* for example, with these lines:

[*Enter* ROMEO.]
ROMEO He jests at scars that never felt a wound.
[JULIET *appears above at a window.*]
But, soft! what light through yonder window
breaks?
It is the east, and Juliet is the sun.
Arise, fair sun, and kill the envious moon,
Who is already sick and pale with grief,
That thou her maid art far more fair than she:
Be not her maid, since she is envious;
Her vestal livery is but sick and green
And none but fools do wear it; cast it off.
It is my lady, O, it is my love!
O, that she knew she were!
She speaks, yet she says nothing: what of that?
Her eye discourses; I will answer it.
I am too bold, 'tis not to me she speaks:
Two of the fairest stars in all the heaven,
Having some business, do entreat her eyes
To twinkle in their spheres till they return.
What if her eyes were there, they in her head?
The brightness of her cheek would shame those
stars,
As daylight doth a lamp; her eyes in heaven
Would through the airy region stream so bright
That birds would sing and think it were not
night.

See, how she leans her cheek upon her hand!
O, that I were a glove upon that hand,
That I might touch that cheek!

JULIET Ay me!

ROMEO She speaks:
O, speak again, bright angel! for thou art
As glorious to this night, being o'er my head,
As is a wingèd messenger of heaven
Unto the white-upturnèd wondering eyes
Of mortals that fall back to gaze on him
When he bestrides the lazy-pacing clouds
And sails upon the bosom of the air.

Notice that line 25 is spoken first by Romeo, then by Juliet, then by Romeo. Notice that lines 1–7, indeed most of Romeo's first speech, contains end-stopped lines (lines ending in some form of punctuation), while Romeo's second speech (lines 26–33) contains only one end-stopped line. In fact, that second speech would probably be *read* like this:

She speaks:
O, speak again, bright angel!
for thou art As glorious to this night,
being o'er my head,
As is a winged messenger of heaven Unto the white-upturned wondering eyes Of mortals that fall back to gaze on him When he bestrides the lazy-pacing clouds
And sails upon the bosom of the air.

Blank verse, then, is really a simple patterning of voice into alternating accented and unaccented syllables. And note, even this regular pattern can be and is subverted, by inverting accented and unaccented syllables (as in the beginning of line 29, ''Unto the white''), adding extra unaccented syllables (as in line 27, ''night, being o'er my head''), or by superimposing other patterns of rhythm or pulse on the iambic pentameter (as in line 26, which would probably be read, '' . . . O speak again, bright angel! for thou art . . . ''). So blank verse turns out at last to be little more than a series of predominately iambic lines—or something very close to normal English prose.

Mending Wall

Something there is that doesn't love a wall,
That sends the frozen-ground-swell under it,
And spills the upper-boulders in the sun;
And makes gaps even two can pass abreast.
The work of hunters is another thing:
I have come after them and made repair
Where they have left not one stone on a stone,
But they would have the rabbit out of hiding,
To please the yelping dogs. The gaps I mean,
No one has seen them made or heard them made
But at spring mending-time we find them there.
I let my neighbor know beyond the hill;
And on a day we meet to walk the line
And set the wall between us once again.
We keep the wall between us as we go.
To each the boulders that have fallen to each.
And some are loaves and some so nearly balls
We have to use a spell to make them balance:
"Stay where you are until our backs are turned!"
We wear our fingers rough with handling them.
Oh, just another kind of out-door game,
One on a side. It comes to little more:
There where it is we do not need the wall:
He is all pine and I am apple orchard.
My apple trees will never get across
And eat the cones under his pines, I tell him.
He only says, "Good fences make good neighbors."
Spring is the mischief in me, and I wonder
If I could put a notion in his head:
"Why do they make good neighbors? Isn't it
Where there are cows? But here there are no cows.
Before I built a wall I'd ask to know
What I am walling in or walling out,
And to whom I was like to give offence.
Something there is that doesn't love a wall,
That wants it down." I could say "Elves" to him,
But it's not elves exactly, and I'd rather
He said it for himself. I see him there
Bringing a stone grasped firmly by the top
In each hand, like an old-stone savage armed.

He moves in darkness as it seems to me,
Not of woods only and the shade of trees.
He will not go behind his father's saying,
And he likes having thought of it so well
He says again, "Good fences make good neighbors."

—*Robert Frost*

1. Examine each and every line of this famous poem for its meter. Where does Frost violate the iambic foot of blank verse? (The poem's first three words are a good place to start here.) Frost has a remarkable ability to make the flattest statements in basic English prose sound poetic; is his success more a result of his violating iambic rhythms or of his ability to find language that conforms to iambic metrical patterns?

2. Frost, as we mentioned in Chapter 3, Section 7, spoke occasionally about the importance of pitch in poetry. Can you find in this poem any examples of lines or phrases where pitch seems especially important? How about rhythms superimposed upon iambic meter?

3. Discuss the character of Frost's neighbor and of the poet as he presents himself in his poem. How are they different? How are they alike? Why does Frost bother to mention the hunters who level his walls to flush hares from hiding?

The Bishop Orders His Tomb at Saint Praxed's Church

Rome, 15—

Vanity, saith the preacher, vanity!
Draw round my bed: is Anselm keeping back?
Nephews—sons mine . . . ah God, I know not! Well—
She, men would have to be your mother once,
Old Gandolf envied me, so fair she was!
What's done is done, and she is dead beside,
Dead long ago, and I am Bishop since,
And as she died so must we die ourselves,
And thence ye may perceive the world's a dream.
Life, how and what is it? As here I lie
In this state-chamber, dying by degrees,
Hours and long hours in the dead night, I ask
"Do I live, am I dead?" Peace, peace seems all.
Saint Praxed's ever was the church for peace;
And so, about this tomb of mine. I fought
With tooth and nail to save my niche, ye know:

—Old Gandolf cozened me, despite my care;
Shrewd was that snatch from out the corner South
He graced his carrion with, God curse the same!
Yet still my niche is not so cramped but thence
One sees the pulpit o' the epistle-side,
And somewhat of the choir, those silent seats,
And up into the aery dome where live
The angels, and a sunbeam's sure to lurk:
And I shall fill my slab of basalt there,
And 'neath my tabernacle take my rest,
With those nine columns round me, two and two,
The odd one at my feet where Anselm stands:
Peach-blossom marble all, the rare, the ripe
As fresh-poured red wine of a mighty pulse.
—Old Gandolf with his paltry onion-stone,
Put me where I may look at him! True peach,
Rosy and flawless: how I earned the prize!
Draw close: that conflagration of my church
—What then? So much was saved if aught were missed!
My sons, ye would not be my death? Go dig
The white-grape vineyard where the oil-press stood,
Drop water gently till the surface sink,
And if ye find . . . Ah God, I know not, I! . . .
Bedded in store of rotten fig-leaves soft,
And corded up in a tight olive-frail,
Some lump, ah God, of *lapis lazuli,*
Big as a Jew's head cut off at the nape,
Blue as a vein o'er the Madonna's breast . . .
Sons, all have I bequeathed you, villas, all,
That brave Frascati villa with its bath,
So, let the blue lump poise between my knees,
Like God the Father's globe on both his hands
Ye worship in the Jesu Church so gay,
For Gandolf shall not choose but see and burst!
Swift as a weaver's shuttle fleet our years:
Man goeth to the grave, and where is he?
Did I say basalt for my slab, sons? Black—
'Twas ever antique-black I meant! How else
Shall ye contrast my frieze to come beneath?
The bas-relief in bronze ye promised me,
Those Pans and Nymphs ye wot of, and perchance
Some tripod, thyrsus, with a vase or so,
The Saviour at his sermon on the mount,
Saint Praxed in a glory, and one Pan

Ready to twitch the Nymph's last garment off,
And Moses with the tables . . . but I know
Ye mark me not! What do they whisper thee,
Child of my bowels, Anselm? Ah, ye hope
To revel down my villas while I gasp
Bricked o'er with beggar's mouldy travertine
Which Gandolf from his tomb-top chuckles at!
Nay, boys, ye love me—all of jasper, then!
'Tis jasper ye stand pledged to, lest I grieve
My bath must needs be left behind, alas!
One block, pure green as a pistachio-nut,
There's plenty of jasper somewhere in the world—
And have I not Saint Praxed's ear to pray
Horses for ye, and brown Greek manuscripts,
And mistresses with great smooth marbly limbs?
—That's if ye carve my epitaph aright,
Choice Latin, picked phrase, Tully's every word,
No gaudy ware like Gandolf's second line—
Tully, my masters? Ulpian serves his need!
And then how I shall lie through centuries,
And hear the blessed mutter of the mass,
And see God made and eaten all day long,
And feel the steady candle-flame, and taste
Good strong thick stupefying incense-smoke!
For as I lie here, hours of the dead night,
Dying in state and by such slow degrees,
I fold my arms as if they clasped a crook,
And stretch my feet forth straight as stone can point,
And let the bedclothes, for a mortcloth, drop
Into great laps and folds of sculptor's-work:
And as yon tapers dwindle, and strange thoughts
Grow, with a certain humming in my ears,
About the life before I lived this life,
And this life too, popes, cardinals and priests,
Saint Praxed at his sermon on the mount,
Your tall pale mother with her talking eyes,
And new-found agate urns as fresh as day,
And marble's language, Latin pure, discreet,
—Aha, ELUCESCEBAT quoth our friend?
No Tully, said I, Ulpian at the best!
Evil and brief hath been my pilgrimage.
All *lapis,* all, sons! Else I give the Pope
My villas! Will ye ever eat my heart?
Ever your eyes were as a lizard's quick,

They glitter like your mother's for my soul,
Or ye would heighten my impoverished frieze,
Piece out its starved design, and fill my vase
With grapes, and add a vizor and a Term,
And to the tripod ye would tie a lynx
That in his struggle throws the thyrsus down,
To comfort me on my entablature
Whereon I am to lie till I must ask
"Do I live, am I dead?" There, leave me, there!
For ye have stabbed me with ingratitude
To death—ye wish it—God, ye wish it! Stone—
Gritstone, a-crumble! Clammy squares which sweat
As if the corpse they keep were oozing through—
And no more *lapis* to delight the world!
Well go! I bless ye. Fewer tapers there,
But in a row: and, going, turn your backs
—Ay, like departing altar-ministrants,
And leave me in my church, the church for peace,
That I may watch at leisure if he leers—
Old Gandolf, at me, from his onion-stone,
As still he envied me, so fair she was!

—*Robert Browning*

1. *Vanity . . . :* Cf. Ecclesiastes, i:2. 14. *St. Praxed's:* the church actually exists in Rome, although it is much smaller than this poem would suggest. 21. *espistle-side:* the right side as one faces the altar. 31. *onion-stone:* a cheap marble prone to peeling. 41. *frail:* basket. 42. *lapis lazuli:* a bluish semiprecious stone. 46. *Frascati:* a town in the hills near Rome. 54. *antique-black:* a more expensive stone than basalt, also black. 57. *wot:* know. 58. *thyrsus:* a staff surmounted with a cone or ivy vines. 60. Note the garish mixture of scenes the Bishop orders. 77. *Tully:* Cicero, whose Latin was impeccable. 79. *Ulpian:* Domitius Ulpian (170–228 A.D.), whose Latin was of a lower quality. 82. *God made and eaten:* the reference is to the celebration of mass. 99. *Elucescebat:* "he was illustrious." The Latin is that of Ulpian, not of Cicero. 108. *vizor:* mask: *term:* bust. 116. *gritstone:* sandstone.

1. This poem is a dramatic monologue, spoken by the Bishop to his two bastard sons as he lies dying. What can you tell about the Bishop's life? About his character? About his old enemy Gandolf, dead before him? About his sons? Be sharp in you analysis, for Browning has managed to suggest a great deal by innuendo only.

2. To what realization(s) does the Bishop come over the course of his speech? About his sons? About his life? About his tomb? What sort of a tomb do you think his sons will give their father?

3. Observe Browning's meter in this poem. Is it more or less regular than Frost's? Than Shakespeare's? Where does Browning obscure the natural iambic meter of his lines? Why? How conscious are you of the structure of this poem as you read it or listen to it?

5. A Structure: Alliterative Structure

As it's possible to pattern accented and unaccented syllables and rhymes into feet and lines, and to create a regular poetic structure, it is also possible to pattern alliteration and assonance into poetic forms. In fact, all English poetry written before 1066 was structured not by accentual meter and rhyme, but by alliterative patterns. Each line of poetry was broken in half by a pause, with each half line containing two beats or pulses or accents (we are not entirely certain how Anglo-Saxon poets counted their rhythm). The poet then alliterated *at least* one pulse or accent in each of the two half lines. Usually he alliterated three, and often he alliterated all four accents or beats. Here, roughly transcribed to make them more readable, are some lines from *Beowulf* (written around the eighth century), followed by a translation of those same lines by Charles Kennedy. Note that these lines contain no regular meter and no rhyme. Note also that Kennedy attempts in his translation to retain the same alliterative pattern of his original, although the alliteration is much stronger in the Anglo-Saxon than in the modern English.

from Beowulf

Gewat that neosian, sythan niht becom,
hean huses, hu hit Hring-Dene
aefter beorthege gebun haefdon.
Fand tha thaer inne aethelinga gedriht
swefan aefter symble; sorge ne cuthon,
wonsceaft wera. Wiht unhaelo,
grim ond graedig, gaero sona waes,
reoc ond rethe, ond on raeste genam
thritig thegna; thanon eft gewat
huthe hremig to ham faran,
mid thaere waelfylle wica neosan.

—*anonymous*

Then, under cover of night, Grendel came
to Hrothgar's lofty hall to see how the Ring-Danes
were disposed after drinking ale all evening;
and he found there a band of brave warriors,
well-feasted, fast asleep, dead to worldly sorrow,
man's sad destiny. At once that hellish monster,
grim and greedy, brutally cruel,
started forward and seized thirty thanes
even as they slept; and then, gloating

over his plunder, he hurried from the hall,
made for his lair with all those slain warriors.

We might note that only in rare cases does there appear to be any correlation between sound and sense: that is, the Old English poet worked consciously to create alliterative structures in his poetry, but he made no effort to make the sound of his alliterations and assonances in any way appropriate to the subject of the lines in which he used them. Probably he had his hands full enough simply finding all those repeated vowel and consonant sounds. Anglo-Saxon poetry, then, is musical, but its music is independent of its meaning.

Alliterative poetry continued to be written in England well into the middle ages, although lettered poets came increasingly to use the rhymed and metered forms introduced by the Norman conquerers from France. Very little alliterative poetry is written today, although Alfred, Lord Tennyson and Ezra Pound used it for their translations of Anglo-Saxon originals, and Richard Wilbur wrote "The Lilacs" in an alliterative form.

The Battle of Brunanburh

I

Athelstan King,
Lord among Earls,
Bracelet-bestower and
Baron of Barons,
He with his brother,
Edmund Atheling,
Gaining a lifelong
Glory in battle,
Slew with the sword-edge
There by Brunanburh,
Brake the shield-wall,
Hew'd the linden-wood,
Hack'd the battle-shield,
Sons of Edward with hammer'd brands.

II

Theirs was a greatness
Got from their grandsires—
Theirs that so often in
Strife with their enemies
Struck for their hoards and their hearts and their homes.

III

Bow'd the spoiler,
Bent the Scotsman,
Fell the ship-crews
Doom'd to the death.
All the field with blood of the fighters
Flow'd, from when first the great
Sun-star of morning-tide,
Lamp of the Lord God
Lord everlasting,
Glode over earth till the glorious creature
Sank to his setting.

IV

There lay many a man
Marr'd by the javelin,
Men of the Northland
Shot over shield.
There was the Scotsman
Weary of war.

V

We the West-Saxons,
Long as the daylight
Lasted, in companies
Troubled the track of the host that we hated;
Grimly with swords that were sharp from the grindstone,
Fiercely we hack'd at the flyers before us.

VI

Mighty the Mercian,
Hard was his hand-play,
Sparing not any of
Those that with Anlaf,
Warriors over the
Weltering waters
Borne in the bark's-bosom,
Drew to this island—
Doom'd to the death.

VII

Five young kings put asleep by the sword-stroke,
Seven strong earls of the army of Anlaf
Fell on the war-field, numberless numbers,
Shipmen and Scotsmen.

VIII

Then the Norse leader—
Dire was his need of it,
Few were his following—
Fled to his war-ship;
Fleeted his vessel to sea with the king in it,
Saving his life on the fallow flood.

IX

Also the crafty one,
Constantinus,
Crept to his North again,
Hoar-headed hero!

X

Slender warrant had
He to be proud of
The welcome of war-knives—
He that was reft of his
Folk and his friends that had
Fallen in conflict,
Leaving his son too
Lost in the carnage,
Mangled to morsels,
A youngster in war!

XI

Slender reason had
He to be glad of
The clash of the war-glaive—
Traitor and trickster
And spurner of treaties—
He nor had Anlaf
With armies so broken
A reason for bragging
That they had the better
In perils of battle
On places of slaughter—
The struggle of standards,
The rush of the javelins,
The crash of the charges,
The wielding of weapons—
The play that they play'd with
The children of Edward.

XII

Then with their nail'd prows
Parted the Norsemen, a
Blood-redden'd relic of
Javelins over
The jarring breaker, the deep-sea billow,
Shaping their way toward Dyflen again,
Shamed in their souls.

XIII

Also the brethren,
King and Atheling,
Each in his glory,
Went to his own in his own West-Saxon-land,
Glad of the war.

XIV

Many a carcase they left to be carrion,
Many a livid one, many a sallow-skin—
Left for the white-tail'd eagle to tear it, and
Left for the horny-nibb'd raven to rend it, and
Gave to the garbaging war-hawk to gorge it, and
That gray beast, the wolf of the weald.

XV

Never had huger
Slaughter of heroes
Slain by the sword-edge—
Such as old writers
Have writ of in histories—
Hapt in this isle, since
Up from the East hither
Saxon and Angle from
Over the broad billow
Broke into Britain with
Haughty war-workers who
Harried the Welshman, when
Earls that were lured by the
Hunger of glory gat
Hold of the land.

—*Alfred, Lord Tennyson*

12. *linden-wood:* shields made of lindenwood. 43. *Mercian:* inhabitant of Mercia, a seventh- and eighth-century Anglo-Saxon kingdom that extended over the middle part of England. 66. *warrant:* reason. 69. *reft:* bereft. 98. *Dyflen:* Dublin. 110. *weald:* forest.

This poem is a translation of an Anglo-Saxon poem by the same title. It was made by Tennyson in 1880, and based somewhat on a prose translation done by his son. What patterns of accent and alliteration can you find in the translation? How regular is Tennyson's structure? How true is it to the four-stress alliterative verse of his original? Does Tennyson seem to drop into an accentual meter (iambic, anapestic, dactylic, trochaic) in some places? The demands of alliteration force Tennyson to use some phrases and words which would, even in 1880, have been pretty obscure. Do you find that "brake the shield-wall," "hewed the linden-wood," "bracelet-bestower," "hammered brands," and many others are confusing and obstructive, or do they help to give the poem a genuine Anglo-Saxon flavor?

The Lilacs

Those laden lilacs
at the lawn's end
Came stark, spindly,
and in staggered file,
Like walking wounded
from the dead of winter.
We watched them waken
in the brusque weather
To rot and rootbreak,
to ripped branches,
And saw them shiver
as the memory swept them
Of night and numbness
and the taste of nothing.
Out of present pain
and from past terror
Their bullet-shaped buds
came quick and bursting,
As if they aimed
to be open with us!

But the sun suddenly
settled about them,
And green and grateful
the lilacs grew,
Healed in that hush,
that hospital quiet.
These lacquered leaves
where the light paddles

And the big blooms
buzzing among them
Have kept their counsel,
conveying nothing
Of their mortal message,
unless one should measure
The depth and dumbness
of death's kingdom
By the pure power
of this perfume.

—*Richard Wilbur*

1. Identify patterns of accent and alliteration in "The Lilacs." How close is Wilbur to the Anglo-Saxon verse tradition? Do his alliterations in any way reinforce the meaning of his lines?

2. The lilacs become, at the poem's conclusion, a symbol—or at least the key to some meaning hidden deep in the nature of things. What symbolic meanings do the lilacs carry? The lilacs' identity is developed from association with a variety of other images. Which seem especially important in this respect? What do those other images, similes, and metaphors have in common? Is this what you usually associate lilacs with?

6. A Structure: Syllabic and Line Count

While the overwhelming preponderence of English and American poets have counted accents or beats when they sought a basis for structuring their poems, it is also possible to count other elements of poetry. Hendecasyllabics, for example, are lines of unrhymed poetry containing eleven syllables to the line. Such poetry is common in Greek and Latin, and something of a standard in Italian, but it is infrequent in English. The haiku, a form introduced into English from the Japanese, also counts syllables: five in the first line, seven in the next, five in the last. While the nature of the Japanese and English languages make haiku in English substantively different from haiku in Japanese, the form has proven so popular that whole magazines are today devoted to publishing haiku. (New rules, incidentally, obtain in some of these magazines, and English poets frequently liberate themselves from the old 5–7–5 syllabic count.) Other poets will occasionally write verse in a form that counts syllables rather than pulses or accents or metrical feet.

Another popular method of creating structure in a poem is simply to make sure that each stanza contains the same number of lines, and that the lines be of approximately the same length. While this is a loose structure indeed by traditional standards, it is relatively rigid for modern poets, who have almost unanimously adopted free verse. Judith Minty considered herself a conservative, a traditionalist, because she standardized the lines of "The End of Summer." She wrote, "I like symmetry. I was/am still convinced that a poem should 'look right' on the page. So, when the first section came out to seven lines and the next fell into the same pattern, I was certain that each subsequent section should be a seven-line stanza."

Hendecasyllabics

In the month of the long decline of roses
I, beholding the summer dead before me
Set my face to the sea and journeyed silent,
Gazing eagerly where above the sea-mark
Flame as fierce as the fervid eyes of lions
Half divided the eyelids of the sunset;
Till I heard as it were a noise of waters
Moving tremulous under feet of angels
Multitudinous, out of all the heavens;
Knew the fluttering wind, the fluttered foliage,
Shaken fitfully, full of sound and shadow;
And saw, trodden upon by noiseless angels,
Long mysterious reaches fed with moonlight,
Sweet sad straits in a soft subsiding channel,
Blown about by the lips of winds I knew not,
Winds not born in the north nor any quarter,
Winds not warm with the south nor any sunshine;
Heard between them a voice of exultation,
"Lo, the summer is dead, the sun is faded,
Even like as a leaf the year is withered,
All the fruits of the day from all her branches
Gathered, neither is any left to gather.
All the flowers are dead, the tender blossoms,
All are taken away; the season wasted,
Like an ember among the fallen ashes.
Now with light of the winter days, with moonlight,
Light of snow, and the bitter light of hoarfrost,
We bring flowers that fade not after autumn,
Pale white chaplets and crowns of latter seasons,

Fair false leaves (but the summer leaves were falser)
Woven under the eyes of stars and planets
When low light was upon the windy reaches
Where the flower of foam was blown, a lily
Dropt among the sonorous fruitless furrows
And green fields of the sea that make no pasture:
Since the winter begins, the weeping winter,
All whose flowers are tears, and round his temples
Iron blossom of frost is bound for ever."

—Algernon Charles Swinburne

This poem is a tone piece, playing back and forth across several of the themes most dear to the Pre-Raephaelite heart: death and impending death, decay, sickness, sorrow, pain. The poem asserts, in a nonrational way, the beauty of decay and the permanence of death. What images strike you as especially representative of this attitude? What images do you find that are normally associated with youth, beauty, and rebirth? How are they redefined in this poem? What devices of voice does Swinburne use to enhance the tone of the poem? What aspects of Swinburne's verse form help (or hurt) the poem?

Thoreauhaiku

the cock is crowing,
let's get up and drink some light,
sleepy-eye musquash

&

morning's sack of wind
breaks the cabin smoke below
a wishbone of geese

&

those aren't locusts
and wild honey, Baptist Partridge,
eating up my peas

&

the caterpillar
   and I mope along waiting
      our resurrection

&

fireflies lacing through
   Spaulding's cranberry meadow:
      Christmas in July

&

above virgin-mould
   by Dismal Swamp, the wild stump
      serves a poet well

&

rest, nervous needle,
   in the shade of my pocket,
      westward I go free

—*Raymond Roseliep*

1. The haiku is, as you can see, a very visual, concrete form. It uses many images, and it has a good, solid appearance on the page. What do Roseliep's images, collectively, connote?

2. What do you know about Thoreau? Why might these images, with these connotations, be appropriate to a "Thoreauhaiku"?

3. In a form as slender as the haiku, every syllable must carry a great deal of weight. There can be no slack. Do you find any extraneous words, any shirking syllables in this poem?

4. How conscious are you, as you read through the poem, of form? How insistent is syllable count as a form—as compared, say, to accentual meter or pulse, or alliterative verse such as you read in "The Battle of Brunanburh"?

The Fish

wade
through black jade.
   Of the crow-blue mussel-shells, one keeps
   adjusting the ash-heaps;
      opening and shutting itself like

an
injured fan.
The barnacles which encrust the side
of the wave, cannot hide
there for the submerged shafts of the

sun,
split like spun
glass, move themselves with spotlight swiftness
into the crevices—
in and out, illuminating

the
turquoise sea
of bodies. The water drives a wedge
of iron through the iron edge
of the cliff; whereupon the stars,

pink
rice-grains, ink-
bespattered jelly-fish, crabs like green
lilies, and submarine
toadstools, slide each on the other.

All
external
marks of abuse are present on this
defiant edifice—
all the physical features of

ac-
cident—lack
of cornice, dynamite grooves, burns, and
hatchet strokes, these things stand
out on it; the chasm-side is

dead.
Repeated
evidence has proved that it can live
on what can not revive
its youth. The sea grows old in it.

—*Marianne Moore*

1. Count the syllables of each line of each stanza in this poem, and describe its structure. How insistent is this structure? As you read through the poem, how conscious are you of form? As you *look* at the poem, how conscious are you of form?

2. The content of this poem is also very visual. What picture does Moore paint? What does she mean by "The sea grows old in it"? What contrasts are set up in this poem?

3. Can you find any correlation between the poem's structure and its meaning? Or has Moore arbitrarily selected a form in which to work?

The End of Summer

1

The old bitch labrador swims
in heavy circles. Under water
her legs run free without their limp.
She stretches brown eyes toward me,
snorting water, and the stick I throw
stirs gray memories of ten Octobers,
ducks that fly at the sun and fall.

2

On the Pere Marquette River, salmon
quiver upstream from the lake: a return
to alpha. At the dam
they leap and throw themselves
through currents, stretch
and spend themselves against the torrent
from the falls, lie torn on rocks.

3

All week the sky has been filled
with orange petals. Monarch butterfies
floating in cycles toward milkweed.
Freed from their jade chrysalis,
they have been waiting for the wind's
current to die. The beach
is covered with torn wings.

4

The merganser carries fire
on his hood. All summer
he has nested in our channel, drifted
with the half-tame mallards. His sharp bill
stabs the water to catch bread I throw.
He belongs by the sea. I want him
to fly now before October and guns.

—*Judith Minty*

1. Each stanza of this poem has seven lines. Can you find any other pattern of meter or rhyme in these stanzas? How conscious are you, as you read or look at the poem, of this structure?

2. What images do you find in the poem? How are the dominant images of each stanza related? In discussing the poem, Ms. Minty spoke of "a strange linking and jumping of imagery," almost as if the poem was built on a series of links. One link she specifically pointed out was the red orange of the merganser's head feathers; what does it link to? What other links can you find in the poem?

3. How do the images of this poem come together? What would you say is the point of the poem?

The Language

Locate *I*
love you some-
where in

teeth and
eyes, bite
it but

take care not
to hurt, you
want so

much so
little. Words
say everything.

I
love you
again,

then what
is emptiness
for. To

fill, fill.
I hear words
and words full

of holes
aching. Speech
is a mouth.

—*Robert Creeley*

Creeley's "structure" in this poem is a "stanza" of three lines. The lines are so short, however (some of them being a single syllable, others containing half words), that they are scarcely recognizable as structure. Is this poem in fact a "free verse" poem (see Chapter 4, Section 8)? Do you care?

7. A Structure: Rhetorical Structure

A favorite and highly effective technique of professional speakers, preachers, and politicians is to pattern language in parallel clauses or phrases—or, better still, to produce a series of parallel phrases beginning or ending (and in some cases beginning *and* ending) with the same word or words. "Seeing is believing" has a nice balance to it that makes the expression hang in our memory. So too does "to know him is to love him." And the longer "You can't always get what you want, but if you try sometime, you might find you get what you need." We could diagram such parallelisms and balances quite simply:

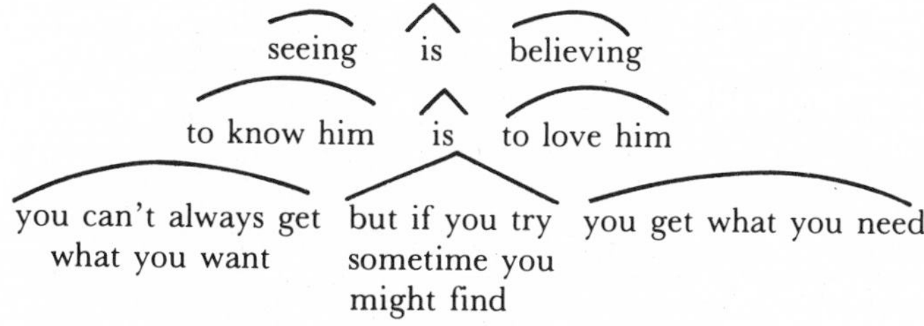

Even the third parallelism, suspended as it is by a relatively long phrase ("but if you try sometime, you might find"), is an effective use of static, balanced rhetoric.

More dynamic than balances are triplets: "I came, I saw, I conquered." "I don't like chocolate ice cream, I never have liked chocolate ice cream, and I never will like chocolate ice cream." When schematized, lines like these look much less static:

I came, I saw, I conquered.

I don't like chocolate ice cream, I never have liked chocolate ice cream,

and I never will like chocolate ice cream.

Sometimes single words can be repeated, to form a series of repeated sounds:

It launched forth filament, filament, filament, out of itself,

Or perhaps a series of similar, although not identical words:

Ceaselessly music, venturing, throwing, seeking the spheres

These rhetorical effects ornament both prose and poetry, and constitute one of every writer's bag full of tricks. Some writers, speakers, and poets weave complex patterns of parallelisms and balances which constitute a fluid, irregular, but undeniable structure. Consider, for example, Winston Churchill's address to Parliament of June 4, 1940, when the war seemed to be going very badly indeed:

> Even though large tracts of Europe and many old and famous
>
> States have fallen or may fall into the grip of the Gestapo and all
>
> the odious apparatus of Nazi rule, we shall not flag or fail. We shall
>
> go on to the end, we shall fight in France, we shall fight on the seas
>
> and oceans, we shall fight with growing confidence and growing
>
> strength in the air, we shall defend our Island, whatever the cost

> may be, we shall fight on the beaches, we shall fight in the hills, we shall never surrender, and even if, which I do not for a moment believe, this Island or a large part of it were subjugated and starving, then our Empire beyond the seas, armed and guarded by the British Fleet, would carry on the struggle, until, in God's good time, the new World, with all its power and might, steps forth to the rescue and the liberation of the old.

This is the kind of prose of which people often say, "That's poetry!" And it is, because the balances, repetitions, parallelisms, alliterations, and even rhymes create structures of sound that make prose indistinguishable, really, from free-verse poetry. Study the web of Churchill's rhetoric carefully. Notice that just when you might be getting weary of a repeated phrase ("we shall fight on . . .") he varies it slightly ("we shall defend our Island") or interrupts the pattern ("we shall fight with growing confidence and growing strength"). Notice too that this structure is not nearly so rigid or predictable as, say, four stanzas of six lines each, every line of five trochaic syllables and a rhyme at the end; or even four stresses to the line, three of the four alliterated.

It is possible to extend the rhetorical structuring of language beyond balanced constructions and parallel phrases into a definite architecture of phrase. Joan Baez, for example, in "Diamonds and Rust," seems to be working in a form composed of five phrases per stanza:

Well I'll be damned   here comes your ghost again
But that's not unusual,   it's just that the moon is full
And you happened to call.

These phrases are not rhetorically similar, except that they can be roughly counted as one "pulse" each. Looked at (or listened to) from this perspective, "Diamonds and Rust" has a very definite structure to it.

Contemporary poets, as we have noted, are not much for metrical verse or traditional stanzaic forms. Sometimes they count syllables or lines, but usually they do not. This is not to say their work lacks all structure: Whitman, Williams, Ginsberg (whose poem "Howl" has exerted an influence over poets of the past twenty years comparable only to what Eliot's "The Waste Land" exerted upon poets of the twenties and thirties) all write poems filled with rhetorical parallelisms and balances, with the structure of rhetorical devices.

I Have a Dream

I say to you today, my friends, that in spite of the difficulties and frustrations of the moment I still have a dream. It is a dream deeply rooted in the American dream.

I have a dream that one day this nation will rise up and live out the true meaning of its creed: "We hold these truths to be self-evident; that all men are created equal."

I have a dream that one day on the red hills of Georgia the sons of former slaves and the sons of former slaveowners will be able to sit down together at the table of brotherhood.

I have a dream that one day even the state of Mississippi, a desert state sweltering with the heat of injustice and oppression, will be transformed into an oasis of freedom and justice.

I have a dream that my four little children will one day live in a nation where they will not be judged by the color of their skin but by the content of their character.

I have a dream today.

I have a dream that one day the state of Alabama, whose governor's lips are presently dripping with the words of interposition and nullification, will be transformed into a situation where little black boys and black girls will be able to join hands with little white boys and white girls and walk together as sisters and brothers.

I have a dream today.

I have a dream that one day every valley shall be exalted, every hill and mountain shall be made low, the rough places will be made plains, and the crooked places will be made straight, and the glory of the Lord shall be revealed, and all flesh shall see it together.

This is our hope. This is the faith with which I return to the South. With this faith we will be able to hew out of the mountain of despair a stone of hope. With this faith we will be able to transform the jangling discords of our nation into a beautiful symphony of brotherhood. With this faith we will be able to work together, to pray together, to struggle together, to go to jail together, to stand up for freedom together, knowing that we will be free one day.

This will be the day when all of God's children will be able to sing with new meaning

My country, 'tis of thee,
Sweet land of liberty,
  Of thee I sing:
Land where my fathers died,
Land of the pilgrims' pride,
From every mountain-side
  Let freedom ring.

And if America is to be a great nation this must become true. So let freedom ring from the prodigious hilltops of New Hampshire. Let freedom ring from the mighty mountains of New York. let freedom ring from the heightening Alleghenies of Pennsylvania!

Let freedom ring from the snowcapped Rockies of Colorado!

Let freedom ring from the curvacious peaks of California!

But not only that; let freedom ring from Stone Mountain of Georgia!

Let freedom ring from Lookout Mountain of Tennessee!

Let freedom ring from every hill and molehill of Mississippi. From every mountainside, let freedom ring.

When we let freedom ring, when we let it ring from every village and every hamlet, from every state and every city, we will be able to speed up that day when all of God's children, black men and white men, Jews and Gentiles, Protestants and Catholics, will be able to join hands and sing in the words of the old Negro spiritual, "Free at last! free at last! thank God almighty, we are free at last!"

—*Rev. Martin Luther King, Jr.*

King's famous "I Have a Dream" speech is, of course, prose, but it is prose which, like Churchill's, approaches poetry in its music and structure. Mark in this speech all the examples you can find of balance, parallelism, and series of words and phrases. Then look for alliteration and assonance. Finally, examine the speech for phrases which seem to be patterned accentually into poetic feet, into musical beats, into poetic rhythms. How far is this speech, really, from poetry?

A Noiseless Patient Spider

A noiseless patient spider,
I mark'd where on a little promontory it stood isolated,
Mark'd how to explore the vacant vast surrounding,
It launch'd forth filament, filament, filament, out of itself,
Ever unreeling them, ever tirelessly speeding them.

And you O my soul where you stand,
Surrounded, detached, in measureless oceans of space,
Ceaselessly musing, venturing, throwing, seeking the spheres to connect them,
Till the bridge you will need be form'd, till the ductile anchor hold,
Till the gossamer thread you fling catch somewhere, O my soul.

—*Walt Whitman*

Sometimes Whitman repeats a word two or even three times. Is this mere rhetoric, or does repetition actually expand the meaning of the word, or its emotional impact upon a reader? Is there any reason why Whitman might find repetition of identical or similar phrases useful in this poem? How much different are Whitman's poem and King's speech? Are the differences those of structure or of content?

Psalm 150

Praise the Lord!
Praise God in his sanctuary;
praise him in his mighty firmament!
Praise him for his mighty deeds;
praise him according to his exceeding greatness!

Praise him with trumpet sound;
praise him with lute and harp!
Praise him with timbrel and dance;
praise him with strings and pipe!
Praise him with sounding cymbals;
praise him with loud clashing cymbals!
Let everything that breathes praise the Lord!
Praise the Lord!

Underline all the repeated phrases in this Psalm, and connect them with lines. Mark the balanced phrases with arcs. Is there any justification, apart from the music and rhetoric of the thing, for such a profusion of repetition?

Diamonds and Rust

Well I'll be damned, here comes your ghost again
But that's not unusual, it's just that the moon is full
And you happened to call
And here I sit, and on the telephone
Hearing a voice I'd known a couple of light years ago
Heading straight for a fall.

As I remember your eyes were bluer than robin's eggs
My poetry was lousy you said. Where are you calling from?
A booth in the midwest
Ten years ago I had bought you some cuff links;
You brought me something. We both know what memories can bring,
They bring diamonds and rust.

Well you burst on the scene already a legend,
The unwashed phenomenon, the original vagabond,
You strayed into my arms.
And there you stayed, temporarily lost at sea;
The madonna was yours for free, yes, the girl on the half-shell
Could keep you unharmed.

Now I see you standing with brown leaves falling all around
And snow in your hair
Now you're smiling out the window of that crummy hotel
Over Washington Square.
Our breath comes out white clouds, mingles and
Hangs in the air.
Speaking strictly for me we both could have died
Then and there.

Now you're telling me you're not nostalgic
Then give me another word for it—you who're so good with
  words
And at keeping things vague.
'Cause I need some of that vagueness now, it's all come back
  too clearly.
Yes, I loved you dearly. And if you're offering me diamonds
  and rust
I've already paid.

—*Joan Baez*

1. Listen to Joan Baez sing this song on the album *Diamonds and Rust.* Where do you suppose the poem gets its five-phrase structure? Does the singer ever have to squeeze to fit her phrases into this pattern? Why do lines 19–26 not fit the pattern of the rest of the song?

2. What do the images "diamonds" and "rust" suggest to you? How are they appropriate to a song on this subject?

3. In Chapter 2, Section 6 we spoke of "confessional poetry," and the poet's own self as subject. This song's subject is the relationship between Joan Baez herself and singer Bob Dylan (calling from a booth somewhere in the midwest). Dylan, for his part, has written songs that appear to be about the same relationship, particularly on his *Blood on the Tracks* album. To what extent does this song transcend biography and the Dylan-Baez relationship and take on significance for you? Do you relate to this song? Would you if Baez and Dylan were not famous?

8. A Structure: Free Verse

It *is* possible to write poetry that has no regular pattern of accentual meter, no rhyme, no regular pulse or beat, no pattern of rhetorical structures and phrases, and no standardized count of line or syllable. This poetry is called "free verse," and it has become increasingly popular in the twentieth century, especially in the last two decades.

How free is free verse? Some critics would call the kinds of poetry we have been discussing in the last few sections—poetry that counts accent or pulse, poetry structured according to rhetorical patterns—free verse, in the sense that it does not conform to traditional metrical forms. Some people would argue that poetry entirely free of structure is prose (and pretty formless prose at that), and thus extremely free verse is just prose poetry (see Chapter 4, Section 9). Clearly there are degrees of freedom, and "free verse" is a relative term.

This much is certain: free verse has the great advantage of liberating the poet from all *demands* of repeated pattern, and thus from the distortions he might otherwise have to make in his poetry for the sake of regular rhyme and meter. There are none of those awkward inversions of subject and verb, or verb and object that rhyme or meter often necessitate:

Three years she grew in sun and shower,
Then Nature said, "A lovelier flower
On earth was never sown. . . ."

—*Wordsworth*

There is none of that filler that bad poets throw into their poetry to flesh out a line or make a rhyme:

An elf-queen will I love, ywis,
For in this world no woman is
Worthy to be my make
In town;
All other women I forsake,
And to an elf-queen I me take
By dale and eek by down!

—*Chaucer, "Sir Thopas," in parody*

There is none of that wrenching of syntax and distorted compression of the language you sometimes find when poets have been forced to squeeze maximum meaning into the confines of metrical form:

as Thou
Art jealous, Lord, so I am jealous now;
Thou lov'st not, till from loving more, Thou free
My soul; whoever gives, takes liberty;

—*John Donne*

Perhaps best of all, there is not the pecking of typewriter keys and the bells of rhyme at the end of each line that you get with poets—even good poets—whose rhythm is too monotonous, whose rhymes are too obtrusive:

"Surely," said I, "surely that is something at my window lattice;
Let me see, then, what thereat is, and this mystery explore—
Let my heart be still a moment and this mystery explore;—
'Tis the wind, and nothing more!"

—*Edgar Allan Poe*

Free verse also has positive advantages. The poet is free to break his lines when and where he wishes, to control the tempo of the poem or for other reasons. Notice, for example, how Jim Morrison uses form to control tempo in the Doors' song/poem ''Horse Latitudes'':

Horse Latitudes

When the still sea conspires an armor
And her sullen and aborted
Currents breed tiny monsters,
True sailing is dead.

Awkward instant
And the first animal is jettisoned,
Legs furiously pumping
Their stiff green gallop,
And heads bob up
Poise
Delicate
Pause
Consent
In mute nostril agony
Carefully refined
And sealed over.

—*Jim Morrison*

There is no rhyme in Morrison's poem, and the lines are of various lengths; but the line lengths and the lack of unifying rhyme are not capricious whims of the poet. The first three lines are all one clause, long and uninterrupted by the pauses that inevitably result from regular perfect rhyme. The free flow of the verse is entirely consistent with the meaning of the lines, and contrasts sharply with the fourth line, which has a static quality to its sound and its sense. Then there is a break in the verse, which signals a break in time as the sailors make the decision to jettison their cargo of horses in order to lighten the ship caught in the dead calm of the doldrums. The poet captures in the next several lines the awkward instant, in reality only a half a minute or so even though it seems an eternity both to the horse and the poet watching this agony, during which the horse struggles, bobs up for the last time, and finally drowns. The length of that moment is conveyed by breaking ''Poise/ Delicate/ Pause/ Consent'' into four one-word lines. And then the horse is gone and the poem and sea move quietly on, as if nothing had happened. The poem ends on the very final and highly effective ''over.''

The form of the poem, then, is an adjunct to conveying the meaning, which is the poet's description of one horrifying, fascinating moment. On the record the poem is read to an eerie, atonal cacophony that builds to a deafening crescendo of feedback, approximating the terror felt by horse and poet—and audience.

This disadvantage of free verse, of course, is that it offers virtually no structure at all. At least its critics claim it is without discipline. Its advocates, however, often claim a structure of sorts, either the rhetorical patterns and patterns of pulse discussed earlier, or the structure of syllables in lines that Charles Olson identified in his essay on "Projective Verse." Borrowing from an old argument of the Romantic poets, Olson said that a poem is energy "transferred from where the poet got it . . . by way of the poem . . . to the reader." He claimed that "FORM IS NEVER MORE THAN AN EXTENSION OF CONTENT" (capital letters his), and he claimed that "ONE PERCEPTION MUST IMMEDIATELY AND DIRECTLY LEAD TO A FURTHER PERCEPTION . . . always one perception must must must MOVE INSTANTER, ON ANOTHER!" Further, Olson stated, poetry proceeds from "the HEAD, by way of the EAR, to the SYLLABLE," and from "the HEART, by way of the BREATH, to the LINE." Exactly what he meant has been the subject of much discussion ever since, but clearly for Olson the line—not the stanza—is the basic rhythmic unit of poetry, and the syllable, the smallest unit of speech, is the basic unit of pulse. Each line defines its own rhythm, its own form, its own structure. One structure follows on another, as one line follows on another, as one perception follows on another.

Charles Tomlinson once wryly observed, "An Englishman, of course, is unwilling to admit Olson writes poetry as well as prose"; to him projective verse, free verse, all verse without basic metered form, is prose. The issue is certainly open to debate—both the desirability of form in poetry and the degree to which "free verse" is actually free. Examine the following poems (a) looking for patterns of structure, and (b) deciding whether you miss whatever you cannot find. Then look at other free verse poems in this book and ask yourself the same questions: do they have any form of structure at all, and do I miss what isn't there?

Looking at Models in the Sears Catalogue

These are our immortals.
They stand around
and always look happy.
Some must do work,

they are dressed for it,
but stay meticulously
clean. Others
play forever,
at the beach, in backyards,
but never move
strenuously. Here
the light is such
there are no shadows.
If anyone gestures,
it is with an open
hand. And the smiles
that bloom everywhere
are permanent, always
in fashion.
                    So
it is surprising to discover
children here,
who must have sprung
from the dark of some loins.
For the mild bodies
of these men and women
have learned to stay
dry and cool:
even the undressed
in bras and briefs
could be saying,
It was a wonderful dinner,
thank you so much.
                                        Yet,
season after season,
we shop here:
in Spring's pages,
no ripe abundance
overwhelms us;
in Winter's pages,
nothing is dying.
It is a kind of perfection.
We are not a people
who abide ugliness.
All the folds in the clothing
are neat folds,
nowhere to get lost.

—*Philip Dacey*

Love Poem

Last night you would not come,
and you have been gone so long.
I yearn to find you in my aging, earthen arms
again (your alchemy can change my clay to skin).
I long to turn and watch again
from my half-hidden place
the lost, beautiful slopes and fallings of your face,
the black, rich leaf of each eyelash,
fresh, beach-brightened stones of your teeth.
I want to listen as you breathe yourself to sleep
(for by our human art we mime
the sleeper til we dream).
I want to smell the dark
herb gardens of your hair—touch the thin shock
that drifts over your high brow when
you rinse it clean,
for it is so fine.
I want to hear the light,
long wind of your sigh.
But again tonight I know you will not come.
I will never feel again
your gentle, sleeping calm
from which I took
so much strength, so much of my human heart.
Because the last time
I reached to you
as you sat upon the bed
and talked, you caught both my hands
in yours and crossed them gently on my breast.
I died mimicking the dead.

—*John Logan*

Howl

for Carl Solomon

I

I saw the best minds of my generation destroyed by madness, starving hysterical naked,
dragging themselves through the negro streets at dawn looking for an angry fix,

angleheaded hipsters burning for the ancient heavenly connection to the starry dynamo in the machinery of night,
who poverty and tatters and hollow-eyed and high sat up smoking in the supernatural darkness of cold-water flats floating across the tops of cities contemplating jazz,
who bared their brains to Heaven under the El and saw Mohammedan angels staggering on tenement roofs illuminated,
who passed through universities with radiant cool eyes hallucinating Arkansas and Blake-light tragedy among the scholars of war,
who were expelled from the academies for crazy & publishing obscene odes on the windows of the skull,
who cowered in unshaven rooms in underwear, burning their money in wastebaskets and listening to the Terror through the wall,
who got busted in their public beards returning through Laredo with a belt of marijuana for New York,
who ate fire in paint hotels or drank turpentine in Paradise Alley, death, or purgatoried their torsos night after night
with dreams, with drugs, with waking nightmares, alcohol and cock and endless balls,
incomparable blind streets of shuddering cloud and lightning in the mind leaping toward poles of Canada & Paterson, illuminating all the motionless world of Time between,
Peyote solidities of halls, backyard green tree cemetery dawns, wine drunkenness over the rooftops, storefront boroughs of teaheads joyride neon blinking traffic light, sun and moon and tree vibrations in the roaring winter dusks of Brooklyn, ashcan rantings and kind king light of mind,
who chained themselves to subways for the endless ride from Battery to holy Bronx on benzedrine until the noise of wheels and children brought them down shuddering mouth-wracked and battered bleak of brain all drained of brilliance in the drear light of Zoo,
who sank all night in submarine light of Bickford's floated out and sat through the stale beer afternoon in desolate Fugazzi's, listening to the crack of doom on the hydrogen jukebox,
who talked continuously seventy hours from park to pad to bar to Bellevue to museum to the Brooklyn Bridge,
a lost battalion of platonic conversationalists jumping down the stoops off fire escapes off windowsills off Empire State out of the moon,

yacketayakking screaming vomiting whispering facts and
memories and anecdotes and eyeball kicks and shocks of
hospitals and jails and wars,
whole intellects disgorged in total recall for seven days and
nights with brilliant eyes, meat for the Synagogue cast on the
pavement,
who vanished into nowhere Zen New Jersey leaving a trail of
ambiguous picture postcards of Atlantic City Hall,
suffering Eastern sweats and Tangerian bone-grindings and
migraines of China under junk-withdrawal in Newark's bleak
furnished room,
who wandered around and around at midnight in the railroad
yard wondering where to go, and went, leaving no broken
hearts,
who lit cigarettes in boxcars boxcars boxcars racketing through
snow toward lonesome farms in grandfather night,
who studied Plotinus Poe St. John of the Cross telepathy and
bop kaballa because the cosmos instinctively vibrated at their
feet in Kansas,
who loned it through the streets of Idaho seeking visionary
indian angels who were visionary indian angels,
who thought they were only mad when Baltimore gleamed in
supernatural ecstasy,
who jumped in limousines with the Chinaman of Oklahoma on
the impulse of winter midnight streetlight smalltown rain,
who lounged hungry and lonesome through Houston seeking
jazz or sex or soup, and followed the brilliant Spaniard to
converse about America and Eternity, a hopeless task, and so
took ship to Africa,
who disappeared into the volcanoes of Mexico leaving behind
nothing but the shadow of dungarees and the lava and ash of
poetry scattered in fireplace Chicago,
who reappeared on the West Coast investigating the F.B.I. in
beards and shorts with big pacifist eyes sexy in their dark
skin passing out incomprehensible leaflets,
who burned cigarette holes in their arms protesting the narcotic
tobacco haze of Capitalism,
who distributed Supercommunist pamphlets in Union Square
weeping and undressing while the sirens of Los Alamos
wailed them down, and wailed down Wall, and the Staten
Island ferry also wailed,
who broke down crying in white gymnasiums naked and
trembling before the machinery of other skeletons,
who bit detectives in the neck and shrieked with delight in

policecars for committing no crime but their own wild cooking pederasty and intoxication,
who howled on their knees in the subway and were dragged off the roof waving genitals and manuscripts,
who let themselves be fucked in the ass by saintly motorcyclists, and screamed with joy,
who blew and were blown by those human seraphim, the sailors, caresses of Atlantic and Caribbean love,
who balled in the morning in the evenings in rosegardens and the grass of public parks and cemeteries scattering their semen freely to whomever come who may,
who hiccupped endlessly trying to giggle but wound up with a sob behind a partition in a Turkish Bath when the blond & naked angel came to pierce them with a sword,
who lost their loveboys to the three old shrews of fate the one eyed shrew of the heterosexual dollar the one eyed shrew that winks out of the womb and the one eyed shrew that does nothing but sit on her ass and snip the intellectual golden threads of the craftsman's loom,
who copulated ecstatic and insatiate with a bottle of beer a sweetheart a package of cigarettes a candle and fell off the bed, and continued along the floor and down the hall and ended fainting on the wall with a vision of ultimate cunt and come eluding the last gyzym of consciousness,
who sweetened the snatches of a million girls trembling in the sunset, and were red eyed in the morning but prepared to sweeten the snatch of the sunrise, flashing buttocks under barns and naked in the lake,
who went out whoring through Colorado in myriad stolen night-cars, N.C., secret hero of these poems, cocksman and Adonis of Denver—joy to the memory of his innumerable lays of girls in empty lots & diner backyards, moviehouses' rickety rows, on mountaintops in caves or with gaunt waitresses in familiar roadside lonely petticoat upliftings & especially secret gas-station solipisisms of johns, & hometown alleys too,
who faded out in vast sordid movies, were shifted in dreams, woke on a sudden Manhattan, and picked themselves up out of basements hungover with heartless Tokay and horrors of Third Avenue iron dreams & stumbled to unemployment offices,
who walked all night with their shoes full of blood on the snowbank docks waiting for a door in the East River to open to a room full of steamheat and opium,
who created great suicidal dramas on the apartment cliff-banks

of the Hudson under the wartime blue floodlight of the moon & their heads shall be crowned with laurel in oblivion,
who ate the lamb stew of the imagination or digested the crab at the muddy bottom of the rivers of Bowery,
who wept at the romance of the streets with their pushcarts full of onions and bad music,
who sat in boxes breathing in the darkness under the bridge, and rose up to build harpsichords in their lofts,
who coughed in the sixth floor of Harlem crowned with flame under the tubercular sky surrounded by orange crates of theology,
who scribbled all night rocking and rolling over lofty incantations which in the yellow morning were stanzas of gibberish,
who cooked rotten animals lung heart feet tail borsht & tortillas dreaming of the pure vegetable kingdom,
who plunged themselves under meat trucks looking for an egg,
who threw their watches off the roof to cast their ballot for Eternity outside of Time, & alarm clocks fell on their heads every day for the next decade,
who cut their wrists three times successively unsuccessfully, gave up and were forced to open antique stores where they thought they were growing old and cried,
who were burned alive in their innocent flannel suits on Madison Avenue amid blasts of leaden verse & the tanked-up clatter of the iron regiments of fashion & the nitroglycerine shrieks of the fairies of advertising & the mustard gas of sinister intelligent editors, or were run down by the drunken taxicabs of Absolute Reality,
who jumped off the Brooklyn Bridge this actually happened and walked away unknown and forgotten into the ghostly daze of Chinatown soup alleyways & firetrucks, not even one free beer,
who sang out of their windows in despair, fell out of the subway window, jumped in the filthy Passaic, leaped on negroes, cried all over the street, danced on broken wineglasses barefoot smashed phonograph records of nostalgic European 1930's German jazz finished the whiskey and threw up groaning into the bloody toilet, moans in their ears and the blast of colossal steamwhistles,
who barreled down the highways of the past journeying to each other's hotrod-Golgotha jail-solitude watch or Birmingham jazz incarnation,
who drove crosscountry seventytwo hours to find out if I had a vision or you had a vision or he had a vision to find out Eternity,

who journeyed to Denver, who died in Denver, who came back to Denver & waited in vain, who watched over Denver & brooded & loned in Denver and finally went away to find out the Time, & now Denver is lonesome for her heroes,
who fell on their knees in hopeless cathedrals praying for each other's salvation and light and breasts, until the soul illuminated its hair for a second,
who crashed through their minds in jail waiting for impossible criminals with golden heads and the charm of reality in their hearts who sang sweet blues to Alcatraz,
who retired to Mexico to cultivate a habit, or Rocky Mount to tender Buddha or Tangiers to boys or Southern Pacific to the black locomotive or Harvard to Narcissus to Woodlawn to the daisychain or grave,
who demanded sanity trials accusing the radio of hypnotism & were left with their insanity & their hands & a hung jury,
who threw potato salad at CCNY lecturers on Dadaism and subsequently presented themselves on the granite steps of the madhouse with shaven heads and harlequin speech of suicide, demanding instantaneous lobotomy,
and who were given instead the concrete void of insulin metrasol electricity hydrotherapy psychotherapy occupational therapy pingpong & amnesia,
who in humorless protest overturned only one symbolic pingpong table, resting briefly in catatonia,
returning years later truly bald except for a wig of blood, and tears and fingers, to the visible madman doom of the wards of the madtowns of the East,
Pilgrim State's Rockland's and Greystone's foetid halls, bickering with the echoes of the soul, rocking and rolling in the midnight solitude-bench dolmen-realms of love, dream of life a nightmare, bodies turned to stone as heavy as the moon,
with mother finally ******, and the last fantastic book flung out of the tenement window, and the last door closed at 4 AM and the last telephone slammed at the wall in reply and the last furnished room emptied down to the last piece of mental furniture, a yellow paper rose twisted on a wire hanger in the closet, and even that imaginary, nothing but a hopeful little bit of hallucination—
ah, Carl, while you are not safe I am not safe, and now you're really in the total animal soup of time—
and who therefore ran through the icy streets obsessed with a sudden flash of the alchemy of the use of the ellipse the catalog the meter & the vibrating plane,

who dreamt and made incarnate gaps in Time & space through images juxtaposed, and trapped the archangel of the soul between 2 visual images and joined the elemental verbs and set the noun and dash of consciousness together jumping with sensation of Pater Omnipotens Aeterna Deus
to recreate the syntax and measure of poor human prose and stand before you speechless and intelligent and shaking with shame, rejected yet confessing out the soul to conform to the rhythm of thought in his naked and endless head,
the madman bum and angel beat in Time, unknown, yet putting down here what might be left to say in time come after death,
and rose reincarnate in the ghostly clothes of jazz in the goldenhorn shadow of the band and blew the suffering of America's naked mind for love into an eli eli lamma lamma sabacthani saxophone cry that shivered the cities down to the last radio
with the absolute heart of the poem of life butchered out of their own bodies good to eat a thousand years.

II

What sphinx of cement and aluminum bashed open their skulls and ate up their brains and imagination?
Moloch! Solitude! Filth! Ugliness! Ashcans and unobtainable dollars! Children screaming under the stairways! Boys sobbing in armies! Old men weeping in the parks!
Moloch! Moloch! Nightmare of Moloch! Moloch the loveless! Mental Moloch! Moloch the heavy judger of men!
Moloch the incomprehensible prison! Moloch the crossbone soulless jailhouse and Congress of sorrows! Moloch whose buildings are judgment! Moloch the vast stone of war! Moloch the stunned governments!
Moloch whose mind is pure machinery! Moloch whose blood is running money! Moloch whose fingers are ten armies! Moloch whose breast is a cannibal dynamo! Moloch whose ear is a smoking tomb!
Moloch whose eyes are a thousand blind windows! Moloch whose skyscrapers stand in the long streets like endless Jehovahs! Moloch whose factories dream and croak in the fog! Moloch whose smokestacks and antennae crown the cities!
Moloch whose love is endless oil and stone! Moloch whose soul is electricity and banks! Moloch whose poverty is the specter of genius! Moloch whose fate is a cloud of sexless hydrogen! Moloch whose name is the Mind!

Moloch in whom I sit lonely! Moloch in whom I dream Angels!
  Crazy in Moloch! Cocksucker in Moloch! Lacklove and
  manless in Moloch!
Moloch who entered my soul early! Moloch in whom I am a
  consciousness without a body! Moloch who frightened me out
  of my natural ecstasy! Moloch whom I abandon! Wake up in
  Moloch! Light streaming out of the sky!
Moloch! Moloch! Robot apartments! invisible suburbs! skeleton
  treasuries! blind capitals! demonic industries! spectral na-
  tions! invincible madhouses! granite cocks! monstrous bombs!
They broke their backs lifting Moloch to Heaven! Pavements,
  trees, radios, tons! lifting the city to Heaven which exists and
  is everywhere about us!
Visions! omens! hallucinations! miracles! ecstasies! gone down
  the American river!
Dreams! abortions! illuminations! religions! the whole boatload
  of sensitive bullshit!
Breakthroughs! over the river! flips and crucifixions! gone down
  the flood! Highs! Epiphanies! Despairs! Ten years' animal
  screams and suicides! Minds! New loves! Mad generation!
  down on the rocks of Time!
Real holy laughter in the river! They saw it all! the wild eyes!
  the holy yells! They bade farewell! They jumped off the roof!
  to solitude! waving! carrying flowers! Down to the river! into
  the street!

III

Carl Solomon, I'm with you in Rockland
  where you're madder than I am
I'm with you in Rockland
  where you must feel very strange
I'm with you in Rockland
    where you imitate the shade of my mother
I'm with you in Rockland
  where you've murdered your twelve secretaries
I'm with you in Rockland
  where you laugh at this invisible humor
I'm with you in Rockland
  where we are great writers on the same dreadful typewriter

I'm with you in Rockland
  where your condition has become serious and is reported on the radio
I'm with you in Rockland
  where the faculties of the skull no longer admit the worms of the senses
I'm with you in Rockland
  where you drink the tea of the breasts of the spinsters of Utica
I'm with you in Rockland
  where you pun on the bodies of your nurses the harpies of the Bronx
I'm with you in Rockland
  where you scream in a straightjacket that you're losing the game of the actual pingpong of the abyss
I'm with you in Rockland
  where you bang on the catatonic piano the soul is innocent and immortal it should never die ungodly in an armed madhouse
I'm with you in Rockland
  where fifty more shocks will never return your soul to its body again from its pilgrimage to a cross in the void
I'm with you in Rockland
  where you accuse your doctors of insanity and plot the Hebrew socialist revolution against the fascist national Golgotha
I'm with you in Rockland
  where you will split the heavens of Long Island and resurrect your living human Jesus from the superhuman tomb
I'm with you in Rockland
  where there are twentyfive-thousand mad comrades all together singing the final stanzas of the Internationale
I'm with you in Rockland
  where we hug and kiss the United States under our bedsheets the United States that coughs all night and won't let us sleep
I'm with you in Rockland
  where we wake up electrified out of the coma by our own souls' airplanes roaring over the roof they've come to drop angelic bombs the hospital illuminates itself imaginary walls collapse O skinny legions run outside O starry-spangled shock of mercy the eternal war is here O victory forget your underwear we're free

I'm with you in Rockland
  in my dreams you walk dripping from a sea-journey on the
  highway across America in tears to the door of my cottage
  in the Western night

San Francisco 1955–56
—Allen Ginsberg

3. *connection:* a dope seller. 10. *Paradise Alley:* a tenement courtyard in the East Village in New York. 12. *Paterson:* Paterson, N.J., Ginsberg's hometown. 14. *Battery to holy Bronx:* termini of the New York subway system; *Zoo:* the Bronx Zoo. 15. *Bickford's:* a cafeteria where Ginsberg worked as a college student; *Fugazzi's:* a bar in Greenwich Village frequented in the fifties by beats. 24. *kaballa:* the mystical tradition of interpretation of Hebrew scripture. 43. *N.C.:* Neal Cassady, also the hero of Jack Kerouac's *On the Road.* 59. *Golgotha:* hill on which Christ was crucified. 70. *Pilgrim's, Rockland's* and *Greystone's:* mental institutions near New York. 74. *Pater Omnipotens Aeterna Deus:* all powerful father, eternal god. 77. *eli eli lamma lamma sabacthani:* "My God, my God, why have you forsaken me?" Christ's last words on the cross. 80. *Moloch:* in the Old Testament, a god to whom children were sacrificed by the Phoenecians and the Ammonities. 95. *Carl Solomon:* a patient, with Ginsburg, at the Columbia Psychiatric Institute in 1949.

It is difficult to say what in this poem shocked the sensibilities of 1950s America more: its collage of half-digested images retched from an overstuffed American stomach, images purged from the "Ozzie and Harriet" mind of the fifties, or the great rambling formlessness of Ginsberg's poetics. "Hold back the edges of your gowns, Ladies," wrote William Carlos Williams by way of introduction to the poem, "we are going through hell."

In retrospect, "Howl" seems less disconcerting than it once did: we are by now familiar with Ginsberg's imagery (it may even seem tame); we hear and read the language he uses every day; we can see the humor as well as the revulsion in "Howl"; and the poetics can be understood as part of a line in American poetry that dates to Walt Whitman and comes to us through Sandburg, Lindsay, Williams, and many others. "Howl" is a poem of images and cadences, and all discussions of the poem may be reduced quite simply to two issues: first, what statement (on the soul of America, on the spirit of the fifties, on the state of Ginsberg and his companions) emerges out of the custard pie of imagery? And second, how do Ginsberg's form and the pulse of his cadences, the stopping and starting and speeding up and slowing down, impact on your ear?

9. A Structure: Prose Poetry

The poet Michael Anania once remarked, "There was a time in my life when I read every scrap of poetry I could get my hands on, everything I saw where the lines didn't go all the way over to the right-hand margin. Even the telephone book." He was joking, of course, playing with popular ideas about poetry—and yet he touched upon a very fundamental issue: as poetry becomes increasingly unstructured, why not simply write it out as prose? In fact, the same question could be asked of regularly metered and rhymed poetry: if the end of one line "spills right over" into the beginning of the next, unchecked by punctuation and obliterating rhymes, why not simply write it out in paragraph form? Early scribes, it should be noted, often wrote poems one line after the other, right on up to the edge of the paper, a new line of manuscript beginning, as often as not, somewhere in the middle of a "line" of poetry. They were trying to save parchment, of course, but why not? Why not print Shakespeare's Sonnet 55 or Whitman's "Noiseless Patient Spider" out in prose:

Sonnet 55

Not marble, nor the gilded monuments of princes, shall outlive this powerful rhyme; but you shall shine more bright in these contents than unswept stone, besmeared with sluttish time. When wasteful war shall statues overturn, and broils root out the work of masonry, nor Mars his sword nor war's quick fire shall burn the living record of your memory. 'Gainst death and all obvious enmity shall you pace forth; your praise shall still find room even in the eyes of all posterity that wear this world out to the ending doom. So, till the judgment that yourself arise, you live in this, and dwell in lovers' eyes.

A Noiseless Patient Spider

A noiseless patient spider, I mark'd where on a little promontory it stood isolated, mark'd how to explore the vacant vast surrounding, it launch'd forth filament, filament, filament, out of itself, ever unreeling them, ever tirelessly speeding them. And you O my soul where you stand surrounded, detached, in measureless oceans of space, ceaselessly musing, venturing, throwing, seeking the spheres to connect them, till the bridge you will need be form'd, till the ductile anchor hold, till the gossamer thread you fling catch somewhere, O my soul.

What has been lost?

Perhaps there is no reason why poetry, especially free verse, should not appear as prose, unless the poet is looking for a visual effect (like cummings) or using the line to control tempo (like Jim Morrison in "Horse Latitudes" or Don L. Lee in "But He Was Cool"). Several modern poets have taken to writing what they call "prose poems": poetry written in prose paragraphs. Here are two examples. Examine them for evidence of structure and pattern. Do you find any? Do you think that these are not really quite poetry because "the lines go all the way over to the right-hand margin"? What other qualities of poetry do they exhibit?

Fall

Because it is the first Sunday of pheasant season, men gather in the lights of cars to divide pheasants, and the chickens, huddling near their electricity, and in some slight fear of the dark, walk for the last time about their little hut, whose floor seems now so bare.

The dusk has come, a glow in the west, as if seen through the isinglass on old coal stoves, and the cows stand around the bar door; now the farmer looks up at the paling sky reminding him of death, and in the fields the bones of the corn rustle faintly in the last wind, and the half moon stands in the south.

Now the lights from barn windows can be seen through bare trees.

—Robert Bly

The Bourgeois Poet #27

Why poetry small and cramped, why poetry starved and mean, thin-lipped and sunken-cheeked? Why these pams, these narrow-shouldered negatives? (The best we can say is that they're seed catalogs.) And why those staring eyes, so carefully fixed on the photographic plate? Why no lips at all but in their stead the practiced line of anger and the clamped jaw? Why always the darkening halo, so seemingly satanic? (The best we can say is that they are trying to mirror our lives. Do they know our lives? Can they read past the symbols of our trade?) Why so much attention to the printed page, why the cosmetology of font and rule, meters laid on like fingernail enamel? Why these lisping indentations, Spanish question marks upside down? Why the attractive packaging of stanza? Those cartons so pretty, shall I open them up? Why the un-American-activity of the sonnet? Why must grown people listen to rhyme? How much longer the polite applause, the tickle in the throat?

What will fatten you, skinny little book? What will put lead in your pencil? All of you dust-collecting seed catalogs, to the Goodwill you go, to the broad stench of the paper mill! Seed catalog, go pulp yourself!

Poems, flowers of language, if that's what you are, grow up in the air where books come true. And you, thin packet, let your seed fly, if you have any.

—*Karl Shapiro*

10. A Structure: Concrete Poetry

One possibility of form has nothing to do with words as spoken sounds. The poet might mold the words and letters of a poem, as they are printed on the page, to create designs or to play a typographical game which in one way or another enhances the meaning of the words. In such cases the poem's structure comes not from the sound of its words, but from the shape of black ink on white page. These games have been going on for some time: George Herbert's "Easter Wings" (a poem in the shape of two pair of wings) was written in 1633:

Easter Wings

Lord, who createdst man in wealth and store,
  Though foolishly he lost the same,
    Decaying more and more
        Till he became
          Most poor:
          With thee
        O let me rise
    As larks, harmoniously,
  And sing this day thy victories:
Then shall the fall further the flight in me.

My tender age in sorrow did begin:
And still with sicknesses and shame
Thou didst so punish sin,
That I became
Most thin.
With thee
Let me combine,
And feel this day thy victory;
For, if I imp my wing on thine,
Affliction shall advance the flight in me.

—*George Herbert*

1. *store:* abundance. 19. *imp:* graft.

Notice here that the *sense* of lines 1–5 and 11–15 is diminishment, and the *sense* of 6–10 and 16–20 is replenishment. The form of the poem, apart from making an interesting design, reflects the content of the poem.

Not until the twentieth century, however, have large numbers of poets begun experimenting seriously in visual poetry. And their experiments admit of several degrees. First, and simplest, are typographical arrangements in which the placement of words and letters forms a visual pun on the meaning of the words, as in cummings's "r-p-o-p-h-e-s-s-a-g-r" (Chapter 1, Section 1). Allen Ginsberg, uncharacteristically (because Ginsberg is nothing so much as an *oral* poet, and you cannot read concrete poetry aloud), was playing the same kind of game in his poem "Funny Death":

Funny Death

```
FFFFF U           U  NN        N
F     U           U  N N       N
FFFFF U           U  N   N     N
F       U       U    N     N N  NY     DEATH
F         U   U      N       NN
F           UU       N         N
```

The music of the spheres—that ends in Silence
The Void is a grand piano
a million melodies
one after another

silence in between
rather an interruption
of the silence
Tho the music's beautiful
Bong Bong Bon——
gnob
gnob
gno——
Bong Bong Bong
o n
n o
g b
b g
o n
n o
obgnobgnobgnob
THE circle of forms
Shrinks
and disappears
back into the piano.
—*Allen Ginsberg*

More sophisticated than "Easter Wings," "Funny Death," and "r-p-o-p-h-e-s-s-a-g-r" are concrete poems which use the arrangement of words on the page to create structures of nonlinear relationships. When a poem is read or sung, one word follows another, one idea follows another sequentially: after word/thought A must come either word/thought B or word/thought C, but not both together, because you can only say or sing one thing at a time. Oral poems have line. But there is no reason why printed poems should necessarily have line, because the eye, in taking in a page of printed words, can read any way it wishes. The eye is not necessarily forced, except by habit, to move left to right, top to bottom across the page. In fact, if encouraged to do so, it can see both word/thought B *and* word/thought C in exactly the same relationship to word/thought A. Or the eye can see no relationships at all, only an arrangement of words or letters. "Silent Poem," by Robert Francis is—as the title suggests—a poem to be seen. "I became so fond of the strong character of solid compounds [backroad, stonewall, etc.]," he wrote, "that I made a list purely for my pleasure. In time I wanted to make a poem out of those words, fitting them together like a patchwork quilt."

Silent Poem

backroad leafmold stonewall chipmunk
underbrush grapevine woodchuck shadblow

woodsmoke cowbarn honeysuckle woodpile
sawhorse bucksaw outhouse wellsweep

backdoor flagstone bulkhead buttermilk
candlestick ragrug firedog brownbread

hilltop outcrop cowbell buttercup
whetstone thunderstorm pitchfork steeplebush

gristmill millstone cornmeal waterwheel
watercress buckwheat firefly jewelweed

gravestone groundpine windbreak bedrock
weathercock snowfall starlight cockcrow

—Robert Francis

The result of Francis's experiment is a poem you can read left to right or right to left, top to bottom or bottom to top, or even diagonally. Or you can *see* it, take it all in, as a field of words.

In concrete poetry, of course, the field is the thing. In fact, concrete poetry is much closer to visual art forms—the collage or the abstract painting—than it is to traditional poetry. What we look for in a concrete poem is only partially related to such qualities of poetry as thing, voice, and statement; we look for artistic considerations such as design, spatial relationships, space itself, rhythm (in the visual sense), light, dark, movement, stasis, geometry. Printed poetry, once the poet begins to insist on the printedness of his medium, is something quite different from oral poetry, almost a new way of thinking and communicating, as the following examples of concrete poetry demonstrate.

On the following pages you will find four examples of concrete poetry by Wisconsin poet Norbert Blei. Notice how they move gradually out of literature and into graphic art. Notice how the meaning of words becomes increasingly subordinated to the shape and placement of words. Is "Look Now Look! Love" a poem or a picture?

WOMAN

being
all
that
you
are

SINGER

of LOVE

soft star dance

& SEA moon

NIGHT-BLOOMING
POPPIES . . .

say NO

to power

For
this
just

YES

In the still of this morning:

EARTH WORMS

Green Grass

Eggplant

doves

A Flutter of Butterflies

Everything's Coming Up

...floating in now

Blai

WIDE OPEN

THE *Hunter* **WIND** *Back*

Night ***Pottery***

the Open Secrets of

DANCES

Ripened *Red*

& **The silent ride**

of *the Sun*

Look
LOOK!
Now
Love

5 A Poem Is a Statement

So a poem is concrete: a person, a place, or an image. It is the voice of the poet: a music of sounds, rhythms, and tones. And it is a structure: a pattern of sounds and words, an organization. What is the purpose of a poem? What does it do? Is it merely a pleasant game people play with words, poetry for its own sake (art for art's sake), or can we learn something from it? Should we expect poetry to change our lives, to *do* things to us? Should we learn from poetry? If so, *what* should we learn?

The extent to which poetry should or should not instruct has been a matter of heated discussion almost as long as people have been writing about art. Plato, considering the matter in his *Dialogues,* was very strong on poets as teachers, and insisted that they present only appropriate, moral models of gods and mortals for their readers to imitate. Aristotle, although more interested in matters of technique in his *Poetics,* never for a moment doubted that the proper *end* of technique was some kind of presumably moral statement on the ways of gods and men. Milton viewed his job in *Paradise Lost* as nothing short of explaining God's ways to men, and it was something of a commonplace during the Renaissance that to be a good artist one must first of necessity be a good (i.e. moral) person. Throughout the seventeenth and eighteenth centuries the function of poetry was to convey the accumulated cultural wisdom of society, to provide instruction in culture. Frequently in these centuries poetry was used, as in Pope's "Essay on Man," as a vehicle for philosophical thought.

Beginning in the nineteenth century, however, another school of thought began to develop in English poetry. Wordsworth argued that poetry was not the expression of culture or morality, or even ideas, but "the spontaneous overflow of powerful feelings," and "emotion recollected in tranquility." Edgar Allan Poe, at the remove of fifty years and several thousand miles from Wordsworth, inveighed against didacticism, a ''heresy'' which he thought had ''accomplished more in the corruption of our Poetical Literature than all its other enemies combined.'' He argued that the proper end of poetry was pleasure caused by beauty and apprehended not by the intellect or the moral conscience, but by ''the soul.'' In fact, Poe thought poetry had ''no concern whatever'' with either duty or truth. So much for instruction in poetry! Although Poe's views were, at the time, idiosyncratic even among other poets, his position was developed by the French symbolists, and carried thence back into the mainstream of English literature, and it is today a commonplace that art exists for its own sake, that didactic art is bad or dull or both, that the poet's obligation is to explore beauty wherever he can find it (even in the ugly), and to hell with societal norms, culture, and morality. Many poets feel that a poem should not even *mean* something, let alone instruct, and write poetry deliberately designed to confound audiences who insist on finding meaning in poetry. ''A poem should not mean,'' wrote Archibald MacLeish in his famous ''Ars Poetics,'' ''but be.''

The argument divides itself really into two separate issues. The first is whether a poem should make any attempt at philosophical statement at all. Should a poet even attempt to talk about truth, justice, the human condition, what is moral and ethical? Or is it sufficient—is it, in fact, all we can legitimately ask—that a poet be true to his own technique? Might not disciplined technique even be a kind of indirect statement, or at least a testimonial to beauty, and indirectly to truth? Norman Mailer expressed this notion at the beginning of his book about the Vietnam War protest march in Washington, *The Armies of the Night:* ''When was everyone going to cut out the nonsense and get to work, do their own real work? One's own literary work was the only answer to the war in Vietnam.''

The second question is whether the poet should be held responsible for the morality of his statement, and if so, by whom, and—most important of all—who should define the standard of morality against which poet and poem are measured? In communist countries, of course, poets, like all artists, are expected to mouth the party morality, with the result that they either speak untruth (not to mention unbeauty) or find themselves silenced. This is an unhappy situation. In western society, poets have until quite recently dissociated themselves from direct social and political commentary, with the results that politics and society have lost their most impartial and moral critics, and degenerated into chaos and spiritual paralysis, and sports and television, and all the other evils of modern America. This is also an unhappy situation.

Both of these issues—whether poetry *should* mean something, and whether it should teach—are perhaps as much a matter of faith as anything. Still it is wise for us to explore the many ways in which a poem can make a statement, or at least comment implicity or explicity on the human condition. And because so many poems are in the last analysis poems about poetry, about the possibility of statement and the relative values of technique and content, a knowledge of this complex aesthetic argument is something of a precondition to absorbing "the statement" of many modern poems. The statement of many poems, often implicit, is a statement on art and the nature of art.

It is the position of this book that no poets, try as they may, can escape the simple fact that words are not mere blotches of ink on the page. Words have meanings, and people *expect* words to mean things, and they will persist in making "D o g" mean a four-footed furry creature that barks and wags its tail, and not a two-legged winged creature that peeps, and there is nothing a poet can do—short of writing in a foreign language that neither he nor his audience understands—to escape the very nature of his medium. If the poet refuses to put a meaning in his poem, audiences will persist in finding a meaning, or several possible meanings, or in being baffled and angered and turning away from poem and poet. And it is finally the position of this book, to be blunt about it, that statement is as important to a poem as a good concrete subject, structure, and voice—and while poems do exist that lack one or even two of those four essential qualities, a poem that disregards statement has as little chance of artistic significance as a poem that ignores the need for concrete subject, a recognizable voice, and deliberate structure.

1. A Statement: Theme

"A sower went out to sow his seed," we read in the thirteenth chapter of Matthew's gospel. "And as he sowed, some seeds fell along the path, and the birds came and devoured them. Other seeds fell on rocky ground, where they had not much soil, and immediately they sprang up, since they had no depth of soil, but when the sun rose they were scorched, and since they had no root they withered away." And so forth. Now in reading this we grasp immediately that here is no simple story about a sower sowing seed, but a story about Christ spreading his teachings. We know this even before Christ explains it to his followers: "When any one hears the words of the kingdom and does not understand it, the evil one comes and snatches away what is sown in his heart: this is what was sown along the path. As for what was sown on rocky ground, this is he who hears the word and immediately receives it with joy; yet he has no root in himself, but endures for a while, and when tribulation or persecution arises on account of the word, immediately he falls away."

The question is *how* do we intuit that this story is not really about a sower, but about Christ? Or, more properly, that it is a story about a sower, all right, but its *theme,* its "hidden meaning," its "allegorical explanation" is about Christ's teachings? How do we know when Aesop begins a fable about two dogs quarreling over a bone, which they lose to a kite who swoops down to steal it from them—how do we know, even before we get to the moral of the fable, that this is really a story about the destructiveness of avarice? How do we know when someone is being sarcastic, when "yes" really means "no," when "well aren't *you* clever" really means "look, dummy, anybody could have figured that out"?

The answer is, it's hard to tell. Some people really do need Christ's explanation of the parable of the sower, and Aesop's moral. Some people do not understand satire and parody and sarcasm. And they are not very good at getting the "hidden meaning," or theme, or broader statement of a poem or short story. There is a certain sensitivity to identifying themes, especially in stating them accurately, without overstatement or oversimplification.

Finding the theme of a work of literature depends a great deal on the sensitivity of the reader, and on the work itself. Explicitly didactic poems, the kind Poe complained about, are pretty difficult to miss. Oliver Wendell Holmes explicates the meaning of his "Chambered Nautilus" like Aesop explicating a fable:

The Chambered Nautilus

This is the ship of pearl, which, poets feign,
   Sails the unshadowed main,—
   The venturous bark that flings
On the sweet summer wind its purpled wings
In gulfs enchanted, where the Siren sings,
   And coral reefs lie bare,
Where the cold sea-maids rise to sun their streaming hair.

Its webs of living gauze no more unfurl;
   Wrecked is the ship of pearl!
   And every chambered cell,
Where its dim dreaming life was wont to dwell,
As the frail tenant shaped his growing shell,
   Before thee lies revealed,—
Its irised ceiling rent, its sunless crypt unsealed!

Year after year beheld the silent toil
  That spread his lustrous coil;
  Still, as the spiral grew,
He left the past year's dwelling for the new,
Stole with soft step its shining archway through,
  Built up its idle door,
Stretched in his last-found home, and knew the old no more.

Thanks for the heavenly message brought by thee,
  Child of the wandering sea,
  Cast from her lap, forlorn!
From thy dead lips a clearer note is born
That ever Triton blew from wreathed horn!
  While on mine ear it rings,
Through the deep caves of thought I hear a voice that sings:—

Build thee more stately mansions, O my soul,
  As the swift seasons roll!
  Leave thy low-vaulted past!
Let each new temple, nobler than the last,
Shut thee from heaven with a dome more vast,
  Till thou at length art free,
Leaving thine outgrown shell by life's unresting sea!

—*Oliver Wendell Holmes*

3. *bark:* ship. 5. *Sirens:* mythological creatures, half woman and half bird, reputed to lure sailors to their deaths by the sweet sound of their singing. 26. *Triton:* son of Poseidon, the God of the sea, who carried a horn made out of a conch shell.

Here, clearly, is a thing, a voice, a structure . . . and statement aplenty (and proof, incidentally, that more is not always better). Poetry need not be quite so explicit to have a clear theme. Carly Simon, for example, took a good long look at marriage in "The Way I've Always Heard It Should Be." Nowhere does she preach against it, the way Holmes sermonized in "The Chambered Nautilus," but the portrait she paints of her own parents' lives and the lives of her friends make it clear that only with great reservation (and perhaps resignation) does she finally agree, "okay, we'll marry."

The Way I've Always Heard It Should Be

My father sits at night with no lights on;
his cigarette glows in the dark.

The living room is still;
I walk by, no remark.
I tiptoe past the master bedroom where
My mother reads her magazines.
I hear her call, "Sweet dreams,"
But I forget how to dream.

But you say it's time we moved in together
And raised a family of our own, you and me.
Well, that's the way I've always heard it should be;
You want to marry me,
We'll marry.

My friends from college, they're all married now;
They have their houses and their lawns.
They have their silent noons,
Tearful nights, angry dawns.
Their children hate them for the things they're not;
They hate themselves for what they are.
And yet they drink, they laugh;
Close the wound, hide the scar.

But you say it's time we moved in together,
And raised a family of our own, you and me.
Well, that's the way I've always heard it should be.
You want to marry me.
We'll marry.

You say that we can keep our love alive;
Babe, all I know is what I see.
The couples cling and claw
And drown in love's debris.
You say we'll soar like two birds through the clouds,
But soon you'll cage me on your shelf.
I'll never learn to be just me first
By myself.

Well, okay, it's time we moved in together,
And raised a family of our own, you and me.
Well, that's the way I've always heard it should be.
You want to marry me.
We'll marry.

—*Carly Simon*

Not all songs, and not all poems either, are as clear as Holmes's and Simon's, and therein lies the problem. Many artists like to be more subtle about their statements, to "lay it between the lines," as Peter, Paul, and Mary once put it in "Rock-n-roll Music." And in subtlety comes confusion. Moreover, many works of art resist reduction to a single statement, or to an easily stated theme: they admit to a range of interpretations, to a variety of possible themes. Most modern poets would take it as an insult if you were to reduce the "meaning" of their poem to a single line or two. In fact, they would probably object to any attempt to paraphrase or abstract the statement of their poems, arguing that the whole poem is its meaning, the statement of the poem is the poem. They might even argue that they were intending no statement at all. What, for example, is the theme of Poe's "The Raven"? It has none. Poe would have told you that. It is a special effects poem, an exercise in beauty apprehended by the soul, and it makes no statement at all, except the implicit argument that special effects poems are worth writing and reading, and the world is a scary place where the supernatural sometimes intrudes upon everyday lives.

So how do we know if a poem is supposed to have a theme, and what that theme might be? First, we look at the connotative and denotative meaning of the words. What does "sleep" connote? Frequently death. Might Robert Frost's poem about picking apples, then, have something to do with death? Perhaps. Second, we look for metaphors and symbols, and for metaphorical possibilities. If a poet says "My love is like a red, red rose," then we know his rose poem is really a love poem. If he hands us a rose unexplained, then we must rifle the files of our brain for metaphoric and symbolic possibilities until we find something that fits the poem; perhaps we'll be able to infer that the poem is not so much a rose poem as a love poem. Or handed woods full of oak, dogwood, and witch hazel by Richard Wilbur, we might survey the metaphorical possibilities of trees and look closely at some of his lines, noting that in closing he makes a statement applicable not only to trees but to people as well. We could conclude that perhaps, just perhaps, the poet is talking about people under the guise of talking about trees. We might look at Chairman Mao's ode to a plum blossom and ask ourselves, "Just what is he saying about this plum blossom?" Having answered that, we might press the matter further: "Is there any chance that what he says about the flower is intended to apply to other things as well?"

We listen carefully for a poet's voice, for tone and meter and music and rhythm, for they can turn the theme of a poem right around and make "yes" mean "no" and "you're really a clever lad" mean "look, you dolt!" Even form may constitute part of the theme of a poem.

Robert Frost's popular poem "Design," for example, questions the nature and even the existence of cosmic design in nature, closing with the line "If design govern in a thing so small." We might find the poem ambiguous until we note that the form of the poem is a perfect sonnet, a very tight sonnet with only four rhyming sounds. And the form suggests an answer: yes, design *does* govern in small things.

Still, identifying themes and restricting the range of possible themes remains a sensitivity cultivated only by practice and experience. You have done much already in this book in the way of finding themes, for almost every discussion has been intended not only to point out that aspect of poetry under discussion, but to take you to an understanding of the poet's statement as well. There is more to come, of course. And here are a few particularly choice poems on which you can practice your sensitivity to the thematic statement of a poem. Begin by asking yourself in each case, "What are the key words and lines in this poem?" Then look for metaphoric possibilities. Try to explain what appears idiosyncratic or odd to you, because the chances are good that it looked odd to the poet as well and is intended to be odd—its oddness is its significance. Listen to the voice of the poet. And in each case be careful not to make your theme more specific or more general than the poem warrants. Then compare your interpretations with those of your friends, argue for and against the various possibilities, and see if you can arrive at a consensual interpretation.

Ode to the Plum Blossom

On reading Lu Yu's Ode to the Plum Blossom, *I countered it with the following lines.*

Wind and rain escorted Spring's departure,
Flying snow welcomes Spring's return.
On the ice-clad rock rising high and sheer
A flower blooms sweet and fair.

Sweet and fair, she craves not Spring for herself alone,
To be the harbinger of Spring she is content.
When the mountain flowers are in full bloom
She will smile mingling in their midst.

—*Mao Tse-tung*

After Apple-Picking

My long two-pointed ladder's sticking through a tree
Toward heaven still,
And there's a barrel that I didn't fill
Beside it, and there may be two or three
Apples I didn't pick upon some bough.
But I am done with apple-picking now.
Essence of winter sleep is on the night,
The scent of apples: I am drowsing off.
I cannot rub the strangeness from my sight
I got from looking through a pane of glass
I skimmed this morning from the drinking trough
And held against the world of hoary grass.
It melted, and I let it fall and break.
But I was well
Upon my way to sleep before it fell,
And I could tell
What form my dreaming was about to take.
Magnified apples appear and disappear,
Stem end and blossom end,
And every fleck of russet showing clear.
My instep arch not only keeps the ache,
It keeps the pressure of a ladder-round.
I feel the ladder sway as the boughs bend.
And I keep hearing from the cellar bin
The rumbling sound
Of load on load of apples coming in.
For I have had too much
Of apple-picking: I am overtired
Of the great harvest I myself desired.
There were ten thousand thousand fruit to touch,
Cherish in hand, lift down, and not let fall.
For all
That struck the earth,
No matter if not bruised or spiked with stubble,
Went surely to the cider-apple heap
As of no worth.
One can see what will trouble
This sleep of mine, whatever sleep it is.
Were he not gone,
The woodchuck could say whether it's like his
Long sleep, as I describe its coming on,
Or just some human sleep.

—*Robert Frost*

Norwegian Wood

I once had a girl,
Or should I say
She once had me;

She showed me her room,
Isn't it good
Norwegian Wood?

She asked me to stay
And she told me to sit anywhere
So I looked around
And I noticed there wasn't a chair.

I sat on a rug
Biding my time,
Drinking her wine.

We talked until two
And then she said
"It's time for bed."

She told me she worked in the morning
And started to laugh,
I told her I didn't
And crawled off to sleep in the bath.

And when I awoke
I was alone,
This bird had flown,

So I built a fire,
Isn't it good,
Norwegian Wood?

—*John Lennon–Paul McCartney*

A Wood

Some would distinguish nothing here but oaks,
Proud heads conversant with the power and glory
Of heaven's rays or heaven's thunderstrokes,
And adumbrators to the understory,

Where, in their shade, small trees of modest leanings
Contend for light and are content with gleanings.

And yet here's dogwood: overshadowed, small,
But not inclined to droop and count its losses,
It cranes its way to sunlight after all,
And signs the air of May with Maltese crosses.
And here's witch hazel, that from underneath
Great vacant boughs will bloom in winter's teeth.

Given a source of light so far away
That nothing, short or tall, comes very near it,
Would it not take a proper fool to say
That any tree has not the proper spirit?
Air, water, earth and fire are to be blended,
But no one style, I think, is recommended.

—*Richard Wilbur*

First Snow in Lake County

All night it fell around us
as if the sky had been sheared,
its fleece dropping forever
past our windows, until our room
was as chaste and sheltered
as Ursula's, where she lay
and dreamed herself in heaven:
and in the morning we saw
that the vision had held, looked out
on such a sight as we wish for
all our lives:
a thing, place, time
untouched and uncorrupted,
the world before we were here.

Even the wind held its peace.

And already, as our eyes
hung on, hung on, we longed
to make that patience bear
our tracks, already our daughter
put on her boots and screamed,
and the dog jumped with the joy

of splashing the white with yellow
and digging through the snow
to the scents and sounds below.

—*Lisel Mueller*

Channel Firing

That night your great guns, unawares,
Shook all our coffins as we lay,
And broke the chancel window-squares,
We thought it was the Judgment-day

And sat upright. While drearisome
Arose the howl of wakened hounds:
The mouse let fall the altar-crumb,
The worms drew back into the mounds,

The glebe cow drooled. Till God called, "No
It's gunnery practice out at sea
Just as before you went below;
The world is as it used to be:

"All nations striving strong to make
Red war yet redder. Mad as hatters
They do no more for Christès sake
Than you who are helpless in such matters.

"That this is not the judgment-hour
For some of them's a blessed thing,
For if it were they'd have to scour
Hell's floor for so much threatening . . .

"Ha, ha. It will be warmer when
I blow the trumpet (if indeed
I ever do; for you are men,
And rest eternal sorely need)."

So down we lay again. "I wonder,
Will the world ever saner be,"
Said one, "than when He sent us under
In our indifferent century!"

And many a skeleton shook his head.
"Instead of preaching forty year,"
My neighbor Parson Thirdly said,
"I wish I had stuck to pipes and beer."

Again the guns disturbed the hour,
Roaring their readiness to avenge,
As far inland as Stourton Tower,
And Camelot, and starlit Stonehenge.

—*Thomas Hardy*

9. *glebe:* ecclesiastical pasture lands. 14. *hatters:* Cf. *Alice in Wonderland.* 35. *Stourton Tower:* an ancient tower in Dorsetshire. 36. *Camelot:* the mythical seat of Arthur's kingdom; *Stonehenge:* a prehistoric temple on Salisbury Plain.

2. A Statement: Allegory

Symbols set moving in a narrative framework, or a story that seems intended to tell another, hidden story, form an allegory, and many narrative poems—especially old poems—are allegories of one sort or another. For example, a character named John Doe is minding his own business while watering the grass one day, when up walks a grim-visaged fellow in a black suit who tells him, "John, you must come with me immediately on a long journey. No time to say good-bye, no need to bring anything with you, we're off. It's very urgent." John says, "Alas, I'd like to say farewell to my wife Mary, because we had an argument last night, and I don't want to leave her angry at me." "No time for that," says the man. "But wait a minute," says John, "because I have some unattended business, some donations I wanted to make to the Salvation Army." "Too late," he is told. "But let me stop by the bank and withdraw my savings; I've got quite a bundle saved up, and it might prove useful." "You won't need money on this journey," his friend tells him. "Gee," says John wistfully, "what a waste of time it's been saving all these years. And I wish I had some time to straighten out a few relationships."

Well. Now what we have here, on the simplest level, is a story of John Doe, his mysterious journey, and a weird stranger. But obviously this story is about death, the suddenness with which it comes, and how people confront the moment of their departure from this life. What we have here is an allegory, a moral allegory in which certain abstract psychological and moral truths are set moving in a concrete story. The name "John Doe" kind of gives the allegory away right from the start, because "John Doe" is a symbolic name. We might have made the tale even more allegorical by calling him "Everyman," and Mary "Wife" and the checkbook "Wealth," and so on; or we might have made the tale less allegorical by giving the literal level—the story of John, the journey, the stranger—a little more realistic treatment.

Other psychological or moral concepts will do nicely for allegory: falling in love, for example, or the battle of good versus evil, or coming of age physically or psychologically. But historical events can be and often are allegorized: Phil Ochs's song "The Crucifixion" is, in one sense at least, an allegory about the rise and assassination of President John F. Kennedy, and Pete Seeger's "Waist Deep in the Big Muddy" is an allegory about the late Lyndon B. Johnson and America's gradual involvement in Vietnam. Personal history as well as public history can be recounted allegorically, although a major biographical reconstruction is usually beyond the patience of most readers, who will simply "miss" a personal allegory.

Allegory was extremely popular during the Middle Ages and early Renaissance, but it fell thereafter into a long period of disrepute from which it has never quite recovered. Recently it has reappeared in popular songs such as "The Crucifixion," "Waist Deep in the Big Muddy," and "Puff, the Magic Dragon" (which can be read as an allegory of a child growing up). Other song writers and poets like to "throw off a vague allegorical hint," as one critic has said of one of Chaucer's tales. "A Horse with No Name" and many of the Moody Blues' compositions are good examples of vaguely allegorical songs. Even the effect of allegory, however, is distasteful to many moderns: despite the fact that allegory has one foot in the real world it tends to fly off into abstraction, which is anathema to most modern poets.

Waist Deep in the Big Muddy

It was back in nineteen forty-two,
I was part of a good platoon;
We were on maneuvers in a-Loozianna,
One night by the light of the moon;
The captain told us to ford a river,
And that's how it all begun.
We were knee deep in the Big Muddy
But the big fool said to move on.

The sergeant said, "Sir, are you sure,
This is the best way back to the base?"
"Sergeant, go on; I once forded this river
Just a mile above this place;
It'll be a little soggy but just keep slogging,
We'll soon be on dry ground."
We were waist deep in the Big Muddy
And the big fool said to push on.

The sergeant said, "With all this equipment
No man'll be able to swim";
"Sergeant, don't be a nervous nellie,"
The Captain said to him;
"All we need is a little determination;
Men, follow me, I'll lead on."
We were neck deep in the Big Muddy
And the big fool said to push on.

All of a sudden, the moon clouded over,
We heard a gurgling cry;
A few seconds later, the captain's helmet
Was all that floated by;
The sergeant said, "Turn around men,
I'm in charge from now on."
And we just made it out of the Big Muddy
With the captain dead and gone.

We stripped and dived and found his body
Stuck in the old quicksand;
I guess he didn't know that the water was deeper
Than the place he'd once before been;
Another stream had joined the Big Muddy
Just a half mile from where we'd gone.
We'd been lucky to escape from the Big Muddy
When the damn fool said to push on.

Well, maybe you'd rather not draw any moral,
I'll leave that to yourself;
Maybe you're still walking and you're still talking
And you'd like to keep your health;
But every time I read the papers
That old feeling comes on:
Waist deep in the Big Muddy
And the Big Fool says to push on.

Waist deep in the Big Muddy
And the Big Fool says to push on;
Waist deep in the Big Muddy
And the Big Fool says to push on;
Waist deep! Neck deep! Soon even a tall
Man'll be over his head!
Waist deep in the Big Muddy
And the Big Fool says to push on!

—Pete Seeger

There could be no doubt in the minds of Americans who heard this song in the late sixties that the "damn fool" captain was none other than President Lyndon B. Johnson, telling all the "nervous nellie" critics of American involvement in Vietnam that all they needed was a little faith and determination. The quicksand, of course, was the quicksand of the war, which kept sucking the country further and further in, threatening to destroy us all. Seeger is circumspect in explaining his allegory in stanza six, but the explanation is really quite unnecessary.

The Corpus Christi Carol

Lully, lullay, lully, lullay,
The faucon hath borne my make away.

He bare him up, he bare him down,
He bare him into an orchard brown.

In that orchard ther was an hall
That was hanged with purple and pall.

And in that hall ther was a bed:
It was hanged with gold so red.

And in that bed ther lith a knight,
His woundes bleeding by day and night.

By that beddes side ther kneeleth a may,
And she weepeth both night and day.

And by that beddes side ther standeth a stoon:
Corpus Christi written theron.

—anonymous

2. *faucon:* falcon; *make:* mate. 6. *pall:* black velvet. 9. *lith:* lies. 11. *may:* maid. 13. *stoon:* stone. 14. *Corpus Christi:* "the body of Christ," the communion host.

"The Corpus Christi Carol" has puzzled readers for centuries, and the key to its allegory is probably now lost in antiquity, buried with the medieval poet who wrote it. It does, however, illustrate how a little research can enlighten puzzling poems. We know from Hopkins's "The Windhover" that the falcon is a traditional symbol for Christ, so the identification of the two here should come as no surprise. The action, though, remains unclear until we know that in some medieval churches it was customary to move the host (the *Corpus Christi*) from the main altar to a side altar hung with purple during the period between Good Friday and Easter Sunday, and to keep a watch constantly over the host at that altar. Although such information does not explain every detail of the story, it does go a long way toward clearing up some of the mystery of the allegory.

anyone lived in a pretty how town

anyone lived in a pretty how town
(with up so floating many bells down)
spring summer autumn winter
he sang his didn't he danced his did.

Women and men (both little and small)
cared for anyone not at all
they sowed their isn't they reaped their same
sun moon stars rain

children guessed (but only a few
and down they forgot as up they grew
autumn winter spring summer)
that noone loved him more by more

when by now and tree by leaf
she laughed his joy she cried his grief
bird by snow and stir by still
anyone's any was all to her

someones married their everyones
laughed their cryings and did their dance
(sleep wake hope and then) they
said their nevers they slept their dream

stars rain sun moon
(and only the snow can begin to explain
how children are apt to forget to remember
with up so floating many bells down)

one day anyone died i guess
(and noone stooped to kiss his face)
busy folk buried them side by side
little by little and was by was

all by all and deep by deep
and more by more they dream their sleep
noone and anyone earth by april
wish by spirit and if by yes.

Women and men (both dong and ding)
summer autumn winter spring
reaped their sowing and went their came
sun moon stars rain

—*e. e. cummings*

1. What sort of people are "anyone" and "noone"? What kind of world do they live in? How do they get along with each other? With their world? Is the death in stanza 7 real or metaphorical? What is the allegorical significance of this poem?

2. The poem contains several cycles: "sun moon stars rain," "autumn winter spring summer," "stars rain sun moon," etc. What do they have to do with the story of "anyone" and "noone"?

3. The meter and rhyme of this poem insist on turning it into a child's nursery rhyme. Why might that be appropriate?

A Poison Tree

I was angry with my friend:
I told my wrath, my wrath did end.
I was angry with my foe:
I told it not, my wrath did grow.

And I water'd it in fears,
Night and morning with my tears;
And I sunned it with smiles,
And with soft deceitful wiles.

And it grew both day and night,
Till it bore an apple bright;
And my foe beheld it shine,
And he knew that it was mine,

And into my garden stole
When the night had veil'd the pole:
In the morning glad I see
My foe outstretch'd beneath the tree.

—*William Blake*

This poem is symbolic (the tree, the apple, the garden). Because it tells a story in symbols, it *sounds* allegorical. Can you put your finger on exactly what Blake is allegorizing? Is it a psychological process, a moral truth, or both?

All Along the Watchtower

"There must be some way out of here," said the joker to the thief,
"There's too much confusion, I can't get no relief.
Businessmen, they drink my wine, plowmen dig my earth,
None of them along the line know what any of it is worth."

"No reason to get excited," the thief, he kindly spoke,
"There are many here among us who feel that life is but a joke.
But you and I, we've been through that, and this is not our fate,
So let us not talk falsely now, the hour is getting late."

All along the watchtower, princes kept the view
While all the women came and went, barefoot servants too.

Outside in the distance a wildcat did growl,
Two riders were approaching, the wind began to howl.

—*Bob Dylan*

Like Blake, Dylan burns with the nuance of allegory here. We *know* that here are no ordinary joker and thief, princes, wildcat, and approaching riders. Symbols are everywhere, and yet it is difficult indeed to explain Dylan's allegorical landscape. "All Along the Watchtower" comes as something of the apocalyptic climax to Dylan's album *John Wesley Harding,* in which Dylan explores the weighty matters of sin, death, guilt, penance, and salvation. It is filled with religious imagery and characters like St. Augustine and Judas Priest. This song immediately follows a lyric of profound spiritual death and immediately precedes a song of grace and rebirth. Does its position give you any clues to the allegory of "All Along the Watchtower"? Listen to the song sung on *John Wesley Harding,* and note how the performance adds to the eerie, apocalyptic, allegorical flavor of the lyrics.

Daniel and the Sacred Harp

Daniel, Daniel and the sacred harp,
Dancin' through the clover;
Daniel, Daniel, would you mind
If I look it over?

I heard of this famous harp long ago
Back in my home town,
But I sure never though old Daniel'd be the one
To come and bring it around.

Tell me, Daniel, how the harp
Came into your possession.
Are you one of the chosen few
Who will march in the procession?
and Daniel said,
"The sacred harp was handed down
From father unto son,
And me not being related,
I could never be the one.

So I saved up all my silver
And took it to a man
Who said he could deliver the harp
Straight into my hand.

Three years I waited patiently
'Til he returned with the harp from the Sea of Galilee.
He said, 'There is one more thing I must ask,
But not of personal greed.'
But I wouldn't listen, I just grabbed the harp and said,
'Take what you may need.'"

Now Daniel looked quite satisfied
And the harp it seemed to go,
But the price that Daniel had really paid
He did not even know.

Right to his brother he took his troubled mind,
And he said, "Dear brother, I'm in a bind."
But the brother would not hear his tale,
He said, "Oh, Daniel's gonna land in jail."

So to his father Daniel did run,
And he said, "Oh father, what have I done?"
His father said, "Son, you've given in;
You know you've won your harp, but you're lost in sin."

Then Daniel took the harp and went high on the hill,
And he blew across the meadow just like a whippoorwill.
He played out his heart just the time to pass,
But as he looked to the ground he noticed no shadow did he
cast.

Daniel, Daniel and the sacred harp,
Dancin' through the clover;
Daniel, Daniel, would you mind
If I look it over?

—*Robbie Robertson*

What does the harp represent? Who is the man who delivered the harp to Daniel? What is the price that Daniel really paid? Someone once said that the story of Elvis Presley was told allegorically in "Daniel and the Sacred Harp." What do you suppose he meant by that?

3. A Statement: Philosophy

In many of their self-appointed roles, poets allow themselves to comment more or less directly on the world around them. As social consciences, as visionaries, as myth-makers and psychologists and sociologists, poets philosophize repeatedly on the human condition, the American Dream (or nightmare), politics, and religion. It's not hard for a poet to fancy himself a philosopher or preacher and feel compelled to speak his piece on truth, justice, and the way of all flesh.

Usually the poet makes his statement indirectly, concealing it underneath some form of concrete subject: a historical event, a person, a place, an image, or a metaphor. But sometimes poets philosophize directly, writing a kind of verse essay in philosophy or sociology. Twentieth-century poets do less naked philosophizing than their predecessors, but you don't need to have Kenny Rogers telling you "every hand's a winner, and every hand's a loser," or Bob Dylan warning you sternly "you've got to serve somebody," to know that there's still a lot of philosophy in modern poetry and song. Unfortunately for both poets and us, some of the philosophy comes second hand and trivialized. "Shelley would have been a much better poet if he had just forgotten Neo-Platonism and stuck to writing poetry" is an argument you frequently hear, with variations, applied to poets from Yeats to Eliot to Bob Dylan. Besides, philosophical poetry always runs the risk of becoming abstract and insubstantial. William Carlos Williams's emphasis on ideas *in things* was partially a reaction against philosophical and emotional abstraction.

Still, in good philosophical poetry the thought is not clichéd and carries with it enough of the other qualities of poetry—thing, voice, structure—to make it more interesting, more beautiful, and ultimately more memorable and forceful than pure prose philosophy. Even today, there are many who would sooner take their philosophy from a poet than from a professor of philosophy, their psychology from a poet than a shrink, their musings on God and man from a poet than from a priest.

Examine carefully the poems and song that follow. Ask yourself in each case these questions: what philosophical argument is being advanced? How fresh, how insightful is that idea? What other devices of poetry does the poet use to advance this argument? Is the poem too abstract, too insubstantial? Is this poetry, or is it idea?

Dust in the Wind

I close my eyes, only for a moment and the moment's gone
All my dreams pass before my eyes, a curiosity.
Dust in the wind, all they are is dust in the wind.

Same old song, just a drop of water in an endless sea
All we do crumbles to the ground, although we refuse to see.
Dust in the wind, all we are is dust in the wind.

Don't hang on, nothing lasts forever but the earth and sky.
It slips away; all your money won't another minute buy.
Dust in the wind, all we are is dust in the wind.

—*Kerry Livgren*

My Mind to Me a Kingdom Is

My mind to me a kingdom is;
  Such present joys therein I find
That it excels all other bliss
  That earth affords or grows by kind.
Though much I want which most would have,
Yet still my mind forbids to crave.

No princely pomp, no wealthy store,
  No force to win the victory,
No wily wit to salve a sore,
  No shape to feed a loving eye;
To none of these I yield as thrall.
For why my mind doth serve for all.

I see how plenty suffers oft,
  And hasty climbers soon do fall;
I see that those which are aloft
  Mishap doth threaten most of all;
They get with toil, they keep with fear.
Such cares my mind could never bear.

Content I live, this is my stay;
  I seek no more than may suffice;
I press to bear no haughty sway;
  Look, what I lack my mind supplies;
Lo, thus I triumph like a king,
Content with that my mind doth bring.

Some have too much, yet still do crave;
  I little have, and seek no more.
They are but poor, though much they have,
  And I am rich with little store.
They poor, I rich; they beg, I give;
They lack, I leave; they pine, I live.

I laugh not at another's loss;
  I grudge not at another's gain;
No worldly waves my mind can toss;
  My state at one doth still remain.
I fear no foe, I fawn no friend;
I loathe not life, nor dread my end.

Some weigh their pleasure by their lust,
  Their wisdom by their rage of will;
Their treasure is their only trust;
  A cloakéd craft their store of skill.
But all the pleasure that I find
Is to maintain a quiet mind.

My wealth is health and perfect ease;
  My conscience clear my choice defense;
I neither seek by bribes to please,
  Nor by deceit to breed offense.
Thus do I live; thus will I die.
Would all did so well as I!

—*Sir Edward Dyer*

4. *kind:* nature. 5. *want:* lack. 12. *for why:* because.

from An Essay on Man

Awake, my St. John! leave all meaner things
To low ambition, and the pride of Kings.
Let us (since Life can little more supply
Than just to look about us and to die)
Expatiate free o'er all this scene of Man;
A mighty maze! but not without a plan;
A Wild, where weeds and flow'rs promiscuous shoot,
Or Garden, tempting with forbidden fruit.
Together let us beat this ample field,
Try what the open, what the covert yield;
The latent tracts, the giddy heights explore
Of all who blindly creep, or sightless soar;
Eye Nature's walks, shoot Folly as it flies,
And catch the Manners living as they rise;
Laugh where we must, be candid where we can;
But vindicate the ways of God to Man.

I.

Say first, of God above, or Man below,
What can we reason, but from what we know?
Of Man what see we, but his station here,
From which to reason, or to which refer?
Thro' worlds unnumber'd tho' the God be known,

'Tis ours to trace him only in our own.
He, who thro' vast immensity can pierce,
See worlds on worlds compose one universe,
Observe how system into system runs,
What other planets circle other suns,
What vary'd being peoples ev'ry star,
May tell why Heav'n has made us as we are.
But of this frame the bearings, and the ties,
The strong connections, nice dependencies,
Gradations just, has thy pervading soul
Look'd thro'? or can a part contain the whole?
  Is the great chain, that draws all to agree,
And drawn supports, upheld by God, or thee?

II.

Presumptuous Man! the reason wouldst thou find,
Why form'd so weak, so little, and so blind!
First, if thou canst, the harder reason guess,
Why form'd no weaker, blinder, and no less!
Ask of thy mother earth, why oaks are made
Taller or stronger than the weeds they shade?
Or ask of yonder argent fields above,
Why JOVE's Satellites are less than JOVE?
  Of Systems possible, if 'tis confest
That Wisdom infinite must form the best,
Where all must full or not coherent be,
And all that rises, rise in due degree;
Then, in the scale of reas'ning life, 'tis plain
There must be, somewhere, such a rank as Man;
And all the question (wrangle e'er so long)
Is only this, if God has plac'd him wrong?
  Respecting Man, whatever wrong we call,
May, must be right, as relative to all.
In human works, tho' labour'd on with pain,
A thousand movements scarce one purpose gain;
In God's, one single can its end produce;
Yet serves to second too some other use.
So Man, who here seems principal alone,
Perhaps acts second to some sphere unknown,
Touches some wheel, or verges to some goal;
'Tis but a part we see, and not a whole.
  When the proud steed shall know why Man restrains
His fiery course, or drives him o'er the plains;

When the dull Ox, why now he breaks the clod,
Is now a victim, and now Ægypt's God:
Then shall Man's pride and dulness comprehend
His actions', passions', being's, use and end;
Why doing, suff'ring, check'd, impell'd; and why
This hour a slave, the next a deity.
  Then say not Man's imperfect, Heav'n in fault;
Say rather, Man's as perfect as he ought;
His knowledge measur'd to his state and place,
His time a moment, and a point his space.
If to be perfect in a certain sphere,
What matter, soon or late, or here or there?
The blest today is as completely so,
As who began a thousand years ago.

—*Alexander Pope*

1. *St. John:* Henry St. John, Viscount Bolingbrooke, prime minister of England under Queen Anne, a friend of Pope's, and a philosophical writer himself. 5. *expatiate:* speak at length. 10. *covert:* a thicket. 14. *manners:* passions, habits, moral conduct. 15. *candid:* lenient. 25. *system:* solar system. 33. *chain:* the great chain of being, in which all things are arranged in a hierarchical order, descending from God at the top to nothingness at the bottom. 34. *supports:* sustains. 42. *Jove's:* here the planet Jupiter. 73. *in a certain sphere:* in heaven.

The Passionate Shepherd to His Love

Come live with me and be my love,
And we will all the pleasures prove
That valleys, groves, hills, and fields,
Woods, or steepy mountain yields.

And we will sit upon the rocks,
Seeing the shepherds feed their flocks
By shallow rivers, to whose falls
Melodious birds sing madrigals.

And I will make thee beds of roses
And a thousand fragrant posies,
A cap of flowers and a kirtle
Embroidered all with leaves of myrtle;

A gown made of the finest wool
Which from our pretty lambs we pull;
Fair-linèd slippers for the cold,
With buckles of the purest gold;

A belt of straw and ivy buds,
With coral clasps and amber studs.
And if these pleasures may thee move,
Come live with me and be my love.

The shepherd swains shall dance and sing
For thy delight each May morning.
If these delights thy mind may move,
Then live with me and be my love.

—*Christopher Marlowe*

2. *prove:* try out, experience.

The Nymph's Reply to the Shepherd

If all the world and love were young,
And truth in every shepherd's tongue,
These pretty pleasures might me move
To live with thee and by thy love.

Time drives the flocks from field to fold,
When rivers rage and rocks grow cold,
And Philomel becometh dumb;
The rest complains of cares to come.

The flowers do fade, and wanton fields
To wayward winter reckoning yields.
A honey tongue, a heart of gall,
Is fancy's spring, but sorrow's fall.

Thy gowns, thy shoes, thy beds of roses,
Thy cap, thy kirtle, and thy posies
Soon break, soon wither, soon forgotten:
In folly ripe, in reason rotten.

Thy belt of straw and ivy buds,
Thy coral clasps and amber studs,
All these in me no means can move
To come to thee and be thy love.

But could youth last and love still breed,
Had joys no date nor age no need,
Then these delights my mind might move
To live with thee and be thy love.

—*Sir Walter Raleigh*

7. *Philomel:* a princess of Athens, who after being raped and having her tongue cut out by Tereus, was transformed into a nightingale by the gods.

The Preacher: Ruminates Behind the Sermon

I think it must be lonely to be God.
Nobody loves a master. No. Despite
The bright hosannas, bright dear-Lords, and bright
Determined reverence of Sunday eyes.

Picture Jehovah striding through the hall
Of His importance, creatures running out
From servant-corners to acclaim, to shout
Appreciation of His merit's glare.

But who walks with Him?—dares to take His arm,
To slap Him on the shoulder, tweak His ear,
Buy Him a Coca-Cola or a beer,
Pooh-pooh His politics, call Him a fool?

Perhaps—who knows?—He tires of looking down.
Those eyes are never lifted. Never straight.
Perhaps sometimes He tires of being great
In solitude. Without a hand to hold.

—*Gwendolyn Brooks*

New Year's Poem

The Christmas twigs crispen and needles rattle
Along the windowledge.
            A solitary pearl
Shed from the necklace spilled at last week's party

Lies in the suety, snow-luminous plainness
Of morning, on the windowledge beside them.
And all the furniture that circled stately
And hospitable when these rooms were brimmed
With perfumes, furs, and black-and-silver
Crisscross of seasonal conversation, lapses
Into its previous largeness.
        I remember
Anne's rose-sweet gravity, and the stiff grave
Where cold so little can contain;
I mark the queer delightful skull and crossbones
Starlings and sparrows left, taking the crust,
And the long loop of winter wind
Smoothing its arc from dark Arcturus down
To the bricked corner of the drifted courtyard,
And the still windowledge.
          Gentle and just pleasure
It is, being human, to have won from space
This unchill, habitable interior
Which mirrors quietly the light
Of the snow, and the new year.

—*Margaret Avison*

A Dialogue of Self and Soul

I

My Soul. I summon to the winding ancient stair;
  Set all your mind upon the steep ascent,
  Upon the broken, crumbling battlement,
  Upon the breathless starlit air,
  Upon the star that marks the hidden pole;
  Fix every wandering thought upon
  That quarter where all thought is done:
  Who can distinguish darkness from the soul?

My Self. The consecrated blade upon my knees
  Is Sato's ancient blade, still as it was,
  Still razor-keen, still like a looking-glass
  Unspotted by the centuries;
  That flowering, silken, old embroidery, torn
  From some court-lady's dress and round
  The wooden scabbard bound and wound,
  Can, tattered, still protect, faded adorn.

My Soul. Why should the imagination of a man
Long past his prime remember things that are
Emblematical of love and war?
Think of ancestral night that can,
If but imagination scorn the earth
And intellect its wandering
To this and that and t'other thing,
Deliver from the crime of death and birth.

My Self. Montashigi, third of his family, fashioned it
Five hundred years ago, about it lie
Flowers from I know not what embroidery—
Heart's purple—and all these I set
For emblems of the day against the tower
Emblematical of the night,
And claim as by a soldier's right
A charter to commit the crime once more.

My Soul. Such fullness in that quarter overflows
And falls into the basin of the mind
That man is stricken deaf and dumb and blind,
For intellect no longer knows
Is from the *Ought,* or *Knower* from the *Known*—
That is to say, ascends to Heaven;
Only the dead can be forgiven;
But when I think of that my tongue's a stone.

II

My Self. A living man is blind and drinks his drop.
What matter if the ditches are impure?
What matter if I live it all once more?
Endure that toil of growing up;
The ignominy of boyhood; the distress
Of boyhood changing into man;
The unfinished man and his pain
Brought face to face with his own clumsiness;

The finished man among his enemies?—
How in the name of Heaven can he escape
That defiling and disfigured shape
The mirror of malicious eyes
Casts upon his eyes until at last
He thinks that shape must be in his shape?

And what's the good of an escape
If honour find him in the wintry blast?

I am content to live it all again
And yet again, if it be life to pitch
Into the frog-spawn of a blind man's ditch,
A blind man battering blind men;
Or into that most fecund ditch of all,
The folly that man does
Or must suffer, if he woos
A proud woman not kindred of his soul.

I am content to follow to its source
Every event in action or in thought;
Measure the lot; forgive myself the lot!
When such as I cast out remorse
So great a sweetness flows into the breast
We must laugh and we must sing,
We are blest by everything,
Everything we look upon is blest.

—*William Butler Yeats*

4. A Statement: Surrealistic Poetry

Surrealism has been very popular with twentieth-century artists, and poets are no exception. Developed in France under the leadership of André Breton in the 1920s, surrealist poetry did not achieve any really widespread popularity in America until the late 1960s and seventies, when a number of poets started experimenting with surrealist verse.

Put simply, surrealist poetry is poetry of the dream world: people, places, images, events swim into and out of the poem without discernible patterns of cause and effect. In fact, the world of the poem seems to be beyond the conscious control of the poet, and you often hear surrealistic poets candidly admit that they don't know what the poem is all about either. "This poem comes out of something so deep in me," said John Judson of "The Lineage of Indian Ponies," "that I don't understand it . . . today." The poet himself struggles to wrest the poem from his subconscious, not even knowing what he's looking for, feeling a tentative way toward a poem that feels right. When asked about meaning in a surrealist poem, the poet is quite likely to turn the question back on the questioner: "You tell me what it means to you."

One justification of surrealist poetry comes, of course, from Freudian and Jungian psychology, from Bergsonian philosophy. The world of conscious reality is important, but no more important than the world of dreams. And conversely, the world of dreams has as much legitimacy as the world around us, which we touch and feel and measure and like to think has a certain rationality to it. To understand the human species, you must probe not only the rational, exterior world, but the interior psychological world. And because the world is subrational, or prerational, you probe it not with reasoned arguments or even rational thought, but with myth and symbol and strange warps of images and metaphors.

Another justification for surrealist poetry comes from life itself, which has become increasingly surreal as one "catch-22" grows out of another. The American experience with the news coverage of the Vietnam war was, as has often been pointed out, totally surrealistic: you'd turn on the television set and see films of the latest battles, followed by a Coca Cola commercial, scenes of the president addressing Congress or kissing babies, an automobile accident, a beautiful young girl trying to sell you a car or a bank account, and football players knocking the daylights out of each other while fans shouted their approval and cheerleaders flaunted their assets. Then there was some serious talk about body counts and the light at the end of the tunnel. The movie *Apocalypse Now,* whatever its faults, caught the incredible surrealism of Vietnam perfectly in the scene where one soldier goes surfing down the river, using the wake of a patrol boat, with Mick Jagger blasting from the radio and the boat's wake upsetting Vietnamese sampans. *That* was surrealism. It may well be that the world of the surreal has not only as much legitimacy, but as much reality as the so-called "real world" of logical causes and consequences.

Surrealist poems, like myth poems, are difficult to discuss in the logical language of criticism. You can't explain them the way you'd explicate a metaphor or even a symbol. You can't weigh their validity the way you can weigh the validity of a myth. If a myth does not explain some aspect of the "real world" in symbolic terms, then it's not a good myth; but a surreal poem does not seek that kind of symbolism. Nor does the surrealist poem deny meaning, like the poetry of antistatement (to be discussed shortly). It asserts a meaning that it cannot articulate in any other language. The surrealist poem *is.* And while you should not expect to translate it into logical explanations, so also you should not dismiss it as nonsense. You intuit a surrealist poem: it must feel right to you as it feels right to the poet who wrote or discovered it. Like a dream, it leaves a persistent impression.

The Lineage of Indian Ponies

I have felt the moss pulse in my left arm,
the woodsmell cover my thoughts,
and in my laugh, the stain of bittersweet
caught in barbed wire.
But there are still the ponies.

Mornings, when the wind comes out of the cottonwoods
with that silver delight that occupied Huck's laughter,
and I hear the sound of the applause
mounting at the Royal Nonesuch,
I have visions of a prize carp,
a puffed up raw fish made dandy on a plate of dandelions,
its smile a carpet-bag full of wild flowers,
its long hair ratty as a stamped field
left by Evangelists on Friday.
But there are still the ponies.

And on Monday,
blue after the sleep of the Sabbath,
when the lone ghost of my father rises from the snow,
looking always toward the leak of daylight,
the hum of his voice snarled in Whitman's beard,
trapped under fields and fields of evergreen,
looking always toward the mountain,

there are still the ponies:
their thighs full of hurtling cloud,
their gray rage spawned by the sun, and my daughters;
their eyes are my sons,
champed by visions of dark green valleys on the moon.

—John Judson

Poet John Judson gave this account of the genesis of this poem: "My father died of a heart attack, and I was called back to Maine. Back in Maine I got off the plane, and I had just been teaching *Huckleberry Finn* and we were going into Whitman, and I realized that he died because he believed the same thing that Whitman believed. And I come back home to all of this going on, and I walk in the front door, and my children are watching two people set foot on the moon. When I was a kid, I used to think of the clouds going west, maybe over Fargo, North

Dakota, in shapes of horses with manes blowing.'' Does this help ''explain'' the poem for you? Or does it explain only its origin? Does the poem have any profound intuitive meaning for you?

Lobsters in the Brain Coral

Freediving thirty to forty feet, only a few seconds to spare
at the bottom of each dive before the death
of my wind, I catch sight of an antenna or front leg-pincer
waving listlessly into the light like a weed-stalk:

the only visible appendage of a tough old bull langouste,
his spiny-thorned carapace of back wedged deep
into a crevice in steep flat near-vertical planes of rock.
His trench lightless, I can only guess his position—

impossible to snare him with a gig-noose, I aim the Hawaiian sling spear, stretched taut on the bow of my forearm.
The spear connects, freezes. I hustle to the surface for air,
hyperventilate, and dive again; hanging upside down,

my legs dangling over my head, I peer deeply into the cleft.
No sign of life. Hah!—he's braced for the fight.
Tugging and tugging at the spear, I yank out his twenty-pound
impaled barrel-shell, his crotchety long legs

wriggling—he looks like a Gargantuan subaqueous spider!
He contracts his muscular powerful tail,
discharging high-pitched cries that seem to emit
from a sphere of sound surrounding him, a queer

distancing remove between the creature and its shrieks.
I compress the tail. He silences. The spear
runs deep into his back, diagonally. I force the point,
flared-open within him, through to the other side

and unscrew the spearhead, his great armored body-
vault
shuddering quietly. Astonished by his suffering,
his austere beauty, I relax my grip—he jerks loose,
scraping his backspikes across my bare wrist,

three streaks inscribing my skin. *The red ink smears,*
runs, thinning off into swirls, a spreading
stain. Slow leaks—painless—from my punctured inner tubes,
I deflate. Oh stop, precious flow. A blowout,

I may go flat, caving-in on my bones. The lobster zooms
backwards, his tail flapping—violent, noiseless—
his body, a single bony claw swiftly clenching,
unclenching,
his whines, a siren wailing softer in the distance.

In pursuit, I chase him below a massive brain coral. I
swim
under a grayish bulge and drift into the interior,
my hand gripping the rim. Am I staring inside
somebody's
dream? In five or six rooms of his skull—

sockets like sinuses, honeycombing the coralhead—stand
lobsters of all sizes: some upside-down,
others on the walls, the floors; always in the dark
corners, favoring the shadows, leaning away

from the light, antennae waving. I move my glove
to the nearest cubicle and tap a pincer.
It falls from the body. The lobster drops out of sight
into a hidden channel. Then, the whole colony

moves in unison: bodies uplifted, legs stretched taut,
unbending, all begin sidling in a slow trot
around the linings of the caverns, a dance of skinless
bones, creakless many-jointed rickety stilts

dragging the glossy-plated bodies this way and that,
somersaulting over and over, sagging
without letting go, until I forget if my feet are under
or over my head. Let me out of your brain,

I command the dreamer. I suffocate in this airless hive
where I lose my mass in your sleep. Awake!
My weight drifts, fades to a gas in your mind.
Do I decompose? *You become an enamelled box*

on spindly crutches. Lay out your fingerprints lengthwise
and braid them into two feelers—antennae.
Fly backwards, snapping your whip of tail; your tail,
the one muscle, the one hatchery, the one edible.

Wail, if attacked. When cornered, back to a wall,
drop off your legs, twiggy stick by stick,
flop in the gravelly bottom-muck, a glum squat egg,
quadruple amputee. A basket case. Give me back

to my jails of skin, to my soaps of blood-suds, to my glands,
lungs and lymphs, to all those emerald birds—
heart, liver, gall bladder and balls. Oh spheres and cubes
of my body, multiply strangely into diamonds

whose many shining stars are eyes, eyes that glow,
eyes that radiate light but admit no spark—
eyes luminous, eyes opaque—a universe of eyes sparkling
in another's dream. Eyes of my flesh, restored!

—*Laurence Lieberman*

5. *langouste:* lobster.

This poem begins realistically enough, with Lieberman spear-fishing for lobster. Where does the poem become surrealistic? What elements in the experience with which Lieberman begins serve to legitimatize the surrealism at the end of his poem? Does Lieberman give us any indication that he too finds the poem surreal?

What does this poem mean to you? How does it compare with, for example, Coleridge's "Rime of the Ancient Mariner"? With Brooker and Reid's "A Whiter Shade of Pale" (Chapter 5, Section 8)?

5. A Statement: Paradox, Ambiguity, and Irony

One reason many poets are reluctant to make broad philosophical pronouncements, especially the affirmative declarations of, say, Longfellow's "A Psalm of Life" (Chapter 1, Section 5), is that so little objective evidence seems these days to justify any hard conclusions at all, either optimistic *or* pessimistic. In moral philosophy "situational ethics" elevates relativism into a moral principle; in physics an "uncertainty principle" makes the impossibility of knowing a scientific law. Even our weather reports predict only the *probability* of rain or snow. Nobody seems to want to say for absolutely sure.

This age of uncertainty has its advantages and disadvantages—accuracy, freedom from dogma on the one hand, a certain confusion and ambiguity on the other—but for better or worse its effect on poetry have been marked. More and more poets have written poetry that offers multiple perspectives about its subject, and thereby, about life; and more and more critics have—by virtue of attention paid—elevated this poetry to significance. Paradox, ambiguity, irony—these are the hallmarks of what we call "modern" poetry, and of poets like Dickinson, Hopkins, and Donne, who have been discovered by readers some years after their deaths and elevated in the modern period to the status of major writers. Paradox, ambiguity, irony—each mode of expression involves a schizophrenic presentation of two or more possibilities, each of which has an equal claim to validity. Each fuzzes the poem's statement. Each leaves us hanging.

Paradox, of course, brings together two contraries, both of which we hold to be true, and places them in head-to-head confrontation, like John Donne's famous restatement of the Christian paradox in his sonnet "Batter My Heart, Three-Personed God":

for I, / Except you enthrall me, never shall be free

A similar sense of paradox underlies the aphorism with which Blake finished his poem "The Marriage of Heaven and Hell":

Enough! or Too much.

But poets need not be so explicit in their use of paradox. John Crowe Ransom built his poem "Bells for John Whiteside's Daughter" around the implicit contradiction between the active, energetic, kenetic little girl he once knew and "her brown study, / Lying so primly propped." The girl, in turn, allows him to examine a fundamental paradox in human existence: life leads invariably and inevitably to death, yet it is this great rushing toward death that defines our lives:

Bells for John Whiteside's Daughter

There was such speed in her little body,
And such lightness in her footfall,
It is no wonder her brown study
Astonishes us all.

Her wars were bruited in our high window.
We looked among orchard trees and beyond,
Where she took arms against her shadow,
Or harried unto the pond

The lazy geese, like a snow cloud
Dripping their snow on the green grass,
Tricking and stopping, sleepy and proud,
Who cried in goose, Alas,

For the tireless heart within the little
Lady with rod that made them rise
From their noon apple-dreams and scuttle
Goose-fashion under the skies!

But now go the bells, and we are ready,
In one house we are sternly stopped
To say we are vexed at her brown study,
Lying so primly propped.

—*John Crowe Ransom*

3. *brown study:* state of reverie or abstraction. 5. *bruited:* rumored.

What images of motion (and commotion) do you find in this poem? What images of stasis? Notice how they come paradoxically together in a phrase like "like a snow cloud / Dripping their snow on the green grass." What connotations do "snow" and "green grass" have that make their conjunction in a single metaphor a miniature of the poem's central paradox? Can you find any other examples of paradoxical imagery in this poem? How does the voice of the final line enhance the sense of the poem?

Batter My Heart, Three-Personed God

Batter my heart, three-personed God; for You
As yet but knock, breathe, shine, and seek to mend;
That I may rise and stand, o'erthrow me, and bend
Your force to break, blow, burn, and make me new.
I, like an usurped town, to another due,
Labor to admit you, but O, to no end;
Reason, Your viceroy in me, me should defend,
But is captive, and proves weak or untrue.
Yet dearly I love You, and would be loved fain,
But am betrothed unto Your enemy.
Divorce me, untie or break that knot again;
Take me to You, imprison me, for I,
Except You enthrall me, never shall be free,
Nor ever chaste, except You ravish me.

—*John Donne*

7. *viceroy:* representative and governor, as in a colony. 9. *fain:* gladly, willingly.

1. What is the condition of Donne's soul? What does he mean when he says "Reason . . . me should defend, / But is captive, and proves weak or untrue"? What is Donne asking for in this poem?

2. What metaphors does Donne use in this poem?

3. What paradoxes does Donne explore in this poem?

4. What is the structure of this poem? How strictly does Donne adhere to his structure?

Crazy Jane Talks with the Bishop

I met the Bishop on the road
And much said he and I.
"Those breasts are flat and fallen now,
Those veins must soon be dry;
Live in a heavenly mansion,
Not in some foul sty."

"Fair and foul are near of kin,
And fair needs foul," I cried.
"My friends are gone, but that's a truth
Nor grave nor bed denied,
Learned in bodily lowliness
And in the heart's pride.

''A woman can be proud and stiff
When on love intent;
But Love has pitched his mansion in
The place of excrement;
For nothing can be sole or whole
That has not been rent.''

—*William Butler Yeats*

What paradoxes does Yeats explore in this poem? What is the position of the Bishop? Of Crazy Jane? Who do you think is right?

Another occasion for multiple perspectives is the ambiguous situation. Instead of defining carefully a pair of mutually exclusive positions, the poet deliberately blurs the statement of the poem, to allow multiple interpretations. In the song ''Angie, Baby'' is Angie a witch, a crazy girl, or what? Does she kill her lover? Shrink him? What? We don't know; the situation is ambiguous. What does ''love'' mean in the Beatles' song ''All You Need Is Love''? The word is open to a variety of interpretations, and musical phrases echoing and reechoing across the song seem to validate anything we can imagine: the teen-age infatuation of ''She loves you, yeah, yeah, yeah,'' the old-fashioned romantic love of ''Greensleeves,'' the sophisticated sex of ''In the Mood,'' the Christian *agape* of the old Christmas carol ''What Child Is This?'' But it's possible, the more we think about it, that what the world needs is all the love it can get, of whatever kind. All you need is *all* these kinds of love. The Beatles' song exploits the multiple meanings of love to make an important, if not especially original, point.

One mark of an intelligent person, F. Scott Fitzgerald is reported once to have said, is the ability to hold two or more contradictory beliefs at the same time. This definition of intelligence, of course, reflects nothing so much as the modern fondness for ambiguity, for seeing things from multiple perspectives. One of Frost's most redemptive qualities is the uncomfortable ambiguity that seeps into so much of his poetry. And it explains the current popularity of Emily Dickinson, who left us some poems so perfectly balanced they refuse even after a century to fall to one side or the other.

These Are the Days When Birds Come Back

These are the days when Birds come back—
A very few—a Bird or two—
To take a backward look.

These are the days when skies resume
The old—old sophistries of June—
A blue and gold mistake.

Oh fraud that cannot cheat the Bee—
Almost thy plausibility
Induces my belief.

Till ranks of seeds their witness bear—
And softly thro' the altered air
Hurries a timid leaf.

Oh Sacrament of summer days,
Oh Last Communion in the Haze—
Permit a child to join.

Thy sacred emblems to partake—
Thy consecrated bread to take
And thine immortal wine!

—*Emily Dickinson*

1. What season of the year is Dickinson portraying? How can you be sure?

2. In lines 6ff, is the poet talking about June or the Indian summer? When she calls the season a fraud, does she mean the false promise of Indian summer or the promise of June? How important is this distinction to the statement she is making in this poem?

3. Toward the end of the poem, Dickinson introduces considerable religious imagery. What comment is made by June and Indian summer on religion? And vice versa? Is the exact identity of that fraud back in line 7 important in deciding what the poem says about religion?

Let It Be

When I find myself in times of trouble
Mother Mary comes to me
Speaking words of wisdom,
Let it be.

And in my hour of darkness
She is standing right in front of me
Speaking words of wisdom,
Let it be.

Let it be,
Let it be,
Let it be,
Let it be,
Whisper words of wisdom,
Let it be.

And when the broken hearted people
Living in the world agree
There will be an answer,
Let it be.

For though they may be parted
There is still a chance that they will see
There will be an answer,
Let it be.

Let it be,
Let it be,
Let it be,
Let it be,
There will be an answer,
Let it be.

And when the night is cloudy
There is still a light that shines on me
Shine until tomorrow,
Let it be.

I wake up to the sound of music.
Mother Mary comes to me
Speaking words of wisdom,
Let it be.
Let it be,
Let it be,
Let it be,
Let it be,
Whisper words of wisdom,
Let it be.

—John Lennon–Paul McCartney

The most clearly ambiguous phrase (to use an oxymoron) is the title, "Let It Be." To what does "it" refer? To an answer? An answer to what question? And just how do we "let it be?" But another and perhaps more important ambiguity may lie in "Mother Mary," who speaks the words of wisdom. In rock lyrics Mary is frequently a personification of marijuana ("Along Comes Mary," "Just Like a Woman," "Proud Mary"), and she may be just that here. But Mother Mary suggests Mary, Christ's mother, and some religious implications are added to the poem. If the figure is deliberately ambiguous, what would be the point of combining the associations of the Virgin Mary and marijuana? Does the rest of the poem assume added meaning in light of this ambiguous Mary? Does it explain what the answers might be, how "it" might be, what "it" might resolve?

The term *irony* has two meanings in literature. One—the simpler and the popular meaning—is saying one thing and meaning another, or telling a story with a conclusion other than what was expected at the beginning of the story. "I love you" means "I hate you." "I guess the Lord must be in New York City" means "This is the most God-forsaken town on the face of the earth." The loser turns out to be a winner. The poor beggar is a king in disguise. A character is going backward when he thinks he's going forward, creating his own destruction at the very moment he thinks he's insuring his future. Harry Chapin's song "Cat's in the Cradle" is ironic in this sense: father has little time for his son when the boy is young; then the son, grown-up, has no time for the father. "My boy was just like me," realizes the unhappy father. Joni Mitchell was ironic in this sense in her song "Big Yellow Taxi": "they pave paradise to put in a parking lot."

In the more literary sense, irony refers to a jarring juxtaposition of two contradictory images. Sarah Cleghorn was being ironic in this sense in her epigrammatic poem on men who play beside children who work:

The Golf Links

The golf links lie so near the mill
   That almost every day
The laboring children can look out
   And see the men at play.

—*Sarah Cleghorn*

Less bitterly, Gwendolyn Brooks was being ironic in her poem of two young ladies, one who went to college and one who stayed home:

Sadie and Maud

Maud went to college.
Sadie stayed at home.
Sadie scraped life
With a fine-tooth comb.

She didn't leave a tangle in.
Her comb found every strand.
Sadie was one of the livingest chits
In all the land.

Sadie bore two babies
Under her maiden name.
Maud and Ma and Papa
Nearly died of shame.

When Sadie said her last so-long
Her girls struck out from home.
(Sadie had left as heritage
Her fine-tooth comb.)

Maud, who went to college,
Is a thin brown mouse.
She is living all alone
In this old house.

—*Gwendolyn Brooks*

A similar juxtaposition, this time between young and old, can be found in this Charles Kingsley poem. At first it appears that the poet finds youth frivolous and deluded (''and every goose a swan''); then we discover that age is no fun either. By the time we're finished with the poem, we are not entirely certain which to prefer, youth or age.

Young and Old

When all the world is young, lad,
  And all the trees are green;
And every goose a swan, lad,
  And every lass a queen;
Then hey for boot and horse, lad,
  And round the world away;
Young blood must have its course, lad,
  And every dog his day.

When all the world is old, lad,
  And all the trees are brown;
And all the sport is stale, lad,
  And all the wheels run down;
Creep home, and take your place there,
  The spent and maimed among:
God grant you find one face there,
  You loved when all was young.

—*Charles Kingsley*

6. A Statement: Poetry as Aesthetic Statement

One result of poetry textbooks like this one, courses in American and English literature, books *about* as well as *of* poetry, and a general awareness of art (in the colleges and universities, if not in American society in general) is a certain self-consciousness among artists of their roles and functions. One important difference between a folk culture and an advanced civilization is precisely this self-conscious professionalism in the artist. Naiveté is found only in amateurs; self-consciousness is the price of sophistication.

In balance it is well that poets have a clear idea of what to do and how to go about it, for in poetry as elsewhere forethought usually makes better. However, this self-consciousness has drawbacks. First, poetry can lose spontaneity and that basic, honest feeling that comes with products of folk culture. "*Anybody* can be spontaneous," claimed academic critics of the beat poetry popular in the late forties and the fifties. But on the contrary, it takes a certain habitual looseness, a certain ingenuousness to be free. And we admire spontaneity, in poetry as elsewhere: as Yeats noted in "Adam's Curse," for all the hours of work invested in a line of poetry, it must seem like a moment's thought, else all the work has gone for nothing. The more labored a line is and the more self-conscious the poet becomes, the harder it is to be spontaneous.

The second problem with artistic self-consciousness is that it leads to art about art and poems about poetry. This may be a subtle distinction, especially if the poems about poetry come disguised as poems about, say, a jar of Tennessee; but it is an important distinction when the poem bumps into its audience. Most audiences are simply not familiar enough with poetic theory, the kinds of issues discussed in this book, to understand a poem that is mainly about poetry. Nor do lay audiences care about poetic theory. They are interested primarily in *what is said.* As poetry (or any other art form) comes increasingly to take itself for a subject, then poetry becomes an in-group art, written by and for poets. And when only poets are listening to poets, society as a whole suffers.

One may even arrive at the state where a poem is written not because the poet has something compelling to express, but to explore an aesthetic possibility or exemplify a theory about poetry. This can be very confusing to audiences, especially when the theory exemplified by the poem is that art should have no meaning.

By the extension of metaphor, of course, a great many poems can be made to pertain to poetry that are in fact statements on other subjects. Is the poem about order? Very well, poetry has order; the poem is about poetry. Is the poem about beauty? Poetry is beauty; the poem can be said to say something about theory. And so forth. By that argument—not, incidentally, lost on the poets who wrote them—many poems in this collection are poems on poetry. Here, however, are a handful of poems that address themselves directly to the matter of aesthetics: what is a poem? What does a poem do? What can we expect from a poet? What statements does each one make about poetry? How does it make those statements?

A High-Toned Old Christian Woman

Poetry is the supreme fiction, madame.
Take the moral law and make a nave of it
And from the nave build haunted heaven. Thus,
The conscience is converted into palms,
Like windy citherns hankering for hymns.
We agree in principle. That's clear. But take
The opposing law and make a peristyle,
And from the peristyle project a masque
Beyond the planets. Thus, our bawdiness,
Unpurged by epitaph, indulged at last,
Is equally converted into palms,
Squiggling like saxophones. And palm for palm,
Madame, we are where we began. Allow,
Therefore, that in the planetary scene
Your disaffected flagellants, well-stuffed,
Smacking their muzzy bellies in parade,
Proud of such novelties of the sublime,
Such tink and tank and tunk-a-tunk-tunk,
May, merely may, madame, whip from themselves
A jovial hullabaloo among the spheres.
This will make widows wince. But fictive things
Wink as they will. Wink most when widows wince.

—*Wallace Stevens*

3. *nave:* the main part of a church. 5. *cithern:* an old, guitarlike instrument. 7. *peristyle:* a court enclosed by columns. 8. *masque:* a lavish, stylized, artificial, quasidramatic enter-

tainment popular during the Renaissance. 15. *flagellants:* medieval European religious fanatics who beat themselves publicly. The practice smacks of sexual perversion.

What analogy does Stevens use in this poem to explain poetry to the high-toned old Christian woman? How appropriate is it? What do you suppose are her views of poetry? Stevens claims that whether you begin with conscience or "the opposing law," by the time the poet gets done you are "palm for palm" where you began. Do you agree? What does "this" in line 21 refer to?

What examples of metaphor, alliteration, imagery, and particularly effective use of rhythm can you find in this poem?

So Long, Frank Lloyd Wright

So long, Frank Lloyd Wright.
I can't believe your song is gone so soon.
I barely learned the tune.
So soon,
So soon.

I'll remember Frank Lloyd Wright.
All of the nights we'd harmonized till dawn.
I never laughed so long.
So long,
So long.

Architects may come and
Architects may go and
Never change your point of view.
When I run dry
I stop awhile and think of you.

So long, Frank Lloyd Wright.
All of the nights we harmonized till dawn.
I never laughed so long.
So long,
So long.

—*Paul Simon*

The architect Frank Lloyd Wright becomes for singer Paul Simon the embodiment of an important aesthetic principle: freshness, spontaneity, new energies and new visions. The key lines to the song are 14 and 15: "When I run dry / I stop awhile and think of you." Thus the architect becomes not only an example, but (like most examples, incidentally) an inspiration. Notice that Simon's song is in the old Tin Pan Alley form; but notice too that his use of that form is quite innovative—as innovative and substantial as Frank Lloyd Wright's buildings.

Jan Jensen
Raku Jar
1977

The jar is without color, except
a pink blush of borax glaze and the
metallic gray of burned ash.

It stands seven inches high and five
inches across the base. It is etched
with a random of smoked lines.

On the lower portion of one side
where the borax glaze did not hold, the
surface is pocked, like the moon.

"This jar will not hold water," you say.
"It is fragile, and in ten years it
may have crumbled to potsherds."

"Why make a jar," I want to know, "that
will not hold flowers? Why make a jar
that oozes like a cheesecloth?"

"Fill it with dried flowers," you tell me.
I can observe its textures. It is
an exercise in technique.

"Art should serve some purpose," I insist.
"I want art that makes me a statement.
A clay jar should hold water."

"Technique is enough," you answer. "Style
testifies to its own honesty.
The jar is its own value."

Well, the facts remain: you made a jar
that holds no water, and I have bought
your jar that holds no water.

Thus the jar becomes
both a statement and
an invitation.

—*Charles Creed*

Raku: a process of firing clay that deliberately burns patterns of smoke, open flame, and cracks into the glaze and into the substance of whatever is being fired. Because of the cracks, raku pottery is extremely fragile.

Implicit in Paul Simon's eulogy to Frank Lloyd Wright was a respect for the integrity of art, for the capacity of art, whether song or architecture or poetry, to make its own statement by virtue of integrity. The idea that fresh, honest art of any form attests, *simply by being fresh and honest,* to freshness and honesty in general is popular with artists, and is expressed in the eighth stanze of this poem, in response to the speaker's demand for "art that makes me a statement." How is this issue related to the raku jar and its ability to perform the jobs for which jars are normally made? What argument about art is the speaker advancing? What view of art is held by the artist who made the jar? Stanza nine suggests a compromise: obviously the artist must believe at least partially in functionalism, because she made a jar and not some other abstract form; and obviously the speaker is willing to put up with nonfunctional art, because he buys the jar. What might this say about art in general? About poetry?

What is the structure of this poem? Is it functional . . . or merely decorative?

Nuns Fret Not at Their Convent's Narrow Room

Nuns fret not at their convent's narrow room;
And hermits are contented with their cells;
And students with their pensive citadels;
Maids at the wheel, the weaver at his loom,
Sit blithe and happy; bees that soar for bloom,
High as the highest Peak of Furness-fells,
Will murmur by the hour in foxglove bells:
In truth the prison, unto which we doom
Ourselves, no prison is: and hence for me,

In sundry moods, 'twas pastime to be bound
Within the Sonnet's scanty plot of ground;
Pleased if some Souls (for such there needs must be)
Who have felt the weight of too much liberty,
Should find brief solace there, as I have found.

—*William Wordsworth*

5. *blithe:* happy. 6. *Furness-fells:* hills around Coniston Water, near Hawkshead, England. 8. *doom:* condemn.

Wordsworth ranges with the bee, nun, and maiden at her loom across a wide range of human experience within the confines of this poem. What statement does he make about art? Is it true? What is the form of this poem? Does the poem prove itself true?

Ars Poetica

A poem should be palpable and mute
As a globed fruit,

Dumb
As old medallions to the thumb,

Silent as the sleeve-worn stone
Of casement ledges where the moss has grown—

A poem should be wordless
As the flight of birds.

A poem should be motionless in time
As the moon climbs,

Leaving, as the moon releases
Twig by twig the night-entangled trees,

Leaving as the moon behind the winter leaves,
Memory by memory the mind—

A poem should be motionless in time
As the moon climbs.

A poem should be equal to:
Not true.

For all the history of grief
An empty doorway and a maple leaf.

For love
The leaning grasses and two lights above the sea—

A poem should not mean
But be.

—*Archibald MacLeish*

Here are more statements about poetry, almost riddles. Some of MacLeish's similes are easily understood: old medallions are worn medallions that would not yield a definite pattern to fingers when touched, even though their image is still visible. In this sense they are dumb to the thumb, and in this sense, MacLeish argues, poems should also be dumb: they should have something to say, but not be explicit about it. Other similes are more enigmatic: "wordless / As the flight of birds," for example. Work out each statement separately, then bring them together into a coherent view of poetry. The poem is titled "Ars Poetica," or "the art of poetry." What does MacLeish say about the art of poetry? Does this poem meet his own criteria for a good poem? Do you agree with MacLeish on what a good poem should be like?

In Memory of W. B. Yeats

1

He disappeared in the dead of winter:
The brooks were frozen, the airports almost deserted,
And snow disfigured the public statues;
The mercury sank in the mouth of the dying day.
O all the instruments agree
The day of his death was a dark cold day.

Far from his illness
The wolves ran on through the evergreen forests,
The peasant river was untempted by the fashionable quays;
By mourning tongues
The death of the poet was kept from his poems.

But for him it was his last afternoon as himself,
An afternoon of nurses and rumours;
The provinces of his body revolted,
The squares of his mind were empty,
Silence invaded the suburbs,
The current of his feeling failed: he became his admirers.

Now he is scattered among a hundred cities
And wholly given over to unfamiliar affections;
To find his happiness in another kind of wood
And be punished under a foreign code of conscience.
The words of a dead man
Are modified in the guts of the living.

But in the importance and noise of tomorrow
When the brokers are roaring like beasts on the floor of the Bourse,
And the poor have the sufferings to which they are fairly accustomed,
And each in the cell of himself is almost convinced of his freedom;
A few thousand will think of this day
As one thinks of a day when one did something slightly unusual.
O all the instruments agree
The day of his death was a dark cold day.

2

You were silly like us: your gift survived it all;
The parish of rich women, physical decay,
Yourself; mad Ireland hurt you into poetry.
Now Ireland has her madness and her weather still,
For poetry makes nothing happen: it survives
In the valley of its saying where executives
Would never want to tamper; it flows south
From ranches of isolation and the busy griefs,
Raw towns that we believe and die in; it survives,
A way of happening, a mouth.

3

Earth, receive an honoured guest;
William Yeats is laid to rest:
Let the Irish vessel lie
Emptied of its poetry.

Time that is intolerant
Of the brave and innocent,
And indifferent in a week
To a beautiful physique,

Worships language and forgives
Everyone by whom it lives;
Pardons cowardice, conceit,
Lays its honours at their feet.

Time that with this strange excuse
Pardoned Kipling and his views,
And will pardon Paul Claudel,
Pardons him for writing well.

In the nightmare of the dark
All the dogs of Europe bark,
And the living nations wait,
Each sequestered in its hate;

Intellectual disgrace
Stares from every human face,
And the seas of pity lie
Locked and frozen in each eye.

Follow, poet, follow right
To the bottom of the night,
With your unconstraining voice
Still persuade us to rejoice;

With the farming of a verse
Make a vineyard of the curse,
Sing of human unsuccess
In a rapture of distress;

In the deserts of the heart
Let the healing fountain start,
In the prison of his days
Teach the free man how to praise.

—*W. H. Auden*

9. *quay:* pier, wharf. 25. *Bourse:* the stock exchange in Paris. 55. *Kipling:* British writer and poet. His views included the benign imperialism of "the white man's burden." 56. *Claudel* (Paul): French diplomat, writer, poet; his writing is strongly colored by an ascetic Christianity.

This poem begins as a commemorative poem, written on the occasion of the death of Irish poet William Butler Yeats. It moves quickly, however, to a statement on the nature of poetry. What does Auden have to say about poetry, its function, its modus operandi? Do you agree with him?

7. A Statement: Wit

"Technique is enough," went one argument in the poem "Raku Jar"; "style / testifies to its own honesty." "Poetry makes nothing happen," said Auden; "it survives, / A way of happening, a mouth." Here are classic justifications. The argument is certainly attractive: a thing of beauty is, as John Keats once noted, a joy forever. We enjoy a beautiful poem as we enjoy a good basketball game, just for the technique of the thing, quite independent of its meaning. And what, we might ask, does ultimately mean anything? Perhaps poetry should simply busy itself with being good, a fun game, an honest game played cleanly and with excitement.

In the matter of technique, of course, the poet confronts a variety of options. There is an art that conceals itself, the art of which Yeats spoke in "Adam's Curse"; and then there is an art that calls attention to itself, shows off its technique, leaves us flushed at the way the poet handles words, by the style and craft of the poem. These poets are somewhat out of fashion these days, when we are suspicious of talent which, like a clever lawyer, sells itself to any purpose that will pay. We want something genuine, and amateur art *looks* more genuine than ostentatious displays of talent. Other ages, however, would have found contemporary poetry quite slovenly and inartistic, not really poetry at all, and pretty threadbare in comparison with the carefully crafted products of their own poets. In fact, much poetry has been written, inspired by the most trivial of circumstances, that is little more than an exercise in craft, a display of technique, style, and wit.

Wit is a word one hears only infrequently these days, but it provides a name for poetry designed mainly to show off, to state everyday thoughts in fine language. As Pope put it:

True wit is Nature to advantage dressed,
What oft was thought, but ne'er so well expressed;

Notice that wit does not mean humor, although finely expressed thoughts may contain an element of cleverness that comes close to surprise, and thus to humor. Style lavished upon trivia, puns or double-entendres, discovering similarities where you could find only differences, all characteristics of poetry that shows off, tend toward a certain levity. Aphorisms like Pope's, or like Cole Porter's "Birds do it, bees do it, even educated fleas do it, let's do it, let's fall in love"—these are so clever they are nearly humorous. But humor is not the central issue: style is.

Once wit is defined simply as language memorable more for the way it says something that what it says, we realize that there's a good deal more wit floating around, even today, than we would at first suspect. It may go unrecognized as art, of course (or, if recognized, relegated to the category of "mere stylistics"), but it's there: the well-turned insult, the aphoristic epigram, the polished compliment or eulogy. Even in popular song, an old folk singer like Paul Simon can sing into the top forty the urbane, witty trifle "Fifty Ways to Leave Your Lover":

Fifty Ways to Leave Your Lover

"The problem is all inside your head," she said to me;
"The answer is easy if you take it logically.
I'm here to help you if you're strugglin' to be free;
There must be fifty ways to leave your lover."

She said, "It's really not my habit to intrude;
I hope my meaning won't be lost or misconstrued,
But I'll repeat myself at the risk of being crude,
There must be fifty ways to leave your lover.

Just skip out the back, Jack,
Make a new plan, Stan,
You don't need to be coy, Roy,
Just get yourself free.

Hop on the bus, Gus,
You don't need to discuss much;
Just drop off the key, Lee,
And get yourself free."

She said, "It grieves me now to see you in such pain,
I wish there was something I could do to make you smile
again."
I said, "I appreciate that, and could you please explain
About the fifty ways?"

Just skip out the back, Jack,
Make a new plan, Stan,
You don't need to be coy, Roy,
Just get yourself free.

Hop on the bus, Gus,
You don't need to discuss much;
Just drop off the key, Lee,
And get yourself free.

She said, "Why don't we both just sleep on it tonight;
I'm sure in the morning you'll begin to see the light."
And then she kissed me, and I realized she probably was right,
There must be fifty ways to leave your lover.

Just skip out the back, Jack,
Make a new plan, Stan,
You don't need to be coy, Roy,
Just get yourself free.

Hop on the bus, Gus,
You don't need to discuss much;
Just drop off the key, Lee,
And get yourself free.

—*Paul Simon*

This remarkable song has a delicacy of tone almost unmatched in popular song, except by the clever (to a fault) "You're So Vain," by Carly Simon. "Back, Jack," "plan, Stan," and all the other short rhymes are examples of a technique called "jive talk," borrowed from the mid-fifties, when "hep cats" rhymed the last syllable of every sentence with a proper name. It was a low form of wit and still is, except that Simon uses the vaguely antique quality of jive talk to flavor his song and to characterize the people in it, and to build into "Fifty Ways" a certain ironic disparity between the way he could think/act/talk back in his youth and the ways he thinks/acts/talks in his middle age. Notice too the simple, almost colloquial lines, somewhere between prose and poetry, until we realize (much to our surprise) that "And then she kissed me, and I realized she probably was right" is almost perfect iambic pentameter, with some very clever rhyming going on as well, and here is a clever, witty poem. Notice finally the way Simon throws away the end of "fifty ways to leave your lover" in line 20, just when the phrase was on the verge of becoming monotonous. Add to this the clever rhyming of "bus, Gus" and "discuss much," and the understated, provokingly flat delivery, and you have a remarkable show of talent.

Here are other displays of wit from the seventeenth and eighteenth centuries. Notice that they are not necessarily humorous poems; in fact, Ben Jonson's elegant, polished, witty "On My First Daughter" is an elegy on the death of his child. Rochester's poem is a witty insult; Dryden's and Cowper's witty compliments.

On My First Daughter

Here lies, to each her parents' ruth,
Mary, the daughter of their youth;
Yet all heaven's gifts being heaven's due,
It makes the father less to rue.
At six months' end, she parted hence
With safety of her innocence;
Whose soul heaven's queen, whose name she bears,
In comfort of her mother's tears,
Hath placed amongst her virgin-train:
Where, while that severed doth remain,
This grave partakes the fleshly birth;
Which cover lightly, gentle earth!

—Ben Jonson

1. *ruth:* sorrow. 7. *whose name she bears:* the child's name was Mary. 10. *that:* the soul, severed from the body, but to be reunited with the body at the Resurrection.

On King Charles

We have a pretty witty king
  And whose word no man relys on:
He never said a foolish thing,
  And never did a wise one.

—John Wilmont, Earl of Rochester

On the Burning of Lord Mansfield's Library

When wit and genius meet their doom
  In all devouring flame,
They tell us of the fate of Rome,
  And bid us fear the same.

O'er Murray's loss the muses wept,
  They felt the rude alarm,
Yet bless'd the guardian care that kept
  His sacred head from harm.

There Memory, like the bee that's fed
  From Flora's balmy store,
The quintessence of all he read
  Had treasured up before.

The lawless herd, with fury blind,
  Have done him cruel wrong;
The flowers are gone—but still we find
  The honey on his tongue.

—*William Cowper*

On the Burning: see also Cowper's poem in Chapter 1, Section 6. 1. *doom:* fate. 5. *Murray:* Lord Mansfield. 10. *Flora's balmy store:* flowers.

Lines: On Dullness

Thus dullness, the safe opiate of the mind,
The last refuge weary wit can find,
Fit for all stations and in each content
Is satisfied, secure, and innocent:
No pains it takes, and no offence it gives,
Unfeared, unhated, undisturbed it lives.
—And if each writing author's best pretense,
Be but to teach the ignorant more sense;
Then dullness was the cause they wrote before,
As 'tis at last the cause they write no more;
So wit, which most to scorn it does pretend,
With dullness first began, in dullness last must end.

—*Alexander Pope*

Epigram on Milton

Three poets, in three distant ages born,
Greece, Italy, and England did adorn.
The first in loftiness of thought surpassed,
The next in majesty, in both the last:

The force of Nature could no farther go;
To make a third, she joined the former two.

—*John Dryden*

1. *three poets:* Homer, Virgil, and Milton.

8. A Statement: Antistatement

Modern poets, as we have noted, have become increasingly dubious about the advisability, even about the possibility of making definite pronouncements, in poetry or elsewhere. Some have turned to irony, paradox, and deliberate ambiguity in an attempt to write poetry whose statement accurately describes the world as they see it. Others have gone a step further. They are convinced that there *is* no meaning that human beings can apprehend with their limited brains or that can be expressed in the hopelessly defective communications system that is the English language . . . and they have intentionally written poetry in which normal patterns of meaning are deliberately obscured or the expectations of an audience that a poem mean something are deliberately frustrated. "Painting is paint," one modern painter once said, emphasizing the substance paint and devaluing such considerations as shape, rhythm, balance, and composition. So we might say "poetry is words," emphasizing the medium of poetry at the expense of character, narrative, image, meaning. The statement of such a poem is a statement against statements, against the capability of words to carry meaning, against the desirability of statement. Poem becomes antipoem, statement becomes antistatement.

Antiart in all forms may be seen as a reflection of the confusions and uncertainties of the modern world, and of the very real uncertainties of modern sciences (linguistics among them), and it is partially a reaction against readers intent on making poetry beautiful thoughts beautifully expressed—or even weighty thoughts to admiration dressed. This reaction was, incidentally, shared by many composer/singers of popular songs back in the late 1960s, when people started reading important messages into every top-forty tune (partially, of course, because some writers were *putting* important statements in top-forty tunes). "It doesn't mean shit to a tree," the Jefferson Airplane titled one song. "And it doesn't," composer Paul Kantner told an interviewer one afternoon; "we didn't even know what we were doing when we wrote it." Song as antisong. Said Beatle John Lennon, "It's nice when people like it, but when they start 'appreciating' it, getting great deep things out of it, making a thing of it, then it's a lot of shit. It proves what we've always thought about most sorts of so-called art . . . It all becomes a big con. We're a con as well. They've given us the freedom to con them. Let's stick that in there, we say, that'll start them puzzling. I'm sure all artists do, when they realize it's a con. I bet Picasso sticks things in. I bet he's been laughing his balls off the last eighty years.'' Art as antiart.

Now it's really quite difficult to make up nonsense, as Lewis Carroll and Edward Lear demonstrated in the nineteenth century. Both composed ''nonsense verse'' that made quite a bit of sense in a weird sort of way. But using techniques of programmed randomness reflecting a spinning radio dial, collages of symbols and phrases, and the fragmentation of words into syllables, some contemporary poets have come very close indeed to pure poetry as words:

A Whiter Shade of Pale

We skipped the light fandango
And turned cartwheels cross the floor.
I was feeling kind of seasick
But the crowd called out for more.
The room was humming harder
As the ceiling flew away
When we called out for another drink
The waiter brought a tray
And so it was that later
As the miller told his tale
That her face at first just ghostly
Turned a whiter shade of pale.

She said, ''There is no reason,
And the truth is plain to see,''
But I wandered through my playing cards
And would not let her be
One of sixteen vestal virgins
Who were leaving for the coast
And although my eyes were open
They might just have well been closed.
And so it was that later
As the miller told his tale
That her face at first just ghostly
Turned a whiter shade of pale.

—*Keith Reid–Gary Brooker*

"A Whiter Shade of Pale" presents an interesting collection of images set to a very un-rock-n-rollish bit of music adapted from J. S. Bach. As a song the thing was popular enough, although the disjunction between the measured, orderly progression of its music and the wild disorder of its lyrics suggests that the song is either highly ironic or totally incoherent. The more you sort through the fragments, Chaucer's Miller and the Vestal Virgins and the waiter with his tray, the more you come to the conclusion that there's no coherence at all here. On the other hand, it may well be that the Procol Harum were deliberately looking for a heap of images, past and present, to work up into a collage disarrayed enough to function as an ironic counterpart to Bach's music. Thus they could juxtapose the modern chaos against Bach's seventeenth-century order. There is deliberate meaninglessness in the poem, then, which becomes a statement on the meaninglessness of life in the twentieth century.

I Know a Man

As I sd to my
friend, because I am
always talking,—John, I

sd, which was not his
name, the darkness sur-
rounds us, what

can we do against
it, or else, shall we &
why not, buy a goddamn big car,

drive, he sd, for
christ's sake, look
out where yr going.

—*Robert Creeley*

Creeley's poem, of course, makes sense in that we understand the meaning of the various phrases and statements he uses. Still, the phrases do not quite fit together, and the statement of the poem is a denial of Meaning with the capital M. "The darkness surrounds us" sounds like a phrase copped from one of the classical modern poets (Eliot, Frost, Yeats), all busy lamenting the disintegration of civilization and the impending night. While darkness may in fact cover the earth, Creeley immediately trivializes such weighty matters with "shall we &/

why not, buy a goddamn big car." Then the existential response to both the trivial and the profound: "drive . . . look/ out where yr going." In the face of meaninglessness, one can only push on, which is all one could do anyway, so there it all is. It is worth noting that in writing his poems, Creeley frequently breaks words in mid-syllable at the end of a line, or phrases in mid-phrase, creating both puns and dislocations. And in reading his poems aloud, he observes those breaks with deliberate and—to an unaccustomed ear—slightly disorienting pauses that destroy the coherence of word and phrase and thus the poem's meaning.

9. A Statement: Poetry of Statement

The tendency of much contemporary poetry is to strip away: strip away metaphor, cut out myth, delete fancy language, images, symbols, rhyme, meter, beautiful thoughts, ironies, ambiguities, wit, allusions—all the things, in other words, that traditionally go into making poetry an elevated art. What these poets are seeking is a comfortable poetry, not so very show-offish, something people can live with and understand and assimilate and not have to be bothering their heads all the time with "What does it *mean?*" or "I wonder if my reaction to this is valid?" or "What am I supposed to be getting out of this?" A lot of poets *aren't* trying to do this, of course, but many are, and in balance it's a pleasant state of affairs, because so much poetry has gone to such excesses of imagery, allusion, flowery language, noble thoughts, ignoble thoughts, experimental forms and languages, and all the rest, that much of the audience has been driven away, and poetry has become a kind of monster that terrifies more than comforts ordinary readers.

The difficulty with such poetry is that it has virtually nothing except its clean simplicity to commend it as fine art, and very little for critic or teacher to explain, elucidate, analyze, footnote, and all the other things that critics and teachers do to poetry, things that keep them in business. So this simple poetry—"poetry of statement" we sometimes call it—goes about its business unheralded, mainly because there isn't much to herald. The poem says its piece and is over. We can say, "That was very nicely put," and that is about all because it's all the poet allows. A. E. Housman writes this kind of poetry and, for all the imagery and thematic complexity of some of their songs, so too do the Beatles and Bob Dylan. Dylan, in fact, has an absolutely uncanny ability to work into his songs and poems the most prosey, mundane lines, and make them work as poetry. One thinks of "Lily, Rosemary, and the Jack of Hearts," with the line "'There's something funny goin' on,' he said, 'I can just feel it in the air.''' That line has metrical regularity, of course, but it's as straight a prose statement as you will find anywhere, the kind of thing you might overhear anybody say in any one of a hundred different situations. Or the Beatles "Oh! Darling," from *Abbey Road* side two; what could be less artsy, less poetic, more clear?

Oh! Darling

Oh! darling, please believe me, I'll never do you no harm.
Believe me when I tell you, I'll never do you no harm.
Oh! darling, if you leave me, I'll never make it alone.
Believe me when I beg you, don't ever leave me alone.
    When you told me you didn't need me anymore,
    Well, you know I nearly broke down and cried.
    When you told me you didn't need me anymore,
    Well you know I nearly broke down and died.
Oh! darling, if you leave me, I'll never make it alone.
Believe me when I tell you, I'll never do you no harm.
    When you told me you didn't need me anymore,
    Well you know I nearly broke down and cried.
    When you told me you didn't need me anymore,
    Well you know I nearly broke down and died.
Oh! darling, please believe me, I'll never let you down,
Oh! believe me when I tell you, I'll never do you no harm.

—*John Lennon–Paul McCartney*

Jim Croce dressed things up a bit in "Time in a Bottle," with the interesting images of putting time in a bottle and wishes in a box, but basically the song, especially its chorus, is simple poetry of statement.

Time in a Bottle

If I could save time in a bottle
The first thing that I'd like to do
Is to save every day
'Til Eternity passes away
Just to spend them with you.

If I could make days last forever
If words could make wishes come true
I'd save every day like a treasure and then,
Again, I would spend them with you.

But there never seems to be enough time
To do the things you want to do
Once you find them.
I've looked around enough to know
That you're the one I want to go
Through time with.

If I had a box just for wishes
And dreams that had never come true
The box would be empty
Except for the memory
Of how they were answered by you.

But there never seems to be enough time
To do the things you want to do
Once you find them.
I've looked around enough to know
That you're the one I want to go
Through time with.

—*Jim Croce*

The poet e. e. cummings may play around with typography, but when you strip away the concreteness of his poems, many of them amount to very simple, plain, and—most significantly—easily *intelligible* statements . . . like this simple statement that war is hell:

plato told

plato told

him:he couldn't
believe it(jesus

told him;he
wouldn't believe
it)lao

tsze
certainly told
him,and general
(yes
mam)

sherman;
and even
(believe it
or

not)you
told him:i told
him;we told him
(he didn't believe it,no

sir)it took
a nipponized bit of
the old sixth

avenue
el;in the top of his head:to tell

him

—*e. e. cummings*

23. sixth avenue el: shortly before the outbreak of World War II, the United States government permitted the sale to Japan of New York City's Sixth Avenue elevated subway as scrap metal.

John Berryman is more sophisticated in the first of his ''Eleven Addresses to the Lord'' in the way he modulates into and out of poetry of statement. Note, for example, that the poem's first stanza leans toward a certain imagery in its descriptions of God: ''craftsman of the snowflake,'' ''endower of Earth so gorgeous & different from the boring moon.'' With the second stanza, however, Berryman eschews eloquence and gets down to the simple fundamentals of speech, only to return to a functional imagery (''this blue chair'' as the poem concludes).

from Eleven Addresses to the Lord, #1

Master of beauty, craftsman of the snowflake,
inimitable contriver,
endower of Earth so gorgeous & different from the boring
  Moon,
thank you for such as it is my gift.

I have made up a morning prayer to you
containing with precision everything that most matters.
'According to Thy will' the thing begins.
It took me off & on two days. It does not aim at eloquence.

You have come to my rescue again & again
in my impassable, sometimes despairing years.
You have allowed my brilliant friends to destroy themselves
and I am still here, severely damaged, but functioning.

Unknowable, as I am unknown to my guinea pigs:
how can I 'love' you?
I only as far as gratitude & awe
confidently & absolutely go.

I have no idea whether we live again.
It doesn't seem likely
from either the scientific or the philosophical point of view
but certainly all things are possible to you,

and I believe as fixedly in the Resurrection-appearances to
  Peter & to Paul
as I believe I sit in this blue chair.
Only that may have been a special case
to establish their initiatory faith.

Whatever your end may be, accept my amazement.
May I stand until death forever at attention
for any your least instruction or enlightenment.
I even feel sure you will assist me again, Master of insight &
  beauty.

—John Berryman

6 Sustained Performances

Frequently poets group individual lyrics together into larger structures of greater or lesser cohesiveness, juxtaposing one poem against another, repeating themes and motifs, linking lyrics together with verbal or imagistic echoes, providing their readers with a sustained performance that can run to the hundreds, even thousands of lines. One way of bringing separate lyrics together in a loosely cohesive structure is to arrange the poems of a single volume so that they develop a central idea, explore various aspects of a single theme, or tell a story. Edgar Lee Masters's *Spoon River Anthology,* for example, contains a series of lyrics depicting characters who all lived in a fictional town on the Spoon River. Over the course of the volume, a portrait emerges not only of the various characters whose stories Masters tells, but of the town itself. A. E. Housman arranged the lyrics of his first volume of poems, *A Shropshire Lad,* to tell the story of a young man, Terence Hearsay, who grew up in and later left the area around Shropshire. We meet him and his friends, watch him mature and develop, and understand something of the confusion he feels when he is torn from the context that has given meaning to his life. The unity of these two volumes is loose, of course, but still quite evident. Most volumes of poetry these days have at least a thematic unity, and one major injustice in anthologies and textbooks like this one is that, in the very process of sampling many poets they obliterate that unity. Once in your life you should read a single volume of poems—not a "collected poems"—by a major contemporary poet.

Some poets prefer something more formal in the way of unifying structures. Sonnet cycles, series of sonnets that tell a story or develop a philosophical meditation, were popular during the Renaissance and are still being written today. Shakespeare, Sidney, and Spenser all wrote sonnet sequences, as did Edna St. Vincent Millay, W. H. Auden, and George Meredith. Donne's "La Corona" is a series of seven sonnets, each linked to the next by repeated lines.

Or a poet may bring lyrics so close together that they act and look more like a unit than individual poems. Tennyson's famous *In Memoriam* is really a long series of over a hundred independent lyrics carefully ordered, numbered, and printed together under one title. Michael Anania's "The Riversongs of Arion" is a similar construct. But although the poems appear under a single title, the various parts retain much of their own integrity: breaks of thought and subject between one section and the next are usually sharp and abrupt, tone and even verse form can vary from one section to the next. Even in cases like "The Riversongs," the place to begin analysis of the whole is with an analysis of each separate unit.

Every sustained performance is unique, and each requires a special set of guidelines for study—but all involve patterns of meaning that extend beyond the boundaries of the individual lyrics or subsections of a large poem. *Sergeant Pepper's Lonely Hearts Club Band* requires a process of analysis not much different from that demanded by "The Riversongs" or a sonnet cycle, because *Sergeant Pepper,* unlike most rock albums, has a linear structural and thematic unity. The individual lyrics are, of course, impressive, and they are a place to begin discussion; but analysis of any one lyric must soon carry one into analysis of the whole album, just as a study of any one of Donne's or Anania's poems ought ultimately to lead to a treatment of the whole. The techniques developed in discussing *Pepper's* should prove quite useful in treating "La Corona" and "The Riversongs," and finally Wordsworth's "Ode," the most unified of the poems in this chapter.

Sergeant Pepper's Lonely Hearts Club Band

I

Sergeant Pepper's Lonely Hearts Club Band

It was twenty years ago today
That Sergeant Pepper taught the band to play.
They've been going in and out of style,
But they're guaranteed to raise a smile.
So may I introduce to you
The act you've known for all these years:
Sergeant Pepper's Lonely Hearts Club Band.
We're Sergeant Pepper's Lonely Hearts Club Band,
We hope you will enjoy the show.
We're Sergeant Pepper's Lonely Hearts Club Band.

Sit back and let the evening go,
Sergeant Pepper's Lonely,
Sergeant Pepper's Lonely,
Sergeant Pepper's Lonely Hearts Club Band.
It's wonderful to be here,
It's certainly a thrill,
You're such a lovely audience,
We'd like to take you home with us,
We'd like to take you home.
I don't really want to stop the show
But I thought you might like to know
That the singer's going to sing a song
And he wants you all to sing along.
So may I introduce to you
The one and only Billy Shears.
Sergeant Pepper's Lonely Hearts Club Band.

II

With a Little Help From My Friends

What would you think if I sang out of tune,
Would you stand up and walk out on me?
Lend me your ears and I'll sing you a song,
And I'll try not to sing out of key.
I get by with a little help from my friends,
I get high with a little help from my friends,
Going to try with a little help from my friends.
What do I do when my love is away?
(Does it worry you to be alone?)
How do I feel by the end of the day?
(Are you sad because you're on your own?)
No I get by with a little help from my friends.
Do you need anybody?
I need somebody to love.
Could it be anybody?
I want somebody to love.
Would you believe in a love at first sight?
Yes I'm certain that it happens all the time.
What do you see when you turn out the light?
I can't tell you, but I know it's mine.
Oh I get by with a little help from my friends.
Do you need anybody?
I just need somebody to love.

Could it be anybody?
I want somebody to love.
I get by with a little help from my friends,
Yes I get by with a little help from my friends,
With a little help from my friends.

III

Lucy in the Sky with Diamonds

Picture yourself in a boat on a river
With tangerine trees and marmalade skies.
Somebody calls you, you answer quite slowly,
A girl with kaleidoscope eyes.
Cellophane flowers of yellow and green
Towering over your head,
Look for the girl with the sun in her eyes
And she's gone.
Lucy in the sky with diamonds,
Lucy in the sky with diamonds,
Lucy in the sky with diamonds.
Follow her down to a bridge by a fountain
Where rocking horse people eat marshmallow pies.
Ev'ryone smiles as you drift past the flowers
That grow so incredibly high.
Newspaper taxis appear on the shore
Waiting to take you away,
Climb in the back with your head in the clouds
And you're gone.
Lucy in the sky with diamonds,
Lucy in the sky with diamonds,
Lucy in the sky with diamonds.
Picture yourself on a train in a station
With plasticine porters with looking glass ties.
Suddenly someone is there at the turnstile,
The girl with kaleidoscope eyes.
Lucy in the sky with diamonds,
Lucy in the sky with diamonds,
Lucy in the sky with diamonds.

IV

Getting Better

It's getting better all the time.
I used to get mad at my school,

The teachers who taught me weren't cool,
Holding me down,
Turning me round,
Filling me up with your rules.
I've got to admit it's getting better,
It's a little better all the time.
I have to admit it's getting better,
It's getting better since you've been mine.
Me used to be angry young man,
Me hiding me head in the sand.
You gave me the word,
I finally heard,
I'm doing the best that I can.
I admit it's getting better,
It's a little better all the time.
Yes I admit it's getting better,
It's getting better since you've been mine.
Getting so much better all the time,
It's getting better all the time,
Better, better, better.
I used to be cruel to my woman,
I beat her and kept her apart from the things that she loved.
Man I was mean,
But I'm changing my scene,
And I'm doing the best that I can.
I admit it's getting better,
It's a little better all the time.
Yes I admit it's getting better,
It's getting better since you've been mine,
Getting so much better all the time.

V

Fixing a Hole

I'm fixing a hole where the rain gets in
And stops my mind from wandering
Where it will go.
I'm filling the cracks that ran through the door
And kept my mind from wandering
Where it will go.
And it really doesn't matter if I'm wrong, I'm right
Where I belong, I'm right
Where I belong.
See the people standing there

Who disagree and never win
And wonder why they don't get in my door.
I'm painting the room in a colourful way,
And when my mind is wandering
There I will go.
And it really doesn't matter if I'm wrong, I'm right
Where I belong, I'm right
Where I belong.
Silly people run around,
They worry me and never ask me
Why they don't get past my door.
I'm taking my time for a number of things
That weren't important yesterday,
And I still go.
I'm fixing a hole where the rain gets in
And stops my mind from wandering
Where it will go,
Where it will go.

VI

She's Leaving Home

Wedn'sday morning at five o'clock as the day begins,
Silently closing her bedroom door,
Leaving the note that she hoped would say more,
She goes downstairs to the kitchen clutching her hankerchief,
Quietly turning the backdoor key,
Stepping outside, she is free.
She (We gave her most of our lives)
Is leaving (Sacrificed most of our lives)
Home (We gave her ev'rything money could buy.)
She's leaving home after living alone for so many years.
(Bye, bye)

Father snores as his wife gets into her dressing gown,
Picks up the letter that's lying there,
Standing alone at the top of the stairs,
She breaks down and cries to her husband, "Daddy, our
  baby's gone.
Why would she treat us so thoughtlessly?
How could she do this to me?"
She (We never thought of ourselves.)
Is leaving (Never a thought for ourselves.)

Home (We struggled hard all our lives to get by.)
She's leaving home after living alone for so many years.
(Bye, bye)

Friday morning at nine o'clock she is far away,
Waiting to keep the appointment she made,
Meeting a man from the motor trade.
She (What did we do that was wrong?)
Is having (We didn't know it was wrong.)
Fun (Fun is the one thing that money can't buy.)
Something inside that was always denied for so many years.
She's leaving home,
Bye, bye.

VII

Being for the Benefit of Mr. Kite

For the benefit of Mister Kite
There will be a show tonight on trampoline.
The Hendersons will all be there
Late of Pablo Fanques fair, what a scene.
Over men and horses, hoops and garters,
Lastly through a hogshead of real fire.
In this way Mister K. will challenge the world.

The celebrated Mister K.
Performs his feat on Saturday at Bishopsgate.
The Hendersons will dance and sing
As Mister Kite flies through the ring. Don't be late.
Messrs. K. and H. assure the public
Their production will be second to none.
And of course Henry the horse dances the waltz.

The band begins at ten to six
When Mister K. performs his tricks without a sound,.
And Mister H. will demonstrate,
Ten somersets he'll undertake on solid ground.
Having been some days in preparation,
A splendid time is guaranteed for all.
And tonight Mister Kite is topping the bill.

VIII

Within You Without You

We were talking about the space between us all
And the people who hide themselves behind a wall of illusion,
Never glimpse the truth. Then it's far too late
When they pass away.
We were talking about the love we all could share,
When we find it to try our best to hold it there with our love.
With our love we could save the world,
If they only knew.
Try to realize it's all within yourself, no one else can make you change,
And to see you're only very small
And life flows on within you and without you.
We were talking about the love that's gone so cold
And the people who gain the world and lose their soul. They don't know,
They can't see. Are you one of them?
When you've seen beyond yourself, then you may find peace of mind is waiting there,
And the time will come when you see we're all one
And life flows on within you and without you.

IX

When I'm Sixty-Four

When I get older, losing my hair,
Many years from now,
Will you still be sending me a valentine,
Birthday greetings, bottle of wine?
If I'd been out till quarter to three,
Would you lock the door?
Will you still need me,
Will you still feed me,
When I'm sixty-four?
You'll be older too.
And if you say the word
I could stay with you.

I could be handy mending a fuse
When your lights have gone;
You can knit a sweater by the fireside,
Sunday mornings go for a ride.
Doing the garden, digging the weeds—
Who could ask for more?
Will you still need me,
Will you still feed me,
When I'm sixty-four?
Ev'ry summer we can rent a cottage
In the Isle of Wight if it's not too dear.
We shall scrimp and save.
Grandchildren on your knee,
Vera, Chuck and Dave.

Send me a postcard, drop me a line
Stating point of view,
Indicate precisely what you mean to say,
Yours sincerely, wasting away.
Give me your answer, fill in a form,
Mine forever more.
Will you still need me,
Will you still feed me,
When I'm sixty-four?

X

Lovely Rita

Lovely Rita, meter maid,
Lovely Rita, meter maid,
Lovely Rita, meter maid,
Nothing can come between us.
When it gets dark I tow your heart away.
Standing by a parking meter,
When I caught a glimpse of Rita
Filling in a ticket in her little white book.
In a cap she looked much older
And the bag across her shoulder
Made her look a little like a military man.
Lovely Rita, meter maid,
May I enquire discreetly,

When you are free to take some tea with me?
Took her out and tried to win her;
Had a laugh and over dinner
Told her I would really like to see her again.
Got the bill and Rita paid it,
Took her home and nearly made it
Sitting on a sofa with a sister or two.
Oh, lovely Rita, meter maid,
Where would I be without you?
Give us a wink and make me think of you.
Lovely Rita, meter maid,
Lovely Rita, meter maid,
Lovely Rita, meter maid.

XI

Good Morning, Good Morning

Good morning good morning good morning good morning
Nothing to do to save his life,
Call his wife in.
Nothing to say but what a day,
How's your boy been?
Nothing to do, it's up to you.
I've got nothing to say but it's O.K.
Good morning good morning good morning
Going to work, don't want to go,
Feeling low down.
Heading for home you start to roam,
Then you're in town.
Ev'rybody knows there's nothing doing,
Ev'rything is close, it's like a ruin,
Ev'ryone you see is half asleep,
And you're on your own in the street.

After a while you start to smile,
Now you feel cool.
Then you decide to take a walk
By the old school.
Nothing has changed, it's still the same.
I've got nothing to say but it's O.K.
Good morning good morning good morning
People running round, it's five o'clock,
Ev'rywhere in town it's getting dark,

Ev'ryone you see is full of life,
It's time for tea and meet the wife.

Somebody needs to know the time,
Glad that I'm here.
Watching the skirts you start to flirt,
Now you're in gear.
Go to a show, you hope she goes.
I've got nothing to say but it's O.K.
Good morning good morning good morning

XII

Sergeant Pepper's Lonely Hearts Club Band
(Reprise)

We're Sergeant Pepper's Lonely Hearts Club Band,
We hope you have enjoyed the show.
We're Sergeant Pepper's Lonely Hearts Club Band,
We're sorry but it's time to go.
Sergeant Pepper's lonely.
Sergeant Pepper's lonely.
Sergeant Pepper's lonely.
Sergeant Pepper's lonely.
Sergeant Pepper's Lonely Hearts Club Band,
We'd like to thank you once again,
Sergeant Pepper's one and only Lonely Hearts Club Band,
It's getting very near the end.
Sergeant Pepper's lonely,
Sergeant Pepper's lonely,
Sergeant Pepper's Lonely Hearts Club Band.

XIII

A Day in the Life

I read the news today, oh boy,
About a lucky man who made the grade.
And though the news was rather sad,
Well I just had to laugh.
I saw the photograph.
He blew his mind out in a car.
He didn't notice that the lights had changed.
A crowd of people stood and stared.

They'd seen his face before.
Nobody was really sure
If he was from the House of Lords.

I saw a film today, oh boy.
The English army has just won the war.
A crowd of people turned away,
But I just had to look,
Having read the book.
I'd love to turn you on.

Woke up, fell out of bed,
Dragged a comb across my head,
Found my way downstairs and drank a cup,
And looking up I noticed I was late.
Found my coat and grabbed my hat,
Made the bus in seconds flat,
Found my way upstairs and had a smoke,
Somebody spoke and I went into a dream.

I read the news today, oh boy:
Four thousand holes in Blackburn, Lancashire,
And though the holes were rather small
They had to count them all.
Now they know how many holes it takes to fill the Albert Hall.
I'd love to turn you on.

—*The Beatles*

The more one listens to *Sergeant Pepper,* the more carefully one analyzes the imagery and the almost infinite variety of rhythm and rhyme, the more one hears other albums by other rock groups, the more stunning this album becomes. Musically and verbally it was impressive when it first appeared; in retrospect it is even more impressive. There can be little doubt that it will be listened to and studied for many years to come, because of both the quality of its music and the variety of its poetry.

The long-playing record imposes itself as a form upon the Beatles' work, of course, and they must work within its context: the performance may not extend much beyond an hour, but at least forty minutes of time must be filled. The public expects a series of single cuts on each side; the first and the last cuts will have emphasis because of their positions. There will be a break at the end of the first side, which may necessitate some form of recapitulation at the beginning of the second. Within these predetermined confines, however, the Beatles are free to develop a narrative (as the Who did with *Tommy*) or thematically related lyrics that work off each other. They compromise: the two "Sergeant Pepper" songs frame a series of distinct studies of great musical and poetic variety, putting the whole album in the context of a stage performance (the illusion is furthered by "A Little Help From My Friends"). The last cut on the second side is parenthetical, outside the performance context, a new perspective on all that has gone before.

The place to begin a consideration of the album is with the individual lyrics, some of which have already been the subject of considerable discussion. Only after one has grasped the songs individually can one begin drawing patterns of meaning from the whole album. "Lucy In the Sky" is widely interpreted as an acid trip and an acrostic for LSD. Certainly both the tonal distortions of the music and the rich sensual imagery of the poem suggest the popular conception of such a trip. Moreover, the boat, the taxi, and the train all suggest "trip" in the literal sense, and the distortions in sense perception evidenced by the tall flowers past which one drifts, the intense awareness of color and taste in tangerine trees and marmalade skies, and the hallucinations hinted at by "rocking horse people" and Lucy's kaleidoscope eyes would seemingly settle the issue. But in an interview in the *Washington Post,* Paul McCartney claimed that the song derived from a picture drawn by John Lennon's little boy, Julian. Although he could not deny the appropriateness of the LSD interpretation, he claimed that in writing the poem they had never thought about that at all. It may, of course, be that the interview rather than the song was a put-on, but one is never sure. "Lucy In the Sky" is a powerful poem: the title image suggests an awareness that the rest of the song develops, an awareness of the most common of things in the most uncommon of contexts, imbueing Lucy with mystical attraction. Perhaps the song is really about the awareness of the extraordinary within the ordinary—but then that is precisely what LSD was reported (perhaps erroneously) to open one's eyes to.

"For the Benefit of Mr. Kite" presents another problem. McCartney claimed it came straight off a wall poster; others remind us that kiff (pot) and hashish—Mssrs. K. and H. whose performance will be second to none—and horse are all slang terms for drugs, and argue for a drug interpretation. After all, H. turns somersets without ever leaving the ground, and K. flies through a ring. Perhaps the circus imagery is but an adjunct to describing a trip. Or perhaps the drug images and the circus images supplement each other, both functioning metaphorically to suggest a further, deeper theme: the loss of one's self (with related anxieties, self-analyses, and doubts) in the magic of a grand performance. Drugs take one away from reality for a moment just as the carnival atmosphere of a circus takes one away; one loses hold of reality in the noise and color and magic of the moment. And certainly Mister Kite's performance is a splendid, colorful, swirling, enchanting thing metrically as well as imagistically.

"A Day in the Life" is, with the possible exception of "Lucy in the Sky," the most haunting and the most ambiguous song on the album. Madison Avenue has managed to make the phrase "turn on" virtually meaningless by applying it to everything from shades of cosmetics to chocolate malts, but the expression always did have a certain ambiguity to it. First, of course, it means drugs, and the man is having a smoke and the Beatles have admitted in various interviews to using various drugs and the B.B.C. was convinced enough of the line's meaning to ban the song from the network. But the other images in the song suggest that we are being asked to turn on to an awareness of the bankruptcy of life as we usually live it in the twentieth century, and to an awareness of what life might be. The man blew his mind out just when he finally made the grade, the war was won but nobody really cared. Life goes on, a collage of nearly missed buses and holes to be carefully counted. If "Lucy in the Sky" was a trip that turned us on to the magic of what is conventional, all that magic has disappeared in "A Day in the Life." The trip is over, and it was a bummer.

The comparison between these two songs brings us to a more important question: what kind of a statement does the album as a whole make? Everyone, including for a change McCartney himself, agrees that yes, it does have a unity, and it is obvious that the unity is intentional: "Sergeant Pepper's Lonely Hearts Club Band" introduces Billy Shears and "With A Little Help"; the record moves without a break from the end of "Sergeant Pepper's (Reprise)" to "A Day in the Life"; the drug motif repeats itself again and again in the "high" of "A Little Help," the weeds of "When I'm Sixty-Four," the tea of "Lovely Rita." Technically, the crescendo at the end of "A Day in the Life" is an analog of the barnyard cacophony at the end of "Good Morning," just as the emptiness of the imagery reflects the same banality implicit in the other. "Within You Without You" proclaims overtly what the previous lyrics suggested indirectly; it is a kind of summary of side one of the album before we begin side two. "When I'm Sixty-Four" balances "She's Leaving Home." And so on. But what kind of a statement does this unity make?

The context of the whole album is provided by the opening two songs: this is a performance by Sergeant Pepper (Ringo Star, alias Billy Shears—he wears the sergeant's stripes on his uniform) and his lonely hearts club band. Two things are important: the band is lonely, and it is performing. Perhaps the two are interrelated: performers are generally lonely people, lonely people perform when they pretend not to be lonely and in an attempt to escape their loneliness. What is especially significant, however, is that Sergeant Pepper and his band are aware of the fact that they are performing, that they are acting out an illusion—others are not as aware, but then again they are probably not as lonely. Some are off into a drug thing; others tell themselves that things are, after all, getting better all the time, or rationalize their disillusionment by excusing themselves. Some withdraw into self-isolation and others drown any misgivings they might have in the noise and excitement of a circus performance. "What we were talking about," says George Harrison bluntly in "Within You Without You," "is what is hypocritical and what is honest, and who hides behind what walls of illusion." But if the lyrics of this song outline inadequate responses people make when they are vaguely aware that something is wrong with their lives, the next three songs present us with a gallery of incredibly shallow individuals. The first proposes the most mundane of marriages to a mail-order bride; the second falls in love with a meter maid he happens to see writing up tickets; the third drives in self-impressed fashion aimlessly around town looking for pick-ups. What makes the whole despicable crowd especially disgusting (and the Beatles' comment especially morose) is the irrepressible high spirits of the music, which ironically mocks the words themselves and piles irony on top of irony. And then the band, Sergeant Pepper's Band, Sergeant Pepper's Lonely Hearts Club Band, breaks in with its initial statement, now made depressingly meaningful: "Sergeant Pepper's lonely." The "l" is lower case; the phrase ends with a period. The band is making a statement: "Sergeant Pepper is lonely," and that's what we've been talking about for the duration of this performance. By now we as listeners have begun to feel a trifle lonely too, and "A Day In the Life," with the alienated, impassive attitude of the observers and its resounding chord dying-out-to-nothing at the end is almost too much. But it is too much not simply because of the song itself, but because the entire weight of the whole album comes crashing down on that final chord. And the whole weight of *Sergeant Pepper* is a lot of weight.

La Corona

I

Deign at my hands this crown of prayer and praise,
Weav'd in my low devout melancholy,
Thou which of good, hast, yea art treasury,
All changing unchang'd Ancient of days;
But do not, with a vile crown of frail bays,
Reward my muse's white sincerity,

But what thy thorny crown gain'd, that give me,
A crown of Glory, which doth flower always;
The ends crown our works, but thou crown'st our ends,
For, at our end begins our endless rest;
The first last end, now zealously possessed,
With a strong sober thirst, my soul attends.
'Tis time that heart and voice be lifted high,
Salvation to all that will is nigh

II

Annunciation

Salvation to all that will is nigh;
That All, which always is All everywhere,
Which cannot sin, and yet all sins must beare,
Which cannot die, yet cannot choose but die,
Loe, faithful Virgin, yields himself to lie
In prison, in thy womb; and though he there
Can take no sin, nor thou give, yet he'will wear
Taken from thence, flesh, which death's force may try.
Ere by the spheres time was created, thou
Wast in his mind, who is thy Son, and Brother;
Whom thou conceiv'st, conceiv'd; yea thou art now
Thy Maker's maker, and thy Father's mother;
Thou'hast light in dark; and shutst in little room,
Immensity cloisterd in thy dear womb.

III

Nativity

Immensity cloisterd in thy dear womb,
Now leaves his welbelov'd imprisonment,
There he hath made himself to his intent
Weak enough, now into our world to come;
But Oh, for thee, for him, hath th'Inn no room?
Yet lay him in this stall, and from the Orient,
Stars, and wisemen will travel to prevent
Th'effect of *Herod's* jealous general doom.
Seest thou, my Soul, with thy faith's eyes, how he
Which fills all place, yet none holds him, doth lie?
Was not his pity towards thee wondrous high,
That would have need to be pitied by thee?
Kiss him, and with him into Egypt go,
With his kind mother, who partakes thy woe.

IV

Temple

With his kind mother who partakes thy woe,
Joseph turn back; see where your child doth sit,
Blowing, yea blowing out those sparks of wit,
Which himself on the Doctors did bestow;
The Word but lately could not speak, and lo
It suddenly speaks wonders, whence comes it,
That all which was, and all which should be writ,
A shallow seeming child, should deeply know?
His Godhead was not soul to his manhood,
Nor had time mellowed him to this ripeness,
But as for one which hath a long task, 'tis good,
With the Sun to begin his business,
He in his ages morning thus began
By miracles exceeding power of man.

V

Crucifying

By miracles exceeding power of man,
He faith in some, envy in some begat,
For, what weak spirits admire, ambitious, hate;
In both affections many to him ran,
But Oh! the worst are most, they will and can,
Alas, and do, unto the immaculate,
Whose creature Fate is, now prescribe a Fate,
Measuring self-life's infinity to'a span,
Nay to an inch. Lo, where condemned he
Bears his own cross, with pain, yet by and by
When it bears him, he must bear more and die.
Now thou art lifted up, draw me to thee,
And at thy death giving such liberal dole,
Moist, with one drop of thy blood, my dry soul.

VI

Resurrection

Moist with one drop of thy blood, my dry soul
Shall (though she now be in extreme degree
Too stony hard, and yet too fleshly,) be
Freed by that drop, from being starv'd, hard, or foul,

And life, by this death abled, shall control
Death, whom thy death slew; nor shall to me
Fear of first or last death, bring misery,
If in thy little book my name thou enroll,
Flesh in that long sleep is not putrified,
But made that there, of which, and for which 'twas;
Nor can by other means be glorified.
May then sins sleep, and deaths soon from me pass,
That wak't from both, I again risen may
Salute the last, and everlasting day.

VII

Ascension

Salute the last and everlasting day,
Joy at the uprising of this Sun, and Son,
Ye whose just tears, or tribulation
Have purely washed, or burnt your drossy clay;
Behold the Highest, parting hence away,
Lightens the dark clouds, which he treads upon,
Nor doth he by ascending, show alone.
But first he, and he first enters the way.
A strong Ram, which hast batter'd heaven for me,
Mild Lamb, which with thy blood, hast mark'd the path;
Bright Torch, which shin'st, that I the way may see,
Oh, with thine own blood quench thine own just wrath,
And if thy holy Spirit, my Muse did raise,
Deign at my hands this crown of prayer and praise.

—*John Donne*

1. *Deign at:* accept from. 2. *melancholy:* pensiveness. 5. *bays:* laurel wreathes bestowed for excellency or achievement. 23. *spheres:* the nine spheres of the Ptolomaic universe, above and beyond which God had his dwelling place. 37. *doom:* judgment, decree. 45. *wit:* wisdom. 47. *The Word:* Cf. John 1:1. 76. *Death . . . slew:* Cf. "Death, be not Proud," Chapter II. 88. *drossy:* wastelike, earthy, impure. 93. *Ram:* an illusion to the ram sacrificed instead of Isaac by Abraham.

The Riversongs of Arion

"The Rule is one, like itself accompanied with stability and rest; if once we go astray from that, there is neither end nor quiet in error, but restlessness and emptiness."

Thomas Hooker (1659)

"This evening Guthrege Cought a White Catfish . . . *tale much like that of a* Dolfin."

Journals of Lewis and Clark
(July 24, 1804)

I

Adrift on an oil-drum raft
I have traveled this river south
past packinghouse spills

with split-bellied watermelons
and castaway chicken heads.
I have seen catfish and bullheads

feed among the scum that eddies
beneath eroded silt shoals
and heard the silver tankers

taxi across crestfallen bluffs
at the fenced bend above the Platte's
mouth and caught, now, at midstream

on a rusted snare of dredge cable
with the slow brown water curling
dark foam against barrel heads,

my fingers track the grain of dry plank,
measuring the dull cadence of bare
feet over a worn poler's tread.

II

The river's wavelets,
thick with sewage, move,
it seems, upstream against

final deposit in some
widening delta. Illusive.
It is the rush beneath

speeding as the deep
channel bends; the surface
moving more slowly, inertial,

is curled back and downward.
So, when catfish feed
in quick channel waters,

they move upstream, angling
into the surface just as
the curling wave is pulled

back. Rivermen call this
the catfish dance because
from the banks they seem

stationary, bobbing up
and down in the dark foam.
Marquette feared the thud

of their bodies against
his canoe; treacherous,
the roiling brown waters,

Pekitanoui, route to
the vermillion sea, with
large branches, whole trees

adrift, floating islands,
the channel blue, called
ponderosa. Goodrich's white?

a common channel cat, up to
four feet, *punctatus.* I wait.
White Catfish Camp—that stretch

of silt, as good as any, any
song, river, now, like furrowed
loam, dendrite bluffs. They leap.

III

(''the always restless, always moving on'')

Some years before set
forth by raft across
the oil-slick sludge
of Angel Lake, SE

off Locust Street
toward Paxton-Vierling
and the U.P. Shops.

He called himself The Kid,
said: Like The Kid don't
take no shit from nobody.
Said: Like don't nobody
fuck with The Kid.

The print of black water
along his arm, each pore
webbed with it, and washed
up over the packing-crate lid,
coming closer each time
he moved—THIS SIDE UP.
Locust Street viaduct behind
him, the freightyard, rail-
head pennies spread like leaves;
to the left, the drive-in movie
angling east; beam crane dead
ahead; windward, the city,
odors of cattle across steel.

The cool he put on
each morning, uneasy,
adjusted all day,
his arduous slouch,
flared cuffs, hair
oiled and arched back.

Somewhat confused, the surface
so much like creosote on wood,
and the evening closing down.
It was not what he had imagined,
night along the cinder shore,
hardly angelic, not a lake at all,
and the movie slivering its wedge
of light against tarnished silver,
his line of sight down the edge
of it—indistinguishable bright
objects, Monument Valley, perhaps,
thin strands of horses spilling
toward him like kelp in the crests

of long, persistent waves—the West,
Terminus, repeated everywhere, light
of the Rockies jostled with these
shadows, "never to be thrown down."

It was in Lincoln County,
the Lincoln County Wars, he
carved his name; in Texas
against carpetbaggers, home-
stead plundered, fiancé
promised to a storekeeper;
in Abilene against Hickok;
greased lightning; Vera Cruz,
that sunny afternoon, a smile;
"two sixes to beat," aces and eights
with his back to the door.

The sun hovers, cloudless sky,
town caught in its shadows,
a mother sweeps her child
away, curtains twitch, unseen
eyes, horseflesh ripples;
thin fingers that dealt smart
faro, cigar cupped in his hand;
it went to his lips, a shade slow,
the other, and fell for a border roll.

"I got no quarrel with you, Kid,"

so pulled her up into the saddle
behind him and rode away. How
sudden that sunset, saguaros.

Nowhere to go, riversump among refuse,
and under a ridge of pebbled glass—
skylights sooted dark as shale—
the Shops' nightsong, Union Pacific
hammered out "its dead indifference."

Dumbass, he said, skidding home,
loose heel-cleat scything his ankle.

IV

Dark-skinned with black hair
drawn tightly back, looking
northward through day-ribbed
bluffs, she stood, I think,
ahead of the polers
in the keelboat's blunt
wet prow with a Yankee
helmsman facing her back,

and the wind, westerly—
out of my own childhood
and that unbroken prairie
where the Pawnee moved
like dust—shook the chewed
fringes of her buckskin dress.

". . . these barbary coasts . . ."

Stiff chokecherry thickets,
quick with sparrows, high
grasses where gray slag cuts
back to rain slides of yellow clay.
The same shores—or not? In time
the river sidewinds its banks.
Never the same soil; here, marks
of the land's uneven flow.

All fancy. She did not pass here,
met them half-a-year north,
already with child—Baptiste,
called Pomp, for Pompey—
with Lewis attending his birth,

". . . having the rattle of a snake by me
I gave it to him and he administered two
rings of it to the woman broken in small
pieces with the fingers and added to a
small quantity of water. . . ."

yet the fringes, like pinfeathers,
her flight, the dream of home,
brown water opening twin petals
at her feet. The movie, that orange
novel, shapes of the river—mud slake
where she stands at some distance.
The campsite ebbs, now returns
like a wave. The treeline pitches
toward me, and there, a chokecherry
springs to a river tern's reach.

Before the empty plains,
spread like flat water
shoaling toward sand hills,
the first slopes, unarable,
of the dividing mountains,
the city squats above the river,
as an Indian woman at her
day's work might squat—
oblivious to the land behind her,
her hands full of the land—
red corn, dried meats, new skins.

At Rulo, Oto, Ponca, and Pawnee
camp on flats between bluffs falls,
move west each morning in open trucks
to get a year's beet sugar in.

V

(as Meriwether Lewis)

Which river is this
the first or the last?

fog like the old South
rising off slow water,
enclosing swamps

Is that a waterthrush
or falling water muted?

without channel markers
we often ran aground,

and it was impossible to
know whether we were lost
until a stream ran out
or we found a landmark,
Great Falls

the deceptive waterthrush
imitating falling water

each night I read my Journals
like a novel, seeking some
inevitability of plot, a hint
of form pointing toward an end

Am I remembering or acting again,
rounding out my own last scene
with a playwright's feel for disorder?

the cabin is filled with smoke,
like a Mandan lodge in winter,
women in the corners working skins,
young men striking flint on flint,
a man of words muttering to children
in the shadows past the firelight,
the brotherhood of wars turning
their faces to the banked fire:
floors of plank, a single table
like a keelboat, but smelling
of tallow, spilt ale, Virginia tobacco,
white smoke lit by the hearth fire,
a roadhouse lost in a river fog

tavern odors and the far-off
drip of water, thin as birdsong;
the swampbird singing of water
as the great waters quickly fall;
fog touched with a hint of
Cyprus standing in still water
and spruce wet with mountain rain

there is a bend in thought
as treacherous as a river's bend
forked at the farthest side;
I have forgotten its meaning,

the lesson it holds for the sailor,
devout in purpose with a mind for home,
or the thinker intent on endings uncharted,
lost in a river fog on a still night

    I am unable to make a homily stick
    and fasten my thoughts, foundering, to it,
    unable to make a sighting certain enough

the river has neither course nor current;
the last point of the relative compass,
upstream/downstream, falls away; the duet
of waterfowl and waterfall, complementary
virtuosi of distances untaken or taken
and forgotten, is joined to dissonance.

Tonight, the Mare Tranquillitatis,
like a thumbprint on silver,
and oddly, like a street name
or an address, the Plain of Jars.

    "This feather stirs . . ."

wind's wing across water,
something brushed aside,
the care taken, her eyes;
what we had imagined in
the trees, as though witnessed
at it and afterwards feared
so many things otherwise
common, the quickness
of small animals, birds,
dragonfly and cicada.

Quiet takes back her
folded fields. Elmshoot,
chokecherry and willow
clamor above shadowed
watermillions, the Leek-
green grass, buffaloberry,
"which strikes & profumes
the sensation," those busy
tides, treacherous sand—
how it swirls and gathers

where rivers join—
the Platte's due payment,
distant soil ''with great
velocity roleing,'' as though
the high plains in visitation . . .
the bitter places, destinations
we already have names for,
all that is said of what
most surely awaits us,
wind and water, this green
tumult, its weathers.

Think of the clouds
as surfaces in time,
the river bank as
a banking of clouds,
that what is seen here
folding over itself
is a gathering of those
pasts we voyage into
and so watch it all
with practiced apprehension.
This peculiar edge of things
wears toward us at its
own pace, the scree
of distant mountains
configured now as leaves.

Marsh of Sleep, Sea of Crises,
Sea of Serenity, Lake of Dreams,

Among the provisions they carried
across tidal drifts of sand
and wind drifts snared with weeds—

hemp-bound faggots dipped in pitch
and flax-bound sheaves of grain;
so the land was parceled first

in cross-stands raised on a salt
beach, each household counting its
remaining necessities, thus counting

the lands they were wedged into—
sweet soils beyond salt bogs
and stiff grasses. Rivers, trails

where Spanish armor rusted into
dark mud. What they had expected
was a magic, wholly accessible, devout

as daylight, gold the western sun
displayed, cities of gold, resplendent
in that holy fire. In a tangle of

purpose—dream and vision—there
were many caught in this soil, clutched
down among their metals, decaying.

VIII

("signs is *signs,* mine I tell you")

Time and time again, snake's
head rising to the doe's
udder, and her, fresh-killed,

hanging over the water
and no great distance from it.
I threw chunks and drove

this snake off Several times;
was so determined, I was
compelld to kill him. Peeled

Some bark to lay down on,
gathered wood to make fires,
Heard the party on shore.

So much always moving away
Be quick about it! Fond
farewell, watery grasp. You

rest your head one evening
against the powdering sand,
say a few words, murmur

to the gathering dark—
umbruliata, the enshadowment,
trees' long slant, hillside

and what lies beyond, that
brightness faltering, as well.
Broad expanse of the river

turned to blood, red hue
drifting into gold or boiled
with rings, many-tinted as

an opal. Graceful, smooth
circles uncoil each syllable;
what was said to her, embossed

in gold, crept by me upon
the waters: colors of departure—
sunset, the stars' terrible retreat.

Centered, now, by all that leaves
us behind, its red calibrations,
our lines of sight played like

taut strings, the present moment
trembles within other durations—
that clay, as though precisely

cut, its remnants swirling fire
at my feet, the galled leaf
flared from a bare stem,

snake's head or flame dancing.
Light-play and murmur acquiesce
to image and parable, that tongue

flicking, our own incessant song,
how carefully the ship's pilot
steers past its raptures, dangers

the beauty shimmers here—
bluff reef, break, changing
channel and dissolving bar—

all that the castaway holds
dear, drifted . . . drifted
precipitate of his bewilderment.

IX

The sunlight on the water,
landfall shadows, treeline
edging down the slow current.

This is the land I made for you
by hand, what was touched once
then misremembered into words,

place where the soil slips out
from under its trees, where
stiff weeds fall like rapids.

It is the made emblem of time,
that only, nothing we have,
nothing we have ever held,

and it is only my arrogance
that calls it mine, this press
of clay on clay, this sluice

for cattlepens and sewers.
So, sunlight yellows on water;
treeforms blacken at dusk.

"Meanwhile the voice continues,"
or several voices, mine, yours,
those others that slide beneath us

among catfish and bullheads
angling in the slime, water voices
that suck the current in and pump it out,

gills that speak back waters the river's
long swirl threads to oblivion,
and her voice somewhere in the rocky

watershed, as yet unformed, thrilling,
who speaks in tongues so quickly, child
at the sunny edge of constant snow.

X

(In and Out)

In came the doctor,
in came the nurse,
in came The Lady
with the alligator purse.

That moving window of rope,
the hazed shape that swings
boundaries or hazards.
Once
he lived here, often taking
a morning walk or afternoon
stroll along this street.

Did you know her once,
forgotten, The Lady?

Surgical implements and appliances
still-lived on the porcelain table,
the delicate tubes that feed and drain,
hang translucent curves, coaxial;
a flexible bedside straw angles from
a smudged waterglass like a cut stem.

She held her gloves in one hand,
the limp fingers spread like petals,
dark and wilted, above her fist;
beneath her dress, where her crossed
legs pressed tightest, she ground
nylon on nylon into another breath.

They count in song
or sing the alphabet,
adding syllables to match
the jostle of their step.
In verses some words
are merely breath;
silences
are sometimes spoken.

Go in and out the window.

The rope's click on the pavement
springs the half-circle out of shape;
the projector loop stutters and
Pasolini dances:
Il mondo salvato dai ragazzini,
toe caught and falling through
the flickering hemp casement.

"the descent beckons . . ."

She cranks the head up
and turns his face to the window—
late light sluiced past
chokecherry across occluded eyes;

the brown water threads its sludge;
the sprung branches of a fallen elm
trail curls of yellow scum, turning
as the catheter bends southward.

"there warn't no home
like a raft, after all"

Each spring the land spills back
with the receding floods, the slag
of the gray flats hooked with rubble,
still weeds strung with drying mud;
the river's harvest bobs in the dark current.

Her hair swings and jostles
the dance the mud encloses—
coagulated drops slowing the turns,
thick chokecherries bead the light.

"At Malvern, the trees . . ."
Thwaites, Jim, Buckeridge,
Gutheridge, the fisherman,
Lewis, the birdman;

the woman, expecting flight,
as she calls the river's slow turns;
the Lady, shifting in her chair,
pulling the strings of her beaded sack,
snapping the florentined, flowered clasp,

click, the recessional: song and dance.

Out went the doctor,
out went the nurse,
out went The Lady
with the alligator purse.

—*Michael Anania*

Michael Anania's Notes to "The Riversongs of Arion"

The Arion of this sequence is a contemporary who sets off on a trip down the Missouri River from Omaha and gets stuck just south of the city. On July 22, 1804, Lewis and Clark proceeded north from the mouth of the Platte River about ten miles and pitched a five-day camp, named, for Silas Goodrich's catch of July 24, White Catfish Camp. This Arion's diversions, complaints, and plaintiff anthems while stranded opposite what he supposes is that campsite comprise the sequence.

I have relied heavily on Reuben Thwaites's *Original Journals of the Lewis and Clark Expedition* and on portions of his *Jesuit Relations* and *Early Western Travels.* The sequence also owes a debt to Paul Russell Cutright's *Lewis and Clark: Pioneering Naturalists* (University of Illinois Press). My personal debt to Henry Nash Smith is deepened here, as well.

Captain Clark was the most prolific diarist in the early stages of the journey, and I have often retained his peculiar spelling as a key-signature of his idiom. The notes that follow deal primarily with matters that grew familiar in the course of this sequence's journey but which are not commonly available.

I. "silver tankers": Offut Air Force Base is situated on the hills over the river near the site of the Lewis and Clark camp.

III. "the always restless . . .": from Conrad Aiken's poem "The Kid."

"Terminus": Both Thomas Hart Benton and Melville (*Clarel*) invoke the Roman god when discussing the end of American expansion at the Rockies.

"Lincoln County . . .": Billy the Kid distinguished himself in the Lincoln County Wars, though the gunslinger here is an amalgam which includes Billy, John Wesley Hardin, Wild Bill Hickok, and a smattering of movie cowboys.

"two sixes to beat": the last words of John Wesley Hardin.

"a border roll": Hardin's favorite trick, in which sixguns extended in surrender were instantly flipped back into firing position.

IV. The conclusion over Sacajawea's first association with the Lewis and Clark expedition has its source in movies and popular novels, which have often presented her as an Indian "maid" who joined the explorers near St. Louis.

V. Whether Lewis was murdered or committed suicide at Grinder's Stand, Tennessee, in October, 1809, is still a matter of speculation. At his death Lewis was governor of Louisiana Territory, enroute to Washington and then Philadelphia, where he was to have edited the *Journals.*

VIII. "*signs is . . .*": Jim to Huck, *Huckleberry Finn* (Chapter "The Last").

The story of the snake and the doe is Captain Clark's (June 23 & 24, 1804).

umbruliata: Calabrian Italian for dusk, enshadowment.

"Broad expanse . . .": cf. Twain, *Life on the Mississippi* (Chapter 9).

X. *Il mondo salvato dai ragazzini* ("The world saved by the children"): Pier Paolo Pasolini.

Much of the identification between the river, death, and the past comes from Confucius. An example is quoted by Mao Tse-tung in his poem "Swimming":

> Here on the river the Master said:
> Dying—going into the past—is like a river flowing.
>
> (Willis Barnstone, tr.)

Ode: Intimations of Immortality from *Recollections of Early Childhood*

> *The Child is father of the Man;*
> *And I could wish my days to be*
> *Bound each to each by natural piety.*

I

There was a time when meadow, grove, and stream,
The earth, and every common sight,
To me did seem
Appareled in celestial light,

The glory and the freshness of a dream.
It is not now as it hath been of yore—
Turn whereso'er I may,
By night or day,
The things which I have seen I now can see no more.

II

The Rainbow comes and goes,
And lovely is the Rose,
The Moon doth with delight
Look round her when the heavens are bare,
Waters on a starry night
Are beautiful and fair;
The sunshine is a glorious birth;
But yet I know, where'er I go,
That there hath past away a glory from the earth.

III

Now, while the birds thus sing a joyous song,
And while the young lambs bound
As to the tabor's sound,
To me alone there came a thought of grief:
A timely utterance gave that thought relief,
And I again am strong:
The cataracts blow their trumpets from the steep;
No more shall grief of mine the season wrong;
I hear the Echoes through the mountains throng,
The Winds come to me from the fields of sleep,
And all the earth is gay;
Land and sea
Give themselves up to jollity,
And with the heart of May
Doth every Beast keep holiday;—
Thou Child of Joy,
Shout round me, let me hear thy shouts, thou happy Shepherd-boy!

IV

Ye blessèd Creatures, I have heard the call
Ye to each other make; I see
The heavens laugh with you in your jubilee;
My heart is at your festival,
My head hath its coronal,

The fulness of your bliss, I feel—I feel it all.
Oh evil day! if I were sullen
While Earth herself is adorning,
This sweet May-morning,
And the Children are culling
On every side,
In a thousand valleys far and wide,
Fresh flowers; while the sun shines warm,
And the Babe leaps up on his Mother's arm:—
I hear, I hear, with joy I hear!
—But there's a Tree, of many, one,
A single Field which I have looked upon,
Both of them speak of something that is gone:
The Pansy at my feet
Doth the same tale repeat:
Whither is fled the visionary gleam?
Where is it now, the glory and the dream?

V

Our birth is but a sleep and a forgetting;
The Soul that rises with us, our life's Star,
Hath had elsewhere its setting,
And cometh from afar:
Not in entire forgetfulness,
And not in utter nakedness,
But trailing clouds of glory do we come
From God, who is our home:
Heaven lies about us in our infancy!
Shades of the prison-house begin to close
Upon the growing Boy,
But He beholds the light, and whence it flows,
He sees it in his joy;
The Youth, who daily farther from the east
Must travel, still is Nature's Priest,
And by the vision splendid
Is on his way attended;
At length the Man perceives it die away,
And fade into the light of common day.

VI

Earth fills her lap with pleasures of her own;
Yearnings she hath in her own natural kind,
And, even with something of a Mother's mind,

And no unworthy aim,
The homely Nurse doth all she can
To make her Foster-child, her Inmate Man,
Forget the glories he hath known,
And that imperial palace whence he came.

VII

Behold the Child among his new-born blisses,
A six years' Darling of a pigmy size!
See, where 'mid work of his own hand he lies,
Fretted by sallies of his mother's kisses,
With light upon him from his father's eyes!
See, at his feet, some little plan or chart,
Some fragment from his dream of human life,
Shaped by himself with newly-learned art;
A wedding or a festival,
A mourning or a funeral;
And this hath now his heart,
And unto this he frames his song:
Then will he fit his tongue
To dialogues of business, love, or strife;
But it will not be long
Ere this be thrown aside,
And with new joy and pride
The little Actor cons another part;
Filling from time to time his "humorous stage"
With all the Persons, down to palsied Age,
That Life brings with her in her equipage;
As if his whole vocation
Were endless imitation.

VIII

Thou, whose exterior semblance doth belie
Thy Soul's immensity;
Thou best Philosopher, who yet dost keep
Thy heritage, thou Eye among the blind,
That, deaf and silent, read'st the eternal deep,
Haunted for ever by the eternal mind,—
Mighty Prophet! Seer Blest!
On whom those truths do rest,
Which we are toiling all our lives to find,
In darkness lost, the darkness of the grave;
Thou, over whom thy Immortality

Broods like the Day, a Master o'er a Slave,
A Presence which is not to be put by;
Thou little Child, yet glorious in the might
Of heaven-born freedom on thy being's height,
Why with such earnest pains dost thou provoke
The years to bring the inevitable yoke,
Thus blindly with thy blessedness at strife?
Full soon thy Soul shall have her earthly freight,
And custom lie upon thee with a weight,
Heavy as frost, and deep almost as life!

IX

O joy! that in our embers
Is something that doth live,
That nature yet remembers
What was so fugitive!
The thought of our past years in me doth breed
Perpetual benediction: not indeed
For that which is most worthy to be blest—
Delight and liberty, the simple creed
Of Childhood, whether busy or at rest,
With new-fledged hope still fluttering in his breast:—
Not for these I raise
The song of thanks and praise;
But for those obstinate questionings
Of sense and outward things,
Fallings from us, vanishings;
Blank misgivings of a Creature
Moving about in worlds not realised,
High instincts before which our mortal Nature
Did tremble like a guilty Thing surprised:
But for those first affections,
Those shadowy recollections,
Which, be they what they may,
Are yet the fountain light of all our day,
Are yet a master light of all our seeing;
Uphold us, cherish, and have power to make
Our noisy years seem moments in the being
Of the eternal Silence: truths that wake,
To perish never;
Which neither listlessness, nor mad endeavour,
Nor Man nor Boy,
Nor all that is at enmity with joy,
Can utterly abolish or destroy!

Hence in a season of calm weather
Though inland far we be,
Our Souls have sight of that immortal sea
Which brought us hither,
Can in a moment travel thither,
And see the Children sport upon the shore,
And hear the mighty waters rolling evermore.

X

Then sing, ye Birds, sing, sing a joyous song!
And let the young Lambs bound
As to the tabor's sound!
We in thought will join your throng,
Ye that pipe and ye that play,
Ye that through your hearts to-day
Feel the gladness of the May!
What though the radiance which was once so bright
Be now for ever taken from my sight,
Though nothing can bring back the hour
Of splendour in the grass, of glory in the flower;
We will grieve not, rather find
Strength in what remains behind;
In the primal sympathy
Which having been must ever be;
In the soothing thoughts that spring
Out of human suffering;
In the faith that looks through death,
In years that bring the philosophic mind.

XI

And O, ye Fountains, Meadows, Hills, and Groves,
Forebode not any severing of our loves!
Yet in my heart of hearts I feel your might;
I only have relinquished one delight
To live beneath your more habitual sway.
I love the Brooks which down their channels fret,
Even more than when I tripped lightly as they;
The innocent brightness of a new-born Day
Is lovely yet;
The Clouds that gather round the setting sun
Do take a sober colouring from an eye
That hath kept watch o'er man's mortality;
Another race hath been, and other palms are won.

Thanks to the human heart by which we live,
Thanks to its tenderness, its joys, and fears,
To me the meanest flower that blows can give
Thoughts that do often lie too deep for tears.

—*William Wordsworth*

Epigraph: the final lines of Wordsworth's "My Heart Leaps Up." 21. *tabor:* a small drum. 40. *coronal:* a garland worn on festive occasions.

A Select Bibliography of Rock Criticism

Items listed below should prove useful in treating song lyrics or, occasionally, poems contained in this anthology. Some give general background of popular music; others contain very specific analyses of individual lyrics or poems. A couple discuss the nature of oral poetry (spoken poetry, as distinct from printed poetry) as it developed during the fifties, sixties, and seventies.

Aldridge, Allen, ed. *Beatles Illustrated Lyrics.* 2 vols. New York: Delacorte Press, 1969, 1971.

Belz, Carl. *The Story of Rock.* New York: Harper and Row, 1973.

Boundary 3 (1976): an entire issue given over to oral poetry.

Bruchac, Joseph. *The Poetry of Pop.* Paradise, California: Dustbooks, 1974.

Campbell, G. M. "Bob Dylan and the Pastoral Apocalypse." *Journal of Popular Culture,* 8 (spring 1975), 696–707.

Christgau, Robert. *Any Old Way You Choose It.* New York: Penguin, 1973.

———. "Rock Lyrics Are Poetry (Maybe)." *Cheetah* (December 1967).

———. "Secular Music." *Esquire,* 71 (April 1969): 62ff.

Dalton, David, ed. *The Rolling Stones.* New York: Music Sales, 1972.

Davies, Hunter. *The Beatles.* New York: McGraw Hill, 1978.

DeMorse, D. E. "Avant-Rock in the Classroom." *English Journal,* 58 (February 1969), 196–200.

DeMott, Ben. "Rock as Salvation." *New York Times Magazine* (August 25, 1969): 49ff.

Dylan, Bob. *The Songs of Bob Dylan.* New York: Knopf, 1978.

———. *Writings and Drawings.* New York: Knopf, 1975.

Economu, George. "Some Notes Towards Finding a View of the New Oral Poetry." *Boundary 2* (1975), 653–63.

Eisen, Jonathan. *Altamount: Death of Innocence in the Woodstock Nation.* New York: Avon, 1970.

——, ed. *The Age of Rock.* 2 vols. New York: Random House, 1969, 1970.

English, Helen. "Rock Poetry, Relevance, and Revelation." *English Journal,* 54 (November 1970), 1122–7.

Ferri, Mary. "Modern Songs as Lyric Poetry: Euphony, Rhythm, Meter and Rhyme." *Style,* 4, 245–51.

Fong-Torres, Ben, ed. *What's That Sound: the Contemporary Music Scene from the Pages of Rolling Stone.* New York: Doubleday (Anchor), 1976.

Gambaccini, Paul. *Paul McCartney: In His Own Words.* New York: Music Sales, 1976.

Gillett, Charlie. *The Sound of the City.* New York: E. P. Dutton, 1970.

Goldberg, Steven. "Bob Dylan and the Poetry of Salvation." *Saturday Review,* 53 (May 30, 1970), 43–6.

Goldman, Albert. *Freakshow.* New York: Atheneum, 1971.

Goldstein, Richard. *The Poetry of Rock.* New York: Bantam Books, 1969.

Gray, Michael. *Song and Dance Man: The Art of Bob Dylan.* New York: Dutton, 1973.

Greenfield, Robert. *A Journey Through America with the Rolling Stones.* London: Granada, 1975.

Gross, Michael. *Bob Dylan: An Illustrated History.* New York: Today Press, 1978.

Herman, Gary. *The Who.* New York: Macmillan, 1972.

Jahn, Mike. *Rock: From Elvis Presley to the Rolling Stones.* New York: Time Books, 1973.

Johnson, Thomas S. "Desolation Row Revisited: Bob Dylan's Rock Poetry." *Southwest Review,* 62 (1977), 135–47.

Kermode, Frank, and Stephen Spender and Art Kane. "Bob Dylan: The Metaphor at the End of the Funnel." *Esquire,* 77 (May 1972), 109–18ff.

Kofsky, Frank. *Black Nationalism and the Revolution in Music.* New York: Path Press, 1970.

Korrall, Burt. "Music of Protest." *Saturday Review,* 51 (November 16, 1968), 26ff.

Landau, Jon. *It's Too Late to Stop Now: A Rock and Roll Journal.* New York: Simon & Schuster, 1971.

Lindstrom, N. "Dylan: Song Returns to Poetry." *Texas Quarterly,* 19 (winter 1976), 131–6.

Lyden, Michael. *Rock Folk.* New York: Dial, 1971.

MacGregor, Craig, ed. *Bob Dylan: A Retrospective.* New York: Morrow, 1972.

Marcus, Griel. *Mystery Train: Images of America in Rock 'n' Roll Music.* New York: Dutton, 1976.

Martin, D. L. "Langston Hughes's Use of the Blues." *CLA Journal,* 22 (December 1978), 151–9.

McConnell, Frank D. "Rock and the Politics of Frivolity." *Massachusetts Review,* 12 (1971), 119–34.

Mellers, Wilfred. *Twilight of the Gods: the Beatles in Retrospect.* New York: Viking, 1974.

Melly, George. *Revolt Into Style.* New York: Garden City (Anchor), 1970.

Meltzer, Richard. *The Aesthetics of Rock.* New York: Something Else Press, 1971.

Monteiro, G. "Dylan in the Sixties." *South Atlantic Quarterly,* 73 (spring 1974), 160–72.

Mosher, Harold F. "The Lyrics of American Pop Music: A New Poetry." *Popular Music and Society,* 1 (1972), 167–76.

Naha, Ed, compiled by. *Lillian Roxon's Rock Encyclopedia,* rev. ed. New York: Grosset and Dunlap, 1978.

Nicholas, A. X. *The Poetry of Soul.* New York: Bantam Books, 1971.

Palmer, Tony. *All You Need Is Love: the Story of Popular Music.* New York: Penguin, 1977.

Peyser, Joan. "The Music of Sound." *Columbia University Forum,* 10 (fall 1967).

Pichaske, David. *A Generation in Motion: Popular Music and Culture in the Sixties.* New York: Schirmer Books, 1979.

———. *The Poetry of Rock: The Golden Years.* Peoria, Illinois: The Ellis Press, 1981.

Poague, L. A. "Dylan as Auteur: Theoretical Notes, and an Analysis of 'Love Minus Zero/No Limit.'" *Journal of Popular Culture,* 8 (summer 1974), 53–8.

Poirier, Richard. "Learning from the Beatles." *Partisan Review,* fall 1967, 526–46.

Rinzler, Alan. *Bob Dylan: an Illustrated Record.* New York: Harmony, 1978.

Rolling Stone Magazine (the single most valuable source of intelligent criticism of rock music and the counterculture in general, especially between 1970 and 1975).

Rolling Stone Magazine. *Knocking on Dylan's Door.* San Francisco: Straight Arrow Books, 1974.

———. *The Rolling Stone Illustrated History of Rock & Roll.* New York: Random House, 1976.

———. *The Rolling Stone Interviews.* New York: Simon and Schuster, 1971.

———. *The Rolling Stone Record Reviews.* New York: Simon and Schuster, 1971.

———. *The Rolling Stone Record Reviews, Number 2.* New York: Pocket Books, 1974.

———. *The Rolling Stone Rock-n-roll Reader.* New York: Bantam, 1974.

Rosenstone, R. A. "Times They Are A-Changin': the Music of Protest," *Annals of the American Academy of Political and Social Sciences,* 382 (March 1969), 131–44.

Sadek, E. "Simon and Garfunkel: The Singers and the Songs." *Saturday Review,* 53 (February 28, 1970), 91ff.

Sarlin, Bob. *Turn It Up (I Can't Hear the Words).* New York: Simon and Schuster, 1973.

Scaduto, Anthony. *Bob Dylan.* New York: New American Library, 1973.

———. *Mick Jagger.* London: Granada, 1975.

Scharf, W. J. "Randy Newman and the Obscure Politics of God." *Theology Today,* 30 (January 1974), 409–13.

Smith, Jack E. "Turning On: the Selling of the Present, 1970." *College English,* 60 (March 1971), 333–8.

Spinner, Stephanie. *Rock Is Beautiful: An Anthology of American Lyrics.* New York: Dell, 1970.

VanWert, William F. "Dylan: A Documentary." *Antioch Review,* 35, 274–82.

Wenner, Jan, ed. *Lennon Remembers.* San Francisco: Straight Arrow Books, 1971.

Williams, Paul. *Outlaw Blues.* New York: Pocket Books, 1969.

Willis, Ellen. "The Sound of Dylan." *Commentary,* 44 (November 1968), 71–8.

Oral Poetry: A List of Recorded Poems and Songs

This book treats poetry as an oral as well as a printed form. As an oral form, poetry must be heard—not only in the reader's inner ear, but aloud, as read by a teacher or a professional reader or the poet himself. Sometimes—quite often, in fact—what seems obscure on the page becomes lucidly simple upon hearing.

In the list below I have given preference to poems read by the poets who wrote them and songs performed by their own composers. For this reason the list is far from complete—poetry on record and tape still has a very limited circulation. Even a few of the items listed here may prove difficult to find in some college libraries. The rewards, however, are worth the effort, for a tape or record will take the reader not only further into the poem or song to be studied, but into a whole new world of poem-as-sound.

Finally, nothing makes poetry come alive like an actual reading by a poet one has already met in a book. Many of these poets are still giving readings all over the country. Attend one. Attend a reading by poets who are not in this book. Bring a poet to your campus. Support your local poet.

Anonymous. "Barbara Allen." *Folksongs of Britain: The Child Ballads, vol. 1.* Caedmon, CT 1145; cass. CDL 51145.

———. "Come All Ye Fair and Tender Ladies." Ian and Sylvia, *So Much for Dreaming.* Vanguard, VRS 79241.

———. "The House of the Rising Sun." Animals, *Best of the Animals.* MGM 4324; Bob Dylan, *Bob Dylan.* Columbia CS–8579.

———. "Lord Randall." *Folksongs of Britain: The Child Ballads,* vol. 1. Caedmon, CT 1145; cass. CDL 51145.

———. "Sir Patrick Spens." *The Poetry of Robert Burns and Border Ballads.* Caedmon TC 1103; cass. CDL 51103.

Arnold, Matthew. "Dover Beach." *Palgrave's Golden Treasury of English Verse.* Caedmon TC 2011; cass. CDL 52011.

Auden, W. H . "As I Walked Out One Morning" and "In Memory of W. B. Yeats." *W. H. Auden Reading.* Caedmon, TC 1019; cass. CDL 51019.

Baez, Joan. "Diamonds and Rust." *Diamonds and Rust.* A&M SP4527.

Beatles, The. *Sgt. Pepper's Lonely Hearts Club Band.* Capital 2653.

Beowulf. *Beowulf.* Spoken Arts 918.

Blake, William. "London," "The Lamb," "Mock On, Mock On, Voltaire, Rousseau," "A Poison Tree," and "The Tyger." *The Poetry of William Blake.* Caedmon TX 1101; cass. CDL 51101.

Bly, Robert. "Where We Must Look for Help." *Robert Bly Reads His Poetry.* Cassette Curriculum 154.

Brooker, Gary & Keith Reid. "A Whiter Shade of Pale." *Procol Harum.* Deram (5) 18008.

Brooks, Gwendolyn. "Sadie and Maud." *Gwendolyn Brooks Reading Her Own Poetry.* Caedmon TC 1244; cass. CDL 51244.

———. "We Real Cool." *Tough Poems for Tough People.* Caedmon TC 1396; cass. CDL 51396.

Browne, Jackson. "The Pretender." *The Pretender.*

Browning, Robert. "The Bishop Orders His Tomb." *The Poetry of Browning.* Caedmon TC 1048; cass. CDL 51048.

———. "My Last Duchess." *My Last Duchess and Other Poems.* Caedmon TC1201; cass. CDL 51201.

Cohen, Leonard. "Suzanne." *Leonard Cohen.* Columbia CS–9533.

Coleridge, Samuel Taylor. "Kubla Khan." *The Poetry of Coleridge.* Caedmon TC 1092; cass. CDL 51092.

———. "Rime of the Ancient Mariner." *English Romantic Poetry.* Caedmon TC 3005; cass. CDL 53005.

Croce, Jim. "Time in a Bottle" and "You Don't Mess Around with Jim." *Jim Croce's Greatest Character Songs.* Lifesong 35571.

cummings, e. e. "anyone lived in a pretty how town," "Buffalo Bill's defunct," "next to God," and "She being Brand." *E. E. Cummings Reads His Collected Poetry.* Caedmon TC 2080; cass. CDL 52080.

Davies, Idris. "The Bells of Rhymney." *Peter Seeger's Greatest Hits.* Columbia CS 9416.

DelaMare, Walter. "Silver." *Anthology of Twentieth Century English Poetry.* Folkways FL 9886.

Dickinson, Emily. "Because I Could Not Stop for Death" and "I Like to See It Lap the Miles." *Poems and Letters of Emily Dickinson.* Caedmon TC 1119; cass. CDL 51119.

———. "Hope Is the Thing with Feathers." *Great American Poetry.* Caedmon TC 2009; cass. CDL 52009.

Donne, John. "Go and Catch a Falling Star." *Palgrave's Golden Treasury of English Poetry.* Caedmon TC 2011; cass. CDL 52011.

———. "Death, Be Not Proud." *Hearing Poetry, vol. 1.* Argo 404.

———. "A Valediction." *The Love Poems of John Donne,* Caedmon TC 1141; cass. CDL 51141.

Dylan, Bob. "All Along the Watchtower," "I Pity the Poor Immigrant," "John Wesley Harding." *John Wesley Harding.* Columbia CS9604.

———. "Desolation Row." *Highway 61 Revisited.* Columbia CL 2389.

———. "The Lonesome Death of Hattie Carroll" and "A Restless Farewell." *The Times They Are A-Changin'.* Columbia KCS 8905.

———. "Sad-Eyed Lady of the Lowlands." *Blonde on Blonde.* Columbia C2S 2841.

———. "Subterranean Homesick Blues" and "Mr. Tambourine Man." *Bringing It All Back Home.* Columbia CS–9128.

Eagles. "Hotel California." *Hotel California.* Asylum 6E103A.

Eberhart, Richard. "The Groundhog." *Caedmon Treasury of Modern Poets Reading Their Own Poetry.* TC 2006; cass. CDL 52006.

Eliot, T. S. "Macavity: the Mystery Cat." *T. S. Eliot Reading the Wasteland and Other Poems.* Caedmon TC 1326; cass. CDL 51326.

Emerson, Ralph Waldo. "The Concord Hymn." *American Patriotism in Poems and Prose.* Caedmon TC 1204; cass CDL 51204; *The Poetry of Ralph Waldo Emerson.* Caedmon TC 1359; cass. CDL 51359; *Prose and Poetry of America.* Enrichment Materials, Inc. (Random House).

Farina, Mimi. "In the Quiet Morning." Joan Baez, *Come from the Shadows.* A&M SP4339.

Frost, Robert. "After Apple Picking," "The Death of the Hired Man," "Mending Wall," and "Provide, Provide." *Robert Frost Reads "The Road Not Taken" and Other Poems.* Caedmon TC 1060; cass. CDL 51060.

Ginsberg, Allen. "Going to Chicago." This poem was read by Ginsberg at the Phil Ochs Memorial Celebration at Madison Garden. Some copies of this tape circulate underground.

———. "Howl." *Allen Ginsberg and Anne Waldman Reading at the Narope Institute, 1975.* Tape available from Poet's Audio Center, P.O. Box 50145, Washington D.C. 20024.

Goodman, Steve. "The City of New Orleans." Arlo Guthrie, *Best of Arlo Guthrie.* Warner BSK 3117.

Guthrie, Woody. "Pretty Boy Floyd." Joan Baez, *The Greatest Songs of Woody Guthrie.* Vanguard VSD 35/36; Woody Guthrie, *Original Recordings Made by Woody Guthrie.* Warner BS 2999.

———. "Tom Joad." Country Joe McDonald, *The Greatest Songs of Woody Guthrie.* Vanguard VSD 35/36.

Hardy, Thomas. "Channel Firing." *Poetry of Thomas Hardy.* Caedmon TX 1140; cass. CDL 51140.

Herreck, Robert. "To the Virgins to Make Much of Time." *Palgrave's Golden Treasury of English Poetry.* Caedmon TC 2011; cass. CDL 52011.

Holmes, Oliver Wendell. "The Chambered Nautilus." *Old Ironsides and Other Poems.* Caedmon TC 1302; cass. CDL 51302.

Hopkins, Gerard Manley. "Carrion Comfort," "Pied Beauty," "Spring and Fall," and "The Windhover." *The Poetry of Gerard Manley Hopkins.* Caedmon TC1111; cass. CDL 51111.

Housman, A. E. "Eight O'Clock," "Loveliest of Trees," and "To an Athlete Dying Young." *A Shropshire Lad and Other Poetry.* Caedmon TC 1203; cass. CDL 51203.

Ian, Janis. "This Must Be Wrong." *Aftertones.* Columbia PC33919.

Jagger-Richards. "Honkey Tonk Women." *Get Yer YaYa's Out!* London NPS5.

———. "No Expectations." *Beggar's Banquet.* London PS539.

Jeffers, Robinson. "Shine, Perishing Republic," and "To the Stone-Cutters." *The Poetry of Robinson Jeffers.* Caedmon, cassette only CDL 51297.

Joel, Billy. "Honesty" and "My Life." *52nd Street.* Columbia 35609.

———. "Only the Good Die Young" and "She's Always a Woman to Me." *The Stranger.* Columbia 34987.

Judson, John. "The Lineage of Indian Ponies." A tape of this poem is available from The Plains Distribution Service, P.O. Box 3112 Fargo, North Dakota 58102 under the title *John Judson Reading at Vitero College.*

Keats, John. "La Belle Dame Sans Merci" and "Ode to a Grecian Urn." *English Romantic Poetry.* Caedmon TC 3005; cass. CDL 53005.

Kinnell, Galway. "The Bear." *Spoken Arts Treasury of 100 Modern American Poets Reading Their Poems,* vol. 16. Spoken Arts SA 1055.

Kristofferson, Kris. "Me and Bobby McGee." Kristofferson, *Songs of Kris Kristofferson.* Columbia 34687; Janis Joplin, *Full Tilt Boogie.* Columbia KC30322.

Lee, Don L. "But He Was Cool." *Don't Cry, Scream.* Tape available from Broadside Press, 12651 Old Mill Place, Detroit Michigan, 48238.

Lennon, John. "Mind Games." *Mind Games.* Apple SW3414.

——. "Working Class Hero." *John Lennon/Plastic Ono Band.* Apple SW 3372.

—— and Paul McCartney. "Eleanor Rigby." *Revolver.* Capitol ST 2576.

—— and ——. "I Am the Walrus." *Magical Mystery Tour.* Capital 5SMAL 2835.

—— and ——. "Let It Be." *Let It Be.* Apple AR 34001.

—— and ——. "Norwegian Wood." *Rubber Soul.* Capitol ST 2442.

—— and ——. "Oh! Darling" *Abbey Road.* Apple SO 383.

—— and ——. "Penny Lane" and "Strawberry Fields Forever." *Magical Mystery Tour.* Capitol 5SMAL 2835.

Lightfoot, Gordon. "Wreck of the Edmund Fitzgerald." *Summertime Dream.* Warner MS2246.

Lindsay, Vachel. "I Have a Little Turtle." *A Gathering of Great Poetry for Children.* Caedmon TC 1235; cass. CDL 51235.

Livgreen, Kerry. "Dust in the Wind." *Two for the Show.* Kirshner (CBS Records) 35660.

Longfellow, Henry Wadsworth. "A Psalm of Life." *The Best Loved Poems of Henry Wadsworth Longfellow.* Caedmon TC 1107; cass. CDL 51107.

Lowell, Robert. "Robert Frost." *Robert Lowell: A Reading.* Caedmon TC 1569; cass. CDL 51569.

MacLeish, Archibald. "You, Andrew Marvell." *Historical Anthology of American Poetry.* Argo RG 245/46.

Marlowe, John. "The Passionate Shepherd to His Love." *Palgrave's Golden Treasury of English Poetry.* Caedmon TC 2011; cass. CDL 52011.

Marvell, Andrew. "To His Coy Mistress." *Metaphysical Poetry.* Caedmon TC 1049; cass. CDL 51049.

Mitchell, Joni. "The Blue Motel Room." *Hejira.* Asylum 7E1087.

——. "Woodstock." Mitchell, *Ladies of the Canyon.* Warner 6376; Crosby, Stills, Nash and Young, *Déjà Vu.* Atco 7200.

——. "You Turn Me On I'm a Radio." *For the Roses.* Asylum SD 5057.

Moore, Marianne. "The Fish." *Marianne Moore Reading Her Poems and Fables from La Fontaine.* Caedmon TC 1025; cass. CDL 51025.

Morrison, Jim. "Horse Latitudes" and "Twentieth Century Fox." *The Doors.* Elektra 74007.

O'Day, Alan. "Angie, Baby." *Helen Reddy's Greatest Hits.* Capitol ST 11467.

Olson, Charles. "Further Completion of Plat." *Maximus Poems IV, V, VI.* Folkways 9738.

Plath, Sylvia. "The Applicant" and "Lady Lazarus." *Spoken Arts Treasury of 100 Modern American Poets Reading Their Own Poems,* vol. 18 Spoken Arts SA 1057.

Poe, Edgar Allan. "Annabel Lee." *The Raven and Other Works.* Caedmon TC 1028; Joan Baez, *Joan.* Vanguard VRS9240.

Ransom, John Crowe. "Bells for John Whiteside's Daughter." *Prose and Poetry of America.* Enrichment Records, album 5 (Random House).

Robertson, Robbie. "Daniel and the Sacred Harp" and "The Rumor." *Stagefright.* Capitol SW 425.

——. "The Night They Drove Old Dixie Down." *Rock of Ages.* Capitol SABB 611045.

Roethke, Theodore. "Elegy for Jane." *Theodore Roethke Reads His Poetry.* Caedmon IC 1351; cass. CDL 51351.

Sandburg, Carl. "Gone." *Carl Sandburg Reading Cool Tombs and Other Poems.* Caedmon TC 1150; cass. CDL 51150.

Seals, Jim, and Dash Crofts. "Summer Breeze." *Summer Breeze.* Warner 2629.

Seeger, Pete. "Waist Deep in the Big Muddy." *Waist Deep in the Big Muddy and Other Love Songs.* Columbia CL 2705.

Shakespeare, William. "Sonnets 18, 55, and 73." *William Shakespeare's Sonnets.* Caedmon SRS 241; cass. CDL 5241.

——. "Spring" and "Winter." *Love's Labors Lost.* Caedmon SRS 207; cass. CDL 5207.

——. "Under the Greenwood Tree." *Songs from the Plays of Shakespeare.* Caedmon SRS 242; cass. CDL 5242.

Shelley, Percy Bysshe. "Ode to the West Wind." *English Romantic Poetry.* Folkways FL 9883.

Simon, Carly. "That's The Way I've Always Heard It Should Be." *Carly Simon.* Elektra EKS 74082.

——. "You're So Vain." *No Secrets.* Elektra EKS 75049.

Simon, Paul. "American Tune." *There Goes Rhymin' Simon.* Columbia KC 32280.

———. "El Condor Pasa" and "So Long, Frank Lloyd Wright." *Bridge Over Troubled Waters.* Columbia KCS 9914.

———. "Fifty Ways to Leave Your Lover." *Still Crazy After All These Years.* Columbia 33540.

Slick, Grace. "White Rabbit." *Surrealistic Pillow.* RCA LSP 3766.

Spender, Stephen. "I Think Continually of Those Who Were Truly Great." *Caedmon Treasury of Modern Poets Reading Their Own Poetry.* Caedmon TC 2006.

Stafford, William. "Now." *William Stafford Reads His Work.* Cassette Curriculum 150.

Stevens, Cat. "Into White." *Tea for the Tillerman.* A&M SP 4280.

Stevens, Wallace. "Fabliau of Florida" and "Nomad Esquisite." *Spoken Arts Treasury of 100 Modern American Poets Reading Their Own Work,* vol. 2. Spoken Arts SA 1041.

———. "The Idea of Order at Key West." *Wallace Stevens Reading His Poems.* Caedmon TC 1068; cass. CDL 51068.

Tennyson, Alfred, Lord. "The Charge of the Light Brigade." *Classics of English Poetry for the Elementary Curriculum.* Caedmon TC 1301; cass. CDL 51301.

———. "The Lotos-Eaters." *Palgrave's Golden Treasury of English Poetry.* Caedmon TC 2011; cass. CDL 52011.

———. "Morte D'Arthur" and "Ulysses." *The Poetry of Tennyson.* Caedmon TC 1080; cass. CDL 51080.

Thomas, Dylan. "Do Not Go Gentle Into That Good Night," "Fern Hill," and "Prologue." *Dylan Thomas Reading His Complete Recorded Poetry.* Caedmon TC 2014; cass. CDL 52014.

Wilbur, Richard. "The Lilacs" and "A Wood." *Richard Wilbur Reads His Poetry.* Caedmon TC 1248; cass. CDL 51248.

Whitman, Walt. "Song of Myself." *Leaves of Grass.* Caedmon TC 1154; cass. CDL 51154.

William, Mason. "Dedication for a Plot of Ground," "Portrait of a Woman in Bed." *Spoken Arts Treasury of 100 American Poets,* vol. 2. Spoken Arts SA 1041.

Wordsworth, William. "Intimations Ode." English Romantic Poetry. Caedmon TC 3005; cass. CDL 53005.

———. "London, 1802." *Palgrave's Golden Treasury of English Poetry.* Caedmon TC 2011; cass. CDL 52011.

———. "Nuns Fret Not" and "Tintern Abbey." *The Poetry of Wordsworth.* Caedmon TC 1026; cass. CDL 51026.

Wright, James. "Autumn Begins in Martins Ferry, Ohio." *The Poetry and Voice of James Wright.* Caedmon TC 1538; cass. CDL 51538.

Wyatt, Sir Thomas. "They Flee from Me." *Palgraves Golden Treasury of English Poetry.* Caedmon TC 2011; cass. CDL 52011.

Yeats, William Butler. "Crazy Jane Talks With the Bishop." *The Poetry of William Butler Yeats.* Caedmon CT 1081; cass. CDL 51081.

———. "Dialogue of Self and Soul" and "Leda and the Swan." *Dylan Thomas Reads the Poetry of W. B. Yeats.* Caedmon TC 1353; cass. CDL 51353.

———. "When You Are Old." *Now, What Is Love?* Argo RG 370.

Index for Authors and Titles of Poems

A

"After Apple Picking" (Frost), 451
"All Along the Watchtower" (Dylan), 461
"All You Need Is Love" (Lennon-McCartney), 55
"Altars in the Street, The" (Levertov), 195
"American Poetry" (Simpson), 244
"American Tune" (Simon), 124
ANANIA, MICHAEL
"The Riversongs of Arion," 526
"Anecdote of the Jar" (Stevens), 215
"Aner Clute" (Masters), 270
"Angie Baby" (O'Day), 163
"Annus Mirabilis," from (Dryden), 52
"Another" (Haining), 260
"anyone lived in a pretty how town" (cummings), 459
"Applicant, The" (Plath), 278
ARNOLD MATTHEW
"Dover Beach," 126
"Ars Poetica" (MacLeish), 492
ASHBERY, JOHN
"Our Youth," 115
"Asian Peace Offers Rejected Without Publication" (Bly), 46
"As I Walked Out One Evening" (Auden), 313, 317
ATWOOD, MARGARET
"A Place: Fragments," 106
AUDEN, W. H.
"As I Walked Out One Evening," 313, 317
"In Memory of W. B. Yeats," 493
"Paysage Moralisé," 363
"Autumn Begins in Martins Ferry,
AVISON, MARGARET
"New Year's Poem," 470

B

BAEZ, JOAN
"Diamonds and Rust," 417
"Ballad of the Goodly Fere" (Pound), 386
BALLOWE, JAMES
"The Doughboy," 213
"Barbara Allan" (anon.), 380
"Batter My Heart, Three Personed God" (Donne), 481
"Battle of Brunanburh, The" (Tennyson), 399
"Bear, The" (Kinnell), 95
BEATLES, THE
"Sergeant Pepper's Lonely Hearts Club Band," 510
"Because I Could Not Stop for Death" (Dickinson), 312, 315
"Bells for John Whiteside's Daughter" (Ransom), 480
"Bells of Rhymney, The" (Davies), 367
"Beowulf," from (anon.), 30, 398
BERRYMAN, JOHN
"Dream Song #1," 272
"Eleven Addresses to the Lord #1," 507
"The Prisoner of Shark Island," 179
"The Bishop Orders His Tomb at Saint Praxed's Church" (Browning), 394
BLAKE, WILLIAM
"The Lamb," 251
"London," 44

BLAKE, WILLIAM *(cont.)*
"Mock On, Mock On, Voltaire, Rousseau," 160
"A Poison Tree," 460
"The Tyger," 252
BLEI, NORBERT
Concrete Poems, 439
"Blue Motel Room" (Mitchell), 178
BLY, ROBERT
"Asian Peace Offers Rejected Without Publication," 46
"Driving Toward the Lac Qui Parle River," 183
"Fall," 434
"Where We Must Look for Help," 98
"Bourgeois Poet #27, The" (Shapiro), 434
"Bridge of Sighs, The" (Hood), 298
"Bring Us in Good Ale" (anon.), 39
BROOKER-REID
"A Whiter Shade of Pale," 502
BROOKS, GWENDOLYN
"I Love Those Little Booths at Benvenuti's," 296
"The Preacher: Ruminates Behind the Sermon," 470
"Sadie and Maud," 486
"We Real Cool," 295
BROWNE, JACKSON
"The Pretender," 134
BROWNING, ROBERT
"The Bishop Orders His Tomb at Saint Praxed's Church," 394
"My Last Duchess," 176
"Bryan, Bryan, Bryan, Bryan" (Lindsay), 332
BRYANT, WILLIAM CULLEN
from "The Iliad" (trans.), 10
"To a Waterfowl," 53
"Buffalo Bill's" (cummings), 112
"But He Was Cool" (Lee), 330

C

"Carrion Comfort" (Hopkins), 358
CARROLL, LEWIS
"You Are Old, Father William," 281
"Chambered Nautilus, The" (Holmes), 446
"Channel Firing" (Hardy), 454
"Charge of the Light Brigade, The" (Tennyson), 200
CHAUCER, GEOFFREY
from "The Parliament of Fowls," 375
CIADRI, JOHN
"Men Marry What They Need. I Marry You," 351
"City of New Orleans, The" (Goodman), 208
CLEGHORN, SARAH
"The Golf Links," 485
COHEN, LEONARD
"Suzanne," 221
COLERIDGE, SAMUEL TAYLOR
"Kubla Khan," 228
"The Rime of the Ancient Mariner," 74
"Come All You Fair and Tender Ladies" (anon.), 239
Concrete Poems (Blei), 439
"Confessional" (d'Orleans), 374
"Constantly risking absurdity" (Ferlinghetti), 38
"Corpus Christi Carol, The" (anon.), 458
COWPER, WILLIAM
"On the Burning of Lord Mansfield's Library," 63, 499
"Crazy Jane Talks with the Bishop" (Yeats), 481
CREED, CHARLES
"Jan Jensen/Raku Jar," 490
CREELEY, ROBERT
"I Know a Man," 503
"The Language," 410
CROCE, JIM
"Time in a Bottle," 505
"You Don't Mess Around with Jim," 159
CUMMINGS, E.E.
"anyone lived in a pretty how town," 459
"Buffalo Bill's," 112
"next to of course god," 358
"plato told," 506
"r-p-o-p-h-e-s-s-a-g-r," 8
"she being Brand," 245

D

DACEY, PHILIP
"Looking at Models in the Sears Catalogue," 421
"Daniel and the Sacred Harp" (Robertson), 462
DAVIES, IDRIS
"The Bells of Rhymney," 367
"Death, Be Not Proud" (Donne), 356

"Death of the Hired Man, The" (Frost), 154
"Dedication for a Plot of Ground" (Williams), 325
DE LA MARE, WALTER
"Silver," 225
"Delight in Disorder" (Herrick), 105
"Desolation Row" (Dylan), 139
DE VENTADORN, BERNART
"To Bel Vezer on Her Dismissal of the Poet," 33
"Dialogue of Self and Soul, A" (Yeats), 471
"Diamonds and Rust" (Baez), 417
DICKINSON, EMILY
"Because I Could Not Stop For Death," 312, 315
" 'Hope' is the thing with feathers," 247
"I Like to See It Lap the Miles," 298
"These Are the Days When Birds Come Back," 482
"This Was a Poet," 111
DONNE, JOHN
"Batter My Heart, Three Personed God," 481
"Death, Be Not Proud," 356
"La Corona," 523
"Song," 349
"A Valediction: Forbidding Mourning," 240
"Do Not Go Gentle into That Good Night" (Thomas), 360
D'ORLEANS, CHARLES
"Confessional," 374
"Doughboy, The" (Ballowe), 213
"Dover Beach" (Arnold), 126
"Dream Song #1" (Berryman), 272
"Driving Toward the Lac Qui Parle River" (Bly), 183
DRYDEN, JOHN
from "Annus Mirabilis," 52
"Epigram on Milton," 500
"Pygmalion and the Statue" (trans.), 71
DUGAN, ALAN
"Love Song: I and Thou," 256
"Dust in the Wind" (Livgren), 464
DYER, SIR EDWARD
"My Mind to Me a Kingdom Is," 465
DYLAN, BOB
"All Along the Watchtower," 461
"Desolation Row," 139
"I Pity the Poor Immigrant," 348
"John Wesley Harding," 73
"The Lonesome Death of Hattie Carroll," 42
"Mr. Tambourine Man," 36
"Sad-Eyed Lady of the Lowlands," 283
"Subterranean Homesick Blues," 291

E

"Easter Wings" (Herbert), 435
EBERHART, RICHARD
"The Groundhog," 216
"Eight O'Clock" (Housman), 238
"El Condor Pasa" (Simon), 243
"Eleanor Rigby" (Lennon-McCartney), 167
"Elegy for Jane" (Roethke), 123
"Eleven Addresses to the Lord, #1" (Berryman), 507
ELIOT, T.S.
"Macavity: The Mystery Cat," 34
EMERSON, RALPH WALDO
"Hymn Sung at the Completion of the Concord Monument," 63
"End of Summer, The" (Minty), 409
"Epigram on Milton" (Dryden), 500
"Essay on Criticism," from (Pope), 368
"Essay on Man, An," from (Pope), 466
ETTER, DAVE
"Green-Eyed Boy After Reading Whitman and Sandburg," 59

F

"Fabliau of Florida" (Stevens), 183
"Fall" (Bly), 434
FARINA, MIMI
"In the Quiet Morning," 172
"Farmer and the Owl" (Knoepfle), 271
FELDER-HENLEY-FREY
"Hotel California," 130
FERLINGHETTI, LAWRENCE
"Constantly risking absurdity," 38
"I have not lain with beauty," 259
"Sometime during eternity," 266
"Fern Hill" (Thomas), 305
"Fifty Ways to Leave Your Lover" (Simon), 497
"First Party at Ken Kesey's with Hell's Angels" (Ginsberg), 28
"First Snow in Lake County" (Mueller), 453

"Fish, The" (Moore), 407
"Fit of Rhyme Against Rhyme, A" (Jonson), 302
"Flower Market, The" (Po-Chu-I), 43
FRANCIS, ROBERT
"Silent Poem," 438
FROST, ROBERT
"After Apple-Picking," 451
"The Death of the Hired Man," 154
"Mending Wall," 393
"Provide, Provide," 276
"Funny Death" (Ginsberg), 436
"Further Completion of Plat" (Olson), 26

G

GINSBERG, ALLEN
"First Party at Ken Kesey's with Hell's Angels," 28
"Funny Death," 436
"Going to Chicago," 68
"Howl," 423
"God's Measurements" (Lieberman), 209
"Going to Chicago" (Ginsberg), 68
"Going to Sleep" (Livesay), 367
"Golf Links, The" (Cleghorn), 485
"Gone" (Sandburg), 169
GOODMAN, STEVE
"The City of New Orleans," 208
"Green-Eyed Boy After Reading Whitman and Sandburg" (Etter), 59
"The Groundhog" (Eberhart), 216
GUTHRIE, WOODY
"Pretty Boy Floyd," 24
"Tom Joad," 383

H

HAINING, JIM
"Another," 260
HARDY, THOMAS
"Channel Firing," 454
"Her Death and After," 148
"Neutral Tones," 275
HARRISON, GEORGE
"Within You Without You," 516
"Hendecasyllabics" (Swinburne), 405
HERBERT, GEORGE
"Easter Wings," 435
"Virtue," 344
"Her Death and After" (Hardy), 148
HERRICK, ROBERT
"Delight in Disorder," 105
"Presence and Absence," 366
"To Blossoms," 240
"To the Virgins, to Make Much of Time," 278
"High-Toned Old Christian Woman, A" (Stevens), 488
HOLMES, OLIVER WENDELL
"The Chambered Nautilus," 446
HOMER
from "The Iliad" (trans. Bryant), 12
"Honesty" (Joel), 390
"Honky Tonk Women" (Jagger-Richards), 275
HOOD, THOMAS
"Bridge of Sighs," 298
" 'Hope' is the thing with feathers" (Dickinson), 247
HOPKINS, GERARD MANLEY
"Carrion Comfort," 358
"Pied Beauty," 288
"Spring and Fall: To a Young Child," 316
"The Windhover," 250
"Horse Latitudes" (Morrison), 420
"Hotel California" (Felder-Henley-Frey), 130
"House of the Rising Sun, The" (anon.), 378
"House on the Hill, The" (Robinson), 360
HOUSMAN, A. E.
"Eight O'Clock," 328
"Loveliest of Trees, the Cherry Now," 5
"To an Athlete Dying Young," 65
"Howl" (Ginsberg), 423
"How the West Was Won" (Woessner), 115
HUGHES, LANGSTON
"October 16," 67
"Little Lyric (Of Great Importance)," 366
"Young Gal's Blues," 389
"Hymn Sung at the Completion of the Concord Monument" (Emerson), 63

I

"I Am the Walrus" (Lennon-McCartney), 226
IAN, JANIS
"This Must Be Wrong," 294
"Idea of Order at Key West, The" (Stevens), 103
"I Have a Dream" (King), 414

"I have not lain with beauty" (Ferlinghetti), 259
"I Know a Man" (Creeley), 503
"Iliad, The," from (Homer, trans. Bryant), 10
"I Like to See It Lap the Miles" (Dickinson), 298
"I Love Those Little Booths at Benvenuti's" (Brooks), 296
"Inauguration Day: January, 1953" (Lowell), 205
"In Memory of W. B. Yeats" (Auden), 493
"In the Quiet Morning" (Farina), 172
"Inviting a Friend to Supper" (Jonson), 61
"I Pity the Poor Immigrant" (Dylan), 348
"I Think Continually of Those Who Were Truly Great" (Spender), 58

J

JAGGER-RICHARDS
"Honkey Tonk Women," 275
"No Expectations," 243
"Jan Jenson/Raku Jar" (Creed), 490
JEFFERS, ROBINSON
"Shine, Perishing Republic," 128
"To the Stone-Cutters," 103
JOEL, BILLY
"Honesty," 390
"My Life," 175
"Only the Good Die Young," 130
"She's Always a Woman to Me," 94
John Wesley Harding" (Dylan), 73
JONSON, BEN
"A Fit of Rhyme Against Rhyme," 302
"Inviting a Friend for Supper," 61
"An Old Colt," 366
"On English Mounsieur," 171
"On My First Daughter," 499
"To Fine Lady Would-be," 171
JUDSON, JOHN
"The Lineage of Indian Ponies," 475

K

"Karma" (Robinson), 162
KEATS, JOHN
"La Belle Dame Sans Merci," 161
"Ode on a Grecian Urn," 214
KING, MARTIN LUTHER, JR.
"I Have a Dream," 414
KINGSLEY, CHARLES
"Young and Old," 486
KINNELL, GALWAY
"The Bear," 95
KIPLING, RUDYARD
"Sestina of the Tramp-Royal," 365
KNOEPFLE, JOHN
"Farmer and the Owl," 271
KRISTOFFERSON, KRIS
"Me and Bobby McGee," 265
"Kubla Khan" (Coleridge), 228
KUZMA, GREG
from "Nebraska," 188

L

"La Belle Dame Sans Merci" (Keats), 161
"La Corona" (Donne), 523
"Lady Lazarus" (Plath), 136
"Lamb, The" (Blake) 251
"Language, The" (Creeley), 410
"Leda and the Swan" (Yeats), 357
LEE, DON L.
"But He Was Cool," 330
LENNON, JOHN
"A Working Class Hero," 45
LENNON-MCCARTNEY
"All You Need Is Love," 55
"Eleanor Rigby," 167
"I Am the Walrus," 226
"Let It Be," 483
"Norwegian Wood," 452
"Oh! Darling," 505
"Penny Lane," 182
"Strawberry Fields," 329
"Let It Be" (Lennon-McCartney), 483
"Letter to an Imaginary Friend," from (McGrath), 196
LEVERTOV, DENISE
"The Altars in the Street," 195
"One A.M.," 226
LIEBERMAN, LAURENCE
"God's Measurements," 209
"Lobsters in the Brain Coral," 476
LIGHTFOOT, GORDON
"The Wreck of the Edmund Fitzgerald," 381
"Lilacs, The" (Wilbur), 403
LINDSAY, VACHEL
"Bryan, Bryan, Bryan, Bryan," 332
"On the Building of Springfield," 50
"The Little Turtle," 35

"Lineage of Indian Ponies, The" (Judson), 475
"Lines: Composed a Few Miles above Tintern Abbey" (Wordsworth), 184
"Lines: On Dullness" (Pope), 500
"Lines: When the Lamp Is Shattered" (Shelley), 331
"Little Lyric (Of Great Importance)" (Hughes), 366
"Little Turtle, The" (Lindsay), 35
LIVESAY, DOROTHY
"Going to Sleep," 367
LIVGREN, KERRY
"Dust in the Wind," 464
"Lobsters in the Brain Coral" (Lieberman), 476
LOGAN, JOHN
"Love Poem," 423
"London" (Blake), 44
"London, 1802" (Wordsworth), 357
"Lonesome Death of Hattie Carroll, The" (Dylan), 42
LONGFELLOW, HENRY WADSWORTH
"A Psalm of Life," 54
"Looking at Models in the Sears Catalogue" (Dacey), 421
"Lord Randall" (anon.), 349
"Lotos-Eaters, The" (Tennyson), 285
"Loveliest of Trees, the Cherry Now" (Housman), 5
"Love Poem" (Logan), 423
"Love Song: I and Thou" (Dugan), 256
LOWELL, ROBERT
"Inauguration Day: January, 1953," 205
"Robert Frost," 173
LU-CHI
"Wen-Fu," 101

M

Macavity: The Mystery Cat" (Eliot), 34
MACLEISH, ARCHIBALD
"Ars Poetica," 492
MARLOWE, CHRISTOPHER
"The Passionate Shepherd to His Love," 468
MARVELL, ANDREW
"To His Coy Mistress," 223
MASTERS, EDGAR LEE
"Aner Clute," 270
"Ode to Autumn," 268
MCGRATH, THOMAS
from "Letter to an Imaginary Friend," 196
"Me and Bobby McGee" (Kristofferson-Foster), 265
"Mending Wall" (Frost), 393
"Men Marry What They Need. I Marry You" (Ciardi), 351
MILTON, JOHN
"On the Late Massacre in Piedmont," 206
MINTY, JUDITH
"The End of Summer," 409
MITCHELL, JONI
"Blue Motel Room," 178
"Woodstock," 204
"You Turn Me On, I'm a Radio" (Mitchell), 246
"Mock On, Mock On, Voltaire, Rousseau" (Blake), 260
MOORE, MARIANNE
"The Fish," 407
MORRISON, JIM
"Horse Latitudes," 420
"Twentieth Century Fox," 4
"Mr. Flood's Party (Robinson), 169
"Mr. Tambourine Man" (Dylan), 36
MUELLER, LISEL
"First Snow in Lake County," 453
"My Galley Charged with Forgetfulness" (Wyatt), 354
"My Last Duchess" (Browning), 176
"My Life" (Joel), 175
"My Mind to Me a Kingdom Is" (Dyer), 465

N

"Nebraska," from (Kuzma), 188
"Neutral Tones" (Hardy), 275
"New Year's Poem" (Avison), 470
"next to of course god" (cummings), 358
"Night They Drove Old Dixie Down, The" (Robertson),194
"No Expectations" (Jagger–Richards), 243
"Noiseless Patient Spider, A" (Whitman), 416
"Nomad Exquisite" (Stevens), 287
"Norwegian Wood" (Lennon–McCartney), 452
"Now" (Stafford), 289

"Nuns Fret Not at Their Convent's Narrow Room" (Wordsworth), 491
"Nymph's Reply to the Shepherd, The" (Raleigh), 469

O

"October 16" (Hughes), 67
O'Day, Alan
 "Angie, Baby," 163
"Ode: Intimations of Immortality" (Wordsworth), 542
"Ode on a Grecian Urn" (Keats), 214
"Ode to Autumn" (Masters), 268
"Ode to the Plum Blossom" (Mao Tse-tung), 450
"Ode to the West Wind" (Shelley), 131
"Oh! Darling" (Lennon-McCartney), 505
"Old Colt, An" (Jonson), 366
"Old Man's Comforts, The" (Southey), 280
Olson, Charles
 "Further Completion of Plat," 26
"One A.M." (Levertov), 226
"On English Mounsier" (Jonson), 171
"On King Charles" (Rochester), 174
"Only the Good Die Young" (Joel), 130
"On My First Daughter" (Jonson), 499
"On the Building of Springfield" (Lindsay), 50
"On the Burning of Lord Mansfield's Library" (Cowper), 63, 499
"On the Late Massacre in Piedmont" (Milton), 206
"Our Youth" (Ashbery), 115
Ovid
 "Pygmalion and the Statue," 71

P

"Parliament of Fowls," from (Chaucer), 375
"Passing of Arthur, The" (Tennyson), 12
"Passionate Shepherd to His Love, The" (Marlowe), 468
"Paysage Moralisé" (Auden), 363
"Penny Lane" (Lennon-McCartney), 182
"Pied Beauty" (Hopkins), 288
"Place: Fragments, A" (Atwood), 106
Plath, Sylvia
 "The Applicant," 278
 "Lady Lazarus," 136
"plato told" (cummings), 506
Po-Chu-I
 "The Flower Market," 43
"Poison Tree, A" (Blake), 460
Pope, Alexander
 from "Essay on Criticism," 368
 from "An Essay on Man," 466
 "Lines: On Dullness," 500
"Portrait of a Woman in Bed" (Williams), 113
Pound, Ezra
 "Ballard of the Goodly Fere," 386
"Preacher: Ruminates Behind the Sermon, The" (Brooks), 470
"Presence and Absence" (Herrick), 366
"Pretender, The" (Browne), 134
"Pretty Boy Floyd" (Guthrie), 24
"Prisoner of Shark Island, The" (Berryman), 179
"Prologue" (Thomas), 322
"Provide, Provide" (Frost), 276
"Psalm of Life, A" (Longfellow), 54
"Psalm 150," 416
"Pygmalion and the Statue" (Ovid, trans. Dryden), 71

R

Raleigh, Sir Walter
 "The Nymph's Reply to the Shepherd," 469
Ransom, John Crowe
 "Bells for John Whiteside's Daughter," 480
"Red Wheelbarrow, The" (Williams), 218
Reid-Brooker
 "A Whiter Shade of Pale," 502
"Rime of the Ancient Mariner, The" (Coleridge), 74
"Riversongs of Arion, The" (Anania), 526
"Robert Frost" (Lowell), 173
Robertson, Robbie
 "Daniel and the Sacred Harp," 462
 "The Night They Drove Old Dixie Down," 194
 "The Rumor," 57
Robinson, E.A.
 "The House on the Hill," 360
 "Karma," 162
 "Mr. Flood's Party," 169
 "Sonnet: Oh, for a Poet," 49
Rochester, John Wilmot, Earl of
 "On King Charles," 174

ROETHKE, THEODORE
"Elegy for Jane," 123
Romeo and Juliet, from (Shakespeare), 230, 391
"Rondel: An Un-Love Song" (Schoonover), 374
ROSELIEP, RAYMOND
"Thoreauhaiku," 406
"r-p-o-p-h-e-s-s-a-g-r" (cummings), 8
"Rumor, The" (Robertson), 57

S

"Sad-Eyed Lady of the Lowlands" (Dylan), 283
"Sadie and Maud" (Brooks), 486
SANDBURG, CARL
"Gone," 169
SCHOONOVER, AMY JO
"Rondel: An Un-Love Song," 374
SEEGER, PETE
"Waist Deep in the Big Muddy," 456
"Sergeant Pepper's Lonely Hearts Club Band" (Beatles), 510
"Sestina of the Tramp-Royal" (Kipling), 365
"Seven Wealthy Towns" (anon.), 367
SHAKESPEARE
from *Romeo and Juliet,* 230, 391
Sonnet 18, 355
Sonnet 55, 102
Sonnet 75, 356
"Spring," 219
"Under the Greenwood Tree," 350
"Winter," 219
SHAPIRO, KARL
"The Bourgeois Poet #27," 434
"she being Brand" (cummings), 245
SHELLEY, PERCY BYSSHE
"Lines: When the Lamp Is Shattered," 331
"Ode to the West Wind," 131
"Sonnet: England in 1819," 45
"She's Always a Woman to Me" (Joel), 94
"Shine, Perishing Republic" (Jeffers), 128
"Silent Poem" (Francis), 438
"Silver" (de la Mare), 225
SIMON, CARLY
"The Way I've Always Heard It Should Be," 447
"You're So Vain," 64
SIMON, PAUL
"American Tune," 124
"El Condor Pasa," 243
"Fifty Ways to Leave Your Lover," 497
"So Long, Frank Lloyd Wright," 489
SIMPSON, LOUIS
"American Poetry," 244
"Sir Patrick Spence" (anon.), 153
SLICK, GRACE
"White Rabbit," 255
"So Long, Frank Lloyd Wright" (Simon), 489
"Sometime during eternity" (Ferlinghetti), 266
"Song" (Donne), 249
"Song of Myself," from (Whitman), 119, 144, 248, 321
"Sonnet: England in 1819" (Shelley), 45
"Sonnet: Oh, for a Poet" (Robinson), 49
Sonnet 18 (Shakespeare), 355
Sonnet 55 (Shakespeare), 102
Sonnet 73 (Shakespeare), 356
SOUTHEY, ROBERT
"The Old Man's Comforts," 280
SPENDER, STEPHEN
"I Think Continually of Those Who Were Truly Great," 58
"Spring" (Shakespeare), 219
"Spring and Fall: To a Young Child" (Hopkins), 316
STAFFORD, WILLIAM
"Now," 289
"The Stick in the Forest," 165
STEVENS, WALLACE
"Anecdote of the Jar," 215
"Fabliau of Florida," 183
"A High-Toned Old Christian Woman," 488
"The Idea of Order at Key West," 103
"Nomad Exquisite," 287
"Stick in the Forest, The" (Stafford), 165
"Strawberry Fields" (Lennon-McCartney), 329
"Subterranean Homesick Blues" (Dylan), 291
"Suzanne" (Cohen), 221
SWINBURNE, ALGERNON CHARLES
"Hendecasyllabics," 405

T

TENNYSON, ALFRED, LORD
"The Battle of Brunanburh," 399
"The Charge of the Light Brigade," 200
"The Lotos-Eaters," 285
"The Passing of Arthur," 12
"Ulysses," 201

"That the Night Come" (Yeats), 6
"These Are the Days When Birds Come Back" (Dickinson), 482
"They Flee from Me" (Wyatt), 272
"This Must be Wrong" (Ian), 294
"This Was a Poet" (Dickinson), 111
Thomas, Dylan
"Do Not Go Gentle into That Good Night," 360
"Fern Hill," 305
"Prologue," 322
"Thoreauhaiku" (Roseliep), 406
"Time in a Bottle" (Croce), 505
"To an Athlete Dying Young" (Housman), 65
"To a Waterfowl" (Bryant), 53
"To Bel Vezer on Her Dismissal of the Poet" (de Ventadorn), 33
"To Blossoms" (Herrick), 240
"To Fine Lady Would-be" (Jonson), 171
"To His Coy Mistress" (Marvell), 233
"Tom Joad" (Guthrie), 383
"To the Stone-Cutters" (Jeffers), 103
"To the Virgins, to Make Much of Time" (Herrick), 278
Tse-tung, Mao
"Ode to the Plum Blossom," 450
"Twentieth Century Fox" (Morrison), 4
"Tyger, The" (Blake), 252

U

"Ulysses" (Tennyson), 201
"Under the Greenwood Tree" (Shakespeare), 350

V

"Valediction: Forbidding Mourning, A" (Donne), 240
"Virtue" (Herbert), 344

W

"Waist Deep in the Big Muddy" (Seeger), 456
"Way I've Always Heard It Should Be, The" (Simon), 447
"Wen-fu" (Lu-Chi), 101
"We Real Cool" (Brooks), 295
"When You Are Old" (Yeats), xii
"Where We Must Look for Help" (Bly), 98
"White Rabbit" (Slick), 255
"Whiter Shade of Pale, A" (Reid-Brooker), 502
Whitman, Walt
"A Noiseless Patient Spider," 416
from "Song of Myself," 119, 144, 248, 321
Wilbur, Richard
"The Lilacs," 403
"A Wood," 452
Williams, William Carlos
"Dedication for a Plot of Ground," 325
"Portrait of a Woman in Bed," 113
"The Red Wheelbarrow," 218
"Windhover, The" (Hopkins), 250
"Winter" (Shakespeare), 219
Woessner, Warren
"How the West Was Won," 115
"Wood, A" (Wilbur), 452
"Woodstock" (Mitchell), 204
Wordsworth, William
"Lines: Composed a Few Miles Above Tintern Abbey," 184
"London: 1802," 357
"Nuns Fret Not at Their Convent's Narrow Room," 491
"Ode: Intimations of Immortality," 542
"The World Is Too Much with Us," 56
"Working Class Hero, A" (Lennon), 45
"World Is Too Much with Us, The" (Wordsworth), 56
"Wreck of the Edmund Fitzgerald, The" (Lightfoot), 381
Wright, James
"Autumn Begins in Martins Ferry, Ohio," 47
Wyatt, Sir Thomas
"My Galley Charged with Forgetfulness," 354
"They Flee from Me," 272

Y

Yeats, William Butler
"Crazy Jane Talks with the Bishop," 481
"A Dialogue of Self and Soul," 471
"Leda and the Swan," 357
"That the Night Come," 6
"When You Are Old," xii
"You, Andrew Marvell" (MacLeish), 257
"You Are Old, Father William" (Carroll), 281

"You Don't Mess Around with Jim" (Croce), 159
"Young and Old" (Kingsley), 486
"Young Gal's Blues" (Hughes), 389
"You're So Vain" (Simon), 64
"You Turn Me On, I'm a Radio" (Mitchell), 246